ISBN 978-1-5283-4837-9
PIBN 10922359

1 MONTH OF
FREE
READING

at

www.ForgottenBooks.com

By purchasing this book you are eligible for one month membership to ForgottenBooks.com, giving you unlimited access to our entire collection of over 1,000,000 titles via our web site and mobile apps.

To claim your free month visit:

www.forgottenbooks.com/free922359

REPORTS OF CASES

SUPREME COURT

OF

NEBRASKA.

SEPTEMBER TERM, 1897—JANUARY TERM, 1898.

VOLUME LIII.

OFFICIAL REPORTER.

LINCOLN, NEB.:
STATE JOURNAL COMPANY, LAW PUBLISHERS.
1898.

Rec. Mar. 24, 1899.

THE SUPREME COURT

OF

NEBRASKA.

1897–98.

CHIEF JUSTICES,

A. M. POST, [*]
T. O. C. HARRISON. [†]

JUDGES,

T. O. C. HARRISON, [†]
T. L. NORVAL,
J. J. SULLIVAN. [‡]

COMMISSIONERS,

ROBERT RYAN,
JOHN M. RAGAN,
FRANK IRVINE.

OFFICERS.

ATTORNEY GENERAL,

C. J. SMYTH.

CLERK AND REPORTER,

D. A. CAMPBELL.

DEPUTY CLERK,

W. B. ROSE.

---

[*]Term expired January 5, 1898.
[†]Became Chief Justice January 6, 1898.
[‡]Elected November 2, 1897, and took his seat January 6, 1898.

DISTRICT COURTS OF NEBRASKA.

JUDGES.

First District—
- C. B. LETTON..Fairbury.
- J. S. STULL............................. ....Auburn.

Second District—
- B. S. RAMSEY..Plattsmouth.

Third District—
- A. J. CORNISH...Lincoln.
- CHARLES L. HALL....................................Lincoln.
- E. P. HOLMES..Lincoln.

Fourth District—
- B. S. BAKER...Omaha.
- CHARLES T. DICKINSON ....Tekamah.
- JACOB FAWCETT....................................Omaha.
- W. W. KEYSOR.......................................Omaha.
- CLINTON N. POWELL................................Omaha.
- C. R. SCOTT..Omaha.
- W. W. SLABAUGH ....Omaha.

Fifth District—
- EDWARD BATES.....................................York.
- S. H. SEDGWICK....................................York.

Sixth District—
- I. L. ALBERT...Columbus.
- WM. MARSHALL.....................................Fremont.

Seventh District—
- W. G. HASTINGS.....................................Wilber.

Eighth District—
- R. E. EVANS..Dakota City.

Ninth District—
- J. S. ROBINSON............................ ....Madison.

Tenth District—
- F. B. BEALL...Alma.

Eleventh District—
- A. A. KENDALL.......................................St. Paul.
- J. R. THOMPSON......................................Grand Island.

DISTRICT COURTS OF NEBRASKA.

Twelfth District—
    H. M. SULLIVAN...Broken Bow.

Thirteenth District—
    H. M. GRIMES...North Platte.

Fourteenth District—
    G. W. NORRIS...Beaver City.

Fifteenth District—
    M. P. KINKAID ....O'Neill.
    W. H. WESTOVER.......................................Rushville.

PRACTICING ATTORNEYS.

ADMITTED SINCE THE PUBLICATION OF VOL. LII

AMES, ERNEST C.
BATTELLE, CHARLES.
BELDEN, OLIVER W.
BOBBITT, CHARLES E.
BOWMAN, G. L.
BRANSON, O. L.
BROWN, JAMES A.
BURCH, N. D.
BUSH, HAROLD D.
COWAN, W. P.
COWIN, W. B.
CUNNINGHAM, M. V.
CURTISS, A. D.
DALY, HUGH.
DAVIS, F. M.
DE FRANCE, CHARLES O.
DENISON, JOHN D.
DERNIER, WILLIAM DELES.
DISNEY, FRANK T.
ELDRED, C. E.
ELY, WILLIAM M.
FISCHER, HARRY.
FISHUE, WALTER C.
FOLSOM, ERNEST C.
FOLSOM, MORRIS W.
GAINES, FRANK H.
GROSVENOR, JOHN H.
GUSTIN, FRANK.
HALLOREN, F. C.
HAMER, F. C.
HANSEN, WALTER A.
HINES, ORPHOSEUS F.
HODDER, ERNEST C.
HUMPHREY, FRED L.
HURLEY, C. C.
IMHOFF, CHARLES HUDSON.
JENNINGS, WILLIAM H.

JOHNSON, VICTOR OSCAR.
KELLEY, GEORGE D.
KEMP, JAMES H.
LADD, CHARLES FRANKLIN.
LEAVITT, HENRY P.
LEE, THOMAS F.
LINDSAY, BENJAMIN.
LYNDES, JOHN C.
McDONALD, N. P.
McGUIRE, E. T.
McININCH, M. S.
MAHER, JOHN G.
MANCK, H. H.
MOYER, L. E.
MYERS, W. A.
POPE, O. G.
PURCELL, J. J.
ROACH, LEONARD E.
SACKETT, HARRY E.
SINCLAIR, NEIL.
SINGHAUS, JOHN.
SLATTERY, ERNEST M.
SMITH, ALIX O.
STAHL, F. A.
STINES, L. B.
SWAIN, ORLANDO.
TROUP, L. M.
VAN DECAR, HERBERT B.
WARFIELD, GEORGE A.
WHIPPLE, HERBERT A.
WILCOX, SHERMAN.
WILLARD, JOHN D.
WILSON, A. P. TONE, JR.
WILSON, BURTON W.
WILSON, L. S.
WINSLOW, LOREN E.
YOCUM, A. C.

SUPREME COURT COMMISSIONERS.

(Laws 1893, chapter 16, page 150.)

SECTION 1. The supreme court of the state, immediately upon the taking effect of this act, shall appoint three persons, no two of whom shall be adherents to the same political party, and who shall have attained the age of thirty years and are citizens of the United States and of this state, and regularly admitted as attorneys at law in this state, and in good standing of the bar thereof, as commissioners of the supreme court.

SEC. 2. It shall be the duty of said commissioners, under such rules and regulations as the supreme court may adopt, to aid and assist the court in the performance of its duties in the disposition of the numerous cases now pending in said court, or that shall be brought into said court during the term of office of such commissioners.

SEC. 3. The said commissioners shall hold office for the period of three years from and after their appointment, during which time they shall not engage in the practice of the law. They shall each receive a salary equal to the salary of a judge of the supreme court, payable at the same time and in the same manner as salaries of the judges of the supreme court are paid. Before entering upon the discharge of their duties they shall each take the oath provided for in section one (1) of article fourteen (14) of the constitution of this state. All vacancies in this commission shall be filled in like manner as the original appointment. *Provided,* That upon the expiration of the terms of said commissioners as hereinbefore provided, the said supreme court shall appoint three persons having the same qualifications as required of those first appointed as commissioners of the supreme court for a further period of three years from and after the expiration of the term first herein provided, whose duties and salaries shall be the same as those of the commissioners originally appointed. (Amended, Laws 1895, chapter 30, page 155.)

See page xlix for table of Nebraska cases overruled.

––––––––––

The syllabus in each case was prepared by the judge or commissioner writing the opinion.

––––––––––

A table of statutes and constitutional provisions cited and construed, numerically arranged, will be found on page lv.

TABLE OF CASES REPORTED.

A.

B.

TABLE OF CASES REPORTED.

E.

F.

G.

2

I.

J.

K.

L.

M.

CASES CITED BY THE COURT.

A.

B.

C.

D.

E.

F.

3

G.

I.

J.

K.

L.

M.

N.

Q.

R.

S.

T.

4

TABLE OF NEBRASKA CASES OVERRULED.

TABLE OF CASES OVERRULED.

STATUTES AND CONSTITUTIONAL PROVISIONS

CITED AND CONSTRUED.

STATE.

CASES

ARGUED AND DETERMINED

IN THE

SUPREME COURT OF NEBRASKA.

SEPTEMBER TERM, A. D. 1897.

PRESENT:

Hon. A. M. POST, Chief Justice.

Hon. T. O. C. HARRISON, } Judges.
Hon. T. L. NORVAL,

Hon. ROBERT RYAN,
Hon. JOHN M. RAGAN, } Commissioners.
Hon. FRANK IRVINE,

F. G. KEENS v. BUFFALO COUNTY ET AL.

FILED DECEMBER 9, 1897. No. 7663.

Review: PROCEEDINGS BEFORE COUNTY BOARD: EVIDENCE. Where error proceedings present no question, except one of fact, and there existed no means by which the evidence upon which such question was determined by an inferior board or tribunal could be preserved upon the hearing before it, the finding of such board or tribunal must be affirmed.

ERROR from the district court of Buffalo county. Tried below before HOLCOMB, J. *Affirmed.*

R. A. Moore, for plaintiff in error.

Norris Brown, contra.

5 (1)

RYAN, C.

This cause was brought into this court upon the petition in error of F. G. Keens for the reversal of a judgment of the district court of Buffalo county affirming the action of the board of county commissioners of said county with reference to the assessment of said Keens in the year 1893. The record of the county board recites the proceedings with reference to the subject-matter just indicated, as follows:

"Consideration of the matter of the assessment of F. G. Keens being in order, his attorney, Mr. Moore, being present, stated that his client, Mr. Keens, would come before the board to be questioned relative to off-set claimed by him, but that he refused to bring books or papers or other evidence to substantiate his word in the matter.

"Moved by Stuckey and seconded by Hoag that this board refuse to allow the prayer of F. G. Keens in the matter of his assessment on the ground that there is not sufficient evidence before them on which to act, and that this board have requested said Keens to appear with his books and his witnesses and be examined under oath as to the nature, extent, and character of said alleged indebtedness, and he refused to do so. Ayes and nays being called for resulted as follows: Ayes—Aron, Brady, Bennett, Collard, Day, Deets, Elliott, Ferris, Fisher, Hoag, Ihde, Johnson, Lambert, Lunger, Mohring, Mortimer, McNeal, Pickett, Pokorny, Richards, Salisbury, and Stuckey; total, 23. Nays—Bowie and Millett; total, 2. Absent—Towers, Fritz, and Jones. Mr. Moore, as attorney for Mr. Keens, then stated that he should take the matter of his assessment to the district court on writ of error."

From this record it seems that the plaintiff in error failed before the board of county commissioners because he adduced no evidence to sustain his claim for the reduction of his assessment. In the record there are found copies of three affidavits certified by the county clerk of Buffalo county as having been filed and offered as evidence before the board. The proceedings sought to be reviewed were had July 16, 1893. At that time there was no provision for the settlement of a bill of exceptions in matters heard by a board of county commissioners, and therefore no means existed for preserving the evidence upon which questions of fact, by such board, had been determined. (*Hopkins v. Scott*, 38 Neb., 661.) The district court for this reason could not consider these affidavits, and, upon the record of the county board, could not do otherwise than sustain its action. The judgment of that court is therefore

AFFIRMED.

JOHN H. WRIGHT V. FRANK MORSE.

FILED DECEMBER 9, 1897.   No. 7649.   *

1. **Review:** CONFLICTING EVIDENCE. The verdict of a jury reached on consideration of merely conflicting evidence will not be disturbed in the supreme court.

2. **Evidence:** OFFER TO COMPROMISE. An offer to compromise a matter in dispute cannot be given in evidence against the party by whom such offer was made.

3. **Execution Sale:** PURCHASE FOR DEFENDANT'S BENEFIT: RIGHTS OF BUYER. Where a party purchased property at an execution sale and paid the purchase price therefor, at the request of the execution defendant to whom such property was subsequently delivered, such party is entitled to recover the amount of such payment from the execution defendant, even though the execution sale, in law, was unauthorized and void.

ERROR from the district court of Boyd county. Tried below before KINKAID, J. *Affirmed.*

H. M. Uttley, for plaintiff in error.

John H. Mosier, contra.

RYAN, C.

This action was brought in the county court of Boyd county, wherein the plaintiff Morse recovered judgment, from which Wright appealed to the district court of said county, wherein a judgment, similar to that appealed from, was rendered, upon the verdict of a jury. By his petition in error Wright seeks the reversal of this judgment.

By his petition in the district court Morse alleged that, upon the oral request of Wright, Morse had attended a certain sale of cattle upon an execution against Wright; had purchased said cattle for the sum of $128, which he had paid, and that Wright, though he had received the said cattle from Morse, had refused to reimburse Morse as said Wright had agreed to when the aforesaid request to purchase was made. The answer of Wright put in issue the averments of the petition and contained averments that the execution sale was a nullity for reasons which hereafter shall be more fully stated. It admits of some doubt whether or not Morse, by his own testimony given in chief, sustained all the averments of his petition, but from a consideration of all the evidence the jury was justified in finding the verdict which it returned. Plaintiff in error complains because he was not permitted on cross-examination of Morse to show that Morse had offered to accept one-half the amount he had paid on his bid if Wright would pay that sum to him. This was evidently an offer to compromise and was properly excluded. It is also urged as error that the trial court refused to permit Wright to show that the court by which judgment had been rendered against him for the satisfaction of which the cattle were sold to Morse had no legal existence at the time such judgment was rendered. We agree with the district court that, if Morse bought the cattle upon the procurement of Wright, it was immaterial whether the sale was authorized by law or not. Morse, as the jury found upon conflicting evidence, purchased these cattle at this sale purely to subserve some unexplained purpose of Wright, and Wright cannot complain that the sale, technically, was without authority of law. Wright in his testimony admitted that, even after the sale had been made, he directed Morse to give his check for the purchase price, but required that it should be made non-negotiable, due in ten days, and that, meantime, payment thereof should be forbidden. From Wright's own testimony it further appears that he himself gave notice not to pay the check, as he claims in pursuance of the advice of one or more lawyers whom he had consulted. Morse, after this, voluntarily paid the amount of his bid to the constable who had conducted the sale on the execution against Wright, and we cannot say that Morse was without justification in doing this, for neither the neighborly sympathy, nor the contract undertakings, disclosed in the trial of this case, required of Morse that he should, as a matter of accommodation, engage in litigation for the benefit of Wright. We have found no error in the record and the judgment of the district court is

AFFIRMED.

WILLIAM J. MAXWELL V. FRANK L. GREGORY.

FILED DECEMBER 9, 1897.   No. 7620.

1. **Vendor and Vendee**: FAILURE TO MAKE TITLE: REPAYMENT OF PURCHASE MONEY. A party who, under the terms of an executory written contract, is conditionally entitled to receive a good title to real property, upon its being made certain that the other party cannot make such title, may recover such payments as he has meantime made pursuant to the terms of the contract to which he is a party.

2. ——: ——: ——: EVIDENCE. It is not competent for a defendant sought to be compelled to make restitution as above indicated, to show his own solvency, or that he has been empowered by virtue of negotiations with the holders of the outstanding title to make a good and sufficient warranty deed, no such ability or readiness having been averred in his answer.

ERROR from the district court of Douglas county.
Tried below before FERGUSON, J. *Affirmed.*

The facts are stated in the opinion.

B. N. Robertson, for plaintiff in error:

A court of equity will allow a reasonable time to perfect a title, and when valid, in the absence of fraud, will compel the vendee to accept it. (See *Frost v. Brunson,* 6 Yerg. [Tenn.], 35; *Bryant v. McCollum,* 4 Heisk. [Tenn.], 520; *Elliott v. Blair,* 5 Cold. [Tenn.], 193.)

Where the vendor is complainant it is not necessary for him to show that he was able to give a good title at the time of making the agreement to sell or at the time of the commencement of the suit. It will be sufficient if he can give a perfect title at the time of the decree. (*Coffin v. Cooper,* 14 Ves. [Eng.], 205; *Hepburn v. Auld,* 5 Cranch [U. S.], 262; *Brown v. Haff,* 5 Paige Ch. [N. Y.], 235; 28 Am. & Eng. Ency. Law, 74; *Jenkins v. Fahey,* 73 N. Y., 355.)

Lake, Hamilton & Maxwell, contra:

Under an agreement by the vendor of lands to execute a good and sufficient conveyance the purchaser may demand a clear title, as well as that it be assured to him by proper covenants. (*Davis v. Henderson,* 17 Wis., 108; *Taft v. Kessel,* 16 Wis., 291; *Davidson v. Van Pelt,* 15 Wis., 375; *Bateman v. Johnson,* 10 Wis., 1; *Falkner v. Guild,* 10 Wis., 563.)

A purchaser under an executory contract may recover the money paid without alleging or proving readiness to perform on his part, where the vendor is unable to perform. (*Clark v. Weis,* 87 Ill., 438; *Runkle v. Johnson,* 30 Ill., 328; *Miner v. Hilton,* 44 N. Y. Supp., 155; *Wright v. Dickinson,* 11 Am. St. Rep. [Mich.], 602; *Linton v. Allen,* 28 N. E. Rep. [Mass.], 780.)

RYAN, C.

Frank L. Gregory filed his petition in the district court of Douglas county alleging that William J. Maxwell, pretending and representing himself to be the owner in fee of lot 3, block 21, in West Omaha, had sold said lot to said plaintiff and had entered into a written agreement with said plaintiff evidencing such sale. By the terms of this agreement, pleaded in the petition, Maxwell agreed to sell to Gregory the whole of the lot above described for the consideration of $1,500, of which consideration $500 was to be paid at the date of the delivery of the contract, which was June 2, 1887, and the balance in three equal annual payments to be made June 1 of each of the years indicated. By this contract Gregory was required to pay and discharge all taxes and assessments imposed on said property from the date of said agreement, within three months from such times as the same should fall due. There was contained in this contract the following provisions: "Forthwith after second payment of said purchase money, taxes, and interest as aforesaid, time being of the essence of this contract, the party of the first part [Maxwell] agrees to execute, or cause to be executed, to the party of the second part a good and sufficient warranty deed for the said lot three, to be delivered on the surrender of the duplicate contract." The petition contained averments that, at the date of the contract, Gregory, relying upon the representations of Maxwell that he could and would make good title, had paid the sum of $500 as required, and in 1888 and 1889 had paid taxes and assessments to the amount of $30.47; that on August 10, 1893, he had tendered to Maxwell the sum of $1,599.52, the amount due under the contract, and requested that a deed be executed in accordance with the provisions of said contract whereby Maxwell had bound himself to make such conveyance. It was alleged that Maxwell had not made the conveyance demanded, and was unable to do so by reason of the fact that he was the owner of but one-half of the lot bargained to be conveyed, as had been adjudicated by a court having jurisdiction of the subject-matter and of the parties, of whom said Maxwell was one. The prayer of the petition was for the recovery of the payments above described as actually having been made and received on the faith of the provisions of said contract, with seven per cent per annum interest thereon from the several dates when the said payments respectively had been made, and for the enforcement of a lien for said amount prayed, against the interest of Maxwell in the real property described in the contract between Maxwell and Gregory. In his answer Maxwell admitted the execution of the contract, but denied that he had made any false representations in respect thereto. He further averred that Gregory, at the time of the making of the written contract described in the petition, had full knowledge of the condition of the title of Maxwell and of the adverse claims of other parties to the lot which was the subject-matter of said contract and of the nature of such claim of adverse title as set forth in the pleadings and decree in Maxwell against Higgins et al., the case to which Gregory had referred in his petition. It was further answered that more than four years had elapsed before this action was begun and that, therefore, the statute of limitations had fully barred it. In the answer it was also alleged that, notwithstanding the duty of Gregory under the provisions of said contract to pay taxes and assessments, he had failed to make such payments, to which failure was attributable the sale of said lot for taxes and in pursuance of such sale the issuance of a tax deed which remains outstanding. There was also a denial of each averment of the petition which had not been admitted in an earlier part of said answer. A reply in denial of each averment in the answer completed the issues upon which a trial was had to the court. There was a judgment as prayed by Gregory, for the reversal of which Maxwell prosecutes these proceedings in error.

In effect, this action was one brought by Gregory for the recovery of money which he had paid on an executory contract which Maxwell, the other party thereto, was unable to carry out. Under these circumstances Gregory was justified in rescinding, and upon such rescission was entitled to recover what he had been compelled to pay in performance of the conditions which by the terms of said contract had been imposed upon him and by the default of the other party had been rendered unavailing, with interest. (*Clark v. Weis*, 87 Ill., 438; *Miner v. Hilton*, 44 N. Y. Supp., 155; *Wright v. Dickinson*, 67 Mich., 580; *Linton v. Allen*, 154 Mass., 432.) On the trial there was an offer to show that Maxwell was able to obtain credit for the sum at least of $10,000. We cannot conceive how this fact, if established or conceded, impaired the right of Gregory to a return of his money with seven per cent interest thereon. It was also attempted to be shown that Maxwell had negotiated with the parties who had prevailed against him with reference to the undivided one-half of the lot he had agreed to sell to Gregory. Following this offer the following question was propounded to Maxwell: "You may state now whether or not these negotiations have given you full power to execute a warranty deed to this lot three to plaintiff." This was answered in the affirmative, but on motion the answer was stricken out. By this ruling the court gave it to be understood that in the decision of the case presented no consideration would be given to the fact that, by virtue of negotiations between Maxwell and the holders of the outstanding title adverse to his claim of title, Maxwell had been given power to execute a warranty deed to Gregory. In this view the court was right. No offer to convey had been made in the answer, neither had there been an averment of a willingness to make a conveyance. The question and its answer did not imply that Maxwell had obtained the outstanding title and was therefore prepared to perform. They elicited merely the fact that Maxwell's late adversaries had given him power to make a warranty deed to Gregory. If by this it was meant that Maxwell, as the agent of these parties, or as their attorney in fact, had power to execute the deed in question, this would not meet the requirements of the contract with Gregory. The question simply called for Maxwell's conclusion as to whether the negotiations conferred power upon him to execute a warranty deed, and hence the answer elicited no material fact. By these considerations we are led to the conclusion that the court properly refused to consider this question and answer.

It is urged that Gregory acquiesced in the delay necessary to settle the litigation between Maxwell and Higgins. An examination of the evidence discloses the facts that he was ready to perform at any time, and repeatedly signified this willingness to Maxwell and Maxwell's agent in this matter, but was put off from time to time by one excuse and another until the final adjudication was had in the case of Maxwell against Higgins. The plaintiff in error cannot be heard to found objections upon this forbearance for his own benefit and at his own instance.

There was no attempt whatever to show the existence of any tax deed, so that we are not called upon to discuss questions which the existence of such a title under the circumstances pleaded in the answer might have raised. The judgment of the district court is

AFFIRMED.

JOSEPH BRINCKLE V. NELLIE STITTS.

FILED DECEMBER 9, 1897. NO. 7662.

1. **Assignments of Error:** MOTION FOR NEW TRIAL. Errors in a petition in error must be assigned separately and this rule is not complied with by an assignment that there was error in overruling the motion for a new trial where such motion embraces several distinct complaints of errors.

2. **Instructions**: EXCEPTIONS: REVIEW. Where a party did not except to the refusal of the trial court to give an instruction requested by such party he cannot be heard to complain of the refusal in the supreme court.

3. **Review**: EXCLUSION OF EVIDENCE: BILL OF EXCEPTIONS. Error alleged as to the exclusion from the jury of the whole or a part of an alleged book of original entries cannot be considered in the supreme court when the book is not to be found in connection with the bill of exceptions.

4. **Depositions**: OBJECTION TO ANSWER. An answer to an interrogatory in a deposition contained both competent and incompetent testimony. *Held,* That an objection was properly sustained to the entire answer.

ERROR from the district court of Fillmore county. Tried below before HASTINGS, J. *Affirmed.*

John D. Carson, for plaintiff in error.

Charles H. Sloan, contra.

RYAN, C.

This was an action for compensation for personal services rendered for plaintiff in error by the defendant in error. There was a verdict as prayed to the amount of $200, for which amount, with costs, a judgment was duly rendered by the district court of Fillmore county. In the petition in error there was no assignment as to the sufficiency of the evidence to sustain the verdict. It is true this was made the ground of one of the several complaints urged in the motion for a new trial, and in the petition in error the overruling of the motion for a new trial in a general way was assigned as error. This, however, presented no question as to any one of the several errors alleged in the motion for a new trial. (*City of Chadron v. Glover,* 43 Neb., 732; *Glaze v. Parcel,* 40 Neb., 732; *Stein v. Vannice,* 44 Neb., 132; *Sigler v. McConnell,* 45 Neb., 598; *Conger v. Dodd,* 45 Neb., 36.)

It is urged in argument that the district court erred in its refusal to give the fourth instruction asked by the plaintiff in error. There was no exception to this ruling; hence we cannot determine whether or not there was error in such refusal. It is urged that an alleged book of original entries was improperly excluded from the consideration of the jury. Unfortunately, this book does not appear in connection with the bill of exceptions, and we therefore cannot determine whether or not there was error in excluding portions of it.

The final assignment is that there was error in excluding as evidence the answer to the fourth interrogatory in the deposition of J. F. Steenrod. In this answer there was some competent testimony, but this was in connection with testimony which was clearly incompetent. The district court therefore properly excluded the entire answer of the witness.

There was assigned no other error, and it follows that the judgment of the district court is

AFFIRMED.

JOSEPH W. SHABATA ET AL. V. JOHN R. JOHNSTON ET AL.

FILED DECEMBER 9, 1897. No. 7615.

1. **Appearance:** JURISDICTION. A defendant who has voluntarily submitted his person to the jurisdiction of a district court cannot afterwards be heard by answer to question such jurisdiction.

2. **Banking Corporations:** EVIDENCE OF EXISTENCE. A finding adverse to the contention that a banking corporation had ceased to exist by lapse of time will be sustained where, on each side, the evidence is of like character with a preponderance in favor of the finding rather than against it.

3. **Set-Off.** A claim on the part of a defendant, which he will be entitled to set off against the claim of a plaintiff against him, must be one upon which such defendant could, at the date of the commencement of the suit, have maintained an action on his part against the plaintiff.

4. **Joint Assignments of Error.** A joint assignment of errors, in a petition in error made by two or more persons, which is not good as to all who join therein must be overruled as to all.

5. **Bills and Notes:** RIGHTS OF PURCHASERS. Where, upon a sufficient consideration moving to himself, a party has given his promissory note to the cashier of a bank to take up the indebtedness of another person due to said bank, such maker will be held liable to one who subsequently purchases said note, even after due; not necessarily because of any right to protection on account of being such purchaser, but because the note could be enforced by the bank for whose benefit it was originally made.

6. ———: ———: ASSETS OF INSOLVENT BANK. In an action by the purchaser of a note sold to him by the receiver of an insolvent bank under an order of court directing such sale, the fact that the entire capital stock of such bank was held by its cashier at the time of the making of such note, or thereafter, constitutes no defense.

ERROR from the district court of Douglas county. Tried below before KEYSOR, J. *Affirmed.*

The opinion contains a statement of the case.

Hastings & McGintie, Hall & McCulloch, F. I. Foss, and *W. R. Matson,* for plaintiffs in error:

The court erred in excluding evidence to sustain the allegations of the answer that the court was without jurisdiction. (*Coffman v. Bradhoeffer,* 33 Neb., 279; *Carlisle v. Corran,* 2 S. W. Rep. [Tenn.], 26.)

The court erred in not considering that the notes sued on were long overdue and were taken subject to all pre-existing equities and defenses. (*Sturges v. Bank of Circleville,* 11 O. St., 153; *Haughton v. First Nat. Bank of Elkhorn,* 26 Wis., 663; *Merchants Bank v. Rudolf,* 5 Neb., 527; *First Nat. Bank of Cedar Rapids v. Erickson,* 20 Neb., 580; *Myers v. Bealer,* 30 Neb., 280; *Clute v. Frasier,* 58 Ia., 268.)

The agreement between Foss on the one side and Stevens and Johnston on the other, that a note should be executed for the full amount of another's indebtedness to the bank and signed by Stevens and Foss as a matter of accommodation to the bank, may be shown by parol evidence. (*Edney v. Willis,* 23 Neb., 56; *Davis v. Neligh,* 7 Neb., 78; *Bridge v. Johnson,* 5 Wend. [N. Y.], 355; *Morgan v. United States,* 113 U. S., 500; *Speck v. Pullman Pal-*

ace Car Co., 121 Ill., 57; *Simons v. Morris*, 53 Mich., 155; *Wood v. McKean*, 64 Ia., 18.)

The court erred in not finding that the charter of the State Bank had expired and that it was not a corporation. (*Louisville Banking Co. v. Eisenman*, 21 S. W. Rep. [Ky.], 531; *Swift v. Smith*, 65 Md., 428.)

The corporation was extinct. (*Sturges v. Vanderbilt*, 73 N. Y., 384; *People v. Walker*, 17 N. Y., 503; *Greeley v. Smith*, 3 Story [U. S. C. C.], 657; *Eagle Chair Co. v. Kelsey*, 23 Kan., 632; *Krutz v. Paola Town Co.*, 20 Kan., 397; *Merrill v. Suffolk Bank*, 31 Me., 57; *Bank of Mississippi v. Wrenn*, 3 S. & M. [Miss.], 791.)

No title passed to the purchaser of the note until the performance of the condition on which it was held. (*Patrick v. McCormick*, 10 Neb., 1; *Roberson v. Reiter*, 38 Neb., 198; *Cincinnati, W. & Z. R. Co. v. Iliff*, 13 O. St., 235; *Worrall v. Munn*, 5 N. Y., 229; *Fairbanks v. Metcalf*, 8 Mass., 230; *Southern Life Ins. & Trust Co. v. Cole*, 4 Fla., 359; *Bank of Healdsburg v. Bailhache*, 65 Cal., 327; *Andrews v. Thayer*, 30 Wis., 228.)

A receiver is not a *bona fide* holder of negotiable instruments. (*Bates v. Wiggin*, 37 Kan., 44; *In re North American Gutta Percha Co.*, 17 How. Pr. [N. Y.], 549; *Lorch v. Aultman*, 75 Ind., 162; *Pittsburgh Carbon Co. v. McMillin*, 119 N. Y., 46; *Hope Mutual Life Ins. Co. v. Taylor*, 2 Rob. [N. Y.], 278; *Litchfield Nat. Bank v. Peck*, 29 Conn., 384.)

The rule of *caveat emptor* applies to receivers' sales. (High, Receivers, sec. 199*b*; Beach, Receivers, sec. 734; *Hackensack Water Co. v. De Kay*, 36 N. J. Eq., 549; *In re Third Nat. Bank*, 9 Biss. [U. S.], 535; *Alexander v. Relfe*, 74 Mo., 495; *Pringle v. Woolworth*, 90 N. Y., 511; *Barron v. Mullin*, 21 Minn., 374; *Foster v. Barnes*, 81 Pa. St., 377; *Manning v. Monaghan*, 23 N. Y., 544; *Arnold v. Weimer*, 40 Neb., 216.)

Charles Offutt, contra:

Defendants entered a general appearance, and proof of

want of jurisdiction was properly excluded. (*Aultman v. Steinan*, 8 Neb., 109; *Raymond v. Strine*, 14 Neb., 236.)

References as to question of escrow: *Wier v. Batdorf*, 24 Neb., 86; *Scott v. State Bank*, 9 Ark., 36; *Massmann v. Holscher*, 49 Mo., 87; *Henshaw v. Dutton*, 59 Mo., 139; *Jones v. Shaw*, 67 Mo., 667; *Walker v. Crawford*, 56 Ill., 449.

References to question of consideration and as to inadmissibility of evidence to show conditions on which the note was held: *Adams v. Wilson*, 12 Met. [Mass.], 138; *Barlow v. Ocean Ins. Co.*, 4 Met. [Mass.], 270; *Russell v. Cook*, 3 Hill [N. Y.], 504; *Yates v. Donaldson*, 61 Am. Dec. [Md.], 290; *Renwick v. Williams*, 2 Md., 356; *Jones v. Berryhill*, 25 Ia., 289; *Thompson v. Shepherd*, 12 Met. [Mass.], 311; *Allen v. First Nat. Bank*, 17 Atl. Rep. [Pa.], 886; *Kaserman v. Fries*, 33 Neb., 427; *Hubbard v. Marshall*, 50 Wis., 322; *Dickson v. Harris*, 60 Ia., 727; *Brouwer v. Appleby*, 1 Sandf. [N. Y.], 158; *Gillett v. Ballou*, 29 Vt., 296; *Brown v. Hull*, 1 Denio [N. Y.], 400; *McSherry v. Brooks*, 46 Md., 103; *Brown v. Spofford*, 95 U. S., 480; *Burnes v. Scott*, 117 U. S., 582.

The pretended escrow agreement was insufficient in law. Even if established it would constitute no defense. Whatever rights the receiver had passed to plaintiff. That plaintiff's purchase was made after maturity is immaterial. Set-off cannot be pleaded against the receiver. (*Harrington v. Connor*, 51 Neb., 214; *Barker v. Lichtenberger*, 41 Neb., 751; *Koehler v. Dodge*, 31 Neb., 337; *State v. Commercial State Bank*, 28 Neb., 677; *State v. Exchange Bank of Milligan*, 34 Neb., 198; *State v. Commercial & Savings Bank*, 37 Neb., 174; *Eastern Bank v. Capron*, 22 Conn., 639; *Haxtun v. Bishop*, 3 Wend. [N. Y.], 13; *Hayes v. Kenyon*, 7 R. I., 136; *Gillet v. Philips*, 13 N. Y., 114; *Alexander v. Relfe*, 74 Mo., 516; *Button v. Hoffman*, 61 Wis., 20; *Winona & St. P. R. Co. v. St. Paul & S. C. R. Co.*, 23 Minn., 359; *Baldwin v. Canfield*, 26 Minn., 43; *Millsups v. Merchants & Planters Bank*, 13 So. Rep. [Miss.], 903; *Louisville Banking Co. v. Eisenman*, 21 S. W. Rep [Ky.], 531; *Swift v. Smith*, 5 Atl. Rep. [Md.], 534; *Pitts-*

burgh Carbon Co. v. McMillin, 119 N. Y., 46; *Foley v. Holtry*,
41 Neb., 563; *In re Penn Bank*, 25 Atl. Rep. [Pa.], 310;
Tuckerman v. Brown, 33 N. Y., 297.)

RYAN, C.

In the district court of Douglas county there were
commenced two actions, in each of which John R. Johnston and Frank H. Connor, receiver of the State Bank of
Nebraska at Crete, Nebraska, were plaintiffs. In one of
these Joseph W. Shabata and Fayette I. Foss were the
defendants, and in the other Mr. Foss was the sole defendant. They were tried to the court upon evidence,
a large part of which was applicable to both cases.
There was a judgment against Mr. Foss and Mr. Shabata
in the sum of $3,014.34 in one case, and against Mr. Foss
in the other case in the sum of $11,638.89. To review
these judgments separate petitions in error have been
filed, but both are argued and submitted as in one case.
We shall not discuss whether the court by the service of
its summons obtained jurisdiction of the defendants, for
there was a voluntary submission to such jurisdiction
before its existence was denied by the answer.

The action against Shabata and Foss was instituted
upon a promissory note alleged to have been made by
the former to the latter and by the latter indorsed, "Demand and notice waived, F. I. Foss," and transferred to
the State Bank of Nebraska. John R. Johnston, by purchase of the assets of the aforesaid bank from its receiver,
became the owner of this note and thereon brought suit
against the maker and the indorser above indicated. It
was contended by the defendants in the district court in
both actions that the State Bank of Nebraska had
originally been organized to exist twenty years and that
this period having expired, the bank had ceased to exist,
and that, therefore, John R. Johnston, by his purchase of
the two notes, had obtained no title. In the first place
we note that there was introduced in evidence no copy

of the original articles of incorporation of the bank in question. By oral evidence it was sought to be shown the ultimate fact above stated as to the organization of the bank; but by testimony of the same character it was shown that by an amendment of the articles of incorporation of this bank the period of its existence was extended so as to cover the transactions involved in this litigation. This latter testimony is corroborated by a copy of a record of the proceedings of the stockholders of said State Bank whereby an amendment extending the term of the existence of said bank was adopted, and it was shown that this amendment had been filed as required by law before the transactions under review took place. Not only was this the case, but it was shown, without question, that the bank had been adjudged insolvent; that a receiver therefor had been appointed, who had duly qualified, and under the direction of this court had sold the assets of the said bank to John R. Johnston, by whom, as such purchaser, the suits had been brought on the notes involved in these proceedings. In this condition of affairs it was proper to find that the transfer vested title in Johnston.

It is complained that the court did not find that Johnston as the purchaser of overdue paper did not stand in the same position as did George D. Stevens to whom Foss transferred the note of Shabata. There could be no question, from a consideration of the evidence, that the district court was fully justified in assuming that a concession of this position would not aid the defendants. It may be conceded, as Mr. Foss testified, that this note was originally placed in the bank with the express understanding between Foss and the cashier that an attorney's fee due Foss from J. R. Johnston and said cashier would be adjusted at a subsequent time instead of being deducted from the amount for which the note was given, but this is immaterial, for, on Mr. Foss' own statement, this fee was not owing to him by the bank. It is, however, insisted that this attorney's fee was properly

pleaded as a set-off to the right of Johnston to recover
on this note against Foss. We shall assume, for the purposes of this case, that when Johnston brought suit on
the note against Foss as an indorser, Foss might properly plead as a set-off against Johnston whatever right
he had to recover attorney's fees due him from Johnston.
It was shown, without leaving room for doubt, that, at
the time the services as an attorney are claimed to have
been rendered for Johnston, Foss was a member of the
firm of Dawes & Foss, under articles of agreement which
required payment of such fees to be made to said firm as
such. Had an action been begun against Johnston it
must have been on behalf of the firm of Dawes & Foss,
for it was due to that firm and not to an individual member thereof. Since Foss could not have maintained an
action in his own name for his own benefit for this attorney's fee, he could not plead and establish it as a set-off
against a cause of action held by Johnston against him.
(*Simpson v. Jennings*, 15 Neb., 671; *Wilbur v. Jeep*, 37
Neb., 604; *Burge v. Gandy*, 41 Neb., 149; *Richardson v.
Doty*, 44 Neb., 73.)

It is complained that the district court excluded proof
that the words "demand and notice waived" were not
on the note of Shabata when Foss placed his indorsement
thereon. There was no motion for a new trial filed by
Shabata. The petition in error was filed by Shabata and
Foss jointly. The assignment that the waiver of demand and notice was not on the note when it was
indorsed and that Foss never consented to those words
being placed over his indorsement was one which was
available to Foss alone. It has been repeatedly held by
this court that a joint assignment of errors in a petition
in error, made by two or more persons, which is not good
as to all who join therein must be overruled as to all.
(*Gordon v. Little*, 41 Neb., 250; *Harold v. Moline, Milburn
& Stoddard Co.*, 45 Neb., 618; *Small v. Sandall*, 45 Neb.,
306.) This assignment, therefore, raises no question
which we can consider. The trial was to the court;

hence the assignments with reference to the admission of incompetent evidence in either of the two cases under consideration will not be considered. This principle is so well settled in this court that it requires no citation of authorities to secure its recognition.

In the case against Mr. Foss alone the recovery was sought upon a promissory note for $10,000, dated June 17, 1892, due three months after date, with interest at ten per cent per annum from maturity, payable to George D. Stevens. It has already been stated how Mr. Johnston became the owner of this note. There is no merit in the contention that Mr. Johnston should have been held to have taken this note subject to whatever defenses existed in favor of the maker against the original payee, for we are satisfied that the district court was justified in finding that this note was enforceable against Foss even in favor of the bank for which Stevens was acting in taking and indorsing it. Mr. Foss had been president and Mr. Stevens cashier of this bank when there had been suffered to accumulate the indebtedness of $10,037 against a customer of the bank. The directors were dissatisfied with this transaction, and it was agreed that Foss and Stevens should take up this claim by giving their note for $7,500, and accordingly the $10,037 note with its chattel mortgage security was assigned to Foss and Stevens. There were renewals of the $7,500 note during the period of several years, sometimes the payment of interest being made, but more often being included in the renewals. There was not an entire uniformity observed in these renewals as to the relations of the parties thereto; hence it was we find that the note sued on was made by Foss & Stevens, whose liability thereon to the bank was apparently that of an indorser. This fact, however, in no degree tended to constitute a defense in favor of Foss in this action.

It was pleaded and sought to be proved that the entire capital stock of the State Bank of Nebraska at Crete was in fact owned by George D. Stevens, and, therefore,

it was urged in argument this action should have been
treated as though the rights of the bank with respect to
this note had never existed.   It was disclosed by the
evidence. that at the time the indebtedness was assumed
by Mr. Foss and Mr. Stevens, then respectively president
and cashier of the bank, its capital stock was held by
various parties, and, as already indicated, its affairs were
supervised by its directors—at least to the extent of
requiring Mr. Foss and Mr. Stevens to assume the payment of an indebtedness, which, as managing officers of
the bank, they had permitted to arise.   At the time this
liability was assumed the capital stock of the bank was
not held by Stevens.   If he ever acquired control of all
the stock, it was after the indebtedness under consideration had been assumed by himself and Mr. Foss.   For
the purposes of this case we shall assume that the acquisition of the entire capital stock by Stevens and his
wife in fact vested the complete ownership of it in Stevens.   When this ownership was acquired he, with Mr.
Foss, was owing the bank nearly, if not quite, $10,000,
and, it seems, the bank was insolvent.   If the result now
contended for should be sanctioned under these circumstances, the rule would be recognized that the cashier of
an insolvent bank, by acquiring its capital stock, could
prevent the collection from himself of any amount which
he might owe the bank, even though such indebtedness
might have arisen from his own dereliction in the performance of his duties as such cashier.   In the case
under consideration the bank was placed in the hands of
a receiver because of its insolvency.   His duties were on
behalf of the creditors of the bank, and except for the
purpose of treating its capital stock as a means of collecting funds for the payment of the creditors of the
bank if resort thereto should be necessary, he had no
concern with such capital stock.   Certainly, under
orders of the court by which he had been appointed as
in this case, he had power to sell the assets of the bank,
thereby conferring on purchasers the right to enforce

payment of evidences of indebtedness to the bank pur-chased, by suits in their own names. In actions of this class it is entirely immaterial how, or by whom, the cap-ital stock of the insolvent bank is owned. Even in actions to recover an ordinary indebtedness this defense pleaded has been held unavailable. (*Harrington v. Connor*, 51 Neb., 214.)

This disposes of all the errors of which complaint is made, except an assignment that the findings are not sustained by sufficient evidence. As there is no good ground for this contention the judgment of the district court is

AFFIRMED.

RAGAN, C., dissenting.

JAMES H. McMURTRY v. COLUMBIA NATIONAL BANK OF LINCOLN.

FILED DECEMBER 9, 1897.   No. 7664.

1. **Execution: APPRAISEMENT: REVIEW.** This court will not review the appraisement made of real estate sold on execution, for the purpose of determining whether such appraisement is too high or too low, unless objections on that ground be made and filed in the court from which the execution issued, before the sale occurred, and such objections be ruled upon by said court.

2. ———: **SALE: REVIEW.** Evidence examined and *held* to sustain the finding of the district court that the execution creditor had not caused the real estate in controversy to be levied upon and sold contrary to a valid agreement existing between himself and the execution defendant.

ERROR from the district court of Lancaster county. Tried below before TIBBETS, J. *Affirmed.*

Field & Brown, for plaintiff in error.

Brown & Leese, contra.

RAGAN, C.

This is a proceeding in error to review a judgment of the district court of Lancaster county confirming an execution sale of real estate.

1. The first assignment is that the value placed upon the property by the appraisers was very much less than its fair value. We cannot review this assignment for the reason that no objections to the appraisal were made and filed in the court from which the execution issued, before the sale occurred. (*Overall v. McShane*, 49 Neb., 64, and cases there cited.)

2. The plaintiff in error insisted in the court below, as a ground for setting aside the sale, that the execution creditor had caused the real estate to be seized and sold contrary to a valid agreement existing between himself and the plaintiff in error, in and by which, for a certain consideration, execution was not to issue until after a year from the date of said agreement; and that the execution on which the sale in controversy was made was issued before the expiration of the year, in violation of the terms of such agreement. The plaintiff in error now insists that the district court erred in finding and holding that no such an agreement existed. To sustain his contention as to said agreement the plaintiff in error filed in the court below his affidavit. The execution creditor in answer to this filed his affidavit, in which he does not deny the making of the agreement claimed by the plaintiff in error, but alleges that it has no reference to the property in controversy here, and specifically points out what property was embraced within that agreement. These two affidavits constitute all the evidence on the subject. We cannot say that the district court reached the wrong conclusion from the evidence before it, and its judgment is

AFFIRMED.

JOHN A. WAKEFIELD ET AL., APPELLEES, V. THEODORE L. VAN DORN ET AL., IMPLEADED WITH FRED MEN-GEDOHT, APPELLANT.

FILED DECEMBER 9, 1897.   No. 7658.

1. **Mechanics' Liens**: FORECLOSURE: PARTIES. Where two contractors furnish labor and material towards the erection of an improvement on real estate in pursuance of separate contracts with the owner therefor, and one of said contractors files his claim for a lien under the statute, and then brings suit to have established and foreclosed such lien, the other contractor is a proper and necessary party to such suit, although at the time the action was brought he had not filed his claim for a lien.

2. ———: ———: ———: DECREE. And the decree rendered in such case is, as to the contractor not made a party, a nullity; and, after completing his contract and complying with the statute, he may bring suit to have established and foreclosed a lien against the real estate upon which the improvement was erected.

3. ———: ———: ———: ESTOPPEL. And in case he does so, the fact that the first suit was pending, to his knowledge, at the time he filed his claim for a lien under the statute does not estop him from maintaining the action.

APPEAL from the district court of Douglas county. Heard below before KEYSOR, J. *Affirmed.*

Joel W. West, for appellant.

Gregory, Day & Day, and *Montgomery & Hall, contra.*

RAGAN, C.

This is an appeal by Fred Mengedoht from a decree of the district court of Douglas county awarding John A. Wakefield a contractor's lien upon certain real estate for labor and material furnished by him for the erection of an improvement thereon in pursuance of a contract therefor with one Theodore Van Dorn, the then owner of said real estate. Mengedoht now owns the said real estate. While Van Dorn was the owner of said real estate he undertook the erection of extensive

buildings thereon, and in the execution of such project
he made a contract with one Specht to furnish certain
labor and material towards the construction of said improvement. Van Dorn also made a contract with Wakefield to furnish the labor and material for the erection
of another part of said improvement. Within four
months of the date of furnishing the last item of labor
or material by Specht he took the steps required by
statute to obtain a contractor's lien against the real estate, and subsequently brought suit to have established
and foreclosed his lien. Wakefield was not made a
party to this action, although his contract with Van
Dorn antedated the bringing of the Specht suit; and
he began furnishing labor and material towards the construction of the improvement before the Specht suit was
brought, and completed his contract, and filed in the
office of the register of deeds an itemized account of the
labor and material which he had furnished toward the
improvement in pursuance of his contract with Van
Dorn, and claimed a lien upon the premises while the
Specht suit was pending. The Specht suit proceeded to
decree in his favor. The real estate of Van Dorn was
appraised, advertised, and sold, Mengedoht becoming the
purchaser. Some time after this sale was confirmed
Wakefield brought the present action to have established
and foreclosed a lien against the premises for the labor
and material which he had furnished Van Dorn toward
the erection of the improvement on said real estate. As
a defense to this action Mengedoht interposed the bringing of the Specht suit; that at that time Wakefield had
not filed any claim for a lien upon the premises in the
office of the register of deeds; that when he did file his
claim for a lien the Specht suit was pending, was notice
to him, and that he was bound by the decree in that
action and estopped from now asserting a lien upon the
premises involved in that decree. This is the argument
relied upon here by Mengedoht for a reversal of the decree appealed from. We think the contention is unten-

able. Since Wakefield, in pursuance of a contract with the owner, began the furnishing the labor and material towards the erection of this improvement prior to the date of the bringing of the Specht suit, his lien, when finally perfected, dated back and attached to the real estate on the date when he furnished the first labor or material. (*Henry & Coatsworth Co. v. Fisherdick*, 37 Neb., 207.) Wakefield, then, was a proper and necessary party to the suit brought by Specht to foreclose his mechanic's lien; and as he was not made a party he was not affected or bound by the decree rendered in the Specht case. (*Steigleman v. McBride*, 17 Ill., 300; *Kelly v. Chapman*, 13 Ill., 530; *Whitney v. Higgins*, 10 Cal., 547; *Jones v. Hartsock*, 42 Ia., 147.) But it is said that Specht, at the time he brought his suit, did not know that Wakefield had furnished any labor or material towards the erection of the improvement; and that, as he had filed no claim in the office of the register of deeds for a lien upon the premises, Specht had no means of ascertaining that Wakefield had a claim upon these premises or a right to perfect a lien against them. The answer to this argument is that Specht was bound to know, at the time he brought his suit, of the claims of all the parties for liens against the premises for labor and material furnished in the erection of the improvement, whether such parties had at that time filed claims for their liens or not. If one mortgage be given to secure the payment of two negotiable promissory notes and the mortgagee assign one of these notes to one person and the other note to a second person and the second person brings suit to foreclose the mortgage for the collection of the note held by him, he is bound to know of the existence of the assignee of the first note and make him a party to the suit or the decree will be void as to such assignee. (*Studebaker Bros. Mfg. Co. v. McCargur*, 20 Neb., 500.) We do not think Wakefield was obliged to intervene in the Specht suit, though he may have had actual knowledge of its pendency at the time he filed his claim for a lien, nor do we know of any principle of law upon which it can be held that his failure to do so estops him from maintaining his present action.

AFFIRMED.

FRANK B. SHELDON, RECEIVER, APPELLANT, V. JAMES D. RUSSELL ET AL., APPELLEES.

FILED DECEMBER 9, 1897.   No. 7625.

Fraudulent Conveyances: EVIDENCE: LIENS ON INSURANCE POLICY: REVIEW. The record examined, and *held* that the findings made and the decree rendered are the only ones that could have properly been made and rendered under the evidence in the case.

APPEAL from the district court of Nemaha county. Heard below before BABCOCK, J. *Affirmed.*

W. H. Kelligar, F. B. Sheldon, and *E. O. Kretsinger,* for appellant.

T. Appelget, G. B. Beveridge, A. W. Field, and *E. P. Brown, contra.*

RAGAN, C.

Frank B. Sheldon, as receiver of the State Bank of Johnson, Nebraska, brought this suit in equity in the district court of Nemaha county alleging in his petition, in substance, that Russell & Holmes, copartners, were indebted to the bank of which he was receiver; that said indebtedness had been reduced to judgment, execution issued and return unsatisfied; that the judgment remained wholly unpaid, and that both Russell and Holmes were insolvent. The petition then alleged that on a certain date Russell & Holmes became the owners of a paid-up life insurance policy for $5,000, which had been issued to one Hickman, and at the same time became the owners of certain promissory notes of said Hickman, calling for a large sum of money; that these notes and this insurance policy were assets of the said copartnership of Russell & Holmes. The petition then alleged that Russell & Holmes, or one of them, wrongfully converted the Hickman insurance policy and notes to his own use and had made a pretended assignment of them to the Farmers & Merchants National Bank of Auburn, Nebraska, and that subsequently said Russell & Holmes, or one of them, had fraudulently assigned said Hickman notes and insurance policy to the First National Bank of Lincoln, Nebraska. The petition contained the usual allegations that these assignments to the banks were fraudulent and made for the purpose of defrauding the creditors of Russell & Holmes and prayed that the assignment might be set aside, and that the said insurance policy and the notes might be decreed assets of the firm of Russell & Holmes, sold, and the proceeds applied to the payment of the receiver's judgment against them. Both said banks and Hickman appeared and answered this petition, and from the decree rendered by the district court the receiver has appealed.

The district court found that Hickman was largely indebted at one time to Russell & Holmes, as an evidence of which he executed to them the notes mentioned by the receiver in his petition, and to secure the payment of these notes he assigned them the insurance policy in controversy; that Russell & Holmes subsequently became largely indebted to the Bank of Auburn, as evidence of which they executed to said bank their notes, and to secure their payment Russell & Holmes assigned to that bank the Hickman notes, together with the insurance policy which secured their payment; and that Russell & Holmes were also largely indebted to the First National Bank of Lincoln, and to secure the payment of that debt they made another assignment of this insurance policy. From these findings the court decreed that Hickman had the legal title to the insurance policy, but that the Bank of Auburn had a first lien thereon to secure the debt of Russell & Holmes to it; that the First National Bank of Lincoln had a second lien upon the insurance policy to secure what Russell & Holmes owed it, and that the receiver was entitled to the equities of Hickman in the insurance policy. These findings and this decree are the only ones that could have properly been rendered under the evidence in the record. The decree of the district court is

AFFIRMED.

ERNEST VAN SKIKE V. DARIUS C. POTTER ET AL.

FILED DECEMBER 9, 1897.　No. 7667.

1. **Physicians and Surgeons:** CONTRACTS WITH PATIENTS: EVIDENCE. The evidence examined and *held* to sustain the findings of the jury that defendants did not contract with plaintiff to effect for him a permanent cure; did not contract to visit and treat him until he was cured; that defendants were not guilty of negligence in the treatment given the plaintiff nor in adopting and pursuing the method of treatment followed by them.

2. ———: DEGREE OF SKILL REQUIRED. The law does not require of a surgeon absolute accuracy either in his practice or his judgment. It does not hold him to the standard of infallibility, nor require of him the utmost degree of care or skill, but that in the practice of his vocation he shall exercise that degree of knowledge and skill ordinarily possessed by members of his profession.

3. ———: MALPRACTICE: PLEADING AND PROOF. A petition alleged that defendants agreed to visit and treat plaintiff until he recovered. The answer was a general denial. The defendants were permitted to testify that, at the date of their last visit to plaintiff, they informed him that they should not return unless they should be requested so to do; that they received no such request and did not revisit plaintiff. *Held,* That this evidence was relevant under the pleadings.

4. **Jurors:** QUALIFICATION: EXAMINATION. In a suit against a surgeon for damages for alleged negligence in operating upon and treating plaintiff's fractured kneecap, the district court refused to permit persons called as jurors to answer, on their *voir dire* examination, whether they were members of any church organization or secret

society. *Held*, That it does not appear, nor can it be inferred from any fact in the record, that the district court abused its discretion or erred in its ruling in this matter.

5. ——: ——: ——. A litigant has the right to examine a person called as a juror for the purpose of ascertaining whether or not there exist grounds for challenging such person for cause; but what questions may be asked such a person, or what range or scope such an examination may take, is a matter committed to the sound discretion of the trial court; and its ruling will not be disturbed unless there has been an abuse of discretion to the prejudice of the party complaining.

6. ——: ——: ——. A juror's *voir dire* examination set out in the opinion, and *held* that the district-court did not err in overruling the plaintiff's challenge lodged against him on the ground of his bias and prejudice.

7. **Physicians and Surgeons**: MALPRACTICE: EVIDENCE. In a suit for damages against a surgeon for alleged negligence in operating upon and treating plaintiff's fractured kneecap, text-books on surgery, though standard authority on the subject, cannot be read to the jury as independent evidence of the opinions and theories therein expressed or advocated.

ERROR from the district court of Seward county. Tried below before WHEELER, J.   *Affirmed.*

The opinion contains a statement of the case.

F. I. Foss, J. D. Pope, Biggs & Thomas, and *W. R. Matson*, for plaintiff in error:

Defendants did not plead that they were discharged. Evidence that the physicians were discharged is not admissible under a general denial. (1 Ency. Pl. & Pr. 849, 850; *Burlington & M. R. R. Co. v. Kearney County*, 17 Neb. 511; *Peet v. O'Brien*, 5 Neb. 362; *Haggard v. Hay*, 13 B. Mon. [Ky.] 175; *Clark v. Finnell*, 16 B. Mon. [Ky.] 329; *Francis v. Francis*, 18 B. Mon. [Ky.] 57; *Curtis v. Richards*, 9 Cal. 33; *Schenk v. Evoy*, 24 Cal. 104; *Lewis v. Coulter*, 10 O. St. 451; *Atchison & N. R. Co. v. Washburn*, 5 Neb. 125; *City of Lincoln v. Walker*, 18 Neb. 244; *Quick v. Sachsse*, 31 Neb. 312; *City of South Omaha v. Cunningham*, 31 Neb. 316; *Smith v. Wigton*, 35 Neb. 460; *Staley v. Housel*, 35

Neb. 160; *Powder River Live Stock Co. v. Lamb*, 38 Neb. 340; *Dinsmore v. Stimbert*, 12 Neb. 434.)

Standard books on medicine and surgery were erroneously excluded from the evidence. (Code of Civil Procedure, sec. 342; *Sioux City & P. R. Co. v. Finlayson*, 16 Neb. 578; *McCandless v. McWha*, 22 Pa. St. 261; *Carpenter r. Blake*, 60 Barb. [N. Y.] 488; *Bowman v. Woods*, 1 Greene [Ia.] 441.)

The court erred in refusing to require jurors upon their *voir dire* to answer questions as to membership in secret societies and church organizations. (12 Am. & Eng. Ency. Law 350; *City of Boston r. Baldwin*, 139 Mass. 315; *Commonwealth r. Moore*, 143 Mass. 136; *Donovan r. People*, 28 N. E. Rep. [Ill.] 964; *Lavin r. People*, 69 Ill. 303; *Monaghan r. Agricultural Fire Ins. Co.*, 18 N. W. Rep. [Mich.] 797; *Pinder r. State*, 8 So. Rep. [Fla.] 837; *Pearcy r. Michigan Mutual Life Ins. Co.*, 111 Ind. 59; *People r. O'Neill*, 16 N. E. Rep. [N. Y.] 68; *People r. Keefer*, 56 N. W. Rep. [Mich.] 105; *Owens r. State*, 32 Neb. 167; *People v. Wheeler*, 55 N. W. Rep. [Mich.] 371; *Omaha S. R. Co. r. Craig*, 39 Neb. 601; *Haugen r. Chicago, M. & St. P. R. Co.*, 53 N. W. Rep. [S. Dak.] 769.)

References as to degree of skill required and as to liability of physicians and surgeons: *Lynch r. Davis*, 12 How. Pr. [N. Y.] 323; *Carpenter r. Blake*, 60 Barb. [N. Y.] 488; *Dale v. Donaldson*, 48 Ark. 188; *Ballou r. Prescott*, 64 Me. 305; *Potter r. Virgil*, 67 Barb. [N. Y.] 578; *Barbour r. Martin*, 62 Me. 536; *Bemus r. Howard*, 3 Watts [Pa.] 255; *Gates r. Fleischer*, 67 Wis. 504; *Hibbard r. Thompson*, 109 Mass. 286; *Wilmot r. Howard*, 39 Vt. 447; *O'Hara r. Wells*, 14 Neb. 403; *Graves r. Santway*, 6 N. Y. Supp. 892; *Carpenter r. Blake*, 10 Hun [N. Y.] 358; *Becker v. Janinski*, 15 N. Y. Supp. 675.

An error of judgment may be so gross as to be inconsistent with reasonable care, skill, and diligence. (*West v. Martin*, 31 Mo. 375; *Howard r. Grover*, 28 Me. 97.)

Physicians and surgeons engaged in practice as partners are all liable for malpractice by a member of the firm. (*Hyrne v. Erwin*, 55 Am. Rep. [S. Car.] 15; *Whittaker v. Collins*, 34 Minn. 299.)

Norval Bros., George W. Lowley, D. C. McKillip, and *J. L. McPheely, contra:*

Evidence that the physicians stated they would not again visit plaintiff unless requested to do so, that they did not receive such request, and did not revisit him, was admissible under the pleadings. (*Omaha & R. V. R. Co. v. Wright*, 49 Neb. 456; 8 Ency. Pl. & Pr. 218, 226, 250; *Smith v. Phelan*, 40 Neb. 765.)

References as to qualification of jurors and as to correctness of the rulings on challenges: *People v. Thiede*, 39 Pac. Rep. [Utah] 845; *People v. Cotta*, 49 Cal. 168; *People v. Fong Ah Sing*, 70 Cal. 8; *People v. McGonegal*, 32 N. E. Rep. [N. Y.] 616; *Spies v. Illinois*, 123 U. S. 131; *State v. Pike*, 49 N. H. 399; *Scott v. Chope*, 33 Neb. 95; *Basye v. State*, 45 Neb. 261; *Detroit W. T. R. Co. v. Crane*, 50 Mich. 182; *Brumback v. German Nat. Bank*, 46 Neb. 540; *Blenkiron v. State*, 40 Neb. 664; *McLain v. Morse*, 42 Neb. 52; *Van Etten v. Test*, 49 Neb. 725; *Wilcox v. Saunders*, 4 Neb. 570; *Garneau v. Palmer*, 28 Neb. 307.

Text-books on medicine and surgery are not books of science, nor competent as evidence. (*Union P. R. Co. v. Yates*, 79 Fed. Rep. 584; *Collier v. Simpson*, 5 Car. & P. [Eng.] 73; *Ashworth v. Kitridge*, 12 Cush. [Mass.] 193; *Ware v. Ware*, 8 Me. 42; *State v. O'Brien*, 7 R. I. 336; *People v. Hall*, 48 Mich. 482; *Gallagher v. Market Street R. Co.*, 67 Cal. 13; *Epps v. State*, 102 Ind. 539; *Commonwealth v. Wilson*, 1 Gray [Mass.] 337; *Melvin v. Easley*, 1 Jones [N. Car.] 386; *Payson v. Everett*, 12 Minn. 216; *St. Louis, A. & T. R. Co. v. Jones*, 14 S. W. Rep. [Tex.] 309; *People v. Donald*, 12 N. W. Rep. [Mich.] 669; *McKinnon v. Bliss*, 21 N. Y. 210; *Morris v. Harmer*, 7 Pet. [U. S.] 558; *Bogardus v. Trinity Church*, 4 Sand. Ch. [N. Y.] 633; *Missouri v. Kentucky*, 11 Wall. [U. S.] 395; *Boehringer v. Richards Medicine Co.*, 29 S. W. Rep. [Tex.] 508; *City of Bloomington v. Shrock*, 110 Ill. 219.)

RAGAN, C.

On July 4, 1890, Ernest Van Skike, while playing baseball, fractured his kneecap. For negligently treating this wound he sued Drs. Potter & Reynolds in the district court of Seward county for damages. The trial resulted in a verdict and judgment in favor of the doctors, to reverse which the plaintiff below has filed here a petition in error.

1. The first assignment of error is that the verdict is not sustained by sufficient evidence. The undisputed facts in the case are that plaintiff's kneecap was fractured at Cordova, Nebraska. One Dr. Doty was immediately called, dressed the wound, and put the plaintiff's leg in a temporary splint; and he was then taken to Beaver Crossing, which appears to have been his home. That night Dr. Greedy was called to treat the plaintiff's wound. He applied adhesive plasters to the knee, put it in roller bandages and a fracture box, and continued to visit and treat the plaintiff. On July 7 the defendants, with Dr. Greedy and at his request, called to see the plaintiff, and made an examination of the plaintiff's wound, and one of the defendants then expressed the opinion that a necessary, or at least a proper, method of treating the plaintiff's wound would be to make incisions in the skin and flesh of the knee and wire the two pieces of the fractured kneecap together with silver wire. On July 10 the defendants, in company with Dr. Greedy and a man named Evans, visited the plaintiff and performed an operation upon his knee. They subjected the plaintiff to the influence of chloroform, made incisions in the skin and flesh covering the kneecap, exposed the same, drilled holes in the two fractured parts thereof, and wired them together with a silver wire. While one of the defendants was drilling a hole in one of the pieces of the kneecap, a movement of the plaintiff's leg occurred, causing the drill to break, leaving the point thereof in the bone. The broken point of this

drill was, by the defendants, left imbedded in the knee-cap. The defendants visited the plaintiff on July 14, 22, 25, and on August 1, but did not return after the last date. The plaintiff, however, did not recover until after the spring of 1891, at which time other surgeons performed another operation upon his knee. At the time this suit was brought, and at the time the trial occurred, the muscles of the plaintiff's leg and thigh were shrunken, and his knee-joint enlarged and stiff. In other words, the plaintiff appears to be permanently injured, and his claim in this suit is that his permanent injury is the result of the negligent treatment given his wound by the defendants.

Under the assignment that the verdict is not sustained by sufficient evidence a specific argument of the plaintiff is that, in consideration of a certain reward promised the defendants, they undertook and promised not only to treat his fractured knee but to effect a perfect cure thereof, so that he should have as healthy a limb and as perfect use thereof as he had prior to the time the injury occurred. The evidence on the part of the plaintiff tends to sustain his contention. The defendants, however, deny that they entered into any contract with the plaintiff in and by which they guarantied to cure him, and the evidence on their behalf tends to support their theory. We cannot say that the jury's finding that the defendants did not undertake or agree to effect a permanent and complete cure of the plaintiff is unsupported by the evidence.

Another special argument of the plaintiff, under the assignment being considered, is that the defendants undertook and promised the plaintiff after performing the operation upon his knee on July 10 to continue to visit him and treat him until he should recover. The evidence on behalf of the plaintiff tends to sustain this contention. The defendants, however, deny that they made such an agreement, and allege that they made no agreement whatever with the plaintiff as to how often or how

long they should visit and treat him, but that they
did visit him in connection with Dr. Greedy, examined
and treated his wound until and including August 1,
at which time they informed the plaintiff that in their
opinion he was doing well, and their further visits would
be unnecessary, and that they should not return again
unless he or Dr. Greedy should request them; and that
they were never requested to visit the plaintiff after said
August 1.   The evidence of the defendants tends to support their contention in this respect, and again we cannot say that the jury's finding in favor of the defendants on this question is not supported by sufficient evidence.

As a part of the assignment under consideration, a
third special argument of the plaintiff is that the defendants were guilty of negligence in adopting and pursuing the method of wiring the plaintiff's fractured
kneecap together with silver wire; and the finding of
the jury that the defendants were not guilty of negligence in adopting and pursuing the method they did
lacks evidence to support it.   On behalf of the plaintiff
numerous physicians and surgeons testified as experts
that the method adopted and pursued by the defendants
in setting the plaintiff's kneecap—that is, by wiring the
fractured portions together—was not the proper method.
On the other hand, the defendants themselves and the
physicians and surgeons called as experts in their behalf testified that the method adopted and pursued by
the defendants in treating the plaintiff's kneecap was a
proper and safe one.   In other words, as is usual, the
experts for the plaintiff agreed with his contention and
the experts on behalf of the defendants agreed with
their contention.   Whether the method adopted and pursued by the defendants was the proper one was a question of fact for the jury, and they, upon conflicting evidence, have acquitted the defendants of negligence in
adopting and pursuing the method they did, and we
cannot say that they reached the wrong conclusion.

Another special argument is that the finding of the jury that the defendants were not guilty of negligence in leaving the broken drill in the bone lacks evidence to support it. Whether leaving this broken drill in the bone was negligence or not was likewise a question of fact for the jury, and the evidence of the surgeons and experts who testified for the plaintiff tends to show that leaving this broken drill in the bone was not good surgery. The evidence of the defendants on the point under consideration was, in substance, that after the operation of wiring the fractured kneecap was completed the plaintiff was suffering greatly; that the temperature of his body was abnormally high, and his pulse abnormally rapid, and that the knee was highly inflamed; that it was impossible to remove the drill point without breaking the bone; that the drill point as well as all other instruments used in the operation had been antisepticized, and it was the unanimous opinion of all surgeons and physicians who testified in behalf of the defendants that under the circumstances the leaving of the drill point in the bone was proper. We cannot say that the jury was wrong in agreeing with the defendant's theory.

A final special argument, under the assignment that the verdict is not sustained by sufficient evidence, is that the defendants were guilty of negligence in not advising the plaintiff of the fact that the drill had been broken and the point left in the bone of his kneecap. This, like the other questions discussed, was a question of fact for the jury. When the defendants found themselves confronted wth the emergency it was a question of professional judgment whether the plaintiff should be advised of the presence of this drill point in his kneecap. It was undoubtedly the honest opinion of the defendants that the plaintiff would receive no harm from the presence of this drill point in his kneecap, and they may have been of opinion that his ignorance of the presence of the drill point could do him no harm while if he knew the fact his anxiety upon the subject might work him an injury.

The jury have found, and the evidence sustains the finding, that the defendants in keeping the plaintiff ignorant
of the presence of the drill point in his kneecap were, in
good faith, exercising their best professional judgment,
and when they did this they cannot be held, as a matter
of law, to have been guilty of negligence, though it afterwards turned out that they were mistaken as to the
effect that the drill point in the bone would have upon
the plaintiff's knee. The law does not require of a physician or surgeon absolute accuracy either in his practice
or his judgment. The law does not hold physicians and
surgeons to the standard of infallibility, nor does it require of them the utmost degree of care or skill of which
the human mind is capable; but that, while in the practice of their vocation, they shall exercise that degree of
knowledge and skill ordinarily possessed by members of
their profession. (*O'Hara v. Wells*, 14 Neb. 403; *Hewitt v.
Eisenbart*, 36 Neb. 794; *Griswold v. Hutchinson*, 47 Neb.
727.)

2.. A second assignment of error is that, on the trial
below, the defendants were permitted to prove that they
were discharged by the plaintiff from further attendance upon him without such discharge being specially
pleaded. After a careful perusal of the entire record
we have failed to find that any such an issue as a discharge was presented to the district court or that the
defendants were permitted to prove a discharge by the
plaintiff. The plaintiff alleged in his petition that he
had employed the defendants to treat him until his injury was healed. This allegation the defendants met
with a general denial. On the trial the plaintiff introduced evidence which tended to support the allegation
of his petition, and the defendants were permitted to
deny this and to state at what times they visited the
plaintiff, and the last time they visited him, to-wit,
August 1, and that they then told the plaintiff that they
should not return again unless he or Dr. Greedy, his
attending physician, should so request them, and that

after that time they were never requested, either by the plaintiff or Dr. Greedy, to revisit the plaintiff. This evidence was all relevant under the issues made by the pleadings.

3. A third assignment of error relates to the refusal of the district court to permit persons called as jurors to answer on their *voir dire* examination certain questions. The plaintiff's counsel propounded to such persons the following questions: "Do you belong to any religious society? Do you belong to any secret society?" Counsel for the defendants objected to these questions and the court sustained the objections, and it is now insisted that in so doing the court committed an error. To sustain their contention counsel cite us to the following authorities:

Donovan v. People, 28 N. E. Rep. [Ill.] 964. In that case the trial judge refused to permit the counsel for the defendant to subject the persons called as jurors to any examination whatever, saying: "Except you examine the jurors for cause through the mouth of the court you cannot examine them at all." The case cited is not in point.

Another case is *Lavin v. People*, 69 Ill. 303. Counsel for the defendant in that case asked the persons called as jurors on their *voir dire* whether they were members of a temperance society or connected with any society or league organized for the purpose of carrying on prosecutions under the temperance laws of the state. The defendant was about to be put on trial under an indictment charging him with selling intoxicating liquors contrary to the statutes of the state, and the supreme court held, and we think properly, that the district court erred in refusing to permit the question asked to be answered.

Another case cited is *Pearcy v. Michigan Mutual Life Ins. Co.*, 12 N. E. Rep. [Ind.] 98. This was a suit upon a life insurance policy, and one of the persons called as a juror was asked on his *voir dire* whether he held a policy issued by the defendant company, and answered "No."

It afterwards turned out that the juror had insured his life in the defendant company for the benefit of his wife, and the court held that the defeated party by reason of this false answer of the juror was entitled to a new trial.

Another case cited is *People v. Wheeler*, 55 N. W. Rep. [Mich.] 371. In this case the people prosecuted Wheeler for keeping a saloon open on Sunday, and a juror testified on his *voir dire* that he had always been "down on liquor selling," and that when sitting as a juror in a case where a liquor seller was interested as a defendant or a witness he had a prejudice against such person. Wheeler then challenged this juror for cause. The trial court over-ruled the challenge and the supreme court reversed the judgment for that reason.

We are unable to see that these cases are authority for the contention of the plaintiff here. In this case was involved, neither directly nor indirectly, any religious or secret society, and we are unable to understand what useful or just purpose of the plaintiff could have been subserved by permitting the jurors to state whether or not they were members of a church organization or a secret society. It is true that a litigant has the right to examine a person called as a juror for the purpose of ascertaining whether or not there exists grounds for challenging such person for cause. But what questions may be asked such a person, or what range or scope such an examination may take, is a matter committed to the sound discretion of the trial judge. No rule can be laid down that would be a safe guide in all cases; and the scope of such an examination, and the pertinency of the questions propounded, are to be determined from the nature of the case on trial. (*Basye v. State*, 45 Neb. 261.) We must not be understood as holding that in no case is it proper to ask a juror on his *voir dire* whether he belongs to a church organization or a secret society. All we decide here is that the district court did not abuse its discretion in this case in refusing to permit the persons called as jurors to state whether they belonged to any secret society or church organization.

4. Another assignment of error argued relates to the action of the district court in overruling a challenge for cause submitted by the plaintiff to one Fuller who was called and examined as a juror, the contention of the plaintiff being that Fuller's examination disclosed that he was biased or prejudiced in favor of the defendants. Fuller stated that he was a married man having a wife and one child; that he was then, and had been for ten years, residing on a farm in Seward county; that he was acquainted with the defendants, but not with the plaintiff; that he was not present at the former trial of this case; that he had heard something about the case from parties who were present at the former trial; that these parties pretended to relate the facts to some extent; that from what he had heard he had not formed or expressed any opinion as to the merits of the case; that the facts related to him made no impression upon his mind, and would not influence his verdict in the present trial; that one of the defendants had been his family physician before his, Fuller's, marriage. The other had been his physician since he was married, but neither of the defendants was his physician at this time. He was then asked by plaintiff's counsel this question:

Would the fact that Dr. Reynolds has been your family physician, and Dr. Potter since you were married, have any effect upon you, if you sit as a juror in this case?

A. It might.

Q. If, after you had all the evidence, the fact of your acquaintanceship with them might be overcome by the same, might it not?

A. It might; yes.

The plaintiff's counsel then challenged the juror for cause. The challenge was resisted by the defendants and their counsel propounded to him the following questions:

Q. Notwithstanding this statement that you have heard, you have formed or expressed no opinion?

A. I have expressed no opinion.

Q. Formed no opinion?

A. I don't think I have formed any opinion.

Q. Have you any opinion now as to the rights of the parties?

A. No; I have not.

Q. Have you any bias or prejudice for or against either of the parties?

A. No; I have not.

Q. Notwithstanding your acquaintance with the defendants in this action, can you render a fair and impartial verdict upon the evidence (the testimony) of the court?

A. I believe I could.

Q. And the fact that you are acquainted with Drs. Reynolds & Potter and that you have employed them in your family, would not interfere with your rendering a fair and impartial verdict on the evidence, would it?

A. Well, I don't hardly believe it would. I believe I said once that it might, but I don't believe it would.

At this point the court took the juror in hand and the following occurred:

Q. You say they are your family physicians at this time?

A. They are not.

Q. How long since either of them was employed by you?

A. About eighteen months.

Q. Have they or either of them been employed frequently by you in your family?

A. Up to that time all the medical assistance we needed.

Q. Your relations were very friendly with them?

A. Yes, sir.

Q. Well, now, what do you say? Would the fact that they have been your family physicians,—would that fact of your relations with them,—have any influence on your verdict in this case?

A. I believe not.

And thereupon the court overruled the challenge. We do not think the examination of this juror disclosed that he was biased or prejudiced either against the plaintiff or in favor of the defendants, and therefore we think the court did not err in overruling the challenge.

5. On the trial the plaintiff offered in evidence extracts from certain standard text-books on surgery. These offers of evidence the district court excluded, and this ruling is the next assignment of error argued. These text-books were offered "for the purpose of showing the practice of reducing fractures of the patella,— simple transverse fractures,"—"and for the purpose of showing that the authors of the books offered in evidence condemn the practice of wiring, and that it should never be resorted to except in cases where the chances of life are equal to that of death, that it is dangerous, and that the results following in the greater portion, and in far more than a majority of the cases, have proved fatally, and of very bad results." It is to be noted that these text-books were offered for the purpose of showing that in the opinion of their authors the wiring of a fractured kneecap was not good surgery. They were not offered for the purpose of fortifying an opinion which had been expressed by an expert upon the witness stand and whose opinion was predicated upon the text-books offered, nor were they offered for the purpose of showing that they contradicted the opinion expressed by such expert. But they were offered as independent evidence to sustain the plaintiff's contention that the wiring of the fractured kneecap by the defendants was not good surgery and therefore negligence. Was this evidence competent? We think that the great weight of authority, both English and American, is to the effect that text-books on surgery, though standard authority, are not competent, independent evidence.

In *Union P. R. Co. v. Yates*, 79 Fed. Rep. 584, it was distinctly held that medical books could not be read to the jury as independent evidence of the opinions therein expressed. The opinion is by Thayer, circuit judge, and, like all that eminent jurist's opinions, it is an able and exhaustive one. Most, if not all, the authorities on the question are cited and reviewed; and we cannot better express our own views on the subject under consideration than to quote that opinion. The learned judge said: "The authorities, both English and American, are practically unanimous in holding that medical books, even if they are regarded as authoritative, cannot be read to the jury as independent evidence of the opinions and theories therein expressed or advocated. One objection to such testimony is that it is not delivered under oath; a second objection is that the opposite party is thereby deprived of the benefit of a cross-examination; and a third and perhaps a more important reason for rejecting such testimony is that the science of medicine is not an exact science. There are different schools of medicine, the members of which entertain widely different views, and it frequently happens that medical practitioners belonging to the same school will disagree as to the cause of a particular disease, or as to the nature of an ailment with which a patient is afflicted, even if they do not differ as to the mode of treatment. Besides, medical theories, unlike the truths of exact science, are subject to frequent modification and change, even if they are not altogether abandoned. For these reasons it is very generally held that when, in a judicial proceeding, it becomes necessary to invoke the aid of medical experts it is safer to rely on the testimony of competent witnesses who are produced, sworn, and subjected to a cross-examination, than to permit medical books or pamphlets to be read to the jury." We cheerfully yield to this case as authority. But it is said in this connection that this evidence was admissible by virtue of section 342, Code of Civil Procedure of this state, which provides that "historical works, books of science or art, and published maps or charts when made by persons indifferent between the parties are presumptive evidence of facts of general notoriety and interest." This is the exact language of section 1906 of the Code of Civil Procedure of the state of California, and in *Gallagher r. Market Street R. Co.*, 6 Pac. Rep. 869, this provision of the Code was construed, and it was held that, by the adoption of this section of the Code, the legislature intended to extend the common-law rule of evidence rather than restrict it, but that the extension was limited by the phrase "facts of general notoriety and interest." The court said: "What are facts of general notoriety and interest? We think the terms stand for facts of a public nature, either at home or abroad, not existing in the memory of men, as contradistinguished from facts of a private nature, existing within the knowledge of living men, and as to which they may be examined as witnesses. It is of such public facts, including historical facts, facts of the exact sciences, and of literature or art, when relevant to a cause, that, under the provisions of the Code, proof may be made by the production of books of standard authority. * * * But medicine is not considered as one of the exact sciences. It is of that character of inductive sciences which are based on data which each successive year may correct and expand so that what is considered a sound induction last year may be considered an unsound one this year, and the very book which evidences the induction, if it does not become obsolete, may be altered in material features from edition to edition, so that we cannot tell, in citing from even a living author, whether what we read is not something that this very author now rejects." We conclude, therefore, that text-books on surgery, though of standard authority, are not competent evidence except as to matters of general notoriety or interest within the meaning of said section 342 of our Code.

6. A final assignment of error argued relates to the

action of the district court in giving and refusing to give certain instructions. The charge of the court is quite lengthy, and it seems to have been prepared with great care, and correctly laid down the law applicable to the facts in evidence in the case on trial. It would subserve no useful purpose to set out the instructions about which complaint is made; and it must suffice to say that after a careful examination of the record we are of opinion that no error, of which the plaintiff has a right to complain, was committed by the district court either in giving or refusing to give instructions. The judgment of the district court must be and is

AFFIRMED.

NORVAL, J., not sitting.

BANKERS LIFE INSURANCE COMPANY, APPELLANT, V. A. M. ROBBINS, EXECUTOR, APPELLEE, ET AL.*

FILED DECEMBER 9, 1897. No. 7628.

1. **Life Insurance:** ACTION ON POLICY: VENUE. A cause of action, or some part thereof, on a life insurance policy arises, within the meaning of section 55 of the Code of Civil Procedure, in the county where the insured died.

2. ———: ———: ———. A life insurance company created under the laws of this state is situated, within the meaning of section 55 of the Code of Civil Procedure, in any county of the state in which it maintains an agent or servant engaged in transacting the business for which it exists.

3. **Principal and Agent:** EVIDENCE OF RELATION. Whether the relation of principal and agent exists between two parties is generally a question of fact, and, while it is not necessary to prove an express contract between the parties to establish such relation, either that must be done, or the conduct of the parties must be such that the relation may be inferred therefrom.

4. ———: ———: INSURANCE COMPANIES. Section 8, chapter 16, Compiled Statutes, declares what conduct on the part of a person shall be conclusive evidence of the fact that he is an agent of a foreign insurance company. The section has no application to an agent of an insurance company created under the laws of this state.

*Rehearing allowed.

5. ——: ——: ——. The fact that a bank collects and remits to a domestic insurance company premiums due from its policyholders, but transacts, and is authorized to transact, no other business for the insurance company, is not evidence which will, of itself, sustain a finding that such bank is the agent of such insurance company within the meaning of section 74 of the Code of Civil Procedure.

6. **Void Judgment:** INJUNCTION: PLEADING AND PROOF. A party against whom a judgment has been rendered by default, which judgment is void for want of jurisdiction over the person of the defendant, is not entitled to an injunction to restrain the enforcement of such judgment unless he makes it appear, both from his pleadings and proof, (1) that he has a meritorious defense to the cause of action on which the judgment is based; (2) that he has no adequate remedy at law; and (3) that his plight is in nowise attributable to his own neglect. .

7. **Adequate Remedy at Law.** An adequate remedy at law within said rule is one that is as practical and efficient to the ends of justice and its prompt administration as the remedy in equity.

8. ——. The remedies at law available to the appellant, the adequacy of such remedies, and whether the plight of appellant was due to his own negligence, discussed in the opinion.

APPEAL from the district court of Lancaster county. Heard below before STRODE, J. *Reversed.*

See opinion for statement of the case.

John H. Ames and *E. F. Pettis,* for appellant:

Service of summons in Valley county was not made upon any agent of the insurance company. There is no evidence that the company ever had an agent in that county, but the contrary is affirmatively shown. The judgment in the district court of Valley county is void. (*Enewold v. Olsen,* 39 Neb. 59; *Chambers v. Bridge Manufactory,* 16 Kan. 270; *Caruthers v. Hartsfield,* 3 Yerg. [Tenn.] 366; *Ridgeway v. Bank of Tennessee,* 11 Humph. [Tenn.] 523; *Bond v. Wilson,* 8 Kan. 228; *Starkweather v. Morgan,* 15 Kan. 274; *Glass v. Smith,* 66 Tex. 548; *Ricketts v. Hitchens,* 34 Ind. 348; *Dobson v. Pearce,* 12 N. Y. 156.)

Relief should be granted when a judgment is shown to be void. (*Blakeslee v. Murphy,* 44 Conn. 188; *Brickley v. Heilbruner,* 7 Ind. 488; *Grass v. Hess,* 37 Ind. 193; *Chambers v. Hodges,* 23 Tex. 110; *Cooke v. Burnham,* 32 Tex. 129; *Glass v. Smith,* 66 Tex. 548; *Collins v. Fraiser,* 27 Ind. 477; *McNiell v. Edie,* 24 Kan. 108.)

Appellant in this action pleaded a sufficient defense to the alleged cause of action in which the void judgment was rendered. The fact that assured, in violation of the policy, concealed the danger to which he was exposed, was sufficient to avoid the contract of insurance. (*North American Fire Ins. Co. v. Throop,* 22 Mich. 146; *New York Bowery Fire Ins. Co. v. New York Fire Ins. Co. of the City of New York,* 17 Wend. [N. Y.] 359; *Hartman v. Keystone Ins. Co.,* 21 Pa. St. 466; *Swift v. Massachusetts Mutual Life Ins. Co.,* 63 N. Y. 186; *Commonwealth Ins. Co. v. Monninger,* 18 Ind. 352; *Goddard v. Monitor Mutual Fire Ins. Co.,* 108 Mass. 56; *Kelsey v. Universal Life Ins. Co.,* 35 Conn. 225; *Ring v. Phœnix Assurance Co.,* 145 Mass. 426; *Jennings v. Chenango County Mutual Ins. Co.,* 2 Denio [N. Y.] 75; *Brady v. United Life Ins. Ass'n,* 60 Fed. Rep. 727; *McFarland v. St. Paul Fire & Marine Ins. Co.,* 46 Minn. 519; *Singleton v. St. Louis Mutual Ins. Co.,* 66 Mo. 63; *Smith v. National Benefit Society,* 123 N. Y. 85; *Dwight v. Germania Life Ins. Co.,* 103 N. Y. 341.)

A. M. Robbins and *Reese & Gilkeson, contra:*

The original action was properly brought in Valley county, and that was the proper place to bring the action. (Code of Civil Procedure sec. 55; *Union Central Life Ins. Co. v. Pyers,* 36 O. St. 544; *Bruil v. Northwestern Mutual Relief Ass'n,* 39 N. W. Rep. [Wis.] 529; *Insurance Co. of North America v. McLimans,* 28 Neb. 657; *Harvey v. Parkersburgh Ins. Co.,* 16 S. E. Rep. [W. Va.] 580.)

There was proper service in Valley county upon agents of the company. (Compiled Statutes, ch. 16, sec. 8; *State v. United States Mutual Accident Ass'n,* 31 N. W. Rep. [Wis.] 229; *Southwestern Mutual Benefit Ass'n v. Swenson,* 30 Pac. Rep. [Kan.] 405; *Voorhees v. People's Mutual Ben-*

efit Society, 48 N. W. Rep. [Mich.] 1087; *Pacific Mutual Life Ins. Co. v. Williams,* 15 S. W. Rep. [Tex.] 478; *Southern Ins. Co. v. Wolverton Hardware Co.,* 19 S. W. Rep. [Tex.] 615; *Reyer v. Odd Fellows' Fraternal Accident Ass'n,* 32 N. E. Rep. [Mass.] 469; *Gibson v. Manufacturers' Fire & Marine Ins. Co.,* 10 N. E. Rep. [Mass.] 730; *St. Louis & S. F. R. Co. v. Deford,* 16 Pac. Rep. [Kan.] 442; *State v. Northwestern Endowment & Legacy Ass'n,* 22 N. W. Rep. [Wis.] 135; *State v. Farmer,* 5 N. W. Rep. [Wis.] 892; *State v. Farmers & Mechanics Mutual Benevolent Ass'n,* 18 Neb., 276.)

The petition for injunction does not state facts sufficient to constitute a cause of action, but does show that appellant had an adequate remedy at law. (*Hurlburt v. Palmer,* 39 Neb. 158; *Anheuser-Busch Brewing Ass'n v. Peterson,* 41 Neb. 897; *Marine Ins. Co. v. Hodgson,* 7 Cranch [U. S.] 332; *Mastick v. Thorp,* 29 Cal. 447; *Englebrecht v. Shade,* 47 Cal. 627; *Hopkins v. Keller,* 16 Neb. 571; 1 High, Injunction secs. 29, 125, 129, 131; *Patterson v. Hill,* 16 N. W. Rep. [Ia.] 599; *Horn v. Queen,* 4 Neb. 108; *Pope v. Hooper,* 6 Neb. 178; *Kittle v. Wilson,* 7 Neb. 76; *Pilger v. Torrence,* 42 Neb. 903; *Paul v. Davidson,* 43 Neb. 505; *Massachusetts Benefit Life Ass'n v. Lohmiller,* 74 Fed. Rep. 23; *Woodward v. Pike,* 43 Neb. 777; *Langley v. Ashe,* 38 Neb. 53; *Norwegian Plow Co. v. Bollman,* 47 Neb. 186; *San Antonio & A. P. R. Co. v. Cockvill,* 10 S. W. Rep. [Tex.] 702.)

Receipt and retention of premiums after loss constitute a waiver of forfeiture of the policy. An insurer cannot hold the fruits of a fraudulent transaction and at the same time plead the fraud of insured. (*Rice v. New England Mutual Aid Society,* 146 Mass. 248; *McGurk v. Metropolitan Life Ins. Co.,* 56 Conn. 528; *Billings v. German Ins. Co.,* 34 Neb. 502; *Farmers Union Mutual Ins. Co. v. Wilder,* 35 Neb. 573; *Zell v. Herman Farmers Mutual Ins. Co.,* 44 N. W. Rep. [Wis.] 829; *Smith v. St. Paul Fire & Marine Ins. Co.,* 13 N. W. Rep. [Dak.] 355.)

There was no competent evidence that statements in

assured's application for insurance were untrue, or that
the risk was hazardous. (*Fraternal Mutual Life Ins. Co.
v. Applegate*, 7 O. St. 297; *Washington Life Ins. Co. v.
Haney*, 10 Kan. 403; *Rawls v. American Life Ins. Co.*, 36
Barb. [N. Y.] 357; *John Hancock Mutual Life Ins. Co. v.
Daly*, 65 Ind. 6.)

RAGAN, C.

The Bankers Life Insurance Company is a corporation
created and subsisting under and by virtue of the laws
of this state, having its domicile and principal place of
transacting its business in the city of Lincoln, in Lancaster county. In October, 1891, it insured the life of
John C. Morrow in the sum of $5,000, payable on his
death to his wife, Anna B. Morrow. Morrow at this time
was a resident of Valley county, Nebraska, in which
county he subsequently died. In the district court of
said county Mrs. Morrow brought suit on said insurance
policy against the insurance company, and a summons
was issued for the insurance company and delivered to
the sheriff of said county for service. This summons
said sheriff duly returned, reciting that he had served
it upon the insurance company in said Valley county by
delivering a true copy thereof to one J. L. McDonough,
the agent of said insurance company in said county, and
that he had served it upon the insurance company in
said Valley county by delivering a true copy of said
summons to J. A. Patton, the cashier of the Ord State
Bank, situate in said county, the chief officer of said bank
not being found in the county, and said bank being then
and there the agent of said insurance company. The
insurance company made no appearance whatever to
this action. In November, 1892, the district court of
said Valley county rendered a judgment by default in
favor of Mrs. Morrow, and against the insurance company, on said insurance policy. Subsequently Mrs. Morrow died testate, and A. L. Robbins was appointed her
executor; and, subsequent to this, Robbins caused an

execution to be issued on said judgment and placed in the hands of the sheriff of Lancaster county, and the insurance company thereupon instituted in the district court of said Lancaster county this action against the sheriff of said county and Robbins, the executor, to enjoin the collection of said execution and the enforcement of said judgment on the ground that the district court of Valley county had no jurisdiction over the person of the insurance company and that the judgment was therefore absolutely void. The trial in the district court of Lancaster county resulted in a dismissal of the insurance company's action and it appeals.

1. Since the insured died in Valley county the cause of action upon the insurance policy, or some part thereof at least, arose in that county within the meaning of section 55 of the Code of Civil Procedure. (*Union Central Life Ins. Co. v. Pyers*, 36 O. St. 544; *Bruil v. Northwestern Mutual Relief Ass'n*, 39 N. W. Rep. [Wis.] 529.) And since the insurance company was a corporation created by the laws of this state, if it was situate in said Valley county within the meaning of said section 55 of the Code of Civil Procedure, then the action of Mrs. Morrow on the insurance policy was properly brought in Valley county, and the insurance company was situate in Valley county within the meaning of said section 55 of the Code of Civil Procedure, if, at that time, it had and maintained in said county a place of business and an agent or servant engaged in conducting and carrying on the business for which it existed. (*Fremont Butter & Egg Co. v. Snyder*, 39 Neb. 632.) And if McDonough, or the State Bank of Ord upon whom the summons was served, or either of them, was then and there the agent or servant of the insurance company in and for said Valley county, engaged in, and conducting and carrying on, the business of the insurance company, the summons was properly served upon such agent or agents, the court had jurisdiction of the insurance company, and its judgment was not void.

8

2. The evidence in the record shows without dispute that at the time this summons was served upon McDonough he was not, and had never been, the agent of the insurance company. He had never taken an insurance application for it, nor had he ever claimed to be the insurance company's agent. At the time Morrow's policy of insurance was applied for an agent of the insurance company was in Valley county and McDonough introduced this agent to a number of persons in that county, and the insurance company desired McDonough to act as its agent in that county, but he never agreed to so act, and he was never appointed by the company, nor did he ever do anything for it from which his agency could possibly be inferred. Whether the relation of principal and agent exists between two parties is generally a question of fact; and while it is not necessary to prove an express contract between the parties to establish such relation, either that must be done, or the conduct of the parties must be such that such relation may be inferred therefrom. Here the record discloses affirmatively that no express contract existed between these parties that would create such a relation, and there is a total want of evidence from which such a relation might be inferred. The district court of Valley county then obtained no jurisdiction over the insurance company by the service of this summons upon McDonough.

3. This brings us to the contention of the appellee that the Ord State Bank was the agent of the insurance company. At all times after Morrow's insurance policy was issued the insurance company would transmit to the Ord State Bank the calls or assessments for the premiums due from its policy holders living in Valley county, at the same time notifying the policy-holder that he could pay his premium, or call, to the Ord State Bank, and that that institution would give him a receipt for such call or premium. The insurance company, when transmitting these calls for premiums to the bank, would forward to it receipts for the policy-holder for the premium, instruct-

ing the bank that when the premium was paid, and it delivered the receipts, to countersign the same. Numerous policy-holders—among them Morrow himself—paid their premiums to this bank under this arrangement between it and the insurance company, and the bank accounted to the insurance company for the premiums thus received. This is the only business or service performed by the bank for the insurance company; and the contention of the appellee is that the conduct of the insurance company and the bank in the matter of the collection and remittance of these premiums is evidence which establishes that the relation of principal and agent existed between them, and that the bank was an agent of the insurance company upon whom service of summons might be had, within the meaning of the statutes of this state. In support of its contention that the bank was such agent of the insurance company the appellee contends that inasmuch as the bank was collecting and remitting the premiums on calls which the insurance company forwarded its policy-holders, section 8, chapter 16, Compiled Statutes, made the bank an agent of the insurance company upon whom service of summons might be had. This chapter 16, Compiled Statutes, is entitled "Corporations," and the first 14 sections of it deal with insurance companies. The first section provides that every insurance company incorporated under the laws of this state shall make specific statements to the auditor of public accounts, which statements shall contain a list of its assets and liabilities, the names of its officers and agents, and their place of residence, etc. The second section makes it the duty of such an insurance company to make these statements to the auditor semi-annually and prescribes what the statements shall contain. The third section denounces a penalty against the president and secretary of any such an insurance company that shall fail to comply with the act. The fifth section of the act provides that no agent of any insurance company created under the laws of any other state or ter-

ritory shall take any risk or transact any business of insurance in the state without first procuring a certificate
of authority from the auditor of public accounts, and before he shall be entitled to such a certificate such an
agent shall furnish the auditor with a statement under
oath, signed by the president or secretary of the foreign
insurance company, showing certain things enumerated
in the section. Section 6 of the act provides, in substance, that no agent of any insurance company created
under the laws of any foreign government other than one
of the states of the nation shall transact any business in
this state without first procuring a certificate of authority
therefor from the auditor of the state, and then the section prescribes what such an agent shall do in order to
obtain such a certificate. Section 7 of the act provides
for an annual renewal of the statements required to be
made to the auditor. Section 8 of the act relied upon by
appellee provides that: "Any person or firm in this state
who shall receive or receipt for any money on account
of or for any contract of insurance made by him or them
* * * or who shall receive or receipt for money from
other persons to be transmitted to any such company or
individual aforesaid, for a policy or policies of insurance
or any renewal thereof, * * * or who shall in anywise directly or indirectly make or cause to be made any
contract or contracts of insurance for or on account of
such company aforesaid, shall be deemed to all intents
and purposes an agent or agents of such company and
shall be subject and liable to all the provisions of this
chapter." Section 10 of said act denounces a penalty of
a fine of $1,000, or imprisonment in the county jail for
thirty days, or both, for violation of the act. Now it is
quite evident that this section 8 simply declares what
conduct on the part of a person shall be evidence of the
fact that he is an agent of a foreign insurance company.
The section was designed to aid the state in prosecuting
agents of foreign insurance companies for transacting
the business of insurance in this state without first hav-

ing procured from the auditor of this state a certificate
of authority therefor. It was never designed nor intended by the legislature by this section that it should
apply to an agent of an insurance company created under
the laws of this state. We conclude, therefore, that if
the fact that a bank collects and remits to a domestic
insurance company premiums due from its policy-holders
is, of itself and alone, evidence which would sustain a
finding that the relation of principal and agent exists
between the parties in such sense that such an insurance
company might be properly served with summons by
leaving a copy of summons with such agent, this result
does not flow from, or depend in any manner upon, said
section 8.

Counsel for the appellee have cited us to numerous
cases which they claim hold that this said section 8, or
statutes in all respects similar, apply alike to persons
or banks acting for foreign and domestic insurance companies. It is not necessary to review these authorities.
Not one of them is in point. They are all cases in which
some person or some bank had received or collected and
remitted premiums due a foreign insurance company
from its policy-holder; and the court simply held, in
accordance with the plain provisions of the statute, that
the receiving and receipting for the premium by the bank
or person, and transmitting the money received to the
insurance company, made such bank or person an agent
of such foreign insurance company upon whom a service
of summons might properly be had. Among the cases
cited is *Southwestern Mutual Benefit Ass'n v. Swenson,* 30
Pac. Rep. [Kan.] 405.

4. A further contention of the appellee in support of
the validity of the judgment of the district court of Valley county is that, independently of said section 8, chapter 16, the Ord State Bank was an agent of the insurance
company within the meaning of section 74, Code of Civil
Procedure. This section is as follows: "When the defendant is an incorporated insurance company, and an

action is brought in a county in which there is an agency thereof, the service may be upon the chief officer of such agency." The argument is that the conduct of the bank in receiving, receipting for, and transmitting the premiums due the insurance company from its policy-holders, with the knowledge and consent of the insurance company, made the bank the agent of the insurance company within the meaning of said section 74. We cannot agree to this contention. It is true that the bank, in doing what it did, was acting as the agent of the insurance company, but it was a special agent for a special purpose. It was not transacting for the insurance company the business for which the insurance company was organized, to-wit, the taking of risks, the issuance of policies, or the renewal of policies. If the insurance company had sent a call against the policy-holder to an attorney in Valley county for collection, that attorney, while engaged in attempting to collect this call or premium, would have been an agent of the insurance company; but he would have been a special agent, and we do not think any one would contend that the insurance company might be brought into the district court of Valley county and subjected to its jurisdiction by a service of summons upon such an attorney as its agent. To sustain his contention that the bank was an agent of the insurance company, within the meaning of said section 74 of the Code, or was situate in said Valley county at the time of the service of the summons upon the bank within the meaning of section 55 of the Code, appellees rely upon *Fremont Butter & Egg Co. v. Snyder*, 39 Neb. 632. But that case is distinguishable from the one at bar. In the Butter & Egg Case the corporation was a domestic one, with its principal place of business in Dodge county. It was a trading corporation engaged in buying, packing, and shipping butter and eggs. It rented a building and had a place of business in Saunders county. It had a man named Darrah there in its employ who was buying and shipping butter and eggs for it and drawing on it for what he paid out on its behalf. Snyder & Co. sued the corporation in Saunders county, and one contention of the corporation was that the district court of Saunders county had no jurisdiction over it, as it could not be sued in that county, its principal place of business being in Dodge county. But this court said, construing section 55 of the Code, that it was situated where it had and maintained a place of business and servants, employés, and agents engaged in conducting and carrying on the business for which it existed. If the Ord State Bank at the time it was served with summons as the agent of the insurance company had been engaged in soliciting insurance the case would be an authority in point. We reach the conclusion that the Ord State Bank, at the time of the service upon it of the summons of the Valley county district court, was not the agent of the insurance company; that the district court of Valley county, by the service of such summons, acquired no jurisdiction over the insurance company, and that the judgment pronounced by it was and is absolutely void.

5. But it does not necessarily follow because this judgment is void for want of jurisdiction over the insurance company that the latter is entitled to an injunction to restrain its enforcement. Injunction suits to restrain the enforcement of judgments have been many times before the courts, as will be seen from an examination of the following cases out of the many in the books: *Horn v. Queen*, 4 Neb. 108; *Scofield v. State Nat. Bank*, 9 Neb. 316; *Colby v. Brown*, 10 Neb. 413; *Young v. Morgan*, 13 Neb. 48; *Gould v. Loughran*, 19 Neb. 392; *Johnson v. Van Clerc*, 23 Neb. 559; *Proctor v. Pettitt*, 25 Neb. 96; *Winters v. Means*, 25 Neb. 241; *Lininger v. Glenn*, 33 Neb. 187; *Janes v. Howell*, 37 Neb. 320; *Langley v. Ashe*, 38 Neb. 53; *Norwegian Plow Co. v. Bollman*, 47 Neb. 186; *Hendrickson v. Hinckley*, 17 How. [U. S.] 442; *Knox County v. Harshman*, 133 U. S. 152; *Massachusetts Benefit Life Ass'n v. Lohmiller*, 74 Fed. Rep. 23; *Fickes v. Vick*, 50 Neb. 401; *Losey v. Niedig*, 52 Neb. 167. Without attempting to review

all or any of these cases we think they are authority for
the following rule: A party against whom a judgment
has been rendered by default, which judgment is void
for want of jurisdiction over the person of the defendant, is not entitled to an injunction to restrain the enforcement of such judgment unless it appears, both from
his pleadings and proof, (1) that he has a meritorious
defense to the cause of action on which the judgment is
based; (2) that he has no adequate remedy at law; and
(3) that his plight is in nowise attributable to his own
neglect. The eminent counsel who represents the appellant in this case concedes that the rule in many
jurisdictions, and in this, is that an injunction will not
be granted to restrain the collection of a judgment void
for want of jurisdiction over the defendant thereto, unless such defendant makes it appear that he had a meritorious defense to the cause of action on which the judgment is based. But the counsel says that the court has
fallen into an error in establishing this rule, and that
he is satisfied, if we will review the authorities and reconsider the principles upon which those cases rest, we
will overrule them. We have re-examined these authorities and reconsidered the principles upon which
they rest and instead of departing from the rule announced by them, we feel satisfied in adhering to it.

One reason for the rule is that equity will not do a
useless thing, and it would subserve no useful purpose
to set aside a judgment void for want of jurisdiction, if
the party asking this had no defense to the action upon
which it was based.

Another reason for this rule is that it is not enough
that the judgment assailed be unlawful. It must be
against conscience as well. We now proceed to apply
the rule just stated to the case at bar, and the first
inquiry is whether the appellant has made it appear
from the pleadings and evidence that he had a meritorious defense to the cause of action upon which this
judgment is based. The district court found that the

appellant had such a defense. This finding is based upon the evidence in the record that Morrow, at the time he made application for and received the insurance policy involved herein, was at enmity with certain persons who had threatened to take his life, and he was then in constant fear and expectation that these parties would murder him; that he fraudulently concealed these facts from the insurance company and thereby induced them to take the risk upon his life which they would not have taken had they been advised of the facts, and that Morrow came to his death at the hands of these parties who had threatened his life. It is true that the finding of the district court is that the appellant had made out a *prima facie* defense. This was all the district court was required to and probably all he should have found on the subject. It was not his duty to go into the merits of the alleged defense of the insurance company any further than to ascertain that the appellant had made out a *prima facie* valid defense, and that it was urging the same in good faith. (*Western Assurance Co. v. Klein*, 48 Neb. 904.) We conclude, therefore, that the finding of the district court that the appellant, both by his pleading and evidence, had made a *prima facie* meritorious defense to the cause of action upon which the void judgment was based is correct.

A second question under the rule is, had the appellant a remedy at law? The insurance company knew that Mrs. Morrow had sued it in Valley county and obtained this information before the time fixed for it to answer by the summons issued in that case. It might have appeared specially in that court and objected to its jurisdiction on the ground that the summons had not been served upon it in that county, nor upon any one who was its agent. After the judgment was rendered it might have prosecuted an error proceeding therefrom to this court, and we think it might have moved the court, under section 602 of the Code of Civil Procedure, to set the judgment aside. If the execution issued on the judgment had been levied upon its personal property, the insurance company might have replevied the same. If the execution had been levied upon its real estate, it might have resisted a suit in ejectment brought by the purchaser at the execution sale. Here, then, is not only a remedy but several remedies at law. But were these remedies adequate ones within the meaning of the rule and the law? In *Welton v. Dickson*, 39 Neb. 707, this court, following the rule laid down by the supreme court of the United States in *Watson v. Sutherland*, 72 U. S. 74, said: "It is not enough that there is a remedy at law. It must be plain and adequate, or, in other words, as practical and efficient to the ends of justice and its prompt administration as the remedy in equity." If the insurance company, on being informed that it had been sued in Valley county, had appeared specially in that court, objected to its jurisdiction over it, and put in the proof that it has in this case, then, had the district court ruled in favor of its jurisdiction, the insurance company might have prosecuted an error proceeding to this court, which would have resulted in a dismissal of the action brought in Valley county. But if the insurance company was not situated in and had no agent in Valley county, within the meaning of sections 55 or 74 of the Code of Civil Procedure, it was entitled to have the suit against it tried in the district court of Lancaster county; and while by appearing specially in Valley county and objecting to the jurisdiction of the court and prosecuting a proceeding in error, if unsuccessful, to this court, it would have obtained the same result that it seeks to obtain by this injunction proceeding, still we do not think the insurance company's remedies by special appearance or motion under section 602 of this Code were adequate ones. A remedy is not adequate, within the meaning of this rule, which compels the citizen to go from the county of his residence into a foreign jurisdiction in which he has never been present and in which he has never been lawfully summoned. The right of the

insurance company to be sued in the county where its
principal place of business was located, or in some
county in which it was situated or had an agent, was
and is a legal right; and it is a strained construction of
language to say that because a litigant may go into a
foreign jurisdiction and enter a special appearance to
an action, that that remedy is adequate, when, beside
the costs, expenses, and time spent in attending court
in the foreign jurisdiction, he is compelled to surrender
valuable legal rights. The insurance company might
have taken this judgment to the supreme court on error
proceeding at any time within one year after its rendition, but that remedy would not have been adequate,
because the record discloses on its face that the insurance company had been duly summoned in Valley
county, and in that proceeding it could not have introduced evidence to show that it in fact had no agent or
agency in that county upon whom service of process
could be made. Had the insurance company waited
until the sheriff levied upon its personal property and
replevied it, or had it waited and resisted an ejectment
suit by the purchaser of its real estate at execution sale,
then the record discloses that it would have had no
redress for the costs expended by it in prosecuting the
replevin action or in resisting the ejectment suit, as the
appellees were wholly insolvent. In this connection we
deem it proper to say we do not think that the provisions
of section 602 of the Code contemplate a void judgment,
but one which is voidable by reason of some fraud or
irregularity. Such a construction indeed has by the
supreme court of the state of Iowa been placed upon a
section of the Iowa Code identical with said section 602.
(See *Leonard v. Capital Ins. Co.*, 70 N. W. Rep. [Ia.] 629.)
Yet, while we think that the provisions of said section
of the Code specially apply to voidable judgments, we
do not doubt that one against whom a judgment has
been rendered, which is void for want of jurisdiction
over it, may have such judgment set aside under the

third subdivision of said section of the Code, as having been irregularly obtained. Our conclusion is, that while the insurance company had a remedy at law, such remedy was not an adequate one; that in order to avail itself of some of these remedies it would have been compelled to sacrifice other legal valuable rights; and to have resorted to others it would have suffered damages for which it could have received no redress.

A final inquiry under the rule is whether the plight or condition in which the insurance company finds itself is in anywise attributable to its own neglect. We do not think it is. It is true that while it had been advised that it had been sued in Valley county it made no move to defend itself; but we are clearly of opinion that this was neither negligence nor evidence of negligence. It was a state corporation domiciled in Lancaster county; and by the very law of its creation could be sued only in that county, unless it had voluntarily established a place of business or appointed an agent in some other county for the transaction of its business. It was not guilty of negligence in failing to take notice of rumors, or even correct information, that it had been sued in a jurisdiction in which it did not reside, in which it was not suable, and in which it had no agent on whom service of process could be made. It was compelled to presume that the district courts knew the law of the land and it had the right to suppose that they would rule in accordance with that law.

The decree of the district court is reversed and a judgment will be entered here decreeing the judgment of the district court of Valley county to be absolutely void for want of jurisdiction over the person of the defendant therein, and perpetually enjoining the appellees and those claiming under them from enforcing, or attempting to enforce, the collection of such judgment.

DECREE ACCORDINGLY.

JOHN P. HIGGINS, APPELLEE, V. KENT K. HAYDEN,
RECEIVER, APPELLANT.

FILED DECEMBER 9, 1897.   No. 7622.

1. **Banks and Banking**: BILL OF EXCHANGE: COLLECTION: TITLE. Evidence examined and *held* to show that a bill of exchange, drawn to the order of a bank by its customer, the amount of which was placed to the customer's credit, became the property of the bank, and was not entrusted to it merely for collection.

2. ———: INSOLVENCY: TRUSTS: PLEADING. A petition seeking to charge a trust on property in the hands of the defendant, the receiver of an insolvent bank, may allege that the bank obtained the property as bailee, and at the same time charge that it was obtained by fraudulent concealment of insolvency, and relief may be granted on the latter ground, although the former be not proved.

3. ———: ———: FRAUD: DEPOSITS. Where a bank remains open and holds itself out as ready to transact business, this is an implied representation of solvency, and for its officers to then receive a deposit, knowing it to be hopelessly insolvent, is a fraud.

4. ———: ———: ———: ———: RESCISSION. The depositor under such circumstances may rescind the contract of deposit and recover back the thing deposited, while it or its proceeds may be distinguished in specie, and before they have become commingled with the general assets of the bank.

5. ———: ———: ———: ———: EVIDENCE. Certain stipulations in the record *held* to justify a finding that the proceeds of the deposit in question had been preserved separate, and not commingled with the general assets.

APPEAL from the district court of Lancaster county. Heard below before TIBBETS, J. *Affirmed.*

The opinion contains a statement of the case.

Cobb & Harvey and *G. M. Lambertson*, for appellant:

The draft was not deposited for collection but for credit, and the only relation between the parties is that of debtor and creditor. (*National Commercial Bank v. Miller*, 77 Ala. 168; *St. Louis & S. F. R. Co. v. Johnston*, 27 Fed. Rep. 243; *Ditch v. Western Nat. Bank*, 10 Banking L. J. 354.)

The alleged insolvency of the bank affords the plaintiff no ground of action. (*Redington v. Roberts*, 25 Vt. 686; *Patton v. Campbell*, 70 Ill. 72; *Smith v. Smith*, 21 Pa. St. 367; *Nichols v. Pinner*, 18 N. Y. 295.)

The court erred in rendering judgment for interest. (*White v. Knox*, 111 U. S. 784.)

A. G. Greenlee, contra:

The draft remained the property of the appellee, as did also the proceeds. (*Freeholders v. State Bank*, 32 N. J. Eq. 467; *Hazlett v. Commercial Nat. Bank*, 19 Atl. Rep. [Pa.] 55; *National Gold Bank & Trust Co. v. McDonald*, 51 Cal. 64; *Scott v. Ocean Bank*, 23 N. Y. 289; *Beal v. City of Somerville*, 50 Fed. Rep. 647.)

The bank did not become the owner of the draft in controversy for the reason that it was hopelessly insolvent at the time, and was known to be so by the president who received this draft. Its receipt for any purpose was such a fraud upon the appellee as would prevent the bank from acquiring title. (*Williams v. Lowe*, 4 Neb. 394; *St. Louis & S. F. R. Co. v. Johnston*, 133 U. S. 576; *Wilson v. Coburn*, 35 Neb. 530.) ·

The appellee is entitled to interest from the time receiver obtained the money. (*Thompson v. Gloucester City Savings Institution*, 8 Atl. Rep. [N. J.] 97; *Moors v. Washburn*, 34 N. E. Rep. [Mass.] 182; *Judd v. Dike*, 15 N. W. Rep. [Minn.] 672.)

IRVINE, C.

The plaintiff, Higgins, was a customer and depositor of the Capital National Bank of Lincoln, and on the morning of January 19, 1893, drew a bill of exchange on George Burke & Frazier, of South Omaha, for $2,000, to the order of the bank, and tendered it to the teller, saying that he had checks outstanding which would overdraw his account and that he desired credit for the draft. The teller referred him to the president of the bank, who at first hesitated to allow credit for the draft, but on plaintiff's informing him of the outstanding checks agreed to do so, saying: "Well, we will give you credit for it, but if Burke & Frazier don't pay it you will be overdrawn just the same. We will take care of your checks." Thereupon a deposit slip was made out, which, with the draft, was handed to the teller, who then gave plaintiff credit on his pass-book for $2,000. Plaintiff's account was that morning overdrawn $5.15. Plaintiff, on obtaining the credit, drew a check for $10, which was cashed, and during the day a check previously drawn for $1,000 was presented and paid,—all against the credit obtained by the draft. The bank was at the time irretrievably insolvent and its president knew that fact. It remained open and transacted business until the afternoon of January 21, but did not open thereafter and was soon placed in the custody of a receiver. On the 20th and 21st there were certain small deposits and checks by the plaintiff, the net effect of which was to leave the bank indebted to the plaintiff at the time of its failure in the sum of $998.20. The bank on receiving the draft had immediately sent it to the South Omaha National Bank, its correspondent. It was accepted, and on the 21st paid to the South Omaha bank, and its amount was then credited by the South Omaha bank to the Lincoln bank. On the failure of the Lincoln bank the plaintiff undertook to arrest the proceeds of the draft, to the extent of the Lincoln bank's debt to him, in the hands of the South Omaha bank. This sum was held by the South Omaha bank for some months and was finally paid to the receiver under some arrangement whereby it was to be held by him to await the result of this case, which was then begun by the plaintiff against the receiver to charge a trust upon the fund. The finding and judgment of the district court were in favor of the plaintiff and the receiver appeals.

The case was presented upon the principal theory that the draft had been entrusted to the Lincoln bank merely for collection, and that it remained the plaintiff's property, subject only to a lien in favor of the bank for the sums advanced on the faith thereof. We think the proof failed to support this theory. The evidence shows, without contradiction, that the plaintiff had drawn checks to the amount of more than $1,000 against an already overdrawn account, and that he realized the necessity of securing a credit at the bank which would protect them. The bank received the draft with the distinct understanding that a credit was to be given which had already been drawn against, it paid outstanding checks in pursuance of that understanding and cashed a check contemporaneously with the deposit. The conduct of the parties is entirely inconsistent with the theory of a bailment for collection. It establishes as clearly as evidence could that the draft was drawn for the benefit of the bank and in consideration of an immediate credit of its face value.

The petition, however, contained averments of the bank's insolvency and of its president's knowledge thereof, and that the draft had been procured through the president's fraudulent concealment of the bank's condition, and relief was asked also on that ground. Appellant urges that the latter theory is inconsistent with that already discussed, and that the plaintiff cannot be heard to urge it in connection therewith. We do not think that the two theories are inconsistent. One may, with perfect consistency, say, "You obtained my property as bailee for a special purpose, and you shall not claim it for your own," and at the same time say, "You obtained possession of my property by fraud, and whether it was by bailment or sale I wish to rescind the contract and recover the property." The bill in the case of *St. Louis & S. F. R. Co. v. Johnston*, 133 U. S. 566, was framed in a very similar manner. The circuit court held that the two theories were inconsistent (27 Fed. Rep. 243), but the supreme court of the United States reversed the decree of the circuit court and granted relief on both grounds, holding that the pleading was regular.

Where a bank remains open, holding itself out as
ready to transact business, this is an implied representation of solvency, and for it to receive a deposit when
its insolvency is known to its officers is a fraud upon the
depositor. (*St. Louis & S. F. R. Co. v. Johnston, supra;
Cragie v. Hadley*, 99 N. Y. 131; *Anonymous*, 67 N. Y. 598;
*American Trust & Savings Bank v. Gueder & Paeschke Mfg.
Co.*, 150 Ill. 336; *Peck v. First Nat. Bank*, 43 Fed. Rep.
357; *Wasson v. Hawkins*, 59 Fed. Rep. 233.)   The depositor may, therefore, at his election, rescind the contract of deposit and recover back the money or property,
but he must do so before the deposit has become commingled with the general assets of the bank. (*Wilson v.
Coburn*, 35 Neb. 530.)   Had in this case such a commingling taken place?

The South Omaha bank was a regular correspondent
of the Lincoln bank and did not remit collections made
for it in specie or as distinct remittances.   It credited
the Lincoln bank with funds as they were collected, and
transferred balances on orders of the Lincoln bank in
round sums as they accrued and the Lincoln bank demanded.   When the draft was received by the South
Omaha bank the account of the Lincoln bank seems to
have been overdrawn, as appears from a memorandum
on the letter acknowledging the draft.   On the morning
of January 21, there was to the credit of the Lincoln
bank $1,025.05.   The $2,000 draft was paid that day and
passed to its further credit, and there was an additional
credit of $1,751.04, making a total credit of $4,776.09.
The Lincoln bank that day drew $3,000, leaving a bal-
ance in favor of the Lincoln bank at the time of the failure, of $1,776.09.   This was certainly evidence tending,
at least, to show that there had been a commingling of
the proceeds of the draft with the funds of the Lincoln
bank, by using such proceeds at least in part for the
payment of drafts of that bank.   This would seem to
follow from the rules laid down in a somewhat similar
case by the supreme court of the United States.   (*Com-*
9

mercial Nat. Bank v. Armstrong, 148 U. S. 50.) We are,
however, embarrassed in the consideration of this question by certain stipulations appearing in the bill of exceptions. At the commencement of the trial it was stipulated "that the money in controversy was in the hands
of the South Omaha National Bank at the time of the
failure of the Capital National Bank, and the appointment of a receiver thereof, and was remitted by the
said South Omaha National Bank to the receiver on or
about the 19th day of July, 1893, and that the fact that
the money was so transferred from the possession of
the South Omaha National Bank to the possession of the
receiver shall not affect or prejudice the rights of the
plaintiff to the same." Giving this stipulation its reasonable effect, it would seem to recognize that the specific money collected on this draft was retained by the
South Omaha bank, and that it was still retained separately by the receiver in such manner as to protect the
rights of plaintiff. Nevertheless, at the close of the bill
of exceptions we find counsel for the receiver making
the following statement: "It is stipulated that the meaning of the words 'money in controversy' as used in the
stipulation at the beginning of this case has reference
to the balance due the Capital National Bank from the
South Omaha National Bank at the date of its remittance to the receiver of the Capital National Bank. The
defendant does not admit, however, that said sum is a
part of the money collected, but claims and reserves the
right to show by competent testimony that it was
mingled with other funds of the Capital National Bank
prior to the date of its remittance to the receiver." This
was followed by a statement by counsel for the plaintiff,
after a formal objection to the introduction of a statement of the account between the two banks which was
of no consequence on this issue because it disclosed no
dates of payments, that "the reservation of the defendant in the stipulation having been made after the case
was tried and argued, the plaintiff will ask leave, if he

so desires, to introduce testimony upon the matters set forth in the reservation." It will be observed that the modification of the stipulation had in view, not the substitution of other facts by agreement for those stipulated, but that it seemed to contemplate merely the withdrawal of any estoppel from proving the facts in this very vital respect to be contrary to those stipulated, that plaintiff did not resist the modification so claimed, but merely claimed the right to himself introduce evidence on the issue so injected. So far as appears from the record neither side availed itself of the privilege of offering further proof, and a reasonable construction of the record is that the stipulation was to stand, except as the defendant by further proof, which it does not appear he adduced, should rebut one feature thereof. In this light it was proper for the district court to consider the stipulation as of full effect in establishing that the fund had been preserved separate by the collecting agent, and that it had gone to the receiver under an agreement to continue its separate custody.

Finally it is contended that the district court erred in allowing interest under the circumstances. In the absence of statute this contention would have much force, but the point has heretofore been determined adversely to the defendant upon a construction of our statute. (Compiled Statutes, ch. 44, sec. 4; *Capital Nat. Bank v. Coldwater Nat. Bank*, 49 Neb. 786.)

AFFIRMED.

UNITED STATES NATIONAL BANK OF OMAHA v. J. H. GEER ET AL.*

FILED DECEMBER 9, 1897. No. 7607.

1. **Negotiable Instruments**: INDORSEMENT: TITLE: INTENT. The question whether title passes to a negotiable instrument delivered to a bank under a restrictive but ambiguous indorsement, without an

*Rehearing allowed.

express contract, but in pursuance of an established usage, is one of fact rather than law, and depends on the intent of the parties.

2. ———: ———: FORM: PAROL EVIDENCE. As between the immediate parties the form of an indorsement is not conclusive, but the nature of the contract may be proved by parol evidence.

3. ———: SALE: BAILMENT. Evidence examined, and *held* to show a sale of the instrument in controversy, and not a bailment for collection.

4. **Sales:** FRAUD: RESCISSION: BANKS: INSOLVENCY. The right to rescind a sale for fraud is lost if not exercised before the vendee transfers the property to an innocent purchaser for value. This rule applies to an attempt to recover a chose in action sold to an insolvent bank in ignorance of its insolvency, as against the claims of a transferee from the bank who has parted with value on the faith of the bank's title.

ERROR from the district court of Nuckolls county. Tried below before HASTINGS, J. *Reversed.*

J. C. Cowin and *W. D. McHugh*, for plaintiff in error.

References: *Metropolitan Nat. Bank v. Loyd*, 25 Hun [N. Y.] 101, 90 N. Y. 530; *First Nat. Bank of Elkhart v. Armstrong*, 39 Fed. Rep. 231; *Cragie v. Hadley*, 99 N. Y. 131; *Ayers v. Farmers & Merchants Bank*, 79 Mo. 421; *Wasson v. Lamb*, 120 Ind. 514; *Titus v. Mechanics Nat. Bank*, 35 N. J. Law 588; *Strong v. King*, 35 Ill. 1; *In re State Bank*, 56 Minn. 119; *Holmes v. First Nat. Bank of Lincoln*, 38 Neb. 326.

O. H. Scott and *Cobb & Harvey*, contra.

References: *National Bank v. Burkhart*, 100 U. S. 692; *Barnard v. Kellogg*, 10 Wall. [U. S.] 390; *Beal v. City of Somerville*, 50 Fed. Rep. 650; *Manufacturers Nat. Bank v. Continental Bank*, 148 Mass. 553; *St. Louis & S. F. R. Co. v. Johnston*, 133 U. S. 566; *Moors v. Goddard*, 147 Mass. 288; *Fifth Nat. Bank v. Armstrong*, 40 Fed. Rep. 46; *St. Louis & S. F. R. Co. v. Johnston*, 27 Fed. Rep. 243, 133 U. S. 566; *Hoffman v. First Nat. Bank of Jersey City*, 46 N. J. Law 605; *Levi v. National Bank of Missouri*, 5 Dill. [U. S.] 107; *Balbach v. Frelinghuysen*, 15 Fed. Rep. 683; *Branch v. United States Nat. Bank*, 50 Neb. 470; *First Nat. Bank of Chicago v. Reno County Bank*, 3 Fed. Rep. 257; *Freeman's Nat. Bank v. National Tube Works Co.*, 151 Mass. 413; *Blaine v. Bourne*, 11 R. I. 119; *City Bank of Sherman v. Weiss*, 67 Tex. 331; *White v. Miners Nat. Bank*, 102 U. S. 659; *Peck v. First Nat. Bank*, 43 Fed. Rep. 357.

IRVINE, C.

This was an action by the United States National Bank of Omaha to recover the amount of a certificate of deposit for $5,500 issued by the defendants Geer and Mease, partners in the banking business at Nelson under the name of the Commercial Bank, to the order of the defendant Craven, by him indorsed and transferred to the defendant the First National Bank of Hebron. It is claimed by the plaintiff that the certificate was by the Hebron bank sold and transferred to the Capital National Bank of Lincoln and by the Lincoln bank to the plaintiff. The Hebron bank, by its answer, asserts ownership in itself, claiming that the Lincoln bank received the certificate merely as the agent of the Hebron bank, for the purpose of collection, and that the indorsement being restrictive, the Lincoln bank could not and did not pass title to the Omaha bank. The right to the certificate as between these two parties is the only matter in contest, there being no issues affecting the other defendants except such as may be incidental to the controversy indicated. The district court found in favor of the Hebron bank and entered judgment accordingly.

Similar questions have been presented to the courts with such frequency and such variety of detail that there now appear in the books an array of opinions which would be hopelessly confusing were they to be considered as tending to establish general rules of law for determining such questions. They range all the way from those holding that, as between the parties even, title passes by the legal import of words used by way of indorsement, regardless of intent, to those practically resting the mat-

ter on the presumed motive of the indorser, disregarding
entirely the form of the transaction and the contractual
intent. While intermediate to these extremes are found
many cases presenting marked resemblances to that before us, and solved in different ways by different courts,
we are saved the necessity of an analysis of such cases
for the purpose of inducing therefrom a general rule of
law, by attention to a very simple proposition recognized
in effect by counsel on both sides. A moment's reflection
will show that the question is not what legal relations
result from a deposit for collection alone, or from a sale
or discount, but it is whether this was such a deposit or
a sale; that is, whether title passed. The solution of this
question rests in determining the common intent of the
parties,—a question of fact and not of law. Among the
cases expressly or by clear implication treating the question as one of fact are *Metropolitan Nat. Bank v. Loyd*, 25
Hun [N. Y.] 101, 90 N. Y. 530; *Titus v. Mechanics Nat.
Bank*, 35 N. J. Law 589; *In re State Bank*, 56 Minn. 119;
Fifth Nat. Bank v. Armstrong, 40 Fed. Rep. 46; *St. Louis &
S. F. R. Co. v. Johnston*, 133 U. S. 566.

There is no conflict in the evidence. Such doubts as
exist arise as to inferences from facts proved, and not as
to the existence of those facts. For ten years preceding
the events in controversy the Hebron bank and the Lincoln bank had a continuous course of dealings with one
another, the Hebron bank keeping an account with the
Lincoln bank, and remitting to it from time to time
drafts, checks, and other instruments, which were either
at once or upon collection placed to the credit of the
Hebron bank. It is said that the banks were not "correspondents," but, so far as the evidence discloses, the
only difference between their relations and those of banks
confessedly occupying the relation in contemplation by
witnesses who use that somewhat ambiguous term was
that while the Hebron bank drew drafts for general banking purposes upon its correspondents at Omaha, and
eastern cities, it drew against its credit at the Lincoln

bank only for the purpose of transferring funds to its so-called correspondents, and not in favor of its customers generally. So far as the treatment of paper sent by the Hebron bank was concerned, there was no difference between its relations with the Lincoln bank and with its Omaha correspondent. We mention this fact merely because in argument some stress seems to be laid on the supposed difference in relations. There is no room for doubt that the motive which influenced the Hebron bank to maintain the account at Lincoln was to secure an economical method of collecting its "foreign paper," or, more accurately, to secure an economical and speedy method of realizing cash, or a credit equivalent thereto, upon such paper. The motive of the Lincoln bank appears only by inference. It collected paper at par, except where it was itself subjected to expense in favor of third parties, and then charged against the paper only the expense so incurred. It paid the Hebron bank interest on daily balances. It seems quite clear that its motive, therefore, was to obtain the temporary use of the property of the Hebron bank so entrusted to it, for banking purposes. Paper remitted was divided into two classes, styled by most of the witnesses "cash items" and "collections," by officers of the Hebron bank as "sight items" and "time items." It is certain, however, that the latter nomenclature was inaccurate, as the distinction was only partly based on the time of payment. In the "cash items" were included all instruments presently payable on solvent banks and between individuals of known solvency. Other paper belonged to the collection class. The classification was determined by the character of the paper and not by the form of indorsement or the terms of the transmitting letter. Thus the form of indorsement on both classes seems to have been "Pay to the order of R. C. Outcault, Cash., for account of First National Bank of Hebron, Nebr." In remitting, printed forms were used, bearing after the address the words "Enclosed please find for collection and ——." The blank was usually filled with the abbreviation "Cr." All witnesses agree that the language so employed was not regarded as of any significance in determining the disposition of the paper. If the paper fell within the "collection" class it was noted on the Hebron bank's collection register as having been sent, and its number on that register was noted on the blank with which it was transmitted. On receipt by the Lincoln bank it was entered on the latter's collection register, and the Hebron bank was by mail notified that it had been received and would obtain "prompt attention." When collected it would be credited to the Hebron bank, and the latter notified of the fact. The Hebron bank would then charge its amount to the Lincoln bank. If the paper was a "cash item," the Hebron bank would charge it to the Lincoln bank at once on remitting it, the Lincoln bank would credit it to the Hebron bank immediately on its receipt, and notify the Hebron bank that it had been so credited. No further notice would be sent the Hebron bank unless the paper should be dishonored, in which event its amount would be charged to the Hebron bank and the latter so notified, the paper being returned. Interest was paid on the general balance, including as it did those cash items which had been credited upon their receipt but not yet collected. It would seem that by the custom of banks in such cases, when a credited item is dishonored, interest thereon is charged to the remitting bank from the time credit was given, and that the Lincoln bank was authorized by such custom to so treat the Hebron bank, but it would also seem that such right was never in fact exercised. During the period referred to certain notes of the Hebron bank were rediscounted by the Lincoln bank, and some of these not being paid at maturity, the Lincoln bank exercised, and the Hebron bank acknowledged, the right to immediately charge them back to the Hebron bank in the same manner as dishonored "cash items." The balance at any time to the credit of the Hebron bank was subject to be drawn upon, including that amount representing credited but uncollected cash items. The officers of the Hebron bank testify that they habitually refrained from so drawing until a reasonable time should elapse for the collection of such items, and that they regarded the privilege of sooner drawing as an act of courtesy and not a legal right; but there can be little doubt that both banks regarded the apparent balance as an available fund and that abstention from drawing by the Hebron bank, prior to the collection of items, was an act of convenience or prudence on its part, rather than the recognition by it that the apparent credit was premature.

On January 20, 1893, the Hebron bank, being then the owner of the certificate of deposit in controversy, remitted it with other items to the Lincoln bank. It was indorsed in the usual manner, "for account of" the Hebron bank, and was transmitted as usual "for collection and credit." It was treated by both banks as a "cash item" in the manner above described. On sending it the Hebron bank charged it to the Lincoln bank, and on receiving it the Lincoln bank credited it to the Hebron bank and notified the latter of that fact. It was received by the Lincoln bank on the 21st and the same day transmitted to the plaintiff, the Omaha bank, under substantially similar circumstances, and in pursuance of similar usages and a similar course of dealing. The Lincoln bank charged it to the Omaha bank and the latter credited it to the Lincoln bank. On the morning of the 21st the account of the Lincoln bank was overdrawn with the Omaha bank some $1,900. Including the amount of the certificate, credits were that day given the Lincoln bank amounting to over $18,000. The Omaha bank that day paid out on checks and drafts of the Lincoln bank nearly $17,000. It thus appears that the whole of the credit obtained by the certificate was the same day exhausted by payments actually made in favor of the Lincoln bank. The Lincoln bank was hopelessly insolvent, to the knowledge of its officers, and was closed on the afternoon of the 21st, never to reopen. On the 23d the certificate was presented to the Nelson bank and payment refused because of the claim interposed by the Hebron bank.   Perhaps certain other facts of which the court takes notice are of some import.   Nelson, where the certificate was payable, is in the county adjoining that in which Hebron is located, to the west, and the two towns are connected by a line of railroad.   Lincoln is a considerable distance to the northeastward of both towns, and Omaha is still farther northeast.   It is not claimed that the diversion of paper from its natural geographical course is in itself any proof that it is being transmitted for other purposes than collection, but the fact that the Hebron bank found it profitable to send the paper through such a course indicates that the purpose of the Lincoln bank was to use the paper otherwise than as a direct collecting agent, and throws some light on the understanding of both parties as to what such use might be.

Certain aspects of the foregoing facts tend, it is argued, to stamp the transaction as one between a principal, the Hebron bank, and its agent for collection.   One of these features is that the Lincoln bank was not what is known as a correspondent of the Hebron bank.   As already indicated, we cannot conceive that any importance attached to this distinction, whatever it may be, because there can be no doubt that their arrangements contemplated the establishment of the relationship of debtor and creditor at one time or another, with reference to this particular instrument or its proceeds.   Next it is argued that the arrangement between the banks was for a collection agency and that therefore the transaction should be treated in the nature of a collection.   The motive of the Hebron bank in entering into its relations with the Lincoln bank was, as stated, undoubtedly to obtain the speedy conversion of foreign paper into cash or its equivalent, but, that this object was not intended to be effected by the specific collection and remission of each instrument forwarded, is attested by every transac-

tion between the two banks for a period of many years.
It was probably immaterial to the Hebron bank whether
it collected the paper through an agent for its own benefit, or in effect sold it and at once obtained credit therefor, and in any event the motive of the Hebron bank is
not the controlling circumstance. It is perfectly clear
that the real understanding between the banks was that
the paper should become that of the Lincoln bank, to
handle in its own way and for its own benefit, else we
must suppose that it was acting in responsible business
matters wholly gratuitously. Nor can we see that the
practice and conceded right of the Lincoln bank, to
charge back dishonored items, can be of any great weight
in determining the nature of the contract. The Hebron
bank was responsible as indorser on all such paper, and
it seems to have been the practice of the Lincoln bank to
take the necessary steps to charge the Hebron bank as
such. That liability alone justified the Lincoln bank in
charging back dishonored paper against any credit then
existing. It is argued that the credit given on receipt of
cash items was, because of such practice, provisional only
and insufficient to bind either party; but it was so far
absolute as to permit the Hebron bank to draw against
such credit,—in other words, to enforce payment by the
Lincoln bank,—and seems only to have been conditional
in the sense that any purchase of negotiable paper is conditional when based on a responsible indorsement, and
with the understanding that in case of dishonor the
holder will look immediately to the indorser. Nor was
the form of indorsement, under all the facts of the case,
indicative of a transfer for collection merely. It is probably true, and we consider the case on this theory, that it
was so restrictive as to charge the Omaha bank with
notice of a reserved title in the indorser if title were
reserved. But, whatever may be the law elsewhere, it
is the law of this state that as between the immediate
parties the true relationship may be shown, notwithstanding the form or terms' of the indorsement itself.

(*Roberts v. Snow*, 27 Neb. 425; *Dusenbury v. Albright*, 31 Neb. 345; *Salisbury v. First Nat. Bank*, 37 Neb. 872; *Holmes v. First Nat. Bank*, 38 Neb. 326; *Corbett v. Fetzer*, 47 Neb. 269.) This being so, when we consider the uniform course of business between these parties, it seems that the real significance of the language of this indorsement was to pass the certificate, not for collection merely, but as the property of the Lincoln bank for the purpose of its amount going forthwith to the credit of the Hebron bank on the account kept therewith. The form of the transmitting letter certainly tends toward a remittance for collection, but in view of the admitted fact that all classes of paper were remitted under this same form and that they were differently treated under this same instruction, we cannot permit this fact to control the more emphatic language conveyed by the acts of the parties. Stress is also laid on a note appearing on the printed form whereon acknowledgments were made by the Lincoln bank of the receipt and credit of such items. This was as follows: "This bank, in receiving collections elsewhere than in Lincoln, acts as your agent, and assumes no responsibility beyond that of due diligence on its part." But this somewhat vague notice applies by its terms to "collections" only, and the blank bore upon it a separate column for collections, on which this certificate did not appear, this, like all "cash items" appearing in a column headed "credited." Thus the notice referred to made even more distinct the practical difference between the two classes of items and showed, if it showed anything, that the "cash items" were not received for collection. On the other hand, there are certain facts which to our mind unmistakably stamp the transaction as a sale, and none is inconsistent with that theory. That there were two classes of items the classification being based manifestly on the practicability of immediately converting the paper into cash, or using it as such, without subjecting it to a process of collection, and that this instrument was treated by both parties as belonging to the cash class; that credit was immediately given before the Lincoln bank had disposed of the paper or collected its proceeds; that interest was paid upon this credit, and that it was subject to draft, all these facts point toward a sale. Mere book-keeping, it is true, does not control the question. Charges and credits may be made merely for convenience in book-keeping; but when the evidence shows that they were not so made, that they were not made at all with items confessedly held for collection, and that when made as to other items, such entries were accompanied by such results as the payment of interest and the honoring of drafts, the matter is no longer one of book-keeping, but is essential to the transaction itself. It is inconceivable that the Lincoln bank would collect gratuitously and pay interest on paper which it did not own, and before it was collected, for the privilege of performing this gratuitous service. It is absolutely certain that the Lincoln bank undertook such service, so advanced credit and paid interest, for the privilege of using the paper for its own purposes and its own profit, as it did in this case by selling it to the Omaha bank, and that the Hebron bank perfectly understood that this was the object and that such paper was so treated. In the light of the usage of the banks the contract was in effect this: The remittance by the Hebron bank was a proposal to sell the certificate for its face, the Lincoln bank to immediately place so much at the disposal of the Hebron bank and to pay interest thereon until the Hebron bank should demand the money or its equivalent; the Hebron bank assuming the ordinary liability of an indorser with the express understanding added thereto that such liability should be subject to immediate enforcement in case of dishonor, by charging the amount against the credit maintained in the Lincoln bank. The mailed acknowledgment was an acceptance of that proposal. No clearer case of a transfer of title could well be contrived. For reasons stated at the outset we do not consider cases adjudicated elsewhere as of any force in determining the facts of this case, but it is believed that all the cases holding under somewhat similar circumstances that title did not pass, present such differences in the facts as to render them readily distinguishable. For instance, in what is perhaps the strongest case cited, *Beal v. City of Somerville*, 50 Fed. Rep. 647, there was no agreement, express or implied, that the checks deposited should be treated as cash or that the credit given might be drawn against. Interest was not paid. Other cases treat an indorsement "for collection" as controlling, and incapable of being extended by extrinsic evidence. Others neglect the fundamental rule that a deposit generally creates simply the relation of debtor and creditor, and is not a bailment.

It is suggested that as the Lincoln bank was at the time insolvent to the knowledge of its officers, it was incapable of taking and consequently transmitting title. This is stating the rule too strongly. The rule invoked is only the application of the general law of fraud in sales induced by false representations, keeping the bank open and holding it out as ready to transact business being an implied representation of solvency. A sale made to such a bank would not be void. It would be, at the most, voidable at the option of the vendor or depositor, and could not be avoided after the rights of innocent third parties had attached. As already intimated, the indorsement may have been so restricted that the Omaha bank could not claim as an innocent purchaser if title had not in fact passed to its vendor, but title did pass and the Lincoln bank owned the certificate unless and until the Hebron bank rescinded the sale. Before this happened it could, and did, pass title to a stranger who parted with value therefor, and it was then too late for the Hebron bank to assert its right to rescind.

REVERSED AND REMANDED.

WILLIAM H. TRITES ET AL. V. HITCHCOCK COUNTY.

FILED DECEMBER 9, 1897.   No. 7647.

1. **Res Judicata:** PROCEEDINGS OF COUNTY BOARD: CLAIMS. A county board, in examining the reports and adjusting the accounts of a county officer, acts ministerially, and an adjustment so made is no bar to an action subsequently brought to recover moneys unlawfully withheld by the officer; but such a board, in auditing and allowing claims, under the power conferred by Compiled Statutes, chapter 18, article 1, section 37, acts judicially, and its judgment is conclusive unless reversed in appellate proceedings.

2. ——: ——: ——: PLEADING. An answer, the nature of which is stated in the opinion, *held* to sufficiently plead an adjudication against the county by the allowance of a claim by the board in its judicial capacity.

ERROR from the district court of Hitchcock county. Tried below before WELTY, J.   *Reversed.*

J. W. Cole and *W. S. Morlan,* for plaintiffs in error.

L. H. Blackledge and *R. O. Adams, contra.*

IRVINE, C.

This was an action by Hitchcock county upon the official bond of Trites, who was formerly treasurer of that county. On the trial, after the county had rested, the court sustained an objection to the introduction of any testimony on behalf of the defendants on the ground that the answers stated no defense. This was logically followed by instructing the jury to return a verdict in favor of the county for the amount by it claimed. These rulings were manifestly erroneous as to the sureties defending, who by their answer merely admitted the election and qualification of Trites, the making and approval of the bond, and denied all other allegations of the petition. Trites and the sureties joined, however, in the motion for a new trial, and also in the petition in error, so that there can be no reversal because of the error affecting the sureties alone unless the rulings complained of were erroneous as to Trites also. The petition, as a breach of the bond, alleged that during Trites' incumbency of the office he, as such officer, received $9,150 from the sale of refunding bonds; that he claimed, as commission for selling said bonds, the sum of $306.60, and held out from the sum so by him received said sum of $306.60, and that he had neglected and refused to pay over to the county said sum. Trites, in his answer, denied that he ever took, received, held out, or otherwise failed to account to the plaintiff for said sum; that he kept, or retained, said sum as fees, commission, or salary, and averred that during his incumbency regular settlements were made as required by law; that at each of said settlements he faithfully and fully accounted for every dollar that came into his hands as treasurer, not in any instance taking, claiming, or deducting any fees, salary, or commission, but that in each instance all fees, salary, or commissions by him received were first audited and allowed by the plaintiff. Further, Trites averred that he had been appointed by the commissioners of the county to negotiate the bonds described in the petition, and that he had fully accounted for and paid into the treasury all the proceeds of the sale of said bonds, without reservation or deduction; that subsequently, and with full knowledge of all the facts, the commissioners allowed and paid to Trites the sum sued for, as salary or commission for his services, and that no appeal was taken from said allowance and payment. The sufficiency of this answer must be determined in the light of a rule now well settled in the jurisprudence of the state. A county board, in examining the reports and approving the accounts of a county officer, acts ministerially, and an adjustment so made is no bar to an action subsequently instituted to recover moneys unlawfully withheld by the officer; but such a board in auditing and allowing claims, under the power conferred by Compiled Statutes, chapter 18, article 1, section 37, acts judicially, and its judgment is conclusive, unless reversed in appellate proceedings. The cases establishing and illustrating the foregoing propositions are collated in the recent case of *Hazelet v. Holt County*, 51 Neb. 716. A case applying them to a state of the pleadings somewhat similar to the present is *Gage County v. Hill*, 52 Neb. 444. The answer, while unnecessarily involved and somewhat verbose, and while lacking much in accuracy of statement, nevertheless fairly pleads that Trites did not withhold the money sued for, but that he, on the contrary, fully accounted therefor, and that what he received was in pursuance of the allowance to him of a claim interposed therefor, and passed upon by the board in its judicial capacity. Trites' answer, therefore, presented a defense, and the district court erred in refusing to permit evidence to be introduced thereunder.

REVERSED AND REMANDED.

PAXTON & GALLAGHER ET AL., APPELLANTS, V. JONATHAN J. SUTTON ET AL., APPELLEES.

FILED DECEMBER 9, 1897. No. 7563.

Homestead Exemption. A debtor may acquire a homestead, and hold it exempt from execution for debts created before its acquisition, but not then reduced to judgment, and this although the homestead was obtained by exchange for property which was liable for the payment of such debts.

APPEAL from the district court of Chase county. Heard below before WELTY, J. *Affirmed.*

Howard M. Kellogg and *Alfred W. Agee*, for appellants.

References: *Riddell v. Shirley*, 5 Cal. 488; *Randall v. Buffington*, 10 Cal. 491; *Pratt v. Burr*, 5 Biss. [U. S.] 36; *Bugg v. Russell*, 75 Ga. 837; *Wedgewood v. Withers*, 35 Neb. 583.

10

A. B. Taylor, contra.

A homestead is not liable for debts contracted before the homestead was purchased. (*Hanlon v. Pollard*, 17 Neb. 368; *Palmer v. Hawes*, 50 N. W. Rep. [Wis.] 341; *Jacobi v. Parkland Distilling Co.*, 43 N. W. Rep. [Minn.] 52; *Dortch v. Benton*, 3 S. E. Rep. [N. Car.] 638; *Tucker v. Drake*, 11 Allen [Mass.] 145; *O'Donnell v. Segar*, 25 Mich. 367; *North v. Shearn*, 15 Tex. 174; *Cipperly v. Rhodes*, 53 Ill. 346; *Culver v. Rogers*, 28 Cal. 521; *Randall v. Buffington*, 10 Cal. 491; *Backer v. Meyer*, 43 Fed. Rep. 702; *Kelly v. Sparks*, 54 Fed. Rep. 70; *Woodward v. People's Nat. Bank*, 31 Pac. Rep. [Colo.] 184; *Hines v. Duncan*, 79 Ala. 112.)

IRVINE, C.

Jonathan J. Sutton was engaged in the mercantile business at Aurora, in Hamilton county. On February 21, 1893, he was indebted to the plaintiffs in divers amounts for goods sold to him to replenish his stock. On that day he exchanged his stock of goods for 160 acres of land in Chase county. The title to 80 acres was taken in himself and to the remaining 80 in his wife. On March 6, 1893, he removed upon the land and has since been occupying it as a homestead. The plaintiffs very promptly reduced their claims to judgment, and on March 6 filed transcripts of their several judgments in the office of the clerk of the district court of Chase county. They then caused executions to be levied upon the land and afterwards filed the petition in this case, alleging that by reason of the conveyance to Mrs. Sutton and the claim of homestead the land could not be sold to advantage, and praying that their levies be declared valid and the land subjected to the payment of the judgments. The pleadings and admissions made on the trial left, so far as the homestead was concerned, really no contested issue except whether the purpose of Sutton in

. making the exchange was to defeat his creditors. There was a finding for the defendants and judgment of dismissal. The court found that the land did not exceed $2,000 in value, so that it was exempt from judgment liens and execution or forced sale unless the special circumstances prevented the operation of the exemption privilege as to these judgments. It is contended that the sole object of Sutton in exchanging his goods for the land and removing upon it was to obtain the benefit of the exemption laws and thereby defeat his creditors. We shall assume that this was shown. Did it constitute such a fraud upon creditors as to estop him from asserting his homestead exemption?

In this state the homestead exemption may be claimed as well against debts existing when the homestead was acquired as against those created thereafter. (*Hanlon v. Pollard*, 17 Neb. 368.) The statute makes no distinction between the two classes of debts and the courts cannot create any. The right here depends upon the situation when judgment is recovered and not when the debt is created. (*Bowker v. Collins*, 4 Neb. 494; *Hanlon v. Pollard, supra.*) The homestead exemption cannot be claimed as against a judgment recovered before the land became a homestead, because in that case the lien of the judgment had attached, and the acquisition of a homestead character does not displace existing liens. And the law generally is so where the statute does not, as many statutes do, except pre-existing debts from the operation of the exemption. It follows that it is the legal right of a debtor to acquire a homestead, and in order to do so he must usually devote to that purpose money or property that is not exempt. Credit is extended or should be extended with a view to that right. If such be the debtor's absolute right then it would seem that his motive is immaterial. As in the case of the alienation of exempt property, it is held that such alienation cannot be set aside as fraudulent, because it cannot operate as a fraud; so here, if the right exists to purchase exempt property with non-exempt, such purchase. cannot operate as a fraud upon creditors. For similar reasons the appropriation of all a debtor's property to pay a favored creditor is not a fraud upon the others except as the statute makes an actual fraudulent intent invalidate the transaction. The fact that the debt was incurred in the purchase of a part of the goods from the sale of which the exempt property was acquired does not affect the case, unless indeed the goods were bought with the intention of not paying for them and of converting them into exempt property for the purpose of accomplishing that object. In that case the goods might be reclaimed if the fraud were seasonably discovered, and it may be that if not discovered until after their exchange, the property for which they were exchanged might then be charged with the debt. Such a case would not be unlike that of one's stealing property and then claiming it as against the owner. But this case presents no such state of facts. It is true that it appears that a small part of the goods out of which some of the debts arose was not delivered until a few days after the sale of the stock, but these goods were not bought in contemplation of the sale or with the intent to defraud, so far as the evidence discloses.

A few cases are opposed to the views we have expressed,—notably *Pratt v. Burr*, 5 Biss. [U. S. C. C.] 36. The reasoning of that case would, however, defeat the exemption as against any pre-existing debt, and is based, as in other cases taking a similar view, on the injustice and apparent immorality of a claim of exemption under such circumstances. Such cases neglect the fundamental principle that the courts cannot set aside valid legislative acts or engraft amendments upon them merely because the judges deem the legislation unwise or even unjust. In all cases of exemptions the creditor suffers because the legislature has deemed the importance of protecting the family in its home and sustenance to be greater than that of enforcing the payment of debts.

The great weight of authority is, however, in accordance with the opinion we have indicated. In *Comstock v. Bechtel*, 63 Wis. 656, the question was squarely presented whether a conversion of non-exempt property into exempt, for the sole purpose of placing it beyond the reach of creditors, would subject the latter property to the payment of debts existing at the time of the conversion, and the court held that it would not, that the property from its character remained exempt and the only remedy of the creditor was by attacking the sale of the non-exempt property. *Cipperly v. Rhodes*, 53 Ill. 346, was a case like the one before us, even to the fact of the conveyance of the homestead to the wife, and the homestead was held exempt because "it was not a fraud on creditors to buy a homestead which would be beyond their reach." So in *Jacoby v. Parkland Distilling Co.*, 41 Minn. 227, the debtor's right was in such case affirmed, because "he is merely exercising a right which the law gives him, and subject to which every one gives him credit." Michigan holds to the same effect, the court saying: "There may be a moral wrong in thus keeping property from creditors, but if so it is one which the statute, on grounds of public policy and to prevent distressing families, has sanctioned in allowing the exemption, and therefore is not legally a fraud." (*O'Donnell v. Segar*, 25 Mich. 367.) And in California, after one decision indicating a contrary view, it is now settled that one may apply non-exempt property to the discharge of incumbrances on a homestead, and claim the whole homestead as exempt. (*Randall v. Buffington*, 10 Cal. 493; *In re Henkel*, 2 Sawyer [U. S. C. C.] 305.) The law is thus stated by Foster, J., in *Kelly v. Sparks*, 54 Fed. Rep. 70: "It seems to be well settled on principle and the preponderance of authority that an insolvent debtor, knowing himself to be insolvent, may acquire a homestead for himself and family, and hold the same exempt from his creditors, although purchased with non-exempt assets, and that fraud cannot be imputed to such an act.

* * * Credit is given the debtor in full view of this comprehensive exemption." (See, too, *First Nat. Bank v. Glass*, 79 Fed. Rep. 706.)

In the view we have taken of the question discussed it follows that all the land would have been exempt if title had been taken in Sutton. He therefore had the right as against creditors to convey or cause to be conveyed a portion thereof to his wife, as the homestead can be claimed from the property of either. (Compiled Statutes, ch. 36, sec. 2.) It is unnecessary, therefore, to consider the special attack and special defense with reference to her right.

AFFIRMED.

PROVIDENT LIFE & TRUST COMPANY, APPELLANT, V.
DANIEL KENISTON ET AL., APPELLEES.

FILED DECEMBER 9, 1897. No. 9273.

Receivers: APPOINTMENT. An application for the appointment of a receiver is addressed to the sound discretion of the court, and where, under all the circumstances of a given case, it appears that a greater injury would ensue from the appointment than from permitting the possession of the property to remain undisturbed, a receiver will not be appointed.

APPEAL from the district court of Douglas county. Heard below before KEYSOR, J. *Affirmed.*

Lake, Hamilton & Maxwell, for appellant.

Gregory, Day & Day, contra.

IRVINE, C.

The plaintiff, the Provident Life & Trust Company, obtained a decree foreclosing a mortgage made by the defendant Keniston. At the sale the plaintiff became the purchaser. Keniston appealed from the order of confirmation and his appeal is still pending. After that appeal had been perfected the plaintiff applied to the district court for the appointment of a receiver of the premises in controversy. The district court denied the application, and this is an appeal by the plaintiff from the order denying it. The case has been advanced in order that the appeal, if well taken, might not be unavailing.

The grounds upon which the application was based were that the property was insufficient in value to pay the mortgage debt with accruing interest and costs, and that the defendants were permitting taxes to become delinquent and had suffered the premises to be sold for taxes. We need not inquire into the first matter. The sale determined the amount to be realized by plaintiff in its capacity of mortgagee. As such it would be entitled to the purchase price, in case of final confirmation, and no more, whatever might be the value of the property. While resisting the setting aside of the sale it could not be heard to say that such sale was bad and that therefore it should be reinstated in its position as an unsatisfied mortgagee, and that the property on a resale would be insufficient to satisfy its debt. The second ground was fully proved and would ordinarily, perhaps, be sufficient to justify the appointment of a receiver on application of the purchaser, where the order of confirmation has been superseded. But the evidence in this case was, we think, sufficient to sustain the action of the trial court in refusing to interfere with defendant's possession. The premises are occupied as a homestead by Keniston and his family, and while we do not determine that this fact would alone in all cases be sufficient to prevent the appointment of a receiver, still it will readily be conceded that it is in all cases a circumstance proper for the consideration of the court in determining whether one should be appointed. To interfere thus summarily with the possession of real property, before the final determination of a cause, is always a somewhat severe, though sometimes a necessary, exercise of judicial power. Certainly the court should be more reluctant to so interfere where a homestead and a home are thereby destroyed, than where its action involves only the disturbance of purely selfish business interests, capable of monetary admeasurement. Such a rule is dictated at once by considerations of humanity, public policy, and well-defined equitable principles. In addition to this there was testimony, contradicted it is true, but sufficient to sustain a finding to that effect, that the property in controversy was situated in a locality where there was very little demand for property of such character, that it was doubtful if it could be rented, and that if rented at all it would not bring more than $25 per month, and at that rate it would be necessary for the lessor to pay the water rents and keep the building in repair; that the hazards of such an administration of the property would cause a depreciation thereof greater than the probable income from rents which might be received, and that Keniston had kept the premises in perfect repair and had exercised great care in the preservation thereof. An application for a receiver is addressed to the sound discretion of the trial court, and while by the statutes and by force of adjudicated cases the exercise of that discretion is to a certain extent governed by general rules, still in each case the particular circumstances must be regarded, and if, considering all the circumstances, "the case be such that a greater injury would ensue from the appointment of a receiver than from leaving the property in the hands now holding it, or if any other considerations of propriety or conveniency render the appointment of a receiver improper or inexpedient, none will be appointed." (*Vose v. Reed*, 1 Woods [U. S. C. C.] 650.) In the light of the foregoing rules and of that aspect of the evidence most favorable to the defendant, which we must here accept in view of the finding below, the district court did not err in refusing plaintiff's application.

AFFIRMED.

ARTHUR PERRY ET AL. V. GERMAN-AMERICAN BANK.

FILED DECEMBER 21, 1897.   No. 7431.

1. **Conversion: EVIDENCE.** Evidence examined and *held* to sustain the finding adverse to the contention of plaintiffs in error.

2. **Trial: LEADING QUESTIONS.** It is within the discretion of the district court in a proper case to allow leading questions, and the exercise of such discretion, in the absence of an apparent abuse thereof, is not the subject of review on appeal. (*St. Paul Fire & Marine Ins. Co. v. Gotthelf*, 35 Neb. 351.)

3. **Evidence: TELEGRAM: PRESUMPTION OF DELIVERY.** A similar presumption of delivery results from the entrusting to a telegraph company for transmission of a message properly addressed to that which follows from the posting of a letter for transmission by the United States mail.

4. ———: ———: ———.   Such presumption results from the office of a telegraph company to the public, which, in this state, is that of a carrier of intelligence with rights and duties analogous to those of carriers of goods and passengers. (*Western Union Telegraph Co. v. Call Publishing Co.*, 44 Neb. 326.)

ERROR from the district court of Douglas county. Tried below before BLAIR, J.   *Affirmed.*

I. R. Andrews, for plaintiffs in error.

J. J. McCarthy, contra.

POST, C. J.

The defendant in error, hereafter called the bank, on May 28, 1893, at the village of Emerson, advanced to one Johnson the sum of $1,200, wherewith to purchase certain cattle.   On the same day the cattle above mentioned were by Johnson shipped to South Omaha, consigned to the plaintiffs in error, who were engaged in business as commission men and live stock brokers, and at the same time, as security for the money so advanced, Johnson drew against the proceeds of the said cattle a sight draft, of which the following is a copy:

"GERMAN-AMERICAN BANK,
"$1,200.00.   EMERSON, NEB., May 29, 1893.

"At sight pay to the order of German-American Bank twelve hundred and no 100 dollars, and charge to the account of   G. G. JOHNSON.

"To Perry Bros. & Co., South Omaha, Neb."

On the upper margin of said draft was written the following words: "21 head cattle shipped May 28, 1893, from Emerson, Neb." It should in this connection be noted that May 28, the day of the foregoing transactions, was Sunday; hence the draft was made to bear date of the 29th. On the 28th the bank, for its further protection, forwarded to plaintiff in error the following telegraphic message:

"EMERSON, NEB., May 28, 1893.

"*To Perry Bros. & Co.:* We have draft on you from G. G. Johnson, twelve hundred dollars, for 21 head cattle shipped to-day.   GERMAN-AMERICAN BANK."

The foregoing message was received at South Omaha at 3:50 P. M. on Sunday, the 28th, and delivered to plaintiffs in error on the day of its receipt or the following day. Johnson accompanied the cattle in question from Emerson to South Omaha, where he arrived Sunday night, and the next morning about 7 o'clock notified plaintiffs in error of the arrival of the cattle. He also at the same time, as appears from his testimony, personally notified plaintiffs in error that "there was a draft of $1,200 on the cattle," which he directed the latter to pay and place the balance of the proceeds of said consignment to his credit. Plaintiffs in error, in the course of their business, sold said cattle, and received the proceeds therefor about 3 o'clock P. M. on Monday, the 29th, but credited the entire amount thereof to Johnson upon an open account for advancements previously made, and refused payment of the draft of the bank when presented in due time. The bank, in an action for the refusal of plaintiffs in error to accept its said draft, and for the conversion of its aforesaid security, recovered judgment in the district court for Douglas county, and which is presented for review by means of this proceeding.

It is first argued that the record fails to disclose a pledge of the cattle in controversy to the bank as security for the money advanced. That contention is without merit. Both Johnson and Moseman, the cashier, testified, in substance, that the bank was to have a lien upon the cattle and the proceeds thereof for the money advanced by it.

It is next complained that the court erred in permitting the bank, over the objection of plaintiffs in error, to ask the witnesses Johnson and Mead certain leading questions. The allowing of leading questions is, as a general rule, within the discretion of the trial court, and its judgment in that regard is not, in the absence of an abuse of discretion, the subject of review on appeal or proceedings in error. (*St. Paul Fire & Marine Ins. Co. v. Gotthelf*, 35 Neb. 351.)

Lastly, it is contended that the district court erred in giving instruction No. 6, relating to the presumption arising from the transmission of the telegram above mentioned. It was by the paragraph complained of in substance charged that the plaintiffs in error having themselves produced the message, which was shown to have been received at South Omaha on the afternoon of the 28th, it is presumed to have been delivered in season, that is, previous to the sale of the cattle on the afternoon of the 29th, and that the burden is upon the plaintiffs in error of proving the contrary. There is certainly no error in the instruction of which plaintiffs in error can complain. There is, indeed, a decided preponderance of authority in favor of the proposition that a similar presumption of delivery results from the entrusting to a telegraph company for transmission of a message properly addressed as that which follows from the posting of a letter duly addressed and stamped for transmission by means of the United States mail. (*Oregon*

Steamship Co. v. Otis, 100 N. Y. 446; *Commonwealth v. Jeffries,* 7 Allen [Mass.] 548; Wharton, Evidence sec. 76; Gray, Communication by Telegraph sec. 136.) Such presumption results naturally, if not necessarily, from the relation of telegraph companies to the public, which, in this state at least, is held to be that of public carriers of intelligence with rights and duties analogous to those of carriers of goods and passengers. (*Western Union Telegraph Co. v. Call Publishing Co.,* 44 Neb. 326.) Plaintiffs in error, in appropriating the price of the cattle sold, claimed to act under and by virtue of a previous understanding with Johnson whereby the proceeds of all stock consigned to them by the latter should be applied in satisfaction of the balance owing by him. But conceding the existence of an agreement such as alleged, the plaintiffs in error have, without objection, been permitted to retain the proceeds of the cattle over and above the claim of the bank. In other words, they have enforced their claim to the extent of Johnson's interest in the property, which, in view of the facts in evidence, is all they are entitled to demand. What would have been their rights in the premises had the sale and appropriation of the proceeds of the cattle been consummated by them in ignorance of the claim of the bank, we are not called upon to consider, since there is in this record abundant evidence to support the finding against them upon that issue. The judgment is clearly right and must be

AFFIRMED.

J. W. TOMBLIN V. JONATHAN HIGGINS.

FILED DECEMBER 21, 1897. No. 7629.

Usury: ACTION FOR INTEREST. The defense of usury is available in an action by a national bank for the recovery of unpaid interest where the rate contracted for by it is in excess of that prescribed by the act of congress. (*Norfolk Nat. Bank v. Schwenk,* 46 Neb. 381.)

ERROR from the district court of Furnas county. Tried below before WELTY, J. *Affirmed.*

W. S. Morlan, for plaintiff in error.

J. H. Broady, contra.

POST, C. J.

This cause was commenced in the county court of Furnas county, where the plaintiff in error sued to recover from the defendant in error as maker of a promissory note for $500, bearing date of March 14, 1891, and payable March 14, 1892, with interest from date, to the order of "J. W. Tomblin, Pt." A trial upon issue joined resulted in a judgment for the defendant, from which an appeal was prosecuted to the district court, where, to the petition in the usual form in like actions, an answer was interposed in which it was alleged that the First National Bank of Arapahoe was the real party in interest, and that in the execution and delivery of the note in suit, as well as in the several antecedent transactions furnishing the pretended consideration therefor, the plaintiff acted as the trustee for said bank. Said allegation was accompanied by a statement in detail of the transactions between the defendant and the bank, resulting in the execution of this note, which are in brief the loaning by the latter to the former of a large sum of money at a usurious rate of interest, the renewal from time to time of the notes given therefor at a usurious rate of interest, and the payment upon said notes and renewals thereof of a sum largely exceeding the money loaned. It was further expressly charged that the note in suit was given for usurious interest which had accrued on the original loan and renewal notes given therefor, and for no other or different consideration whatever. The plaintiff replied, (1) denying the allegations of the answer except such as were therein confessed; (2) alleging that the note in suit was given for a part of the balance found to be due from defendant upon final settlement previously had of all matters of difference between the parties. A trial was had of the issues thus presented in the month of October, 1893, resulting in a verdict for the plaintiff, which was, however, set aside on motion of the defendant. Subsequently the plaintiff, by leave of court, filed an amended petition alleging the execution of the note to him as agent and president of the bank above named and in its behalf. To this petition the defendant . answered, (1) admitting the execution of the note, and, in effect, denying the other allegations thereof; (2) alleging the usury of the original loan and renewals thereof, including the note in suit; (3) alleging that the bank, if the party in interest in said transaction, is now estopped to assert any right in that behalf, for the reason that said note was taken by said bank in the name of plaintiff with the fraudulent purpose of evading the penalty imposed by act of congress for the taking or reserving of usurious interest by national banks. In the reply subsequently filed, after a denial of the new matter in the answer, it is alleged, in substance, that the security held by the bank for the indebtedness of defendant being deemed insufficient, an arrangement was made whereby the notes representing such indebtedness should be reduced to the extent of $500, and a new and separate note executed for that amount that pursuant to such agreement the note in suit was executed as payment *pro tanto* and the sum of $500 credited upon defendant's notes so held by the bank. A second trial was had to the court without the assistance of a jury, resulting in a finding and judgment for the defendant, from which the plaintiff prosecutes error to this court.

It is, in the view we take of the record, necessary to notice a single one of the several questions argued by counsel, viz., that of the consideration for the note which is the subject of this controversy. If, as contended by defendant, the sole and only consideration therefor is interest on his apparent indebtedness to the bank, being a balance of principal and interest of a loan confessedly usurious, it follows that the judgment should be affirmed, since the utmost that can be claimed in behalf of the plaintiff under the averments of his pleadings, is that he stands as the representative of the bank.   It has been settled by repeated decisions of this court that the plea of usury is good in an action by a national bank as to unpaid interest where the contract rate exceeds that prescribed by the national banking act.   (*Hall v. First Nat. Bank of Fairbury,* 30 Neb. 99; *McGhee v. First Nat. Bank of Tobias,* 40 Neb. 92; *Norfolk Nat. Bank v. Schwenk,* 46 Neb. 381.)

The evidence bearing upon the question under discussion is somewhat confusing, and involves transactions so numerous and intricate as to render even the briefest possible synopsis thereof impracticable in this connection.   There certainly is evidence tending to sustain the contention that the note represents interest on the usurious loan, and positive proof that it is otherwise without any consideration whatever.   We are unable to perceive any sufficient ground for interference with the finding of the district court.

JUDGMENT AFFIRMED.

CHICAGO, BURLINGTON & QUINCY RAILROAD COMPANY V.
ANGELINE STEEAR.

FILED DECEMBER 21, 1897.   No. 7665.

1. **Carriers: LOSS OF BAGGAGE: EVIDENCE: CHECKS.** A check for baggage is *prima facie* evidence that the baggage it represents has been delivered to the issuing company by the person to whom the check is issued. The introduction of the check in evidence is such proof of the fact of the delivery of the baggage as to cast the burden on the party contesting the fact of proving to the contrary or showing the nondelivery.

2. **Conflicting Evidence: REVIEW.** The finding of fact by a trial court based on conflicting evidence will not be disturbed on error to this court unless clearly wrong.

ERROR from the district court of Clay County. Tried below before HASTINGS, J. *Affirmed.*

The opinion contains a statement of the case.

J. W. Deweese, L. G. Hurd, and *F. E. Bishop,* for plaintiff in error:

A passenger's check for baggage is only *prima facie* evidence that the carrier received the baggage, and may be rebutted by proof that the carrier did not, in fact, receive it. (*Ringwalt v. Wabash R. Co.,* 45 Neb. 760; *Marquette, H. & O. R. Co. v. Kirkwood,* 45 Mich. 51; *Isaacson v. New York C. & H. R. R. Co.,* 16 Am. & Eng. R. Cas. [N. Y.] 193; *Michigan Southern & N. I. R. Co. v. Meyres,* 21 Ill. 631; *Chicago, R. I. & P. R. Co. v. Clayton,* 78 Ill. 616.)

The carrier is not liable, as the evidence shows that the loss was due to the agents of the passenger. (*Ringwalt v. Wabash R. Co.,* 45 Neb. 760; *Missouri P. R. Co. v. McFadden,* 154 U. S. 155.)

Thomas H. Matters, contra.

References: *Davis v. Michigan S. & N. I. R. Co.,* 22 Ill. 278; *Thornton Check v. Little M. R. R. Co.,* 2 Disn. [O.] 238; *Davis v. Cayuga & S. R. Co.,* 10 How. [N. Y.] 330; *Atchison, T. & S. F. R. Co. v. Brewer,* 20 Kan. 669; *Dill v. South Carolina R. Co.,* 62 Am. Dec. [S. Car.] 407.

HARRISON, J.

This action was commenced by the defendant in error to recover damages which she alleged were occasioned by the loss, by the company, of her valise and its contents, of which the company had taken possession and charge as a part of her baggage, she being at the time a passenger, by its line of road, on a trip from Chicago,

Illinois, to Inland, Nebraska. The company defended on the ground that it had never received the valise, and, from a judgment in favor of defendant in error for the value of the valise and its contents, has prosecuted error proceedings to this court. The trial was to the court without a jury.

The defendant in error, who, it appears, in October, 1893, was journeying from some place in Michigan to her home in Inland, Clay county, this state, detailed in a portion of her evidence that on October 12, 1893, she started from Muskegon, Michigan, and went to St. Joe, Michigan; from there she travelled by boat to Chicago. She had with her a trunk and the valise, or, as she styled it, a "satchel." It is of the non-delivery to her by the company of the latter that she complains in this suit. She further stated as follows:

Q. State what you did with the trunk and satchel.

A. In the morning after I got to Chicago, I went out of the cabin, and there was a man sitting there with a lot of checks upon his arm. I was going to the fair, and I did not want to carry the satchel; so I went to him and I asked him if I could not have that satchel checked with my trunk, and transferred to the Union Depot. He said I could. I asked him how long I could leave it there. He said I could leave it there a month if I wanted to, but I did not leave it there that long.

Q. Well, state what you did.

A. I sat the satchel down in front of him and he put a check upon it and then he said show me your trunk. I showed him my trunk and he put a check upon that, and he gave me two checks. This was Thursday morning. On Saturday I went to the Union Depot to get my baggage to get it checked to Inland. When I went there, and they asked me to show my ticket and show my check, I gave them the two checks. He went off and then came back and gave me two checks for Inland.

Q. How long was he gone?

11

A. I cannot tell. It was quite a while. I should think maybe half an hour; maybe longer.

Q. Is that one of the checks he gave you (offering check to witness)?

A. Yes, sir; it looks like it.

(The plaintiff offers the check in evidence, being No. 42017.)

Q. When did you arrive in Chicago?

A. On the 12th, in the morning.

Q. When did you check your baggage at the depot?

A. On Saturday.

Q. What month was that?

A. October.

Q. What day of the month,—about how many days after you arrived in Chicago?

A. It was three days. It was the third morning.

Q. When did you arrive at Inland?

A. I arrived there the 17th day of October.

A witness for the company stated, as a portion of his evidence, that during October, 1893, he was in the employ of the McBride Express Company in charge of one of its wagons in Chicago, and undertook to transfer the trunk and valise of defendant in error from the "Graham & Morton Dock" to the Chicago, Burlington & Quincy Railroad Depot, issuing to her check numbered 590, evidencing the delivery to the express company, and its possession, of the valise. This witness also said that when he finally arrived at the depot, he did not have the valise, and thought he had lost it,—had left it at some other than the proper place. He had made several stops to deliver baggage on the way from the dock to the depot. In the deposition of the baggage-master at the Union Passenger Depot in Chicago,—the depot used by the plaintiff in error company,—he testified that he issued the check which the defendant in error had at the time of the trial; that he did it without the baggage then in his possession, giving it in exchange for check 590 of the McBride Express Company which the defendant in error delivered to him. In this connection we will revert to the evidence of the expressman in which occurred the following passage:

Q. What, if anything, did you say to the party in charge at the Union Passenger Station when you delivered the other baggage on that day?

A. At first I didn't notice this valise was short, and the baggageman told me how many pieces I had. The baggageman asked me where the valise was, and I looked all over, and I could not find it; and I told the baggageman I would go along to some other depots, that maybe I left it by mistake. So I did. I went to all the other depots and I could not find it.

From this it appears that the baggage-master asked the expressman for a valise of the existence of which it is not disclosed by the evidence he had any prior knowledge,—which seems at least somewhat unlikely. Three days later, notwithstanding this information which it is claimed had been imparted to, and received by, the baggage-master, he delivered to defendant in error a check of the company evidencing to her, and to all others, that the valise was in the possession of the company. The check delivered to the defendant in error was evidence of the delivery of the baggage it represented to the company, and, when introduced in evidence, established, *prima facie*, the fact of the delivery of the valise to the company, and threw the burden of proof on the company to show a non-delivery. (*Atchison, T. & S. F. R. Co. v. Brewer*, 20 Kan. 669; *Chicago, R. I. & P. R. Co. v. Clayton*, 78 Ill. 616; 4 Lawson, Rights, Remedies & Practice par. 1951, and cases cited; *Davis v. Michigan S. & N. I. R. Co.*, 22 Ill. 278.) The check is *prima facie* evidence of receipt and non-delivery. (3 Am. & Eng. Ency. Law [2d ed.] 580, and cases cited in note 3; *Cleveland, C., C. & St. L. R. Co. v. Tyler*, 35 N. E. Rep. [Ind.] 523; 3 Wood, Railway Law sec. 403; Thompson, Carriers 514; *Oakes v. Northern P. R. Co.*, 26 Pac. Rep. [Ore.] 230.) In the case at bar the check proved, *prima facie*, the receipt of the valise by

the company, and the evidence introduced to show the
contrary was in direct conflict therewith; and it was for
the trier of facts to weigh and determine which should
be given the greater credence. In view of all the evidence we cannot say the conclusion reached was manifestly wrong; hence it will not be disturbed. (*Stein-
kraus v. Korth,* 44 Neb. 777; *Thompson v. Field,* 45 Neb.
146.) The judgment of the district court is

AFFIRMED.

HENRY OTIS V. HANS CLAUSSEN.

FILED DECEMBER 21, 1897.   No. 7660.

1. **New Trial:** ASSIGNMENTS OF ERROR: REVIEW. If a motion for a new
   trial assigns several grounds for a new trial, an assignment in a
   petition in error that the court erred in overruling the motion for
   a new trial is too general and indefinite to present anything for
   consideration or review. (*Sigler v. McConnell,* 45 Neb. 598.)

2. **Replevin:** COSTS: RULINGS ON EVIDENCE: REVIEW. Alleged errors
   of the trial court in the admission and exclusion of evidence examined and the actions of the court in regard to the assigned particulars *held* not erroneous, or not prejudicially so.

ERROR from the district court of Fillmore county.
Tried below before HASTINGS, J. *Affirmed.*

John Barsby and *John D. Carson,* for plaintiff in error.

Charles H. Sloan, contra.

HARRISON, J.

In an action of replevin by the defendant in error in
the district court of Fillmore county, he asserted the
special ownership and right to the immediate possession of a span of mules by virtue of a chattel mortgage
executed and delivered to him of date September 12, 1888,
by one D. C. McLeese. The plaintiff in error admitted
the execution and existence of the mortgage under which

defendant in error claimed ownership of the property, the right to possession of which was in dispute in the suit, but pleaded that, long prior to the commencement of this action, by an agreement or transaction between D. C. McLeese and defendant in error, the note, the payment of which the mortgage was given to secure, was satisfied and the lien of the mortgage became inoperative; also, that subsequent to the agreement, the effect of which was the release of the mortgage to defendant in error, the property was mortgaged to Aultman, Miller & Co., and in default of payment of the debt secured by the mortgage to Aultman, Miller & Co. the mortgage was foreclosed and at the sale the property was purchased by the plaintiff in error, who was in possession of the property under the title or ownership acquired by such purchase. A trial of the issues resulted in a verdict and judgment for defendant in error, and the cause has been removed to this court by error proceedings on the part of the unsuccessful party in the trial court.

The petition in error contains three assignments as follows:

"1. The court erred in excluding from the jury the bill of sale from D. C. McLeese to John Barsby, marked 'Exhibit F' in the bill of exceptions.

"2. The court erred in admitting to the jury the transcript of proceedings in the case of Hans Claussen against Henry Thompson had before J. E. Curtis, justice of the peace in and for Fairmont township, Fillmore county, Nebraska, and marked 'Exhibit 4' in the transcript.

"3. The court erred in overruling the motion for a new trial.

The motion for a new trial contained several grounds for a new trial. This being true, the third assignment of error is too general and indefinite to present anything for review. (*City of Chadron v. Glover*, 43 Neb. 732; *Sigler v. McConnell*, 45 Neb. 598.)

One assignment of error relates to the exclusion from evidence of an offered bill of sale which purported to

convey the property in dispute from D. C. McLeese to
John Barsby, executed of date subsequent to the alleged
transaction between McLeese and defendant in error, by
which it was claimed the mortgage or lien of defendant
in error was satisfied, and also after the date of the mortgage to Aultman, Miller & Co., to which reference has
hereinbefore been made. It is stated that the object of
this offer was to show that it was the understanding of
the parties thereto that the mortgage to defendant in
error had been, in effect, canceled by the transaction
which, it was pleaded, had occurred between defendant
in error and McLeese. It appears from the evidence
that Barsby was present at the time of the alleged agreement between McLeese and defendant in error, to which
we have just referred, and was assigned the duty of
attending to the fulfillment of some of its conditions.
It is further contended that it would have appeared, had
the evidence been admitted that the bill of sale had been
recorded, that the defendant in error was charged with,
or had full knowledge of, its existence, and was estopped
to assert any rights in the property. The bill of sale,
while it may have embodied some idea or understanding
of the immediate parties to it, could not, and did not,
show any ideas of the defendant in error, and, in the
sense or import claimed for it, could have no force or
effect as to him or his rights in or to the property. He
was in no manner or degree a party in or to its execution and delivery, and could not be charged by it in the
ideas or understandings embodied in it; nor was there
anything in the fact of the existence of the bill of sale
or the defendant in error's knowledge of its existence
which could in any manner or to any extent work an
estoppel as against his assertion of his rights, if any, he
still had under and by virtue of the mortgage of the property to him. There was no error in the exclusion from
the evidence of the offered bill of sale; hence the first
assignment of error must be overruled.

Of the matters which it was set forth in the answer

were included in the agreement between defendant in error and McLeese by which it was claimed the former's rights under his mortgage were extinguished, was one in reference to a bill of costs in a case before J. E. Curtis, justice of the peace, which, it was also pleaded, D. C. McLeese agreed to assume as his debt and pay. The bill of costs referred to was charged against the defendant in error and the transcript from the justice docket which was admitted in evidence had in, or on it, a short statement that the costs had been paid by Hansen, the defendant in error. This was not evidence competent in this action to prove the payment of the costs in that action by Hansen. The statement, as it appeared in the transcript, could not bind plaintiff in error or have any force or effect as to him or his rights; hence could not be received here to affect him or such rights. As between the justice and the defendant in error, the entry in the docket, as shown by the transcript, might have possessed some significance, but it was not substantive evidence in this case as against plaintiff in error that such costs had been paid, and by defendant in error; hence the evidence should have been excluded, but the error of its admission was harmless, for the defendant in error had testified that he had paid these costs and the testimony was not disputed.

This disposes of all of the assignments of error, and it follows from the conclusions announced that the judgment of the district court will be

AFFIRMED.

EDWARD JOHNSON v. STATE OF NEBRASKA.

FILED DECEMBER 21, 1897.   No. 9383.

1. **Information:** VERIFICATION: OBJECTION. It is too late to object to the verification of an information after the accused has been arraigned, and pleaded not guilty, unless such plea has been withdrawn.

2. ———: PARTICIPANTS IN CRIME: DEFENDANTS. All participants in a
   crime may be jointly charged in the same information, or they
   may be informed against separately, as the prosecutor may elect.
   It will not defeat a criminal prosecution for the evidence to show
   that all perpetrators of the crime were not made defendants.

3. **Criminal Law**: SUFFICIENCY OF EVIDENCE. To warrant a conviction
   in a criminal prosecution it is not essential that the evidence adduced on the trial should exclude every possible hypothesis but the
   guilt of the accused.

4. ———: INSTRUCTIONS. Mere non-direction by the trial court will not
   work a reversal where proper instructions covering the point were
   not requested.

ERROR to the district court for Douglas county. Tried
below before BAKER, J. *Affirmed.*

I. J. Dunn, for plaintiff in error.

C. J. Smyth, Attorney General, and *Ed P. Smith, Deputy
Attorney General,* for the state.

NORVAL, J.

The defendant was tried upon an information charging him with the felonious breaking and entering, in the
night-season, the dwelling of one Charles E. Taylor with
the intent to steal, and also with the larceny therefrom
of, one church communion set and other chattels belonging to said Taylor. The trial resulted in a conviction of
the crime of burglary.

The information was verified before the deputy clerk
of the district court, and a motion to quash the information on that ground was denied by the court, which
ruling is assigned for error. The objection to the verification is not available, for the reason the motion to
quash was filed and presented after the accused had been
arraigned and his plea of not guilty to the charges in
the information had been entered, without a withdrawal
of such plea. (*Davis v. State,* 31 Neb. 247; *Hodgkins v.
State,* 36 Neb. 160; *Bailey v. State,* 36 Neb. 808; *Korth v.
State,* 46 Neb. 631; *Davis v. State,* 51 Neb. 401.)

Complaint is made of the giving of the seventh paragraph of the court's charge, which was in this language: "You are instructed that if you find from the evidence that there were others connected with or participated in the burglary jointly with the defendant, then you would be warranted in finding the defendant guilty. The evidence must satisfy you that the defendant is guilty individually or in conjunction with others, and that there is no other reasonable hypothesis that any other person or persons committed the crime."

The information charges that the defendant committed the burglary and larceny, while the evidence adduced on the trial tended to show that he was aided and assisted in the commission of the offenses by at least one other person. It is argued that the instruction was erroneous in that it authorized a conviction of the defendant without the other participant in the crimes being made a co-defendant with him; in other words, that under an information charging one person with a burglary, there can be no conviction unless the evidence discloses that the defendant alone perpetrated the offense. To this doctrine we cannot yield assent. When two or more persons jointly participate in a crime, they may be prosecuted therefor together under one information or indictment, or they may be informed against separately, in the discretion of the prosecutor; and it will not defeat a criminal prosecution that the evidence shows all participants in the crime were not made defendants. (1 Bishop, Criminal Procedure sec. 463.) In *Walbridge v. State*, 13 Neb. 236, it was decided that to justify a conviction upon circumstantial evidence, the proofs must be so conclusive as to leave no reasonable doubt that the accused and no other person committed the offense. But that case does not hold there can be no conviction unless it is established by the evidence that the defendant alone committed the crime charged, without the assistance of any one else. The question we are now considering was not involved or determined in *Wal-*

bridge v. State, supra, and counsel for the defendant is in
error in supposing that it has any bearing upon the point
under consideration.   The seventh instruction correctly
stated the law, and there was no error committed in
refusing the first request to charge tendered by the defendant, since it enunciated principles confessedly in
conflict with the rule laid down in the instruction quoted
above.

It is next insisted that it was prejudicial error to
refuse to give to the jury the second instruction tendered
by the defendant, which is as follows:

"2. You are instructed that if the facts and circumstances of the case, as detailed by the witnesses upon
the stand, can be accounted for or explained upon any
other hypothesis than the guilt of the defendant, then
your verdict should be not guilty."

This instruction was faulty, because it did not contain
the word "reasonable" preceding the word "hypothesis."
The defendant was not entitled to an acquittal merely
because the evidence or criminating circumstances may
have been explained upon some possible theory of innocence of the accused of the crime charged.   In *State v.
Mathews,* 66 N. Car. 106, it is said: "The rule   *   *   *
requiring proof beyond a reasonable doubt does not require the state, even in a case of circumstantial testimony, to prove such a coincidence of circumstances as ex-
cludes every hypothesis except the guilt of the prisoner.
The true rule is that the circumstances and evidence
must be such as to produce a moral certainty of guilt, and
to exclude any other reasonable hypothesis." In line with
that case are *State v. Schoenwald,* 31 Mo. 147; *People v.
Murray,* 41 Cal. 66; 1 Bishop, Criminal Procedure sec.
1077.   All the law required to authorize a conviction of
the prisoner was that the facts should be consistent with
his guilt and inconsistent with any other reasonable or
rational conclusion, and this is true though circumstantial evidence is relied upon to establish guilt.   The above
request to charge, had it been given, would have per-

mitted an acquittal upon mere conjecture, or some ill-supported theory that the defendant may be innocent of the crime charged, which is not the law.

Objection is made because the jury were not instructed upon the law of circumstantial evidence. As no proper request to charge upon that point was submitted to the court below by the prisoner, he cannot urge the non-direction of the court as a ground for reversal. (*Hill v. State,* 42 Neb. 503; *Housh v. State,* 43 Neb. 163; *Pjarrou v. State,* 47 Neb. 294.)

It is also insisted that the evidence is insufficient to sustain the verdict, because, it is alleged, that it was not shown the accused broke and entered the dwelling-house in question in the night-season. This contention is devoid of merit. Charles E. Taylor, the prosecuting witness, testified, and his testimony is uncontradicted, that he locked the doors of his residence and left the house after dark between 6 and 7 o'clock P. M. of January 17, 1897, and returned home with his wife about 10 o'clock the same night, when it was discovered that the dwelling had been broken into and burglarized during his said absence. This testimony, not having been contradicted, was ample to justify the jury in finding that the crime was committed in the night-time. The defendant was not prejudiced by the trial court asking the witness Charles Orleans whether his place was a repository for articles stolen by Johnson, inasmuch as the witness answered the interrogatory in the negative. Moreover, without this question and answer, the previous examination of the witness might have left an impression on the minds of the jurors that Orleans had been secreting stolen chattels for the defendant. He was accorded a fair and impartial trial. The judgment is

AFFIRMED.

SARPY COUNTY STATE BANK, APPELLANT, V. H. M.
HINKLE & SON ET AL., APPELLEES.

FILED DECEMBER 21, 1897. No. 7528.

Chattel Mortgages: SALE OF PROPERTY: PROCEEDS: LIENS ON SUR-
PLUS: ATTACHMENT. The decree of the court below is without evidence to support it.

APPEAL from the district court of Sarpy county.
Heard below before BLAIR, J. *Reversed.*

H. C. Lefler, and *Kennedy, Gilbert & Anderson,* for appellant.

W. W. Morsman, contra.

NORVAL, J.

There is no controversy over the material facts in this
case, which may be summarized as follows: On July 17,
1893, the defendants H. M. Hinkle & Son were engaged in
the mercantile business at Springfield, Sarpy county, and
were indebted in large sums to numerous creditors,
among others the plaintiff and appellant herein, the
Sarpy County State Bank, and the defendants Cyrus K.
Spearman, McCord-Brady Company, and the Kilpatrick-
Koch Dry Goods Company. On said date H. M. Hinkle
& Son, being indebted to Spearman in the sum of $3,870,
to secure the payment thereof executed and delivered
to said Spearman a chattel mortgage on their stock of
merchandise, which mortgage was duly filed for record
at 5:30 o'clock in the afternoon of the same day, and
Spearman took immediate possession of the mortgaged
chattels. Subsequently, on the same day, the said H. M.
Hinkle & Son executed another mortgage upon the same
goods, in favor of plaintiff, the Sarpy County State Bank,
to secure the payment of a *bona fide* indebtedness of
$1,394, which mortgage was delivered to the bank, and
by it filed in the office of the county clerk of Sarpy county

on July 18, 1893. Afterwards, on the same day, the said mortgagees executed two chattel mortgages upon the same goods, one to McCord-Brady Company and the other to the Kilpatrick-Koch Dry Goods Company. Mc-Cord-Brady Company repudiated the mortgage given to it, and on July 20, 1893, sued out a writ of attachment against said H. M. Hinkle & Son, and caused the sheriff to levy the same upon said stock of goods, which at the time was in the possession of Spearman, under his said chattel mortgage. The property was likewise seized upon other writs of attachment. Spearman thereupon replevied the goods from the sheriff, and after obtaining possession thereof sold the property under the terms of his mortgage, realizing therefrom the sum of $1,559.11, above the amount of his lien and the costs and expenses of the sale. The Kilpatrick-Koch Dry Goods Company intervened in the replevin suit and made claim to the property by virtue of its chattel mortgage. Upon the trial of the cause Spearman obtained judgment against the sheriff, and the dry goods company recovered judgment against Spearman in the sum of $1,559.11. The sheriff prosecuted error to this court, where the judgment was affirmed. (See *Whitney v. Spearman*, 50 Neb. 617.) The present action was brought by the Sarpy County State Bank against H. M. Hinkle & Son, Cyrus K. Spearman, the Kilpatrick-Koch Dry Goods Company, McCord-Brady Company, and other creditors of said H. M. Hinkle & Son, plaintiff praying a decree establishing its said mortgage as the first and best lien upon the surplus funds in the hands of Spearman, notwithstanding the said judgment in favor of the Kilpatrick-Koch Dry Goods Company; that Spearman be required to pay the surplus funds in his hands, or so much thereof as shall be necessary to satisfy the amount of plaintiff's mortgage, with interest and costs; and that, pending this suit, the Kilpatrick-Koch Dry Goods Company be restrained from enforcing its judgment against Spearman; and that the latter be enjoined from paying said judgment, until the rights and equities of plaintiff can be determined by the court; and for such further or other relief as the court shall deem just and equitable. McCord-Brady Company and the Kilpatrick-Koch Dry Goods Company filed separate answers to the petition, but Spearman and the other defendants made default. There was a reply filed to each of said answers, and upon the trial the court dismissed the petition of plaintiff and dissolved the restraining order. Plaintiff appeals.

It is very plain that the decree of the court below cannot stand. Plaintiff had a lien on the property second only to Spearman's mortgage, and it is evident that plaintiff, under the undisputed facts, was entitled to a decree against the latter for the amount of surplus remaining in Spearman's hands after satisfying the amount of his mortgage debt. It is true that in the replevin suit the Kilpatrick-Koch Dry Goods Company obtained a judgment against Spearman for this identical money, but that is of no importance here, since the bank was not a party to the replevin litigation, and is not in the least affected by the judgment entered therein. As between the bank and the dry goods company their rights are to be determined as though the judgment in favor of the latter in the replvin action had never been obtained. H. M. Hinkle & Son were justly indebted to the bank in $1,394, and to secure the payment thereof the mortgage in question was executed and recorded prior, in point of time, to the mortgage given to the dry goods company. Plaintiff has a first lien, for the amount of its debt remaining unpaid, upon the surplus money in the hands of Spearman, and the dry goods company is entitled to a lien upon said surplus, subject to the lien of plaintiff. The decree is reversed and the cause remanded to the district court with directions to render a decree in accordance with this opinion.

REVERSED AND REMANDED.

●

HENRY LUBKER ET AL. V. GRAND DETOUR PLOW
COMPANY.

FILED DECEMBER 21, 1897.   No. 7610.

1. **Judgment:** FINDING: EVIDENCE. Judgment based upon a finding
   without sufficient evidence to sustain it is merely erroneous, but
   not void.
2. **Pleading and Proof:** VARIANCE: REVIEW. There must exist a material variance between the allegations and the proof to work a reversal of a cause.

ERROR from the district court of Platte county. Tried
below before SULLIVAN, J. *Affirmed.*

Albert & Reeder, for plaintiffs in error.

McAllister & Cornelius, contra.

NORVAL, J.

The Grand Detour Plow Company filed a petition in
the court below against Henry Lubker, W. J. Welch, and
Gus R. Krause to obtain the revivor of a certain dormant
judgment recovered before one John Rickley, a justice
of the peace in and for Columbus township, in Platte
county, a transcript of which judgment had been duly
lodged in the office of the clerk of the district court of.
said county. The answer was a general denial, and on
the hearing an order of revivor was entered.

It is insisted that the judgment sought to be revived
is void upon its face. The transcript of said judgment
shows that it was recovered upon a promissory note
signed "Krause, Lubker & Welch." The summons issued
in the case by the justice was served on William J.
Welch, Gus R. Krause, and Henry Lubker, the persons
who were the defendants in the court below in the proceedings to revive, and the justice entered judgment
against them, and not against the firm of which they
were members. It may be that the justice erred in entering judgment against the defendants, upon the mere
production of the note, without additional proofs show-

ing that they were members of the firm who executed the obligation sued on. There may not have been sufficient evidence before the justice to authorize the finding, but if that be the case it does not render the judgment void. At most it is an error for which, in a proper proceeding, a reversal might have been obtained. Furthermore, the transcript of the justice's docket shows that the defendants have recognized the validity of the judgment by paying $34 thereon within a year after its rendition.

The only other ground urged for a reversal is that the finding of the district court is without evidence to support it. The transcript of the justice's judgment was introduced on the hearing, which agreed with the averments of the petition for revivor as to date, amount, and the names of parties, plaintiff and defendants, as well as the name of the justice who pronounced the judgment. There were variances between the allegations and the proofs in the following respects: The petition alleged that the judgment sought to be revived was recovered before John Rickley, a justice of the peace of the city of Columbus, Platte county, and that a transcript of the same was filed in the office of the clerk of the district court on November 11, 1887, while the transcript received in evidence is indorsed as having been filed November 29, 1887, and is of a judgment rendered by John Rickley, a justice of the peace of Columbus township, Platte county. The variance in the two particulars stated relates to matters not of sufficient importance to require a reversal of the cause, since the judgment sought to be revived was otherwise definitely described in the petition. The defendants could not have been misled. No objection to the admission of the transcript was raised in the court below. Had the point now urged been made at the time of the trial doubtless the defect would have been remedied. The order reviving the judgment is

AFFIRMED.

THOMAS E. WILSON, COUNTY CLERK OF GAGE COUNTY, ET AL. V. STATE OF NEBRASKA, EX REL. JAMES PLASTERS.

FILED DECEMBER 21, 1897. No. 7567.

1. **Counties**: ALLOWANCE OF CLAIMS: ITEMS. A claim against a county cannot be audited and allowed in advance of the furnishing of the items or the rendition of the services therein charged.

2. ———: ———: COUNTY BOARD. A county board may not delegate to its chairman and clerk the power to audit claims against the county.

3. ———: ———: WARRANTS. It is only after the allowance of a claim upon the treasury of a county that a warrant in payment thereof may be properly drawn.

ERROR from the district court of Gage county. Tried below before BABCOCK, J. *Reversed.*

R. W. Sabin and *J. A. Smith,* for plaintiffs in error.

George A. Murphy, contra.

NORVAL, J.

James Plasters was the duly appointed and qualified deputy county clerk of Gage county, and acted as such during the month of January, 1894, from the 4th day of said month. On the 1st day of the month following he filed in the office of the county clerk a bill for his services as deputy during the preceding month, at the rate of $800 per annum, to-wit, in the sum of $75.08, and demanded of the respondents Thomas E. Wilson and Edward B. Sherman, respectively the county clerk and the chairman of the board of supervisors of said county of Gage, that they countersign and issue to him a warrant on the county general fund for the amount of said bill. Respondents having failed and refused to comply with said demand, relator instituted this action for a peremptory writ of mandamus commanding them to issue a warrant in his favor, in the sum last aforesaid, for his salary as deputy county clerk. To obtain a reversal of the judgment of the court below rendered in favor of the relator is the purpose of this proceeding.

By section 42, chapter 28, Compiled Statutes 1893, each county clerk of a county containing a population of over 25,000 inhabitants may be allowed one deputy at a salary of $1,000 per annum, which compensation, it seems, said section requires to be paid out of the fees of the office. After the adoption of said section the legislature of 1893 passed sections 46*d* and 46*c* of said chapter 28 (Session Laws 1893, ch. 18, secs. 1, 2), which read as follows:

"Sec. 46*d*. That in all counties in the state of Nebraska having twenty-five thousand (25,000) inhabitants or over, the county clerk shall be supplied by the board of county commissioners or supervisors with the help necessary for the use of such office, said clerk or help to be paid in the manner hereinafter provided.

"Sec. 46*e*. The salary of such clerks or assistants shall be fixed, allowed, and paid monthly, by the county commissioners or supervisors out of the general fund of the county."

It is under and by virtue of the foregoing provisions that relator claims the right to have his salary paid out of the county general fund. Respondents argue that a deputy county clerk is not a "clerk" or "assistant" within the purview of said sections, and further, that said sections are obnoxious to various constitutional provisions, and therefore void. In our view it is unnecessary at this time to pass upon any of those contentions, since relator is not entitled upon his own showing to the relief demanded. This claim against Gage county for salary has never been allowed by the county board thereof. Not until after a claim is duly audited and allowed is the county clerk and chairman of the county board authorized to draw and issue a warrant therefor. (Compiled Statutes, ch. 18, art. 1, secs. 33, 37. See also section 46*e* quoted above.)

Relator relies upon the following resolution adopted by the board of supervisors of Gage county on July 15, 1893, which was several months before the services were rendered, or the appointment of relator as deputy county clerk was made:

"WHEREAS, Owing to the fact of the infrequent meeting of the board of supervisors, it works a great hardship upon the various employés of the county officers, in getting their pay, who are entitled to receive it from the general fund of the county, by reason of having to discount their accounts and time in advance, in order to get their salaries to live upon, be it therefore

"*Resolved*, That the chairman of the board of supervisors and the clerk of said board are hereby empowered to issue monthly warrants for the amounts due those employés of the various offices of the county who are entitled to receive their pay from the general fund of the county commencing on the first day of August, 1893.

"This applies also to the janitor, county superintendent, and the county attorney at such times that their salaries are due. This resolution does not apply to the salaries of any employés who do not receive their salaries from the general fund of the county.

"*Provided*, That no warrants as aforesaid shall be drawn by the chairman for any salaries unless the same is fixed by the statute or has been fixed by this board."

The foregoing falls very far short of meeting the requirements of the statute relating to the auditing and adjusting of claims by county boards. The law does not contemplate the auditing of a demand until after the items or services therein charged have been actually furnished or rendered. Manifestly such is the import of said section 37. Moreover, a county board cannot delegate to its chairman and clerk, jointly or singly, the power to examine and pass upon claims against the county, any more than the board can confer the authority to do so upon the sheriff or the janitor of the court house. The action upon a claim must be by the county board when in lawful session. We must not be understood as deciding that the board of supervisors of a county may not refer claims to a committee composed of one or more of its members for investigation and report; but in such case the board itself must take final action thereon by adopting or rejecting the report or recommendation of the committee. For the reasons stated the writ should have been denied. The judgment is

REVERSED.

GERTRUDE T. EDNEY ET AL. V. JAMES E. BAUM ET AL.

FILED DECEMBER 21, 1897. No. 9188.

Executors and Administrators: REVOCATION OF LETTERS: EFFECT ON ACTION. Where the letters of an administrator or executor have been revoked, such *quondam* personal representative has no standing in the supreme court to question the correctness of a judgment rendered by the district court in an action wherein he was a party when such revocation took place.

ERROR from the district court of Lancaster county. Tried below before HALL, J. *Proceeding in error dismissed.*

Richard Cunningham and *Lamb & Adams,* for plaintiffs error.

Burr & Burr and *C. E. Magoon, contra.*

RYAN, C.

On questions differing widely from those now presented an opinion has been filed in this case. (*Edney v. Baum,* 44 Neb. 294.) After the case had been remanded to the district court of Lancaster county an amended petition was filed in which "Gertrude T. Edney and Patrick Cavanaugh, as executors of the last will of James A. Edney, deceased," alone were named as plaintiffs.

The defendants were James E. Baum, David Baum, and
Daniel Baum. The relief prayed was a judgment for the
amount of damages alleged to have been sustained by
the estate of James A. Edney by reason of the fraudulent
representations of the value of certain lots made by defendants, whereby said personal representatives of
James A. Edney had been induced to accept said lots as
part payment for a certain stock of goods constituting a
part of said estate, which stock, by said executrix and
executor, had been sold to the defendants. While the
jury were deliberating upon the verdict to be rendered
upon the issues which had been joined between said
litigants the defendants by their supplemental answer
alleged that before the trial had begun the said executrix
and executor had been finally discharged upon their
petition, whereby there had been a representation and
showing made by them that the estate of their testator
had been fully settled. There was a prayer for a dismissal of this action and that it might be abated. On
April 6, 1896, being the day on which the above described
supplemental answer was filed, there was returned a
verdict for the plaintiffs in the sum of $3,000, and, within
three days thereafter, the defendants filed their motion
for a new trial. In October, 1896, there was filed by
plaintiffs in said court a paper described as "Reasons
why motion for new trial should not be granted." In
this paper the objections to sustaining the motion for a
new trial were that the discharge of the executrix and
executor had been made improvidently and against the
wishes of said executrix and executor. The district
court filed its special findings on December 11, 1896, and
thereon dismissed the action because of the discharge of
said personal representatives of James A. Edney and because the petition failed to state a cause of action. As
the conclusion reached with reference to the first of these
propositions must dispose of this proceeding in this
cause, we shall refrain from the expression of any opinion with reference to the merits of the second. Upon

the issues of fact presented by the supplemental answer there was a finding by the district court adversely to the contentions of the plaintiff. No bill of exceptions was settled, for which reason this finding must be recognized as conclusive. In this proceeding, therefore, we are bound to assume that the proper probate court, acting within the scope of its powers and with jurisdiction of the subject-matter, regularly entered an order whereby the executrix and executor of the estate of James A. Edney were discharged. The consequences of this discharge must now be considered and determined.

Section 336, chapter 23, Compiled Statutes, provides: "When an executor or an administrator shall die, be removed from office, or resign, or when his letters shall be revoked, during the pendency of any suit in which he is a party, the suit may be prosecuted by or against the executor or administrator appointed in his place, if any shall be appointed, in like manner as if it had originally been commenced by or against such last executor or administrator." The defendants in error have insisted very strenuously in argument that the removal of the executrix and executor caused an abatement of the action, but it will be noticed upon a careful consideration of the language just quoted that no such result is therein contemplated. This is significant in view of the sections of the Code of Civil Procedure, which we shall now consider. It is provided in section 45 that "An action does not abate by the death, marriage, or other disability of a party, or by the transfer of any interest therein, during its pendency, if the cause of action survive or continue. In the case of the marriage of a female party, the fact being suggested on the record, the husband may be made a party with his wife; and, in the case of the death or other disability of a party, the court may allow the action to continue by or against his representative or successor in interest." Sections 466 and 467 of said Code provide that actions may be revived in the names of the representatives and successors of plaintiffs within a year from the time the order of revivor might first have been made, and not later without the consent of the opposite party. The provisions of section 468 are as follows: "When it appears to the court by affidavit that either party to an action has been dead, or where a party sues or is sued as a personal representative, that his powers have ceased for a period so long that the action cannot be revived in the names of his representatives or successor, without the consent of both parties, it shall order the action to be stricken from the docket." We have referred to the above statutory provisions, not for the purposes of determining whether or not the action of the district court was in accordance with the provisions of the statute, but to illustrate our views, which are, that by the removal of the executrix and executor the action did not, *ipso facto*, abate, but remained in suspension until there should appear a party authorized to take further steps for its prosecution. While this condition of suspension existed there was no power in the *quondam* executrix or executor to prosecute error proceedings to this court, nevertheless we are asked by these very representatives to recognize them as still existing parties and at their instance to set aside an order of which they alone complain. This we are powerless to do, for the very obvious reasons that the district court, in the proper exercise of its jurisdiction, found as a fact that these alleged personal representatives had ceased to be such,—a conclusion we are bound to assume was correct, because we have not presented to us the evidence on which it was reached. From these considerations it results that as no order granting or denying relief on the application of these alleged personal representatives as plaintiffs in error can be made, their petition in error must be, and accordingly it is,

DISMISSED.

ANDREW L. UNDELAND ET AL. V. FRANK S. STANFIELD
ET AL.

FILED DECEMBER 21, 1897.   No. 7674.

1. **Chattel Mortgages:** FORECLOSURE SALE: RIGHTS OF BIDDERS. One
who claims an interest in chattels by virtue of his bid therefor
upon the foreclosure of a mortgage thereon by sale at public auc-
tion cannot be heard to question the regularity of a subsequent
sale of the same chattels rendered necessary by his own refusal, by
payment, to make good his bid.

2. **Amendment of Pleading During Trial.** It is within the discretion
of the trial court to allow an amendment of a petition in the
course of a trial where such amendment does not change the
original cause of action stated by the plaintiff.

ERROR from the district court of Douglas county.
Tried below before AMBROSE, J. *Affirmed.*

Weaver & Giller, for plaintiffs in error.

Lawrence Rath and *Charles Offutt, contra.*

RYAN, C.

This was replevin for the possession of certain barber's supplies, tools, etc., which had been mortgaged by
the firm of A. L. Undeland & Co. to various parties to
whom that firm was indebted. As a purchaser under
the foreclosure of certain of these mortgages, Frank S.
Stanfield, originally as owner, began this action in the
district court of Douglas county. Subsequently, with
leave of said court, Stanfield amended his petition so
as to claim the replevied property as owner and as agent
and custodian of one Annie Bradbury, who, as was alleged, had a special interest in, and by reason thereof
was entitled to the immediate possession of, said property. The nature of this special interest claimed for
Annie Bradbury will appear in the further statement
of the facts of this case. The firm of A. L. Undeland &
Co. was composed of Andrew L. Undeland and Nels,

Steffenson.   This firm executed the chattel mortgages at the dates, for the several amounts, and to the respective parties, following, to-wit: January 15, 1894, to Theodore A. Kochs, for $250; January 16, 1894, to Mrs. Annie Bradbury, for $265; January 17, 1894, to E. E. Bruce & Co., for $71.54; January 19, 1894, to Graef Cutlery Co., for $365.25; January 19, 1894, to J. B. Williams Co., for $118.12.   On January 19, 1894, the mortgage to Theodore A. Kochs was assigned to Mrs. Bradbury and at some time in January, 1894, the mortgage to E. E. Bruce & Co. was assigned to Frank S. Stanfield.   These two parties therefore were the owners of the mortgages to secure the aggregate amount of $586.54.   On January 17, 1894, Stanfield went into possession of the mortgaged property upon the request of Mrs. Bradbury and continued in such possession until the date of the sale hereinafter described.   On February 20, 1894, pursuant to the foreclosure notices which had been duly published by Mrs. Bradbury in her own right and as assignee and by Frank S. Stanfield as assignee, the mortgaged property was offered for sale.   By this time other mortgages had been filed of record.   There was competitive bidding until the final bid was made by Jacob B. Emminger of $1,925 for the whole of the property mortgaged.   In satisfaction of this bid Emminger refused to pay more than $704, insisting that this would be sufficient to discharge the mortgages advertised for foreclosure, and all proper and reasonable costs attendant upon the sale, and even this offer was coupled with the requirement that the mortgages should be assigned to the bidder.   After an hour and probably more spent in attempting to obtain payment of the bid above described the agent of the parties foreclosing declared that the bid not being complied with was rejected and forthwith again offered the property for sale, and there being no other bidder, it was struck off to Stanfield for $1,300.   Emminger thereupon, with the aid of Undeland, Weaver, and Giller, took possession of the property which he claimed to have pur-

chased and this replevin suit was brought against these
parties to recover the possession to which Stanfield
claims to be entitled by virtue of his bid on behalf of
himself and Mrs. Bradbury.

The arguments of Mr. Emminger will now be considered separately.   He urges that, as the excess above
the mortgages held by Stanfield and Mrs. Bradbury was
payable to the mortgagors, he should not have been
required to pay the amount of his bid.   One matter of
dispute between Stanfield and Emminger when the latter
refused to make good his bid was that the expenses of
foreclosure, as estimated by Stanfield, were not approved
by Emminger as being necessary as to two items and
were not reasonable as to a third.   As a mere purchaser
these matters were no concerns of Emminger.   His
proposition was to take the property at the price fixed
by himself, and if he wished to get this property there
was but one thing for him to do, and that was, to pay
what by his bid he had offered.   He undertook to justify
his refusal not only on the above ground, but also because, as he claimed, Stanfield was not financially
responsible for the sum of $1,925.   Mr. Emminger had
no justification for offering to pay this sum unless he
intended to pay it if accepted, and having made the bid,
it was no concern of his whether Stanfield would account
faithfully to his principal or not.   Again, Mr. Emminger
insists that the sale to Stanfield was made after 4 o'clock,
and, therefore, no title thereby was vested in Stanfield.
Emminger is in no position to raise this question.   He,
at least, has no title, and his dispossession of Stanfield
by force gave him no rights by virtue of possession.   The
other plaintiffs in error in the district court filed as their
answer a disclaimer of title and denied that they ever
had been in possession of the goods in controversy.
They, therefore, cannot be heard at this late stage of the
proceedings to urge that Stanfield should not be entitled to possession because of irregularities in the sale,
even if we should concede that the sale to Stanfield was

irregular,—a concession not necessary to be taken into account.

The amendment did not change the cause of action and was, therefore, permissible. (*Stratton v. Wood*, 45 Neb. 629.) There is found no error in the record and the judgment of the district court is

AFFIRMED.

53 123
53 127

GRANITE STATE FIRE INSURANCE COMPANY V. BUCK-STAFF BROTHERS MANUFACTURING COMPANY.

FILED DECEMBER 21, 1897.   No. 7765.

1. **Insurance:** PROOF OF LOSS: CLASSIFICATION OF PROPERTY. The general allegation in a petition that certain insured property, otherwise fully described, was real property, does not require that the insured, in making proofs of loss in an action on a policy, should show that the property was real property and totally destroyed and thereupon rely upon the provisions of the valued policy law; but he may show the value as it was just before the fire, and its value just after, as affording data for the assessment of his damages, without attempting to classify the property as real or personal.

2. ———: VALUE OF PROPERTY: EVIDENCE. Where there was evidence which showed that the property had been totally destroyed and that its value before such destruction was of a certain amount, the jury was justified in accepting this testimony as the basis for a recovery by the plaintiff, notwithstanding the fact that there was evidence contradictory of each of these propositions.

ERROR from the district court of Lancaster county. Tried below before HALL, J.   *Affirmed.*

Sylvester G. Williams and *Stevens, Love & Cochran,* for plaintiff in error.

Charles O. Whedon, contra.

RYAN, C.

On October 14, 1892, the Buckstaff Brothers Manufacturing Company, a corporation, effected an insurance of its property with the Granite State Fire Insurance Company. The three several items insured, as well as the insurance thereon, were described in the policy as follows:

"$1,000 on the following property hereinafter described and situated on block 105, Lincoln, Nebraska, to-wit:

"$225 on its one-story gravel and board roof buildings, all adjoining and communicating and occupied by the assured as a boiler and engine house, brick machinery room, clay mixing rooms, and dry tunnels building; $13,500 total insurance permitted on above item;

"$75 on boilers, foundations, settings, and iron smoke stack, engines, foundations and settings, pumps and all their immediate connections while contained therein; $4,500 total insurance permitted on above item;

"$700 on fixed and movable machinery of all kinds (except engines, boilers, and pumps), shafting, belting, gearing, hangers, pulleys, conveyers, brick machines, clay crushers, pug mills, iron cars, trucks, tracks, pallets, blowers and fans, tools, implements, millwright work, steam and water pipes, while contained therein; $42,000 total insurance permitted on above item."

On February 16, 1893, while this policy was in force, the property insured was greatly damaged and, as insisted by the insured, was totally destroyed. In an action brought on this policy in the district court of Lancaster county there was a judgment upon a verdict for the total insurance, $1,000, with interest at seven per cent per annum from the date of the loss.

In the petition in the district court there were the allegations: "That on the date last aforesaid and continuously from that time (October 14, 1892) to the time of the fire and the loss hereinafter mentioned said property was used for the purpose of manufacturing brick, and said property was real property and was all used by the plaintiff in the process and business of manufacturing brick at the time of the fire hereinafter mentioned and prior

thereto, and said property constituted a brick manufactory when burned." Plaintiff in error, all through the
trial, insisted, and now insists, that the averment that
the property destroyed was real property necessarily so
qualifies the right to recover that no recovery could be
had for the loss of personal property. In the petition
the property alleged to have been destroyed was described in the same language employed in the policy
descriptive of that insured. Plaintiff in error asked the
district court to instruct the jury that there was no dispute as to the amount payable under the first item in
the policy, provided the insurance company was liable.
We shall therefore omit further reference to this item.
In his testimony J. A. Buckstaff, president of the defendant in error, said that the entire property was destroyed,
was burned up, that everything combustible was burned
except a part of the shed over a part of the kilns, and
that the fair market value of the second item just before the fire was $7,000, and of the third item was $46,-
000. There was no effort made by the company of which
Mr. Buckstaff was president to describe what parts of
the second item were personal, as distinguished from
real property, neither was there such an effort with reference to the constituent parts of the third item. The
contentions of the plaintiff in error that a recovery could
be had for only so much of the loss as affected real property is with respect to an immaterial matter. If the
insured had shown that the entire property covered by
the policy was real property and had been totally destroyed, he might have rested upon the presumption
raised by statute that the value fixed in the policy was
the amount for which a recovery should be had. But
this right did not prevent the insured from showing, as
independent facts, the actual losses, whether to real or
personal property, and this we think was done by the
above evidence to such a degree of certainty that the
jury was warranted in acting upon it notwithstanding
testimony of a contradictory character. The amount of

concurrent insurance, including that evidenced by the policy issued by the plaintiff in error, was $49,500. The loss, if we accept Mr. Buckstaff's testimony as correct, was $53,000. The fact of concurrent insurance, therefore, did not serve to prevent a recovery for $1,000, the total amount of the insurance under the policy of plaintiff in error, with interest thereon.

It is urged that there should have been submitted to the jury 24 requests for special findings. It has been held by this court, repeatedly, that the submission of interrogatories, for the purpose of eliciting special findings, is largely a matter of discretion resting with the trial court. (*Floaten v. Ferrell,* 24 Neb. 353; *Nebraska & Iowa Ins. Co. v. Christiensen,* 29 Neb. 581; *Atchison, T. & S. F. R. Co. v. Lawler,* 40 Neb. 356; *Hedrick v. Strauss,* 42 Neb. 485.) We have not been able to see in what respect there was an abuse of the discretion of the trial court in its refusal to require the jury to make the special findings requested.

It is not necessary to review the alleged errors in overruling challenges to proposed jurors, for the answers of each, on his *voir dire* examination, fully justified the trial court in its assumption that the proposed juror could determine this case independently of ideas entertained with reference to another case, arising out of the same fire, in which some of the proposed jurors had served as jurors.

There is discovered no error in the record and the judgment of the district court is

AFFIRMED.

PROVIDENCE-WASHINGTON INSURANCE COMPANY V. BUCK-
STAFF BROTHERS MANUFACTURING COMPANY.

SPRING GARDEN INSURANCE COMPANY V. BUCKSTAFF
BROTHERS MANUFACTURING COMPANY. ·

WESTERN ASSURANCE COMPANY V. BUCKSTAFF BROTH-
ERS MANUFACTURING COMPANY.

COMMERCIAL UNION ASSURANCE COMPANY V. BUCKSTAFF
BROTHERS MANUFACTURING COMPANY.

FILED DECEMBER 21, 1897.   Nos. 7669, 7670, 7671, 7672.

Insurance: PROOFS OF LOSS: CLASSIFICATION OF PROPERTY: VALUE.

ERROR from the district court of Lancaster county.
Tried below before HALL, J. *Affirmed.*

Sylvester G. Williams and *Stevens, Love & Cochran,* for
plaintiffs in error.

Charles O. Whedon, contra.

RYAN, C.

The four cases above described were submitted on the
record and argument in *Granite State Fire Ins. Co. v. Buckstaff Brothers Mfg. Co.,* 53 Neb. 123. It being conceded
that the decision in the case last named must determine
the result in each of said four cases, the judgment in
each is likewise

AFFIRMED.

MARY ANDRESEN, ADMINISTRATRIX OF THE ESTATE OF
DORA WITTE, V. LEDERER & STRAUSS.

FILED DECEMBER 21, 1897.   No. 7653.

1. **Courts**: POWER TO CORRECT RECORDS. A court of record has the inherent power to correct its own records, even after an appeal, so
that such amended record may show correctly the history of the
proceedings in the district court before the appeal therefrom.

2. ———: ———. A trial court, after an appeal has been perfected
therefrom, has no power to so correct its records, that, in fact, a
modification of the judgment already appealed from shall be
effected. NORVAL, J., dissenting.

3. **Amendment of Records**: REVIEW. The ruling of the district court
in this case is reversed in view of the fact, on the one hand, that,
if the amendment reciting that the judgment was "upon agreement
of parties" was tantamount to a substantive order after appeal it
was void and should not have been considered by the district
court, and if, on the other hand, it was a mere recitation of events
which had occurred during the progress of the trial in the county
court, the district court should not have held the appeal necessarily to have been vitiated by the amendment, as it did by dismissing the appeal because of the recitation of such amendment.
NORVAL, J., dissenting.

ERROR from the district court of Lancaster county.
Tried below before HALL, J. *Reversed.*

Bochmer & Rummons and *W. E. Stewart,* for plaintiff in
error.

Roscoe Pound and *Burr & Burr, contra.*

RYAN, C.

These error proceedings are prosecuted for the reversal
of an order of the district court of Lancaster county
whereby was sustained a motion of Lederer & Strauss
to dismiss an appeal from the allowance in favor of said
Lederer & Strauss of a claim recited in the transcript as
having been heard "upon agreement of parties" in the
county court of said county. The history of the case in
the county court is as follows: On December 4, 1893, the

claims of the State Savings Bank, John L. Carson, and Lederer & Strauss, respectively, against the estate of Dora Witte came on in said county court for hearing. The claimants were represented by counsel, and the administratrix of the estate of Dora Witte, with her counsel, also appeared. The record recites the same proceedings to have been had on each claim, but, as we are now considering that of Lederer & Strauss alone, the portion of the history pertaining thereto in the various stages of the case will be stated. In the record of the county court it is recited that "Upon consideration of the agreement of parties the court finds," etc. The allowance thus appears to have resulted from, and to have been founded upon, the agreement of the parties concerned, made in open court while this claim was under consideration. On January 6, 1894, the administratrix of the estate of Dora Witte filed her motion in the county court asking that the record above referred to be amended so as to conform to the facts as she alleged them to be. This motion was, on the date last mentioned, sustained, and accordingly the record was thereupon made to recite that the order of allowance of date December 4, 1893, had been entered "upon consideration of the evidence introduced." While an appeal from the allowance of this claim was pending in the district court upon the record of the county court in the condition indicated, Lederer & Strauss, having notified the said administratrix that application would be made, presented in the county court, on February 20, 1894, a motion asking, in effect, that the record on the hearing of the claim in that court might be restored to the conditions existing before the amendment procured by the administratrix had been made. This was sustained and accordingly the record was again made to show that the allowance of the claim was "upon agreement of parties." Before another move was made in the county court the last of its amendments was, upon suggestion of a diminution of the record, allowed to be filed in the district court. Very soon

13

thereafter Lederer & Strauss filed a motion to dismiss
the appeal from said district court because the judgment
appealed from had been rendered by agreement of
parties. This motion was sustained. There was another ground stated in the motion which need not be
considered, for the reason that the' ruling of the district
court must be justified, if at all, upon the ground above
stated.

It has been held that the district courts of this state
have power to correct at a subsequent term of court any
errors or defects which may have occurred through the
mistake or neglect of the clerks of said district courts
so as to make the judgment entry correspond to the judgment actually rendered. (*Brownlee v. Davidson*, 28 Neb.
785; *Hoagland v. Way*, 35 Neb. 387; *School District v.
Bishop*, 46 Neb. 850; *Wachsmuth v. Orient Ins. Co.*, 49 Neb.
590.) It scarcely admits of doubt, under the authorities
cited and the current of decisions of the courts of this
country, that this power to make amendments may be
exercised without reference to the mistake or inaccuracy
having arisen through the carelessness of a clerk. As a
general rule, this right of amendment continues even
after an appeal has been taken for a review of the judgment rendered by a court of record. (*Welch v. Damon*,
11 Gray [Mass.] 383; *De Kalb County v. Hixon*, 44 Mo.
341; *Jones v. St. Joseph Ins. Co.*, 55 Mo. 342; *Gamble v.
Daugherty*, 71 Mo. 599; *City Bank v. Exchange Bank*, 97
N. Y. 645; *Guernsey v. Miller*, 80 N. Y. 181; *Chichester v.
Cande*, 3 Cowen [N. Y.] 42; *Chestnutt v. Pollard*, 77 Tex.
87; *Cowan v. Ross*, 28 Tex. 228; *McNairy v. Castleberry*, 6
Tex. 286; *Kelly v. Chicago & N. R. Co.*, 70 Wis. 335; *State
v. Supervisors of Delafield*, 69 Wis. 264.) The correctness
of this rule, as an abstract proposition, is attended with
no difficulty; but, as with many others, the difficulty
arises when we attempt to treat it as of universal applicability. There is recognized by the courts another rule
of very general applicability, and that is, that when an
appeal is taken, all power of the court appealed from, to

change its judgment or modify its orders, ceases to exist until the cause or some part of it is remanded by the appellate court. When there arises a conflict in the operation of these rules it is often difficult to formulate any general proposition fairly deducible from the adjudicated cases. In Iowa it has been held that if a defective return of service of the original notice, answering the purpose of our summons, had been amended before an appeal had been perfected, the decree was binding, but that, if the amendment was made after appeal from the court whose jurisdiction had been determined by the appeal, the amendment was void. (*McGlaughlin. v. O'Rourke*, 12 Ia. 459.) This inflexible rule was invoked and rigidly enforced in *Levi v. Karrick*, 15 Ia. 444, and *Turner v. Bank*, 30 Ia. 191. In *Carmichael v. Vandebur*, 51 Ia. 225, it was held that where an appeal had been taken, the jurisdiction of the trial court was suspended so that it had no power to entertain a motion to correct an error in its proceedings.

In *Chestnutt v. Pollard*, 77 Tex. 86, it was said by Gaines. J., delivering the opinion of the court: "It is true that after an appeal or writ of error has been perfected, the district court has no further jurisdiction in the cause until it be remanded; but a court has authority, upon proper proof, to correct its minutes at any time so as to make them present a faithful record of its action. (*Cowan v. Castleberry*, 6 Tex. 286; *Russell v. Miller*, 40 Tex. 495.)" In this case the correction in the trial court was the substitution of the correct number of the case wherein the decree had been rendered for an incorrect number which originally had been therein inserted. This false number was the sole ground for the contention that the decree had, in reality, not been rendered in the appealed case. The authority of this case is, however, greatly impaired by the fact that it was held that the amendment not being misleading in view of the fact that otherwise than by number the case was sufficiently identified, the correction was with reference to an immaterial matter. As we understand the opinion in *Gerard v. State*, 10 Tex. App. 690, the amendment consisted in giving the names of twelve jurors, the record before correction having named but eleven. In this opinion there was used this language: "We cannot consider for any purpose the attempted correction of the record, made subsequently to the perfection of the appeal and after the jurisdiction had attached on appeal. After an appeal has been taken and the jurisdiction of the appellate court has attached, the case has passed out of the jurisdiction of the trial court and it can make no further order in the case. The effect of an appeal is to suspend and arrest all further proceedings in the case in the court in which the conviction was had until the judgment of the appellate court is received by the court from which the appeal was taken." The value of this case as a precedent is greatly impaired by the fact that it was held that other portions of the record probably sufficiently disclosed that there were twelve jurors, though in giving a list of them there were but eleven persons named as having served as such. We have found no other adjudicated case bearing upon this question in the courts of Texas, and must therefore leave the question in that state in the unsatisfactory condition above indicated.

In *De Kalb County v. Hixon*, *supra*, the syllabus, which reflects correctly the only point determined, was in this language: "Where, a cause having been appealed to the district court, the record showed a dismissal as to a certain defendant, but no final judgment, and a writ of *certiorari* in the cause showed that the judgment had been ordered, but the clerk had omitted to enter it of record, the court below properly ordered its records amended *nunc pro tunc*, so as to show that final judgment followed the order of dismissal. The court had lost jurisdiction of the case, but not of its records."

In *Kelly v. Chicago & N. W. R. Co.*, 70 Wis. 335, the trial court, upon its own motion, on November 30, 1885, had ordered "That the said special verdict be and the same is hereby set aside as inconsistent and a retrial ordered." After this order had been entered an appeal was taken, and, still later the trial court, on motion of plaintiff, amended the above portion of the order by inserting the words "and contrary to the evidence," immediately following the word "inconsistent." Lyon, J., prefaced the opinion of the court which he delivered with these remarks: "It was competent for the defendant to appeal from the order of November 30, 1885, before the same was corrected. It did so appeal and it has the right to have its appeal determined as the order then was, without regard to the subsequent correction thereof. It was so held under very similar circumstances in *State v. Supervisors of Delafield*, 69 Wis. 264." It would seem from this adjudication to be the rule that the trial court has no right to prejudice an appeal already perfected by the insertion in its record of an amendment importing that a trial had been had in such a manner as to imply, for the first time, that questions of fact had been considered in that court. We presume this holding was influenced by a consideration of the well recognized presumptions · which obtain in favor of the correctness of findings of fact made upon the evidence offered by the parties. An illustration of the hopelessness of an attempt, upon principle, to reconcile the decisions of the courts of this country with regard to what is permissible as showing merely what was done in the trial court as distinguished from what was tantamount to an order involving the retention by that court of jurisdiction after an appeal perfected therefrom, the *National City Bank v. New York Gold Exchange Bank*, 97 N. Y. 645, may profitably be examined in connection with *State v. Delafield, supra*. The case between the two banks was determined upon a motion to amend a return, and it was held that an amendment of a record which merely recited that the judgment had been reversed by inserting after the word "reversed" the qualifying words "upon questions of fact and law" was such an amendment as could properly be made in the trial court after an appeal from its judgment, and that a motion to correct the return to show the amendment with a view to its consideration by the appellate court should be sustained. This was in direct conflict with the holding of the supreme court of Wisconsin in *State r. Supervisors of Delafield, supra,* and, on principle, cannot be reconciled with the views entertained by the courts of Iowa and Missouri, and probably Texas.

In the supreme court of California a case resembling that under consideration was determined. (*San Francisco Savings Union r. Myers,* 72 Cal. 161.) The syllabus of this case was as follows:

"1. A motion was made to dismiss the appeal on the ground that the judgment appealed from was entered upon the mutual consent of the parties. The only evidence of consent contained in the transcript consisted of a written indorsement made in the margin opposite to the copy of the judgment as follows: 'Indorsed in lead pencil on the back of the original judgment is the following: Agreed to. Pillsbury & Blanding, Lewis Shearer, William F. Herrin.' The answer of the appellant was subscribed, 'Wallace, Greathouse and Blanding,' as his attorneys, for whom, after the entry of the judgment, was substituted Edward Lynch, by whom the notice of appeal was signed. Held, that the motion should be denied.

"2. The superior court cannot deprive the supreme court of jurisdiction of an appeal from a judgment by amending it while the appeal is pending."

With reference to the first paragraph of the syllabus above quoted it is quite evident that the court proceeded upon the theory that the facts recited did not justify the assumption that any agreement had been made. A portion of the language of the opinion should be read with reference to the subject-matter of the final paragraph, for by that means we are enabled more satisfactorily to realize the attitude of the supreme court of California with respect to the question we now have under consideration. Referring to a former motion to dismiss on the ground described in the first paragraph of the syllabus, the opinion proceeded thus: "It is urged, however, that the new motion is based upon evidence of facts not presented nor relied upon when the former motion was made. The only new fact submitted on the hearing of the present motion is that, after the order denying the former motion to dismiss, the court below, on application of plaintiff, amended, or attempted to amend, the judgment appealed from by inserting therein, 'Pillsbury and Blanding, attorneys for the defendant, M. L. Mc-Donald, * * * agreeing thereto.' If it be conceded the court below had power to amend the judgment, the amended judgment was substituted for the original, and, from the time of its entry, became the 'final judgment' in the superior court. We think it very plain that the superior court cannot deprive this court of jurisdiction of an appeal from a judgment by amending the judgment while the appeal is pending here." It is clear from the final paragraph of the syllabus, considered in connection with the language of the court above quoted, and the order which denied the motion to dismiss the appeal, that the supreme court of California was of the opinion that the insertion in the records of the superior court of words showing that the judgment appealed from had been entered by agreement had no effect upon such appeal, and that the amendment in question was not a mere correction of the recitations of a record, but was rather a prejudicial attempted modification of the judgment which had already been appealed from, which should not be tolerated in the appellate court. As we have already intimated, it is not difficult to formulate abstract general rules, which, applied to many cases, operate very satisfactorily. The difficulty is in the universal application of these rules, especially where, as in this case, they seem to conflict. The district court was evidently of the opinion that the amendment in the county court, whereby the transcript from that court of record was made to show that the hearing had been entirely upon the agreement of parties, was more than a mere amendment of a recitation of facts which had transpired, for the motion to dismiss the appeal because of the judgment being founded upon such an agreement was by said district court sustained. If the district court correctly assumed that it should dismiss the appeal because the amendment was one which destroyed the right to a hearing in the appellate court, this amendment was in its effect more than a mere correction of the record to show the history of the case in the trial court, consequently the order dismissing the appeal must be reversed, for, under all the authorities, an attempted exercise of jurisdiction by the trial court after an appeal from that court cannot be suffered to prejudice the rights of the appellant. On the other hand, if, in fact, the amendment accomplished no more than correctly to recite what had transpired during the trial, and in no degree impaired the rights of the appellant to be heard in the district court on the record in the condition it was when the appeal was taken, then the district court erred in holding the amendment of such controlling force that, upon its being shown to exist, the appeal must be dismissed. In any event, therefore, the judgment of the district court must be, and accordingly it is,

REVERSED.

MARY ANDRESEN, ADMINISTRATRIX OF THE ESTATE OF DORA WITTE, v. JOHN L. CARSON.

FILED DECEMBER 21, 1897. No. 7652.

Courts: POWER TO CORRECT RECORDS: APPEAL.

ERROR from the district court of Lancaster county. Tried below before HALL, J. *Reversed.*

Boehmer & Rummons and *W. E. Stewart*, for plaintiff in error.

J. H. Broady, contra.

RYAN, C.

This case involves the identical questions involved in *Andresen v. Lederer*, 53 Neb. 128, and none others, and, accordingly, the judgment of the district court in this case is

REVERSED.

NORVAL, J., dissenting.

JOHN LENZEN V. JOHN A. MILLER.

FILED DECEMBER 21, 1897.   No. 7334.

1. **Payment**: APPLICATION. Where a debtor remits money to his creditor without a request or instruction on what particular debt to apply the same, the creditor may apply the money upon any debt of his debtor which he chooses.

2. **Action on Notes**: EXCESSIVE VERDICT: REMITTITUR. Verdict of the jury *held* to be excessive and remittitur ordered.

REHEARING of case reported in 51 Neb. 855. *Judyment below held excessive, and remittitur ordered.*

Leslie G. Hurd, for plaintiff in error.

C. L. Richards, S. W. Christy, and *Stewart & Munger, contra.*

RAGAN, C.

This is a rehearing of *Lenzen v. Miller,* 51 Neb. 855. Of the arguments relied on here for reversing the judgment of the district court, we shall notice only two,—that the verdict is not sustained by sufficient evidence, and the

amount awarded by the jury to the plaintiff below is
excessive.

1. This suit was brought by Miller against Lenzen to
recover on three promissory notes bearing date January
17, 1876. The defense of Lenzen, so far as material here,
was the statute of limitations. Miller claimed in avoidance of this defense that Lenzen had paid him various
sums of money on these notes from the year 1879 to 1891,
both inclusive, part of which money so paid had been
indorsed on the notes and the last indorsement made
within five years before the suit was brought. Lenzen's
answer to this was that the moneys remitted by him
to Miller were so remitted with instructions by him·to
Miller to apply the remittances on an account which he
owed Miller, and had owed him since the year 1866. Miller's rejoinder to this was that at no time did Lenzen ever
instruct him, Miller, that the moneys remitted were to
be applied on the account and in fact gave him no instructions at all, and that as Lenzen owed him an
account, and also owed him the notes, he applied the
moneys received from Lenzen on the notes in suit. This
statement serves to illustrate the theory upon which
the case was presented to the jury. The finding of the
jury in favor of Miller embraces a finding that Lenzen
did not direct Miller on what debt to apply any remittances of money made to him; and this is the finding
which plaintiff in error insists is not supported by the
evidence. We think it is. Miller testified positively
that from the year 1879 to 1891, both inclusive, Lenzen
remitted him by checks and drafts, and sometimes by
private parties, various sums of money, aggregating
$1,330; that at no time did Lenzen ever direct, advise,
or request him, Miller, to credit the remittances made
to him upon any particular debt owing to Miller by
Lenzen. Lenzen, while on the stand in his own behalf,
failed to testify that he ever at any time directed or
instructed Miller to apply the remittances of money
made to him on the account owing to him; but he did

testify that, as he was owing him an account, he made the remittances to him that he did for the purpose of having them applied on the account; that, as a matter of fact, he had forgotten the existence of the notes. Here then is sufficient evidence to sustain the finding of the jury that the remittances or payments of money made to Miller by Lenzen were so made without instructions as to where Miller should apply them, and, as the remittances were so made, Miller might apply them as he pleased,—either upon the notes or the account of Lenzen.

We understand the rule to be that, where a debtor remits money to his creditor without request or instruction on what particular debt to apply the same, the creditor may apply the remittances upon any debt of his debtor which he chooses. (*State v. Hill*, 47 Neb. 456; *Crane v. Keck*, 35 Neb. 683.) But if the evidence in the bill of exceptions was not sufficient to sustain the finding of the jury under consideration, we would probably be unable to disturb that finding for the reason that the bill of exceptions discloses that the deposition of one Christie was read to the jury on behalf of Miller, and this deposition is not in the bill of exceptions brought here. It is said in *Storz v. Finkelstein*, 48 Neb. 27, that this court would not weigh the evidence to ascertain if it sustained a verdict when the bill of exceptions discloses that a deposition introduced in evidence and read upon the trial had been omitted therefrom.

2. Defendant in error has offered to file a remittitur from the judgment, and on this offer we have looked into the bill of exceptions solely for the purpose of ascertaining how much such a remittitur should be on defendant in error's testimony alone, and we now proceed to inquire. The principal of the three notes sued on is $1,500. Computing simple interest at 10 per cent per annum on these notes from their date, January 17, 1876, to November 8, 1893,—the first day of the term of court at which the judgment at bar was rendered,—we find the

time to be 17 years 9 months and 21 days, and the interest $2,671.25, or a total of $4,171.25. Miller testified on the stand in behalf of himself that from 1879 to 1891, both inclusive, he had received from Lenzen $1,330 to apply on these notes; that when he received the payments from Lenzen he entered them in an account-book, and, at his convenience, thereafter he indorsed the payments on the notes in suit; that he never received any instructions from Lenzen to apply any of these payments on his account; that the moneys remitted to him by Lenzen were remitted to him for the purpose of being applied upon the notes; and Miller does not testify that he ever applied one cent of the $1,330 received from Lenzen upon the account owing to him by Lenzen. For some reason, not disclosed by the record, Miller indorsed on these notes $790 only of the moneys received from Lenzen. He did indorse or attempt to indorse $375 of the moneys on a note which Lenzen owed his, Miller's, wife. What disposition Miller made of the remaining $165 is not disclosed by the record; but we think that Miller must be charged with the full amount of money which he admits and swears Lenzen remitted to him, which he received, and which he says was remitted to him to be applied upon the notes. This $1,330 with interest amounts to $2,194.80, which, deducted from the principal and interest of the notes in suit, leaves $1,976.45; but the verdict was for $3,704.11, or $1,727.66 too much. The defendants in error may, within thirty days from this date, and as of the date of the judgment, remit $1,727.66 therefrom, and, if they do so, the judgment of the district court for the remainder will be affirmed. If not, the judgment will be reversed and the cause remanded.

JUDGMENT ACCORDINGLY.

BERNARD SICKEL ET AL. V. JOHN S. BISHOP, ADMINIS-
TRATOR.

FILED DECEMBER 21, 1897. No. 7696.

1. **Action on Note:** EVIDENCE OF RELEASE OF SURETY: VERDICT FOR
   PLAINTIFF. Evidence examined, and *held* to sustain the finding of
   the jury.
2. **Review:** ASSIGNMENTS OF ERROR: SET-OFF. Under an assignment
   that "the verdict is not supported by sufficient evidence" this court
   cannot deduct from the award made by the jury the amount of a
   counter-claim or set-off existing in favor of the defendant, and
   against the plaintiff, where the same was not interposed as a defense to the action.

ERROR from the district court of Lancaster county.
Tried below before STRODE, J. *Affirmed.*

Don L. Love, for plaintiffs in error.

John S. Bishop, contra.

RAGAN, C.

In the district court of Lancaster county John S.
Bishop, administrator, sued Bernard Sickel and Luther
P. Ludden upon a promissory note. Bishop had a verdict and judgment, and Sickel and Ludden bring the
same here for review on error.

1. One argument relied upon here for a reversal of
the judgment is that the verdict of the jury is not sustained by sufficient evidence. The execution and delivery of the note are admitted. It seems that the consideration for the note was some personal property sold
by Bishop's intestate to Sickel, and Ludden signed the
note as surety. Ludden's defense was that some time
after the note was given a chattel mortgage was executed to Bishop on the property for which the note was
given, and that Bishop agreed that in consideration of
the securing of the note by this mortgage Ludden should

be released from the note. The evidence on behalf of
Ludden tended to support his defense, while the evidence
on behalf of Bishop tended to overthrow such defense.
In other words, the evidence on the issue was conflicting,
and all we can say upon the subject is that the finding
of the jury that Ludden had not made out his defense
has sufficient evidence for its support. The defense of
Sickel was that he surrendered the mortgaged property
to Bishop upon an agreement, then and there made between them, that Bishop should take the property in
discharge of the debt evidenced by the note. The evidence on behalf of Sickel tended to support this defense,
while the evidence on behalf of Bishop tended to overthrow it. Here again the evidence was conflicting; but
it supports the finding of the jury that Sickel had not
established his defense.

2. Another argument made here is that the award
made by the jury to Bishop is excessive. This contention of plaintiff in error is based upon another contention of his,—that Bishop seized and sold the property
which was mortgaged to secure the payment of the note
sued upon, and that the note should be credited with the
value of that property. The answer to this contention is
that if the fact existed, it was a matter of defense for
the plaintiffs in error, and they should have filed a counter-claim or set-off for the value of such property. No
such an issue as this is made in the pleadings or was
litigated on the trial, and, under an assignment that
"the verdict is not supported by sufficient evidence," we
cannot reduce the award made by a jury by the amount
of a counter-claim or set-off which existed in favor of the
defendant against the plaintiff when it was not interposed as a defense to the action. The judgment of the
district court is right and is

AFFIRMED.

53 1
53 1

JOHN WARLIER V. CHARLES WILLIAMS ET AL.

FILED DECEMBER 21, 1897.　No. 9120.

1. **Injunction**: REMEDY AT LAW. A litigant cannot successfully invoke the extraordinary remedy of injunction to enforce a legal right unless the facts and circumstances in the case are such that his ordinary legal remedies are inadequate,—i. e. that the pursuit of those remedies, or some of them, will not afford him as prompt and efficacious redress as the remedy by injunction.

2. ——: TRESPASS: EJECTMENT. A plaintiff is not entitled to a mandatory injunction to remove from his real estate one who has without color of title unlawfully and forcibly entered and wrongfully remains thereon, though such trespasser be insolvent.

ERROR from the district court of Burt county. Tried below before FAWCETT, J. *Affirmed.*

McCoy & Olmsted, for plaintiff in error.

H. E. Carter, contra.

RAGAN, C.

In the district court of Burt county John Warlier brought this suit in equity against Charles Williams and others, alleging, in substance, in his petition that he was the owner, and in the actual possession, of a certain tract of land described in said petition; that, at the time of the conveyance of said land by the government of the United States to his grantor, the Missouri river constituted one of its boundaries; that the tract conveyed by the United States government since that time had been enlarged by accretions from said river; that the parties made defendants, against his protest and without any right or color of title or authority, had forcibly entered into possession of the lands formed by said accretion; had "squatted" thereon; and, at the bringing of the suit, were using and cultivating said lands and appropriating to themselves the crops grown thereon; that said defendants and each of them were wholly insolvent; that if they were permitted to remain in possession of said

land for ten years they would acquire title thereto by
adverse possession. The prayer was that the defendants might be enjoined from continuing in possession
of said lands. To this petition the district court sustained a general demurrer and dismissed Warlier's action, and he brings this judgment here for review on
error.

This proceeding is, in effect, an application to a court
of equity for a mandatory injunction to remove the defendants in error from the real estate of the plaintiffs
in error upon which they have forcibly and wrongfully
entered and are wrongfully occupying. Counsel for the
plaintiff in error has cited us to numerous cases which
he claims sustain his right to this extraordinary remedy; but an examination of all these cases discloses that
not one of them is in point. A litigant cannot successfully invoke the extraordinary remedy of injunction to
enforce a legal right unless the facts and circumstances
in the case are such that his ordinary legal remedies
are inadequate,—that is, that the pursuit of those remedies, or some of them, will not afford him as prompt and
efficacious redress as the remedy by injunction. This
we understand to be elementary law. (*Richmond v. Dubuque & S. C. R. Co.*, 33 Ia. 422; *Jerome v. Ross*, 7 Johns.
Ch. [N. Y.] 315; Pomeroy, Equity Jurisprudence secs,
221, 275, 1346, 1347, 1357.) Now the facts stated in the
petition of the plaintiff in error show simply this: That
the defendants in error have forcibly entered upon and
are occupying his real estate. The plaintiff in error has
the legal title and is in possession of this real estate.
He might then institute against these defendants in
error an action of forcible entry and detainer under
chapter 10 of the Code of Civil Procedure, section 1020
of which expressly provides that such an action may be
brought against a defendant who is a settler or occupier
of lands without color of title and to which the complainant in the forcible detainer suit has the right of possession. Here, then, is a plain statutory remedy for the

wrong of which the plaintiff in error complains in this
action. Is this remedy an adequate one? The statute
provides that this action of forcible entry and detainer
may be brought before a justice of the peace after giving
the parties in possession of the lands three days' notice
to quit; that no continuance for more than eight days
shall be granted in the case unless the party made defendant shall give bond for the payment of rent, and if
the judgment shall be entered in favor of the plaintiff,
a writ of restitution shall be awarded in his favor, unless appellate proceedings are taken by defendants, in
which case they shall give a bond to pay a reasonable
rent for the premises while they wrongfully detain the
same. This remedy is not only an adequate one but it is
a summary and a speedy one. The relief demanded by
the plaintiff in error in this injunction proceeding is the
ousting of the plaintiff in error from his real estate so
that he may have the exclusive possession of it. A judgment and a writ of restitution in a forcible entry and
detainer suit would afford him the same and a more
speedy redress than a proceeding by injunction. But
it is said by the plaintiff in error that he is entitled to
pursue the injunction remedy because of the insolvency
of the defendants in error. This argument, as applied
to this case, is untenable. If the defendants in error
are insolvent, then the plaintiff in error has no redress
for the costs and expenses that he may incur in prosecuting either an injunction suit or a forcible entry and
detainer suit. Another argument is that the proceeding
by injunction will avoid a multiplicity of suits. This
argument we also think untenable. We do not understand the mere fact that there exist divers causes of
action which may be the foundation of as many different
suits between the parties thereto is a ground upon which
equity may be called upon to assume jurisdiction and
settle all such matters in one suit. (Chief Justice Beck
in *Richmond v. Dubuque & Sioux City R. Co., supra.*) The
district court was right and its decree is

AFFIRMED.

14

WALLIE GILLICK ET AL. V. WILSON WILLIAMS ET AL.

FILED DECEMBER 21, 1897. No. 9121.

Injunction: REMEDY AT LAW. On the authority of *Warlier v. Williams*,
53 Neb. 143, the decree of the district court is affirmed.

ERROR from the district court of Burt county. Tried
below before FAWCETT, J. *Affirmed.*

McCoy & Olmsted, for plaintiffs in error.

H. E. Carter, contra.

RAGAN, C.

The facts in this case are in all respects the same as
in *Warlier v. Williams*, 53 Neb. 143, and, on the authority
of that case, the decree of the district court in this is

AFFIRMED.

A. L. BAKER V. ELIZA E. SAVIDGE ET AL.

FILED DECEMBER 21, 1897. No. 7621.

Action by Vendee After Eviction: LIABILITY OF VENDOR. No cause
of action arises in favor of a grantee of land, who has been evicted
under title paramount, against his vendor who made no covenants
or representations as to title and was guilty of no fraud.

ERROR from the district court of Dakota county. Tried
below before NORRIS, J. *Reversed.*

Lynn, Sullivan & Foley and *J. Fowler,* for plaintiff in
error.

R. B. Daley and *W. E. Gantt, contra.*

IRVINE, C.

This is a proceeding in error to review a judgment
recovered by Eliza E. Savidge and D. J. Savidge against

A. L. Baker. The bill of exceptions was at a former
term quashed, so that we can consider no questions
requiring an examination of the evidence. The argument of plaintiff in error, while chiefly addressed to the
evidence, is, however, equally applicable to the sufficiency of the petition,—a question always open for
consideration. We do not think that the petition states
a cause of action, and the judgment must for that reason
be reversed.

The petition, in brief, alleges that the Savidges were
the owners of certain land in Dakota county and conveyed it by warranty deed to Baker. In consideration of
said conveyance Baker agreed to convey to Eliza Savidge
certain lots in South Sioux City by good and sufficient
warranty deed with the usual covenants and agreements
in such deeds contained. At the time of the exchange
of deeds Baker represented to plaintiffs that he held a
deed to the lots from certain persons named Clark, which
deed contained the usual covenants of warranty, which
deed had been by the Clarks placed in the hands of defendant with authority to insert the name of any grantee
to whom he might wish to convey the property, and that
it would save expense and convey as good title as a deed
from Baker himself, to insert plaintiffs' names in the
Clark deed. Plaintiffs accepted said deed, gave Baker
possession of their land, and entered into possession of
the South Sioux City lots. The Clarks did not have a
good title to the lots, but plaintiffs were later dispos-
sessed of six of them by persons claiming under title
paramount. The Clarks are insolvent.

This is clearly not an action for breach of covenant.
There was no covenant by the defendant. While it is
charged that his first agreement was to convey by warranty deed, it is then pleaded in effect that the contract
was changed in this particular and the deed and covenant of third persons were taken in lieu of defendant's.
For the same reason there is pleaded the breach of no
implied covenant. Whether or not covenants are ever

implied under our forms of conveyancing, it is quite evident that none can be implied against a party who was not a party to the conveyance. There is not pleaded any contract to furnish a good, a marketable, or any particular title. As finally stated, the contract was merely to exercise a sort of power of appointment, possessed by holding the "blank deed" from the Clarks, in favor of plaintiffs. It appears affirmatively that the contract was in this respect fully complied with. It is not charged that the representations made as to Baker's authority to fill the blank and deliver the deed were not true. These are the only representations pleaded. It is not alleged that Baker represented that the Clarks had good title; nor is it pleaded that Baker represented them to be solvent, so that the allegation that they were insolvent is immaterial; nor can the action be treated as one for money had and received. The transaction was an exchange and not a sale, and there is no attempt to rescind. Moreover, the consideration did not fail. The contract was for a conveyance of the lots, with covenants of warranty by the Clarks. This plaintiffs obtained. For all that appears they were fully aware of the condition of the title and were buying on the hazard of sustaining it. At all events they got just what they contracted for, according to the averments of their petition, and have no cause of action against Baker from the bare fact that they were evicted, in the absence of fraud or some covenant or agreement on his part whereby he would be charged.

REVERSED AND REMANDED.

EX PARTE TRESTER.

FILED DECEMBER 21, 1897. No. 9493.

Criminal Law: FAILURE TO FILE INFORMATION: DISCHARGE OF PRISONER. One who has been admitted to bail after a preliminary examination on a criminal charge, and who becomes a fugitive, is not, after his return or apprehension, entitled to be discharged because no information was filed against him at the term at which he was recognized to appear, and while he was a fugitive.

ERROR from the district court of Lancaster county. Tried below before HALL, J. *Affirmed.*

Macfarland & Altschuler and *C. H. Bane*, for petitioner.

C. J. Smyth, Attorney General, and *Ed P. Smith, Deputy Attorney General,* for the state.

IRVINE, C.

William P. Trester was convicted in the district court of Cherry county of an assault with intent to kill, and sentenced to imprisonment in the penitentiary for a term of three years. Application was thereafter made to the district court of Lancaster county for a writ of habeas corpus, directed to the warden of the penitentiary, it being alleged that the confinement of Trester was unlawful, because no indictment was found or information filed against him at the term of the district court to which he was bound to appear, and none until the second term thereafter. The district court held adversely to the contention of the prisoner and remanded him to the custody of the warden. From this order error is prosecuted.

The case was heard upon an agreed statement of facts, from which it appears that on March 26, 1896, Trester, as the result of a preliminary examination, was held to appear before the district court of Cherry county at the term thereof to be held April 20, 1896. He was then released upon bail, and, about the first of April, became a fugitive, and remained such until in January or February, 1897, when he voluntarily returned. During his absence two terms of court had been held. He was informed against soon after his return and apprehension, and proceeded against thereafter with due dispatch. At the April term, 1896, to which he had been recognized to appear, his recognizance was forfeited.

The statutes upon which the prisoner bases his claim to be discharged are sections 389 *et seq.* of the Criminal Code, being chapter 38 thereof, and sections 583 and 585, being a portion of the law relating to prosecutions by information. Section 389 is to the effect that "Any person held in jail charged with an indictable offense shall be discharged if he be not indicted at the term of the court at which he is held to answer," with certain exceptions then stated. Section 390 provides for the discharge of one committed to prison if he be not brought to trial before the end of the second term after indictment, and section 391 for the discharge of one who has given bail if not brought to trial before the end of the third term after indictment found. Section 392 excepts from the operation of the two preceding sections cases where the court shall be satisfied that the state, after reasonable exertions, has been unable to secure material evidence which there is just ground to believe may be secured at the succeeding term. Sections 390 and 391, in addition, each contains an exception of cases where the delay happens on the application of the prisoner. It will hardly be controverted that these provisions do not promulgate any general policy on behalf of the public interest for the speedy prosecution and termination of criminal proceedings, but they are enactments for the benefit of the accused, for the purpose of securing to him his constitutional right to a speedy trial, and their provisions are therefore leveled against delays occasioned by the inaction of the state's officers. He would be a bold defender, more to be commended for zeal than discernment, who would contend that one who breaks jail, or violates his recognizance by flight, could claim the protection of either section, if the indictment had been found before his escape. There can be no doubt that these provisions are applicable, under the present law, to prosecutions by information, but they are not applicable to cases where the accused is a fugitive and out of reach of the court while the successive terms elapse. They do not by any analogy aid this applicant. Section 389 requires in certain cases the indictment to be found at the term at which the accused is held to appear, but the terms of the law extend only to cases where the accused has been held in jail. There is reason for a distinction in this respect, and for requiring a more speedy prosecution of one committed to jail than of one released on bail; but without deciding that the section is applicable only to prisoners, or rather without deciding that aside from this section the same diligence is not in ordinary cases required where the accused has been admitted to bail, we think it clear that one admitted to bail cannot, on fleeing from justice, take advantage of the failure of the state to proceed against him in his absence. The letter of the statute does not extend to him, and he is certainly not within its spirit. In *Ex parte Two Calf*, 11 Neb. 221, there appears in the syllabus a statement so general that it gives color to the prisoner's contention in this behalf, but on reading the opinion it will appear that the relators were held in jail, so that the statute was in terms applicable. That also was the state of facts in *State v. Miller*, 43 Neb. 860, and the opinion and syllabus are in that case carefully confined to cases where the accused is held in jail. Neither case is then authority in support of relator's argument.

Section 583 makes it the duty of the county attorney to make examination of the facts connected with any case of preliminary examination, where the offender shall have been committed to jail or recognized or held to bail, and if he shall determine that an information ought not to be filed, to subscribe and file with the clerk a statement containing his reasons in fact and in law for not filing an information, "and such statement shall be filed at and during the term of court at which the offender shall be held for his appearance." It is then provided that if the court shall not be satisfied with the reasons so filed the prosecutor shall be directed to file an information and bring the case to trial. The plain object of this section, enacted as a part of the act permitting prosecution by information, was to preserve a method whereby a fruitless or improper prosecution might be discontinued before information filed. Such a step might frequently be necessary, as, for instance, where, after the examination required to be made into the law and the facts, the prosecuting attorney finds he cannot make or advise another to make the oath whereby an information must be verified. The requirement that the statement must be filed at the term to which the offender is held to appear gives countenance to the argument that in ordinary cases an information must be filed at that term, but it is far from conclusive on that point, and in any event it affords no argument in favor of the duty of a prosecutor to so proceed against one who has become a fugitive, who is not being held in custody or restrained by the requirements of bail, and who is not seeking but evading the action of the court.

Section 585 enacts that no information shall be filed against any person who has not had or waived a preliminary examination, but provides as an exceptional case that informations may in such cases be filed against fugitives from justice. This only establishes the right to file an information against a fugitive from justice without a preliminary examination. The object was, as appears from the closing clauses of the section, to so permit for the purpose of aiding in process for extradition. The statute is permissive and not mandatory, and had that for its object and not the enforcement of the prosecutor to proceed by information against all fugitives.

None of the statutes relied upon by the relator entitles him to the right claimed, and it is one which he plainly does not possess in the absence of statute.

AFFIRMED.

CLEMENT L. HART ET AL. V. MEAD INVESTMENT COMPANY.

FILED DECEMBER 21, 1897.   NO. 7661.

1. **Action on Bond:** ANSWER: CONDITIONAL SIGNING. In a suit on a bond, an answer pleading that a defendant signed on condition that others named should also sign before the bond should be delivered and that such others did not sign, is insufficient unless it further alleges that plaintiff had notice of the condition.

2. ——: ——: DEFENSE NOT PLEADED. One of several defendants, sued on a bond, obtaining a favorable verdict on the ground that her signature had been secured by fraud, the other defendants, against whom verdict is at the same time rendered, cannot be heard to complain of the judgment because the release of the successful defendant also released them, they not having pleaded the invalidity of her obligation as a defense for themselves.

ERROR from the district court of Douglas county. Tried below before BLAIR, J.   *Affirmed.*

D. L. Cartan, E. C. Page, Estabrook & Davis, and *J. E. Nevin,* for plaintiffs in error.

William A. Redick, contra.

IRVINE, C.

In the district court the defendant in error recovered judgment against the plaintiffs in error on a bond signed by the plaintiffs in error and one Carrie Parker, and conditioned for the payment of any deficiency judgment which should be rendered the Mead Investment Company against a corporation known as the Northside Building Association, in a foreclosure suit pending at the time the bond was made. Broadly stated, the defense relied on by the plaintiffs in error was that they had each signed the bond on condition that others should sign, and that the condition was not complied with. The district court peremptorily directed a verdict against Hart, Sherman, Nevin, and Parrott. As to defendant Riley the case was submitted to the jury on certain issues, including that

presented by the defense alluded to.   The defendant
Carrie Parker had apparently, although her answer does
not appear in the record before us, interposed a separate
defense that her signature had been procured by fraud,
and that issue was also submitted to the jury and by it
determined in her favor.

While there are in the petition in error numerous special assignments, the case is argued only on the broad
ground that the court erred in directing a verdict in
favor of the plaintiff against the four defendants above
named, and erred in permitting a verdict to be returned
against Riley.

From the pleadings as well as from the evidence it
appears that the defendants were, or were alleged to be,
stockholders or members of the Northside Building Association, which had given to the plaintiff a mortgage
on a number of lots in Omaha, to secure the payment
of a debt on which there remained due about $15,000.
Suit was pending to foreclose this mortgage and an arrangement was made whereby the greater part of the
debt was secured on other property or paid, and all the
mortgaged property released except two lots.   As to
these lots the foreclosure was to proceed to decree and
sale without the interposition of any defense or exercise
of the right of stay, and the building association agreed,
in the terms of the contract, to "procure the execution
and delivery to second party, by Charles R. Sherman,
and C. L. Hart and others, of a bond in the sum of $1,500,
conditioned for the payment of any deficiency arising
upon said sale, within ninety days from the entry of
judgment for said deficiency."   The theory of the defense was that all the members of the building association were to join in the bond.   The defendants other
than Riley pleaded that the condition was not complied
with, in that one Livingston did not sign.   Riley claimed
that the condition was further unperformed in that one
Meadimber did not sign.   The district court in directing
the verdict seems to have proceeded on the theory that

such a defense as the one urged is available only to sureties, and that by the terms of this bond all the defendants except Riley were principals. It is argued that the rule on which the defense is based is not restricted to sureties, and that even if it were, it appears from the face of the bond that the obligation was in the nature of a guaranty of the debt of the building association, and that therefore the defendants would fall within the rule. It would be fruitless to enter into an examination of the questions argued, so far as they relate to these propositions, because in the condition of the pleadings and evidence the judgment was on other grounds correct. The answers are substantially, and in their essential portions verbally, alike. They aver that the building association through its officers came to the defendants with a copy of the contract for a settlement and presented a bond; that the defendants examined these papers, "and upon consideration of the performance of the conditions of said contract, by the parties thereto, and upon the consideration of the signing of said bond by all of the persons named in the body of the bond, this defendant consented, at the request of said Northside Building Association, to sign the document referred to." Further, that the defendants, when they signed said bond, did so "upon the consideration and with the express understanding that one John R. Livingston, named in the bond, would also sign the said bond." To render the defense sought to be interposed available the plaintiff must have had notice of the condition that the bond was not to be delivered until signed by others. (*Cutler v. Roberts*, 7 Neb. 4; *Owen v. Udall*, 39 Neb. 14; *Mullen v. Morris*, 43 Neb. 596; *Brumback v. German Nat. Bank*, 46 Neb. 540.) There is really no distinction in this respect between a bond complete on its face and one bearing in its body the names of persons who have not signed it. In the latter case it has been sometimes held that the fact that names appear in the body of the bond which are not signed thereto is notice to the plaintiff of the condition attached to its delivery, but this is merely an evidential fact and does not change the rule of law. In *Mullen v. Morris, supra,* it was held that such an incomplete bond is *prima facie* good, that the burden remains on the defendants to establish the conditional delivery. There is in none of the answers any allegation that the plaintiff knew of the condition. Indeed, from the manner of pleading, the inference is that the understanding was between the defendants and the building association alone, and that the plaintiff had no part therein. If we look at the evidence we find sufficient, aside from the fact that the name of Livingston appeared in the body of the bond, to justify submitting to the jury the question of plaintiff's knowledge; but, on the other hand, it is more than doubtful whether there was sufficient to go to the jury on the question of the condition itself. It seems rather that the signing by all the members of the association was a matter insisted upon at first by the plaintiff itself for its own better security, than that any of the defendants attached any condition of that character to his signing, or regarded it as a matter affecting materially his own interest.

It is also contended that, inasmuch as it has been determined by the verdict that Carrie Parker's signature was procured by fraud, all the others are released. It is on this point sufficient to say that none of the plaintiffs in error pleaded any defense of that character.

AFFIRMED.

HERMAN OLDIG v JOHN L. FISK.

FILED DECEMBER 21, 1897. No. 7631.

1. **Ejectment:** ADVERSE POSSESSION: PLEADING: EVIDENCE. In ejectment evidence to prove adverse possession is admissible under a general denial of plaintiff's title.

Oldig v. Fisk.

2. ——: ——: EVIDENCE. The purchase or attempt·d purchase of an outstanding title by one in adverse possession, and before the expiration of the statutory period, is not alone sufficient to break the continuity of possession or divest it of its adverse character, although the occupant may believe that he is thereby acquiring the true title. RAGAN, C., dissenting.

3. ——: ——: ——.. One who claims under a tax deed or by adverse possession does not, by causing to be recorded the patent from the United States to another, acknowledge title paramount in that other.

ERROR from the district court of Douglas county. Tried below before AMBROSE, J. *Reversed.*

O. Hollenbeck and *Frick & Dolezal,* for plaintiff in error.

N. H. Tunnicliff and *Elmer E. Thomas, contra.*

IRVINE, C.

This action was ejectment by Fisk against Oldig for eighty acres of land in Douglas county. At the close of the evidence, by agreement of the parties, the jury was discharged and the cause submitted to the court, which entered judgment for the plaintiff on special findings of fact. With regard to the point chiefly controverted these findings are as strongly in favor of the defendant in error as the evidence warrants, and we accept them as affording a proper basis for the examination of the case. From them it appears that in 1857 the land in controversy was pre-empted by Fisk, and a patent was thereafter issued to him. In 1871 Wilson Reynolds obtained a tax deed to the land and thereafter received other tax deeds. Oldig claims under Reynolds. Possession was taken under the tax deeds and the court found that the defendant, Oldig, and his grantors had held adverse possession for more than ten years prior to the beginning of the action, except for the fact that in 1889, and before the bar of the statute had become complete, Reynolds, being then in possession, employed a man named Price to search for the patentee and purchase

from him; that Price produced a deed purporting to be
executed by Fisk, and Reynolds paid Price $900 therefor.
In so doing Price believed that he was dealing with
Fisk and acquiring his title to the premises. While it
is not so specially found, it was clearly proved that the
deed obtained by Price was a forgery.

Defendant in error contends that the defense of adverse possession was not open to the plaintiff in error.
for want of a sufficient plea. We shall not examine into
the sufficiency of the special plea interposed, because we
think that evidence of adverse possession was admissible
under the general denial of Fisk's title. True, the statute of limitations, as a general rule, must be pleaded to
be made available, but there are two reasons why that
rule is not applicable to the defense of adverse possession
in an action of ejectment. The first is that sections 626
and 627 of the Code provide specially for the pleadings
in actions of ejectment, and as to the answer it is enacted
that it shall be sufficient to deny generally the title
alleged in the petition. Under such a denial it has
always been here held that the defendant may show
any facts negativing the plaintiff's right of possession.
(*Franklin v. Kelley*, 2 Neb. 79; *Dale v. Hunneman*, 12 Neb.
221; *Staley v. Housel*, 35 Neb. 160; *Wanser v. Lucas*, 44
Neb. 759.) The other reason is that adverse possession
is more than a defense of the statute of limitations.
Such possession, for the statutory period, not only bars
the remedy, but it vests in the occupant an absolute title
to the land. In support of that rule we have a long and
unbroken line of decisions, beginning at least as early as
Gatling v. Lane, 17 Neb. 77, and extending down to *Fink
v. Dawson*, 52 Neb. 647. Proof of adverse possession
goes therefore directly to disprove plaintiff's title, and
is admissible under the general issue. (*Fink v. Dawson,
supra; Hogan v. Kurtz*, 94 U. S. 773; *Kyser v. Cannon*, 29
O. St. 359; *Donahue v. Thompson*, 60 Wis. 500; *Miller v.
Beck*, 68 Mich. 76; *Stocker v. Green*, 94 Mo. 280; *Trow-
bridge v. Royce*, 1 Root [Conn.] 50; *Wade v. Doyle*, 17 Fla.

522.) What has been said is not opposed to the case of *Alexander v. Meyers*, 33 Neb. 773, which was a suit to foreclose a lien and, therefore, did not present a similar question.

The record then presents, and succinctly presents, the question whether an attempt by one in the adverse possession of land, and before the statutory period has expired, to purchase from the true owner, operates to divest his possession of its adverse character. Title by adverse possession is acquired by ten years' open, continuous, exclusive occupancy under claim of ownership. Whatever may be the law elsewhere, here that claim need not be well founded in law or in fact, it need not be under a *bona fide* belief that it is well founded, it need not even be under color of title. (*Omaha & Florence Land & Trust Co. v. Hansen*, 32 Neb. 449; *Lantry v. Wolff*, 49 Neb. 374; *Gatling v. Lane*, 17 Neb. 80.) Accordingly it has been held that one in adverse possession does not impair his right to rely upon the statute, by purchasing the land at tax sale and taking and recording a tax deed, and that such acts do not create a break in the running of the statute. (*Griffith v. Smith*, 27 Neb. 47.) This rule was followed in *Omaha & Florence Loan & Trust Co. v. Hansen*, *supra*, the court saying: "Neither does the purchase of a tax deed break the continuity of possession. (*Griffith v. Smith*, 27 Neb. 47.) Cases may be found which hold that the purchase of such title breaks the continuity. We cannot agree, however, that such is the case. A party in possession of land as owner certainly has a right to protect that possession by the purchase of any outstanding claim or lien against the property. There is not thereby any break in the possession, nor does the adverse occupant rely upon his purchased title in preference to the one which he previously possessed. He joins the two together and possesses whatever title both may .give him." These decisions logically, if they do not in direct terms, control the present case. They have stood unquestioned for some years and may justly be regarded as founding a rule of property. They certainly should not be departed from in the absence of the most convincing reason, or controlling necessity.

Rather than there being such reason, we think that principle and precedent both favor the rule expressed in the cases cited. While there is some conflict of authority it is to be observed that the cases holding that the benefit of the statute is lost by the purchase or attempted purchase of an outstanding title, are uniformly based on the rule that any act recognizing a superior title in another, at least before the bar of the statute has become complete, defeats its operation. This court has several times enforced that rule, as in *Hull v. Chicago, B. & Q. R. Co.*, 21 Neb. 371, where a railroad company sought the benefit of the statute after having, while in possession, but within ten years, instituted condemnation proceedings against the true owner, thus by a solemn admission of record acknowledging his title. In *Roggencamp v. Converse*, 15 Neb. 105, the occupant, claiming the protection of the statute, had taken a lease from the true owner and thereby not only recognized his title but estopped himself from denying it. The general rule cannot be doubted. The error is not in declaring that rule, but in applying it to the facts before us. A vendee is not estopped to deny his vendor's title. In the purchase of an outstanding title there is nothing inconsistent with the former claim of ownership. It is generally conceded that one may purchase an outstanding title to "buy one's peace" or prevent threatened litigation. There is no room to distinguish in this behalf, between litigation threatened by word of mouth, and litigation threatened by the fact that the title is outstanding,—a constant menace from the very fact of its existence. As in adverse possession the motive of the occupant is immaterial, and the claim of ownership need have no legal foundation, there is no reason why one may not at any time buy in an outstanding title and protect oneself against the probability of disastrous litigation. The fact that one believes the outstanding title to be superior so long as he does not yield thereto cannot affect the question, because the character of one's possession depends upon the fact of a claim of ownership and not its real or supposed validity. In buying what is outstanding there is nothing partaking of the nature of an acknowledgment of the superiority of that title or an abandonment of one's former claim. The old title is not conveyed away or lost. Such an act admits, and admits only, that the occupant deems it worth while to get rid of the outstanding title and unite it to the one under which he has been holding. It does not prove, and alone it does not even tend to prove, a change in the character of the possession or a recognition of a title paramount. In support of these views are the following cases, many of them being cases where the outstanding title was bought while the statute was running, and none recognizing any distinction between that case and one of a purchase after the expiration of the statutory period: *Jackson v. Newton*, 18 Johns. [N. Y.] 355; *Northrop v. Wright*, 7 Hill [N. Y.] 476; *Chapin v. Hunt*, 40 Mich. 595; *Mather v. Walsh*, 107 Mo. 121; *Dean v. Goddard*, 55 Minn. 290; *Clark v. Peckenpaugh*, 46 Ill. 11; *Elder v. McClaskey*, 70 Fed. Rep. 529; *Jackson v. Given*, 8 Johns. [N. Y.] 137*; *Cannon v. Stockmon*, 36 Cal. 535; *Hayes v. Martin*, 45 Cal. 559; *Singer Mfg. Co. v. Tillman*, 21 Pac. Rep. [Ariz.] 818; *Johnstone v. Scott*, 11 Mich. 232; *Headrick v. Fritts*, 93 Tenn. 270; *O'Neal v. Boone*, 53 Ill. 35; *Owens v. Meyers*, 20 Pa. St. 134.

It appears that while the patent was issued to Fisk in due season after his pre-emption, he did not receive it from the land office, and that Reynolds, in 1890, obtained it from the land office and caused it to be recorded. It is claimed that this was a recognition of Fisk's title, or at least that it is evidence tending to show such recognition. It must be remembered that Reynolds entered under a tax deed and that his claim of title was based thereon. In order, then, to lay a foundation for such a

15

claim, Reynolds must show that the land was subject to taxation, and this must be by showing that the legal or equitable title had passed out of the United States. Furthermore, in order to found a claim of title by adverse possession, it was necessary to show title out of the United States. The recording of the patent was consequently an act going as much to support the original claim of title, as in support of that supposed to have been derived from Fisk.

REVERSED AND REMANDED.

RAGAN, C., dissenting.

The general rule is said to be that any act of recognition or acknowledgment of a superior title in another, during the period of adverse possession, will amount to an interruption of the continuity of possession, and defeat the operation of the statute. (See the rule stated and the authorities collated in 1 Am. & Eng. Ency. Law [2d ed.] p. 838.) The precise question here then is, what act, or what conduct on the part of an adverse occupant, is such a recognition or acknowledgment of the paramount title as will stop the running of the statute of limitations in favor of such adverse occupant? In the case at bar, the evidence shows conclusively that Reynolds, while holding the real estate adversely before the statute had run so as to complete his title, voluntarily offered and attempted to purchase the paramount title to this real estate from Fisk, the owner thereof. The authorities hold that such conduct on the part of an adverse holder is evidence which will support a finding that at that time the occupant, then at least, was not occupying adversely to the holder of the paramount title. See *Lovell v. Frost*, 44 Cal. 471, where it was distinctly held: "If a party in possession of land offers to purchase it from the true owner, and this offer is made, not merely to buy an outstanding or adverse claim in order to quiet his possession or protect himself from litigation, the offer is a recognition of the owner's title, and will stop the running of the statute." To the same effect see *Litchfield v. Sewall*, 66 N. W. Rep. [Ia.] 104, and cases there cited, in which it is said: "It seems to be well settled that an offer by defendant to purchase the property, which he is holding adversely from the plaintiff, within the statutory time, is a clear recognition of plaintiff's title, and will interrupt the running of the statute."

At the time Reynolds made this attempt to purchase Fisk's title, the statute had not so run as to perfect his own title to the real estate by the adverse occupancy thereof. Clearly, then, Reynolds was not trying to buy an outstanding or adverse claim existing against this **real estate** in order to quiet his possession to the same or protect him from threatened litigation in reference thereto. He believed, if he did not know, that the paramount legal paper title was in Fisk, and he desired to acquire it so as to vest in his grantee, Oldig, a perfect title to the real estate. The fact that, after receiving and recording the forged deed, he procured the patent issued by the United States to Fisk from the land office and caused it to be spread upon the records is another circumstance which tends at least to show that, at that time and from that time, he was not occupying adversely to the Fisk title but in subordination thereto. The district court concluded from Reynolds' conduct in attempting to purchase the real estate from Fisk that from that time forth he did not claim title to the real estate as against Fisk, nor hold possession nor occupy the same adversely to him, and we think the evidence sustains this conclusion. The judgment of the district court should be affirmed.

CORDELIA W. HARMON, ADMINISTRATRIX, ET AL., APPEL-
LEES, V. CITY OF OMAHA ET AL., APPELLANTS.

FILED DECEMBER 22, 1897. No. 7676.

1. **Void Taxes:** INJUNCTION. "A party who is not guilty of laches may invoke the aid of a court of equity to restrain the collection of a void tax or assessment." *Morris v. Merrell,* 44 Neb. 423, followed.

2. **Taxation:** SPECIAL ASSESSMENTS: CITIES. Where special taxes or assessments against property to pay expenses of improving the streets of a city are void, they cannot be enforced solely on the ground of the benefits of the improvements to the owners of the abutting lots or lands.

APPEAL from the district court of Douglas county. Heard below before KEYSOR, J. *Affirmed.*

W. J. Connell and *E. J. Cornish,* for appellants.

Charles S. Elgutter, contra.

HARRISON, J.

On June 1, 1892, the council of the city of Omaha passed an ordinance by which there was created improvement district No. 470, in said city. The district included a portion of Ninth street from the point of intersection of it and Pacific street and extending north to the alley, or to where, in fact, it abutted the tracks and grounds of the Union Pacific and Burlington railroads. On July 2, 1892, the portion of Ninth street to which we have just referred was, by ordinance then enacted, ordered paved with Colorado sandstone, and between May 10 and June 10, 1893, the work of paving was done under contract with the city authorities. Subsequently, and during the year 1893, a special assessment and levy of taxes were made on the properties included in the district to raise the funds to pay for the paving and curbing. This action was instituted in the district court of Douglas county by the appellees of the property owners in said district to enjoin the collection of the taxes, and from a decree in their favor the city and its officer necessarily involved in the action have appealed to this court.

It was alleged in the petition filed for appellees in the district court, "That no petition praying for said improvement aforesaid signed by the owners of the lots or land abutting upon said street within said improvement district, and representing a majority of the feet frontage thereon, as provided by the laws of the state of Nebraska governing cities of the metropolitan class, has ever been presented or submitted to the city council of the city of Omaha. * * * And plaintiffs further allege that the said mayor and city council were without jurisdiction, and without power or authority of any kind to levy on the property of these plaintiffs, described as aforesaid, the alleged taxes for paving and curbing of said Ninth street, levied as aforesaid, and that said alleged taxes were null and void." The answer of appellants denied the allegations of the portion of the petition which we have quoted, and alleged that "These defendants, further answering said petition, allege that said paving in said district was done with the knowledge and consent and by the permission and authority of the owners of the lots and real estate in said paving district and without objection or protest on the part of said plaintiffs, or either of them, and without objection on the part of any owner of any lot or real estate in said paving district. The said defendants further say that the paving done in said district specially benefited said lots to the full amount, and more than the amount, of the said special assessment levied thereon to cover the cost of said paving." To this answer, so far as is disclosed by the record, there was no reply. The decree rendered in the cause, after the statement that the cause "came on to be heard on the petition, answer, and the evidence and argument of counsel," continues as follows:

"That no petition of the owners of the lots and lands

abutting upon that part of Ninth street within said improvement district No. 470 representing a majority of the feet frontage was ever made, presented, or filed with the mayor or city council asking or requesting to have said street improvement district created or said part of Ninth street in said district paved. The court further finds that said plaintiffs had personal knowledge of the doing of said work of paving at and before the commencement thereof and while the same was being done, and made no objection or protest to said paving being done to the authorities of said city by written protest or otherwise.

"The court further finds that the only protest ever made to or filed with the city authorities of the city of Omaha relating to said paving were the protests filed with the city council, sitting as a board of equalization, of which copies have been introduced in evidence.

"The court further finds, as a matter of law, that by reason of no petition having been made or filed by the owners of the lots and real estate abutting upon said part of Ninth street in said district representing a majority of the feet front thereon asking or petitioning to have said paving done, the said defendant, the city of Omaha, by its mayor and council, were without jurisdiction to do said paving or to levy a special tax or assessment on said lots or real estate to cover the costs of said paving, and that for such reason the said special taxes in plaintiffs' petition described are null and void."

It was adjudged that the assessments and taxes were null and void, and appellants were perpetually enjoined from their enforcement or any attempt at their collection.

Counsel for appellants, in the brief filed, state: "We have, * * * in this case but one question, to-wit, Can a property owner who knows that a city of the metropolitan class is about to pave a street in front of his premises stand by while said improvement is being constructed, making no complaint or protest of any kind to the city until his property is about to be assessed to raise funds to pay the costs of said improvement, and then, for the first time, with full knowledge of all the proceedings from the beginning, admitting that the special benefits to his property by reason of said improvement equal or exceed the amount assessed against his property, obtain a decree in a court of equity enjoining the collection of said taxes and canceling the same, without offering to do equity by paying an amount equal to the special benefits received, not to exceed the amount assessed against his property?" In regard to the character or quality of the assessment and levies of taxes, a question which arises as a part or element of the main question, the authority to make such street improvements and levy the taxes on abutting lots or lands to pay the expenses of the same was conferred in section 69 of chapter 12a of Complied Statutes 1891, one of the sections of the act passed for the government of cities of the metropolitan class, and, prior to its exercise by the officers of the city, there must have been presented to them a petition by the owners of the' majority of the feet frontage of the lots or land abutting on the street praying or requesting that the improvements be made. Without the petition the officers could not move in the premises,—could not order the improvements and levy taxes on the abutting properties for the payment of the whole of the expenses. (*Von Steen v. Beatrice*, 36 Neb. 421; *State v. Birkhauser*, 37 Neb. 521.) There was no such a petition asking for the improvements in district 470 on the portion of Ninth street included in such district; hence the officers were not warranted in the exercise of the authority, the order for the improvements was illegal, and the levy of taxes based thereon was void. It is a familiar rule that enactments by which authority for special assessments or levies of taxes is conferred are to be strictly construed. It is also a familiar doctrine that in order to sustain such assessments, the record must affirmatively show a compliance with all the conditions essential to a valid exercise of the taxing power. (*Smith v. City of Omaha*, 49 Neb. 883; *Hutchinson v. City of Omaha*, 52 Neb. 345; *Stenberg v. State*, 50 Neb. 128.) The proceedings being without the condition necessary at their inception, they were without authority and the taxes levied were void. (*Hurford v. Omaha*, 4 Neb. 352; *Hanscom v. Omaha*, 11 Neb. 44; *Von Steen v. Beatrice, supra; State v. Birkhauser, supra; State v. Irey*, 42 Neb. 186; *Touzalin v. Omaha*, 25 Neb. 824; *Mc-Gavock v. Omaha*, 40 Neb. 85; *Hutchinson v. City of Omaha, supra*.)

It is said in the opinion in the case of *Mulligan v. Smith*, 59 Cal. 206, wherein a question similar to the one we are now discussing was under consideration: "Now the statute made the petition an essential initiative of the proceedings," and further: "When, therefore, the legislature prescribed that a petition from the owners of a majority in frontage of the property to be charged with the cost of the improvement was necessary to set the machinery of the statute in motion, no step could be taken under the provisions of the statute until the requisite petition was presented. It was the first authorized movement to be made in the opening of the avenue. When taken, officers who were to constitute and organize a board of public works were authorized to organize. Until it was taken they had no such authority. They could not legally act at all; or if they acted their proceedings would be unauthorized and void. The presentation of the petition required by the statute was therefore essential. It was, as other courts in construing similar statutes have expressed it, a jurisdictional fact that may not be presumed or inferred, upon which rested all the subsequent proceedings authorized by the statute." (See also *Steckert v. East Saginaw*, 22 Mich. 104; *Tone v. Columbus*, 39 O. St. 281; *Zeigler v. Hopkins*, 117 U. S. 684; *City of Dallas v. Ellison*, 30 S. W. Rep. [Tex.] 1128.)

Reverting now to the main proposition argued for appellants that appellees were not entitled to a decree enjoining the collection of the taxes because they did not take some action before the improvement of the street, it may be said that the finding of the court that the appellees "had personal knowledge of the doing of said work of paving at, and before, the commencement thereof and while the same was being done," is a fair conclusion on the subject drawn from the facts which appear in the record. Was this sufficient to preclude them from obtaining relief by injunction against the enforcement of the void taxes or to bar them of such relief until the payments of the benefits, if any, which accrued to their properties from the improvement of the streets?

In *Steckert v. East Saginaw City, supra,* it was stated that knowledge of the proceedings and of the improvements and of the illegality of the proceedings which rendered the assessments void did not estop the parties or bar them of the relief prayed, an injunction against the collection of special taxes levied to pay the expenses of paving a street, and this was applicable relative to parties who had signed the petition by which the improvement was requested. To the same effect see *City of Dallas v. Ellison, supra.*

In the decision in the case of *Tone v. Columbus, supra,* it was stated: "In regard to proceedings by public officers, preliminary to levying a special assessment for the improvement of a public highway, it is only when the duty to speak is imperative, that mere silence on the part of a land owner will operate as an estoppel. (Cooley, Taxation, 573; *Counterman v. Dublin Township,* 38 O. St. 515.) To sustain an estoppel because of omission to speak, there must be both the opportunity and the duty to speak; the party maintaining silence must be in a situation to know that some one was relying thereon, and acting, or about to act, as he would not have done had he spoken and asserted his right. (*Viele v. Judson,* 82 N. Y. 32.) We think the true rule is this: When the improvement is of a public street upon which the owner's property abuts, before the duty to speak can be said to exist, which is so imperative that if he keeps silent then, he shall not afterwards be heard, it must be shown:

"First—That he knew the improvement was being made. (*Teegarden v. Davis*, 36 O. St. 601; *Stephan v. Daniels*, 27 O. St. 544.)

"Second—That he had knowledge that the public authorities intended and were making the improvement upon the faith that the cost thereof was to be paid by the abutting property owners and that an assessment for the purpose was contemplated. (*Hagar v. City of Burlington*, 42 Ia. 661.) Because cities may improve the public streets out of the general fund and without a special assessment.

"Third—That he knew of the infirmity or defect in the proceedings, under which the improvement was being made, which would render such assessment invalid and which he is to be estopped from asserting. 'At least, in the absence of any evidence of previous knowledge on his part of their unlawful action, he is in time with his protest, when they proceed to deprive him of his rights under such proceedings.' (Cooley, J., 22 Mich. 104; *Davenport C. R. Co. v. Davenport Gas Light Co.*, 43 Ia. 301.)

"Fourth—Some special benefit must have accrued to the owner's property distinct from the benefits enjoyed by the citizens generally. (*Stephan v. Daniels*, 27 O. St. 544; 30 Ind. 194.)" (See also *City of Terre Haute v. Mack*, 38 N. E. Rep. [Ind.] 468.)

In this state the rule has been stated thus: "A party who is not guilty of laches may invoke the aid of a court of equity to restrain the collection of a void tax or assessment." (*Morris v. Merrel*, 44 Neb. 423; *Hutchinson v. City of Omaha*, 52 Neb. 345; *Touzalin v. City of Omaha, supra; Bellevue Improvement Co. v. Village of Bellevue*, 39 Neb. 876; *Thatcher v. Adams County*, 19 Neb. 485.)

The appellees had knowledge of the commencement and progress of the work, and, doubtless, must be charged with knowledge of the provisions of the law under which it was being done; but it will not do to say that they will be charged with notice of the illegal actions of the city officers in relation to the improvements because of the fact that the work was ordered done without the petition required by the statute on the subject, and of this latter it is not of the record that they possessed actual knowledge. It must rather be said that they were warranted in assuming, in the absence of actual information that the officers would and were acting and proceeding legally in all respects as required by statute and to rest their rights on such assumption, and in so doing they were not guilty of laches. This being true, they were entitled to call for the aid of the court in the restraint of the enforcement of the void taxes, and this without prior payment or tender of alleged benefits to their properties. Where special taxes or assessments against property for the payment of expenses of the improvement of streets of a city are void they cannot be enforced solely on the ground of the benefits received by the owners of the abutting lots or lands. (*Buckley v. City of Tacoma*, 37 Pac. Rep. [Wash.] 441.)

Under the facts as they appear in the record before us, the appellees were entitled to the relief afforded them in the decree of the district court. The decree is right and is

AFFIRMED.

PHILETUS PECK V. REUBEN R. TINGLEY ET AL.

FILED DECEMBER 22, 1897. No. 7538.

1. **Instructions:** ASSIGNMENTS OF ERROR. Alleged errors in giving instructions should be separately assigned in the motion for a new trial, as well as in the petition in error.

2. **Partnership Note:** EVIDENCE. A note executed by a member of a firm or partnership in the firm name, where it does not appear on its face to have been executed by the firm in any other capacity

than as a principal debtor, and the partnership is a commercial one, is presumptive evidence that the note is the note of the partnership, and shows a valid claim against it.

3. **Conclusion of Witness on Vital Issue: ERROR.** A portion of the evidence examined, *held* objectionable and erroneously admitted.

ERROR from the district court of Lancaster county. Tried below before STRODE, J. *Reversed.*

John H. Ames and *E. F. Pettis*, for plaintiff in error.

C. E. Tingley and *E. J. Burkett, contra.*

HARRISON, J.

This action was commenced in the district court of Lancaster county by Reuben R. Tingley of the defendants in error against E. W. Hovey, Fred A. Hovey, and Philetus Peck to recover the amount alleged to be his due on a promissory note of date September 22, 1896, for the sum of $1,200, and having thereon the signatures of E. W. Hovey and Hovey & Peck. It appears that E. W. Hovey was the father of Fred A. Hovey and Philetus Peck the father-in-law; that at the time the note in suit was executed there was a partnership doing business in Lincoln under the firm name and style of Hovey & Peck, of which firm Fred A. Hovey and Philetus Peck were members, the former the active managing member and in charge of the business. Answer was filed for some of the parties whom it was sought to charge with the payment of the debt evidenced by the note, that of Philetus Peck being the only one which needs any particular notice, as he is the only party actively prosecuting error proceedings from the adverse judgment of the district court. His answer was as follows:

"Comes now the above named defendant, Philetus Peck, and having obtained leave of court to file this, his second amended answer herein, answering for himself alone to the petition of the plaintiff, says that he has not sufficient knowledge whereon to base a belief as to the truth of the allegations contained in plaintiff's petition, and therefore denies the same.

"And by way of first defense herein, this answering defendant avers that at the date mentioned in plaintiff's petition, upon which date plaintiff claims the said note was executed, this answering defendant, together with the defendant Fred Hovey, were a copartnership duly organized and formed under the laws of the state of Nebraska, having their principal place of business in the city of Lincoln, Nebraska, and were at that time carrying on their partnership business. That said partnership was formed for the sole purpose of carrying on the general business of wholesale and retail dealers in stoves, farm implements, hardware, and other goods of a like character, and for no other purpose whatsoever; and that neither of the partners, by terms of the said partnership agreement, had the power or right to pledge the credit of the said partnership for any other purpose than that of carrying on its said business as aforesaid; and that the signing of notes by the said partnership for purposes other than the purchase of goods necessary and usual for the carrying on of their said business, as hereinbefore set out, was expressly prohibited by the terms of the partnership agreement; and that neither the said copartnership nor this answering defendant at any time received any benefit from, or consideration for, the said pretended signature to the said pretended note set out in plaintiff's petition; and that the said pretended note, and the pretended signature of Hovey & Peck thereto, was not made for the purpose of carrying on the mercantile business of the said Hovey & Peck, and that no person whomsoever had any authority whatever to sign the said name of Hovey & Peck to the said pretended note, and of all of which said matters and facts the said plaintiff had full and complete notice at the time of the delivery to him of the note set out in his petition.

"By way of further defense this answering defendant

avers that at the time of the pretended execution of the pretended note set out in plaintiff's petition, he was, and for a long time past had been, a resident of the state of California, of all of which matters and facts the plaintiff at the time of the delivery to him of the said pretended note well knew; and that he never heard of the pretended execution of the said pretended note until after this action was brought, and at no time between the time the said pretended note set out in plaintiff's petition became due, until after the beginning of this action upon the said pretended note, did this answering defendant have any knowledge or notice whatsoever of the existence of any such pretended note."

To this answer the reply was a general denial of all the new matter therein, and further as follows:

"Plaintiff especially denies that the signing of said note by Hovey & Peck was without consideration, but avers that said loan was made for the express benefit of said firm, in that prior to April, 1885, said firm of Hovey & Peck was indebted to P. P. Mast & Co. on an overdue account amounting to about $1,736.50. In order to save said firm from suit on said account, defendant E. W. Hovey became surety for said firm of Hovey & Peck for said amount and secured said debt by giving a mortgage on his farm and home to said P. P. Mast & Co. At the time of making said loan and giving said note sued on in plaintiff's petition, said debt was not yet paid, and plaintiff avers that the proceeds of said loan for which said note was given went to pay off said indebtedness of Hovey & Peck to P. P. Mast & Co., which was secured by said mortgage on defendant E. W. Hovey's farm, or to make necessary improvements upon said farm so that said defendants Hovey & Peck would not be pushed for said indebtedness, the real facts of which this plaintiff is ignorant.

"Plaintiff further especially denies that defendant Philetus Peck was without knowledge of the firm's liability on said note in question before action thereon was commenced, but avers that all the defendants herein were duly notified of said note upon the day said note became due and payable."

Of the issues there was a trial to the court and a jury, resulting in a verdict and judgment for Reuben R. Tingley.

Some objections to paragraphs of the trial court's charge to the jury are presented in the argument in brief filed for plaintiff in error. In the motion for a new trial the portions of the charge to the jury which it was desired to assail as erroneous were grouped in one assignment. Of one of these it is stated in the brief that it was proper and correct, with which statement we will not take issue. This being determined, we need give the objections to these paragraphs of the charge no further consideration. (*Graham v. Frazier*, 49 Neb. 90; *Johnston v. Milwaukee & Wyoming Investment Co.*, 49 Neb. 68; *Denise v. City of Omaha*, 49 Neb. 750.)

It is urged that the trial court erred in refusing at the close of introduction of evidence in chief for defendant in error to instruct the jury, at request of counsel for plaintiff in error, to return a verdict in his favor. We do not think the trial court erred in its ruling on the request of counsel. At the time it was made the note in suit had been received in evidence, and was shown to have been executed by a member of a firm. There was nothing on its face from which it appeared that it purported to be executed by the firm of Hovey & Peck in any other capacity than as a principal debtor. This being true, and the partnership being a commercial one, in the business of which it is usual or at times necessary to borrow money and to issue notes, the presumption arose and prevailed that the note was the note of the partnership, given for a partnership debt, and was a valid claim against the partnership. (*Schwank v. Davis*, 25 Neb. 196; *Whitaker v. Brown*, 16 Wend. [N. Y.] 507; *Van Dyke v. Seelye*, 52 N. W. Rep. [Minn.] 215.)

Reuben R. Tingley, while testifying in his own behalf,

was told by his counsel, "You may state to the jury, in
your own language, for what purpose and on what consideration that note was given." (The reference in the
foregoing was to the note in suit.) To this an objection
was interposed, which was overruled, when counsel for
Tingley said, "Just state the facts." Mr. Tingley then
said, "Well, the consideration was to Hovey & Peck."
This was immediately objected to, but the objection was
overruled. In this we think the trial court erred. The
matter of the consideration for the execution and delivery of this note, to whom it moved or by whom
received, was a vital question of the issues, and one on
which the evidence was conflicting and somewhat evenly
balanced. The allowance of this statement by the witness may have furnished the turning point for the jury.
The testimony was but a conclusion and of a nature to
directly affect the rights of plaintiff in error, and its
admission prejudicial. It follows that the judgment of
the district court will be reversed and the cause remanded.

REVERSED AND REMANDED.

HOLT COUNTY V. BARRETT SCOTT ET AL.

FILED DECEMBER 22, 1897.   No. 7483.

1. County Treasurer: ADDITIONAL BOND: COUNTY BOARD. By Compiled
    Statutes, chapter 10, section 21, a county board is empowered, ac-
    cording to circumstances, to require the treasurer either to give an
    additional bond, or to give additional sureties on the subsisting
    bond.

2. ———: ———: SURETIES. Sureties executed a county treasurer's
    bond with the above provision in contemplation and forming a
    part of their contract, and they are not released from liability on
    the bond by the board's requiring additional sureties.

3. Evidence of Admitted Facts: REVIEW. It is not error to exclude
    from evidence a written instrument, the making and contents
    whereof are admitted by the pleadings.

4. **Qualification of Officer:** OFFICIAL BOND: APPROVAL. To entitle one elected to an office requiring an official bond to be inducted into office, his bond must be approved and filed for record before his induction, and within the time fixed by statute.

5. ———: ———: ———. While the rule last stated prevails in actions in which it becomes necessary for the claimant of the office to prove his strict legal title to the office to show that he is the officer *de jure*, such as actions of quo warranto, or to recover the fees from a party who, during the term for which the officer was elected, held the office as a *de facto* officer, and received such fees, in actions on official bonds for alleged breaches of the conditions thereof, a very different doctrine prevails and is applicable.

6. **Official Bonds:** APPROVAL: LIABILITY OF SURETIES. The requirements of the statutes in regard to approval of official bonds is for the benefit and convenience of the public, and not directly for the treasurer or his sureties; and, where the bond has been executed and delivered within the time prescribed by the law, though not approved, or not until a date after the time prescribed, and by virtue of the bond and its delivery the treasurer has obtained possession of the office, and received the fees and emoluments thereof, the sureties cannot escape liability for any breaches of the conditions of the bond by their principal, because the bond was not approved or not so until a date without the time prescribed by law.

7. ———: ———: ———. The official bond of a county treasurer with the oath indorsed thereon was filed within the statutory limit for such act. It had not then been approved, and was not approved until a date beyond the limit prescribed. He entered upon the duties of the office and during the time he continued therein, received the fees and emoluments appertaining thereto. In an action on the bond for an alleged breach of its conditions, *held*, that the fact of the lack of approval at the time prescribed by law was not matter of forceful defense for the sureties on the bond.

8. **Officers:** QUALIFICATION. One who holds and performs the duties of an office and receives the fees and emoluments thereof by virtue of an election or appointment thereto or under color of right, is a *de facto* officer and not a mere intruder.

9. **County Treasurer:** APPROVAL OF BOND: SURETIES. A person who was holding the office of county treasurer, and was re-elected, or elected for a second and the succeeding term, filed a bond with the oath of office indorsed thereon within the time fixed by law. The bond then, however, lacked approval, and was not approved until a date without the time fixed by law for such action. The treasurer continued in the office. *Held*, That he was in the office as of the new term under color of right, and was an officer *de facto*, and the sureties on the bond were precluded or estopped from denying that he was in possession of the office of the second term and *de jure*.

10. ———: ———. The fact that an official bond has been approved
    does not of itself constitute or evidence the delivery and acceptance
    of the bond.

11. ———: ———: RELATION. *Quære:* Are approval, taking and sub-
    scribing the oath of office indorsed on the bond, and its filing for
    record constituent elements of its delivery, the filing being the
    dominant one; and if it is within the limit of time prescribed by
    statute, and the approval of a later date, and beyond that of the
    limit, does the approval relate back to the filing?

12. **Principal and Surety:** BONDS. The decision in the case of *Cutler v.
    Roberts*, 7 Neb. 4, examined and distinguished.

ERROR from the district court of Holt county.   Tried
below before CHAPMAN, J.   *Reversed.*

. The facts are stated in the opinion.

H. E. Murphy and *M. F. Harrington,* for plaintiff in
error.

References: *Manley v. City of Atchison,* 9 Kan. 364;
Supervisors of Richmond County v. Wandel, 6 Lans. [N. Y.]
33; *Sullivan v. State,* 23 N. E. Rep. [Ind.] 150; *State v.
Lincoln County,* 18 Neb. 283.

*John H. Ames, E. F. Pettis, E. M. Bartlett, John C. Wat-
son, H. M. Uttley,* and *R. R. Dickson, contra.*

In support of arguments in favor of the contentions
that the bond was properly excluded as evidence against
the sureties, and that the court properly directed a verdict for defendants, reference was made to the following cases: *State v. Lansing,* 46 Neb. 514; *United States v.
Le Baron,* 19 How. [U. S.] 73; *Broome v. United States,*
15 How. [U. S.] 143; *Bruce v. State,* 11 Gill & Johns.
[Md.] 382; *Winneshiek County v. Maynard,* 44 Ia. 15;
Young v. State, 7 Gill & Johns. [Md.] 253; *State v. Jarrett,*
17 Md. 310; *Davis v. Haydon,* 3 Scam. [Ill.] 35; *State v.
Cosgrove,* 34 Neb. 386; *State v. Lynn,* 31 Neb. 770; *McMillin v. Richards,* 45 Neb. 786; *Commonwealth v. Yarbrough,*
2 S. W. Rep. [Ky.] 68; *Commonwealth v. Magoffin,* 25 S.

W. Rep. [Ky.] 599; *Mayo v. Renfroe*, 66 Ga. 408; *City of Chicago v. Gage*, 95 Ill. 593; *Archer v. State*, 74 Md. 443; *Harwood v. Marshall*, 9 Md. 103; *County Commissioners of Dorchester County v. Meekins*, 50 Md. 45; *McPherson v. Leonard*, 29 Md. 377; *Thomas v. Owens*, 4 Md. 220; *United States v. Boyd*, 15 Pet. [U. S.] 187; *Gunther v. State*, 31 Md. 29; *Union Bank of Maryland v. Ridgely*, 1 Harr. & G. [Md.] 231; *State v. Wayman*, 2 Gill & Johns. [Md.] 279; *Falconer v. Shores*, 37 Ark. 386; *State v. Carneall*, 10 Ark. 156; *Basham v. Commonwealth*, 13 Bush [Ky.] 36; *Rounds v. City of Bangor*, 46 Me. 541; *Blake v. Sturterant*, 12 N. H. 569; *Rounds v. Mansfield*, 38 Me. 586; *Wood v. State*, 40 S. W. Rep. [Ark.] 87.

HARRISON, J.

This action was instituted for the county of Holt on what was claimed to be the bond of Barrett Scott, as treasurer of said county. It was alleged in the petition that at a general election held on a stated day of November, 1891, Barrett Scott was duly elected county treasurer of Holt county for the term of two years, the term having its inception on the first Thursday after the first Tuesday of the month of January, 1892; that on December 29, 1891, Barrett Scott, as principal, and his co-defendants, as sureties, executed and delivered the bond in suit, and that the principal on the same day was duly qualified or took the oath of office. It was further averred that the bond was approved March 1, 1892; that Scott, on the day designated by law for the commencement of the term of office of county treasurer, assumed such office, and entered upon the discharge of the duties thereof, in which he continued until August 18, 1893, on which date the office was assumed by one R. J. Hayes, who had been duly appointed Scott's successor. The default alleged, or breach of the conditions of the bond, was that the principal therein had failed to account for and pay over and had converted funds of the county which he had received as its treasurer in the sum of

$90,000. There was an answer filed for the principal in the bond, but against him the county recovered a judgment of which there is no complaint here, and his plea may be passed without further notice. The co-defendants, the sureties, all joined in a plea of their defenses, except Joseph S. Bartley, for whom there was filed a separate answer. The answer of all the sureties except Bartley admitted the allegation of the petition relative to the election of Barrett Scott to the office of county treasurer of Holt county, and it was alleged for each of these answering defendants that Barrett Scott, soon after his election, prepared and presented to them, respectively, a bond similar to the one declared upon in the petition in the action, and requested them to sign the same as his sureties, with which request they complied of date December 17, 1891, and then delivered the instrument to the principal therein; that Barrett Scott had been and was, during the term terminating in January, 1892, the county treasurer of Holt county, and his selection for the office at the election in November, 1891, entitled him to become his own successor, and it was of the duties of the county board to approve any bond he might present prior to the 'inception of the term of office, if approved at all, and before approval to require and compel an accounting for and production of all funds in his hands as treasurer or with which he was then chargeable; that the board wholly failed to perform its duty in either particular, which operated to discharge the answering defendants, since they had executed the bond with a full reliance on the strict performance by the board of such duties; and, further, that the failure to approve the bond before the time by law fixed for the commencement of the term of office operated a vacancy of the office; also, if said bond ever became of effect, Barrett Scott was ordered, on March 1, 1892, removed from the said office, and a vacancy in said office declared to exist, and, if any responsibility had attached to defendants by reason of their executing the bond, it then wholly ceased. It was further averred that the board, with full knowledge that Barrett Scott had failed to account for the funds received during his first term as county treasurer, had not compelled an accounting, but had wholly failed so to do, allowed him to retain the office, perform its duties, and collect moneys, and on March 1, 1892,—long after the proper time for such action,—fraudulently approved the bond, with the intention then entertained of thereby rendering the defendants responsible for the past acts of the principal in the bond. The answer of Bartley, in addition to pleas similar to those contained in the pleading of his co-defendants, alleged that at some date in the month of February, 1892, the county board had a pretended accounting with Barrett Scott, at which certain moneys and property were produced and represented as belonging to Holt county, which in truth and in fact were not the moneys and property of said county,—all of which facts were then known by the board; and that, regardless of such facts and its knowledge thereof, the board, on March 1, 1892, approved the bond; that the defendant signed the bond in good faith and in ignorance of the facts set forth in this portion of his plea, and also of the further fact that Barrett Scott had not fully adjusted the accounts and charges of his first term; that in so signing the bond the defendant relied on the county board to compel the proper adjustment of the accounts and charges of the prior term of office of the treasurer, which duty was wholly neglected and purposely disregarded by the board. It was also of Bartley's answer that during the month of July, 1892, the board, without the knowledge or consent of the answering defendant or his co-defendant sureties, procured two persons to then sign said bond as additional sureties (the persons so signing are not parties to this suit); that such signing constituted a material alteration of the bond, and operated a release of defendants from liability on the bond. There were in the answers for all

defendants general and special denials of the execution
of the bond, of the principal therein having ever taken
the office for the second term; also, of any failure on
his part to fully perform any and all duties of the office.
Just how much force and significance, in view of some
express or implied admissions of the answers, such denials possessed, we need not now notice or discuss. The
replies were general denials.

The trial of the issues was before a jury. The signature of the principal on the bond was identified and the
instrument offered in evidence. An objection was made,
but the bond was received as against the principal and
ruling was withheld as to the other defendants. During the further course of the trial all further objections
to the admission of the bond on the ground of lack of
proof of the signatures of the sureties was cured by an
admission as to each and all of them, but the bond was
not then admitted as against the sureties. What was
the final action in this regard we will relate in what we
conceive to be its proper connection. During the further progress of the trial there was offered for the county
evidence of the acts of the county board, Barrett Scott,
and some other parties who, in one way or another, became participants in the matter of the office of county
treasurer at that time. Such evidence tended to show
that the bond in suit had been delivered to the county
clerk and by him filed; that, probably some weeks after
the expiration of Scott's first term as county treasurer,
there was an attempted adjustment of the accounts and
affairs of the office between him and the board, when
(this was during the month of February, 1892) it was
discovered that Scott was chargeable with $70,000.04;
that there was on hand a very small sum in cash or
money, and the balance was claimed by Scott to be on
deposit in certain banks, of which he at the time furnished a list by which was shown the amount asserted
as on deposit in each of the banks named in the list.
This was not satisfactory to the board, and a production

of the funds was insisted upon. To comply with this demand Scott requested ten days, which was granted by the board, and the treasurer did, at the time designated, have in the vault of the office an amount of money which, combined with a sum represented by a receipt from the state treasurer, made the amount with which he was then chargeable. Some considerable time afterward the board again demanded that the treasurer produce the money, and allow it to be again counted by the board or its committee appointed for the purpose, but this was met with a refusal or a failure to comply.

On March 1, 1892, the bond in suit was approved, and on the same day Scott was charged in impeachment proceedings before the board, and on the fourth day of the same month was adjudged guilty, and his removal from office decreed or ordered. This action of the board was reviewed in the district court in error proceedings, and on March 31 was reversed, so far as the record before us discloses. (And we will say here that in reference to any fact at this time we but state what the record now presented shows.) Scott continued in the possession and performed the duties of the office. No further steps were taken until July 14, 1892, at which time, by resolution of the board, the insufficiency of the treasurer's bond was declared, and he was ordered "to give additional freehold sureties for the better protection of the taxpayers." In an attempted compliance with this order, on or about July 16, Barrett Scott procured William McWhorter and Milo Pickering to sign the bond. After this a committee appointed by the board, presumably after an examination of the bond and an inquiry of the financial responsibility of the proffered additional sureties, reported on August 31 that the bond was still insufficient. It was then ordered that Scott be required to have his bondsmen certify on his bond to the amount of $200,000. On September 1 the board, by resolution then carried, declared that after ten days' notice Scott had failed to give sufficient sureties, and the office of treasurer was vacant. An appointment was then made, and, to the extent we are informed by this record, the appointee gained possession of the office in August, 1893, by the aid of the courts. There was also evidence received which tended to prove the treasurer's failure to account for the funds of the county in a stated sum. When, at the close of the introduction of its evidence in chief, the plaintiff rested, the objection for the defendants, the sureties, to the admission of the bond was renewed and sustained. A motion was then made for the sureties that a verdict in their favor be directed. This was done. Such a verdict was rendered and judgment entered thereon.

The assignments of error have for their burden the exclusion of the bond from evidence, and the giving the peremptory instruction. One—probably the main—ground of the objection to the introduction of the bond in evidence was that there was a variance between the instrument declared upon and the one the county offered, and it is apparent, from what occurred and what was said by the court at the time, that this was the ground on which the objection was sustained. The difference between the bond stated in the petition and the one offered was that on the latter appeared the two names written thereon in July, 1892. It is contended that these additional sureties were not disapproved or rejected, were in fact accepted, or became responsible as bondsmen, which rendered the bond offered essentially different from the one on which the petition was based. The facts, as they are before us, will not bear out this contention. The action of the board on September 1, 1892, after these names had been added to the bond, in declaring the office vacant was a clear and direct refusal of the parties as additional sureties. A rejection or disapproval of the sureties rejects the bond, or bars its becoming of force. (*Apthorp v. North*, 14 Mass. 166; *State v. Fredericks*, 8 Ia. 553; *Marshall v. Hamilton*, 41 Miss. 229.) Was the signing of these two names on the bond, under the circumstances of such signing, a material alteration, or even a spoliation? It is not claimed that the defendants had knowledge of this action, or consented to it. It is provided in section 21 of chapter 10, Compiled Statutes: "The county commissioners of any one of the counties of this state may require the county treasurer· to give additional freehold sureties whenever in the opinion of a majority of said commissioners the existing security shall become insufficient, and said commissioners are hereby also authorized and empowered to demand and receive from said county treasurer an additional bond as required by law, with good and sufficient freehold security in such sum as said commissioners or a majority of them may direct, whenever in their opinion more money shall have passed or is about to pass into the hands of said treasurer than is or would be recovered by the penalty in the previous bond, and if any county treasurer shall fail or refuse to give such additional security or bond for and during the time of ten days from and after the day on which said commissioners shall have required said treasurer so to do, his office shall be considered vacant, and another treasurer shall be appointed agreeably to the provisions of law." The board was empowered by this provision to require additional sureties to the bond then in existence, or to demand an additional or new bond to be executed and delivered to them. This provision was of the law at the time the bond was executed, and entered into it, and became a part of the contract evidenced by it, as much and as fully as if it had been of its written terms, hence the order that additional sureties be given was but the exercise by the board of one of their rights authorized by the contract, and the signing by the two additional sureties was not a material alteration of the bond, and certainly not a spoliation. It must be concluded from what has been said on this branch of the case that these parties, being rejected as sureties, never became liable as such. Their names had been signed to the instrument legally or pursuant to authorization by law. The effect of the instrument in suit was not changed; and the bond offered and that declared on in the petition were, in legal effect, the same; and the bond should not have been excluded on the ground or for the reason given for such action. At first glance it might be said that the decision in the case of *Stoner v. Keith County*, 48 Neb. 279, seems to express a doctrine contrary to the views just stated on the subject of the additional names on the bond, but on looking into that case it will be discovered that the additional sureties had been adjudged liable on the bond by the district court. Whether they had been approved or rejected did not appear, and the case was tried in the district court and presented in this court on the theory that such signers had rendered themselves liable, and were so unless certain subsequent occurrences had worked their discharge; and further, that the first signers were released by the addition of the other names was a conceded fact, from all of which it is clear that the subject herein discussed was not then presented or involved.

We will turn now to the answers, and what they established in relation to the bond and its execution. We have hereinbefore stated that there were in them denials of the execution of the bond and of its being of the meaning and effect pleaded in the petition. Notwithstanding these denials, a careful reading of the answers convinces us that there are contained in each of them statements which are admissions of these facts. It is unnecessary to quote from the pleadings in question. Their true import, when they are subjected to a critical inspection, is unmistakable, and fully supports the conclusion which we have just announced. This being true, these questions in regard to the bond, the execution and text of the bond, were not in issue,—were admitted facts, hence it was not error to exclude the bond from evidence.

It remains to consider the other ground of alleged

error,—the giving of the peremptory instruction. This action was but a sequel to the exclusion of the bond from evidence, and followed it as a matter of course; and, as we have seen, the reason which moved the trial court to reject the bond was not a true one, and, if it was all the reason which existed for the court's directing the verdict, the judgment would be reversed; but, if there was anything in the case which, though not assigned as a basis for what the court did, was sufficient to sustain such action, the judgment should not be reversed. There was but one of the main and determinable issuable matters which, at the close of the evidence in chief on behalf of the plaintiff as to proof, was left in such condition as would warrant the action of the court in giving the peremptory direction in regard to the verdict. The one matter to which we refer was in relation to the approval of the bond. It did appear that the bond was filed December 29, 1891; that Scott had qualified, and his oath of office was indorsed on the instrument as filed. These things were done within the time prescribed by law for their doing, but the approval was without the fixed time. It will now be in order to notice particularly some of the provisions of our statute with reference to official bonds, more especially the portions which relate to the approval of such instruments. Section 1 of chapter 10 of the Compiled Statutes provides that all officers designated therein, including county officers, shall, before entering upon their respective duties, take and subscribe an oath of which the form is given, which shall be indorsed on their bonds if the officers are required to give bonds. Section 5 of the chapter is as follows: "Official bonds, with the oath indorsed thereon, shall be filed in the proper office within the times as follows: Of all officers elected at any general election, on or before the first Thursday after the first Tuesday in January next succeeding the election." By section 7 it is provided that all bonds of county officers, except commissioners and supervisors, shall be

approved by the county board, and, except the bonds of
the county clerk and members of the county board, shall
be filed and recorded in the office of the county clerk.
In section 11 it is provided that "the approval of each
official bond shall be indorsed upon such bond by the
officer approving the same, and no bond shall be filed
and recorded until so approved." Section 15 reads as
follows: "If any person elected or appointed to any office
shall neglect to have his official bond executed and approved as provided by law, and filed for record within
the time limited by this act, his office shall thereupon
ipso facto become vacant, and such vacancy shall thereupon immediately be filled by election or appointment
as the law may direct in other cases of vacancy in the
same office." Section 17 reads: "When the incumbent
of an office is re-elected or reappointed he shall qualify
by taking the oath and giving the bond as above directed; but when such officer has had public funds or
property in his control, his bond shall not be approved
until he has produced and fully accounted for such funds
and property; and when it is ascertained that the incumbent of an office holds over by reason of the non-
election or non-appointment of a successor, or of the
neglect or refusal of the successor to qualify, he shall
qualify anew within ten days from the time at which
his successor, if elected, should have qualified." Barrett
Scott had been treasurer by election for the term of two
years immediately prior to the term which the bond in
suit was given to entitle him to enter upon and hold.
He had been elected for the second term. Of what is
required of a re-elected officer in regard to qualifying,
giving bond, etc., it was announced by this court in
State v. Lansing, 46 Neb. 514, that "sections 7, 15, and 17,
chapter 10, Compiled Statutes, should be construed together, and when so construed the effect of section 17
is to require one who has been re-elected or reappointed
to an office to qualify therefor by taking the oath and
filing the bond, where a bond is required, in the same

manner and within the same time as one for first time
elected." Section 15, herein quoted, was construed in
that decision and by its requirements relative to execution, approval, and filing official bonds was held to create
a condition precedent to the right of a person elected or
appointed to be inducted into office; and the provision
was also held to be self-executing and on failure of compliance therewith by the elected or appointed person,
the right to the office was extinguished or lost, and the
office vacant and subject to be at once either filled by
appointment or election as by law in each case provided.
The decision in that case, also that in *McMillin v. Richards*,
45 Neb. 786, *State v. Cosgrove*, 34 Neb. 386, and *State v.
Lynn*, 31 Neb. 770, are cited as establishing that the bond
of an officer has no force or validity unless approved by
the person or persons and in the manner prescribed by
law, in any and all cases where approval is required.
Whatever may be our ultimate conclusion relative to
the exact question herein involved and for discussion,
we cannot agree that the cases last referred to reached
the length claimed. The cases of the *State v. Lansing*,
State v. Cosgrove, and *State v. Lynn* were all applications
for writs of quo warranto, the object aimed at in each
case being to oust a party from an office, and, in such
cases, the party whose right to hold the office is attacked,
in order to retain the office, must show strict compliance
with the conditions precedent required to entitle him to
enter upon and hold the office. All such cases are distinguishable from actions on official bonds. As was well
stated in *State v. Lansing*, 46 Neb. 522: "Actions upon
bonds given out of time and direct proceedings to oust an
officer for failing to qualify according to law present very
different questions for consideration." And on page 520:
"There is another class of cases which were suits on official bonds tendered and approved after the statutory
time. The best considered of these cases hold the bond
valid, not because the statute fixing the time was directory merely, but because the officer became a *de facto* offi-

cer or because the officer and his sureties were estopped
from asserting the invalidity of the bond, they having
tendered it and it having been accepted, and the officer
having acted under it." The case of *McMillin v. Richards, supra,* was an action by the plaintiff to recover the
fees and emoluments of the office of county treasurer of
a county in this state, which it was claimed had been
received by the defendant during his incumbency of said
office as treasurer *de facto.* It was therein held that the
plaintiff, in order to recover, must have proved that he
possessed the full legal title to the office, had fulfilled all
the requirements of the law necessary to constitute him
on officer *de jure.* That case clearly presented different
questions governed by different reasons and principles
than appear in an action like the case at bar on an official bond.

The direct question to which our attention will now
be given is, did the bond in suit, by reason of its non-
approval within the time prescribed by statute, remain
inoperative, and never become of any force or effect?
If so, the obligation of the sureties had no life, did not
charge them, and the peremptory instruction to the jury
was correct. We will here again call to notice the rule
that, when these parties defendant herein signed this
bond as sureties, they did it, or it must be presumed or
considered that they acted, in contemplation of all the
laws then existing which were applicable to and governing transactions of the nature of the one in hand, and
with knowledge that all such laws and rules of law
entered into and became a part of the contract, which,
by the signing, they indorsed as their agreement.

Turning now to some of the regulations prescribed by
the statutory law in regard to official bonds, and to
which we have hereinbefore called attention, in what
position does a fair and reasonable construction and
enforcement of them place these defendants? Section
15 clearly makes it the duty of the prospective officer to
have his bond approved and filed. His neglect to per-

form these duties operates his forfeiture of the right to
claim or hold the office. It cannot, by any process of true
reasoning, be said to apply to the bond, and render it
any the less effective or operative, if it ever became so.
The latter was not its intention, and is not of its import.
It was not intended to and does no more than prescribe
what shall be done by the prospective officer, and assign
the results of a neglect on his part to do what is required.
The other sections to which we have hereinbefore referred, in relation to approval of the bond, are of the
duties of certain of the county officers, and doubtless of
the ones to whom it is allotted that they shall approve
such bonds as the one in suit; also of the officer whose
duty it was to file and record it after its approval; it
may be said that they were derelict in the performance
of their duties, or the bond would not be in its present
condition; but can or does the fact that they were negligent, render the obligation signed by the sureties of
none avail where it has been delivered, and the principal
has assumed the office, the proper and faithful performance of the duties of which it was designed to secure?
We think not. These provisions relative to approval of
the bond were not for the benefit of the sureties of bonds,
but for the convenience and better security of the public
and the parties who may be directly interested. The
sureties had signed the bond and delivered it to the
principal therein for the purpose for which it was used,
and they have no reasonable or tenable ground for complaint in that some matters which were not of their
concern, or not to be exercised in their behalf, were
neglected and not observed. Nor do we think, by adopting this view, we do not administer the law with fairness
and with as nearly equal justice to all as may be. The
sureties executed the bond and gave it to the principal
to be delivered to the county, by which act he was to
obtain and hold possession of the office, and receive and
enjoy its fees and emoluments. The principal delivered
the bond, neglecting a prescribed duty,—that of procur-

ing it to be approved. He took possession of the office and received and enjoyed its fees and privileges, and it is asserted much more. Whether the last is true or not, we, in the present hearing, have no concern, and need not definitely determine or discuss. To hold that the bond became of effect on its delivery and the assumption of the office by its principal signer, is to do no more than enforce the contract, to require of the sureties what they had in contemplation when they executed and gave the bond to their principal, and by so holding we but do justice to the other party to the bond,—the public, nominally the county. It certainly seems right and consistent with fairness to adopt the course which will be just to all and inflict no injustice on any.

Our conclusion is not new or novel, or unsupported by the opinions of other courts and of text writers. Provisions which require the approval of official bonds are for the benefit of the obligee who alone can take advantage of a failure to observe them. Such failure is never ground upon which the obligor or his sureties can escape liability after a breach of the conditions of a bond.' (4 Am. & Eng. Ency. Law [2d ed.] 669; Murfree, Official Bonds sec. 48; Mechem, Public Officers sec. 313.) "Approval being thus for the protection of the public only, it is well settled that where, by virtue of the bond, the officer has been inducted to the office his sureties cannot escape liability for his defaults because the bond was not approved by the proper officer, or was not approved at all." The case of *People v. Johr*, 22 Mich. 462, was an action against Johr and his sureties on his bond as treasurer of a county in Michigan to recover damages for alleged breach of the bond in not accounting for and paying over moneys received for sales of lands for taxes. The law required the execution and approval of the bond as conditions precedent to the officer's right to make the sales. The bond, as in the case at bar, was excluded from the consideration of the jury in that case for the reason that it was not executed and approved as required by statute. In the opinion in the supreme court on error it was said: "It is doubtless true that, without the approval of the prosecuting attorney and the other circuit court commissioner, the auditor general might have refused the bond, and declined to allow the county treasurer to make the tax sales, and it may be admitted that, as between the auditor general and the people, it was his duty to have done so, and to have appointed another person to make the sales. But the precise question here is whether the county treasurer, who, on the faith of this bond, was allowed to make the sale and receive the money, or his sureties, can now be heard to make the objection that the bond executed by them and accepted and received by the auditor general as and for the bond required by the statute, and on the faith of which he has allowed the treasurer to sell the lands and receive the money, was not approved by all the officers whose approval it was the duty of the treasurer to have obtained. For whose benefit, and for what purpose, did the statute require the approval by the officers mentioned? Certainly not for the benefit or protection of the county treasurer or his sureties, but solely for the security and protection of the public, that the state might not be in danger of losing the public funds by insufficient sureties. And, after the county treasurer and his sureties have had all the benefits they could possibly have enjoyed had the approval been obtained, it is not for his sureties even—much less for him—to object that the state or its officers should have exercised more caution in ascertaining their sufficiency as sureties; for this, upon final analysis, is the whole force of the objection, the bond itself, in all its provisions, being in strict compliance with the statute. Such, we think, must be the result both upon logical and legal principles. It is so well settled as long ago to have become a maxim of law, that any one may waive the benefit of a provision of a law, or a contract introduced for his own benefit. * * * And though, as between the people of the

17

state and the auditor general, the latter may have had
no right to waive the required approval of the sureties in
this case, yet, when the people in their corporate capacity
sue upon the bond, under the circumstances of this case,
there is no principle of justice or common sense, and we
are aware of no principle of law, which prohibits them,
so far as the defendants are concerned, from waiving the
approval, or which can give the defendants the right to
insist upon it for the purpose of defeating their liability.
* * * We think, therefore, the bond in this case, as between the people and the defendants, is to be treated in
all respects as a statute bond, and that the circuit court
erred in excluding it from the jury." (See also *Mc-
Cracken v. Todd*, 1 Kan. 148; *Auditor v. Woodruff*, 2 Ark.
79; *Marshall v. Hamilton*, 41 Miss. 229; *Stevens v. Treasurers*, 2 McCord [S. Car.] 67; *People v. Edwards*, 9 Cal.
286; *Sprowl v. Lawrence*, 33 Ala. 674; *Jones v. State*, 7
Mo. 46; *Apthorp v. North*, 14 Mass. 166; *State v. Fredericks*, 8 Ia. 553; *Boone County v. Jones*, 54 Ia. 699; *Men-
docino County v. Morris*, 32 Cal. 145; *State v. Hampton*, 14
La. Ann. 736; *Young v. State*, 7 Gill & J. [Md.] 253; *Dutton v. Kelsey*, 2 Wend. [N. Y.] 615; *Skelinger v. Yendes*, 12
Wend. [N. Y.] 306; *Ring v. Gibbs*, 26 Wend. [N. Y.] 502.)
Some of the cases cited may not be in all respects entirely in point, but such as are not support the doctrine.
It may be said, if we give full force to the decision in
State v. Lansing, supra, that Barrett Scott did not possess
a full indefeasible title to the office, since his bond had
not been approved. If this be conceded, he was a *de
facto* officer, demanded, obtained, and held the office by
reason of his election thereto. He was not a mere intruder, but was acting under color of right, and in this
action his sureties are estopped. They cannot be heard
to assert that he was no officer. In *Jones v. Scanland*, 6
Humph. [Tenn.] 195,—an action upon an official bond,—
it was said: "Although the election of a person as
sheriff was void, and his induction into office illegal by
reason of his having then been a defaulter to the treas-

ury, and he did not thereby become sheriff *de jure*, yet he became sheriff *de facto*, and those who voluntarily bound themselves for the faithful performance of his duties, as sureties, cannot absolve themselves from their obligation by insisting that he was no sheriff." In the case of *State v. Rhoades*, 6 Nev. 352, it was announced: "Where a state treasurer, re-elected in 1866, accepted a new commission, and took a new oath, and continued to discharge the duties of the office, but failed to file a new official bond within the time prescribed by law, held, that he was an officer *de facto*, and holding as of the new term; and that the sureties on the new bond afterwards filed were estopped from denying that he was holding as of the new term *de jure*. * * * A person discharging the duties of a public office under color of right is an officer *de facto* and not a mere intruder. * * * Where a person discharges the duties of an office as an officer *de facto* and not as a mere intruder he and his sureties are estopped by the recitals in his official bond from denying that he is entitled to the office." After quoting at length from a number of authorities, it is said in the opinion: "These authorities are squarely opposed to the ground taken here that the failure to execute the bond within the statutory time released the sureties. They have precluded themselves from saying that the person for the faithful discharge of whose official acts they became sureties was not of right entitled to perform such acts. The authorities cited on behalf of defendants are not adverse to this conclusion. It will be found upon examination, either that the person for whom the bond was given was a mere intruder, not deemed an officer *de facto*, and consequently not estopped from showing that he was not an officer either in fact or of right, or where the bond was given under circumstances rendering it utterly null, but still free from all elements estopping the parties to it from showing such to be the case. Bonds like this are sustained upon a strong current of authorities holding that a per-

son being an officer *de facto* is not permitted to show or
rely upon the fact that he was not an officer *de jure*, for
the purpose of attacking or setting aside anything which
he may have done in his official capacity. And upon
like reason his sureties are also estopped. Where there
is no element of estoppel, or the reason for the rule does
not exist, of course it should not be applied. The absence of the circumstances constituting an estoppel is
the distinguishing feature between the cases cited for
the defendants and those sustaining the conclusion at
which we have arrived." (See also *Green v. Wardwell*, 17
Ill. 278; *City of Chicago v. Gage*, 95 Ill. 625; *Nunn v. Goodlett*, 10 Ark. 89; *Stevens v. Treasurers*, 2 McCord [S. Car.]
67; *Boone County v. Jones*, 54 Ia. 699; *Plymouth v. Painter*,
17 Conn. 585; *Pier County v. Hannam*, 3 Barn. & Ald.
[Eng.] 266; *Bucknam v. Ruggles*, 15 Mass. 180; *People
v. Collins*, 7 Johns. [N. Y.] 549; *Monteith v. Commonwealth*,
15 Grat. [Va.] 172; *State v. Bates*, 36 Vt. 387; *Town of
Lyndon v. Miller*, 36 Vt. 329; *Marshall v. Hamilton*, 41
Miss. 229; *Norris v. State*, 22 Ark. 524; *People v. Jenkins*,
17 Cal. 500; *People v. Slocum*, 1 Ida. 62; *Ford v. Clough*,
8 Me. 334; *Reed v. Hedges*, 16 W. Va. 194.) For decisions of this court in which the doctrine of estoppel is
recognized and held applicable to sureties on bonds see
Gudtner v. Kirkpatrick, 14 Neb. 347; *Adams v. Thompson*,
18 Neb. 541; *Dunterman v. Storey*, 40 Neb. 447; *Flannagan v. Cleveland*, 44 Neb. 58.

In the case of *Cutler v. Roberts*, 7 Neb. 4, it was held:
"A statutory bond must conform substantially to the
requirements of the statutes in respect to its penalty,
conditions, form, and number of sureties. The statute
in such case enters into and forms a part of the contract, and a surety may insist, as a defense in an action
on such a bond, signed by but one surety where two are
required, that he is not liable thereon, the bond not
being perfect on its face, unless he waive the defect."
The facts of the case were, in substance, as follows: A
judgment in an action on a promissory note was rendered

against one John Rouse.   In an effort to stay an execution of the judgment, the debtor procured a bond to be signed by one surety who, when he signed it, told Rouse that the law required two sureties on such a bond. Rouse promised to get the signature of another surety on the bond but did not do so.   He sent the bond to the probate judge before whom the judgment had been obtained, who, on its receipt, did not approve it, but marked it filed of the date received.   An execution was procured to issue for the enforcement of the judgment and levied on property of the debtor, and in an action to restrain the officer from selling the property, the doctrine, a statement of which we have quoted, was announced.   The law in force then in regard to stay bonds was as follows: "On all judgments for the recovery of money only, except those rendered in any court on appeal or writ of error thereto, or against any officer or person or corporation or the sureties of any of them, for money received in a fiduciary capacity, or for the breach of any official duty, there may be stay of execution, if the defendant therein shall, within twenty days from the rendition of judgment, procure two or more sufficient freehold sureties to enter into a bond, acknowledging themselves security for the defendant for the payment of the judgment, interest, and costs," etc.   The court stated in its opinion written by MAXWELL, J.: "The law in such a case enters into and forms a part of the contract, and a surety may insist as a defense, in an action on a bond signed by but one surety, that he is not liable thereon, the statute being notice to all parties concerned that two sureties were required, unless the surety waived the condition prescribed by the statute,"—from which it appears that the decision was in part, at least, based on the ground that the provision of the statute, by which two sureties were required to make the instrument a statutory bond, was one for the protection and benefit of a surety thereon and with which he could demand a compliance.   The case is not an authority which can govern or influence in a determination of the questions in the case at bar, for reasons: First, the provision herein invoked by the sureties relative to approval of bonds is not designed for the security or benefit of a surety or the sureties, as was the one involved in that case. Second, in the case at bar the purposes for which the bond was executed and delivered were accomplished; hence the consideration passed. In that case, from the very nature of the object sought to be attained by the execution and delivery of the bond, it could not be effected by the bond as filed, nor could its filing produce or induce such conditions as would work an estoppel of the surety to plead or assert the nonoperativeness of the bond. The fact that the bond under consideration in the case of *Cutler v. Roberts* was never approved was not noticed further than to merely state it in the opinion, and it was not an element of the basis for the decision. In the case of *United States v. Maurice*, 2 Brock [U. S.] 96,—an action on an official bond decided by Chief Justice Marshall as circuit judge, —which, while probably not strictly in point in the case at bar, is quite so, and supports the rules herein announced, there will be found some very instructive and wholesome reading on the subjects herein involved.

There is another branch of the question which we think deserves notice. It may be urged that, as there was no approval of the bond in time, there was no acceptance of it by the county, hence it is not binding on the sureties. This is not tenable. The law contemplates that the officer will have the bond approved and afterward filed and recorded. If he secured its approval, and did not file it or deliver it, it would be no more binding because of the approval than it would without it. The approval does not work the acceptance of the bond. It purports to evidence an investigation by the proper person or persons into the reliability and responsibility of the signers of the bond, and the other matters as to which an examination usually does, and always should, precede the approval; and if the bond is approved, this fact also shows that the investigation has disclosed everything to be satisfactory, but the approval does not constitute or evidence a delivery and an acceptance.

There is another argument which might be urged as establishing the validity and potency of the bond in suit, viz., that, when filed in time, as was this one, a later approval relates back to the time of filing, and will be considered as done of that date. This is on the ground that where there are several acts which may be said to be concurrent, required to be done to make or complete a matter or thing, then the dominant act in this case,— the delivery,—shall be preferred, and to it the other acts have relation. Supporting this doctrine are *State v. Tool*, 4 O. St. 553; *Drew v. Morrill*, 62 N. H. 23. This point was not discussed by counsel and as to whether it should prevail or not, we will merely indulge in a query; but if there ever were cases in which the doctrine of relation should be invoked and apply, it is probably in actions of the nature of this.

It follows from the conclusions herein stated that the sureties were not entitled to the peremptory instruction. It should not have been given. The judgment must be reversed and the cause remanded.

REVERSED AND REMANDED.

IRVINE, C., dissenting.

While concurring for the most part in the opinion of the court, I cannot concur in the conclusion that the bond sued on became operative, and desire, as briefly as possible, to express my views on the two principal points on which the court bases that conclusion. I understand the court to hold, in the first place, that the approval of an official bond, at least within the time limited by law, is not essential to the consummation of the contract between the obligors and the public; and, in the second place, that because Scott was suffered to assume the duties and receive the emoluments of the office, and be-

came a *de facto* officer, the sureties are estopped to deny
his title to the office.

It is not, in my opinion, necessary to consider whether,
under any circumstances, an official bond can become
operative until it has been approved. Many cases, it is
true, proceed upon the theory adopted in the opinion of
the court, that provisions for approval are solely for the
benefit of the public, and may be waived, and that therefore the sureties cannot set up a want of approval as a
defense. On the other hand other cases hold that where
an approval is required, it is the act, or one of the
acts, designated by law as requisite to an acceptance,
and that in the absence of approval there has been no
acceptance and therefore no technical delivery. (*United
States v. Le Baron*, 19 How. [U. S.] 73; *Bruce v. State*, 11
Gill & J. [Md.] 382; *State v. Jarrett*, 17 Md. 310; *Crawford
v. Meredith*, 6 Ga. 552; *Commonwealth v. Yarborough*, 2 S. W.
Rep. [Ky.] 68; *Commonwealth v. Magoffin*, 25 S. W. Rep.
[Ky.] 599.) It may be added that every utterance of this
court in the past, and several have been very direct and
emphatic, favors this view. (*State v. Lynn*, 31 Neb. 770;
State v. Cosgrove, 34 Neb. 386; *McMillan v. Richards*, 45
Neb. 786.) However, treating that as an open question,
or as one which should be resolved in favor of the
county's contention, it must be conceded that by force
of our statutes the approval of the bond within the time
limited is essential to entitle the person elected or appointed to enter upon the office. The cases last cited
certainly are authority for that statement, and the case
of *State v. Lansing*, 46 Neb. 514, is absolutely conclusive
of the question. So long as that case stands without
being expressly overruled there can be no doubt on the
subject. The opinion of the court recognizes this principle, and thereby admits that Scott lost all title to the
office when the Thursday after the first Tuesday in January passed without an approval of the bond. Scott
nevertheless remained for ten days a *de jure* officer, holding over under his first election because his successor had

not qualified, and then lost even that title through his failure to requalify under the tenure so acquired. (*State v. Cosgrove, supra.*) Thereafter he was at most a *de facto* officer. It follows that he never occupied the office under his election, by virtue of the right acquired by that election, or for the term contemplated by that election. Being already in office he there remained, solely because the county board neglected to perform its duty by choosing his successor, and subject to be by that board at any minute summarily ousted. The bond had been by the sureties executed in due season, and had by Scott been presented to the county authorities in due season. This is an important and perhaps a controlling fact, the legal effect of which the opinion of the court entirely ignores. The bond contained no recitals except that Scott had been elected for the term mentioned, and its condition is for the faithful performance of the duties of the office. It contemplates that he should hold the office under the election recited, and for the term fixed by law, that he should, in a word, hold as treasurer *de jure,* as it was practicable for him to do when the bond was made. It was not conditioned for his good conduct as an officer holding over his former term, or as a *de facto* officer by sufferance of the county board. (*Winneshiek County v. Maynard,* 44 Ia. 15.) It was given for one purpose, and by the opinion of the court it is made to bind the sureties for an entirely different purpose. The condition of the bond, when read in the light of the facts existing when it was executed, and of the law, was that Scott should faithfully discharge the duties of his office as the county treasurer of Holt county elected for the term of two years beginning the Thursday after the first Tuesday in January, 1892. The court holds the sureties liable upon a bond conditioned for the faithful discharge of the duties of county treasurer, provided the county board should wrongfully suffer him to remain in office, or if by hook or crook he could manage to remain there. It will not do to say that the end in view was his acting

as county treasurer, and that it made no difference by
what right or in what absence of right he so acted. The
sureties are entitled to have their contract construed as
it is and not as the court may think they would, under
other circumstances, have been willing to make it. Moreover it by no means follows, because a man is willing to
become surety for the acts of a *de jure* officer, that he is
willing to stand responsible for the acts of one who in-
trudes himself into an office and may at any moment be
unceremoniously evicted,—one charged with all the burdens of a *de jure* officer, but entitled to none of his rights.
I think the bond is void, not directly for the reason that
it was not approved in time, but because for that reason
Scott lost all title to the office, and the event never occurred whereby, according to the terms of the contract
and the contemplation of the parties, it was to be rendered operative.

Passing now to the other point referred to, the supposed estoppel of the sureties, I cannot see upon what
fact that estoppel can be predicated. If the bond had
recited facts inconsistent with the averment of Scott's
forfeiture of the office, then an estoppel would arise by
deed. If there were any covenant on the subject a liability might arise thereon. If the sureties, after Scott
lost his right to office, had done any act furthering his
claim or inducing the county to admit him into or retain
him in office, an estoppel might arise *en pais*. But there
was, as already said, no recital in the bond except of
Scott's election, and the sureties are not seeking to controvert that fact. There was no covenant binding them
for anything but a lawful holding. No fact had occurred
when they signed the bond or when it was presented to
the county, whereby Scott's right had been defeated or
impaired. After the act of forfeiture they did no act
recognizing his continued right or inducing the county
to recognize it. I can understand that the defendants
would be estopped to assert any fact contrary to recitals
or covenants contained in the bond, and I can understand

that they might be estopped, even in the absence of express recitals, to assert any defect in Scott's title existing at the time the bond was signed or presented. So
if the bond had been presented after the time limited by
law for Scott's qualification it may be that the sureties
could not thereafter allege the forfeiture of right as a
defense, at least if the facts creating the forfeiture were
known to them, or if Scott had been permitted to enter
upon the office in reliance upon the waiver of the irregularity by the defendants. But to create an estoppel by
deed there must be some recital or covenant contrary to
the fact which it is sought to establish by proof; and to
create an estoppel *en pais* there must have been some
act or omission of duty, in reliance whereon the other
party has altered his position to his disadvantage, so
that it would be inequitable to permit the fact to be
shown. In this case there is not the semblance of any
one of these essential elements. The court, on the other
hand, seems to raise the estoppel from the fact that
after the defendants had in good faith presented the bond
for a timely approval, the county board neglected its
duty and permitted Scott to wrongfully hold office; to
raise it from facts occurring after the sureties had done
all their part in making the contract, and facts in which
they had no part and over which they had no control.
The judgment of the court, it seems to me, substitutes for
the contract of the parties one made for them without
their consent or authority by other persons. It holds
them liable, not for the misconduct of Scott as an elected
treasurer. but for his misconduct as an intruder, and in
effect adds to that liability a responsibility for the negligence of the county board. Finally, it estops them by
recitals and covenants they did not make, and by facts
not only unknown to them but nonexistent at the time
of the contract and created by the adverse party and not
by them.

RYAN and RAGAN, CC., concur in the foregoing dissenting opinion.

204|
867|

COMMERCIAL INVESTMENT COMPANY V. JOHN M. PECK
ET AL.

FILED DECEMBER 22, 1897.   No. 7517.

Payment of Mortgage Debt to Clerk of Court: FORECLOSURE. After
the commencement of an action to foreclose a real estate mortgage
for the entire debt, but before judgment, the mortgagors, in vacation, without an order of court or plea, deposited with the clerk of
the court the full amount of the mortgage debt and all costs. The
clerk embezzled the money and absconded. *Held,* That the clerk
did not receive the money by virtue of his office, but in his individual capacity as the mere agent of the mortgagor, and that such
deposit of the money did not extinguish the mortgage. IRVINE
and RAGAN, CC., dissenting.

ERROR from the district court of Dawes county. Tried
below before BARTOW, J. *Reversed.* ·

W. W. Wood and *Stewart & Munger,* for plaintiff in
error.

C. H. Bane and *D. B. Jenckes,* contra.

NORVAL, J.

The action was to foreclose a real estate mortgage for
the entire amount of the debt. The mortgagors, after·
the service of a summons upon them, in vacation, and
without the knowledge and consent of the mortgagee
or its attorney, paid to the clerk of the district court the
full amount due on the mortgage, and all costs. No
entry of such payment was entered by the clerk upon
the books of his office, nor did he pay the money to the
plaintiff or its attorney, but embezzled the same and
absconded. Subsequently a decree of foreclosure was
entered, the defendants being in default of an answer,
an order of sale was issued, and the mortgaged premises
were sold thereunder. Neither the plaintiff nor its attorney was apprised of the deposit with the clerk until
after the sale, when, for the first time, the defendants

ascertained that the clerk had embezzled the money, and that a decree of foreclosure had been entered in the cause. At a term subsequent to the rendition of the decree, the court, on application of the defendants, vacated the decree and set aside the sale, which order is here for review.

We are unable to assent to the proposition that the clerk, by virtue of his office, was authorized to receive the money in this case, and that the payment thereof constituted a payment "into court" and extinguished the mortgage debt. The legislature of this state has provided (Code of Civil Procedure, sec. 889): "The clerk of each of the courts shall exercise the powers and perform the duties conferred and imposed upon him by other provisions of this code, by other statutes, and by the common law. In the performance of his duties he shall be under the direction of his court." The clerk of the district court of Dawes county did not receive the money under and by virtue of any order of the court below requiring the payment to be made, for the very obvious reason no such order was ever entered. Moreover, the money was not received by the clerk during term time, or under such circumstances as to admit of an inference that the payment was made under the court's direction; but the clerk received the money in vacation and without the sanction of the court, either expressed or implied. At common law, payment to the clerk in vacation during the pendency of an action, before judgment and without an order of court, of the amount due plaintiff, was not authorized, and no statutory enactment in this state can be found which empowers a clerk of the district court to receive money under the circumstances disclosed by this record. The law did not constitute the clerk the agent of this plaintiff to receive the amount of its mortgage. After judgment, a clerk of court may receive payment, even in the absence of any express statute upon the subject. (*McDonald v. Atkins*, 13 Neb. 568; *Moore v. Boyer*, 52 Neb. 446.) The authority

of a clerk of a court to receive payment of a judgment in
his office existed at common law, and has been recognized
by long usage. The official power of the clerk is cir-
cumscribed by the extent of his duties, and he ceases
to act by virtue of his office whenever he steps beyond
the boundary of his power. It was no part of the official
duty of the clerk to receive the money from these mortgagors. He did not act officially, but in his individual
capacity as the mere agent of those who entrusted him
with the money. (*Durant v. Gabby*, 2 Met. [Ky.] 91;
Baker v. Hunt, 1 Wend. [N. Y.] 103; *Currie v. Thomas*, 8
Porter [Ala.] 293; *Windom v. Coates*, 8 Ala. 285; *Ball v.
Bank of State*, 8 Ala. 590; *Governor v. Read*, 38 Ala. 253;
Alexandria v. Saloy, 14 La. Ann. 326; *Hammer v. Kaufman*,
39 Ill. 87.)

In *Mayzk v. M'Ewen*, 2 Bailey [S. Car.] 28, it was decided that where money is paid to a clerk of the court he
receives it as the private agent of the party making the
payment, unless accompanied by a plea of tender, or the
deposit has been made in pursuance of an order of court
to do so.

In *Keith v. Smith*, 1 Swan [Tenn.] 92, it was ruled that
money paid into court is unavailing as a tender if not
made upon an order of court authorizing it to be done.

In *Hammer v. Kaufman*, 39 Ill. 87, it was held that a
clerk of court is not, by virtue of his office, authorized
to receive money as a deposit except by order of the
court; that money paid to him without such order may
be withdrawn by the depositor at any time before the
other party has manifested a willingness to accept it,
or the court has recognized it as a fund at its disposal,
and that in case the money is lost by the clerk the one
making the deposit must sustain the loss, instead of the
person for whose benefit the money was received.

In *Levan v. Sternfeld*, 55 N. J. Law 41, it was decided
that payment of money to a clerk of court after the commencement of an action and before judgment, without a
rule, may be disregarded by the party for whom the same

was deposited. Reed, J., in the course of his opinion, says: "Now, the money paid into court in this case, so far as the record shows, was not paid in under any rule. The clerk has no authority to receive money without a rule of court. (1 Sellon, Practice sec. 18, p. 277; *Baker r. Hunt*, 1 Wend. [N. Y.] 103.) The doctrine is obviously sound, therefore, which is said by Campbell in a note to *Rucker v. Palsgrave*, 1 Campbell [Eng.] 557, to have been laid down by Lord Ellenborough, that if, after action brought, the moneys sought to be recovered are paid without a rule of court, the plaintiff must have a verdict."

Currie v. Thomas, 8 Porter [Ala.] 293, was a suit upon a promissory note where the defendant pleaded that a prior suit had been brought on the same note, and that he had paid the full amount due thereon to the clerk of the court. It was held that payment to the clerk did not prejudice the plaintiff. The court in disposing of the question observed: "There are several stages in the proceedings of a case, in which the clerk of a court is by law authorized to be the holder of the moneys which may be paid into court. Thus, on plea pleaded, when the cause of action is admitted to a partial extent, and denied as to the residue. So in the case of a tender. So, also, when money is paid into court in satisfaction of a judgment. In all these cases, however, the money is presumed to be brought before the court, and as it can have no custody of money, it of necessity remains with the clerk, as the fiduciary of the court. But independent of statutory enactments no case is remembered in which money can be lawfully paid to the clerk in vacation, or in any other manner than as the officer of the court in term time, and the receipt of which is always shown by some record of the court, or some proceeding yet on paper, but progressing to a record. To permit this officer to receive demands which have not been reduced to judgment would bring about consequences of a most mischievous tendency, unless received at a time when he

is presumed to be under the immediate control of the
court,—that is, in term time,—and then only in those
cases where the performance becomes a duty imposed by
the peculiar organization of the court."

After diligent search we have been unable to find a
single authority which sustains the proposition that the
deposit of the money with the clerk under the admitted
facts disclosed by this record extinguished the indebtedness, or that plaintiff must look to the clerk for its
money.

Section 856 of the Code of Civil Procedure declares
that "whenever a petition shall be filed for the satisfaction or foreclosure of any mortgage, upon which there
shall be due any interest or any portion or installment
of the principal, and there shall be other portions or
installments to become due subsequently, the petition
shall be dismissed upon the defendant bringing into
court, at any time before the decree of sale, the principal
and interest due with costs." This section is not applicable here for more reasons than one. · In the first place,
the mortgage sought to be foreclosed herein is not embraced within the provisions of the law, since the whole
indebtedness was past due, and no portion or installment
could mature subsequent to the bringing of the suit.
Again, the money was not paid "into court," but was
deposited with the clerk, in vacation, without any rule
or order of court permitting it to be done, and payment
was not accompanied by an answer pleading the same.
Under the authorities already alluded to, such order or
plea was necessary to make the payment available. The
clerk in receiving the deposit was the private agent of
the mortgagors, and the loss must fall upon them. It
follows that the court below erred in treating the mortgage debt as paid, and in vacating the decree of foreclosure and setting aside the sale. Decree reversed and
action dismissed.

REVERSED AND DISMISSED.

HARTFORD FIRE INSURANCE COMPANY V. ANNA F. COREY
ET AL.

FILED DECEMBER 22, 1897.   No. 7650.

1. **Continuance.** The overruling of an application for continuance of a cause, based on the absence of a witness, is without prejudice when the person whose presence was desired was in court during the trial, placed on the witness stand, and was examined by the parties.

2. ——: AFFIDAVITS: REVIEW. Affidavits used in the court below on the hearing of a motion for continuance are not available on review, unless embodied in a bill of exceptions.

3. ——: PLEADING: LACHES. A defendant who, by leave of court, has been permitted to answer after the time fixed therefor by statute, is in no position to object to the case being placed on trial on the ground that the plaintiff has not replied, no order in reference to a reply having been made by the court.

4. **Leave to File Pleadings:** LACHES. The granting of permission to file a reply out of time, or during the trial, rests largely in the legal discretion of the trial court.

5. **Costs:** MOTION TO RETAX: REVIEW. A motion to retax costs is essential to obtain a review of a mistake, neglect, or omission of the clerk of the trial court in the taxation of costs, but such motion is unnecessary where the court has determined that a party is liable for certain costs and rendered judgment against him therefor. *Burton v. State*, 34 Neb., 125, followed.

6. ——: ATTORNEY'S FEES: INSURANCE: PLEADING. Where an attorney's fee is sought to be recovered in an action upon an insurance policy issued under the valued policy act of 1889, the same should be demanded in the petition, and the matter presented to the trial court. *German Ins. Co. v. Eddy*, 37 Neb., 461, followed.

7. ——: ——: ——: ——. In case an attorney's fee is not specifically prayed for in the petition, but the same is demanded in writing by plaintiff at the time of the rendition of the judgment, such act will be treated as an amendment of the prayer of the petition.

ERROR from the district court of Greeley county. Tried below before THOMPSON, J. . *Affirmed.*

Fyke, Yates & Fyke and *T. P. Lanigan,* for plaintiff in error.

M. B. Gearon, J. R. Hanna, and *T. J. Doyle, contra.*

NORVAL, J.

Action by Anna F. Corey and Dora Corey upon a fire insurance policy. There was a trial by jury, and a verdict and judgment for the plaintiff. The defendant prosecutes error.

Immediately preceding the trial the defendant below applied for a continuance in order to procure the attendance of one Ethel Corbett as a witness, which application was denied. Complaint is now made of this ruling. The record discloses that the person above named was present at the trial, was placed upon the witness stand, and examined by plaintiff below and cross-examined by defendant. The court also informed counsel for the company that they might make Miss Corbett a witness for the defense, and when she was excused from the stand the court asked: "Do any of the parties want this witness any further during the trial?" To this inquiry counsel for plaintiffs and defendants, respectively, replied in the negative. It is obvious that there was no error commited in refusing to postpone the trial to procure the attendance of Miss Corbett.

After the impaneling of the jury the defendant a second time sought a continuance of the cause until the next term of court because of the absence of George Brewer, which motion was denied. This decision cannot be reviewed, for the reason the affidavit filed in support of the motion has not been embodied in the bill of exceptions. It is an inflexible rule that affidavits used in the trial court are not available in this court, unless preserved by means of a bill of exceptions. (*Ray v. Mason,* 6 Neb. 101; *Walker v. Lutz,* 14 Neb. 274; *Tessier v. Crowley,* 16 Neb. 372; *Graves v. Scoville,* 17 Neb. 593; *Burke v. Pepper,* 29 Neb. 320; *Strunk v. State,* 31 Neb. 119; *Korth v. State,* 46 Neb. 631; *Minick v. Minick,* 49 Neb. 89.)

On the answer day, which was March 4, 1895, the defendant filed a general demurrer to the petition, which was overruled on the third day thereafter, and on application of the defendant it was given until the morning of March 8 to answer. On request for further time to plead, it was ordered that answer be filed by the coming in of the court on the morning of March 9, at which time a general denial to the averments of the petition was filed. Two days later, the day on which the trial began, an amended answer was filed, by leave of court, which pleaded affirmative matters as a defense. It is insisted that the defendant was forced to trial before the statutory time for making up the issue had elapsed. The argument is based upon the false assumption that the statute relating to the period in which a reply shall be filed in a cause is applicable to the facts disclosed by this record. A demurrer wholly frivolous and intended for the evident purpose of delay was filed on the day which the statute designated for answering. Subsequent to the overruling of this demurrer, a general denial was filed, which formed the issues of fact to be tried, and no reply was necessary. That the court in its discretion subsequently allowed an amended answer to be filed raising other and different issues, did not give the defendant the right to object to the case being placed on trial at the time it was heard because the plaintiffs had not replied, since no order in reference to a reply had been made by the trial court. Plaintiffs did not ask that time be fixed in which they should plead, and defendant was in no position to insist that time should be given them for that purpose.

. Complaint is made because the court allowed a reply traversing the averments of the amended answer to be filed after the selection of the jury. The granting of permission to reply out of time, or during the trial, rests largely in the legal discretion of the trial court. (*Storz v. Finklestein*, 48 Neb. 27, and cases cited.) No abuse of discretion in the ruling just indicated is perceptible. No continuance was asked, or suggested, by the defendant

on the ground that it had been taken by surprise by
reason of the filing of the reply.

At the rendition of the judgment, on written motion
of plaintiff, an attorney's fee of $200 was allowed them
by the court and taxed as part of the costs, which action
is assailed on the ground that an attorney's fee was not
specially asked in the petition, the prayer being merely
for a judgment in a sum certain as damages, and for
costs.   It is true no motion to retax the costs was made
in the trial court, but that does not foreclose a review of
the decision of the court under consideration.   It has
been frequently asserted that a motion to retax costs
in a trial court and a ruling thereon are essential to
review the taxation of costs.   This rule, however, cannot
be invoked in this case, for the obvious reason that a
retaxation of the costs is not sought on account of any
mistake, neglect, or omission of the clerk of the district
court, but the action of the court itself is assailed in
allowing an attorney's fee.   As was said by POST. J., in
the opinion in *Burton v. State*, 34 Neb. 127, where the
identical question was involved and decided: "Ordinarily the taxing of costs is a clerical act performed by
the clerk and the presumption is that the action of the
clerk has not been called to the attention of the court;
hence this court will not, as a rule, review an order taxing costs until a motion to retax has been made and the
trial court given an opportunity to correct the errors,
if any have been made.   In this case the court has considered the question of the liability of plaintiff in error
and deliberately determined that he is liable for costs of
prosecution.   Here the reason of the rule is wanting.   It
would be an idle and useless form to ask the court to
correct on the theory of a mistake or inadvertence of the
clerk that which the record shows to have been a deliberate act of the court."   In actions like the present one
the statute makes it the duty of the court, and not the
clerk, to determine the amount of attorney's fees which
shall be paid by the insurer to the insured.   The clerk

is the mere arm of the court, and could not of his own accord allow an attorney's fee in the case. It requires judicial action. The court below has spoken. It awarded an attorney's fee to plaintiffs, and determined the amount thereof, and to review its decision upon the question no motion to retax was necessary. This view is contrary to *Insurance Co. of North America v. Bachler*, 44 Neb. 549; but the discussion in the opinion in that case upon the question was not necessary to a decision, because the order of the court allowing an attorney's fee was not assigned as error in the petition in error, which omission alone was sufficient reason for the refusal of this court to review the ruling of the trial court upon the subject of attorney's fees.

The policy declared on insured plaintiffs below against loss or damage by fire in the sum of $2,000 upon their two-story frame hotel building situate in the town of Greeley. The insured building having been wholly destroyed by fire, without the criminal fault of the insured, plaintiffs, under the valued policy law, were entitled to recover the amount of insurance named in the policy, and in addition thereto a reasonable sum, to be fixed by the court, as an attorney's fee. (Compiled Statutes, ch. 43, secs. 43, 45; *German Ins. Co. v. Eddy*, 37 Neb. 461; *German Ins. Co. v. Gustin*, 40 Neb. 828.) In the first of those cases it was said that attorney's fees in an action on a policy issued under the valued policy act of 1889, must be demanded in the petition, and the question of allowance of such fees be presented to the trial court and a ruling obtained thereon in order to present the question in the appellate court. That case having been unchallenged for so long a time, should be adhered to. It is not in conflict with *Insurance Co of North America v. Bachler*, 44 Neb. 549, but harmonizes therewith, as an examination of the transcript of the Bachler case reveals that the petition therein specially prayed for the allowance of an attorney's fee. In *Hanover Fire Ins. Co. v. Gustin*, 40 Neb. 828, the question whether the petition on

a valued policy must ask for an attorney's fee was not
presented, considered, or decided.   In the case at bar the
petition on the face disclosed that the suit was upon an
insurance policy covering real estate, and it is in said
pleadings averred that a complete loss of the property
has been sustained without the criminal fault of the insured.   These averments being sustained by the proofs
adduced on the trial, upon a recovery by plaintiffs, the
law authorized the court to award them a reasonable
sum as an attorney's fee to be taxed as costs.   The court
below has complied with the plain requirements of the
law.   It is true the allowance of such fees was not specifically asked in the prayer to the petition, but at the
time of the rendition of the judgment on the verdict.
plaintiffs, by written request, demanded that they be
awarded an attorney's fee in the sum of $300, to be taxed
as a part of the costs as provided by statute.   This was.'
in effect, and should be so treated, as an amendment of
the prayer of the petition.   So regarded, the case at bar
is within both the letter and spirit of the decision in the
Eddy Case.   There being no prejudicial error in the
record, the judgment is

AFFIRMED.

P. C. DURFEE V. STATE OF NEBRASKA.

FILED DECEMBER 22, 1897.   No. 9469.

1. **Criminal Law:** REFUSAL TO APPOINT COUNSEL FOR ACCUSED: RE-
   VIEW.   The action of the trial court in overruling a motion for the
   assignment of counsel to defend a prisoner cannot be reviewed
   here, where the evidence adduced on the hearing was not preserved
   by a bill of exceptions.

2. **Bill of Exceptions:** RECORD OF VOIR DIRE EXAMINATION.   The certificate of the trial judge to a bill of exceptions "that the foregoing
   is all the evidence offered by either party on the trial of the cause"
   is not sufficient to embrace the *voir dire* examination of a juror, or
   the evidence adduced on the hearing of a challenge to the whole
   panel or array of jurors.

3. **Intoxicating Liquors:** UNLAWFUL SALE: EVIDENCE. In a prosecution under section 20, chapter 50, Compiled Statutes, for keeping intoxicating liquors for sale in violation of law, the possession of such liquors by the accused is presumptive evidence of guilt in the district court, as well as before the examining magistrate, unless the accused "shall satisfactorily account for and explain the possession thereof, and that it was not kept for an unlawful purpose."

ERROR to the district court for Furnas county. Tried below before NORRIS, J. *Affirmed.*

L. H. Alberti and *McClure & Anderson,* for plaintiff in error.

C. J. Smyth, Attorney General, Ed .P. Smith, Deputy Attorney General, and *John Stevens, Jr.,* for the state.

NORVAL, J.

This was a prosecution under section 20, chapter 50, Compiled Statutes, for unlawfully keeping for purpose of sale, without a license, certain intoxicating liquors. The accused was convicted, and from the sentence imposed upon him, error is prosecuted to this court.

Application was made to the district court for the appointment of counsel to defend the accused, which request was denied. A reversal cannot be had on account of this ruling for several reasons: First—The assignment of counsel to make the defense was based upon the alleged poverty of the accused. The bill of exceptions contains no evidence tending to establish that he had neither money, property, nor funds with which to employ or secure counsel to make his defense. So far as this record discloses it may have been proven to the satisfaction of the court below that the prisoner possessed ample means with which to procure the assistance of an attorney. It is true the transcript contains an affidavit of poverty, but it cannot be considered. since it is not incorporated in the bill of exceptions. (*Minick v. Minick,* 49 Neb. 89; *Roscrans v. Asay,* 49 Neb. 512; *First Nat. Bank of Madison v. Carson,* 48 Neb. 763; *Hudson v. Pennock,* 48 Neb. 359.)

Second—The accused does not appear to have been prejudiced by the ruling, inasmuch as the record discloses that
he was assisted in making his defense by three able law-
yers.   Third—The statute has made no provision for the
assignment of counsel for pauper or indigent prisoners in
prosecutions for misdemeanors. (Criminal Code, sec. 437.)

The accused challenged the entire panel or array of
petit jurors for the term of court at which he was tried,
on the ground that they were not apportioned among the
several precincts of the county as provided by law, which
motion was overruled, as were likewise the several challenges of jurors for cause made by the accused.   Those
rulings are now complained of but they are not available,
because the evidence adduced regarding said matters is
not properly preserved by the bill of exceptions.   What
purports to be the *voir dire* examination of the jurors,
the challenge to the array, and certain affidavits and
certificates of the county clerk, are included in the bill of
exceptions, but they are not authenticated by the certificate of the trial judge.   He merely certifies "that the
foregoing is all the evidence offered or given by either
party on the trial of the cause." This is insufficient to
show that the bill of exceptions contained either the
testimony on the hearing of the challenge to the panel,
or the *voir dire* examination of the jurors.   Those matters did not occur during, but preceded, the trial.

The giving of the following instruction is alleged as
error:

"7. You are instructed under the statute governing
this case, and heretofore quoted to you in these instructions, it is only necessary for the state to show that the
defendant had the liquors described in the information,
or some of them, in his possession.   After this has been
shown by the prosecution, the law presumes that such
liquors were kept in violation of the law, unless the defendant satisfactorily accounts for, and explains, the
possession of such liquors; and if the prosecution has
shown that the liquors, or any of them, described in the

information were found in the possession of the defendant, as alleged in the information, the burden of proof is then upon the defendant to satisfactorily account for and explain his possession of such liquor or liquors."

Three criticisms upon this instruction are made by counsel, viz.: (1.) That section 20, chapter 50, Compiled Statutes, shows that the legislature intended that the presumption of guilt arising from the possession of intoxicating liquors should be indulged alone before the examining magistrate, and such presumption does not obtain in the district court. (2.) The instruction is erroneous because it shifts the burden of proof from the state to the accused. (3.) The instruction is in conflict with number 5 given by the court on its own motion. The first two objections, for convenience, will be considered together.

Section 20 of said chapter 50 provides: "Hereafter it shall be unlawful for any person to keep for the purpose of sale without a license any malt, spirituous, or vinous liquors in the state of Nebraska; and any person or persons who shall be found in possession of any intoxicating liquors in this state with the intention of disposing of the same without license in violation of this chapter, shall be deemed guilty of a misdemeanor and, on conviction thereof, shall be fined or imprisoned as provided in section 11 of this chapter." The section, after providing for the filing of a complaint for a violation of its provisions, the issuing of a warrant for the search of the premises, and for the arrest of the person described in such complaint and warrant, and what the officer shall do under the writ, declares that "the possession of any of said liquors shall be presumptive evidence of a violation of this chapter and subject the person to the fine prescribed in section 11, unless after examination he shall satisfactorily account for and explain the possession thereof, and that it was not kept for an unlawful purpose." The instruction criticised correctly stated the effect of the foregoing provisions of the law under which the prosecution was instituted. The legislature has made the keeping of intoxicating liquors for sale, without a license, a crime, and has declared that the possession of such liquors shall be presumptive evidence of guilt; and, the statute not having designated any particular forum wherein such presumption shall obtain, it is manifest that the statutory presumption of guilt arising from the possession of intoxicating liquors should be indulged in the district and supreme courts, as well as upon the preliminary hearing before the examining magistrate. The presumption, however, is not conclusive, but may be overcome if the accused shall satisfactorily account for and explain the possession of the liquors, and show they were not kept for an unlawful purpose. The effect of the statute under consideration was to cast the burden upon the person having intoxicating liquors in his possession to establish that they were not kept for sale in violation of law; and the jury were properly so advised. *Robb v. State*, 35 Neb. 285, has no bearing upon the question. That was a prosecution for larceny in which the trial court charged that "the possession by an accused person of property proved to have been recently stolen is sufficient to fasten the guilt of its larceny upon the accused *prima facie* and calls upon him to prove the innocence of his possession." This instruction was held erroneous for the reason it failed to state that it is only when the possession is unexplained that the inference of guilt may be indulged, and because it also casts the burden of proof upon the accused. There exists in this state no statute relating to larceny which makes the possession of stolen property presumptive evidence of the theft, or which requires the accused "to satisfactorily account for and explain the possession thereof and that he did not steal the property." The decision mentioned does not conflict with the views already expressed.

Instruction No. 7 in no manner conflicts with the principles announced in the fifth paragraph of the charge of the court, but one is in perfect harmony with the other.

It is finally insisted that there was reversible error in giving the instruction which is in the following language: "The jury are instructed that it is not incumbent on the state to prove any specific sale to any individual on any particular date, but that the jury may consider any evidence of sale together with any other circumstances which tend to prove that the defendant was keeping in his possession in the building charged in the information either beer or whiskey, with the intent of disposing of the same without first having procured a license for the sale of the same, if any such facts are proved. And you are further instructed that if you find from all the facts proved, if any such is proved, that the defendant was on the 25th day of December, 1895, keeping in his possession in the building described in the information in this case either beer or whiskey, with the intention of disposing of the same without a license, then and in that case you will find the defendant guilty as charged in the information." A single infirmity is imputed to the foregoing, which is that it directed the jurors they were not, in arriving at their verdict, confined to evidence alone, but might consider any fact or circumstance within their own knowledge which would aid them in reaching a conclusion that the accused was guilty. This criticism is very unfair. The language of the instruction will not justify the inference that the jury were warranted in going outside of the evidence adduced on the trial in deciding upon the prisoner's guilt or innocence. On the contrary. the trial court, in the language employed, confined the jury to the considering of the evidence in the case.

No reversible error appearing on the record, the judgment is

AFFIRMED.

GEORGE W. HAYWOOD, APPELLANT, V. WILLIAM MAR-
SHALL, APPELLEE.

FILED DECEMBER 22, 1897. No. 7682.

Aliens: COUNCILMEN OF CITY: QUALIFICATIONS: ELECTIONS: CONTEST.
In cities of the second class of less than 5,000 inhabitants it is required that a councilman shall be an elector of this state. *Held*,
That while a mere declaration of intention to become a citizen
conformably with the naturalization laws of the United States
may, under the constitution of Nebraska, constitute a resident
alien an elector, provided other required conditions exist, yet that,
by implication, this status cannot be extended to the son of such
alien merely because the declaration above referred to was made
before such son had attained his majority.

APPEAL from the district court of Cass county. Heard
below before CHAPMAN, J. *Reversed*.

J. H. Haldeman, for appellant.

A. M. Russell, contra.

RYAN, C.

On April 24, 1894, George W. Haywood filed in the
county court of Cass county a petition in which he
alleged that he was an elector and resident of Weeping
Water, a city of the second class having less than 5,000
inhabitants, situated in said county; that this action
was brought on behalf of said Haywood and the other
qualified electors of said city; that on April 3, 1894, a
municipal election had been held in said city at which
William Marshall, the defendant, John Donelan, and
J. H. Haldeman had been candidates against each other
for the office of councilman for the second ward of said
city; and that the result of said election was that said
Marshall had received 43 votes, Donelan had received 27
votes, and Haldeman had received 24 votes, and accordingly a certificate of election had been issued to said
Marshall. These averments were admitted by the an-

swer, but in said answer there was a denial of the following allegations of the petition: "5. Plaintiff further alleges that the defendant was before, and on said election day was, and since then has been, a foreigner, a subject of Great Britain, and not a citizen of the United States, and he is ineligible to hold the office of councilman of the second ward in said city." Following the above and other averments, which need not be described because no effort was made to establish them by proof. there was a prayer for the issuance of a writ of ouster against the defendant; that his election might be declared void, and for other proper relief and costs. There was a judgment for the defendant on a trial in the county court, and upon appeal in the district court there was a like judgment which is presented for consideration in this court. The pleadings in the district court were like those already described as having been filed in the county court. The trial in the district court began with the following stipulation, to-wit: "It is admitted that William Marshall, the contestee, is the son of John Marshall; that John Marshall came to this country from Great Britain in the year 1872, and that the contestee at that time was an infant minor of the age of nine years; that the father, John Marshall, declared his intentions to become a citizen of the United States October 17, 1875, and has since that time resided in Cass county, state of Nebraska, exercising the rights of an elector in Cass county, and state of Nebraska, where he has resided all of said time; that they have never been elected or held any office in the state of Nebraska except William Marshall the office of councilman for which he is now contesting; and that he was elected as a councilman from the second ward of the city of Weeping Water, Cass county, Nebraska, in April, 1894, and that, as such councilman, he took the oath of office and entered into the duties of such office. It is admitted further that the contestee, William Marshall, has never declared his intention to become a citizen of the United States, he having relied upon the

fact that he was a minor when he came to this country."
There was other evidence, but it was not of a nature
which would present a question other than that indicated by the above stipulation.

In a simpler form than already made use of, this question may be said to depend upon the facts that John Marshall, a citizen of Great Britain, in 1872, brought with
him to this country his son, the contestee, who was then
but nine years of age. In 1875 the father declared his
intention to become a citizen of the United States, and,
although he has ever since resided in this state and exercised the rights of an elector, he has never taken any
further step with reference to becoming such a citizen.
The son, William Marshall, has, since becoming of age,
exercised the rights of an elector, but whether rightfully
or not depends upon the correctness of the assumption on
which he acted. This assumption involves the sole question presented, and that is, whether or not the mere
declaration of the father, during the minority of his son,
of an intention to become a citizen of the United States
constituted such son an elector when he attained his
majority. By section 3, article 1, chapter 14, Compiled
Statutes, it is required that a councilman in a city of the
class in which Weeping Water is embraced shall be an
elector. Section 1, article 7, of the constitution of this
state is in this language: "Every male person of
the age of twenty-one years or upwards belonging to
either of the following classes, who shall have resided
in the state six months, and in the county, precinct, or
ward for the term provided by law, shall be an elector:
First, citizens of the United States; second, persons of
foreign birth who shall have declared their intention to
become citizens conformably to the laws of the United
States on the subject of naturalization, at least thirty
days prior to an election." John Marshall never became
a citizen of the United States; hence the status of his son,
dependent upon the alien father becoming a citizen
under the federal naturalization law, is a matter of no

importance. Upon the taking of the first step toward becoming a citizen, an alien is declared by our constitution to be an elector, and, as such elector, under the laws of this state, he may enter upon the discharge of the duties of councilman of a city of the class in which Weeping Water is included, if elected to such office. If John Marshall had been elected, he could have served as councilman, because he had declared his intention to become a citizen of the United States, but without more, this declaration is not effective to constitute his son such an elector, for there exists neither a constitutional nor a statutory provision to that effect. The judgment of the district court, therefore, must be, and accordingly it is, reversed and the cause is remanded for further proceedings not inconsistent with the views above expressed.

REVERSED AND REMANDED.

ISAAC R. ALTER ET AL. V. BANK OF STOCKHAM ET AL.

FILED DECEMBER 22, 1897. NO. 7189.

1. **Sale of Cattle:** EVIDENCE OF FALSE WEIGHT. Evidence examined, and *held* not to support the finding of the jury that plaintiffs in error had falsely weighed certain cattle sold one of the defendants in error. NORVAL, J., and IRVINE and RYAN, CC., dissenting.

2. **Fraud.** Fraud is not to be presumed; it must be proved.

3. ———: EVIDENCE. If, from the entire evidence on the subject, good faith or an honest mistake may be as rationally and reasonably inferred as fraud, then the law leans to the side of innocence.

4. ———: ———. Direct evidence is not essential to establish fraud. It may be inferred from circumstances; but such inference must not be guesswork or conjecture, but the rational and logical deduction from the circumstances proved.

5. **Equity:** QUESTIONS OF FACT FOR JURY. A district court while sitting as a court of equity is clothed with the inherent power to submit to a jury any question of fact in the case.

6. **Actions:** FORMS: PLEADING. To maintain a civil action under our

Code, it is not essential that the action be denominated either an action at law or in equity, nor that it be given any particular name. If the litigant pleads the facts, and they constitute a cause of action or defense, the courts are bound to award the relief due.

7. **Chattel Mortgages**: SALE OF CHATTELS: CONVERSION BY MORTGAGOR: TRUSTS: REMEDY OF MORTGAGEE. Evidence examined and *held* that the district court erred in dismissing the action of the plaintiffs in error.

8. ———: ———: ———: ———: ———. Where a mortgagor of chattels converts the same into cash, at their full value, and deposits the money with his agent, who has notice of the mortgage lien, an action will lie at the suit of the mortgagee against such agent, for the proceeds of such property; and the fact that the mortgagee did not pursue and seize the mortgaged property does not, of itself, afford such agent a defense to such action.

REHEARING of case reported in 51 Neb. 797. *Reversed.*

Hainer & Smith, for plaintiffs in error.

A. W. Agee and *H. M. Kellogg, contra.*

RAGAN, C.

This is a rehearing of *Alter v. Bank of Stockham,* 51 Neb. 797. In their petition in the district court Alter & Glover alleged the sale by them on September 26, 1889, of 309 head of cattle, to one Wiens, at an agreed price of $8,500; that, as an evidence of said indebtedness, Wiens executed to Alter & Glover his note for said sum of money drawing interest at the rate of ten per cent from date, and due April 1, 1890, and secured the payment of the same by a chattel mortgage upon all said cattle; that said chattel mortgage was duly filed in the office of the county clerk of Hamilton county, soon after its execution,—that being the county in which Wiens lived and kept said cattle; that there was due and unpaid on said note $1,606.65, with interest at ten per cent per annum from May 21, 1890; that Wiens subsequent to the purchase of said cattle executed to said bank two chattel mortgages covering the same cattle; that said mortgages were taken by the Bank of Stockham subject to Alter &

Glover's mortgage; that on January 8, 1890, the bank
took possession of 41 head of said mortgaged cattle,
shipped them to Martin Bros., commission merchants in
South Omaha, Nebraska, and caused them to be there
sold on the open market, and the net proceeds of said
sale,—$1,330,—to be deposited to its credit in a bank
there; that, on March 8, 1890, the Bank of Stockham
took possession of 127 head of the cattle, on which Alter
& Glover held a mortgage, shipped them to South
Omaha, Nebraska, to said Martin Bros., caused the cattle to be there sold in the open market, and the proceeds
of said sale, amounting to $4,907.55, to be deposited to
the credit of the Bank of Stockham in the Union Stock
Yards Bank of South Omaha, and the said Bank of Stockham converted to its own use the said proceeds of $4,-
907.55, except the sum of $2,000 of said proceeds, which
it then and there remitted, or caused to be remitted, to
Alter & Glover to apply on the Wiens note; that the
shipments and sales of the Wiens cattle made by the
Bank of Stockham on January 8 and March 9, 1890, were
made without the knowledge or consent of plaintiffs;
that they had demanded of the Bank of Stockham a return of said cattle or a delivery of the proceeds of their
sale, or so much thereof as would satisfy their mortgage
debt against Wiens; that the Bank of Stockham had
refused to deliver the cattle or pay over the proceeds, or
any portion of them, but had retained said proceeds
and had converted them to their own use; that since
the sale of the cattle the plaintiffs had been unable to
discover their whereabouts, and unable to pursue them,
and subject them to the payment of their mortgage debt;
that the Bank of Stockham, at the time it received and
converted the proceeds of the cattle sold in January
and March, 1890, to its own use, did so with the intent
to defraud the plaintiffs out of their lien on said cattle,
and took the proceeds of said sale and retained them,
with full knowledge of plaintiffs' lien on the cattle. The
petition then alleged the insolvency of Wiens, and

19

prayed that an account might be taken of the amount
due them on the Wiens note and mortgage; that the
priorities of liens of the plaintiffs and the Bank of Stockham should be determined by the court; that the amount
found due the plaintiffs and Wiens might be adjudged a
first lien upon the mortgaged property, and that the
Bank of Stockham might be decreed to hold the proceeds
of the sale of the cattle in trust for the use and benefit
of the plaintiffs and decreed to pay the same over to the
plaintiffs. The answer of the Bank of Stockham, so far
as material here, was a general denial of the averments
of Alter & Glover's petition, coupled with the averment
that Alter & Glover, from the proceeds of the sale of a
part of the mortgaged cattle shipped and sold by them
in May, 1890, had realized more than sufficient to pay
the amount of their mortgage debt. Wiens intervened
in the action and filed an answer in the nature of a cross-
petition, in which he alleged that he purchased the 309
head of cattle from Alter & Glover, and gave his note
for $8,500 for the purchase price; that Alter weighed
these cattle, announcing the weights to be 364,330
pounds, or an average of 1,179 pounds per head; and
that he, Wiens, relied on the honesty of Alter in weighing the cattle, and that the latter falsely and fraudulently weighed them; that their total weight did not
exceed 287,080 pounds, or an average of 929 pounds each;
that the actual value of the cattle, had they been correctly weighed, was $6,688.38; and that the note was
given for $1,811.62 too much. The answer then alleged
that what was justly due on the note had been paid, and
the debt overpaid $454.85, for which sum Wiens asked a
judgment against Alter & Glover. The trial resulted in
the district court pronouncing two judgments: (1.) That
there was due to Alter & Glover from Wiens on his note
$828.91,—about one-half of what Alter & Glover claimed
was due upon it; and this judgment was based upon the
finding of the jury that Alter & Glover falsely weighed
the cattle at the time they sold them to Wiens. (2.) The

second judgment pronounced by the court was one dismissing the plaintiffs' action against the Bank of Stockham. It is to reverse both these judgments that Alter & Glover have prosecuted here a petition in error.

1. Is the finding of the jury that Alter & Glover falsely weighed these cattle at the time they were sold by them to Wiens supported by sufficient evidence? Wiens, to sustain his contention that the cattle were falsely weighed, introduced evidence which showed, or tended to show, the following state of facts: He purchased the cattle from Alter & Glover September 26, 1889. At that time the cattle were at a railway station some miles from the city of Grand Island. The cattle were then driven to Grand Island, and there weighed on the scales in the stock yards of the Union Pacific Railway Company. Wiens and his son were both present at the scales while the cattle were being weighed, though Alter did the actual weighing, calling off the weights of each bunch to Wiens. Wiens, after receiving the cattle, on that day or the next, drove them to his farm in Hamilton county, where he kept them in lots, or in a field, fed them an abundance of hay and corn, and furnished them plenty of water. In other words, he took proper care of the cattle, and properly fed them and watered them. On January 8, 1890, 41 head of the cattle were shipped to South Omaha, and there sold, and these cattle there weighed 48,800 pounds at that time. On March 9, 1890, 127 head of the cattle were shipped to South Omaha, and sold, and there at that time weighed 153,100 pounds; and on May 21, 1890, 126 head of the cattle were shipped to South Omaha, and there sold, and these cattle there at that time weighed 154,840 pounds. In other words, 309 head of the cattle purchased of Alter & Glover at the time of their purchase weighed 364,330 pounds, and 294 head of the same cattle, when sold in January, March, and May, 1890, weighed only 356,740 pounds, or 7,590 pounds less than all the cattle weighed at the time they were purchased; that the scales on which the cattle

were weighed in Omaha were of the Fairbanks manufacture, were in good order, and weighed correctly, and the party who weighed the cattle there weighed them honestly. Wiens also introduced the evidence of a number of farmers and cattle feeders, who testified as experts, to the effect that they were acquainted with these cattle, saw them at the time Wiens was feeding them, and that in their opinion the cattle had gained in weight after Wiens purchased them, and that taking into consideration the character of the cattle, the care taken of them by Wiens, and the feed which they had consumed, these cattle should have gained, and did probably gain, from the time they were purchased by Wiens until they were shipped, an average of 250 to 300 pounds per head. On behalf of Alter & Glover, the evidence tended to show that they were in the business of buying and selling cattle, and had been for some years prior to the time they sold these cattle to Wiens; that they had sold him cattle the year previous to this sale, and that those cattle, after being fed some months by Wiens, had showed a gain in weight; that Alter himself personally weighed these cattle to Wiens, and that he honestly and correctly noted the weight of each bunch of cattle, and honestly and correctly reported the weight of each bunch to Wiens; that Wiens and his son were both present at the time the cattle were weighed,—each one of them being within a few feet of the scale beam and each one of them having the opportunity to see for himself what weight the scale indicated for each bunch of cattle weighed out; that these cattle were known as "Southwestern cattle," or "half-breeds,"—some of them being "scalawags;" that they were very wild; that in driving them from Grand Island over to Wiens' farm in Hamilton county 30 head of them escaped, some of which were never recovered; that, after Wiens had put the cattle into his feed lots on his farm, they broke out of it, broke into a field of corn, and he permitted them to remain in that cornfield; that he dehorned something over 200 of these cattle, and would have dehorned the remainder if they had not been so wild he could not catch them; that cattle so wild as these did not fatten and gain in flesh so readily as tame or domestic cattle; that the cattle were liable to be foundered and injured so as not to fatten when allowed to run in a field of corn, as by so doing they were liable to eat too much, and that the dehorning of cattle had a tendency to prevent their fattening and gaining in weight. Alter & Glover also showed that these 309 head of cattle sold Wiens were part of a bunch of 616 head of cattle; that they had sold 307 of this bunch to a man named Nordgreen, while they were at the railway station, some distance from Grand Island, and that they divided these cattle into two equal bunches, as near as might be, before Wiens' cattle were weighed and delivered; that the 307 head of cattle taken by Nordgreen, after remaining for two weeks on a grass pasture, were brought into Grand Island, weighed upon the same scales that Wiens' cattle were weighed on, and the 307 head of Nordgreen cattle weighed 363,650 pounds, or that Nordgreen's cattle weighed 680 pounds less than Wiens' 309 cattle; that Wiens never made any complaint about the weight of these cattle until after this suit was brought, and that a large number of these cattle, when sold in Omaha, were very lean.

Our opinion is that the evidence does not sustain the finding made by the jury that Alter falsely weighed these cattle, or any of them, when he sold them to Wiens. It is not claimed or pretended by anybody that there was any mistake made; that the scales at Grand Island were not good scales, and in good order; but the jury finds from the evidence, which we have just quoted, that Alter falsely weighed these cattle, and committed a crime. Fraud is not to be presumed. It must be proved; and, while it may be established by circumstantial evidence, yet if the reasonable inference from all such evidence does not preponderate toward the conclusion of fraud, then such evidence will not sustain such finding. In other words, if, from the entire evidence on the subject, good faith or an honest mistake even may be as rationally and reasonably inferred as fraud, then the law leans to the side of innocence. While, to prove fraud direct evidence is not essential, and the inference of fraud may be drawn from facts and circumstances, such inference must not be the guess-work or conjecture of a jury, but the inference must be the rational and logical deduction from the facts and circumstances from which it is inferred. There is just as much evidence in this record to convict the man who weighed these cattle at Omaha of fraud in weighing them as there is to convict Alter of a fraud, and the evidence will not sustain the conviction of either of them of that offense. We reach the conclusion therefore that the judgment pronounced by the district court in favor of Alter & Glover against Wiens must be reversed because the finding on which it is based is unsupported by sufficient evidence.

2. There was much contention in the district court— and the contention is renewed here—as to whether the petition of Alter & Glover states a cause of action at law or in equity; and plaintiffs in error complain here because the district court submitted to a jury the issues of fact made by the pleadings. It is insisted here by the plaintiffs in error that their petition is one in equity for an accounting of the amount due them from Wiens on their mortgage debt, and to hold the Bank of Stockham liable to it as trustee. On the other hand the bank contends that the action was one at law, being simply a suit for conversion of the proceeds of the sale of the Wiens cattle. Under our Code there is but one form of action, namely, a civil action; and the distinction heretofore existing between actions at law and actions in equity, so far as the form of such actions is concerned, is abolished. But, if the action of Alter & Glover is one in equity, we cannot reverse the judgment of the district court solely because of the fact that it submitted questions of fact to a jury. A chancellor was always invested

with the discretion to submit to a jury issues of fact and
the Code has not deprived the courts, when sitting as
courts of equity, of that discretion, and the district courts
of the state, while sitting as courts of equity, are vested
with the discretion to submit to a jury any disputed question of fact. We cannot conceive how a district court
can in any case commit a reversible error simply by submitting a question of fact to a jury. It is wholly immaterial whether the petition of Alter & Glover here be
one in equity or one at law. The Code requires the
pleader to state the facts which constitute his cause of
action or defense, and if he state these facts,—not conclusions,—and they constitute a cause of action or defense,
the law will award him the relief to which he is entitled,
whether the facts make a case in equity or at law. The
litigant does not need to designate his action one for
conversion, or to give it any name. If the pleading
states the facts, and the proof sustains the plea, the court
is bound to afford the relief due, whether the action be
one which at common law was known as an "action of
conversion," or whether it be of such a character that
no name can be found for it in the books of pleading and
practice.

3. This brings us to the consideration of the judgment
of the district court dismissing Alter & Glover's action
against the Bank of Stockham. After Alter & Glover
had put in their evidence, the district court instructed
the jury to return a verdict in favor of the Bank of
Stockham, which it did, and thereupon the court entered
a judgment dismissing Alter & Glover's action against
that bank. The evidence introduced by Alter & Glover
against the Bank of Stockham was as follows: The deposition of one Sears, a bookkeeper for Martin Bros., commission merchants of South Omaha. He testified:

Q. You may state if they [Martin Bros.]received any
cattle for sale during the month of January, 1890, from
one Wiens.

A. Yes, we received two loads of cattle on January 8
from Wiens.

Q. What was done with those cattle?

A. They were sold there at South Omaha.

Q. What disposition was made of the proceeds of the sale of those cattle?

A. The proceeds were deposited in the Union Stock Yards Bank of South Omaha, to the account of the Bank of Stockham, to the credit of Wiens, amount, $1,330.

Q. You may state whether any cattle was received by them [Martin Bros.] from Wiens during the month of March, 1890.

A. Yes; we received six loads on March 8, 1890; six car loads.

Q. What was done with the proceeds of the sale?

A. The proceeds were disposed the same as those of January 8; deposited in the same manner. The amount was $4,907.55.

Q. You may state whether this deposit was made by the direction of Wiens.

A. Yes, sir.

Q. Do you remember whether Mr. Wiens was present at the time of these sales, or either of them?

A. He was present at one of them, and I think he was at both, but I am not positive.

Another deposition read in Alter & Glover's behalf was that of William Wallace, cashier of the Omaha National Bank, of Omaha. He testified as follows:

Q. You may state whether the Bank of Stockham had an account with the Omaha National Bank during the months of January and March, 1890.

A. It had.

Q. You may state whether any deposits were made to that account by the Union Stock Yards Bank of South Omaha during the month of January, 1890.

A. Yes, sir.

Q. Are you able to state the date of such deposit?

A. Yes, sir.

Q. What date?

A. January 9, 1890.

Q. What was the amount of the deposit made to the credit of the Bank of Stockham by the Union Stock Yards Bank on the 9th of January, 1890?

A. $1,330.

Q. You may state whether that deposit was made for the credit or for the account of anybody else besides the Bank of Stockham.

A. It was not.

Q. State whether or not a deposit was made in your bank by the Union Stock Yards Bank during the month of March, 1890.

A. There was.

Q. You may give the date and the amount of that deposit.

A. March 10, $4,907.55.

Q. Was this deposited for the credit of any other person or firm?

A. No, sir.

Q. You may state if this account was subject to check by any other person or corporation except the Bank of Stockham.

A. No.

Q. Does the Bank of Stockham still keep an account with your bank?

A. Yes, sir.

Q. Was the money so deposited on the 9th of January and the 10th of March subject to its check, the same as other funds in your hands?

A. Yes, sir.

Q. State whether or not this money was deposited to any special account with that bank or to its general credit.

A. It was deposited to its general credit.

Cross-examination:

Q. State whether it was drawn upon by that bank, the same as any other money deposited to its credit.

A. Just the same as any other moneys.

Q. This money that was placed to their credit in January, 1890, was sent to the Omaha National Bank by some bank in South Omaha, was it?

A. Yes, sir.

Q. What bank was it that sent it?

A. Union Stock Yards.

Q. And it was the same with the deposit that was made on the 10th of March?

A. Yes, sir.

Q. Just sent to your bank by the Union Stock Yards of South Omaha?

A. Yes.

Q. To be placed to the credit of the Bank of Stockham?

A. Yes, sir.

Another deposition read on behalf of Alter & Glover was that of Carson, assistant cashier of the Union Stock Yards Bank of South Omaha. He testified as follows:

Q. You may state whether any moneys were deposited by them [Martin Bros.] with you for the credit of the Bank of Stockham during that month.

A. On the 8th of January they deposited with us to be remitted to the Omaha National Bank, to the credit of the Bank of Stockham, $1,330 for the use of Wiens.

Q. They deposited money with you for them with instructions to remit to Omaha for the credit of that bank?

A. Yes sir; on March 8th they deposited with us, to be remitted to the Omaha National Bank, $4,907.55, for the credit of the Bank of Stockham, and the use of Wiens.

We think the district court was mistaken in concluding from this evidence that Alter & Glover had no cause of action against the Bank of Stockham. None of this evidence was disputed. Wiens was indebted to Alter & Glover. To secure that indebtedness the latter held a chattel mortgage upon Wiens' cattle. The Bank of Stockham held mortgage liens against the same cattle which were, by their terms, made subject to Alter & Glover's mortgage, and the Bank of Stockham at all times had notice of the existence of Alter & Glover's lien upon the Wiens' cattle. Wiens, the mortgagor, shipped these cattle to South Omaha and sold them at their full value in the public markets and thereby dissipated and destroyed, or at least deprived the mortgagees of, the subject-matter of the property covered by their mortgage and paid the proceeds of the sale over to the Bank of Stockham. This proof followed the allegations of Alter & Glover's petition, and established, as plain as anything could be established, that the Bank of Stockham had in its possession when this suit was brought, the proceeds of the sale of the Wiens cattle, upon which cattle Alter & Glover had a first mortgage lien, the mortgagor having converted the mortgaged property into money. The bank introduced no evidence, nor did it attempt to introduce any evidence, to show that it had any right, title, or claim to the proceeds of the sale of these cattle by reason of any fact whatsoever. So far as the record shows the bank held the moneys as the agent or bailee or debtor of Wiens, and, without doubt, Wiens could not hold the proceeds of the sale of these cattle as against the claim of Alter & Glover; and, if he could not hold them, his bailee could not. *Cone v. Ivinson,* 33 Pac. Rep. [Wyo.] 31, is a case almost identical with the one at bar, and in that case it was held that where a mortgagor of chattels sells the mortgaged property and pays the proceeds thereof to his creditor, the creditor at the time having knowledge of the existence of the chattel mortgage, such creditor was liable to the mortgagee for the proceeds of the sale of the mortgaged property. That case was decided on May 19, 1893. A rehearing was granted and the case was reconsidered and another opinion written adhering to the former conclusion, and reported in 35 Pac. Rep., 93. But the principle of the Wyoming case has been much extended by this court in *Cady v. South Omaha Nat. Bank,* 46 Neb. 756. In that case the owner of some cattle shipped them to a commission merchant in South

Omaha for sale. The commission merchant sold the cattle and deposited the proceeds to his own credit in a
bank in South Omaha, with which he was doing business, the bank at the time having no knowledge or notice
of the relation existing between the commission man and
the owner of the cattle; and yet the court held that,
irrespective of the question of notice, the bank held the
proceeds of the sale of the cattle in trust for their owner.
We are not deciding that the action of Alter & Glover
is an action at law for conversion as against the Bank
of Stockham, nor that it is a bill in equity seeking to
have the Bank of Stockham declared a trustee and to
hold the proceeds of the sale of the Wiens cattle in
trust for Alter & Glover. What we do decide, and all
we decide, is that from the uncontradicted evidence it
appears that the mortgagor converted the mortgaged
property into money and placed it in the hands of his
agent, the Bank of Stockham, it then and there knowing
of the existence of Alter & Glover's lien upon the cattle;
and, as against the mortgagees, Wiens himself was not
entitled to such proceeds; that the bank, on the evidence
in this record, has no better title to the money than
Wiens had, and is liable and should account to Alter &
Glover for such proceeds, whether such a result will
have the effect of making the action at bar one at law
or in equity.

The judgment of the district court in favor of the Bank
of Stockham and against Alter & Glover, and the judgment in favor of Alter & Glover and against Wiens, and
each of them, are reversed and the cause remanded.

REVERSED AND REMANDED.

RYAN, C., adheres to the views already expressed.

CHICAGO, BURLINGTON & QUINCY RAILROAD COMPANY V.
OLIVER EMMERT.

FILED DECEMBER 22, 1897.   No. 7578.

1. **Railroad Companies**: EMBANKMENTS: NEGLIGENCE: TIME ACTION
ACCRUES. Where an injury to the crops and lands of one is caused
by the negligent construction of a railway embankment, which arrested and held upon said lands the flood waters of a natural
stream, such party's cause of action accrues at the date of the injury and not at the date of the negligent construction of the improvement.

2. ———: ———: INJURY TO CROPS: MEASURE OF DAMAGES. In such
case the injured party's measure of damages to his crops is their
fair value at the time of their destruction; and his measure of
damages as to his land is the difference in its value immediately
before and after such flooding.

3. **Surface Water.** This court does not attempt a definition of surface
water. Whether or not it is such should be determined from the
facts of the case in which the question is presented.

4. ———. The flood water of the Nemaha river involved in this case
held not to be surface water, but a constituent part of such stream,
—a natural water course.

5. **Special Damages**: PLEADING. Special damages to be recovered must
be specially pleaded.

6. **Waters**: DAMAGES: EVIDENCE. The ruling of the district court in the
admission and rejection of evidence as to the plaintiff's measure of
damages examined and *held* prejudiciously erroneous.

7. ———: ———: PLEADING. An allegation that the plaintiff's farm
has been damaged by the construction of a railway embankment
near thereto, because the farm has thus come to be known in the
neighborhood as one liable to overflow, does not state a cause of
action.

ERROR from the district court of Richardson county.
Tried below before BUSH, J. *Reversed.*

The opinion contains a statement of the case.

J. W. Deweese and *F. E. Bishop,* for plaintiff in error:

The railroad company acquired the right to build its
railroad where it did, and constructed it in a manner

proper for railroad purposes. The injuries complained of resulted from surface waters, and the company did not incur liability for the damages. (*Bunderson v. Burlington & M. R. R. Co.*, 43 Neb. 545; *Missouri P. R. Co. v. Lewis*, 24 Neb. 848; *Hannaher v. St. Paul, M. & M. R. Co.*, 37 N. W. Rep. [Dak.] 717; *Morrissey v. Chicago, B. & Q. R. Co.*, 38 Neb. 406; *Hoard v. City of Des Moines*, 17 N. W. Rep. [Ia.] 527; *McCormick v. Kansas City, St. J. & C. B. R. Co.*, 57 Mo. 438; *Bell v. Norfolk S. R. Co.*, 36 Am. & Eng. R. Cas. [N. Car.] 652; *Chicago & A. R. Co. v. Benson*, 20 Am. & Eng. R. Cas. [Mo.] 102; *Abbott v. Kansas City, St. J. & C. B. R. Co.*, 83 Mo. 271; *Moyer v. New York C. & H. R. R. Co.*, 88 N. Y. 355; *Johnson v. Chicago, St. P., M. & O. R. Co.*, 80 Wis. 641; *Shelbyville & B. T. Co. v. Green*, 99 Ind. 205; *Wilson v. Bumstead*, 12 Neb. 1; *Ogburn v. Connor*, 46 Cal. 346; *McDaniel v. Cummings*, 23 Pac. Rep. [Cal.] 797; *Collier v. Chicago & A. R. Co.*, 48 Mo. App. 399; *Taylor v. Fickas*, 64 Ind. 173; *Baltimore & O. R. Co. v. Sulphur Springs Independent School District*, 2 Am. & Eng. R. Cas. [Pa.] 169.)

In building embankments on the right of way, railroad companies have the rights of a land owner with reference to obstructing surface water, and may obstruct the flow upon their land, or turn the water back onto the land of others, without incurring liability for damages. (*O'Brien v. City of St. Paul*, 25 Minn. 331; *Hogenson v. St. Paul, M. & M. R. Co.*, 31 Minn. 226; *Pye v. City of Mankato*, 36 Minn. 373; *Alden v. City of Minneapolis*, 24 Minn. 262; *Chicago, K. & N. R. Co. v. Steck*, 33 Pac. Rep. [Kan.] 601; *Missouri P. R. Co. v. Renfro*, 34 Pac. Rep. [Kan.] 802; *Missouri P. R. Co. v. Keys*, 40 Pac. Rep. [Kan.] 277; *Brown v. Winona & S. W. R. Co.*, 55 N. W. Rep. [Minn.] 123; *New York C. & St. L. R. Co. v. Speelman*, 40 N. E. Rep. [Ind.] 541; *Edwards v. Charlotte, C. & A. R. Co.*, 18 S. E. Rep. [S. Car.] 58; *Champion v. Town of Crandon*, 84 Wis. 405; *Anheuser-Busch Brewing Ass'n v. Peterson*, 41 Neb. 904; *O'Connor v. Fond du Lac, A. & P. R. Co.*, 52 Wis. 526; *Walker v. Old Colony & N. R. Co.*, 103 Mass.

10; *Gould v. Booth*, 66 N. Y. 62; *Pflegar v. Hastings & Dakota R. Co.*, 28 Minn. 510; *Omaha & R. V. R. Co. v. Moschel*, 38 Neb. 281; *Chicago, B. & Q. R. Co. v. O'Connor*, 42 Neb. 90; *Bell v. Norfolk S. R. Co.*, 36 Am. & Eng. R. Cas. [N. Car.] 651; *Blakeley v. Chicago, K. & N. R. Co.*, 25 Neb. 207.)

Plaintiff's cause of action, if he has any, arose at the time the road was built, and is, therefore, barred by the statute of limitations. (*Chicago & E. I. R. Co. v. Loeb*, 27 Am. & Eng. R. Cas. [Ill.] 415; *Chicago & A. R. Co. v. Maher*, 91 Ill. 312; *Kansas P. R. Co. v. Mihlman*, 17 Kan. 224; *Smith v. Point Pleasant & O. R. R. Co.*, 23 W. Va. 451; *Powers v. City of Council Bluffs*, 45 Ia. 652.)

There were erroneous admissions of evidence as to the measure of damages. (*Drake v. Chicago, R. I. & P. R. Co.*, 17 Am. & Eng. R. Cas. [Ia.] 49; *Ward v. Chicago, M. & St. P. R. Co.*, 63 N. W. Rep. [Ia.] 1104; *Fremont, E. & M. V. R. Co., v. Marley*, 25 Neb. 145; *Sullens v. Chicago, R. I. & P. R. Co.*, 74 Ia. 666; *Gentry v. Richmond & D. R. Co.*, 16 S. E. Rep. [S Car.] 893; *Chase v. New York C. R. Co.*, 24 Barb. [N. Y.] 273.)

Reavis & Reavis and *C. Gillespie*, contra.

References: *Drake v. Chicago, R. I. & P. R. Co.*, 19 N. W. Rep. [Ia.] 215; *O'Connell v. East Tennessee, V. & G. R. Co.*, 4 Am. R. & C. Rep. [Ga.] 448; *Fremont, E. & M. V. R. Co. v. Crum*, 30 Neb. 70; *Fremont, E. & M. V. R. Co. v. Marley*, 25 Neb. 138; *Omaha & R. V. R. Co. v. Standen*, 22 Neb. 343.

RAGAN, C.

The Nemaha river is one of the natural water courses of the state, and drains a large area of territory. When floods or freshets occur the channel of this river overflows, and the stream then becomes very much widened, extending and flowing at such times from the foot-hills upon one side to the foot-hills upon the other side of the river's valley. In the valley of this river, in Richardson county, is situate the farm of Oliver Emmert. In 1883 the Chicago, Burlington & Quincy Railroad Company, hereinafter called the railroad company, constructed a road at right angles across the valley of this river near said Emmert's farm. For the purpose of laying its ties and track thereon, the railroad company across this valley constructed an embankment of earth, and left no openings or culverts in the same through which the waters of this river, when out of its banks, might flow as they did prior to the construction of such embankment. In 1889 and 1892 freshets occurred, the channel of the river overflowed, and the waters spread out over the valley. The embankment arrested their progress, turned them back, and held them upon the lands of Emmert,—situate just up the river from the embankment,— and destroyed, as he alleges, his grass crops and pasture, a crop of standing corn, and permanently injured or depreciated in value his farm. To recover compensation for these injuries, he sued the railroad company in the district court of Richardson county, alleging that the railroad company, in omitting to construct culverts or openings in its embankment for the passage of the waters of the river in times of flood, had been guilty of negligence that had caused the injury to his property. The trial resulted in Emmert's obtaining a verdict and judgment, to review which the railroad company has instituted in this court error proceedings.

1. As already stated the embankment was constructed in 1883. The injuries sued for occurred in 1889 and 1892, and one proposition relied upon here for a reversal of the judgment of the district court is that Emmert's cause of action arose at the time of the negligent construction of the embankment, or more than four years before the bringing of this action, and hence was barred when brought. This precise question was presented to this court in *Fremont, E. & M. V. R. Co. v. Harlin,* 50 Neb. 698, and we there held that the cause of action arose when the injury sued for occurred, and not at the time of the completion of the improvement negligently constructed

which caused the injury.   The authorities bearing upon
the question under consideration are somewhat exten-
sively examined in that case and we see no reason for not
adhering to the conclusion then reached.

2. Another contention of the railroad company is that
its embankment was properly constructed for railroad
purposes; that the overflow or flood water of this river
was surface water; and, if Emmert was damaged by the
construction of the embankment at the place and in the
manner that it did, the railroad company is not liable
therefor, as it owed no duty to an adjoining proprietor as to the manner in which it should exercise its right
to build its railroad and protect its property from such
surface water.   But is the assumption of the railroad
company that the flood or overflow water of this river
was surface water, correct?   It must be conceded that
many cases hold the flood or overflow of a natural stream
is surface water.   See the rule stated and the authorities collated in 24 Am. & Eng. Ency. of Law [1st ed.],
p. 903.   But we are by no means satisfied with the doctrine of these cases nor with the reasoning on which
they are based.   Though they are in the majority, we
do not think they are right.   We shall not attempt to
lay down a rule as a guide in all cases for determining
whether waters are surface waters.   Whether water is,
or is not, surface water within the meaning of that term,
must be determined from the peculiar facts in the case
in which the question is presented.   But to say that the
flood or overflow water of this Nemaha river, when out
of its banks, and flowing from foot-hill to foot-hill, is
not a part of the river itself, not part of the natural
water course, but mere surface water, is to contradict
ordinary common sense.   In one sense of the word, all
the water of this river was at one time, perhaps, surface
water.   When this water was falling upon the watershed of this stream, when it was millions of aqueous
threads, flowing toward the stream covering the surface
of the watershed, then it was surface water; but when

20

it reached the stream, became a part thereof, whether
the stream was then flowing between its ordinary banks
and in its ordinary channel, or whether it had extended
beyond its channel, and was flowing from one foot-hill
to the other, then this water ceased to be surface water
and became a constituent part of the natural stream.

In *Crawford v. Rambo*, 44 O. St. 282, the supreme court
of Ohio, in discussing the question under consideration,
said: "It is difficult to see upon what principle the flood
waters of a river can be likened to surface water. When
it is said that a river is out of its banks, no more is implied than that its volume then exceeds what it ordinarily is. Whether high or low, the entire volume at
any one time constitutes the water of the river at such
time; and the land over which its current flows must be
regarded as its channel, so that, when swollen by rains
and melting snows, it extends and flows over the bottoms
along its course, that is its flood-channel, as when by
drought it is reduced to its minimum, it is then in its
low-water channel. Surface water is that which is dif-
fused over the surface of the ground, derived from falling rains or melting snows and continues to be such until
it reaches some well-defined channel in which it is accustomed to, and does, flow with other waters, whether
derived from the surface or springs; and it then becomes
a running water stream and ceases to be surface water."
To the same effect see *Byrne v. Minneapolis & St. L. R. Co.*,
38 Minn. 214; *O'Connell v. East Tennessee, V. & G. R. Co.*,
4 Am. R. & C. Rep. [Ga.] 449; *Sullens v. Chicago, R. I.
& P. R. Co.*, 38 N. W. Rep. [Ia.] 545; *Moore v. Chicago,
B. & Q. R. Co.*, 39 N. W. Rep. [Ia.] 390. These cases express our views and we cheerfully yield to them as authority on the subject under consideration.

But it is said that in *Morrissey v. Chicago, B. & Q. R. Co.*,
38 Neb. 406, this court committed itself to the doctrine
that the flood or overflow water of a natural stream was
surface water. But counsel are mistaken. RYAN, C.,
speaking for the court in that case used this language:

"The evidence in the case under consideration fails to show that the water complained of was a part of Yankee creek before crossing the right of way now occupied by the defendant's embankment, though there is evidence from which it might be inferred. It seems, too, that it was ultimately discharged into the Nemaha river independently of Yankee creek. * * * It does not satisfactorily appear from the evidence that it was a part of the flood water of Yankee creek; neither is it shown that but for the railroad embankment it would have sought an outlet by way of that creek. This water, therefore, under any of the definitions above given, was but surface water * * *." Further, the commissioner says: "Our conclusions are that the district court correctly concluded from all the evidence adduced on the trial of this case that the water, the flow of which was interfered with by the railroad embankment, was surface water. It flowed in no defined water course and overflowed only when there were extraordinary freshets. It was not shown that in its undiverted course it originated from or returned to the channel of Yankee creek. Its existence was directly traceable to falling rains. Its course was along the valley but not as a part of the stream." We reach the conclusion, therefore, that the flood or overflow waters of the Nemaha river that were arrested and turned back in 1889 and 1892 by the embankment of the railroad company were not surface waters but were a part of the water of the Nemaha river,—a natural stream.

3. Another error assigned and argued by the railroad company here relates to the rule as to the measure of damages enforced by the trial court. Emmert's proper measure of damages under the issues made by the pleadings as to his crop of corn, was the fair value of the corn destroyed at the time of its destruction. The measure of damages for the grass pasture destroyed was the fair value of the timothy and clover constituting the pasture at the time of its destruction; and the measure of his

damages as to the injury caused to his real estate by the embankment turning back and holding thereon the flood waters, was the difference in the fair market value of his real estate immediately before and immediately after such event. (See *Fremont, E. & M. V. R. Co. v. Crum,* 30 Neb. 76; *Kansas City & O. R. Co. v. Rogers,* 48 Neb. 653; *Fremont, E. & M. V. R. Co. v. Harlin,* 50 Neb., 698.)

On the trial Emmert was asked, and over the objections of the railway company answered, questions as follows: "Q. What was the use of that meadow,—the pasture land,—that year worth to you? State in round numbers what loss it was to you,—the loss of your pasture that year." To which he answered that he was compelled to procure other pasture that year for his stock and that he considered the loss was at least $150. "Q. In its matured state, as you had it before the fall of 1889, what was the actual value of that meadow to you?" To which he answered that it was worth $10 an acre. These questions all called for incompetent and irrelevant evidence under the issues. In his petition Emmert made no claim for any special damages, but claimed damages generally for the destruction of his corn and timothy and clover growing upon the lands on which the embankment of the railroad company held the flood-waters of the river. The question was not what the use of the meadow or the value of the meadow was to Emmert, but the question was: What was the actual fair value of this crop of timothy and clover at the time it was destroyed, and what was the fair value of the crop of corn destroyed? As to the depreciation in value of the land caused by the embankment's arresting the flood waters of the river the petition alleged "that said plaintiff has been further damaged in the sum of $2,000 by reason of the depreciation of the market value of said farm in this: that in consequence of such overflow in the year 1889, and the flooding of his farm by said railroad grade holding and damming the water back upon it, and by subsequent overflows of like character, his said farm has come to be known in the neighborhood as one liable to overflow, and consequently has lessened the market value of the land two-fifths of its value before it was flooded by said negligently constructed railroad, in August, 1883." This allegation of the petition did not state a cause of action. Under this allegation Emmert was not entitled to introduce any evidence to show that his real estate had been damaged or depreciated in value by the construction of this embankment; yet Emmert was, on the trial, over the objection of the railway company, permitted to testify that, after the recession of the high waters, the land was left wet and in a bad condition to cultivate; that the use of it in the year following the flood was of less value by one-half than it was previous to the flood; that the crops grown on the premises in the year succeeding the flood were only half the value they would have been had the flood not been there; that this value amounted to five dollars an acre. The admission of all this evidence was error, as it violated the rule of damages applicable to the case. We cannot say that the admission of this evidence was not prejudicial to the railroad company, as under it the jury may have, and probably did, charge the railroad company with the sum of money which Emmert testified he was compelled to pay for having his cattle pastured during the autumn succeeding the flooding of his land in August, 1892. The jury may have and probably did estimate the value of the crop grown on the premises in the year succeeding the flood of 1892, and concluded that crop was not worth as much by $5 an acre as it would have been had the lands of Emmert not been overflowed in that year. As already stated, Emmert was not suing for any of these things. He alleged generally in his petition his ownership of these lands; that on part of the land was a crop of growing corn, and on other parts of the land there was a pasture composed of timothy and clover, and that these grasses and this corn crop in 1889 were destroyed by the holding of the flood waters of the river on his lands by the railroad company's embankment. What he had been compelled to pay or had paid for pasturing his cattle by reason of the presence of the water on his lands in 1889 was not an issue in the case. Whether the crop succeeding the flood of 1889 and 1892 was as good as it would have been had such an overflow not occurred, was not an issue in the case. We are constrained to say that we think the admission of this evidence was prejudicially erroneous. The judgment is reversed and the cause remanded to the district court with instructions to grant the railroad company a new trial.

REVERSED AND REMANDED.

NEBRASKA LOAN & TRUST COMPANY, APPELLANT, V. LINCOLN & BLACK HILLS RAILROAD COMPANY, APPELLEE.

FILED DECEMBER 22, 1897. No. 7958.

Eminent Domain: REVIEW OF PROCEEDINGS: ERROR AND APPEAL. The method of bringing to this court for review judgments of the district court in proceedings by railroads for the exercise of the right of eminent domain is by petition in error and not by appeal.

APPEAL from the district court of Howard county. Heard below before KENDALL, J. *Appeal dismissed.*

J. B. Cessna, W. H. Thompson, John A. Casto, and *George F. Work,* for appellant.

O. A. Abbott, J. W. Deweese, and *F. E. Bishop, contra.*

IRVINE, C.

The Lincoln & Black Hills Railroad Company instituted proceedings in Howard county for the appropriation of land of the Nebraska Loan & Trust Company. From the report of the appraisers an appeal was taken

to the district court. Within six months after the rendition of judgment in the district court a transcript of
the proceedings was lodged in this court, but more than
a year has elapsed and no petition in error has been filed
or summons in error issued. It is plain that the case is
here, if at all, by appeal and not on error. The railroad
company now interposes objections to the jurisdiction,
presenting the question whether an appeal lies from the
district court to this court in such cases.

For many years it has been generally assumed that
cases of this character, being legal rather than equitable
in their nature, should be brought here on error and not
by appeal. At the same time there is no constitutional
inhibition against providing for an appeal in such cases,
and the Nebraska Loan & Trust Company contends that
the legislature has provided such a remedy. The question is one of technical rather than substantial importance, in view of the equal advantages now afforded by
the two methods of review. The statute, after providing
how condemnation proceedings by railroad companies
shall be instituted, appraisers appointed, damages ascertained and reported to the county judge, and for an appeal from the report of the appraisers to the district
court, further provides that "either party may appeal
from the decision of the district court to the supreme
court of the state, and the money so deposited shall remain in the hands of the county judge until a final decision be had, subject to the order of the supreme court."
(Compiled Statutes, ch. 16, sec. 97.) This section was
adopted as a portion of the first statute regulating railroads, approved February 8, 1864. (Session Laws, p.
130.) It has remained in this respect unchanged, except
by the substitution of "state" for "territory" and "county
judge" for "probate judge." It is by virtue of the use
of the word "appeal" in this section that appellant here
claims the right.

It has frequently been remarked that the word "appeal" is used in many different senses, owing to the di-

versity of statutes regulating appellate procedure. In at least four senses has it been used in this state with reference to proceedings in the supreme court alone. In one sense, and a very frequent one, it denotes all kinds of proceedings for the review of cases,—all proceedings commonly known as appellate. (Vide 2 Am. & Eng. Ency. Law 425, and all the English dictionaries.) In its special and technical sense it designates the particular form of review, dependent upon statute for its existence (Wilcox v. Saunders, 4 Neb. 569; State v. Ensign, 11 Neb. 529; State v. Bethea, 43 Neb. 451), whereby a case is transferred, after decision, to a higher court for a re-examination of the whole proceeding, and final judgment or decree in accordance with the result of such re-examination. (State v. Doane, 35 Neb. 707; Western Cornice Mfg. Co. v. Leavenworth, 52 Neb. 418.) In the latter sense, as applied to proceedings in this court, it can now only refer to the technical appeal provided for by the present "Title 21" of the Code of Civil Procedure. Unless in the statute under consideration it was used in this sense, this case is not properly before us. To determine the question an examination of the history of the various laws on the subject is necessary.

The first territorial legislature, as its first act, adopted portions of the statutes then in force in Iowa. Among these provisions, appearing as section 552, was the following: "From the decision of the district court an appeal lies to the supreme court." Immediately following, but under a separate caption, were a number of sections providing the manner, time, and effect of taking such appeal, very different from the law now in force. This was the only method of review except by certiorari then provided, and the only one known in civil cases until 1858. This was not our present technical appeal, whereby equity cases are reviewed, but a general and exclusive method of review. In 1858 a Code of Civil Procedure was adopted which, with amendments by subsequent legislatures, forms our present code of practice.

Title 16 of that Code provided for proceedings in error, and evidently contemplated making that the sole method of review by the supreme court. A number of the former provisions were then expressly repealed and there was also a general repealing clause, against which there was then no inhibition. Throughout the history of the territory the distinction between law and equity was observed in regard to procedure, and February 15, 1864, there was approved an act to regulate the practice in chancery. Section 45 of that act provided for the appeal of chancery cases, and the following sections regulated the time, manner, and effect of such appeals. These provisions were carried into the Revised Statutes of 1866 as Title 24 of the Code. They were repealed in 1867 (Session Laws, p. 71) by the act whereby the distinctions were abolished between actions at law and suits in equity. Thus we see that the general appeal provided for in 1855 had been superseded in 1858 by the creation of proceedings in error, and while the sections following the caption line and providing not for the right but the method of appealing seem not to have been expressly repealed, the Code of 1858 rendered them obsolete. (*Irwin v. Calhoun*, 3 Neb. 453.) No such thing as an appeal was thereafter known to our law until February 15, 1864, when a new kind of appeal was created for chancery cases alone. The repeal of this law, in 1867, entirely abolished appeals to the supreme court. (*Irwin v. Calhoun, supra.*) There again followed a period wherein appeals did not exist, until March 3, 1873, when the present law was passed, providing for appeals in equity cases, and which has been inserted into the Code as Title 21, in place of the long obsolete sections regulating the manner of proceeding in the early form of appeals, adopted from Iowa. *Wilcox v. Saunders*, 4 Neb. 569.) In the two cases last cited will be found interesting reviews of the legislation we have been considering, by judges who were for the most part personally cognizant of its history.

The section which it is claimed gives the right of ap-

peal in this case was, it will be observed, enacted at a
time when for six years no appeals to the supreme court
had been known to the law, and a week before the same
legislature created anew the right to appeal, and confined it to chancery cases. It follows then that the word
"appeal" in the proviso quoted could not have referred
to the present technical appeal, which was not created
until nine years thereafter, and then confined to equity
cases; nor to the early appeal provided for in 1855, for
that method had been for six years superseded; nor again
did it anticipate and contemplate the appeal provided
for one week later, else that appeal would not, by the
terms of the statute, have been restricted to chancery
cases. A retrospective glance will show that appellate
procedure was still in a formative state and had not in
the minds of the legislature yet assumed a fixed character. The word used could not have referred to any
special method of review then known, and must have
been used in its broad sense for the purpose of conferring
generally the right to a review by the supreme court,
leaving the practice and method of review to be determined by the legislation in force at the time of any
particular proceeding. So interpreted we have no hesitation in saying that under present statutes the method
must be by petition in error. The action is essentially
legal and is not within the cases which the act of 1873
permits to be brought here by appeal.

It is contended that a technical appeal must have been
contemplated by the final clause of the statute, whereby
the condemnation money is to be held by the county
judge "until a final decision be had, subject to the order
of the supreme court." This can mean no more than
that the money is to be held subject to the final decision
as ordered by the supreme court; but if it be true as
claimed that it contemplates the entry of a final judgment by the supreme court, this is insignificant, because
section 594 of the Code, inasmuch as error was to be
made the only method of review, expressly provided that

in error cases the supreme court may itself enter the judgment the district court should have entered.

APPEAL DISMISSED.

RAGAN, C., not sitting.

PHILIP M. CRAPO V. H. C. HEFNER ET AL.

FILED JANUARY 3, 1898.   No. 7704.

Notes: RATES OF INTEREST. Where a note or bond provides for interest at a lawful rate from date until maturity, and for a higher lawful rate thereafter, the latter provision is not in the nature of a penalty, but is authorized by section 3, chapter 44, Compiled Statutes, and accordingly enforceable in an action on the contract. (*Havemeyer v. Paul*, 45 Neb. 373.)

ERROR from the district court of Lancaster county. Tried below before HALL, J. *Reversed.*

Samuel J. Tuttle, for plaintiff in error.

W. E. Stewart and *E. H. Wooley, contra.*

POST, C. J.

There is presented by the record of this case a single question, viz., the rate of interest recoverable upon the note in suit, which in terms provides for interest at seven per cent per annum, payable annually, with the further proviso that "this note is to draw nine per cent interest per annum after default in payment of principal or interest." There was due at the commencement of the action, in addition to the principal note of $3,000, one interest coupon for $210, which also provided for interest at the rate of nine per cent after maturity. The district court allowed interest at seven per cent only and denied the plaintiff's prayer for the higher rate contracted for after default, and which is the ruling now assigned as error.

The precise question here involved was, in *Havemeyer v. Paul*, 45 Neb. 373, determined adversely to the ruling of the district court. It was in the case cited held, overruling *Richardson v. Campbell*, 34 Neb. 181, that where a note provides for a lawful rate of interest from date until maturity and a higher lawful rate thereafter, the latter provision is not in the nature of a penalty, but is authorized by section 3, chapter 44; Compiled Statutes, and accordingly enforceable in an action on the contract. It follows from the reasoning in that case that the judgment of the district court must be reversed and the cause remanded.

REVERSED.

GUY MATHEWS V. H. B. MULFORD.

FILED JANUARY 3, 1898. NO. 7436.

1. **Bill of Exceptions:** ALLOWANCE: LACHES. The fact that the party excepting was diligent, and the delay in serving a bill of exceptions was caused by the official reporter's default in preparing a transcript of the testimony, does not authorize the submission of the bill after the expiration of the time fixed by law and the order of the court.

2. **New Trial:** BILL OF EXCEPTIONS: NEGLECT OF STENOGRAPHER. A court of equity will grant a new trial in a proper case where a party has been deprived of a bill of exceptions by reason of the inability of the stenographic reporter to furnish a transcript of the testimony in time.

ERROR from the district court of Douglas county. Tried below before SCOTT, J. *Affirmed.*

Smith & Sheean, for plaintiff in error.

I. R. Andrews, contra.

POST, C. J.

This action was instituted in the court below by Guy Mathews, an infant, by Mellon L. Mathews, his next friend, to recover for personal injuries. At the close of plaintiff's testimony the jury, under the directions of the court, returned a verdict for the defendant, and to reverse the judgment entered thereon is the purpose of these proceedings.

The cause was tried at the September, 1893, term of the district court of Douglas county, which adjourned *sine die* on January 5, 1894. Forty days from the rising of the court was allowed for the preparation and service of a bill of exceptions. The trial judge extended the time an additional forty days. The official stenographer furnished the plaintiff with a transcript of the evidence . on May 29, 1894, with his certificate attached to the effect that owing to the large amount of official business in his hands, he was unable sooner to complete the transcript of the evidence. The proposed bill of exceptions was served upon counsel for defendant two days later, which was considerably more than eighty days from the rising of the court. The draft of the bill was returned to plaintiff with the indorsement thereon objecting to the allowance thereof on the ground that the same was not served in time. The bill was allowed by the trial judge, subject to the foregoing objections. Under the foregoing facts can the bill of exceptions be considered for any purpose? Plaintiff argues the affirmative of the proposition and cites in support of his contention *Richards v. State*, 22 Neb. 145. The cases are substantially alike, but the opinion in *Richards v. State, supra*, upon the question before us was in express terms overruled in *Horbach v. City of Omaha*, 49 Neb. 851, in which last case it was decided that a bill of exceptions not presented to the adverse party within the time fixed by law and the order of the court cannot be considered, over objection, notwithstanding the delay in the presentation was caused solely by the default of the official reporter in preparing a transcript of the evidence. Following that decision the bill of exceptions must be disregarded. The remedy, if any, is by application to a court of equity for a new trial.

(*Curran v. Wilcox*, 10 Neb. 449; *Holland v. Chicago, B. & Q. R. Co.*, 52 Neb. 100.) Being unable without a consideration of the testimony to determine whether any error was committed in directing the verdict, the judgment is

AFFIRMED.

NICHOLAS HALMES, APPELLANT, V. GEORGE E. DOVEY, APPELLEE.

FILED JANUARY 3, 1898. No. 7565.

Review: CONFLICTING EVIDENCE. Decree appealed from *held* to be sustained by sufficient, although conflicting, evidence.

APPEAL from the district court of Cass county. Heard below before CHAPMAN, J. *Affirmed.*

Byron Clark, for appellant.

A. N. Sullivan, contra.

POST, C. J.

This was an action in the district court for Cass county, the purpose of which was to compel the defendant Dovey to execute an alleged agreement for the release of certain lands from the operation of a judgment previously recovered by him against one Thomas, the plaintiff's grantor. A final hearing in the district court resulted in a finding and decree adverse to the plaintiff's contention, and from which an appeal has been prosecuted in this court.

Appellant frankly concedes that the evidence, so far as it relates to the principal question at issue, viz., the agreement alleged as the foundation of the action, is conflicting and irreconcilable, but seeks to prove that the finding is so decidedly against the weight of the evidence as to require a reversal of the decree upon that ground, while counsel for appellee, with equal plausibility, defends the finding as the logical and necessary result of the proofs adduced. It is clear, from a reading of the entire record, that the case is governed by the rule many times asserted by this court, viz., that a judgment or decree, unless manifestly wrong, will not be disturbed although the evidence may seem sufficient to support a finding for the adverse party. A statement of the evidence would in this connection be without profit to any of the parties concerned and will accordingly not be attempted.

DECREE AFFIRMED.

PATRICK D. McCORMICK, ADMINISTRATOR, v. MRS. S. A. McCORMICK.

FILED JANUARY 3, 1898.   No. 7689.

Executors and Administrators: ALLOWANCE OF CLAIMS: ORDERS: RECORDS. The order of allowance of a claim against an estate by the county court, and its entry thereof, examined, and *held* sufficient, both in form and substance; and further, that the entry was not fatally defective by reason of its lack of the signature of the county judge.

ERROR from the district court of Sarpy county. Tried below before BLAIR, J. *Reversed.*

J. J. O'Connor and *I. J. Dunn,* for plaintiff in error.

Anthony E. Langdon and *Martin Langdon, contra.*

HARRISON, J.

From the record filed in this matter, we discover that during the year 1891 Margaret L. McKenna, of Sarpy county, this state, died intestate. Application was made to the county court by the defendant in error, mother of the deceased, for the appointment of an administrator of the estate, and she named in her petition Daniel Morrison for such position. Clement L. McKenna appeared and requested the appointment of Patrick D. McCormick. This request was granted, and, in August, 1892, McCormick was appointed administrator, and was allowed one year within which to settle the estate. By order of the court, duly published, creditors were allowed six months within which to present claims for adjustment, and September 20, 1892, October 28, 1892, and December 26, 1892, were designated as the days for hearing and adjustment of claims. On September 20, of the days fixed by such order, the defendant in error presented a claim against the estate; and of what was done in regard to her claim the record discloses as follows: On the back of the claim was indorsed: "Allowed Sept. 20, 1892. Edward B. Hoyt, Co. Judge." And in the files of the county court there appeared what was headed a "Schedule of Claims," one of which was:

Claimant.	Amount of claim.	Nature of account.	When allowed.
Mrs. S. A. McCormick.	$739.50	....	Sept. 20, 1892.

There was a column in which as to the other claim (there was but one other scheduled) there appeared the amount allowed. Of the claim here in question there was no entry in said column.

Of the exhibits in the record presented to this court was this:

"Copy of Entry Book C, page 446. Exhibit C.

"In the Matter of the Estate of Maggie McKenna. Schedule of Claims Allowed by the Court. September 20, 1892.

"F. A. Harrison, legal notice................. $6 00
"Mrs. S. A. McCormick, as per bill on file...... 739 50
"Allowed September 20, 1892................ 739 50 '

During the month of January, 1894, on an application for the purpose on behalf of defendant in error, a citation was issued to the administrator by which he was required to appear and show cause why he did not, or should not, pay the claim of defendant in error. The administrator appeared and made a showing in the matter, a hearing was had, and the matter taken under advisement. A short time afterward, and seemingly before the decision in the submitted controversy, there was filed for defendant in error a motion that the court correct or amend the docket entry of the allowance of her claim. Of this motion there was a hearing, after which it was overruled. The court in its decision on the motion made findings in effect that the claim had never been allowed, and that no hearing had ever been had thereon, and ordered a hearing on the claim, fixed a time within which it was to be done, and appointed commissioners to examine and adjust it. On error to the district court of Sarpy county, the order of the county court was reversed, and the journal entry states further of what was done: "It is ordered that this cause be remanded for further proceedings by said court in accordance with law, and that the motion and application be sustained and a judgment entered *nunc pro tunc*, as of the 20th day of September, 1892." The matter is presented here in error proceedings on the part of the administrator.

As we view the questions raised, their proper solution requires a reference to, and application of, some of the statutory provisions relative to the county court and its jurisdiction in the settlement of estates of deceased persons. It is directed in the chapter which regulates the settlement of such estates that a time shall be fixed within which claims against the estate must be presented for adjustment; also that times and places shall be designated for examining and passing on claims of which notice shall be given in the prescribed manner. It is also provided that the judge of the county court

21

shall examine, adjust, and allow or reject claims. (See Compiled Statutes 1891, ch. 20.) In the chapter relative to county courts, the section in regard to the probate books which was in force at the times of the occurrences out of which arose this controversy, was as follows: "The probate books shall consist of a record, entry, estate, and fee book, which shall be kept as follows: 1. The record book shall contain a full record of all wills, testaments and codicils, and the probate thereof, all letters testamentary, of administration and guardianship, and all bonds of executors, guardians and administrators. The original papers shall be filed and preserved in the office. 2. There shall be entered in the estate book all inventories, appraisements, sale bills, and other exhibits and reports received by the court, relative to the settlement or disposition of estates, showing the amount of all such estates, as shown by such instruments. 3. The entry book shall contain a fair statement of all the matters, controversies, and suits that may have arisen for decision and adjudication before said court, with the names of the parties, dates of each entry, and the judgment or opinion of the court, and all orders thereof, and a full record of all determinations of the district or supreme court upon appeal or petition in error in such matters, controversies, and suits. 4. The fee book shall contain an exact account of all fees allowed and paid in each case, showing the names of the persons receiving the same, and for what such fees were paid." (See Compiled Statutes 1891, ch. 20, sec. 32.)

It is conceded that the entry in book "C," which we have hereinbefore set forth in terms, was in the handwriting of the judge who was in office at the date it states the account or claim was allowed (he had died before this proceeding was instituted), and we think it may be said, from what appears in the record, and it is not controverted, that this entry, such as it was, appeared in the proper book for such an entry,—in what is designated by the section of the statutes just quoted as the "entry book." If so, was it such an entry as constituted the claim an allowed one? We think the answer must be in the affirmative . All the preliminaries prescribed in the statute, such as fixing the dates for the presentment and adjustment of claims, publication of notice, etc., had been observed and fulfilled. The entry on the record, while lacking in some recitals such as the appearances of parties and the hearing and contest over the claim, if any, was sufficient to show an allowance of the claim and was complete as an allowance in fact, and also as an entry of the act. (*Yeatman v. Yeatman*, 35 Neb. 422.) That the county judge did not sign the record of the order of allowance did not invalidate or render the allowance of no force. The lack of the signature is not fatal. (*Scott v. Rohman*, 43 Neb. 618.) It follows that the judgment of the district court by which the adjudication of the county court was reversed will be affirmed and the order to the county court to make a *nunc pro tunc* entry of the order of allowance of the claim will be

REVERSED.

ALICE V. ANDERSON v. JERUSHA E. STORY, GUARDIAN.

FILED JANUARY 3, 1898.   No. 7728.

1. **Review:** JURISDICTION: CONSENT. If there is a lack of jurisdiction of the subject-matter, acquiescence or consent of the parties that it be assumed will not confer it, and an appeal in the case or proceeding from the adjudication therein vests no jurisdiction in the appellate tribunal.

2. **Courts:** ACCOUNTS OF FOREIGN GUARDIAN: JURISDICTION. A guardian appointed by a surrogate of a county in New York after removal to this state, and residence here by herself and the ward, applied to a county court of this state to be allowed to render an account as guardian, and to be discharged. The application was acted upon by the county judge, and the guardian presented her report and account. The ward appeared and contested the allowance of portions of the account, without objection or challenge to the jurisdiction of the court. *Held*, That the

county court had no jurisdiction of the subject-matter, and consent or acquiescence of the parties did not give it, and the district court to which an appeal was taken acquired no jurisdiction.

ERROR from the district court of Saline county. Tried below before HASTINGS, J. *Reversed.*

Abbott, Selleck & Lane, for plaintiff in error.

Abbott & Abbott, contra.

HARRISON, J.

It appears herein, from a statement in one of the briefs, which is stated in the other to be substantially correct, that the defendant in error was, during a few months of the year 1874, and prior thereto, the wife of John H. Underwood, who died during the year 1874 in Virginia, where he and his wife were then residing. The plaintiff in error, the daughter of the couple, was born about three months after the death of the father. Soon after the birth of the daughter, the mother removed to Chautauqua county, New York, and there applied to the proper court to be, and was, appointed guardian of her child and its estate. This was done of date May 6, 1876. The defendant in error received as such guardian some $482, the child's share of its father's estate. After about seven years of widowhood, the defendant in error was married to Andrew J. Story, and some three years afterward they removed to Saline county, this state. The daughter, soon after she became of age, was married to one Perry Anderson. The defendant in error had never accounted as guardian, and the daughter, after her marriage, urged that such an accounting be made. After some attempted settlements of the matter, but without anything definite being accomplished, during the year 1892, the defendant in error filed what was styled a petition in the county court of Saline county, in which the facts relative to her appointment as and acts as guardian were set forth, and in which she prayed as follows: "Your petitioner prays that you will request the honorable county judge of said Chautauqua county, New York, to certify all the proceedings heretofore and in said matter to the county court of said Saline county, Nebraska, to the end that said matter may be finally settled where the jurisdiction thereof is vested by reason of the residence of all the parties interested therein. And your petitioner will ever pray," etc. The county judge of Saline county sent the following to the surrogate of Chautauqua county, New York: "The county judge of Saline county, Nebraska, to the Hon. judge of Chautauqua county, New York, greeting: Whereas, Mrs. Jerusha E. Story (formerly Underwood), now resident of this county, has filed her petition in this court, a copy of which is hereto attached, setting forth that in the year 1876 she was duly appointed guardian of Alice Underwood (now by marriage Anderson), by the then judge of your court, and that herself and ward and all persons interested have since become, and. now are, *bona fide* residents of this county; and that said matter of guardianship has never been settled, and praying that said matter may be removed to this court for final settlement because of the residence of all parties within the jurisdiction of this court: Now, therefore, you are hereby respectfully requested to transmit to this court, at your convenience, a certified transcript of all the proceedings had in said matter in your court, together with a certified copy of the bond, to the end that final settlement of the matter may be made. All unpaid fees will be collected and transmitted to your court with receipt for transcript." Pursuant to the request, the surrogate forwarded the papers in the guardianship matter to the judge of the county court of Saline county. The county judge then made an order that the accounting be had and heard on September 9, 1892, at a stated hour, and caused a copy of the order to be published. The ward (the plaintiff in error) appeared and contested the matter to the extent of certain allowances which

the guardian in her report claimed to be her due. After
a hearing on the matter it was adjudged that the guardian was not entitled to the credits claimed in her report
or account, and, further, that she had received the sum
of $481.95; and it was "ordered by the court that said
guardian pay to said minor the sum of $481.95, and,
upon complying with the order of this court, she will
be discharged from said trust and her letters of guardianship cancelled and annulled." The matter was, on
behalf of Mrs. Story, appealed to the district court
where, as the result of a trial to the court, it was disposed of as follows: "And the court being fully advised
in the premises finds for the guardian Jerusha E. Story,
and finds that she is entitled to have her account for
the maintenance of said ward allowed out of said ward's
estate. It is therefore considered by the court that the
guardian Jerusha E. Story, be, and she is hereby, discharged, and that she have and recover of and from
Alice U. Anderson her costs expended in this court."
The matter is presented to this court in error proceedings on the part of the ward.

It is stated in one of the briefs that all parties acquiesced in the jurisdiction of the county court of Saline
county, and that no question is raised touching such
jurisdiction; but however this may have been, it is clear
that the county court of Saline county, though it had
jurisdiction of probate matters and of the matters of
guardianships, did not have jurisdiction to entertain an
accounting by a guardian appointed by a surrogate
court of New York to hear and adjudicate the matters
arising on such accounting, and to discharge or refuse
to discharge the guardian. This was all clearly without
its jurisdiction, and acquiescence or consent of the parties could not and did not confer jurisdiction, if it did
not exist. If the county court had no jurisdiction, the
appellate courts obtained none. (*Brondberg v. Babbott*, 14
Neb. 517; *Union P. R. Co. v. Ogilvy*, 18 Neb. 638; *Moise
v. Powell*, 40 Neb. 671; *Johnson v. Parrotte*, 46 Neb. 51;

Keeshan v. State, 46 Neb. 155; *Stenberg v. State*, 48 Neb. 299.)   As the county and district courts were without jurisdiction in the matter, their adjudications were void and of none effect.   The judgment of the district court is reversed and a dismissal of the matter will be entered.

REVERSED AND DISMISSED.

BENJAMIN D. MILLS V. STATE OF NEBRASKA.

FILED JANUARY 3, 1898.   No. 9234.

1. **Information:** COMPLAINT: VARIANCE.   In a prosecution by information, the complaint and information must charge the same offense, but it is sufficient if the charge in the information is substantially the same as that alleged in the complaint.   If this is so, a plea of no preliminary examination on the ground of a variance between the complaint and information is without force. (*Cowan v. State*, 22 Neb. 519; *Hockenberger v. State*, 49 Neb. 706.)

2. ——: ——: ——.   If the identity of the offense charged is preserved, the statement of it in the information or counts thereof may be varied from that of the complaint to meet a possible state of the proof.

3. ——: UNCERTAINTY: EMBEZZLEMENT.   The word "embezzle" includes within its import the "conversion to his own use" as alleged in an information against one accused of embezzlement, and it does not constitute an information fatally defective, for uncertainty as a plea, that the two are joined by the copulative "and."   The same is also true of the first and any other word or set of words used to express a manner of the commission of the crime.

4. **Embezzlement:** INFORMATION: ALLEGATION OF VALUE.   In an allegation of an information of the crime of embezzlement it was stated that the embezzlement was of the sum of $6,000 in money. *Held*, To be a sufficient expression of the value, the presumption being that it was lawful money.

5. ——: PUBLIC MONEY: OFFICERS AND OTHERS.   By section 124 of the Criminal Code, any person who advises, aids, or participates in the embezzlement of public money by the officer or person charged with the collection, receipt, safe-keeping, transfer, or disbursement of such money is himself guilty of embezzlement. The words "any person" refer to all, and are not confined in

meaning to a person or persons or officer or officers in some manner intrusted with the collection, handling, or care of public
money.

6. **Instruction Defining Crime.** An instruction which consisted of
quotation of the main portions of the section of the Criminal
Code under which the prosecution was instituted *held* not improper or misleading.

7. **Instructions:** CRIMINAL LAW: CIRCUMSTANCES. An instruction in
this cause in regard to consideration of circumstances *held*
proper, and when construed with the other instructions not
misleading.

8. ———: REVIEW. Instructions to the jury are to be considered together and construed as a whole; and if, so considered and construed, they are correct, it is sufficient.

9. ———: EMBEZZLEMENT: EVIDENCE. Certain instructions examined
and *held* applicable to the evidence herein, and proper.

10. ———: NON-DIRECTION: REVIEW. Mere non-direction does not furnish sufficient reason for reversal on review unless proper instructions have been requested and refused. (*Hill v. State*, 42 Neb.
503; *Pjarrou v. State*, 47 Neb. 294.)

11. **Embezzlement:** EVIDENCE: RECEIPT. Objections to the admission
of evidence examined and *held* properly overruled.

12. **New Trial:** NEWLY-DISCOVERED EVIDENCE. To entitle a party to
a new trial on the ground of newly-discovered evidence, it must
appear that the applicant for the new trial could not with reasonable diligence have discovered and produced such evidence at
the trial. (Criminal Code secs. 490, 492.)

13. **Embezzlement:** CONVICTION. Evidence *held* sufficient to sustain
the verdict.

ERROR to the district court for Harlan county. Tried
below before THOMPSON, J. *Affirmed.*

The facts are stated in the opinion.

James McNeny and *Thomas Darnall,* for plaintiff in
error:

The court erred in overruling the plea in abatement
as to the fourth count in the information. For the
crime sought to be charged therein the plaintiff in error
had neither had nor waived a preliminary hearing.
There was a fatal variance between the complaint and

the information. (*Yaner v. People*, 34 Mich. 286; *People v. Jones*, 24 Mich. 214; *People v. Fairchild*, 48 Mich. 31; *People v. Wallace*, 94 Cal. 497; *People v. Parker*, 91 Cal. 91.)

The first count of the information is invalid for uncertainty. (*United States v. Cruickshank*, 92 U. S. 558; *State v. Benjamin*, 49 Vt. 101; *Commonwealth v. Chase*, 125 Mass. 202.)

The first count of the information is insufficient because it fails to state the value of the money alleged to have been embezzled. (*Bork v. People*, 16 Hun [N. Y.] 476; *State v. Stimson*, 4 Zab. [N. J. Law] 9; *Commonwealth v. Smith*, 1 Mass. 245.)

It is absolutely essential to establish the principal's guilt, beyond a reasonable doubt, before the accessory can be convicted. (*Ogden v. State*, 12 Wis. 592; *Pettes v. Commonwealth*, 126 Mass. 242; *Hatchett v. Commonwealth*, 75 Va. 925; *Goins v. State*, 46 O. St. 457; *Ulmer v. State*, 14 Ind. 52; *Buck v. Commonwealth*, 107 Pa. St. 486.)

The evidence does not establish the crime of embezzlement against the principal, and plaintiff in error was not lawfully convicted. (*Hamilton v. State*, 46 Neb. 284; *Fitzgerald v. State*, 50 N. J. Law 475; *People v. Royce*, 106 Cal. 173; *Chapin v. Lee*, 18 Neb. 440; *Fleener v. State*, 58 Ark. 98; *Commonwealth v. Este*, 140 Mass. 279; *State v. Hebel*, 72 Ind. 361; *State v. Munch*, 22 Minn. 75; *People v. Galland*, 55 Mich. 628.)

The fourth count of the information does not state facts sufficient to constitute a crime under the laws of the state. Stripped of its legal phraseology, this count simply charges plaintiff in error with having borrowed the money of the county treasurer, knowing the same to be the money of Harlan county. Is this an offense within the meaning of the statute? We contend it is not. (*State v. Teahan*, 50 Conn. 100; *Commonwealth v. Kimball*, 21 Pick. [Mass.] 373.)

Instruction No. 8 was erroneous in directing the jury

that guilt could be established not only by direct evidence, and other competent evidence, but by "circumstances." (*Long v. State*, 23 Neb. 33; *Thompson v. State*, 30 Ala. 28.)

C. J. Smyth, Attorney General, and *Ed P. Smith, Deputy Attorney General*, for the state.

References: *State v. King*, 81 Ia. 587; *Rhodes v. State*, 27 N. E. Rep. [Ind.] 866; *United States v. Bryne*, 44 Fed. Rep. 188; *State v. Fain*, 106 N. Car. 760; *State v. Knox*, 17 Neb. 683.

HARRISON, J.

The plaintiff in error was by an information filed in the district court of Harlan county charged in the seven counts thereof with the crime of embezzlement. After some preliminary pleas were heard and decided in accordance with motions presented and sustained, the objects of which were that the state be required to elect on which count or counts of the information it would stand and proceed with the prosecution, the state elected to proceed under the first and fourth counts. The plaintiff in error pleaded not guilty, and a trial resulted in his conviction and sentence to a term of imprisonment in the penitentiary, and to pay a fine in double the amount which by the verdict he was adjudged guilty of embezzlement. The prosecution was instituted for an alleged violation of the provisions of section 124 of the Criminal Code, which, to the extent we need notice it, is as follows: "If any officer or other person charged with the collection, receipt, safe-keeping, transfer, or disbursement of the public money, or any part thereof, belonging to the state, or to any county, or precinct, organized city or village, or school district in this state, shall convert to his own use, or to the use of any other person or persons, body-corporate, association or party whatever, in any way whatever, or shall use by way of investment in any kind of security, stock, loan, property, land, or merchandise, or in any other manner or form whatever, or shall loan, with or without interest, to any company, corporation, association, or individual, any portion of the public money, or any other funds, property, bonds, securities, assets, or effects of any kind, received, controlled, or held by him for safe-keeping, transfer, or disbursement, or in any other way or manner, or for any other purpose; or, if any person shall advise, aid, or in any manner participate in such act, every such act shall be deemed and held in law to be an embezzlement of so much of the said moneys or other property, as aforesaid, as shall thus be converted, used, invested, loaned or paid out as aforesaid, which is hereby declared to be a high crime, and such officer or person or persons shall be imprisoned in the penitentiary not less than one year nor more than twenty-one years, according to the magnitude of the embezzlement, and also pay a fine equal to double the amount of money or other property so embezzled as aforesaid." It was charged in the first count of the information: "That Ezra S. Whitney, late of said county, on the 31st day of December, 1894, in the county of Harlan, state of Nebraska, being an officer, to-wit, being the county treasurer for the said county of Harlan, being charged as such officer with the collection, receipt, safe-keeping, transfer, and disbursement of the public moneys belonging to said county, certain of said moneys, to-wit, six thousand dollars of the public moneys belonging to said county, did unlawfully and fraudulently embezzle and convert to his own use, which said moneys had come into the possession and custody of the said Ezra S. Whitney, by virtue of his said office, and in his discharge of the duties thereof. And before said embezzlement, conversion, and felony was committed as aforesaid by the said Ezra S. Whitney, to-wit, on the 31st day of December, 1894, in the county of Harlan aforesaid, one Benjamin D. Mills unlawfully, purposely, fraudulently, corruptly, and feloniously did then and there procure, advise, incite, aid, and abet the said Ezra S. Whitney in

the perpetration of said embezzlement and conversion in
the manner and form aforesaid, contrary to the form of
the statute in such case made and provided, and against
the peace and dignity of the state of Nebraska." And
in the fourth: "That the said Ezra S. Whitney, late of
said county, on the 31st of December, 1894, in the county
of Harlan, and state of Nebraska, being an officer, to-wit,
being the county treasurer for the said county of Harlan,
and being charged as such officer with the collection,
receipt, safe-keeping, transfer, and disbursement of the
public moneys belonging to said county, certain of said
moneys, to-wit, six thousand dollars of the public moneys
belonging to said county, did unlawfully and fraudulently loan and convert to the use of the said Benjamin
D. Mills, which said money had come into the possession
and custody of the said Ezra S. Whitney by virtue of his
said office, and in his discharge of the duties thereof, and
had been received and was controlled and held by him,
the said Ezra S. Whitney, for safe-keeping, transfer, and
disbursement, as county treasurer as aforesaid. And the
said Benjamin D. Mills, then and there being, did then
and there, unlawfully, knowingly, and feloniously, advise and procure the said Ezra S. Whitney, county treasurer as aforesaid, to loan him, the said Benjamin D.
Mills, said six thousand dollars of said public money,
and the said Benjamin D. Mills, did then and there receive from and of Ezra S. Whitney, treasurer of said
Harlan county as aforesaid, said six thousand dollars,
he, the said Benjamin D. Mills, then and there well knowing the same to be the public money of said Harlan
county, received and held as aforesaid, with intent to
embezzle and convert to the use of him, the said Benjamin D. Mills, contrary to the form of the statute in
such case made and provided and against the peace and
dignity of the state of Nebraska."

By plea in abatement the point was raised and presented in the trial court that the fourth count contained
a charge of a crime which was not alleged in the com-

plaint filed in the examining court; hence the plaintiff in error had never had or waived a preliminary examination on such accusation. There were four counts in the complaint filed with the justice of the peace, and when arrested and taken before the justice, the plaintiff in error waived an examination. The first count of the complaint, after statements that Ezra S. Whitney was county treasurer of Harlan county, Nebraska, and of his duties in regard to collection, disbursement, etc., of the public moneys, charged that he did fraudulently, unlawfully, and feloniously convert to his own use and embezzle the sum of $700 of said public money, and that Benjamin D. Mills, plaintiff in error, unlawfully, purposely, fraudulently, corruptly and feloniously did procure, advise, incite, aid, and abet the said Ezra S. Whitney in the perpetration of said embezzlement and conversion. The second count was in substance the same, except as to the amount alleged to have been embezzled, which was $600; also the third, except as to amount, which was stated to be $6,000; and likewise the fourth, except in it the sum was fixed at $11,190. The fourth count in the information filed in the district court, it will be borne in mind, charged the conversion of the public money, in the sum of $6,000, to the use of Benjamin D. Mills, and that it was by his advice and procurement that it was done. Under the system of prosecution by information it may be said the complaint and information should charge the same offense; but it may be added, when it appears that the charge in the complaint is substantially the same as that set forth in the information, the plea of the want of a preliminary examination, or a variance between the complaint and the information is unavailing. (*Cowan v. State,* 22 Neb. 519; *Hockenberger v. State,* 49 Neb. 706.) In the case of *State v. King,* 81 Ia. 587, wherein the defendant had been treasurer of a county in Iowa and was indicted for embezzling the funds of the county, it was charged in the pleading, after the usual averments, that he "did * * * embezzle and convert to his own use without authority of law," a stated sum; that "he did * * * convert said money to his own use by expending the same in his private business, and by permitting persons, whose names are to this grand jury unknown, to use and expend said money in their private business transactions, and by using said money to pay his own private debts." The court in review, in passing on the question of whether the indictment was bad for duplicity, observed: "We are of opinion that the indictment is sufficient. The gist of the offense is the wrongful conversion of the public money, and it is wholly immaterial and mere surplusage to state whether the defendant used it in paying his debt, in purchasing property, had it on deposit in bank, carried it on his person, or loaned it to others; and the fact that three different modes of concealing the money are set forth in the indictment is wholly immaterial." The case of *State v. Spaulding*, 24 Kan. 1, is one in which the defendant was convicted in the trial court of the crime of embezzlement. It is stated in one paragraph of the head-notes: "A preliminary examination was had upon a complaint charging defendant with the embezzlement, as city clerk, of certain moneys of the city of Leavenworth. Afterward an information was filed containing several counts, each charging the embezzlement of the same moneys at the same time, and as the property of the same party, but differing in this: that one charged him with embezzling as clerk, another as agent, another as servant, and so on. Held that a special plea that defendant had had no preliminary examination, except upon the charge of embezzlement as clerk, and that, therefore, all the other counts should be stricken out, was properly overruled." And in the body of the opinion it was said: "In reference to these counts, it will be noticed that they charge the embezzlement of the same money, at the same time, and as the property of the same party. The only difference between them is in the relation which the defendant is charged to have sus-

tained to the party whose money was embezzled. In one
he is called an officer,—its clerk; in another, an agent;
in another a bailee, and so on. It is the same act—the
same wrong—which is complained of in each count." In
the case at bar, the fourth count of the information
charged the embezzlement of the same money, of the
same party, and at the same time as did the complaint,
the sole difference being the manner or method alleged
of the commitment of the crime. It was not a charge of
a different offense, but the allegation of the manner in
which the crime was committed was varied,—no doubt,
to meet a possible contingency in the evidence. This was
allowable. (*State v. Spaulding, supra*; 1 Wharton, Criminal Law [6th ed.] secs. 424, 425; 7 Ency. Pl. & Pr. 446.)

It is urged that the first count of the information is
bad for uncertainty, in that it states that Ezra S. Whitney "did * * * embezzle and convert to his own
use the public moneys of the county." It is claimed that
this alleges the crime to be charged, generally by the
use of the term "embezzle," and specifically by the use
of the words "convert to his own use." Of the form and
substance of the charge in the first count of the information, it may be said: "Embezzle includes in its meaning·
appropriation to one's own use, and, therefore, the use
of the single word embezzle, in the indictment or information, contains within itself the charge that the defendant appropriated the money or property to his own
use." (*State v. Wolff*, 34 La. Ann. 1153; *Hamilton v. State*,
46 Neb. 284.) "Embezzlement" includes "conversion to
his own use," and it is proper to use them, in a charge
of the crime, connected by the copulative "and." The
same is also true of other words included in the term
"embezzle." (7 Ency. Pl. & Pr. 448.) That in proof of
this charge it might be shown that the money was also
converted to the use of another party, would not be repugnant. It might be to the use or benefit of the person
holding the office, and also to the benefit of another. In

this there would be no inconsistency. It would be but
one manner of the commission of the crime charged.
(*State v. Manley,* 17 S. W. Rep. [Mo.] 800.) We do not
think it can, with soundness, be asserted that the allegations of the count under consideration did not inform
the party to be charged, of the crime, with sufficient
clearness to enable him to prepare his defense.. It was
sufficiently definite if it did this.

It is also claimed that the first count of the information is defective because it does not state in specific
terms the value of the money averred to have been embezzled. The point here raised has been determined by
this court adversely to the contention of counsel for
plaintiff in error. In the case of *State v. Knox,* 17 Neb.
683, in considering the sufficiency of the charge of the
crime of embezzlement of money, in a complaint, it was
said of one of the objections: "That an allegation of
value is indispensable. This would be necessary if property or bank bills, not a legal tender, had been embezzled; but, where the allegation is the embezzling of $35
in money, the amount designated expresses the value,
the presumption being that it was lawful money." (See
· *Bartley v. State,* 53 Neb. 310; *Hildreth v. People,* 32 Ill.
36. See also 7 Ency. Pl. & Pr. 432.) The charge in the
case at bar was of the embezzlement of a stated number
of dollars, and was sufficient.

It is insisted that the fourth count of the information
does not state facts sufficient to constitute a crime under
the laws of the state. If it does so, it is under the provisions of section 124 of the Criminal Code, a portion of
which we have hereinbefore quoted. The argument for
plaintiff in error is based, in part at least, on the proposition that this count of the information charges no more
than that Mills borrowed the money of the county with
knowledge that it was the county's money, and that this
is not an offense; and proceeding from this standpoint,
among other matters urged in support of the position

taken, states that section 124 of our Criminal Code is largely copied from an act of congress passed in 1846, and that it is a significant fact that the original act of congress has since been amended to include a borrower of public money, from which the conclusion is drawn that the act as originally passed did not include such a party; hence, the amendment; and the further conclusion is drawn in argument that our section, being largely a copy of the original act of congress, cannot, or should not, be construed to include the borrower. We will say here that we can by no means agree that the fourth count of the information charges against the plaintiff in error a mere naked borrowing of the money of Harlan county from its treasurer with knowledge that it belonged to the county. It charges an embezzlement of such money, its misappropriation or unlawful and felonious conversion, and that plaintiff in error did advise and procure the same, or. in other words, actively participated by words or deeds in the act charged. But leaving this, at least for the present, if not entirely, we will turn to another phase of the question.

Section 124 of the Criminal Code embodies many of the constituent elements of the act of congress to which reference has been made; but it bears a strong resemblance to, and is, in fact, with some few necessary changes and omissions,—the first to meet a difference in conditions and political subdivisions in this state,—a reproduction of section 15 of an act passed by the legislature of the state of Ohio, April 12, 1858. (2 Swan & Critchfield Revised Statutes 1606, sec. 15.) In the case of *Brown v. State*, 18 O. St. 496, which was a prosecution instituted for an alleged violation of the provisions of said section 15, the indictment contained six counts, of which the first and second were abandoned. On the trial of each of three of the other counts it was charged that the treasurer of one of the Ohio counties had converted the money thereof to the use of Brown, and that Brown aided in the act; and, in each of two of them, that he

22

also participated in the act. In one count it was charged
that Brown, by and with the assistance of the treasurer,
took the money of the county from the treasury, it being
then in the possession of the treasurer. Brown was convicted, and on review in the supreme court it was held:
"By the act of April 12, 1858 (2 Swan & Critchfield Revised Statutes, 1606, sec. 15), the party advising, aiding,
or participating in an embezzlement of public money, by
an officer or person intrusted with it, is himself guilty of
embezzlement, although he be not himself an officer, or
person intrusted with public money. * * * The crime
of advising, aiding, or participating in an embezzlement
by a public officer is made by said act a distinct and
substantive offense, and the party guilty of it may be
put upon his trial and convicted, before the conviction
of the embezzling officer." And it was stated in the
opinion: "In the first place, it is claimed that the indictment is bad as to Brown, because it does not allege that
he was a public officer or person intrusted with public
money. The argument seems to be that, as the statute
declares the aider or participator guilty of embezzlement,
it must refer to, and mean, a person having charge of the
public money, or in some way connected with its keeping
or control; otherwise, it is said, he could not be guilty of
embezzlement. We do not so understand the statute.
It is true that the statute makes the act of aiding or participating in embezzlement itself an act of embezzlement.
But that is a mere statutory name for the offense. The
statute defines two substantive offenses. One is the conversion of public money by the party intrusted with it.
The other is the advising, aiding, or participating in the
act of conversion by any person. Each act is declared by
the statute to be an 'embezzlement' and a 'misdemeanor,'
in as unequivocal and direct language as could be employed for the purpose. Its plain declaration is, that
'any person' who advises, aids, or participates in the conversion of public money by a party intrusted therewith,
is himself guilty of embezzlement." In section 124 it is

stated: "If any person shall advise, aid, or in any manner participate." This clearly includes all persons—officers or others—intrusted with the custody or care of
money or any other funds. The count contained a sufficiently definite and specific charge of an embezzlement
as set forth in the section 124 of the Criminal Code; hence
it stated a crime known to our law.

It is asserted that instruction numbered 3, especially
when that which immediately followed it was read in
connection with it, was erroneous and prejudicial. Number 3 was a quotation of almost the whole of section 124
of the Criminal Code, inclusive of the portion in which it
is recited that if certain facts are proved of the acts, or
failures to act, of the officer or persons who have the
collection, care, and disbursement of public money, they
shall constitute *prima facie* evidence of the embezzlement.
Whether the quotation, in an instruction, of a section or
a part or parts of it, in order to convey to the jury knowledge of certain matters stated therein, is the best or
proper method to accomplish such purpose, we are not
called upon to decide; but there were some statements
in the section copied in the instruction, of which it was
necessary the jury should have correct information, and
the manner in which it was given doubtless served the
purpose; but it is urged that all that portion which relates
to the acts, or failures to act, of officers, and their weight
as evidence had application to the treasurer and no direct application to plaintiff in error or his acts. This is
no doubt true; but that Whitney, the treasurer, had been
guilty was a necessary portion of the proof in the establishment of the charge against the plaintiff in error;
hence it was not improper to instruct the jury in regard
to the portion of section 124 relative to evidential matters. But it is further complained that the jury should
have been specifically charged, that this portion of the
instruction must not be applied to the branch of the case
which related directly to plaintiff in error, and the proof
as to him, where it was without direct reference to or

connected with that in regard to the treasurer. It might
have been better so to do, but it was not requested to be
done by counsel for plaintiff in error. But, regardless of
this fact, the matter given in the instruction to which
objection is urged was plain in its import and not obscure
in its designation of the persons as to whom it was pertinent; and we cannot believe that the jury can have
been misled or confused by it, or that it was in any degree
harmful to the rights of the plaintiff in error.

It is complained that the eighth paragraph of the instructions was erroneous and misleading. It was as follows: "The court further instructs the jury that while
they must be convinced of the guilt of the defendant beyond a reasonable doubt, from the evidence, in order to
warrant a conviction, still the proof need not be direct
testimony of persons who saw the offense committed.
The acts constituting the crime may be proved by circumstances and any other competent evidence." It is
said in argument that the effect of this was to allow the
jury to consider any circumstances regarding the alleged
offense, whether shown in evidence or not. It was
proper to instruct the jury in this case relative to the
significance or weight to be given to any pertinent circumstances of which there was proof. Whether the instruction was carefully prepared and worded in the
particular portion indicated by the objection, we need
not determine. In an instruction which preceded this
one in the order of giving, and also in one which followed it, the jury was specifically directed that it must
be governed by what had appeared in evidence in the
cause, in view of which we cannot believe that the jury
was misled by any statement contained in paragraph 8.

Objections are urged against paragraphs 9 and 10 of
the charge to the jury. The first of these was devoted
to stating certain questions to which the jury was to
seek answers in the evidence, and if in the affirmative,
the verdict of guilty was to follow, and if in the negative
as to either of the stated propositions, the verdict was

directed to be, "Not guilty." This instruction referred
to the first count of the information. The one numbered 10 was much the same in terms except that it was
framed with reference to the fourth count of the information. It is possibly true that either of these paragraphs
of the instructions, detached from the others, and so read
and construed, may be in some respects and in some
degree defective. Indeed, it is questionable whether instructions framed as questions—as were these—to be
answered by the jury, and in the event of one answer the
jury instructed to return a verdict of guilty or, on an
opposite finding, the opposite verdict, are in cases of
this nature proper, or should be given; but these, when
read and construed in connection with the others given,
could not have prejudiced the rights of the plaintiff in
error. Of the failure to state in them that the findings
must be from the evidence, it may be said that it is not
necessary, though it may be better, that this should be
stated in every instruction, or in every proposition. It
is sufficient if the jury are informed that all the findings
must be from the evidence. This was done in the instructions in this case.

It is claimed that instruction number 12 was erroneous
and wholly unwarranted. It reads as follows: "You
are instructed that before you can find defendant Benjamin D. Mills guilty of the offense charged in the information, you must find from the evidence beyond a
reasonable doubt that said sums were not deposited in
said bank under the depository bond, or if so deposited
they, or some of them, were drawn out of said depository
by said Benjamin D. Mills upon the checks of Ezra S.
Whitney, as treasurer of said Harlan county." When
this is read in connection with the one which immediately precedes it in the charge to the jury, in which the
jury was informed of the provision of the law in regard
to banks furnishing bonds and being designated by the
county boards as depositories for county funds, and in
the light of the evidence relative to the subject, it is

apparent that the reference in instruction numbered 12
was to a bank or banks so designated, and the import of
its reference to said banks is clear and pertinent. It is
further insisted that this instruction was erroneous, in
that it told the jury that, as one of the elements of the
guilt of plaintiff in error, if it appeared that the money
had been deposited in a designated bank, it must further
appear that it was drawn therefrom by plaintiff in error
by means of checks of Ezra S. Whitney as county treasurer of Harlan county, in that it did not refer to the fact
that the money might have been drawn out of the bank
or banks of deposit on checks issued to pay debts of the
county evidenced by its warrants. This portion of the
instruction would have been prejudicially erroneous if
there had been any evidence to the effect that the money
was drawn in payment of debts of the county, or rather
if there had not been such a condition of the proof in
the case as precluded any idea, or even an inference,
that any of this money was drawn for payment, or paid
on properly evidenced or any indebtedness of the county.
In view of the status of the evidence on this point, there
was no available error in giving the instruction.

Complaint was made of the giving of the fourteenth
paragraph of the charge to the jury, which reads as follows: "You are instructed that the receipts and other
writings introduced in evidence in this case are *prima
facie* evidence of the receipt of the money, and are not
conclusive, and may be qualified and explained by other
competent evidence; and in determining the truth in relation thereto you will take into consideration all the
evidence introduced bearing upon this point." It is insisted that there were some of the writings to which this
paragraph of the instructions evidently referred, which
could not be considered as, in any manner or degree,
tending to establish the guilt of the plaintiff in error.
If competent to be in evidence,—and we must presume
in this discussion that they were,—they must have been
so as matters of proof. In the whole case it must be

borne in mind that to establish the commission of the crime with which the plaintiff in error was charged, it was also necessary to show that Treasurer Whitney had been guilty of embezzlement; and these writings were, some of them, doubtless introduced in the branch of the proof which had a direct bearing on the question of Whitney's commission of the crime, and were thus a portion of the proof on the charge against the plaintiff in error, and it was proper to instruct the jury in regard to them; but it is further urged that the jury was told by this paragraph what weight might be accorded these items of the proof, and the burden was cast on the plaintiff in error of qualifying or explaining them. The court in the instruction did no more than inform the jury of the significance of the evidence to which reference was made, merely stated its effect, and that it was not conclusive in its nature, and might be qualified or explained. There was nothing unfair or erroneous in such action. It was entirely proper. Without such an instruction, the jury might, to the prejudice of the plaintiff in error, have considered these matters as conclusive; nor did the court by its instructions cast the burden on the plaintiff in error of qualifying or explaining these evidential writings. He stated that it might be done by other competent evidence, not from any particular person or source, but that came into the cause from any source. This was the true meaning of the instruction and it was without error.

It is urged that the court wholly failed to instruct the jury in regard to one material fact,—an element of the crime charged. We think a close scrutiny of the whole of the instructions will disclose that this criticism is not wholly merited. There are portions of them where some reference to it would have been proper, and should have been made; but, in view of the state of the evidence relative to the fact, the failure, where it occurred in the instructions, could have no other effect than a non-direction. It devolved upon the counsel for plaintiff in error to prepare and submit proper instructions, failing in which there is no ground for reversal. (*Pjarrou v. State,* 47 Neb. 294; *Hill v. State,* 42 Neb. 503; *Johnson v. State,* 53 Neb. 103.) It may be further said that in regard to the fact as to which it is claimed there was a failure to instruct, there was no dispute or conflict in the evidence. while not admitted it was established and undisputed; hence there could have been but one finding as to it if based on the evidence, and if there was error in the failure to instruct, it was without prejudice.

It is assigned for error that the trial court admitted in evidence a receipt for $6,000, which appears in the record as Exhibit F. The ground of the complaint is that it was not properly identified,—that it was not shown that it was written or signed by plaintiff in error whose receipt on its face it purported to be. During the trial there was produced an envelope which was fully identified as having been received by the treasurer by mail through the post office, and its enclosures, one of which was a letter, was fully identified as being the handwriting of the plaintiff in error. The other enclosure was the receipt in question. The letter was as follows:

"STATE BANK OF REPUBLICAN CITY, NEB.

"Correspondents: American Exchange National Bank, N. Y.; Merchants National Bank, Omaha, Neb.; First National Bank, Lincoln, Neb.

"REPUBLICAN CITY, NEB., Jan. 2, 1894.
"*E. S. Whitney, Treas., Alma, Neb.*—DEAR SIR: Herein I hand you rect. for the $6,000. I do not believe we had better put this on deposit for it will raise such a howl as we never heard.
"Yours as ever, MILLS."

The address to Treasurer Whitney on the envelope was shown to be the handwriting of the plaintiff in error. The receipt read:

"STATE BANK OF REPUBLICAN CITY, NEB.
                                    "Dec. 30, 1894.
"Received of E. S. Whitney, treas., six thousand dollars to hold for deposit.   B. D. MILLS.
"$6,000."

From all this it appears that the letter was written to the treasurer by plaintiff in error addressed by him and received by the treasurer through the post office. The letter had the receipt enclosed with it, and it was referred to therein and recognized by the writer of the letter, the plaintiff in error, as his receipt. This, we think, constituted a sufficient identification for its reception in evidence.

For the plaintiff in error there was presented a motion for a new trial, one of the grounds of which was newly-discovered evidence. This branch of the motion was supported by affidavit. There were filed for the state some affidavits to controvert the facts presented for plaintiff in error in the affidavit in support of the motion. The motion was overruled, and such action, as to this branch thereof, is assigned for error. After an examination of these affidavits, we cannot say the court erred. Its reason for overruling the motion is not in the record, but in view of all the facts as set forth in the several affidavits, it cannot be said that there was newly-discovered evidence which plaintiff in error could not with reasonable diligence have discovered and produced at the trial. This must appear. (See Criminal Code, secs. 490, 492.)

It is also urged that the evidence was wholly insufficient to sustain the verdict. It would serve no useful purpose to quote it at length or summarize it in a statement here. After a careful examination of it we must say that while, from it, it might be said that the money alleged to have been the subject of embezzlement may have, a portion or all of it, gone into the hands and care of the plaintiff in error for the probable purpose of being deposited in the bank, a designated depository for such funds, it is clear that subsequently this purpose was changed, and the money of the county was, in direct violation of the law on the subject (Criminal Code, sec. 124), allowed by the treasurer to be retained by the plaintiff in error for use, and not for deposit, and this by and through the advice and procurement of the latter. That such subsequent action by which the money was so retained by plaintiff in error was in pursuance of an agreement to such effect, between the parties, we think the evidence warranted such conclusions, and, if so, it was sufficient to sustain the verdict rendered. It follows from the conclusions herein reached that the judgment must be

AFFIRMED.

CHARLES B. CONGDON ET AL., APPELLEES, V. NERIAH B. KENDALL ET AL., APPELLEES, AND E. P. ALLIS & COMPANY, APPELLANTS.

FILED JANUARY 3, 1898. No. 7604.

1. **Mechanics' Liens:** MATERIALS: PLACE OF DELIVERY: TIME TO FILE CLAIM. Under a contract to make certain machinery and deliver it "free on board of cars" at a designated place for a stipulated sum, the machinery is furnished, within the meaning of our mechanics' lien law, when it is delivered in accordance with the contract on board the cars at the place named, without expense to the purchaser; and to obtain a lien therefor, the claim for a lien must be filed within four months from that time. (*King v. Ship-Building Co.*, 50 O. St. 320.)

2. ——: ——: ——: ——. The time for so perfecting the lien cannot be extended by the manufacturer supplying gratuitously certain brushes in place of defective ones previously furnished and charged for.

APPEAL from the district court of Lancaster county. Tried below before STRODE, J. *Affirmed.*

Ames & Pettis, for appellants.

References: *Merriam v. Hartford & N. H. R. Co.*, 20 Conn.

354; *Packard v. Getman*, 6 Cow. [N. Y.] 757; *Buckman v. Levi*, 3 Camp. [Eng.] 414; *Frith v. Barker*, 2 Johns. [N. Y.] 327; *Foster v. Dohle*, 17 Neb. 631; *Marriner v. Paxton*, 17 Neb. 634; *Irish v. Pheby*, 28 Neb. 231; *Weir v. Barnes*, 38 Neb. 875; *Pond Machine Tool Co. v. Robinson*, 37 N. W. Rep. [Minn.] 99; *McIntyre v. Trautner*, 63 Cal. 429; *Hubbard v. Brown*, 90 Mass. 590; *Watts-Campbell Co. v. Yeungling*, 125 N. Y. 1; *Badger Lumber Co. v. Mayes*, 38 Neb. 830.

Ricketts & Wilson and *S. L. Geisthardt, contra.*

NORVAL, J.

Kendall & Smith being the owners of a flouring mill at Woodlawn, this state, on May 10, 1893, executed a mortgage thereon to C. B. Congdon & Co. to secure a sum of money certain.   Prior to the making of the mortgage Edward P. Allis & Co. furnished Kendall & Smith machinery for the reparation and reconstruction of said mill, and subsequently a claim for a mechanic's lien was filed in the office of the register of deeds of Lancaster county.   The decree was entered in the court below foreclosing the mortgage.   The court refused Allis & Co. a mechanic's lien upon the ground that the claim for the lien was not filed within four months from the furnishing of the machinery.   The sole contest in this court is between Congdon & Co. and Allis & Co., and if the claim of the latter for a mechanic's lien was not filed within the statutory period, the decree should be affirmed; otherwise it should be reversed.

In November, 1892, Allis & Co., manufacturers of mill machinery at Milwaukee, Wisconsin, entered into a contract with Kendall & Smith, under which the machinery in question was furnished.   The contract contained, among other things, the following provision: "The foregoing list of items comprises all that we are to furnish to you delivered free on board cars, at our shop in Milwaukee, Wis., for the sum of five thousand five hundred dollars," etc.   There is in the record testimony tending

to show, and the trial court found, that the last portion
of the machinery was delivered by Allis & Co. on board
of cars, at their shops, to the Chicago & Northwestern
Railway Company in Milwaukee on January 21, 1893.
The machinery reached Woodlawn on the first day of the
following month and was placed in the mill. The claim
for a lien was not filed until May 23, 1893.

It is argued by appellants that the machinery was not
delivered on board the cars to the railway company until
January 23, 1893. The evidence discloses that the cars
were loaded and placed in the hands of the carrier by
Allis & Co. on Saturday, January 21, and the railway
company on the same day executed and delivered to the
consignors receipts for the goods. It is true the bills of
lading for two of the cars bear date of January 23,
1893, from which fact it is argued that the machinery
was not furnished until that time. The loaded cars
were in the actual charge of the carrier on January
21, received by it for the purpose of forwarding and delivering the goods at the place of destination. The title
passed to Kendall & Smith on said date, since the delivery to the carrier was delivery to the vendees. This is
the effect of the decision in *Union P. R. Co. v. Metcalf,* 50
Neb. 452, where it was held that a consignor was not
entitled to sue a carrier for a failure to deliver goods in
the absence of an averment that he was the owner of the
goods, was liable for their loss or had sustained special
damages. (*McKee v. Bainter,* 52 Neb. 604.)

In *Swanke v. McCarty,* 51 N. W. Rep. [Wis.] 92, the
court uses this language: "Indeed, it is elementary that,
where the vendor is bound to send the goods to the purchaser, delivery to a common carrier is a delivery to the
purchaser himself, the carrier being, in contemplation of
law in such cases, the bailee of the person to whom, not
by whom, the goods are sent, the latter, when employing
the carrier, being regarded as the agent of the former for
that purpose." While the decisions upon the subject are
not in accord, the weight of the authority sustains the

proposition contained in the foregoing quotation, where there is no agreement to deliver the goods to vendee at place of destination. (Benjamin, Sales, secs. 181, 693; *Kelsea v. Ramsey*, 26 Atl. Rep. [N. J.] 907; *Leggett v. Collier*, 56 N. W. Rep. [Ia.] 417; *Barr v. Borthwick*, 25 Pac. Rep. [Ore.] 360; *Sarbecker v. State*, 65 Wis. 174; 21 Am. & Eng. Ency. Law 497, 499, 529; *Kessler v. Smith*, 44 N. W. Rep. [Minn.] 794; *Sullivan v. Sullivan*, 70 Mich. 583; *Falvey v. Richmond*, 13 S. E. Rep. [Ga.] 261; *Bacharach v. Chester Freight Line*, 19 Atl. Rep. [Pa.] 409.) Had the agreement of the manufacturers been to deliver the machinery free on board cars at Woodlawn, a different rule might obtain.

The claim of Allis & Co. for a mechanic's lien was not filed within four months from the delivery of the machinery to the carrier, but was filed within that period from the arrival at Woodlawn. The question is presented whether, within the meaning of the mechanic's lien law, the machinery was furnished as of the date of its delivery to the carrier. Upon principle we do not see how it can be otherwise. Allis & Co., under the contract with Kendall & Smith, had nothing to do with the machinery after its delivery for shipment on board of cars in Milwaukee, and it is plain that the title to the property vested in the vendees immediately upon such delivery to the transportation company. The legal effect is precisely the same as if Kendall & Smith had personally received the machinery from Allis & Co. at their shop in Milwaukee, in which case there could be no doubt that, as between the vendors and vendees, the machinery would be regarded as furnished on the day of its delivery in Milwaukee, for the purpose of fixing the time within which the lien of the manufacturers should be filed. Of course, no mechanic's lien attaches where the materials for which the lien is claimed do not enter into the improvement. As between a lienor and a subsequent purchaser of the premises, or mortgagee in good faith, the time when the materials are delivered upon the premises

would be regarded the time when the lien attached.
(*Badger Lumber Co· v. Mayes*, 38 Neb. 830.) The question
here is whether Allis & Co. are entitled to a lien upon
the property as against Kendall & Smith. If no such
right to a lien exists it is patent there is no priority of
liens to be adjudicated.

In *Great Western Mfg. Co. v. Hunter Bros.*, 15 Neb. 32,
this court decided that the delivery of machinery to a
common carrier in Kansas, to be used in a building in
Nebraska, was the furnishing and delivery of such machinery within the meaning of our mechanics' lien law.
(See *Mallory v. La Crosse Abattoir Co.*, 80 Wis. 170; *Thompson v. St. Paul City R. Co.*, 45 Minn. 13; *Fagan & Osgood
v. Boyle Ice Mach. Co.*, 65 Tex. 324.)

The precise question here involved was decided by the
supreme court of Ohio in *King v. Cleveland Ship Building
Co.*, 50 O. St. 320. The statute of that state is similar to
our own. A mechanic's lien was claimed for an engine
built by the vendor and delivered on board the cars at
Cleveland for shipment to the purchaser at Middleport,
under a contract requiring the vendor to deliver the
engine "f. o. b." cars in Cleveland. The validity of the
lien was contested on the ground that it was not perfected within four months from the time the engine was
delivered on the cars ready for shipment. It was decided
that when the delivery on the cars was complete the engine was furnished within the purview of the statute,
and the claim for lien must be filed within four months
from that time, or the right to a lien will be lost.

The case of *Pond Machine & Tool Co. v. Robinson*, 37 N.
W. Rep. [Minn.] 99, is not in point because the question
here involved was not decided.

In the case at bar Allis & Co. agreed to construct the
machinery and deliver the same free of expense on board
of the cars at Milwaukee. They fully complied with the
contract and furnished the machinery within the contemplation of the statute the moment the delivery on the cars
was complete, and the time in which to perfect the lien
commenced to run from that date.

It was disclosed that after the machinery was set up
in the mill certain brushes furnished under the contract
proved to be defective and Allis & Co. supplied others in
lieu thereof without additional charge or cost to Kendall
& Smith.   It is urged that the furnishing of these brushes
extended the period for perfecting the lien.   The articles
mentioned were furnished gratuitously for the purpose
of making good their contract, and did not operate to
extend the time for filing the lien.   (*Woman's Association
v. Harrison*, 120 Pa. St. 28; *Harrison v. Woman's Association*, 19 Atl. Rep. [Pa.] 804; *McKelvey v. Jarvis*, 87 Pa.
St. 414; *King v. Cleveland Ship Building Co.*, 50 O. St. 320.)
The decree refusing Allis & Co. a lien is

AFFIRMED.

EZRA S. WHITNEY V. STATE OF NEBRASKA.

FILED JANUARY 3, 1898.   No. 9250.

53
159

1. **Embezzlement:** INFORMATION: ALLEGATION OF OWNERSHIP. The
information, with sufficient particularity, avers that Harlan
county, in this state, was the owner of the money alleged to have
been embezzled by the defendant.

2. **Criminal Law:** EVIDENCE: ORDER OF INTRODUCTION. The order in
which testimony shall be introduced rests largely in the discretion of the trial court.

3. **Review:** TRIAL: EVIDENCE. Error cannot be predicated on the
admission of testimony, where the fact sought to be established
by it is subsequently admitted during the trial upon the record
by the parties.

4. ——: ——: RECORD. Error in the proceedings of a trial will
not be presumed, but must affirmatively appear from an inspection of the record.

5. **Embezzlement:** EVIDENCE. Under section 124 of the Criminal Code
the failure and refusal of a county treasurer to promptly pay to
his successor in office any of the public moneys in his hands is
prima facie evidence of embezzlement.

6. **Secondary Evidence:** FOUNDATION. Secondary evidence of the contents of an instrument is admissible upon proof that it once ex-

isted, and was last seen in the possession of the adverse party, where he under oath on the trial has denied the existence of such instrument.

7. **Statutes**: DEPOSITORIES: EMBEZZLEMENT. The act of the state legislature providing for the deposit of state and county funds in banks (Session Laws 1891, p. 347, ch. 50) did not repeal section 124 of the Criminal Code relating to the embezzlement of public moneys.

8. **Embezzlement**: DEPOSIT OF PUBLIC FUNDS. The mere depositing of county funds in depository banks by a county treasurer in strict compliance with the requirements of section 6, chapter 50, Laws 1891, is not an embezzlement of such funds by the treasurer.

9. **Instructions**: REASONABLE DOUBT. Instructions set out in the opinion defining a reasonable doubt *held* correct.

10. ———: HARMLESS ERROR. A conviction will not be reversed for the giving of an instruction, though erroneous, where the defendant was not prejudiced thereby.

11. **County Treasurers**: ACCEPTANCE OF CHECK. An incoming county treasurer accepting a bank check in payment of public funds due from his predecessor is chargeable with the amount of such payment, where the check is surrendered by the incoming officer to the bank which issued it, the amount deposited therein in open account under the depository law, other deposits of county funds are likewise made therein from time to time, checks against the account drawn by the treasurer aggregating a sum in excess of said first deposit are honored and paid by the depository bank, and said acts have been ratified by the county.

.2. **Instructions**: REPETITIONS. It is not error to refuse an instruction where the substance thereof is contained in some paragraph of the charge already given.

13. **Embezzlement**: EVIDENCE. Evidence *held* sufficient to authorize a conviction for the crime of embezzlement.

14. **Criminal Law**: ACCOMPLICE: STATE'S EVIDENCE. The fact that an accomplice turns state's evidence and testifies to such facts as are within his knowledge, under and in pursuance of a promise of immunity from punishment made by the prosecuting officer, without the consent or advice of the court, does not constitute a legal defense to a prosecution against such accomplice.

ERROR to the district court for Harlan county. Tried below before THOMPSON, J. *Affirmed.*

The facts are stated in the opinion.

John Everson, William O. Woolman, and *D. S. Hardin,* for plaintiff in error:

The information does not sufficiently describe the owner of the money alleged to have been embezzled. (*State v. Potter,* 28 Ia. 554; *Smith v. State,* 21 Neb. 556; *Ex parte Eads,* 17 Neb. 145; *Grant v. State,* 17 So. Rep. '[Fla.] 225.)

The court erred in making improper remarks concerning evidence. (*Bowman v. State,* 19 Neb. 527; *State v. Tickel,* 13 Nev. 502; *People v. Bonds,* 1 Nev. 33; *Crutchfield v. Richmond & D. R. Co.,* 76 N. Car. 320; *People v. Wood,* 27 N. E. Rep. [N. Y.] 362; *Sharp v. State,* 51 Ark. 147; *State v. Jacob,* 8 S. E. Rep. [S. Car.] 698; *State v. Stowell,* 60 Ia. 535; *State v. Harkin,* 7 Nev. 377.)

The court gave an erroneous instruction containing an improper definition of a reasonable doubt. (*Cowan v. State,* 22 Neb. 520.)

The motion to suspend sentence on the ground that the prosecuting attorney promised accused immunity from punishment upon his giving state's evidence in another prosecution, should have been sustained. (*Camron v. State,* 32 Tex. Crim. Rep. 180; *United States v. Ford,* 99 U. S. 594; *Newton v. State,* 15 Fla. 610; *State v. Graham,* 41 N. J. Law 15.)

C. J. Smyth, Attorney General, and *Ed P. Smith, Deputy Attorney General, contra:*

In failing to assail the information by motion and in pleading not guilty, accused waived the alleged defect in the description of the owner of the money embezzled. (*Korth v. State,* 46 Neb. 631.)

The records of the treasurer's office were properly admissible in evidence as tending to prove facts therein stated, and not as admissions on part of accused. (*Strong v. State,* 75 Ind. 440; *State v. Ring,* 29 Minn. 78; *People v. Flock,* 59 N. W. Rep. [Mich.] 237; *Stanley v. State,* 88 Ala. 154; *Osborn v. State,* 27 N. E. Rep. [Ind.] 345.)

23

Embezzlement consisting of a continuous series of acts committed at different times, but with a common purpose, may constitute a single offense. (*Bolln v. State*, 51 Neb. 581, and cases cited.)

Presumption that the entire amount was embezzled at the close of the second term: *Heppy v. Johnson*, 73 Cal. 270; *Stoner v. Keith County*, 48 Neb. 279.

The depository law did not repeal section 124 of the Criminal Code relating to embezzlement of public money. (*Korth v. State*, 46 Neb. 631.)

A reasonable doubt was correctly defined in the instructions. (*Willis v. State*, 43 Neb. 102; *Lawhead v. State*, 46 Neb. 607; *Langford v. State*, 32 Neb. 782; *Barney r. State*, 49 Neb. 515; *Polin v. State*, 14 Neb. 540; *Davis r. State*, 51 Neb. 301.)

Accused was properly chargeable with the amount of the check received from his predecessor. (*Bush v. Johnson County*, 48 Neb. 1; *State v. Hill*, 47 Neb. 456.)

NORVAL, J.

Ezra S. Whitney was convicted of embezzlement of public money of Harlan county, while he was the treasurer thereof, and sentenced to a term of two years and six months imprisonment in the penitentiary, and that he also pay a fine in double the sum embezzled. The information alleges that the defendant, "Ezra S. Whitney, was the county treasurer of Harlan county, Nebraska, from the 5th day of January, 1894, to the 9th day of January, 1896, and as such officer was charged with the collection, receipt, safe-keeping, transfer, and disbursement of the public moneys of Harlan county, Nebraska; that the said Ezra S. Whitney, on the 8th day of January, 1896, in said county and state, then and there being, and then and there, as such officer, being charged with the collection, receipt, safe-keeping, transfer, and disbursement of the public money of Harlan county, did then and there unlawfully and feloniously convert to his own use and embezzle a large sum of said money, to-wit, eleven thousand one hundred and ninety dollars, belonging to Harlan county, which said money had then and there come into the possession and custody of the said Ezra S. Whitney by virtue of said office and the discharge of the duties thereof."

The first point made by the defendant is that the information does not allege the money embezzled belonged to Harlan county, this state, and therefore no crime is charged. This objection is exceedingly hypercritical. Undoubtedly an indictment or information cannot be aided by intendment, nor can omissions be supplied by construction. But every act essential to constitute the crime must be averred. Tested by this rule the crime of embezzlement is charged. Stripped of its legal verbiage, the information plainly alleges that the defendant was the county treasurer of Harlan county, Nebraska, and as such officer was charged with the collection, receipt, safe-keeping, transfer, and disbursement of the public money of such county, and did embezzle and convert to his own use $11,190 of the moneys of said county which he had collected by virtue of his said office. The words "said money," as used in the information, refer to the public funds belonging to the county of Harlan, in this state, which it was alleged it was the duty of the defendant to collect and disburse, and which had theretofore come into his possession and custody by virtue of his said office. It is alleged with sufficient particularity that the money converted and embezzled was owned by Harlan county, Nebraska, and the information, therefore, is not defective in substance.

Error is assigned in the admitting in evidence of Exhibit 2. This paper was on file in the county clerk's office of Harlan county, and purports to be a statement made by the defendant, as county treasurer, showing the receipts and disbursements of the treasurer's office for a specified period, together with the amount of public money in his hands to the credit of the several funds at the close of business on January 8, 1896, the date of

the expiration of the defendant's official term. The first
objection urged against the admission of this document
is that no legal foundation for its introduction had been
made. Samuel Roberts, the county clerk of Harlan
county, produced the exhibit, and testified that he had
frequently seen the defendant write; was familiar with
his writing, and that the document objected to was in
the handwriting of the accused. Other or further iden-
tifying proof was not required.

Another objection urged against the reception of said
exhibit in evidence is that the *corpus delicti* had not been
proved, and that the admissions or statements of the
defendant cannot be received to establish that the offense charged has been committed. Whether the rule
contended for is applicable in a prosecution for embezzlement where it is sought to introduce the official reports made by the accused in pursuance of law may
well be doubted. But it is unnecessary to decide the
question at this time, because the defendant was not in
the least prejudiced by the receipt in evidence of Exhibit 2. The order in which parties shall introduce their
proofs rests largely in the discretion of the trial judge.
(*Basye v. State*, 45 Neb. 261; *Consaul v. Sheldon*, 35 Neb.
247; *McCleneghan v. Reid*, 34 Neb. 472; *Rema v. State*, 52
Neb. 375.) The record in this case discloses that shortly
after the ruling in question was made, the following
stipulation, in open court and before the jury, was
entered into:

"For the purposes of this action it is admitted that
the records in the office of the county treasurer of Harlan county during the term of office of the defendant,
Ezra S. Whitney, as treasurer of said county, commencing on the 5th day of January, 1894, and ending on the
8th day of January, 1896, both days inclusive, show that
at close of said term of office the said Ezra S. Whitney, as such treasurer, had on hand and in his charge as
such treasurer, the sum of forty-six thousand three hundred seventy-three dollars and thirty-seven cents ($46,-

373.37), and that he has turned over and paid thereon to his successor in office since January 8, 1896, the sum of seventeen thousand six hundred fifty-three. dollars and thirty-thrée cents ($17,653.33), and to the state treasurer the sum of four thousand four hundred twenty-six dollars and twenty-one cents ($4,426.21)."

The foregoing was an admission of record of the very matter sought to be established by Exhibit 2, viz., that the defendant had in his hands, as treasurer, at the close of his term of office, public funds aggregating the sum of $46,373.37; hence no prejudice resulted in allowing the contents of said exhibit to go to the jury. (*Lamb v. State*, 40 Neb. 312; *Rightmire v. Huntcman*, 42 Neb. 119; *McGavock v. City of Omaha*, 40 Neb. 64; *Hickman v. Layne*, 47 Neb. 177.)

The following question was put by the state to D. A. McCulloch, one of the witnesses for the prosecution, and who succeeded the defendant as county treasurer: "Q. Along in June or July, 1895, sometime, did you have a conversation or hear a conversation or statement made by Mr. Whitney in regard to some money that could not be accounted for?" The defendant objected "as incompetent, irrelevant, immaterial, no proper foundation made, the *corpus delicti* in this action not having been proven, or the fact that there is a shortage in the county treasurer's office." The court thereupon made this statement: "The court admits this upon the account that the attorney for the defense in stating his case to the jury admitted that the books showed a shortage." To this language the defense excepted, and the witness answered, "I did." Complaint is made of permitting said question to be asked and answered, and the quoted remarks of the trial judge are assailed. The question propounded was in its nature merely preliminary, and did not seek to elicit any substantive fact bearing upon the guilt or innocence of the accused, and the answer being within the range of the question was not prejudicial to the rights of the defendant. Moreover, the embezzlement of the money of Harlan county was subsequently established by the stipulation or admission already set .forth, in connection with other evidence. Whether the remarks of the trial judge were prejudicial is not disclosed. If counsel for the prisoner made the statement imputed to them, then the language of the court was pertinent and proper, otherwise it was prejudicial in its character. To have the point established the defendant should have had the opening statement of his counsel preserved in a bill of exceptions, or at least had set forth therein what remarks, if any, were made by counsel to the jury relating to the shortage of the defendant in his accounts with the county. Error is never presumed, but must affirmatively appear from an inspection of the record, is a familiar doctrine, and is quite applicable here. It is for the person who desires a ruling or any fact preserved by a bill of exceptions to procure one to be settled and allowed.

The witness D. A. McCulloch, over the objection of the defendant, was allowed to state that Mr. Whitney informed him that the books were correct, and that he did not have the money or cash to put up which the books called for. C. A. McCloud, who checked up the books of the defendant, testified substantially to a similar conversation and admission of the defendant. It is urged that these admissions should have been excluded, inasmuch as the *corpus delicti* had not been then established. This seems to have been a frequent objection urged during the progress of the trial of the cause, and, if we understand counsel correctly, it is still insisted that the crime of embezzlement has not been proven in this case. The contention is devoid of merit. Prior to the time the objected testimony was received, it had been stipulated or admitted in open court that the records in the county treasurer's office disclosed that the defendant, when he turned over his office to his successor, was chargeable with $46,373.37; that he paid to his successor $17,653.21, and to the state treasurer $4,426.21.

There was evidence tending to show that no other payments have been made by the defendant; that he had at the close of his term on deposit in the State Bank of Republican City, a county depository, county funds to the amount of $14,153.27. Thus it was in evidence that the accused had not accounted to his successor for all the public funds in his hands, and a *prima facie* case of embezzlement was made out against Whitney. (*Bolln v. State*, 51 Neb. 581.) It was, therefore, competent for the state to prove defendant's voluntary admission as to the fact of there being a shortage.

It is insisted that the court erred in requiring the defendant to answer the following question, propounded by the state on cross-examination: "Now, commencing January 1, 1893, what did you put in the bank?" The criticism is that it called for facts which antedate any time that could be charged in the information, and was barred by the statute of limitations. However well taken may have been the objection to the question, the criticism does not apply to the answer of the defendant to the interrogatory. This prosecution was instituted on June 4, 1896, and the first deposit of money in the bank, which the defendant testified to, was made on June 21, 1893, or less than three years preceding the prosecution.

The defendant was a witness in his own behalf, and on his examination in chief he testified to the depositing at various times county funds in the State Bank of Republican City, which was an approved depository bank with a bond of $25,000, and under the law entitled to have on deposit at any time county moneys not to exceed $12,500; and that he deposited moneys of the county in the bank largely in excess of the lawful limit. On cross-examination the defendant, over objections of his counsel, was asked this question: "Why did you put so much money in this depository?" The defendant answered, "Why, I don't know that I can give any explanation why I put so much there." The question was within the limit of proper cross-examination, and was competent as bearing upon the question of intent or motive which actuated the accused at the time he placed the funds in the bank.

It is urged that the court erred in allowing James A. Cline to testify, on rebuttal, to the contents of a certain deposit slip purporting to be evidence of the deposit of $6,000 by the defendant in the State Bank of Republican City. The objection to the ruling of the court is that no foundation for the introduction of secondary testimony had been laid. Mr. Cline, as one of the state bank examiners, examined the affairs of the State Bank of Republican City, and for the purpose of verifying the account between the said bank and defendant as county treasurer, in January, 1895, called upon the latter and asked to see his pass-book. Mr. Cline testified that the request was complied with, and in the pass-book was the deposit slip in dispute, that the witness made a copy thereof, left the original with the defendant, and had not seen it since. The accused, while on the witness stand, denied the existence of such a deposit slip and of all knowledge thereof. This laid sufficient foundation for the admission of parol proof of the contents of the paper.

Complaint is made of the giving of the third paragraph of the court's charge to the jury, which is a copy of section 124 of the Criminal Code, and under the provisions of which law this prosecution was brought and conducted. It is argued that said section was repealed by the legislative enactment entitled "An act to provide for the depositing of state and county funds in banks." (Session Laws 1891, ch. 50; Compiled Statutes, ch. 18, art. 3, secs. 18-23.) The identical point was made and decided adversely to the contention of the defendant, in *Korth v. State*, 46 Neb. 631. With the conclusion therein reached we are content.

It is urged that the giving of the entire section was prejudicial error, because it makes the commission of any one of several specific and different acts a crime, while the defendant is charged with the felonious conversion of the funds of Harlan county to his own use, and in no other way. The section defines a single crime, although it specifies various modes in which the offense may be committed. No prejudice could have resulted in repeating this section to the jury, for by the fourteenth paragraph of the charge they were, in plain and unequivocal language, told that unless the prosecution established by the evidence beyond a reasonable doubt that Whitney converted the money of the county to his own use there must be an acquittal. So that, instead of the jury being turned loose in the field of conjecture, as argued by the counsel for the defense, they were confined in their investigation to the identical charge set up in the information. A verdict of guilty could not have been returned, without disregarding the instructions, even had the proofs shown, which they did not, that the money of the county was embezzled in some other mode or manner than that described in the information.

Instruction No. 5 is an exact copy of section 6, chapter 50, Laws 1891, and relates to the deposit of county funds in depository banks. By the fourth instruction the jury were directed, in substance, that the depositing of moneys in a county depository in compliance with the provisions of section 6 of said depository law did not constitute embezzlement. Instead of the accused being prejudiced by the instruction, the direction of the court ought to, and doubtless did, inure to his benefit. It was shown that several thousand dollars of money of Harlan county were deposited from time to time, by the defendant, in certain depository banks in strict compliance with the law. Had it not been for instructions 4 and 5 the jury might have concluded that the defendant was guilty of the embezzlement of the money which he had lawfully placed in the depository banks.

The court gave the following instructions on the subject of a reasonable doubt:

"8. You are instructed that a reasonable doubt is an actual, substantial doubt arising from the evidence or want of evidence in the case.

"9. That by reasonable doubt is not meant that the accused may possibly be innocent of the crime charged · against him, but it means some actual doubt having some reason for its basis. A reasonable doubt that entitles to an acquittal is a doubt reasonably arising from all the evidence, or want of evidence, in this case. The proof is deemed to be beyond a reasonable doubt when the evidence is sufficient to impress the reason and understanding of ordinarily prudent men with a conviction on which they would act in the most important concerns or affairs of life."

The foregoing states the law correctly. Instructions, either in the identical language, or in substance the same, have been approved by this court in the following cases: *Polin v. State*, 14 Neb. 540; *Langford v. State*, 32 Neb. 782; *Lawhead v. State*, 46 Neb. 607.

The tenth instruction ennunciated that to warrant a conviction the guilt of the accused need not be established by direct evidence, but that the acts constituting the crime might be proven by circumstances and other competent testimony. The criticism made against this instruction is that there is no circumstantial evidence in the case. No witness testified to having seen the defendant embezzle the money or convert it to his own use. But many facts and circumstances are disclosed by the bill of exceptions from which the inference could be very properly drawn that the defendant committed the crime charged in this information. It was therefore not erroneous to instruct the jury on the law of circumstantial evidence.

By the eleventh paragraph of the charge the jury were told that if the defendant, as county treasurer, deposited in a depository bank, subject to check, moneys in excess of the amount allowed by law, that fact alone would not establish that he was guilty of the crime charged; but the depositing of county funds in the bank in violation of the law might be considered, in connection with all the other evidence adduced, for the purpose of ascertaining whether or not the defendant was guilty of the crime of embezzlement. This instruction was quite favorable to the accused, since it was established beyond dispute that the defendant had deposited in at least one of the depository banks county funds in excess of the statutory amount. The instruction fell far short of authorizing a verdict of guilty, in case the jury found that he had violated the depository law. On the contrary, the triers of fact were expressly cautioned that the mere depositing of public funds in violation of said law would not alone establish that the defendant embezzled the money, but that the fact of such illegal deposit of funds might be considered in arriving at a verdict. If the instruction was bad, it was not an error of which the prisoner had any ground to complain. (*Debney v. State*, 45 Neb. 856.)

In instruction No. 12 the court informed the jury that the presumption was that the defendant deposited the money of the county as required by the depository law, and unless they found beyond a reasonable doubt that he did not so deposit said moneys, "but converted the same to his own use or benefit as alleged," they should find him not guilty. The defendant has no substantial foundation for complaint in the giving of this instruction. It was clearly expressed that the presumption was the defendant had performed his duty as a treasurer. How the jury could have been misled by the failure to use the words "in the information," following the words "as alleged" in the latter part of the paragraph, we fail to comprehend. It was not relegated to the domain of conjecture to ascertain what the court intended, but that the jury, possessing ordinary intelligence, must have readily understood that the court had reference to

the charge of embezzlement set forth in the information.

The eighteenth instruction is excepted to, which is in
the language following: "You are instructed that if you
find from the evidence that Ezra S. Whitney, as treasurer of Harlan county, received a check from his predecessor for $7,000 on the State Bank of Republican City.
and that Mr. Whitney deposited the same in said bank,
and it was afterwards credited to Harlan county on open
account under the depository law as herein mentioned,
and the county of Harlan accepted a credit on its open
account for such amount against said bank, this made
the bank Harlan county's debtor for such sum, and
should be charged the same as if the sum had been received by the treasurer in money instead of a check, and
then deposited upon such account in said bank."

In January, 1892, the defendant received from his
predecessor, the former treasurer of Harlan county, a
check on the State Bank of Republican City for $7,000.
in lieu of cash, for that amount of county funds; this
bank was shortly thereafter designated as a county depository, and on January 11, 1892, the defendant surrendered said check to the bank and received credit as
treasurer for the amount thereof, on open account.
Other county funds were deposited in said depository
bank from time to time by this defendant, and which
sums were credited in like manner in the same accounts.
Checks were also drawn by the defendant against the
account aggregating more than $7,000, which were hon-
ored and paid by the said depository bank. At the close
of defendant's term as county treasurer he had a balance
to his credit in said bank, subject to check, of over
$1,500 in excess of the amount which the bank was enti-
tled to receive of county moneys under the depository
law. The theory of the defendant was that inasmuch as
no money was received from his predecessor in office,
but a check, and that the same was deposited the day
preceding the approval of the bond of the bank as a de-

pository of county funds, the amount of said $7,000 could not be taken into account. In the light of these contentions and the facts already detailed, the instruction we are now considering was timely and proper. If the contention of the defendant was sound, then the defendant did not have moneys of the county on deposit in the State Bank of Republican City at any one time in a sum in excess of $12,500, the limit allowed by the statute as a depository bank. The amount of the $7,000 check was not only deposited to the credit of the county on the account, but more than said sum was thereafter drawn by the defendant, as county treasurer, from said bank upon his checks against said account. Under the circumstances disclosed by this record the defendant was required to account to the county for said sum of $7,000 to the same extent as though he had received that sum in lawful money from his predecessor instead of by means of a bank check. (*State v. Hill*, 47 Neb. 456; *Bush v. Johnson County*, 48 Neb. 1.) The defendant concedes, under the cases cited, that he was liable on his bond for the amount of said check, but he argues that he is not guilty of the embezzlement thereof. A ready answer to this is that the state makes no claim to the contrary. This prosecution is not based upon the conversion of any portion of the moneys represented by said $7,000 check. The state gives him credit for the amount thereof on the accounting. The prosecution is for the embezzlement of other funds of Harlan county.

Instructions 19 to 24. inclusive. are assigned for error, but we fail to see anything in them which justifies comment. much less reversal.

Objection is made to paragraph 27 of the instructions, which reads: "You are instructed as a matter of law if the money or any part thereof mentioned in the information is shown by the evidence, beyond a reasonable doubt, to have been received by the defendant and by him appropriated to his own use and benefit, or that he, by his acts, deprived the county of Harlan of such money by the misappropriation of the same in manner and form as alleged, then he is guilty of the crime charged; and unless you do so find you should find him not guilty." Substantially the same criticism is offered upon the foregoing as was urged against the 11th paragraph of the instructions already alluded to, namely, that the omitting from the instructions the words "in the information" after the word "alleged" made the instruction misleading. Stated differently, it permitted the jury to return a verdict of guilty if the accused in any way misappropriated the money, whether it was converted to his own use or not. By the first paragraph of the charge the jury were explicitly advised of the acts which the information alleged the defendant had committed, or the manner of the conversion of the money. So the jury must have understood that the phrase in instruction 27, "in manner and form as alleged," had reference solely to the mode of conversion set forth in the information, and that there could be no conviction unless it was established beyond a reasonable doubt that the prisoner converted to his own use and benefit the moneys of Harlan county; that there should be an acquittal if the county was deprived of the money in any other manner.

The defendant asked a peremptory instruction to return a verdict of not guilty. It was conceded this request was presented upon the theory that section 124 of the Criminal Code had been repealed by the enactment of the depository law. As we have already determined adversely to this contention, the tendered instruction need not be further considered.

The defendant requested this instruction, which was refused:

"7. The jury are instructed that if you find from the evidence that an amount of money in excess of the amount allowed by law to be deposited in the State Bank of Republican City, Nebraska, the public money of Harlan county, was so deposited by the defendant, Ezra S. Whitney, in said bank, and that the board of super-

visors of said county requested additional security to secure the deposit of said sums, and afterwards accepted
additional security from said bank or its bondsmen to
secure the same, in such case the defendant could not be
guilty of embezzling such sums or any part thereof; unless you further find from the evidence, beyond a reasonable doubt, that the said defendant withdrew a part
of said moneys and converted the same to his own use."

This instruction lays down a monstrous doctrine. The
substance of it all is that if the defendant embezzled the
money of the county when he deposited in the bank an
amount in excess of the sum authorized by law, he is not
liable therefor criminally, in case the county authorities
subsequently accepted security for the sum so embezzled.
This is not, and never was, the law. The fact that a
person who has stolen money afterwards returns the
same to the owner, or gives security for its payment, will
not relieve him from criminal liability. So if the owner
of a stolen horse should follow the thief and recover the
horse, or payment of the value of the animal, it would
not defeat a criminal prosecution against the thief. The
same principle governs the case at bar. (*People v. Royce,*
106 Cal. 175; *Thalheim v. State,* 38 Fla. 169.) The criminal
law was not enacted for the purpose of enforcing civil
liabilities, as the instruction requested implies.
Whether or not Harlan county has been successful in
collecting or securing the payment of the money which
the defendant is charged with having embezzled is of
no consequence in this case. Two instructions requested
by the defendant were given, while the others refused
were fully covered by the charge of the court. It was
not error to decline to repeat those which were rejected.
(*Olive v. State,* 11 Neb. 1; *Korth v. State,* 46 Neb. 631.)

Another argument is that the verdict is without sufficient evidence to sustain it. The state established
beyond question that the defendant, at the close of his
official term, was chargeable with the sum $46,373.82, of
which $12,500 was lawfully on deposit in the State Bank

of Republican City, and for which last named sum the defendant is entitled to receive credit. When he turned the office over to his successor he had in his hands, exclusive of said bank deposit, the sum of $33,873.37, which was unaccounted for. The defendant has since paid on account thereof $17,653.33 to his successor in office, and to the state treasurer the further sum of $4,426.21. No other payments have been made by the defendant. The evidence shows that the amount of his shortage still existing is over $11,000, and that he is guilty of embezzlement of more than that amount of the moneys of Harlan county. Instead of there being a total lack of proof to sustain the finding of the jury, the evidence contained in the record is ample to support the verdict.

It is finally insisted that the court below erred in not suspending the sentence. The application in that regard was made after the return of the verdict and before judgment had been entered thereon, being based upon an alleged agreement between the defendant and the prosecuting officer whereby the former, in consideration that he was not to be prosecuted, was to testify on behalf of the prosecution in the case of the State against Benjamin D. Mills, then pending in the district court of Harlan county, for the embezzlement of the same money described in the information herein. The application was supported by affidavits, and resisted by counter-affidavits filed by the state. The counter-showing is sufficient to exonerate the county attorney from having made the agreement alluded to. It is undisputed, however, that some such arrangement was made by the accused with the attorney who was employed by the county as special counsel for the state in the two cases, and that thereafter Whitney, in pursuance thereof, testified on behalf of the state in the prosecution against Mills. In Texas an agreement to turn state's evidence made by the defendant with the prosecuting attorney alone is enforceable if the accused had testified thereunder in good faith. (*Bowden v. State*, 1 Tex. App. 137; *Hardin v. State*, 12 Tex.

Miles v. State.

App. 186; *Camron v. State*, 32 Tex. Crim. Rep. 180.) But this rule does not prevail generally elsewhere. The practice which usually obtains in case of a contract with a prisoner for immunity from prosecution for his offense, entered into with the prosecuting attorney, with the consent of the trial court, is to either enter a *nolle prosequi* or continue the cause to permit the defendant to apply for a pardon. The decided weight of authority sustains the doctrine that an agreement to turn state's evidence made with the prosecuting officer alone, without the court's advice or consent, affords the defendant no protection in the event he is placed on trial in violation of the agreement. (*United States v. Ford*, 99 U. S. 594; *State v. Graham*, 41 N. J. L. 15; *People v. Peter*, 48 Cal. 250; *State v. Lyon*, 81 N. Car. 600.) The rule last stated meets our approval. That the defendant kept his agreement and testified in the case against Mills to such facts as were within his knowledge constitutes no legal defense to this prosecution. The judgment of conviction is

AFFIRMED.

JOSEPH H. MILES ET AL. V. STATE OF NEBRASKA, EX REL. THOMAS McLANE.

FILED JANUARY 3, 1898.   No. 7609.

1. **Intoxicating Liquors:** REVOCATION OF LICENSE. A city council of a city of the second class having less than 5,000 inhabitants, when authorized by ordinance so to do, has the power to entertain a complaint for the revocation of a liquor dealer's license on the ground that he had sold intoxicating liquors to minors and habitual drunkards, and, upon due notice to the licensee of such proposed action, and proof that the complaint was true, to revoke such license, notwithstanding the holder thereof had not been convicted of the violation of the law pertaining to the sale of intoxicating liquors.

2. **Mandamus:** REVIEW OF ORDER REVOKING LICENSE. Mandamus will not lie to review the decision of a city council in revoking a liquor license, where it has not exceeded its jurisdiction, although such order may be clearly erroneous.

24

ERROR from the district court of Richardson County.
Tried below before BABCOCK, J. *Reversed.*

Edwin Falloon, for plaintiffs in error.

Isham Reavis, contra.

NORVAL, J.

On May 13, 1893, the relator, Thomas McLane, was
granted a license by the city of Falls City to sell malt,
spirituous, and vinous liquors for the municipal year,
which license was revoked and canceled by the mayor
and city council on March 24, 1894. Thereupon he instituted this action for mandamus to compel the respondents to restore said license, alleging in his application
as grounds therefor that relator had never been convicted of the violation of any law or ordinance, and therefore the revocation of the license was without authority
and void. The respondents answered the application,
alleging the passage, approval, and publication of ordinance No. 64 of the city of Falls City, entitled "An ordinance to regulate the license and sale of malt, spirituous,
and vinous liquors," etc., and that said ordinance contained among other provisions the following: "That
whenever it shall be brought to the notice of the city
council, by affidavit filed with the city clerk, or otherwise,
that any person holding a license or permit under the
provisions of this ordinance has violated any of the provisions of this ordinance, it shall be the duty of the city
to at once proceed and give such person not less than
three days', nor more than ten days', notice of the time
and place where said matters will be considered by said
city council, and if upon such hearing the council shall
be satisfied that a violation of this ordinance has been
committed by the person so charged, then the council
shall revoke, cancel, and annul the license held by such
party, and upon such hearing said council may examine

witnesses under oath in said matter, and may consider
such other evidence as may be offered by either party.
Every person licensed as herein provided who shall give
or sell any malt, spirituous, or vinous liquors, or any
intoxicating drinks, to any minors shall, upon conviction
thereof, be fined in any. sum not less than $25 nor more
than $100." That in addition to the above provisions
said ordinance prohibited, under fine, any licensed person
from selling to an habitual drunkard, keeping the bar
obstructed from the public view, and allowing his saloon
to remain open after 11 o'clock P. M.; that said city has
ordinances against gambling and houses of prostitution.
The answer further averred that on March 21, 1894, one
W. E. Noonan filed a complaint in writing under oath
with the city clerk of said city, charging, among other
things, substantially that relator knowingly, during the
existence of his license, sold intoxicating liquors to
habitual drunkards and to certain named minors; that
relator procured and permitted prostitutes to remain in
his saloon, on certain specified dates, where evil disposed
persons were permitted to resort to commit adultery and
fornication; that he obstructed the bar from public view;
permitted persons to become grossly intoxicated in his
place of business, and allowed the saloon to remain open
after 11 o'clock at night.   It is also alleged in the answer
that on March 21, 1894, notice was personally served on
relator to appear before the city council March 24, 1894,
at 8 o'clock P. M. and show cause why his license should
not be revoked; that at the appointed time he personally
appeared, a hearing was had, and upon a consideration
of the evidence the said city council found the charges
in said complaint of Noonan to be true, and by resolution
unanimously adopted, the ayes and noes being called,
revoked and annulled relator's license.   A general demurrer to this answer was filed, which the court below
sustained, and awarded a peremptory writ of mandamus
as prayed.   Respondents bring the case for review.

By section 25, chapter 50, Compiled Statutes, the power

to license, regulate, and prohibit the traffic in intoxicating liquors in cities of the class to which Falls City belongs is confided in the corporate authorities of all such cities, and in granting licenses they are required to comply with and observe all of the provisions of said act. Section 5 of said chapter declares that "Any license granted under this chapter may be revoked by the authority issuing the same whenever the person licensed shall, upon due proof made, be convicted of a violation of any of the provisions of this act." The contention of relator is that, under the provision just quoted, respondents had the power to revoke his license upon the single ground that relator had violated some provisions of said act, and not then until there had been first a conviction in some court of competent jurisdiction. The legislature has made the conviction of the licensee of any violation of the laws of the state pertaining to the sale of intoxicating liquors a sufficient ground for a revocation of the license, and it is made the imperative duty of the body or board which granted the license to annul the same, when the fact of such conviction is duly certified to it, without giving notice of such proposed action to the licensee. (*Martin v. State*, 23 Neb. 371.) But the above provision of said section 5 does not preclude the proper city or village authorities from revoking a liquor license upon other sufficient grounds. The statutes have empowered cities of the second class having less than 5,000 inhabitants, in their corporate capacities, to enact ordinances licensing, regulating, and prohibiting the sale of any intoxicating liquors. (Compiled Statutes, ch. 14, art. 1, sec. 69.) In pursuance of the power thereby conferred ordinance No. 64 of the city of Falls City was adopted, which provides, in effect, that when an affidavit is filed with the city clerk charging that a licensed liquor dealer has violated any of the provisions of said ordinance, not less than three nor more than ten days' notice shall be given to the licensee of the time and place where the complaint will be investigated, and if the city council upon such hearing "shall be satisfied that a violation of this ordinance has been committed by the person so charged, then the council shall revoke, cancel, and annul the license held by such party." The provision conferred power upon the city council to revoke a liquor license upon charges preferred, was ample authority for the proceedings taken to cancel relator's license, and justified the revocation of his license without the prior conviction of the licensee.

We do not perceive anything in *Martin v. State, supra,* in conflict with the conclusion already expressed. In that case the license was revoked without a hearing before the council, on the ground that the licensee had been convicted before a police magistrate of selling intoxicating liquors on Sunday in violation of law. There was no necessity for a trial in that case. All the city council had to do was to revoke the license in obedience to the positive requirements of the law. Here there had been no prior conviction of relator of the commission of any offense whatever, so his license could be forfeited only upon a charge duly made and established by the proofs that he had broken some condition or restriction upon which the license was issued. The city council having been given jurisdiction by said ordinance over proceedings to revoke licenses to liquor dealers, and the complaint to the council being sufficient, its decision cannot be reviewed by mandamus. (*State v. Laflin,* 40 Neb. 441; *State v. Cotton,* 33 Neb. 560.)

The judgment of the district court is reversed and the action dismissed.

REVERSED AND DISMISSED.

JOSEPH S. BARTLEY V. STATE OF NEBRASKA.

FILED JANUARY 3, 1898. No. 9347.

1. **Indictment and Information:** MOTION TO QUASH. On a motion to quash an information, the district court will not inquire into the validity of the warrant of arrest issued by the examining magistrate.

2. **Criminal Law:** ABATEMENT: EMBEZZLEMENT. In a prosecution for the crime of embezzlement, the pendency against the accused of a former information in the district court of another county charging him with the embezzlement of the same property within that county, is no ground for abatement.

3. ————: INFORMATION: DEMURRER TO COUNT. Error cannot be predicated upon the overruling of a demurrer to a count in the information, where a *nolle prosequi* is subsequently entered to such count.

4. ————: ————: CAPTION: VENUE. An information, in the caption and venue of which a given county and state are named, which charges that the defendant "in the county aforesaid, then and there being in said county," did commit a given crime, sufficiently alleges that the offense was committed in the county stated in the caption and venue.

5. ————: ————: VENUE. The place of the commission of an offense charged in one of the counts of the information is sufficiently set forth by averment that the defendant, "in the county aforesaid," did commit the acts constituting the offense, when in a former count the county and state are definitely stated.

6. ————: ————: ELECTION AS TO COUNTS. An election by the prosecutor to proceed alone under one count does not so far take the other counts out of the information as to destroy the effect of a reference to them as to time and place.

7. **County Attorney:** RIGHT TO INSTITUTE CRIMINAL PROCEEDING. A county attorney of the proper county may institute a criminal proceeding against a state treasurer for the embezzlement of the moneys of the state, notwithstanding such prosecutor had received no direction from the auditor of public accounts to take such step.

8. **Embezzlement:** INFORMATION. An information for embezzlement is sufficient if it sets forth the crime in the language of the statute creating it, without averring the particular acts in which the offense consisted.

9. ————: ————: STATE TREASURER. An indictment against a state treasurer, which charges the embezzlement to his own use of a certain sum of money belonging to the state, is sufficient without

an allegation that a demand for the money was made upon him by his successor in office.

10. **Information:** ELECTION AS TO COUNTS. Where different felonies of the same general character or grade are charged in different counts of an information, it is within the discretion of the trial court to require the prosecutor to elect as to counts. (*Korth v. State,* 46 Neb. 632.)

11. ———: ———. No election is required between counts charging the same offense.

12. **Jury:** CHALLENGE: REVIEW. Error cannot be predicated upon the overruling of a challenge to a juror for cause, where the record fails to disclose that the complaining party exhausted his peremptory challenges.

13. **Embezzlement:** CONVICTION: EVIDENCE. The evidence in the case is sufficient to sustain a conviction for the embezzlement of the moneys of the state.

14. **Negotiable Instruments:** WARRANTS. Warrants drawn by the auditor of public accounts upon the state treasury are not negotiable instruments.

15. **Banks and Banking:** PAYMENT OF CHECK: CREDIT. The giving of credit as a deposit for the amount of a check, by the bank upon which it is drawn, is, in contemplation of law, a payment of the check in money, to the same extent as though the currency had been paid over the counter on the check and immediately redeposited by the payee.

16. **Embezzlement:** EVIDENCE: STATE TREASURER. A state treasurer who, for an unauthorized purpose, draws a check on a state depository bank having money of the state therein, which he delivers to the payee with intent to defraud the state, and the bank on presentation of the check places the amount thereof to the credit of a third party whom the payee represents in the transaction, and at the same time charges the account of the state with a like sum, is guilty of the embezzlement of the money of the state, within the meaning of section 124 of the Criminal Code.

17. **Evidence:** EMBEZZLEMENT: CORRESPONDENCE. Where a state treasurer employed a bank to negotiate the sale of a warrant which was the property of the state, the correspondence of such bank necessary to effect such sale is admissible in evidence in a prosecution of the treasurer for embezzlement of the amount subsequently used to take up such warrant, where there exists such a relation between the sale and the payment of the warrant that the motive in the latter transaction is illustrated by the facts incident to the former.

18. **Officer:** EMBEZZLEMENT: ESTOPPEL. In a prosecution for embezzlement, one who has filled out his entire term of office cannot be

heard to urge as a defense that when the embezzlement took place he was not an officer *de jure*. It is immaterial in such case whether he was an officer *de jure* or *de facto*.

19. **Evidence:** EXPERT ACCOUNTANT: BOOKS. In a prosecution for embezzlement or other crime, where the books, records, papers, and entries are voluminous and of such a character as to render it difficult for the jury to arrive at a correct conclusion as to amounts, an expert accountant may be allowed to examine such books, etc., and testify as to the result of his examination, when such books, etc., are in the court room subject to inspection by the accused.

20. **Instructions:** CONSTRUCTION. Instructions must be construed together, and if then they correctly announce the rule applicable to the issues and evidence, they will be upheld, even though a single paragraph, standing alone, might be faulty.

21. ———: REASONABLE DOUBT. *Held,* That the instruction defining a reasonable doubt did not deny to the accused the benefit of a reasonable doubt arising from the lack of evidence in the case, and that it was not error to state in such instruction: "You are not at liberty to disbelieve as jurors if from all the evidence you believe as men. Your oath imposes on you no obligation to doubt where no doubt would exist if no oath had been administered."

22. ———: ———. The court charged the jury that: "The law raises no presumption against the defendant. On the contrary, the presumption of law is in favor of his innocence. This presumption of innocence continues through the trial until every material allegation in the information is established by the evidence to the exclusion of all reasonable doubt." *Held,* Equivalent to the rule that the presumption of innocence is a matter of evidence, to the benefit of which the accused is entitled.

23. **Embezzlement:** MONEY: FINDING OF VALUE. In case of conviction under an information charging the embezzlement of money, a verdict finding the amount of money embezzled to be a specified number of dollars is a sufficient finding of value.

ERROR to the district court for Douglas county. Tried below before BAKER, J. *Affirmed.*

The facts are stated in the opinion.

Charles O. Whedon and *T. J. Mahoney,* for plaintiff in error:

The warrant under which the arrest was made was invalid and the information should have been quashed.

(*Rafferty v. People*, 69 Ill. 111; *Garcia v. Sanders*, 35 S. W. Rep. [Tex.] 52.)

The plea in abatement should have been sustained on the ground that another criminal action charging defendant with the same offense was pending in another county. (*State v. North Lincoln S. R. Co.*, 34 Neb. 634; *Monroe v. Reid*, 46 Neb. 331; *Gamsby v. Ray*, 52 N. H. 513; *Commonwealth v. Churchill*, 5 Mass. 174; *Coaldale Brick & Tile Co. v. Southern Construction Co.*, 19 So. Rep. [Ky.] 45; *Parker v. Colcord*, 2 N. H. 36; *Demond v. Crary*, 1 Fed. Rep. 480; *Curtis v. Piedmont Lumber, Ranch & Mining Co.*, 13 S. E. Rep. [N. Car.] 944.)

The information fails to allege that the warrant was lawfully issued or that it was of any value, and is therefore insufficient. (*State v. Babcock*, 22 Neb. 38; *State v. Moore*, 37 Neb. 507.)

The information is defective in failing to allege that the warrant was issued upon a proper voucher. (*State v. Moore*, 36 Neb. 579; *Moore v. Garneau*, 39 Neb. 511.)

The count upon which defendant was convicted does not mention the county wherein the crime was alleged to have been committed, and the count naming the county was abandoned. The state and county are mentioned in the caption, but the caption is no part of the information. The information is therefore insufficient, and will not support a conviction. (*People v. Jewett*, 3 Wend. [N. Y.] 319; *State v. McCarty*, 54 Am. Dec. [Wis.] 150; *Commonwealth v. Stone*, 3 Gray [Mass.] 453; *Rose v. State*, 1 Ala. 28; *State v. Freeman*, 21 Mo. 481; *Mitchell v. State*, 8 Yerg. [Tenn.] 514; *English v. State*, 4 Tex. 125; *Allen v. State*, 5 Wis. 329; *State v. Emmett*, 23 Wis. 632; *McCoy v. State*, 22 Neb. 418.)

An information must charge explicitly all that is essential to constitute an offense and cannot be aided by intendment. (*Smith v. State*, 21 Neb. 552; *Commonwealth v. Smart*, 6 Gray [Mass.] 15.)

Whatever is to be proven must be pleaded in the information. (*State v. Hebel*, 72 Ind. 361; *State v. Hayes*, 78 Mo. 307.)

The manner in which the money was used should have been stated for the purpose of showing whether the use was illegal. The charge that defendant converted the money to his own use was a legal conclusion rather than a statement of fact. (*State v. Brandt*, 41 Ia. 593; *State v. Parsons*, 54 Ia. 405; *Hoyt v. State*, 50 Ga. 313.)

No demand is alleged in the information, and for that reason it fails to show an improper neglect or refusal to pay. (*State v. Munch*, 22 Minn. 67; *Bolln v. State*, 51 Neb. 581.)

The indictment contained several counts for the same act and the prosecuting attorney should have been compelled to elect. (*State v. Lawrence*, 19 Neb. 307; *Aiken v. State*, 41 Neb. 263; *Blodgett v. State*, 50 Neb. 121.)

Challenges to jurors having opinions as to defendant's guilt should have been sustained. (*Curry v. State*, 4 Neb. 545; *Carroll v. State*, 5 Neb. 31; *Olive v. State*, 11 Neb. 1; *Cowan v. State*, 22 Neb. 519; *Miller v. State*, 29 Neb. 437; *Owens v. State*, 32 Neb. 167.)

The misconduct of the prosecuting attorney in referring, in presence of jurors, to attempts at bribery is ground for reversal. (*Thompson v. People*, 4 Neb. 531.)

References to error in the conduct of the trial judge in asking questions and in making remarks during the trial: *State v. Harkin*, 7 Nev. 377; *State v. Ah Tong*, 7 Nev. 148; *Hudson v. Hudson*, 16 S. E. Rep. [Ga.] 349; *Fager v. State*, 22 Neb. 340; *Chicago, R. I. & P. R. Co. v. Archer*, 46 Neb. 914.

The evidence was insufficient to sustain a verdict against defendant, and the motion to direct a verdict in his favor was erroneously overruled. (*State v. McFetridge*, 84 Wis. 473; *State v. Hill*, 47 Neb. 456; *Suydan v. Merrick County*, 19 Neb. 159; *Miller v. Wheeler*, 33 Neb. 765; *Miller v. State*, 16 Neb. 179; *Commonwealth v. Shepard*, 83 Mass. 575; *Hamilton v. State*, 60 Ind. 193; *Pryor v. Commonwealth*, 2 Dana [Ky.] 298; *Garner v. State*, 5 Yerg. [Tenn.] 160; *Thalheim v. State*, 20 So. Rep. [Fla.] 938; *Commonwealth v. Merrifield*, 4 Met. [Mass.] 468;

Lewis v. State, 28 Tex. App. 140; *Commonwealth v. Howe*, 132 Mass. 250; *Carr v. State*, 16 So. Rep. [Ala.] 155; *Territory v. Marinez*. 44 Pac. Rep. [Ariz.] 1089; *Queen v. Brady*, 26 U. Can. Q. B. 13; *Tucker v. State*, 16 Ala. 670; *Lindsay v. State*, 19 Ala. 560; *State v. Copp*, 15 N. H. 212; *State v. McDonald*, 24 Pac. Rep. [Mont.] 628; *Turley v. State*, 3 Humph. [Tenn.] 323; *Jordt v. State*, 31 Tex. 571; *Banks v. State*, 28 Tex. 644; *Johnson v. State*, 11 O. St. 324.)

The state treasurer's bond, not having been approved within the time fixed by statute, was erroneously admitted in evidence. (*State v. Lansing*, 46 Neb. 514.)

The treasury warrant introduced in evidence was different from that copied in the information and should have been excluded. (*State v. Owen*, 73 Mo. 440; *Sharley r. State*, 54 Ind. 168; *Haslip v. State*, 10 Neb. 590; *Prehm r. State*, 22 Neb. 676; *Williams v. People*, 101 Ill. 382.)

The depository bond of the Omaha National Bank was erroneously admitted in evidence. It was not executed according to the requirements of statute. (*Richardson r. Woodruff*, 20 Neb. 137; *Reed v. Merriam*, 15 Neb. 325; *Sutton v. Stone*, 4 Neb. 319; *Hendrix v. Boggs*, 15 Neb. 469; *Baldwin v. Merriam*, 16 Neb. 199; *Shelley v. Towle*, 16 Neb. 194; *Sullivan v. Merriam*, 16 Neb. 157; *Seaman v. Thompson*, 16 Neb. 546; *Bendexen v. Fenton*, 21 Neb. 184; *Gue r. Jones*, 25 Neb. 634; *Adler v. Green*, 18 W. Va. 201; *Easton r. Ormsby*, 27 Atl. Rep. [R. I.] 218; *Williams v. State*, 6 L. R. A. [Fla.] 821; *Chilton v. People*, 66 Ill. 501.)

Because the jury did not ascertain and declare in their verdict the value of the property embezzled, the court had no authority to render a judgment. (*Armstrong r. State*, 21 O. St. 357; *Highland v. People*, 1 Scam. [Ill.] 391; *Sawyer v. People*, 3 Gil. [Ill.] 54; *Tobin v. People*, 104 Ill. 565; *Thompson v. People*, 125 Ill. 256; *Shines v. State*, 42 Miss. 331; *Ray v. State*, 1 G. Greene [Ia.] 316; *State r. Redman*, 17 Ia. 329; *Locke v. State*, 32 N. H. 106; *McCoy r. State*, 22 Neb. 418; *McCormick r. State*, 42 Neb. 866; *Fox v. Phelps*, 17 Wend. [N. Y.] 400; *State v. Doepke*, 5 Mo. App. 590; *Cannon v. State*, 18 Tex. App. 172.)

The seventeenth instruction was erroneous because it gave undue prominence to the testimony of one class of witnesses. (*Markel v. Swobe*, 11 Neb. 213; *Kersenbrock v. Martin*, 12 Neb. 376; *City of Lincoln v. Beckman*, 23 Neb. 677; *First Nat. Bank of Denver v. Lowrey*, 36 Neb. 290; *Rising v. Nash*, 48 Neb. 597.)

By the twenty-first instruction the jury was told that a reasonable doubt must be one arising from a candid and impartial investigation of all the evidence in the case. This is not a correct statement of the law. A doubt may arise from want of evidence. (*Carr v. State*, 23 Neb. 749; *Cowan v. State*, 22 Neb. 519; *Childs v. State*, 34 Neb. 236; *Garrison v. People*, 6 Neb. 274; *Long v. State*, 23 Neb. 33.)

C. J. Smyth, Attorney General, and *Ed P. Smith, Deputy Attorney General*, for the state:

The warrant of arrest contained a sufficient recital of the substance of the offense. (*State v. Hallback*, 18 S. E. Rep. [S. Car.] 919; *Gay v. De Werff*, 17 Ill. App. 417; *Murphey v. State*, 55 Ala. 252; *Rhodes v. King*, 52 Ala. 272; *Jennings v. State*, 13 Kan. 80.)

If the warrant of arrest was defective accused should have moved to quash it before proceeding further. He waived any defect in the warrant. (*Redmond v. State*, 12 Kan. 138; *Alderman v. State*, 24 Neb. 97; *State v. Downs*, 8 Ind. 42.)

The pendency of an information in one court is no ground for a plea in abatement to another information in the same court, or another court of concurrent jurisdiction, for the same cause. (*Commonwealth v. Drew*, 3 Cush. [Mass.] 282; *Hardin v. State*, 22 Ind. 349; *Commonwealth v. Murphy*, 11 Cush. [Mass.] 472; *Commonwealth v. Berry*, 5 Gray [Mass.] 93; *O'Meara v. State*, 17 O. St. 87; *Smith v. Commonwealth*, 104 Pa. St. 339; *Eldridge v. State*, 9 So. Rep. [Fla.] 448; *Commonwealth v. Cody*, 42 N. E. Rep. [Mass.] 575.)

The reference in the third count of the information to the county already named in the first count and in the caption sufficiently designated the county wherein the offense was committed, though a conviction under the first count was abandoned. (*Rema v. State*, 52 Neb. 375; *Smith v. State*, 21 Neb. 552; *Moore v. Fedewa*, 13 Neb. 379; *Alderman v. State*, 24 Neb. 97; *Mount v. State*, 14 O. 295; *State v. McKee*, 1 Bailey [S. Car.] 651; *United States v. Farring*, 4 Cranch [U. S. C. C.] 465; *United States v. Shoemaker*, 2 McLain [U. S.] 114; *Reynolds v. State*, 3 Kelly [Ga.] 53; *Commonwealth v. Wade*, 17 Pick. [Mass.] 395; *Evans v. State*, 24 O. St. 209; *Fisk v. State*, 9 Neb. 63; *Boles v. State*, 13 Tex. App. 650; *Hutto v. State*, 7 Tex. App. 44; *Wills v. State*, 8 Mo. 45; *Commonwealth v. Clapp*, 16 Gray [Mass.] 237; *Phillips v. Fielding*, 2 H. Bl. [Eng.] 131; *Rex v. Dent*, 1 C. & K. [Eng.] 249; *United States v. Hendric*, 2 Sawyer [U. S.] 477; *State v. Nelson*, 29 Me. 329; *State v. McAllister*, 26 Me. 374.)

The information alleges all the statutory ingredients of the offense charged, and the objection that it does not state the facts showing the alleged conversion is without merit. (*Whitman v. State*, 17 Neb. 224; *Smith v. State*, 4 Neb. 277; *Wagner v. State*, 43 Neb. 5; *Hodgkins v. State*, 36 Neb. 160; *State v. Jamison*, 74 Ia. 602; *Claassen v. United States*, 142 U. S. 140; *Hoyt v. State*, 50 Ga. 313; *Gibbs v. State*, 41 Tex. 491; *Reed v. McRill*, 41 Neb. 207; *Sanford v. Jensen*, 49 Neb. 766.)

Before resting its case the state elected as to counts. There was therefore no prejudicial error in the order overruling accused's motion to require plaintiff to elect. (*Korth v. State*, 46 Neb. 631.)

Accused's peremptory challenges not having been exhausted, error, if any, in overruling challenges to jurors was without prejudice. (*Brumback v. German Nat. Bank of Beatrice*, 46 Neb. 540; *Jenkins v. Mitchell*, 40 Neb. 664.)

References in reply to charges of misconduct on part of the prosecuting attorney: *Vaughn v. Crites*, 44 Neb. 812; *Gandy v. State*, 13 Neb. 445; *Hoover v. State*, 48 Neb. 184.

The motion to direct a verdict for defendant was properly overruled. (*State v. Harwood*, 36 Kan. 237; *Stevens v. Parks*, 73 Ill. 388; *Oddie v. National City Bank of New York*, 45 N. Y. 735; *State v. Krug*, 12 Wash. 288; *People v. McKinney*, 10 Mich. 54; *Commonwealth v. Moore*, 44 N. E. Rep. [Mass.] 613; *People v. Bringard*, 39 Mich. 22; *State v. Baumhager*, 28 Minn. 226; *State v. Palmer*, 40 Kan. 474.)

The official bond was competent evidence. (*Commonwealth v. Logue*, 160 Mass. 551; *State v. Goss*, 69 Me. 22; *State v. Minns*, 26 Minn. 183.)

Admission of the treasury warrant in evidence was not prejudicial error. (*Davis v. State*, 51 Neb. 301.)

There was no error in admitting in evidence certain pages of the book of account of the Omaha National Bank. (*Bunker v. Shed*, 49 Mass. 150; *Nicholls v. Webb*, 8 Wheat. [U. S.] 326; *Nourse v. McCay*, 2 Rawle [Pa.] 70; *Mathias v. O'Neill*, 94 Mo. 520; *Imhoff v. Richards*, 48 Neb. 590; *Larabee v. Klosterman*, 33 Neb. 150.)

There was no error in admitting the depository bond in evidence. (*Luce v. Foster*, 42 Neb. 818.)

The books, records, and other public documents kept in the office of the state treasurer, and the official statement filed by him with the auditor of public accounts are competent evidence to prove the receipts and disbursements of such officer. (*State v. Ring*, 29 Minn. 78; *Humphrey v. People*, 18 Hun [N. Y.] 393; *People v. Flock*, 59 N. W. Rep. [Mich.] 237; *Stanley v. State*, 88 Ala. 154; *Osborne v. State*, 27 N. E. Rep. [Ind.] 345; *Strong v. State*, 75 Ind. 440; *Coleman v. Commonwealth*, 25 Gratt. [Va.] 865.)

It was proper to permit the expert accountant to testify to the result of his examination of the books of the state treasury. (*State v. Findley*, 101 Mo. 217; *Hollingsworth v. State*, 111 Ind. 289; *Masonic Mutual Benefit Society v. Lackland*, 97 Mo. 138.)

The statement in the verdict of the amount of money embezzled was a·sufficient finding as to value. (*State v. Hood*, 51 Me. 363; *Cook v. State*, 49 Miss. 8; *State v. White*, 25 Wis. 359; *Schoonover v. State*, 17 O. St. 294; *Smith v.*

State, 60 Ga. 430; *Commonwealth v. Butler*, 144 Pa. St. 568; *State v. Knox*, 17 Neb. 683; *Gady v. State*, 83 Ala. 51.)

Other references: *Norris v. State*, 25 O. St. 217; *Connor v. State*, 29 Fla. 455; *Commonwealth v. Taylor*, 105 Mass. 172; *Commonwealth v. Wood*, 142 Mass. 459; *Commonwealth v. Karpowski*, 167 Pa. St. 225; *State v. Moore*, 50 Neb. 88; *Willis v. State*, 43 Neb. 102; *Roberts v. People*, 9 Colo. 458; *Hemingway v. State*, 8 So. Rep. [Miss.] 317; *State v. Cowan*, 74 Ia. 53.

NORVAL, J.

The defendant, Joseph S. Bartley, was convicted in the district court of Douglas county of embezzlement of moneys belonging to the state while he was the treasurer thereof. Besides a fine in double the amount found by the jury to have been embezzled, a term of twenty years in the penitentiary was the punishment imposed, and to obtain a reversal of said judgment and sentence is the purpose of this proceeding.

The information filed in the court below by the county attorney was in eight counts, the first and second of which charged the embezzlement of a certain warrant, drawn by the auditor of public accounts upon the state treasury for the sum of $180,101.75. The remaining six counts set forth, in different forms, the embezzlement on the 2d day of January, 1897, of $201,884.05 of the moneys belonging to the state, which defendant received by virtue of his said office of state treasurer. At the close of the testimony for the state, the county attorney entered a *nolle prosequi* as to the first two counts of the information, and upon the trial the accused was found guilty under the third count, but was acquitted as to all the other counts upon which the prosecutor elected to rely for a conviction.

At this time it is not deemed essential to mention the various pleas, motions, and demurrers filed preceding the selection of the jury, or to give a history of the trial, or any statement of the facts revealed by the record.

Such matters will be stated as we proceed with the investigation of the grounds urged for a reversal, at least so far as the same may seem necessary to an understanding of the propositions argued.

The first contention made in the brief of counsel for the accused is that the information under which the conviction was obtained should have been quashed, because of the alleged invalidity of the warrant on which the arrest was made. The original complaint was filed with the police judge of the city of Omaha, and the warrant in question was issued thereon, which recited that a complaint had been made under oath before said judge charging that "Joseph S. Bartley, on or about the 25th day of April, A. D. 1895, within said county and within the city of Omaha, did commit the offense of embezzlement." The argument is that the warrant of arrest does not recite the substance of the accusation against the prisoner as required by section 288 of the Criminal Code, and therefore is void. The warrant of arrest was not assailed before the magistrate, but the defendant waived a preliminary examination, and entered into a recognizance for his appearance in the district court to answer the charges preferred against him in the complaint. Objection to the sufficiency of said warrant was made for the first time in the trial court after the filing of the information therein by the county attorney. The question with which we have to deal is not whether the warrant of arrest should have been quashed on a proper objection before the magistrate, but whether the defects in said warrant have been waived by the failure to seasonably take advantage of the same. There is no room for doubt that if the warrant of arrest was bad, the defect was not available to the defendant after he waived his preliminary examination, and had entered into a recognizance for his appearance in the district court. He was not thereafter held by the writ, as that instrument had already performed its office, but stood upon his recognizance. Whether this warrant of arrest was good or bad was not a proper subject of inquiry in the district court. (*Alderman v. State*, 24 Neb. 97; *State v. Downs*, 8 Ind. 42; *Williams v. State*, 88 Ala. 80; *State v. Stredder*, 3 Kan. App. 631; *State r. McManus*, 4 Kan. App. 247.)

In the first case cited this court decided that the district court, upon a motion to quash an information, will not inquire into the validity of the complaint upon which the preliminary examination before the magistrate was had, the crime alleged being the same. The court in the opinion say: "We know of no rule of law which would entitle a person accused of a crime to attack the complaint upon which his preliminary examination was had, after the return of the indictment or information. So far as the power of the court to hold its jurisdiction over him is concerned, the complaint had served its purpose, and could not then be made the subject of attack." It follows from the doctrine enunciated in that case that the defects in this warrant, which might have been fatal if seasonably presented before the magistrate, but which were not there raised, are not available in the district court on motion to quash the information. The two cases cited by counsel for the accused are not in point. They tend to support the proposition that the warrant is fatally defective, but have no bearing whatever upon the question whether such objection can be urged for the first time on motion to quash the information.

The record discloses that the defendant was arraigned before the county court of Lancaster county on the 19th day of April, 1897, upon a complaint charging the accused with the embezzlement of the same auditor's warrant and identical moneys mentioned in the information herein; that the defendant waived examination and entered into a recognizance for his appearance before the district court of said county at the next term thereof; that a transcript of the proceedings was lodged in the office of the clerk of said court on the following day, where on May 27 the information was filed by the county attorney, who on the same day entered a *nolle prosequi;*

25

that the transcript of the proceedings before the police judge of the city of Omaha was filed in the district court of Douglas county on April 29, and that the information upon which the accused was tried was filed therein by the county attorney on May 15. A plea in abatement was filed on May 27, the county attorney replied thereto, and the plea in abatement was overruled by the trial court, which decision we are called upon to review.

In civil cases the rule is that the pendency of a former suit between the same parties may be pleaded in abatement where the judgment in such action would be a bar to a judgment in the second suit brought in another court of concurrent jurisdiction. (*State v. North Lincoln S. R. Co.*, 34 Neb. 634; *Monroe v. Reid*, 46 Neb. 316.) The attorney general argues that this doctrine is not extended to prosecution for crimes. A former indictment or information pending in the same court for the same criminal offense constitutes no ground of abatement. In *O'Meara v. State*, 17 O. St. 515, Welch, J., observed: "It is insisted, in the first place, that the indictment under which the defendant was convicted is a nullity because of the pendency of a former indictment for the same offense, at the time it was found. We know of no such law. The last indictment is as valid as the first. Two indictments for the same offense are often pending at the same time. The state can only proceed upon one of them, but may elect upon which it will proceed. Of course, the right of election implies that both are good and lawful indictments." Chief Justice Shaw, in delivering the opinion of the court in *Commonwealth v. Drew*, 57 Mass. 279, used this language: "It appears to us to be a settled rule of law, that the pendency of one indictment is no good plea in abatement to another indictment for the same cause. Whenever either of them—and it is immaterial which— is tried, and a judgment rendered on it, such judgment will afford a good plea in bar to the other, either of *autrefois convict* or *autrefois acquit*. But where it is found that there is some mistake in an indictment, as a wrong name or addition, or the like, and the grand jury can be again appealed to, as there can be no amendment of an indictment by the court, the proper course is for the grand jury to return a new indictment, avoiding the defects in the first; and it is no good ground of abatement, that the former has not been actually discontinued, when the latter is returned." The authorities are quite uniform in holding that the pendency of a former indictment for the same offense in the same court is no ground for abatement. (Wharton, Criminal Pl. & Pr. sec. 452; *Dutton v. State*, 5 Ind. 533; *Hardin v. State*, 22 Ind. 347; *Smith v. Commonwealth*, 104 Pa. St. 339; *Commonwealth v. Murphy*, 65 Mass. 472; *Commonwealth v. Berry*, 71 Mass. 93; *Commonwealth v. Cody*, 42 N. E. Rep. [Mass.] 575; *Eldridge v. State*, 9 So. Rep. [Fla.] 448; *State v. Security Bank*, 51 N. W. Rep. [S. Dak.] 337; *State v. Curtis*, 29 Kan. 386; *State v. Hastings*, 86 N. Car. 596; *State v. Lambert*, 9 Nev. 321; *Bailey v. State*, 11 Tex. App. 140.)

Counsel for the accused insist the doctrine that a former indictment in the same court is no ground for abatement is not applicable to prosecutions for the same offense in two courts having concurrent jurisdiction thereof. We think this is true. Undoubtedly, where two courts have concurrent jurisdiction of a crime, the court first obtaining jurisdiction acquires exclusive control to the exclusion of the other. (Wharton, Criminal Pl. & Pr. sec. 452, and cases there cited.) It logically follows that the pendency of a prior indictment or information in another court having jurisdiction of the identical offense may be pleaded in abatement of the second prosecution. (See 1 Wharton, Criminal Law sec. 521; *State v. Tisdale*, 2 Dev. & Bat. [N. Car.] 160.) The justices and district courts have concurrent-jurisdiction of misdemeanors committed in their respective counties. Therefore, if an indictment should be returned by the grand jury to the district court charging the defendant with an assault and battery and during the pendency thereof, and before trial, the defendant should be arrested upon a complaint filed before a justice of the peace of the same county charging him with the commission of the identical offense, there is no reason why the pendency of the indictment should not be ground for abating the prosecution before the justice. Both tribunals have concurrent jurisdiction of the same criminal act. The complaint and information filed against Bartley in Lancaster county charged the crime of embezzlement as does the information herein, but the same criminal acts were not alleged. The jurisdiction of the district courts of Lancaster and Douglas counties is not concurrent in criminal actions, in such a sense as to give each original jurisdiction over offenses committed in either county. It is clear the pendency of the criminal action against the defendant in the Lancaster district court was not a bar to this prosecution. Manifestly this is true, both upon reason and authority. Neither a conviction nor acquittal of the offense charged in one information would have constituted a bar to the prosecution under the other information, since in one the venue was laid in Douglas county, while in the other the offense is stated to have been committed in Lancaster county. This being true, unquestionably the fact that an information was pending against the accused in Lancaster county for the embezzlement of the same auditor's warrant and moneys of the state described in the information herein would not abate this prosecution. The authorities cited by counsel for the defendant are easily distinguishable. All are civil cases except *Commonwealth v. Churchill*, 5 Mass. 174, which last case states that the pendency of a prior information or indictment for a crime will not abate a subsequent prosecution for the same offense.

It is argued that the court below erred in not sustaining the demurrer interposed to the first count of the information, which charged the embezzlement by the defendant of a certain warrant drawn by the auditor of public accounts upon the state treasury. This ruling is not available, since it was not prejudicial to the rights of the accused, owing to the fact that the county attorney at the close of the state's testimony entered a *nolle prosc- qui* as to the first and second counts of the information. (*Davis v. State*, 51 Neb. 301.)

It is suggested, if the demurrer had been sustained, no evidence in support of the first count of the information would have been adduced. Doubtless this is true; but the admission of the testimony with respect to the warrant was equally competent to establish the charge contained in the count of the information under which the conviction was had, since the embezzlement of the moneys therein mentioned is predicated upon the fact that the accused paid said warrant out of the moneys belonging to the state. The facts surrounding the issuance of this warrant, and the disposition thereof by the defendant, were admissible to show the guilty intent of the accused in the commission of the crime of embezzling the money which was used to pay the warrant, as will hereafter more fully appear. (*Commonwealth v. Shepard*, 83 Mass. 575.)

It is strenuously insisted that the third count of the information,—the one upon which the accused was convicted,—is fatally defective, inasmuch as the county and state in which the embezzlement was committed are not mentioned in said count. It is therein averred: "That the said Joseph S. Bartley, on the 2d day of January, A. D. 1897, in the county aforesaid, then and there being in said county," etc. These words unquestionably referred to the county of Douglas named in the venue at the top of the information, and set forth in the first count thereof. This is conceded by counsel for the accused, but they argue that such reference is not permissible, because the venue—"The State of Nebraska, County of Douglas, ss."—is no part of the information, and that, the prosecutor having entered a *nolle* as to the first count, such count cannot be considered for any purpose, but the information must be treated precisely the same as though the first count never had been inserted.

Whether the caption is or is not a part of an information, it is unnecessary to determine. The venue given at the top of this information, it is very evident, was made a part thereof by reference had thereto in the third count of the information. This doctrine was recognized and applied, with respect to a criminal complaint before a justice of the peace, in *Rema v. State*, 52 Neb. 379. (See *Rivers v. State*, 144 Ind. 16; *State v. Assmann*, 46 S. Car. 554.) Moreover, the third count of the information with sufficient particularity designates the county where the offense charged was committed, when read in connection with the first count of the information, where it is specifically alleged that the offense therein described was committed in the county of Douglas, in the state of Nebraska, no other county being referred to in the information. In the third count the averment is "In the county aforesaid, then and there being in said county." This clearly indicates that the embezzlement stated in said count was committed in the same county mentioned in the first count, to-wit, Douglas county, in this state. It was unnecessary that the venue should have been therein more distinctly laid. Where an information contains two or more counts, in the first of which the county and state are specifically stated, it is sufficient to allege in the other counts that the offense therein set forth was in the county aforesaid committed. (Criminal Code, sec. 412; *Fisk v. State*, 9 Neb. 62.)

The fact that the county attorney entered a *nolle prosequi* as to the first count is not important. That act did not have the effect to strike said count from the information or record. The entering of the *nolle*, after the commencement of the trial, was equivalent to an acquittal of the offense charged in the first count; but the count still remained a part of the information, and it was competent, if it could, to supply the deficiencies, or aid the allegations, in the other counts. (*Fisk v. State*, 9 Neb. 62; *Evans v. State*, 24 O. St. 208; *Commonwealth v. Clapp*, 82 Mass. 237; *State v. McAllister*, 26 Me. 374; *State v. Nelson*,

29 Me. 329.) In *Wills v. State*, 8 Mo. 52, the indictment contained two counts, on the first of which a *nolle prosequi* was entered, and the time of committing the offense was only shown by reference to that count. It was held that said count was not stricken, and a conviction could be properly had upon the second, although, without reference to the first, it was defective. To the same effect are *Hutto v. State*, 7 Tex. App. 44; *Boles v. State*, 13 Tex. App. 650.

Section 4, article 3, chapter 83, Compiled Statutes, declares: "It shall be the duty of the auditor: * * * Seventh. To direct prosecutions in the name of the state for all official delinquencies, in relation to the assessment, collection, and payment of the revenue, against all persons who by any means become possessed of public money or property, due or belonging to the state, and fail to pay over or deliver the same, and against all debtors of the state." The proposition is advanced that this information is bad because it does not allege that the prosecution was instituted under the direction of the auditor of public accounts. To this we cannot agree. The statute makes it the duty of a county attorney to prosecute all criminal actions in his county, as well as to file in the district court all informations for crimes; and he may institute criminal proceedings against a public officer who is guilty of some official delinquency relating to payment of the revenues, whether directed by the auditor to do so or not. It will not do to say that the county attorney cannot institute such a prosecution until he has been so directed by the auditor. The most that can be claimed for the provision of the statutes already quoted is that it is the duty of the county attorney to institute and prosecute a criminal action against a public officer who has made default in the assessment, collection, or payment of the public revenues, and not that the county attorney is powerless to take any steps towards instituting criminal prosecution against a defaulting state treasurer until after the auditor has given him instructions to act.   The state was not required to prove that this prosecution was brought by direction of the auditor; hence, it was wholly unnecessary for the information to aver such fact.

The count under which the conviction was obtained is assailed on the ground that the particular acts constituting the embezzlement of the moneys of the state are not therein alleged.   The offense is set forth in the information in the language of section 124 of the Criminal Code, which creates the crime of embezzlement by a public officer, and provides the punishment therefor. This was sufficient.   It was not necessary for the prosecutor to set out the evidence relied upon to sustain a conviction, nor allege the particular act or acts in which the crime consisted. (*Whitman v. State*, 17 Neb. 224; *Hodgkins v. State*, 36 Neb. 160; *State v. Jamison*, 74 Ia. 602; *Claassen v. United States*, 142 U. S. 140; *Gibbs v. State*, 41 Tex. 491; *Bennett v. State*, 62 Ark. 516; *State v. Isensee*, 12 Wash. 254.)   The three authorities cited by the defendant do not support a contrary doctrine, as a cursory examination will disclose.

Hoyt v. State, 50 Ga. 313, was a prosecution for embezzlement.   The indictment charged the defendant with the fraudulent conversion to his own use of certain moneys of the state of Georgia without detailing the manner by which the embezzlement was committed, and the court in passing upon the sufficiency of the averments held that "an indictment charging a defendant with having received a certain amount of money to be applied for the use or benefit of the bailor, with an allegation that on a certain day the defendant fraudulently converted a specific portion thereof to his own use, is not demurrable on the ground of its being general, vague, and indefinite, and that it does not put the accused on notice of what he is called on to answer."

In *State v. Brandt*, 41 Ia. 593, the question involved was whether an indictment which charged the crime of embezzlement in the language of the statute was sufficient. The court was equally divided in opinion.

In *State v. Parsons*, 54 Ia. 405, an indictment for embezzlement of public money was held bad, under the statutes of Iowa, because it omitted to charge that the defendant had failed to account for the money. The question we have been considering was not decided in that case.

State v. King, 81 Ia. 587, was a conviction of a county treasurer for the embezzlement of county funds. The indictment therein, in addition to charging that the defendant did "unlawfully and feloniously embezzle and convert to his own use, without authority of law," the money which he had received by virtue of his office, averred that he committed the crime by expending the money in his private business, and by permitting others to use and expend it in their private business transactions, and by using the money to pay the defendant's own private debts. It was urged that each of those acts constitutes a separate offense, and that the indictment was therefore bad for duplicity, as charging three distinct crimes. The supreme court held otherwise, saying: "We are of the opinion that the indictment is sufficient. The gist of the offense is the wrongful conversion of the public money, and it is wholly immaterial and mere surplusage to state whether the defendant used it in paying his debts, in purchasing property, had it on deposit in bank, carried it on his person, or loaned it to others, and the fact that three different modes of concealing the money are set forth in the indictment is wholly immaterial." We do not entertain the least doubt that the information in the case at bar is not defective, because the evidential facts constituting the crime are not alleged.

The objection that the information is bad, inasmuch as it does not aver that a demand had been made upon the accused for the money which came into his custody by virtue of his office of state treasurer, is without merit. It might be different if the information had been framed upon the theory that the defendant was guilty of the crime of embezzlement by reason of his having failed to account and pay over the public moneys, which came into his hands, to his successor. This prosecution is conducted upon the specific charge that the defendant converted and embezzled to his own use during his official term certain of the moneys of the state; therefore no demand upon him for the money by his successor was necessary to be alleged, or proven upon the trial. We quite agree with the attorney general wherein he says: "If a demand were necessary, then a prosecution could not be maintained until demand was made, and compliance with the demand, within a reasonable time, would defeat the prosecution. On this theory the treasurer of the state could do with the money of the state what he pleased,—could invest it in mines, or on the board of trade,—and be guilty of no crime, provided he accounted for the money within a reasonable time after demand. The statute says otherwise; and there is no warrant either in the statutes or decisions for a theory so pernicious." The question under consideration was not passed upon in *Bolln v. State,* 51 Neb. 581. *State v. Munch,* 22 Minn. 67, cited by counsel for defendant, does not support their contention, but is in harmony with the conclusion we have reached. There were two indictments before the court in that case. In one, the defendant, as state treasurer, was charged with the embezzlement and conversion to his own use, of certain moneys belonging to the state of Minnesota, which he had received by virtue of his office. This indictment was sustained, although it contained no averment of a demand. The other indictment charged an embezzlement by reason of the failure of the defendant to pay the money over to his successor in office, and was held defective because it did not allege that a demand for the money had been made upon the defendant by the successor in office.

.Another contention is that the trial court erred in not requiring the county attorney to elect, before entering upon the trial, upon which of the several counts of the information he would rely for a conviction. In *Korth v. State*, 46 Neb. 631, it was ruled that where different felonies of the same general character or grade are charged in separate counts of an information it is within the discretion of the trial judge to require the state to elect among the several counts, and his ruling in that regard will not be molested, unless there has been an abuse of discretion. In the case at bar, as in the one to which reference has just been had, the county attorney made his election as to counts after the testimony for the state had been introduced. No abuse of discretion or prejudicial error is perceptible. The prosecutor elected to rely upon the six counts relating to the embezzlement of money, and, they having charged the same offense, he was not obliged to elect among them. (*Candy v. State*, 8 Neb. 482; *Furst v. State*, 31 Neb. 403; *Aiken v. State*, 41 Neb. 265; *Hill v. State*, 42 Neb. 503; *Hurlburt v. State*, 52 Neb. 428.

Alfred D. Cox, W. F. Church, Fred A. Tompkins, and George S. Mack were severally challenged by the defendant for cause, as being incompetent to serve as jurors, which challenges were overruled by the court, and the rulings are assigned for error. The question of the competency of the persons named to sit as jurors we are relieved of the necessity of considering, since the record fails to disclose that the accused exhausted all of his peremptory challenges. If he was not required to exhaust his peremptory challenges to exclude them from the panel, he was not prejudiced by the overruling of his challenge for cause. (*Bohanan v. State*, 15 Neb. 209; *Palmer v. People*, 4 Neb. 68; *Jenkins v, Mitchell*, 40 Neb. 664; *Blenkiron v. State*, 40 Neb. 11; *Brumbach v. German Nat. Bank of Beatrice*, 46 Neb. 540.)

Error is alleged in the overruling of the motion of the defendant, made at the close of the testimony advanced by the state, to direct a verdict of not guilty. For convenience this ruling will now be considered in connection with the assignment that the proofs are insufficient to sustain the verdict.

There is no controversy as to the facts. During the two years immediately preceding the 6th day of January, 1897, the defendant was state treasurer, and exercised the duties of said office. The Omaha National Bank had been designated, under the laws of the state, for the depositing of the public funds, and the defendant kept on deposit in said bank, in pursuance of law, certain of the money which came into his hands by virtue of his office. The legislature at the session thereof held in 1895, for the purpose of making good to the state sinking fund the amount of loss it had sustained by reason of the failure of the Capital National Bank of the city of Lincoln, passed a law appropriating out of the state general fund the sum of $180,101.75, which appropriation is in the language following: "For state sinking fund, one hundred eighty thousand and one hundred and one and seventy-five one-hundredths ($180,101.75) dollars, to reimburse said fund for same amount tied up in Capital National Bank." (Session Laws 1895, ch. 88, p. 404.) Immediately upon the approval and taking effect of said appropriation, the defendant on the 10th day of April, 1895, made out in his own name, and presented to the auditor of public accounts, a voucher for the sum of money so appropriated for the replenishing of the state sinking fund, and caused the state auditor to issue on that date a warrant upon the state treasury for the payment of $180,101.75, which the defendant countersigned as state treasurer, the warrant being in words and figures following:

"$180,101.75.　　STATE OF NEBRASKA.　　No. 95,241.

"OFFICE OF THE AUDITOR OF PUBLIC ACCOUNTS,

"LINCOLN, NEBR., Apr. 10, 1895.

"Treasurer of Nebraska,

"Pay to J. S. Bartley ......, or order, one hundred eighty thousand one hundred one & 75-100 Dollars. For to Reimburse State Sinking Fund. In accordance with legislative appropriation approved April 10th, 1895; and charge General Fund.

"Countersigned: EUGENE MOORE,
    "J. S. BARTLEY   Auditor of Public Accounts.
    "State Treasurer.   P. O. HEDLUND,
                                        "Deputy."

This warrant was delivered to the defendant on the day it bears date, and he at once registered the same in the proper book in his office for payment, but omitted to enter upon said book, in the proper column, the name of the person presenting the warrant for payment. Almost immediately thereafter the defendant indorsed his name upon the back of said warrant, and placed the same in the hands of the Omaha National Bank, or J. H. Millard, its president, for negotiation, and the latter, as agent for the defendant, sold the same to the Chemical National Bank of New York city for the face value. Pursuant to the directions of the defendant, the Omaha National Bank opened an individual account with him, and entered therein a credit to defendant on the 26th day of April, 1895, for the amount of the proceeds of said warrant. This money was subsequently drawn out of the bank on the personal checks of the defendant. In November, 1896, the warrant was transmitted by the Chemical National Bank to the Omaha National Bank for collection. It was called for payment in order of registration, and on the 2d day of January, 1897, the defendant went to the city of Omaha, and into the Omaha National Bank, drew his check as state treasurer against the depository account of the state in said bank for the sum of $201,884.05, payable to the order of J. H. Millard, Pt., and delivered said check to the bank in payment of said auditor's warrant, which instrument he then and there received, and at the same instant of time the account of the state was charged on the books of said bank with the amount of said check, and the Chemical National Bank was credited with a like sum.

The state relies for a conviction upon the redemption
and payment of said auditor's warrant by the defendant
out of the public funds of the state on deposit in the
Omaha National Bank. The theory of the attorney general is that the warrant was void and therefore the state
treasurer had no right or authority to redeem it. On
the other side, it is insisted that the instrument was a
valid and binding obligation of the state, which the law
required the defendant to pay upon the receipt by him
of sufficient funds for that purpose. In our view it is
wholly immaterial whether the warrant in question was
valid or void. If invalid, the defendant was not justified
in paying it out of the money of the state under the circumstances disclosed by this record. It is argued, if it
was not a valid instrument, it never has been paid. That
the state is minus $201,884.05 by the transaction is an
assured fact. Whether the state may or may not be able
to recover the money from the Omaha National Bank, the
Chemical National Bank, or any other corporation or person, is not material to the present inquiry. Doubtless, it
is the duty of a state treasurer to pay, when he has available funds, a legal warrant drawn upon the treasury by
the proper officer, to the person entitled thereto, and cannot be convicted of embezzlement for having done so.
Had the defendant paid the warrant in question to the
proper person, the case would present an entirely different
aspect. The appropriation upon which the warrant was
drawn was not made in favor of the defendant individually. The purpose of the legislature in passing the act
was to transfer from the state general fund the sum appropriated to the state sinking fund, to reimburse the latter to the extent it had been depleted by the collapse of
the Capital National Bank, and not to pay any debt it
owed the defendant or to make a present to him of the
said sum. The warrant did not belong to him, notwithstanding it was drawn payable to himself in his individual capacity, but he received it officially, in trust for
the state, for and on behalf of the state sinking fund, as he

well knew. The title to the warrant never vested in him, and he could not transfer to another by indorsement that which he never possessed. He could not divest the title of the state in the warrant by the sale thereof to the Chemical National Bank, since he possessed no power to sell or negotiate the instrument. Nor was the bank an "innocent purchaser" within the meaning of that term as applied to commercial paper, inasmuch as the warrant disclosed on its face the purpose and object for which it was drawn, and the bank was bound to know at its peril that the defendant had no title to the instrument. Moreover, warrants issued upon the state treasury by the auditor of public accounts are not negotiable instruments, in the sense that the indorsee thereof may become a *bona fide* purchaser. (*School District v. Stough,* 4 Neb. 357; *Union P. R. Co. v. Buffalo County,* 9 Neb. 452; *Burlington & M. R. R. Co. v. Clay County,* 13 Neb. 370; *State v. Sabin,* 39 Neb. 570; *State v. Cook,* 43 Neb. 318.) The foregoing authorities hold that school district orders and county warrants are not negotiable instruments, and, upon principle, warrants drawn by the state auditor are within the same category. Therefore, it cannot be successfully asserted that the state was required to pay the warrant to the indorsee, as the latter was not an innocent holder. The defendant had actual knowledge of the facts surrounding the issuance and attempted transfer of the warrant. He knew that it was the property of the state, and that he was not legally or morally required to pay the money called for therein to any person other than himself. When the money was in the treasury to meet this warrant, his sole duty in the premises was to take the money out of the general fund and turn the same into the sinking fund,—credit one fund with the amount, and charge the other fund with a like sum. He knowingly disregarded his duty in the premises, paid the money to a party not entitled thereto, and defrauded the state to the extent of the sum so paid. This constituted an embezzlement of the public moneys. (*Bork v. People,* 1 N. Y. Cr. Rep. 368.)

We know judicially that the state, on April 1, 1891, issued 190 relief bonds, each of the denomination of $1,000, payable in five years; that the money belonging to the permanent school fund of the state was invested in those bonds; that the same were retained by the state treasurer for safe-keeping, and that six of them were actually redeemed, paid, and canceled by the defendant as state treasurer on October 31, 1896. Suppose these bonds had been stolen from the treasury, and subsequently paid by defendant to the holder thereof, or defendant had sold the bonds after their maturity to the Omaha National Bank, applied the proceeds to his own use, and subsequently redeemed the same by taking the money out of the state treasury and paying the face of the bonds and accrued interest to said bank; could there be a shadow of doubt that the defendant would have been guilty of the embezzlement of the money of the state, notwithstanding the bonds were legal and binding instruments? We think not. There is no difference between the supposed cases and the one at bar, providing the warrant in question was paid with the moneys of the state, which proposition will now receive attention.

As already stated, the accused was convicted of embezzling a certain sum of public money. Section 124 of the Criminal Code, under the provisions whereof this prosecution was instituted, expurgating all words that are not essential to the present inquiry, provides that "If any officer * * * shall convert to his own use * * any portion of the public money, or any other funds, property, bonds, securities, assets, or effects of any kind, received, controlled, or held by him for safe-keeping, transfer, or disbursement, * * * every such act shall be deemed and held in law to be an embezzlement of so much of the said moneys or other property, as aforesaid, as shall thus be converted, used," etc. At the bar, as well as in the briefs of counsel, the proposition was argued with marked ability whether or not the word "money," as employed in said section is a generic or specific term. For the purposes of this case, we shall assume that the construction of the statute contended for by the defendant is the proper one, namely, that the term "money" was used by the legislature in a specific sense. In other words, it means legal-tender coin, and also paper issued by the government, or by banks by lawful authority, and intended to pass and circulate as money. It is insisted on behalf of the accused that, under the foregoing definition, he did not embezzle money—actual coin or currency—belonging to the state. It is true the state had no specific coins or currency in the possession of the Omaha National Bank, as it had made no special deposit of money in said bank. The state, at the time of the delivery of the check in question to the bank, had on deposit therein, under the depository law, money in excess of the amount found by the jury to have been embezzled, which constituted the bank the debtor of the state to that amount. (*State v. Bartley*, 39 Neb. 353; *In re State Treasurer's Settlement*, 51 Neb. 116.) It was conceded on the argument by counsel for the accused that if the latter had drawn from the depository bank the actual cash and then redeemed the warrant therewith, proof thereof would be sufficient to sustain the charge of embezzlement of money. As we view it the legal effect of the transaction, as it actually occurred, is not materially different. The defendant, as state treasurer, drew his check upon the Omaha National Bank for $201,884.05, payable to the order of the president thereof, and delivered the same to the payee, which, in connection with the acceptance of the check by the bank, the entry of the transaction upon the books thereof, and the surrender of the warrant to the defendant, constituted a segregation or separation of the amount of dollars expressed in the check from the general mass of money in the bank as the portion belonging to the state, and passed the title to the latter. In contemplation of the parties, and in the eye of the law, the segregation was as full and complete as though Mr. Mil-

26

lard, the president of the bank, upon the delivery of the
check to him had stepped into the vault, counted out
$201,884.05, placed it upon the counter, charged the state
with that amount on the bank books, credited the Chemical National Bank with a like sum, delivered the warrant to the defendant, and then returned the money to
the vault from whence it came; or as if the check had
been made payable to the defendant's own order, by himself presented to the paying teller at the bank for payment, who selected from the mass of money in the bank
the sum represented by the check, placed the same in a
pile on the counter, and then, by direction of the defendant, applied the same in payment of the warrant. To
constitute embezzlement it was not necessary that the
defendant himself should have acquired the physical or
manual possession of the money. He, by his check, authorized and directed the bank to pay the money called
for therein to "J. H. Millard, Pt." The bank was
thereby empowered to select and transfer the money to
the payee, which in contemplation of law it did, although
there was no actual handling of a dollar in the entire
transaction. In the language of Morse, Banks and
Banking, sec. 451: "A credit given for the amount of a
check by the bank upon which it is drawn is equivalent
to, and will be treated as, a payment of the check. It is
the same as if the money had been paid over the counter
on the check, and then immediately paid back again to
the acount or for the use for which the credit is given."
(See *Oddie v. National City Bank of New York*, 45 N. Y. 735.)

State v. Baumhager, 28 Minn. 226, was a conviction of
the crime of embezzling public moneys intrusted to the
defendant as county treasurer. The only proof to sustain the charge was that the defendant had $5,000 of
county funds in his hands; that he caused the county
auditor to give him credit on the auditor's books for the
amount of a county order which had been redeemed
by the defendant's predecessor in office, although he had
never returned it to the auditor or obtained credit there-

for.   There was no evidence of an actual conversion by the defendant, nor that there was a shortage in his accounts as county treasurer.   The proofs were held sufficient to sustain the conviction.

State v. Palmer, 40 Kan. 474, was a prosecution for obtaining moneys under false pretenses.   The evidence disclosed that one Critwell drew his check on a certain bank in favor of the defendant for $75; that the latter presented the check, and the bank paid it out of moneys deposited by Critwell, and charged the same to his account. This was held to be the obtaining of the money of the prosecuting witness, although he had no specific money on deposit in the bank.   It is true the defendant then obtained physical possession of the money.   But suppose, instead of receiving the actual cash, he had deposited the check and received credit for the amount on the books of the bank; proof of the commission of the offense of obtaining money under false pretenses would have been none the less complete, since the check was authority to the bank to segregate the amount of the money called for from the funds of the bank, and, when made, such portion at the same instant became the specific property of the prosecuting witness.   Likewise, the very moment the money represented by the check drawn in payment of the warrant in question was separated from the general mass of money in the Omaha National Bank, the title to the money thus segregated passed from the bank to the state for an instant of time.

Roberts v. People, 9 Colo. 458, was a conviction for obtaining the moneys of Arapahoe county under false pretenses.   The proofs showed that the defendant procured a false claim against the county to be audited, and a warrant drawn on the treasury for the same, which was paid. There was no evidence to show that the defendant presented the warrant for payment or received the money thereon.   The court held this omission immaterial, saying: "It was not necessary that defendant should himself present it to the treasury in order to realize the money, or in order that the county should be defrauded of its money by the acts of the defendant."

In *People v. McKinney*, 10 Mich. 54, the doctrine was announced and enforced that any act by a state treasurer, by which the money of the state should be abstracted from the treasury, or diverted from its proper use, with intent to apply it to his benefit, constitutes the crime of embezzlement. The contention was that the defendant was not present when the misappropriation took place. Christiancy, J., as the mouthpiece of the court, used this language: "The whole force of this objection, therefore, rests upon the assumption that the treasurer could perform no act by which the money could be thus abstracted or converted to his own use or benefit, unless at the time of the act he were personally present where the money happened to be. This assumption is so manifestly unfounded in law or fact, as to require no comment." (See in this connection *People v. Bringard*, 39 Mich. 22.)

Bork v. People, 16 Hun [N. Y.] 476, was a conviction of the defendant for embezzlement of $1,000 of the money of the city of Buffalo, in his hands as treasurer of said city. Smith, J., delivering the opinion of the court, observed: "The funds which the treasurer is alleged to have embezzled in the present case may have been a mere credit in a bank, and not money at all, and yet if he treated the credit as cash in his hands belonging to the city, proof that he embezzled it would support an indictment for embezzling money. The rule requiring certainty in an indictment is not to be so applied as to defeat the ends of public justice."

A case precisely in point is *State v. Krug*, 12 Wash. 288, which was a prosecution for the embezzlement of the moneys of the city of Seattle by the treasurer thereof. The evidence disclosed that the defendant, as such officer, drew a check for $10,000 in favor of one Fuhrman upon a bank having funds of the city on deposit in excess of said amount. The payee presented the check and received in payment thereof New York exchange. The bank charged on its books the money to the city, and lessened its credit in said sum. The jury were instructed that the transaction constituted a payment of money, and that they should construe the check or instrument merely as the instrumentality by which the money of the city was transferred from the possession of the defendant. In reviewing the instruction, the supreme court in the opinion say: "Under these facts the appellant claims there was only an exchange of credits and no money was paid. The instruction of the court is based upon the theory that, in contemplation of law at least, this was money. It would be a travesty upon the administration of the law, if treasurers who are the custodians of the funds of the people should be allowed to escape the penalty of embezzlement by any such subterfuge as this theory would protect. * * * The practical result of the transaction in this case was that, when this check was given to Fuhrman, and was paid to Fuhrman by the New York exchange, and that amount charged to the account of the city, the city of Seattle had its account decreased to the amount of the check, and it was just as much a disposition of that $10,000 by the treasurer as though he had gone to the bank and got the money himself, and paid it to Fuhrman, or had loaned him that amount of money out of specie which he received, before it had been taken to the bank." Argument is unnecessary to show that the principle enunciated in that decision, if followed, controls the case at bar.

An examination of the authorities relied upon by counsel for defendant reveals that they do not support their contention. Without unduly extending this opinion, we can do no more than to make a brief reference to the leading cases cited by them.

In *Hamilton v. State*, 60 Ind. 193, it was held that proof of the larceny of national bank notes did not sustain the charge of the larceny of a certain sum "of lawful money of the United States." In *Tracy v. State*, 46 Neb. 361, this court held the contrary to be true.

In *Williams v. State*, 12 S. & M. [Miss.] 58, it was decided that a charge for betting money was not sustained by proof of the betting of United States treasury warrants. Of the same import are *Pryor v. Commonwealth*, 2 Dana [Ky.] 298; *Garner v. State*, 5 Yerg. [Tenn.] 158.

In *Carr v. State*, 16 So. Rep. [Ala.] 155, a banker was indicted for the embezzlement of a certain special deposit of money, and it was ruled that the averment was not sustained by proof of the embezzlement of a bank check.

Thalheim v. State, 20 So. Rep. [Fla.] 948, was a prosecution for the embezzlement of money. It was held that assets generally and property generally were not included in the term "money."

In *Banks v. State*, 28 Tex. 644, it was decided that proof of the theft of a mare would not sustain an indictment for larceny of a "horse," since the statute of Texas did not employ the word "horse" in a generic sense. Of like purport are *Turley v. State*, 22 Tenn. 323; *Jordt v. State*, 31 Tex. 571.

In *Commonwealth v. Howe*, 132 Mass. 250, the indictment was for obtaining a certain sum of money by false pretenses, which charge, it was ruled, was not sustained by proof of obtaining a certificate of deposit of a bank. Had the certificate been presented to the bank and paid, the case might have some bearing upon the question here.

Lindsay v. State, 19 Ala. 560, is to the point that an indictment for selling whiskey is not supported by proof of the sale of any other kind of liquor.

Lewis v. State, 28 Tex. App. 140, was a prosecution for the misappropriation of public money. It was held that the term "money" within the meaning of the Criminal Code, is "legal-tender metallic coins, or legal-tender currency of the United States." In the preceding discussion we have assumed that to be the rule in this state.

Both upon reason and authority we are constrained to hold that the charge of embezzlement of money contained in the third count of the information herein is sustained by the evidence adduced, and that it was not error to decline to direct a verdict of not guilty.

It is insisted that there was error in the admission of evidence of certain letters between the president of the Omaha National Bank and the president of the Chemical National Bank of New York. The earliest portion of this correspondence was a letter from the president of the Omaha National Bank inclosing the auditor's warrant in question, offering to accept therefor its proceeds on the basis of a rate of interest at 6 per cent, if a greater rate would not be allowed. The answer to this letter was dated April 23, 1895. It advised the president of the Omaha National Bank of a credit of said bank with the Chemical National Bank of the sum of $180,550.77, as the proceeds of t' · sale of said warrant, pursuant to the offer contained in the letter of Mr. Millard. Mr. Balch, the assistant cashier of the Omaha National Bank, testified that he saw the defendant at that bank about 5 o'clock in the evening of the same day, or of the one immediately preceding that, on which he saw the letter first above referred to, and that between the day the warrant was sent to New York and the time the advice of the credit was received witness had a conversation · with defendant, in which the former asked the latter what disposition should be made of the proceeds of the warrant when the Omaha National Bank got returns on it, and that defendant replied to open an account and pass it to his own individual credit. The witness further testified that, when the credit was given for the proceeds of the warrant by the Chemical National Bank, he carried out the instructions of defendant and placed the said proceeds to the personal credit of the latter on the books of the Omaha National Bank. A copy of his personal account was introduced in evidence, which showed the credit was given as above indicated. It is unnecessary to go further into details to show that there was sufficient evidence to justify the conclusion that in disposing of the warrant Mr. Millard, the president of the Omaha National Bank, and the bank itself, were the agents of defendant. The evidence above and hereinafter detailed are portions of the proofs which established a common purpose between the defendant and his agency in Omaha, which was the sale of the warrant to the Chemical National Bank. Whatever correspondence was necessary and proper for the consummation of this common design was admissible against the defendant, the party at whose instance we must assume, from the evidence, this correspondence was carried on. (*Brown v. Horr*, 21 Neb. 113.) This principle we think none the less applicable because the transaction entered into with a common purpose was not the ultimate fact sought to be established, but was relied upon to show the motive with which a subsequent act growing out of and intimately connected with it, was done.

It is strenuously insisted that the county attorney unnecessarily made public, in the presence of members of the regular panel of jurors in open court, the alleged fact that there had been an attempt to bribe jurors to find in favor of the accused, and that from this prejudice must have been sustained by the defendant. From the affidavits submitted by defendant it might be concluded that the county attorney did make the statement attributed to him. On the other side, there were affidavits which corroborated the affidavit of Mr. Baldrige, the county attorney, to the effect that his statement in open court was as follows: "I have been informed by a juror on the regular panel that he has been approached by some outside party with a view to influencing his verdict in a case for trial in this court. I deem it my duty to bring this matter to the attention of the court in order that the court may make whatever order it deems necessary or proper in the premises, and that such punishment may be meted out to the guilty party as the court thinks warranted." As to whether there was the alleged misconduct of the county attorney, or whether his conduct was as proper as above indicated, was a question of fact, which, upon conflicting evidence, was settled adversely to the accused. Under such circumstances the ruling of the trial court will not be disturbed. (*Lindsay r. State*, 46 Neb. 177; *Grossman v. State*, 46 Neb. 21; *McMahon v. State*, 46 Neb. 166; *Carleton r. State*, 43 Neb. 373.)

The trial court upon consideration of conflicting evidence concluded that there had been no misconduct on the part of alleged detectives in shadowing or in attempting to communicate with or influence jurors while in charge of a bailiff of the court, and the principle just invoked must likewise preclude a consideration of the question of fact.

In respect to rulings of the court in denying the demand of the defendant that one of the detectives should be compelled to submit to an oral examination in open court touching the matters of fact just considered, and the denial of the demand that the county attorney should answer orally with reference to alleged interviews concerning the conduct of the trial and other like matters, in some of which it was claimed the presiding judge had taken part, it is not deemed necessary to indulge in an extended discussion, for rulings of a like nature have been sustained by this court in *Kountze v. Scott*, 52 Neb. 460, and in *Hamer v. McKinley-Lanning Loan & Trust Co.*, 52 Neb. 705.

In the progress of the examination of Mr. Millard, the president of the Omaha National Bank, he was interrogated with reference to the check drawn by Bartley on said bank for the amount which by the information he was charged with embezzling. In this connection the testimony and conduct complained of, omitting objections and the rulings thereon, were as follows:

"Q. You may state, Mr. Millard, how long that check was in your possession at that time?

"A. I don't think it was ever in my possession,—personal possession.

"Q. How long was it in the bank?

"A. I think it was there two days.

"Q. Do you know what became of it afterwards?

"A. It was returned to Mr. Bartley.

"Q. And that was how long ago?

"A. I would think about two months, or possibly three months ago—perhaps two and a half months ago.

"Q. Did Mr. Bartley come for it at that time to the bank?

"A. No, sir.

"Q. Have you seen the check since?

"A. No, sir.

"Mr. Baldrige: I want to make in open court a formal demand upon the defendant and his attorneys to produce——

"Mr. Whedon: I object to any proceedings of this kind in the presence of the jury. There is no law for it and it is unprofessional.

"Mr. Baldrige: The state in this case——

"Mr. Whedon: I object to any demand being made in the presence of this jury during the trial.

"By the court: The jury may retire to my room in charge of the bailiff. [Jury retired.]"

It is unnecessary to describe what transpired during the absence of the jury from the court room, and we shall, therefore, transcribe from the bill of exceptions the description of the proceedings, in the presence of the jury as we assume, when Mr. Millard, again having been called to the witness stand, was testifying with reference to this check. This part of the record is as follows:

"Mr. Baldrige: I want to say that the state proposes to offer in evidence a notice given by the state of Nebraska to the defense to produce the check about which the witness is interrogated.

"Mr. Whedon: I move to strike out of the testimony and out of the record the statement of counsel, following the ruling of the court on the objection made by counsel, and except to the statement that has been made as improper and irrelevant.

"By the court: The objection overruled and the motion to strike out overruled.

"Mr. Mahoney: The defendant excepts.

"By the court: Before the witness answers I want to ask counsel for the state if they have the check in their possession.

"Mr. Baldrige: No, sir; we have not.

"Mr. Whedon: The defendant objects to this testimony and questions of the court and to the giving of testimony by Mr. Baldrige, on the ground that the counsel for the state's names are not upon or indorsed on the information as witnesses, and they are not competent to testify in the case, and move the court to strike out the testimony, for the reason counsel is not sworn to give the testimony.

"By the court: Objection overruled. It is not a matter of evidence. It is a question for the court's benefit. The jury will not consider any statement between counsel and the court in any manner in forming their verdict.

"Mr. Mahoney: The defendant excepts."

In a later stage of the trial the notice to produce the aforesaid check was offered in evidence in the presence of the jury, and an objection thereto was sustained, whereupon Mr. Baldrige said: "The offer was made generally and more particularly for the purpose of advising the court of the fact that due notice had been served upon the defense requesting them to deliver over to the state for their use in the trial the checks and papers set out in the paper marked 'Exhibit 12.'

"Mr. Mahoney: Defendant objects to putting into the record any offer of an offer and objects to incorporating into the record the statement of counsel of the purpose of the offer, the offer being of a written instrument and defendant moves to strike out what the county attorney has placed in the record.

"The court: The objection to the offer is sustained. The document may be retained as a paper of the files and may be filed in the case, but not received as a matter of evidence. The motion to strike out is overruled. Defendant excepts."

This portion of the record has been copied for the reason that, perhaps, an attempt to describe it in a narrative form might work an injustice, for we confess our inability to imagine in what respect the accused could have been prejudiced by what was said or done. It is disclosed by the bill of exceptions that secondary evidence descriptive of the check in question was offered, and it seems to us that in the preliminary steps leading thereto there was no misçonduct on the part of counsel for the state or of the presiding judge. Whatever unfavorable inference to the accused could have been drawn by the jury from the transaction before them was corrected by the admonition that the jury were not to consider any statements between counsel and the court in any manner in forming their verdict. (*Thalheim v. State*, 20 So. Rep. [Fla.] 945; *Hoover v. State*, 48 Neb. 184.)

There were monthly statements made by the treasurer during defendant's term to the auditor of public accounts offered in evidence, with respect to one of these, defendant's deputy was asked what, if any, means Bartley would have for knowing the correctness of the report as to its details. To this question Mr. Baldrige objected and remarked: "Mr. Bartley might know everything that was in that report; he is the treasurer and is presumed to know it. If he does not he himself should say so." To this last remark Mr. Mahoney objected and excepted as improper, whereupon the court said: "It is improper and that language should not be indulged in in any manner or form as to what the defendant ought to say." It may be conceded that the remark was improper and yet this was just how it was characterized by the court in its remark to the jury, and we cannot assume that this suggestion was ignored. It would unnecessarily prolong this opinion to attempt to describe the several instances wherein it is insisted that the court improperly propounded questions to witnesses under examination. It must suffice to say that each of these alleged infractions of propriety has been carefully considered, and that we have found nothing which justifies an inference that from the course criticised in this respect any prejudice could have resulted to the accused.

It is urged that there was error in the admission in evidence of the official bond of defendant, for the reason the instrument in question, to render it valid, should have been approved on or before January 3, 1895, whereas in fact there was no approval till six days beyond said statutory limit. In support of this contention there is cited the case of *State v. Lansing*, 46 Neb. 514. In the case cited the contention was between parties each of whom claimed that he was county judge of Lancaster county. Lansing, the incumbent, was in possession, and it was asserted in the information, wrongfully so, for the reason that the mandatory requirement of the statute with reference to the approval of his bond had not been complied with. The statutory provision relied upon to sustain this contention was section 15, chapter 10, Compiled Statutes, which is in this language: "If any person elected or appointed to any office shall neglect to have his official bond executed and approved as provided by law, and filed for record within the time limited by this act, his office shall thereupon *ipso facto* become vacant, and such vacancy shall thereupon immediately be filled by election or appointment as the law may direct in other cases of vacancy in the same office."

At the general election following that at which Lansing had been elected to the office of county judge for which he had failed to qualify, it was assumed that the office was vacant and the relator was accordingly nominated to fill this vacancy and received the highest number of votes cast for that office. The action in which the opinion of this court in *State v. Lansing, supra*, was filed was therefore one in which the title to the office was the subject-matter in dispute. Whether there was a vacancy by reason of Lansing's failure to qualify was the pivotal question, and it was held that this failure was a fatal defect in his title. In the case at bar no one ever questioned the right of the defendant to hold the office

of state treasurer for the term for which he was elected.
That term, with all its honors and emoluments he has
enjoyed, and after its expiration there is for the first time
raised a question whether his incumbency was rightful,
which question is raised by himself when charged with
malfeasance in the performance of its duties.   That the
opinion of this court in *State v. Lansing, supra*, has no
tendency to support this contention of the defendant
requires no elaboration to render perfectly clear.
Whether defendant was an officer *de jure* or *de facto*, he
was required to perform the duties which the law imposed upon him with integrity and loyalty to the state,
and his failure in this respect should subject him to punishment regardless of his technical right to be inducted
into office. (*State v. Goss*, 69 Me. 22; *State v. Mims*, 26
Minn. 183; *People v. Cobler*, 108 Cal. 538; *State v. Findley*,
101 Mo. 217.)

It was urged that there were material variances between the auditor's warrant which, it was charged, had
been embezzled, and that which was offered in evidence.
These alleged variances were that the warrant offered
in evidence had certain figures in the upper left hand corner, and on its face the words: "Paid Jan. 2, 1897.   State
of Nebraska.   Treasurer's office," and on the back the
words: "Presented and not paid for want of funds and
registered for payment Apr. 10, 1895.   Number 27932.
J. S. Bartley, State Treasurer, Lincoln, Nebraska." As
to the counts whereby was charged the embezzlement
of the warrant a *nolle* was entered, so that these alleged
variances became immaterial.   The figures consisted of
two amounts which added together made up the amount
with the embezzlement of which Mr. Bartley was
charged.   The other alleged variances were placed upon
the warrant by defendant, in one instance at least, and
if not by himself the other was stamped upon the face
of the warrant by one of the employés in his office.   In
neither case was there what would amount to a spoliation and the warrant therefore was competent evidence

of the facts in proof of which it could be considered by the jury, and these have already been sufficiently noted.

On several of the exhibits offered in evidence there were stamped the words: "Otto Helbig, accountant. Examined. 501 Tacoma Bldg., Chicago." These were explained by Mr. Helbig to have been placed upon the several exhibits to show that in making up his statement of the condition of the office of state treasurer he had used the information conveyed by such exhibits. The exhibits themselves contained statements made by defendant as treasurer and only these were submitted to the jury. The words stamped by Mr. Helbig were not given in evidence, consequently they could not have operated to the prejudice of the accused.

For the defense, Mr. Bartlett, the deputy treasurer, testified on his direct examination that the keeping of the books in the treasurer's office was under his supervision and that the manner in which the sinking fund account was carried was in pursuance of the direction of defendant. On cross-examination Mr. Bartlett testified as follows:

Q. The check referred to was the check in payment of the warrant, was it not?

A. Yes, sir.

Q. But my question is as to the proceeds of the warrant when it was sold.

A. I never knew it was sold. * * *

Q. When did you first know that the warrant was sold?

A. Not until I wrote the stub for the payment of the warrant.

It is complained that the question and answer last quoted were not in the line of cross-examination. We think otherwise. The item referred to was one which under certain conditions, according to the evidence of Mr. Bartlett, would have been entered in the sinking fund account. It did not there appear, and it was proper to ask Mr. Bartlett why the account showed no pro-

ceeds of the sale of the warrant and in this connection
when he first learned of the fact of the sale. His answer was that he learned of this sale on or about the
date of the check, which was January 2, 1897, and this
certainly was a circumstance proper to be considered by
the jury in connection with his direct examination which
showed that his entries were in accordance with the directions of defendant.

It is insisted there was error in permitting E. E. Balch,
assistant cashier of the Omaha National Bank, on cross-
examination, to answer that prior to the date of the
check designated as "Exhibit 49" all the money realized
from the sale of the warrant in New York had been
drawn out of the Omaha National Bank by defendant.
This check bore the date of June 4, 1896. Of the same
date was a deposit slip showing a deposit by defendant
of his individual check to the credit of himself as treasurer in the sum of $50,000. As this check corresponded
with that designated as "Exhibit 49" it was not an abuse
of discretion for the court to permit the cross-examination of the witness to anticipate a possible argument
founded on the above noted coincidences by his testimony
that the proceeds of the sale of the warrant, previous to
June 4, 1896, had been withdrawn from the bank by defendant. In this connection it is proper to remark
there was no abuse of discretion in admitting in evidence,
for the purposes first indicated, the portion of the general
fund account of Mr. Bartley with the Omaha National
Bank of date about June 4, 1896, and certain exhibits
connected with the same subject-matter. (*People v. Mc-
Kinney*, 10 Mich. 54.)

Exhibit 35 was a statement showing the receipts and
disbursements of the state treasury in June, 1896, filed
in the department of the auditor of public accounts of the
state of Nebraska. This statement was signed "J. S.
Bartley, State Treasurer." It was urged that there was
error in refusing to permit the deputy treasurer to testify
whether or not this statement was prepared by the sub-

ordinate force in the treasurer's office. It is not claimed that any of these items in fact was incorrect, and therefore there was no admission by which the defendant would not be bound as well when written by a clerk as when written by himself. If there had been any claim of mistake or oversight this might be different. But even then, when it had been shown that the statement had been signed by defendant, it devolved on him to rebut the presumption that the statement was correct.

We cannot understand what proper purpose could have been subserved if the defendant had been permitted to prove the usual media by which remittances were made to the state treasurer by county treasurers. It seems to be intimated in argument, as we understand it, that if it had been permitted to be shown that these were usually in drafts, checks, etc., that this fact might have justified the deposit in banks other than depositories. The statute on this subject prescribes where deposits must be made and must govern, and no excuse can dispense with its provisions.

Mr. Helbig, an expert accountant, on rebuttal, was permitted to testify that he had made an examination of the books of the treasurer's office, and that from the examination he had ascertained the amount of the general fund on hand at different times, as well as the several amounts of expenditures and disbursements therefrom, together with other items as to various other accounts disclosed by said books. He further testified that all the said books, together with the memoranda he had consulted in connection with them, were present in the court room at the time his testimony was given. Thereupon the court permitted the witness to testify with reference to the conditions above indicated, and this, it is insisted, was prejudicial error. In his discussion of exceptions to the rule requiring the production of the best evidence, Prof. Greenleaf said: "A further relaxation of the rule has been admitted, where the evidence is the result of voluminous facts or of the inspection of many

27

books and papers, the examination of which could not
conveniently take place in court." (1 Greenleaf, Evidence sec. 93.) This exception has been recognized in
Masonic Mutual Benefit Society v. Lackland, 97 Mo. 137, and
in *State v. Findley*, 101 Mo. 217, and by the supreme court
of Oregon in *State v. Reinhart*, 38 Pac. Rep. 822. In
Hollingsworth v. State, 111 Ind. 289, it was held that in a
prosecution for embezzlement, or other crime, where the
books, records, papers, and entries are voluminous and
of such a character as to render it difficult for the jury
to arrive at a correct conclusion as to amounts, expert
accountants may be allowed to examine such books, etc..
and testify to the result. No adjudicated case in opposition to this exception to the general rule requiring the
production of the best evidence has been cited, and we
are satisfied that where, as in this instance, the sources
from which the expert accountant derived his knowledge
were present in the court room subject to inspection he
was properly permitted to testify as he did with reference to what was shown by such books and documents.

In the act entitled "An act to provide for the depositing of state and county funds in banks" (Session Laws
1891, p. 347) it was provided that the depository bond
should be, in substance, of the form set out in said act.
This form closed with the words: "Sealed with our seals
and dated the —— day of ——, A. D. ——." There was
no seal opposite the signatures to the depository bond
which was given by the Omaha National Bank, from
which consideration it is urged that the bond was invalid, and therefore the bank was not legally a depository. · In this case this failure to attach seals is unavailable to defendant, for whether the seals are essential
and whether from the want of them the bank was not
entitled to receive state deposits are immaterial matters.
If defendant entertained doubts as to whether the bank
was in fact a depository he might have been justified in
satisfying himself upon that point before making deposits, but he cannot now be heard to stultify himself

by asserting when the matter becomes a collateral issue
that he deposited the money of the state during his term
of office in a bank wherein by law he was forbidden to
make such deposits.

We pass to the consideration of the instructions given
and refused. It is insisted the trial court erred in its
third paragraph of the charge in saying to the jury that
the information charged the defendant with the embez
zlement of certain public money in the county of Doug
las. This contention is predicated upon the fact that
the counts relating to the misappropriation of the money
contain no specific statement that the crime was committed in Douglas county. The place of the offense, as
shown elsewhere in this opinion, was sufficiently averred
by proper and suitable reference to the first count of the
information and the venue, in each of which the county
of Douglas is set forth, and that such reference was permissible even though a *nolle* to the first count of the information had been entered. This is a sufficient answer
to the foregoing criticism made upon the instructions.

Objection is made to the eighth instruction, which
reads: "The state having entered a *nolle* of the first and
second counts of the information you will not consider
the testimony relative to the warrant, known as 'Exhibit
4,' or any transaction concerning the same, except only
and for the purpose of showing the criminal intent of
the defendant of and concerning the charge of the embezzlement of the $201,884.05." No error prejudicial to
the accused is perceptible in the foregoing language of
the court. It contained no assumption that the defendant acted with a criminal intent, but advised the jury,
and properly so, that they might consider the evidence
of and concerning the warrant for the purpose of ascertaining whether the defendant was actuated by a guilty
intent or motive in appropriating the money alleged to
have been embezzled. The evidence tended to show
that the negotiation of the warrant and the subsequent
payment thereof were parts of the same common design

and purpose, parts of the same transaction, although not transpiring at the same time, and when construed together make manifest the purpose of the defendant to misappropriate to his own use the money of the state. (*People v. Cobler*, 108 Cal. 538.)

The eleventh instruction reads thus: "If you find from the evidence that the Omaha National Bank executed a bond to the state of Nebraska, asking to be designated as a state depository of public money of the state, and that such bond was approved by the governor, secretary of state, and attorney general, then you should find the Omaha National Bank was a state depository of the current funds of the state." It is argued that this instruction is faulty because the jury were not advised as to the form of the bond necessary to be given by the Omaha National Bank to constitute it a state depository. If the defendant desired the jury instructed on that point he should have tendered one to the trial judge. Mere non-direction of the court is no ground for reversal. (*Hill v. State*, 42 Neb. 503; *Housh v. State*, 43 Neb. 163; *Pjarrou v. State*, 47 Neb. 294.)

By the twelfth instruction the jury were told that: "The term 'conversion of money' means an unauthorized assumption and exercise of the right of ownership over the moneys belonging to another, and the alteration of its condition to the exclusion of the owner's right; and such conversion must be with the intention to use or dispose of the said moneys for the benefit of the person converting it, or to the benefit of some other person or corporation than the owner thereof; and it would be a conversion in law even though the party intended at the time of the appropriation at some future time to repay the money so appropriated." The only criticism upon the language is the use of the words "appropriation" and "appropriated." The prefix "mis" should have preceded each of those words in order to have made the expression technically accurate. We are, however, satisfied that the omission thereof was not prejudicial to the accused, since the instruction as a whole when read in connection with the remainder of the charge made plain to the jury that there could be no conviction unless there was a misappropriation of the public money,—in other words, that the appropriation must have been wrongful. It is a rule of universal application that instructions must be considered together, and if then they correctly announce the rule, they will be upheld. (*Davis v. State*, 51 Neb. 301; *Ford v. State*, 46 Neb. 390; *Carleton v. State*, 43 Neb. 373.)

The thirteenth instruction requires no discussion, since it raises the question whether to prove the offense charged it was necessary that specie should have been received on the check given in payment of the auditor's warrant. The instruction is in harmony with the views expressed in another part of this opinion upon the motion to direct a verdict and the sufficiency of the evidence to sustain the conviction. Further elaboration of the point would be superfluous.

It is urged that the court erred in assuming in the tenth, eleventh, and fifteenth paragraphs of the charge the validity of the depository law. An elaborate argument is made in the briefs against the validity of that piece of legislation on grounds other than those heretofore considered by this court. We must be excused from entering upon a discussion of the subject at this time, as the defendant is in no position now to assert that the public moneys of the state were not rightfully on deposit in the Omaha National Bank. He recognized the validity of the statute by placing the moneys of the state in said bank, and it would indeed be a reproach upon the law to permit him to assail the depository law in a prosecution for the embezzlement of the public funds so deposited by him. It was the money of the state that went into the bank, and it was likewise the money of the state that paid the check, whether the bank was a lawful state depository or not.

Complaint is made of the fourteenth instruction. It,

in effect, told the jury that if the defendant disposed of
the warrant in question, or caused it to be done, or secured credit for the same, in his individual capacity and
for his own use, or for the use of any other person except
the state, and if, as state treasurer, he paid the warrant
with state funds, that would constitute embezzlement of
the money with which the warrant was paid. The argument is that the warrant was valid, and it was the duty
of the defendant to pay it in the order of registration.
The position is unsound as we have already demonstrated, at least to our own satisfaction. It is further
said this instruction authorized the jury to find the defendant guilty of embezzling the warrant, although the
counts charging the misappropriation of that instrument
had been *nolled*. There is no merit in this contention.
If certain facts were established, it permitted a conviction for the conversion of the money alone.

The fifteenth instruction is in this language: "If you
find from the evidence that the Omaha National Bank
was a state depository, and if you further find the defendant drew a check upon said bank against the funds
of the state therein deposited to the credit of the state,
and that said check was paid at said bank, that would
constitute a taking of public money of the state by the
defendant at the bank, whether the defendant was present at the time of payment of the check or not; nor
would it be material whether the check was drawn in
favor of the defendant or not, or by whom presented."
It is suggested by counsel that under this instruction it
would be a conversion by defendant, had a check drawn
by him in his official capacity on said bank, but not delivered, been stolen from the defendant, the name of the
payee forged thereon, and then presented to and paid by
the bank. If there were any evidence tending to show
any such state of facts there might be some foundation
for the criticism directed against the instruction. But
no such testimony was admitted on the trial, while it
was established beyond dispute that the defendant in

person presented the check to the bank for payment. The instruction, therefore, could not have misled the jury by reason of the matter suggested, nor because it stated that it was immaterial whether defendant was present or not when the check was paid. Moreover, we do not think it was necessary for the defendant to have been in Douglas county when the check was presented and paid to make the offense complete in that county. Had he sent the check by mail or messenger to take up the warrant, still the misappropriation of the funds would have taken place in that county on the payment of the check there. (*People v. McKinney*, 10 Mich. 54; *Norris v. State*, 25 O. St. 217; *Commonwealth v. Taylor*, 105 Mass. 172; *Commonwealth v. Wood*, 142 Mass. 459; *Commonwealth v. Karpowski*, 167 Pa. St. 225.)

The sixteenth instruction is not incoherent, but is logical and easily understood. The seventeenth instruction related to the testimony of expert accountants, the substance thereof being that the testimony of such witnesses should be given such weight as the jury considered them entitled to. This was not giving undue prominence to the testimony of that class of witnesses.

The twenty-first instruction is criticised, which reads as follows: "'A reasonable doubt,' as used in these instructions, to justify an acquittal, must be a reasonable one arising from a candid and impartial investigation of all the evidence in the case. A doubt produced by an undue sensibility in the mind of any juror in view of the consequences of his verdict is not a reasonable doubt, and the juror is not allowed to create sources of materials of doubt by resorting to trivial or fanciful suppositions and remote conjectures as to a possible state of facts differing from those established by the evidence. You are not at liberty to disbelieve as jurors if from all the evidence you believe as men. Your oath imposes on you no obligation to doubt where no doubt would exist if no oath had been administered. If after a careful and impartial examination and consideration of all the evidence

in the case you can say that you feel an abiding conviction of the guilt of the defendant and are fully satisfied
to a moral certainty of the truth of the charge made
against him, then you are satisfied beyond a reasonable
doubt." Two objections are urged against the above
instruction, first, that the opening sentence incorrectly
states the law. True, the accused had the right to the
benefit of any doubt arising from the want of evidence
in the case. This was not taken from him in the instruction quoted. The court did not say that a reasonable
doubt, to authorize an acquittal, must be one arising
from the evidence alone, but merely told the jury that
to produce an acquittal it must be a reasonable doubt
arising from a candid and impartial investigation of all
the evidence in the case. If the jury did that, it would
reveal to them any lack of evidence to sustain a conviction, and if any such want of evidence was found there
could be no conviction. The other criticism is upon the
language: "You are not at liberty to disbelieve as jurors
if from all the evidence you believe as men. Your oath
imposes on you no obligation to doubt where no doubt
would exist if no oath had been administered." An expression almost in the foregoing language was approved in the
celebrated case of *Spies v. People*, 122 Ill. 1, and *Nevling v.
Commonwealth*, 98 Pa. St. 322, and by this court in at least
two cases, *Willis v. State*, 43 Neb. 102, and *Davis v. State*,
51 Neb. 301. With those decisions we are content. A
discussion of the subject anew would be profitless.

The court declined to give the second instruction requested by the accused, which is as follows: "You are
instructed that the law presumes the defendant innocent
in this case and not guilty as charged in the information.
This presumption of innocence is not a mere form, which
may be disregarded by the jury at pleasure, but it is an
essential, substantial part of the law of the land binding on you as jurors in this case. You are to regard this
presumption of innocence in this case as a matter of evidence in favor of the defendant, to the benefit of which

he is entitled during your entire deliberations." The request is in accord with the holding in *Long v. State*, 23 Neb. 33, where it was stated, following *Garrison v. People*, 6 Neb. 285, that the legal presumption of innocence was a matter of evidence to the benefit of which the accused was entitled. The same principle embraced in this request was laid down in the sixth instruction given in the case at bar by the court on its own motion, which reads thus: "The law raises no presumption against the defendant; on the contrary, the presumption of law is in favor of his innocence. This presumption of innocence continues through the trial until every material allegation in the information is established by the evidence to the exclusion of all reasonable doubt." (*Garrison v. People, supra.*) The instruction in that case to which the defendant took exception read: "And if after you shall have carefully examined the evidence in this case, you shall be able to reconcile it with the innocence of the prisoner, it will be your duty, as no doubt it will be your pleasure, to acquit him." This court held that the language quoted fully recognized the rule that the legal presumption of innocence is a matter of evidence. The twenty-first instruction in the case at hand is no less favorable to the accused than the one requested by him; hence he was not injuriously affected by the refusal to give the instruction tendered.

Defendant's tenth instruction was framed upon the theory that to constitute embezzlement the accused must have obtained the actual physical possession of the money misappropriated. The fallacy of this proposition has already been shown.

The fourteenth and fifteenth instructions refused were to the effect that the auditor's warrant introduced in evidence was a valid instrument and that the defendant could not be convicted of the crime of embezzlement of the money used in payment of such warrant. This doctrine being opposed to the views we have expressed upon another question in the case, the requests were properly refused by the trial court.

It was not error to refuse the other requests of the defendant to charge, since, in so far as they stated the law correctly, they were fully covered by the instructions given. This rule that it is not error to refuse to repeat instructions has been so frequently stated by this court as to make unnecessary the citation of the authority to sustain the proposition.

It is finally insisted that the jury did not ascertain and state in their verdict the value of the money embezzled, and, therefore, the finding was insufficient upon which to base the judgment and sentence. . Section 488 of the Code of Criminal Procedure declares: "When the indictment charges an offense against the property of another by larceny, embezzlement, or obtaining under false pretenses, the jury, on conviction, shall ascertain and declare in their verdict the value of the property stolen, embezzled, or falsely obtained." The foregoing provision makes it mandatory upon the jury, in case of conviction of either of the offenses named in the section, that they fix and return in their verdict the value of the property stolen, embezzled, or falsely obtained. (*McCoy v. State*, 22 Neb. 418; *McCormick v. State*, 42 Neb. 866; *Fisher v. State*, 52 Neb. 531.) The jury in the case at bar, after finding the defendant guilty as charged in the third count of the information, did ascertain and declare "the amount embezzled to be $15188.445," which was a substantial compliance with the requirements of the statute. The meaning of the verdict returned cannot be misunderstood. The accused was convicted upon the charge of embezzling a specified sum of money, and the finding by the jury of the amount embezzled is equivalent to an ascertainment of its value. The words "amount" and "value" when applied to money are synonymous terms. Therefore, when the jury determined the amount of money embezzled, they also ascertained its value.

In *Grant v. State*, 55 Ala. 201, it was ruled that in a prosecution for the embezzlement of money no averment or proof as to the value thereof is necessary, since the

court will take judicial notice that the same is worth its
face value. To the same effect are *Duvall v. State,* 63 Ala.
12; *Gady v. State,* 83 Ala. 51; *State v. Barr,* 38 Atl. Rep.
[N. J.] 817.

In *Hildreth v. People,* 32 Ill. 36, the defendant was prosecuted for larceny of $1,270 in current bank bills. The
jury returned the following verdict: "We, the jury, find
the defendant guilty of larceny, of twelve hundred and
seventy dollars, as charged in the indictment." It was
there argued, as here, that the verdict was defective, because the value of the money was not ascertained by the
jury. The court, in the opinion, say: "It is true the verdict does not, in terms, find the value of the money
stolen. But it finds that he was guilty of stealing a certain number of dollars, and as dollars indicate a fixed
and precise value, the verdict is as certain in that respect as if they had found the worth of the money. The
indictment charges that the defendant stole so many
dollars in bank bills, and the jury find that he was guilty
of the larceny of that number of dollars. This was, although not strictly in form, sufficient in substance."

A question quite analogous to the one under discussion was before the court in *State v. Knox,* 17 Neb. 683,
where it was decided that a complaint for the embezzlement of $35 of the public moneys was sufficient, although
it contained no specific allegation of value. The court,
in speaking of the contention that an averment of value
was indispensable, observed: "This would be necessary
if property, or bank bills not a legal tender, had been
embezzled; but where the allegation is the embezzling of
thirty-five dollars in money, the amount designated expresses the value, the presumption being that it was lawful money." The same principle must control here.
Money is the standard or measure of values; therefore,
when a specified number of dollars or amount of money
is stated or given, that sum is presumed to represent the
value thereof. The legal effect of the verdict is the same
as if the jury had said they found the value of the money

embezzled to be $151,884.45. It is somewhat informal, nevertheless it is sufficient in substance. An examination of the authorities cited upon this point by counsel for the defendant will show that not one of them can properly be enrolled in support of the proposition that this verdict is not sufficient, since in none of the cases was either the amount or value of the property ascertained and stated by the jury in their verdict.

We have scrutinized this record, and given the questions thereby presented the most careful investigation at our command, and the conclusion is irresistible that no reversible error is disclosed. The judgment is accordingly

AFFIRMED.

IRVINE and RAGAN, CC., expressing no opinion.

ANDREW HOEFER v. JULIUS A. LANGHORST.

FILED JANUARY 8, 1898. No. 7694.

Review: PLEADING AND PROOF: VARIANCE: FACTORS AND BROKERS.
Where the claim of an agent for compensation was for finding a purchaser for the land of the defendant ready and willing to purchase, and, without objection, proof was made of the ability to purchase, as well as of the alleged readiness and willingness, the variance cannot be urged as error for the first time in the supreme court.

ERROR from the district court of Cass county. Tried below before CHAPMAN, J. *Affirmed.*

H. D. Travis, for plaintiff in error.

A. N. Sullivan and *J. H. Haldeman, contra.*

RYAN, C.

The defendant in error recovered judgment against the plaintiff in error for the sum of $150, with interest as

prayed, in the district court of Cass county. The claim
on which the judgment was rendered was for procuring
a purchaser of certain land of plaintiff in error in accordance with an agreement so to do made by the defendant in error, for which service the sum of $150 was
to be paid by the plaintiff in error. The evidence justified the jury in finding that the service rendered was that
defendant in error had procured a purchaser, ready and
able to buy the land which the plaintiff in error had
authorized defendant in error to sell. It is true it was
merely alleged in the petition that the party procured as
a purchaser was ready and willing to purchase on the
required terms, but, on the trial, there was no objection
to proof being made of the ability, as well as of the alleged readiness and willingness of the proposed purchaser. It is now too late to raise this question of a variance for the first time. It is possible that this might
have been raised upon one or more of the instructions, if
the assignments with respect to them had been so made
as to admit of the consideration of the instructions independently of each other; but these assignments were
as to groups, in each of which there was an instruction
not open to criticism. We cannot, therefore, inquire
whether or not other instructions were faulty.

The verdict was sustained by the evidence, and the
judgment of the district court is therefore

AFFIRMED.

STATE OF NEBRASKA, EX REL. ROCK COUNTY, V. GEORGE
N. SHELDON ET AL.

FILED JANUARY 3, 1898. No. 9685.

Counties: TAXES: DISCRETION OF COUNTY BOARD: MANDAMUS. Where
county authorities have levied taxes to provide for the current expenses of a certain year to the constitutional limit, courts have no
authority to control the action and discretion of such county
board. Following *Young v. Lane*, 43 Neb. 813.

ERROR from the district court of Rock county. Tried below before KINKAID and WESTOVER, JJ. *Affirmed.*

J. A. Douglas, for plaintiff in error.

E. M. Davisson, contra.

RYAN, C.

In the district court of Rock county there was denied a mandamus to compel the county commissioners of Brown county to levy a tax on the taxable property in Brown county of sufficient amount to pay an existing judgment in favor of the former county against the latter. This proceeding presents for review the correctness of this action of the district court.

It was stipulated that certain portions of the alternative writ and certain parts of the answer were true. Thus there were established the following facts: The judgment of which satisfaction is sought by means of the writ prayed was affirmed in the supreme court in May, 1897, and in January of said year no amount was included in the estimate of expenses for that year for the payment of said judgment, neither was there any levy for that purpose. The amount of revenue which will be realized from the taxes levied by the respondents in and for the year 1897, for ordinary expenses of Brown county, is insufficient to meet and pay the current expenses of said county for the year 1897 and also pay any part of said judgment. The assessors' books of Brown county show that the total taxable property of Brown county is $543,024. The respondents have already made a levy on said taxable property in the sum of one and one-half dollars on each hundred dollars valuation. The case of *Young v. Lane,* 43 Neb. 813, is determinative of this case, for therein it was held that where county authorities have levied taxes to provide for the current expenses of a certain year to the constitutional limit, courts have no authority to control the action and discretion of such county board. The stipulation admits the levy to this limit, which, by section 5, article 9, of the constitution of this state, is $1.50 on each $100 valuation. The judgment of the district court is therefore

AFFIRMED.

JOHN D. TUTT, APPELLANT, v. GEORGE C. HAWKINS, APPELLEE.

FILED JANUARY 3, 1898.   No. 7719.

Elections: BALLOTS: INTENTION OF ELECTOR. The intention of an elector must be ascertained from his ballot, and any inaccuracies in the preparation of such ballot cannot be urged for the first time after an election, to defeat the clearly expressed intention of the voter.

APPEAL from the district court of Cass county. Heard below before CHAPMAN, J. *Reversed.*

Matthew Gering, for appellant.

A. J. Graves, contra.

RYAN, C.

There was filed in the office of the clerk of the district court of Cass county a petition in which the plaintiff John D. Tutt alleged that at the municipal election held in the city of Plattsmouth on April 3, 1894, the whole number of votes cast for councilman of the Fifth ward was 194, of which 79 were for William Slater, 49 were for George C. Hawkins, the contestee, 40 were for said John D. Tutt, and 26 were for Edwin Bates; that upon a canvass of said votes made by the city council of said city William Slater and George C. Hawkins were declared elected. It was futher alleged in the petition that the whole number of votes counted for councilman to fill a vacancy was 66, of which Tutt received 40 and Edwin Bates 26. By the answer of the contestee it was asserted that the votes cast for councilman for the Fifth ward were not canvassed with reference to filling a vacancy, but it was alleged that the four candidates were competitors for the office of councilman for said ward, without reference to whether the candidacy was for the entire or for the unexpired term, and that, relying upon precedent, the candidate receiving the highest number of votes held the full term and the candidate receiving the next highest vote held the unexpired term. We need not consider the issues at greater length, for the question to be determined is whether or not it was proper to follow the alleged precedent. The official ballot with reference to councilman for the Fifth ward was printed as follows:

"Edwin Bates (to fill vacancy)　Republican
"George C. Hawkins　　　　　　Republican
"Wm. Slater　　　　　　　　　Democrat
"J. D. Tutt (to fill vacancy)　Democrat"

It was correctly recited in the petition that Hawkins received 49 while Tutt received but 40 votes; but a reference to the form of ballot cast shows that the electors were not voting for them as rivals for the same office. The intention of the voter must be gathered from the ballot which he actually casts and cannot be defeated by evidence that the ballots were not prepared in accordance with the intention of a political convention by which one of the nominations was made. After an election held without objection to the form of the ballot it is too late to question the result. (*State v. Norris*, 37 Neb. 299.) The district court erred in reaching the conclusion which it did and its judgment is accordingly reversed.

REVERSED AND REMANDED.

W. W. HOUSE v. W. F. WREN ET AL.

FILED JANUARY 3, 1898. No. 7738.

Review: SUFFICIENCY OF EVIDENCE. The judgment in this case, being sustained by sufficient evidence, is affirmed.

ERROR from the district court of Lancaster county. Tried below before TIBBETS, J. *Affirmed.*

J. L. Caldwell, for plaintiff in error.

William G. Clark, contra.

RYAN, C.

This was an action of replevin by plaintiff in error as owner, for the possession of a horse, against the defendants in error holding possession by virtue of a chattel mortgage made by one R. D. Plowman to W. F. Wren. There was a conflict in the evidence as to the correctness of the respective theories advanced by the parties. By the plaintiff's evidence it was made to appear that, accompanied by Mr. Plowman, plaintiff had purchased the horse and given his note therefor. It was rather unfortunate for this theory that Plowman's name was affixed to this note before that of House. It was testified by House, however, that this signature of his was merely as surety, and that the possession of the horse taken and held by Plowman was solely as his bailee. Opposed to this there was evidence which justified the conclusion that the purchase was by Plowman and that the horse, therefore, was his to mortgage and dispose of as he saw fit. The trial was to the court. The judgment was adverse to House, and as it did not lack the support of sufficient evidence it must be, and accordingly is,

AFFIRMED.

28

CONWAY & KNICKERBACKER V. WILLIAM H. MAGILL, SHERIFF, ET AL.

FILED JANUARY 3, 1898. No. 7705.

Sheriff's Liability for Failure to Make Levy: ACTION: EVIDENCE. In order for an execution or attachment creditor to recover his debt against a sheriff, because of the latter's failure to seize under the writ sufficient property of the debtor to satisfy the same, the burden is upon such creditor to plead and prove that, during the life of the writ, his debtor was possessed of property liable to be seized under the writ, and that the sheriff negligently failed to seize such property.

ERROR from the district court of Brown county. Tried below before BARTOW, J. *Affirmed.*

Macfarland & Altschuler and *J. C. McNerney,* for plaintiffs in error.

P. D. McAndrew, contra.

RAGAN, C.

G. A. Sargent & Co. was a copartnership engaged in mercantile business at Ainsworth, Nebraska, and indebted for goods purchased of Conway & Knickerbacker. On the 29th of November, 1892, before the county judge of Brown county sitting as a justice of the peace, Conway & Knickerbacker brought suit against Sargent & Co. and caused an attachment to be issued and delivered to the sheriff of said county commanding him to seize a sufficient amount of the goods and chattels of Sargent & Co. to satisfy the claim of Conway & Knickerbacker in the sum of $180 and the probable costs of the suit, not to exceed $50. Under this order of attachment the sheriff seized the property of the attachment defendants, which the appraisers appointed by the sheriff then and there appraised and valued at $240.79. On the 23d of December, 1892, the attached property was sold at public vendue by the sheriff to satisfy the attachment and brought the sum of $143. Conway & Knickerbacker then instituted this suit in the district court of Brown county against William Magill, the sheriff thereof, and the sureties on his official bond to recover the balance due them from Sargent & Co., basing their action against the sheriff upon his alleged neglect to seize sufficient property of Sargent & Co. to satisfy their, Conway & Knickerbacker's, debt, Sargent & Co. being then and there possessed of sufficient property which could have been seized by the sheriff on the attachment writ. The trial in the district court resulted in a verdict and judgment for the sheriff and his sureties, and Conway & Knickerbacker bring the same here for review on error.

There is not in the record one syllable of evidence which shows or tends to show that Sargent & Co. were possessed of any property of any name or description which the sheriff could have seized on the attachment writ save and except the property he did seize. In order for an execution or attachment creditor to recover his debt against a sheriff because of the latter's failure to seize under the writ sufficient property of the debtor to satisfy the same, the burden is upon such creditor to plead and prove that during the life of the writ his debtor was possessed of property liable to be seized under the writ and that the sheriff negligently failed to seize such property. The judgment of the district court is

AFFIRMED.

WEBER BROTHERS V. EDWARD WHETSTONE.

FILED JANUARY 3, 1898.   No. 7683.

1. **Instructions: REQUESTS: REVIEW.** Before error can be predicated upon the failure of a district court to instruct the jury on some particular feature of a case the party complaining must have by a proper instruction requested the court to instruct upon such feature.

2. **Animals**: AGISTER's LIEN. One who feeds and takes care of live stock in pursuance of a contract therefor with the owner has a lien on such stock to secure his recompense for such feed and care. (Compiled Statutes, ch. 4, art. 1, sec. 28.)

3. ——: ——. An agister cannot be deprived of his lien upon live stock except by his voluntary relinquishment thereof or by such conduct on his part as estops him from asserting it.

4. ——: ——. The taking by the owner of live stock from the possession of his agister without the latter's consent does not divest his lien.

5. ——: ——. If a lien exists against live stock for its feed and care a purchaser of such stock is charged with notice of such lien. That he purchased such stock for value without actual notice of such lien affords him no protection against the same.

ERROR from the district court of Dawes county. Tried below before BARTOW, J. *Affirmed.*

C. Dana Sayrs and *John S. Murphy,* for plaintiffs in error.

E. S. Ricker, contra.

RAGAN, C.

This is an action in replevin brought in the district court of Dawes county by Weber Bros. for certain cattle. The defendant Edward Whetstone claimed that he was entitled to possession of the cattle and had an agister's lien thereon to secure a compensation of $20 agreed to be paid him by the owner of the cattle for herding, feeding, and caring for the same. The trial resulted in a verdict and judgment in favor of Whetstone, and Weber Bros. prosecute error.

1. The first argument is that the court erred in giving to the jury the following instruction: "The jury are instructed that, as a general rule of law, the purchaser of personal property in good faith for value, where delivery of the property accompanies the purchase, is protected against the claims of third parties, but that the owners of stolen property have a right to pursue the same and recover it wherever and in whomsoever's possession it

may be found, regardless of the circumstances under which such possession may have been acquired. So, if property rightly in the possession of any person, and where the law makes such possession the basis of a lien, is, over his protest and forcibly, taken from him,—not necessarily with force and arms, but in such a manner as the person in possession could not prevent,—the possessor's right would not thereby be lost; and under such a statute as the one quoted from in Number 5 of these instructions, purchasers would be put upon inquiry before they can be protected as innocent purchasers from the assertion of such lien." The criticism upon this instruction is the reference of the court therein to the rights of the owner of stolen property to reclaim it. Counsel correctly say that there was no evidence in this case that any of the property in controversy had been stolen.   The evidence shows that the owner of these cattle employed Whetstone to herd and take care of them and for that purpose put them in his possession and agreed to pay him for herding them $20; and while the cattle were so in Whetstone's possession the owner sold them to a man named Hubbard, and he, with force and arms, or at least over the objection and protest of Whetstone, took the cattle out of the latter's possession and sold and delivered them to Weber Bros. On the trial Weber Bros. contended that they were purchasers of the cattle without notice of Whetstone's lien and, therefore, entitled to take the cattle discharged from said lien. In view of this evidence we think that while the instruction may be open to the criticism made upon it by counsel, their clients could not have possibly been prejudiced by it.

2. A contention of the plaintiffs in error on the trial was that Whetstone by his conduct had estopped himself from asserting his lien upon these cattle as against the plaintiffs in error; and another argument here is that the court erred in not giving to the jury an instruction on the law of estoppel as applied to the facts of this case.

A sufficient answer to this argument is, if counsel desired an instruction given to the jury on the question of estoppel, he should have prepared and presented to the court an instruction on that feature of the case with the request that it be given. Not having done this, he cannot now be heard to insist that the court erred because it neglected to give such an instruction. (*German Nat. Bank v. Leonard*, 40 Neb. 676; *Barr v. City of Omaha*, 42 Neb. 341.)

3. A third argument is that the court erred in refusing to give to the jury the following instruction: "The court instructs the jury that if they find from all the evidence that the firm of Weber Bros. purchased the cattle in question on the 11th of October, 1894, without notice of any lien that the defendant Edward Whetstone had upon said cattle, if any he had, then you will find for the plaintiffs and return a verdict in their favor." Whetstone having herded, fed, and cared for these cattle in pursuance of a contract with their owner, and being in possession of the cattle for such purpose under such contract, and having performed the contract, or a part of it, was vested by statute (Compiled Statutes, ch. 4, art. 1, sec. 28) with a lien upon the cattle to secure his compensation for their care, and any one who dealt with those cattle or purchased them was bound to take notice of this lien; and Hubbard, when he purchased the cattle of their owner, took the cattle charged with that lien. They were then in the actual possession of Whetstone, and when Hubbard sold them to Weber Bros., the latter took them charged with Whetstone's lien. True, at that time they were not in the actual possession of Whetstone, but had been taken from him that day by Hubbard by force. The rule of *caveat emptor* applies to one who purchases personal property, and though such purchaser may pay a valuable consideration for such property and at the time have no knowledge that another has a lien upon it for its feed or care, he cannot protect himself as against an agister's lien simply because he is an inno-

cent purchaser of the property without notice of the lien. The agister cannot be deprived of his lien except by his voluntary relinquishment of it or by some act or omission upon his part which would estop him from asserting it as against a purchaser.   He does not lose his lien upon the property simply because°of the fact that it is taken from his possession without his consent and sold to another who has no notice of the lien. (*Kroll v. Ernst*, 34 Neb. 482.)

The court did not err in refusing to give the instruction, and its judgment is right and is

AFFIRMED.

EMILY MOTLEY, APPELLANT, V. GEORGE MOTLEY ET AL., APPELLEES.

FILED JANUARY 3, 1898.   No. 7736.

1. **Dower:** RIGHTS OF WIDOW. The statutes of the state expressly provide how a widow may be lawfully barred of dower in the lands of which her husband died seized, and this bar is made to depend upon her voluntary act.

2. ———: EFFECT OF HUSBAND'S DEBTS: DESCENT. The lands of an intestate descend to his heirs subject to his unsecured debts; but his widow's dower estate in such lands is not incumbered with such debts.

3. ———: RIGHTS OF WIDOW. The lands of a husband during his life are subject to his wife's inchoate right of dower therein; and, at the instant of his death intestate, the law transmutes the inchoate dower lien into an absolute dower estate, subtracts it from the lands of the intestate and vests the right thereto in his widow.

4. **Administrator's Sale:** DOWER. The sale of the lands of his intestate by an administrator. made in pursuance of a license therefor to pay debts allowed against his estate, does not, of itself, divest the widow's dower estate in such lands.

5. ———: ———. A sale of lands by an administrator to pay the debts of his intestate is a judicial sale, and the doctrine of *caveat emptor* applies to a purchaser thereat.

6. ———: ———: NOTICE TO PURCHASER. Where the record of a proceeding, which resulted in a district court's licensing an admin-

istrator to sell the lands of his intestate, discloses that such intestate left a widow, this is, of itself, notice to a purchaser at such sale of such widow's dower estate in such lands.

7. ——: PARTIES TO PROCEEDING: DOWER: ESTOPPEL. A widow made party to a proceeding by her husband's administrator to sell the lands of which he died seized to pay debts allowed against his estate does not estop herself from claiming her dower estate in the lands sold solely because she neglected to appear in such proceeding.

8. ——: ——: ——: ——. Nor does she estop herself from claiming her dower estate in such lands because she attended the administrator's sale, made no objections thereto, and neglected to advise the bidders thereat that she had a dower estate in such lands.

9. ——: ——: ——: ——. Nor is such widow estopped from claiming her dower estate in the lands so sold because she received a part of the proceeds of such sale as her "distributive share of such estate;" such payment not having been made to nor received by her in lieu of her dower estate.

APPEAL from the district court of Adams county. Heard below before BEALL, J. *Reversed.*

See opinion for references to authorities.

Batty, Dungan & Burton, for appellant.

Capps & Stevens, contra.

RAGAN, C. -

John Motley died intestate in Adams county seized in fee-simple of certain real estate situate therein, leaving a widow and four children. In pursuance of a license granted therefor by the district court of said county Motley's administrator sold such real estate for the purpose of paying the unsecured debts of the intestate which had been proved and allowed against his estate in the county court of said county. Subsequently Emily Motley, the widow, brought this proceeding, under the statute, in the county court of said county to have her dower assigned in the lands of which her husband died possessed. The county court rendered a judgment assign.

ing Mrs. Motley her dower, from which George Motley, the purchaser of the real estate at the administrator's sale, appealed to the district court. The action was there tried to the court without the intervention of a jury and resulted in a judgment dismissing Mrs. Motley's action. This judgment of the district court is now before us for review.

1. In support of the judgment of the district court it is insisted that the sale of the lands to pay debts made by the administrator of itself divested the widow's dower. Section 1, chapter 23, Compiled Statutes, provides: "The widow of every deceased person shall be entitled to dower or the use during her natural life of one-third of all the lands whereof her husband was seized of all [an] estate of inheritance at any time during the marriage unless she is lawfully barred thereof." Other sections of this statute prescribe what causes shall operate to bar the widow of dower in the lands of which her husband was seized during the coverture. Section 2 of the chapter provides that if the husband exchange lands of which he is seized for other lands, his widow shall not have dower in both tracts, but may elect to take her dower out of either tract, provided she begins proceedings to have her dower assigned in one tract or the other within one year after her husband's death; and if such a proceeding is not brought within such time, she shall then have dower only in the land received by her husband in the exchange. Section 3 bars the widow of dower in lands mortgaged by her husband prior to the marriage as against the mortgagee and those claiming under him. Section 4 bars the widow of dower in lands purchased by the husband during coverture and mortgaged to secure the purchase money, as against such mortgagee and those claiming under him, even though she may not have united in such mortgage. Section 12 provides that a married woman residing in this state may bar her right of dower in the land of her husband by joining in a conveyance thereof and acknowledging the same. Section

13 provides that a woman may be barred of her dower
in the lands of her husband by a jointure settled on her
with her consent before the marriage, provided such
jointure consists of a freehold estate in lands for the life
of the wife at least to take effect in possession or profit
immediately on the death of the husband. Section 15
provides that if any pecuniary provision shall be made
for the benefit of an intended wife, and in lieu of dower,
and assented to by her in the manner provided by statute,
this shall bar her right of dower in the lands of her husband. Section 17 provides that if lands be devised to a
wife, or other provision be made to her in the will of her
husband, then she may elect to either take under the will
or to claim her dower, but she cannot have both; and by
accepting the benefits of the provisions of the will she
forfeits her right of dower.

These statutes expressly provide how a widow may be
lawfully barred of her dower; and it is to be observed
that no one of these provisions deprives a widow against
her consent of dower in the lands of which her husband
died seized; but her loss of dower is made to depend upon
her voluntary act. The statute does not prescribe, either
expressly or by implication, that the sale by an administrator of his intestate's lands for the payment of his
debts shall have the effect of divesting the widow's dower
in such lands; and while the lands of an intestate descend to his heirs subject to his debts (Compiled Statutes,
ch. 23, sec. 30), and the title which the heirs take to such
lands may be divested by a sale thereof for the payment
of the debts of the intestate allowed against his estate
by the county court, the dower of the widow in such
lands does not come to her charged or incumbered with
such debts or claims. On the death of her husband her
inchoate right of dower, which up to that time was a
mere lien charge or incumbrance upon the real estate of
the husband, ceased to be such lien or charge, and became an estate, carved out of the lands of the intestate
and exempted during her life from the payment of the

ordinary unsecured debts of the intestate. This dower estate the moment it existed became the widow's property; it was not liable for and could not be sold without her consent for the payment of her husband's debts. The language of our statute is not that a widow shall be entitled to dower in the lands of which her husband died seized, but that she shall have dower in all the lands of which her husband was seized as an estate of inheritance at any time during the coverture. This is the law of most of the states of the Union, and in construing this statute the courts are all agreed that, when the lawful marriage of a man and woman and the ownership of real estate by the former concur, an inchoate dower right at once attaches; that this is in the nature of a charge or incumbrance upon the real estate; and, when such right has once attached, it remains and continues a charge upon the real estate, unless released by the voluntary act of the wife or be extinguished by operation of law; and upon the death of the husband the inchoate right is merged into a dower estate. And the authorities are agreed that a judicial sale made of the husband's real state during his lifetime for some obligation of his not secured by a lien upon the real estate in which the wife had joined does not extinguish the wife's inchoate dower, and upon the death of her husband the widow is entitled to her dower estate in the lands so sold. (*Sisk v. Smith*, 1 Gil. [Ill.] 503; *Grady v. McCorkle*, 57 Mo. 172; *Blevins v. Smith*, 16 S. W. Rep. [Mo.] 213; *Vinson v. Gentry*, 21 S. W. Rep. [Ky.] 578; *Porter v. Lazear*, 109 U. S. 84; *Butler v. Fitzgerald*, 43 Neb. 192.) Had the lands involved in this action been sold on execution during the life of the intestate to satisfy the debts for which his administrator sold, such a sale would not have divested the wife's inchoate dower rights nor barred the widow's dower in the lands. How then can it be said that the sale of these lands by the intestate's administrator to pay the latter's debts, of itself, took away the widow's dower in such lands? It is true that the administrator was licensed by the district court to sell the land of the intestate to pay his debts, but the district court by this license or order did not attempt to authorize the administrator to sell the dower estate of the widow in said lands. We need not inquire whether the district court had such authority; it is sufficient that nowhere in any paper in the proceedings of the administrator's sale is the dower estate of the widow referred to.

As we have already seen, the dower estate of the widow was not liable for the debts of the husband which had been allowed against his estate by the county court; and no statute of the state authorizes the district courts, when granting a license to sell the real estate of the intestate to pay his debts, to include therein the widow's dower. Indeed, it is clear from a reading of the statute on the subject of the sale of lands for the payment of the debts of an intestate (Compiled Statutes, ch. 23) that these statutes contemplate only the sale of the intestate's interest in the lands of which he died seized. But his interest in those lands, even during his lifetime, was subject to his wife's inchoate right of dower, and, at the instant of his death, the law transmuted the inchoate dower lien into an absolute dower estate, subtracted it from the lands of the intestate, and vested the right thereto in his widow. By section 82 of said chapter it is provided that such a license may be so framed as to authorize the sale of the reversion of the dower of the widow, and if not so framed, that such reversion may be sold after the expiration of the widow's life estate. In the case at bar the administrator described the lands of which the intestate died seized, procured a license for their sale to pay his debts, and sold them without any more specific description. Nowhere in the proceedings was it stated, in so many words, that he was selling merely the interests of the intestate in those lands; that he was or was not attempting to sell the dower estate of the widow in those lands, nor that he was or was not selling or attempting to sell the reversion of the dower of the widow.   We are not called upon at this time to say whether the purchaser at this administrator's sale acquired the fee-simple title to all these lands subject to the dower estate of the widow therein, or whether such purchaser acquired the fee-simple title to only two-thirds of such lands; but we are quite clear that the administrator was not authorized by the district court to sell the dower estate of the widow in the lands of his intestate and that the widow's dower in these lands was not affected by that sale.   We have not been cited to any case, nor have we been able to find one, which holds that a sale made by an administrator of his intestate's lands to pay ordinary unsecured debts proved against his estate bars the widow of the intestate from dower.   So far as we have examined the cases the uniform holding is the other way.   (See, among others, *Kent v. Taggart*, 68 Ind. 163; *Elliott v. Frakes*, 71 Ind. 412; *Armstrong v. Cavitt*, 78 Ind. 476; *Compton v. Pruitt*, 88 Ind. 171; *House v. Fowle*, 29 Pac. Rep. [Ore.] 890; *Whitcaker v. Belt*, 36 Pac. Rep. [Ore.] 534; *Toledo, P. & W. R. Co. v. Curtenius*, 65 Ill. 120.)

2.   A second argument of the purchaser at the administrator's sale in support of the judgment of the district court is that he is an innocent purchaser of this real estate without notice of the rights of the widow to a dower estate in these lands; that when he purchased them at the administrator's sale he believed he was acquiring a perfect title to all the lands described in the license granted by the district court to the administrator. . But the administrator's sale was a judicial sale.   It was made and approved by authority of the district court of the county where the lands were situate, and the doctrine of *caveat emptor* applies to a purchaser of lands at a judicial sale.   The purchaser was bound to take notice of the authority of the administrator, and this authority was to sell only the interest which the intestate had at his death in the lands sold.   He was purchasing real estate, and it was his duty to examine the title and he had no right to rely upon statements of the adminis-

trator, if any were made, as to the character of the title
which he was selling.   But the record of the proceedings
under which the administrator sold disclosed upon its
face that John Motley had died intestate, seized of certain lands in Adams county; that he left a widow and
certain children and that the administrator was making
the sale of these lands to pay debts allowed by the county
court of Adams county against the intestate's estate.
The purchaser at this administrator's sale was charged
with notice of all that this record discloses, and it was
of itself notice that this widow had a dower estate in
the lands which were being sold.   (See *Norton v. Nebraska Loan & Trust Co.*, 35 Neb. 466; *Butler v. Fitzgerald*,
43 Neb. 192; *Whiteaker v. Belt*, 36 Pac. Rep. [Ore.] 534.)

3.   The widow of the intestate was made a party to the
proceedings of the administrator for the sale of these
lands.   Notice, as required by the statute, was served
upon her to appear and show cause, if any she had, why
such license should not be granted, but she made no
appearance whatever to that proceeding.   Another argument of the purchaser at this administrator's sale, in support of the judgment of the district court, is that the
widow cannot now maintain this action to have her
dower assigned, inasmuch as she neglected to appear in
the district court in the proceeding by the administrator
to sell the lands of her husband and set up her dower
estate in that proceeding.   We do not think any adjudicated case can be found which will sustain this contention.   The writer at least, after a patient and protracted
search, has been unable to find any such case.   Whether
the district court is invested with jurisdiction to assign
dower in any case we do not determine, but certainly
that was not the object of the proceedings by the administrator in seeking a license to sell the real estate of his
intestate.   The application of the administrator in that
proceeding alleged the death of his intestate, described
certain lands of which he died seized, that certain claims
had been proved against his estate in the county court,

and that the personal estate of the intestate was insufficient to pay these allowed claims and the expenses of administration, and prayed the district court for a license to sell the intestate's real estate to pay those claims. If the widow had appeared in that proceeding it would have been no defense to the application for her to allege that she had a dower estate in those lands. Such an answer would have stated no defense to the application of the administrator. The only defense that could have been made to the application would have been one which traversed some of its allegations; and, if we consider that the widow by not appearing confessed the allegations of the administrator's petition, it was not a confession that she had no dower estate in this real estate, but a confession that she had no cause to urge why the license should not be granted as prayed. And when the district court found that the allegations of the application of the administrator were true and adjudged that the license should be granted as prayed, he neither found nor adjudged that the widow of the intestate had no dower estate in the lands licensed to be sold. On the other hand, the application of the administrator and the evidence introduced by him in support of it informed the district court that the intestate had left a widow, and that was of itself notice to the court granting the license to sell that the widow had a dower estate in the e lands; and it would be doing an injustice to the intelligence of the court to indulge the presumption that by granting the license to sell he adjudged that the widow had no dower estate therein or that he intended to include in such license the widow's dower estate.

The question as to whether a widow is barred from prosecuting an action for the assignment of dower in lands which had been sold under a judicial proceeding to which she was a party, but made no appearance, was presented to the supreme court of Illinois in *Shaeffer v. Weed*, 3 Gil. 511, in 1846, Abraham Lincoln appearing for the widow. Shaeffer had furnished material and labor towards the erection of an improvement on the husband's real estate during the latter's lifetime. After the husband's death he brought suit to have established and foreclosed a mechanic's lien upon the real estate for the labor and material furnished the husband. To this proceeding the widow was made a party, but she did not appear in the action; and it was insisted that the judgment rendered in that proceeding upon her default estopped or barred her right of dower in the lands involved in that proceeding. The contention, however, was overruled.

A statute of the state of Illinois provided that one who had mortgaged his real estate should be deemed to have waived or released his homestead right in the real estate therein if there was inserted in the mortgage the following: "Hereby releasing and waiving all rights under and by virtue of the homestead exemption laws of this state." A man and his wife executed a mortgage upon their homestead, but the mortgage did not contain the release of the homestead right as provided by statute. Suit was brought to foreclose this mortgage. The husband and wife were made parties and duly served with process, but made default. A decree of foreclosure was entered, the real estate sold, and the sale confirmed. In *Hoskins v. Litchfield*, 31 Ill. 137, the supreme court of Illinois held that the husband and wife were not barred from asserting their homestead rights in the mortgaged premises because of their failure to appear and set up that right in the foreclosure proceeding, and that the decree pronounced in that action did not have the effect to take away the homestead right of the husband and wife. The court said: "This mortgage as to homestead right is like a mortgage in which the wife has not released her right of dower, when sought to be enforced in defiance of that right. Suppose in such a case the wife were made a party to a bill to foreclose a mortgage, without any averment that any right of dower existed or that the wife had released her dower, and a decree passed against the husband and wife, foreclosing the mortgage and ordering a sale of the premises. No one would contend that the right of dower would be affected by such decree, or that a sale under it could convey the premises freed from the right of dower, for the simple reason that the law has provided a different and an only mode for the release of dower." To the same effect see *Moore v. Titman*, 33 Ill. 357, where it was held that the right secured by the homestead act can only be lost by release or abandonment in the mode pointed out by statute. A mere failure to claim the right by answer or cross-bill in a suit to foreclose a mortgage wherein the right is not released, will not have the effect to bar the right or be considered as a relinquishment of the benefits of the statute. A decree by default and a sale thereunder will not operate to bar the right. To the same effect see *Mooers v. Dixon*, 35 Ill. 208; *Wing v. Cropper*, 35 Ill. 256.

In *Grady v. McCorkle*, 57 Mo. 172, the owner of real estate entered into a contract to convey the same and died. After his death the contractee brought suit against his widow and heirs for the specific performance of this contract. The widow was duly served with process in that suit, but made no appearance therein, and a decree of specific performance was entered as prayed by the contractee. Subsequently the widow instituted a proceeding to have her dower assigned in this real estate and the contractee interposed the decree entered in the specific performance suit as a bar to the widow's claim for dower; but the court held: "In a suit for specific performance of a contract to convey land, brought against the widow and heirs of the owner, where the dower of the widow is not in any manner determined or litigated, or drawn in question by the proceedings, a decree for plaintiff will not estop the widow from afterward recovering her dower." The statute of Missouri, like ours, provided that the widow should be endowed with a third part of all the lands whereof her husband was seized of an estate of inheritance at any time during the

29

marriage. Construing this statute the court said: "The right of dower attaches whenever there is a seizin by the husband during the marriage, and, unless it is relinquished by the wife in the manner prescribed by law, it becomes absolute at the husband's death. After the right of dower has once attached, it is not in the power of the husband alone to defeat it by any act in the nature of an alienation or charge. It is a right in law, fixed from the moment the facts of marriage and seizin concur, and becomes a title paramount to that of any person claiming under the husband by subsequent act." Discussing the effect of the decree in the specific performance suit the court said: "The whole object, extent, and scope of that proceeding was to have the agreement and undertaking of William Grady specifically performed. The rights against the widow and heirs were precisely the same as they would have been against William Grady, had he been alive and made a party to the suit. But a suit against him would not have affected his wife's right to dower without any concurring act on her part. * * * The question of the plaintiff's right of dower was neither raised nor decided and was not made a subject of adjudication in the suit for specific performance. The plaintiff did not answer, and although she was perhaps properly made a party, my conclusion is that she is not barred from claiming her dower interest in the land—she having done nothing to relinquish the same."

A case exactly in point here is *Compton v. Pruitt*, 88 Ind. 171. In that case an administrator was licensed to sell the lands of his intestate to pay debts proved against his estate. His widow was made a party to this proceeding, but did not appear therein. The widow then brought suit to have her dower assigned and the proceedings of the administrator by which the lands of the intestate were sold and conveyed were pleaded in bar of the widow's action; but the court overruled the plea and summed up its conclusion in the syllabus as follows: "An administrator cannot, without a widow's consent, sell her interest in lands of which her husband died seized, to make assets to pay debts. If a widow be made defendant to a proper petition to sell such lands, her default gives no power to sell her interest, and a purchaser does not acquire even color of title against her, and any attempt to sell her interest is a nullity." The court said: "In this case the petition [that is, of the administrator for leave to sell to pay debts] stated that the decedent died seized of the land, etc., leaving a widow. That was equivalent to a statement that only two-thirds of it was liable to be made assets. It notified the court and all parties in interest to that effect as fully as if the language * * * stated expressly that the land to be sold was two-thirds of the land described. So the notice of the application to sell stated that the administrators had filed their petition to sell the real estate of the decedent, nothing more. Such a petition and notice did not inform the widow of an intended attack upon her rights and she was guilty of no laches in failing to appear in the proceeding. She had a right to presume that the land liable to be made assets was the only subject of the petition and against such a petition she had no defense." To the same effect see *Elliott v. Frakes*, 71 Ind. 412.

In *Merchants Bank v. Thomson*, 55 N. Y. 7, it was held: "Where the wife of a mortgagor has not joined in the mortgage and has an inchoate right of dower in the mortgaged premises, the making of her a party to an action of foreclosure without allegations in the complaint that the mortgage is prior, superior, or hostile to her interest does not affect that interest, nor does the general clause in the judgment foreclosing defendants of all right in the premises."

In *Parmenter v. Binkley*, 28 O. St. 32, D. and M. instituted proceedings to foreclose a mortgage executed by B. alone, making B.'s wife a party. The wife did not answer or appear in the case. A decree of foreclosure was rendered and the land sold, and the court held that the foreclosure proceeding did not bar B.'s wife of her right of dower in the land sold.

Hooper v. Castetter, 45 Neb. 67, was a suit brought to foreclose a mortgage executed by both husband and wife. The mortgagor and his wife were made parties and duly served with process, but made no appearance to the action. Certain judgment creditors of the mortgagor were also made parties. They filed answers setting up their judgments and claiming that they were liens upon the mortgaged real estate subject to the mortgage. The court so found and decreed. The land was sold and after the mortgage was discharged there was a surplus paid into court. The judgment creditors claimed that this surplus should be applied on their judgments. The mortgagor and his wife claimed that they were entitled to the surplus in lieu of their homestead. It was contended in that case that the mortgagor and his wife were estopped from claiming the surplus proceeds of the sale because of their failure to set up their homestead rights in the foreclosure suit; but this contention was by this court overruled, and it was held that the question of the homestead rights of the mortgagor was not involved nor litigated in the foreclosure suit, and that the decree rendered in that suit was not a bar to the mortgagor's application to have the surplus paid to him in lieu of the homestead.

4. A fourth argument of the purchaser is that the widow has estopped herself by her conduct from now claiming her dower estate in the lands in controversy. The averment of the purchaser's answer on this subject is as follows: "That said plaintiff [that is, the widow] was present in person and attended the sale of said real estate and heard the bids made therefor and knew what said real estate sold at and never at any time made any objections thereto." The evidence sustains this averment of the answer. But the widow has not estopped herself from claiming her dower estate, because she attended the administrator's sale and made no objections thereto. The administrator was not selling or attempting to sell her property. She had no objection to the

sale of her husband's interest in the lands of which he died seized, and therefore she kept silent. It was not her duty to speak and advise the bidders at that sale of the laws of the state. The bidders, as well as the widow, were bound to know those laws. The answer of the purchaser does not allege, nor do the proofs show, that he was induced to purchase this real estate because of anything done or omitted to be done by the widow. His sole complaint is that she kept silent. But a complete answer to this is that she did not keep silent under circumstances when it was her duty to speak.

Scribner, discussing the question under consideration and citing the authorities, says: "Where the widow has done nothing to mislead the purchaser, and the circumstances are such that she is not required by good faith to disclose her claim, her mere silence in regard to it does not affect her right. Thus, her failure to give notice of her claim when the land in which she has 'dower is advertised for sale is no bar to her recovery. So, where lands are sold by a commissioner under an order of court, obtained by the widow as administratrix, but nothing is said or done to induce the belief that she will waive her dower, a simple omission on her part to announce at the sale that the land will be sold subject to her dower will not estop her from asserting that right. * * * In order to constitute an *estoppel in pais* not only must the widow by her words or conduct have caused the purchaser to believe that he would acquire a title discharged from dower, but he must also have acted upon that belief in making his purchase and paying the purchase money." (2 Scribner, Dower [2d ed.], p. 271.)

The same question was presented in *House v. Fowle*, 29 Pac. Rep. [Ore.] 890, and there the court said: "A widow is not estopped to assert her dower in land sold by order of court to satisfy decedent's debts because she assured the purchaser that the title was good and did not intimate her intention to claim the same—her dower. * * The defendant's next contention is that under the particular facts in this case the plaintiff is estopped from claiming her dower. The facts relied upon to create the estoppel are fully set out in the defendant's answer, but we think they are entirely insufficient. It may be conceded, and no doubt is true, that the defendant acted in the most perfect good faith. There is nothing shown indicating bad faith on either side. The defendant was chargeable with notice of what the statutes contain and of the nature of the title he would acquire at such sale. In addition to this the rule of *carcat emptor* applies to all judicial sales in this state. It was the defendant's privilege and his duty to investigate the title before the sale and for that purpose to employ such assistance as he might deem necessary; but he did not resort to the usual methods to ascertain the state of the title. An unlearned woman, unacquainted with the forms of conveyancing or the methods of business, could not be regarded as a safe guide or source of information from whom the true state of the title could be learned. It will be noticed that the defendant did not ask the plaintiff at either of the conversations he had with her whether she had or claimed any interest in the lands as dower or otherwise. What she told him was that the title was good. That statement was literally true, but it is not equivalent to the statement that she had no dower in the land and that if he would purchase at the sale he would acquire a fee-simple title free from all incumbrances. It does not anywhere appear that the defendant relied upon the statements or representations of the plaintiff and was thereby induced to make the purchase." To the same effect is *Whitcaker v. Belt*, 36 Pac. Rep. [Ore.] 534.

The question under consideration was presented to the supreme court of Illinois in *Toledo, P. & W. R. Co. v. Curtenius*, 65 Ill. 120, and the court said that a widow was not estopped from asserting her claim for dower because she had consented to and advised a guardian's sale of the real estate of which her husband died seized.

. The cases cited by the purchaser here do not sustain his contention that the widow in this action by her conduct has estopped herself from claiming her dower estate. In the first case, *Smiley v. Wright,* 2 O. 506, the widow was not only present at the administrator's sale, but she expressly and publicly asserted that the sale of the lands about to be made would include her dower interest. The license to sell in that case provided that the lands should be sold subject to her dower estate, and after the sale had begun she caused it to be suspended in order that the administrator might announce her agreement that the sale should include her dower estate. The sale was then resumed, and in consequence of this agreement upon her part the bids for the real estate were largely increased and the administrator, with the consent of the widow, then and there attempted to sell, and did sell, her dower interest in her presence; and under these circumstances the court held that she could not afterwards claim her dower in the lands as against the purchaser at that sale. The other case cited by the purchaser here is *Pepper v. Zahnsinger,* 94 Ind. 88. In that case the administrator, who had been licensed to sell the real estate of his intestate to pay debts, was requested, in writing, by the widow to sell her dower estate at the same time that he sold the estate of his intestate. He did so, and then paid to the widow in lieu of dower one-third of the entire proceeds of the sale and the court held that the widow was estopped from afterwards claiming her dower estate. But the facts of these two cases are far away from the facts of the case at bar. They were doubtless correctly decided, but they do not support the contention here that the widow has estopped herself from claiming dower solely because she was present at the administrator's sale and kept silent in regard to her dower estate in the lands being sold.

5. The final contention of the purchaser here is that the widow is estopped from claiming her dower estate because she received a part of the proceeds of the land

sold by the administrator in lieu of her dower estate. This is the allegation of the answer, but it is wholly unsustained by the proofs. The only evidence offered to sustain this allegation is that the administrator, on a final settlement and distribution of the assets of the estate, paid to the widow, by order of the county court, $117.01 1-3, and that this sum was receipted for by the widow as her distributive share of her husband's estate. There is not a word in the record which shows that this money was paid to this widow in lieu of her dower estate, or that she accepted it as such. On the contrary, the undisputed evidence is that this payment was made to and received by the widow in full of her distributive share of her husband's estate, not in lieu of her (dower) estate, or in consideration of her release or conveyance of her (dower) estate. On the coming into the county court of the administrator's final report it appeared that, after the payment of all the claims allowed against the estate of the intestate, and the costs and expenses of administration, there remained in his hands a small sum of money. It was out of this residue that the administrator paid, by order of the county court, the $117 to the widow. With the question as to whether this payment was legally made we are not concerned, as we are not reviewing the judgment of the county court. If that tribunal regarded the surplus in the administrator's hands as part of the personal effects of the intestate, though it arose from the sale of his real estate, and considered that the widow was entitled to a child's share of such residue, the county court may have been mistaken, as the intestate's real estate belonged to his heirs, subject to his debts, and after they had been discharged by sale of the real estate, the surplus remaining from the proceeds of such sale may have belonged to the heirs and not to the widow; but that is a matter between the heirs and the widow. The fact that the widow received a part of the residue of the proceeds of the sale of her husband's real estate is no defense to the purchaser here

against the widow's claim for her own estate. Furthermore, this payment to the widow was made long after
the purchase of the real estate at the administrator's sale,
and we are not informed by the record, nor are we able
to conjecture, how the purchaser was induced to change
his status and buy this land by a payment made to, and
accepted by, the widow after the purchase. In order to
estop the widow from claiming her dower estate as
against the purchaser he must show that he was induced
to change his status by something that she did or omitted
to do. If the county court, the administrator, and the
heirs erroneously supposed, on final settlement of the
estate, that the widow was entitled to part of the money
remaining in the administrator's hands, and on that supposition that money was paid to her, how can the purchaser claim that he was induced to make the purchase
he did by this conduct of the widow, administrator, heirs,
and county court after he made his purchase? The precise question under consideration was presented to the
supreme court of Indiana in *Compton v. Pruitt*, 88 Ind.
171, and the court held that the receipt by the widow
of part of the proceeds of the sale of lands made by the
administrator to pay the debts of the intestate, such payment to the widow having been made as her distributive
share of her husband's estate, did not estop her from
claiming her dower in the lands sold.

We reach the conclusion that in the case at bar the
widow has been illegally and unjustly denied her dower
estate in the lands of her deceased husband. The judgment of the district court is reversed and the cause remanded for further proceedings in accordance with this
opinion.

REVERSED AND REMANDED.

JAMES PALMER V. MRS. P. L. CARPENTER.

FILED JANUARY 3, 1898.   No. 7721.

1. **Usury**: ACCOMMODATION NOTE: RENEWAL.   Where one executes his
   negotiable note payable to the order of a debtor and delivers it
   to him as an accommodation, and the debtor indorses and delivers
   the note to his creditor in payment of a usurious note due the
   creditor from the debtor, such accommodation note is not a renewal of the usurious note; and, in a suit on the accommodation
   note against the maker, he cannot interpose, as a defense thereto,
   the usurious contract existing between the creditor and debtor.

2. **Lost Instruments**: RECOVERY: INDEMNITY.   Where a negotiable
   promissory note payable to order is lost before its maturity, never
   having been indorsed or transferred, the execution of an indemnity bond by the owner to the maker is not an essential prerequisite in order to a recovery upon such note.

ERROR from the district court of Saline county.   Tried
below before HASTINGS, J.   *Affirmed.*

Joshua Palmer and *Abbott & Abbott*, for plaintiff in error.

John B. Scott and *John D. Pope*, contra.

RAGAN, C.

In the district court of Saline county Mrs. P. L. Carpenter recovered a judgment on a promissory note
against James Palmer and the latter has filed here a
petition in error to review that judgment.

1. There is little if any dispute as to the material facts
of the case and they are briefly as follows: Joshua and
James Palmer were brothers and Joshua became largely
indebted to Mrs. Carpenter for money borrowed for which
he executed to her his note and by the contract between
them Joshua was to pay interest on the money borrowed
at the rate of 18 per cent per annum.

In 1890 Joshua and Mrs. Carpenter had a settlement
and at that time Joshua paid to her quite a large sum of
money and still owed her $300.   To pay this sum Joshua

induced his brother James to execute his note for $300 drawing interest at 10 per cent per annum payable to the order of Joshua Palmer, and he indorsed and delivered this note to Mrs. Carpenter and she accepted the same in payment of the debt which he owed her.

When the $300 note became due $100 was paid thereon and James Palmer then executed his two notes of $100, each drawing 10 per cent interest, payable to the order of Mrs. Carpenter, and delivered them to her and she surrendered the $300 note. One of these $100 notes matured on January 1, 1893, and appears to have been paid. The other matured on January 1, 1894. This is the note on which this suit is based. Mrs. Carpenter lost this note before its maturity, but it had never been indorsed nor transferred to any one by her.

In the district court James Palmer set out the usurious loan of money made by Mrs. Carpenter to his brother Joshua, the amount of money that had been paid by Joshua on that loan, and claimed that by reason of the usurious nature of that contract and payments made thereon Joshua had been discharged, and that therefore there was nothing due on the note sued upon, his contention being that the note sued upon was in effect a renewal of the usurious note given by his brother Joshua to Mrs. Carpenter, and that therefore he might successfully interpose the usurious nature of that contract as a defense to the action upon this note.

The district court took a different view of the matter, and it is this action of the court of which James Palmer first complains. The district court was right. The $300 note executed by him to his brother and by the latter indorsed and delivered to Mrs. Carpenter was not a renewal of the note which Joshua Palmer had given to Mrs. Carpenter, but was indorsed by Joshua Palmer to Mrs. Carpenter and accepted by her in payment and discharge of the usurious note, and it operated to pay that usurious debt. (*Culver v. Wilbern Bros.*, 48 Ia. 26.)

Since, therefore, this suit was not upon a usurious contract, nor upon any renewal of such contract, the defense
of usury to the action was not available to James Palmer.
James Palmer was not a party nor a privy to the usurious
contract existing between his brother and Mrs. Carpenter.

2. A second complaint of James Palmer is that the
district court permitted Mrs. Carpenter to recover a
judgment on the lost note without first executing and
delivering to him an indemnity bond to protect him from
loss and damage by reason of the loss of the note sued
upon. But this note was a negotiable note, payable to
the order of Mrs. Carpenter, lost before maturity, and
had never been indorsed or transferred by her. Under
these circumstances is the execution of an indemnity
bond by the owner of the note an essential prerequisite
to a recovery thereon?

In *Mowery v. Mast*, 14 Neb. 510, it was said that where
a negotiable note was lost after maturity a recovery
might be had thereon without the execution of an indemnity bond.

In *Means v. Kendall*, 35 Neb. 693, it was said: "Where
a negotiable note is lost before it becomes due the
court will require the plaintiff to give an indemnifying
bond to the maker as a condition of recovering judgment; but where the instrument is lost after it becomes
due no bond ordinarily would be required." But the
opinion does not disclose whether the lost note sued upon
was lost before or after maturity, and the case can be
regarded as an authority only for the proposition that an
indemnity bond is not necessary to recovery upon a
negotiable promissory note lost after its maturity, not
having been previously indorsed or transferred. The
question was again presented to the court in *Kirkwood v.
First Nat. Bank*, 40 Neb. 484, where the authorities upon
the subject were reviewed at some length, and the conclusion was there reached that where an instrument
negotiable by delivery is lost before maturity a bond of

indemnity should be required as a condition for recovery thereon; but where it was clearly shown that the instrument was payable to order and not indorsed, or that it was lost after maturity, no indemnity bond should generally be required. This case, we think, controls the decision of the case at bar, and following it we hold that where a negotiable promissory note payable to order is lost before its maturity, never having been indorsed or transferred, the execution of an indemnity bond by the owner to the maker is not an essential prerequisite in order to a recovery upon such note.

The judgment of the district court is

AFFIRMED.

53
54

53
●59　1
●59　1

MARSHALL FIELD ET AL. V. D. A. LUMBARD ET AL.

FILED JANUARY 3, 1898. No. 7729.

Replevin: JUDGMENT: BOND: LIABILITY OF SURETIES. Where, in a replevin suit, the defendant recovers and judgment is entered absolutely for the value of the property, and not in the alternative, for a return, or its value if a return cannot be had, the sureties on the replevin bond are not liable for the satisfaction of such judgment.

ERROR from the district court of Dodge county. Tried below before MARSHALL, J. *Affirmed.*

Montgomery & Hall and *Fred W. Vaughan,* for plaintiffs in error.

W. J. Courtright, contra.

IRVINE, C.

This was an action on a replevin bond, in which a judgment of dismissal was obtained by the defendant. In the replevin action there had been a finding or verdict for the defendants therein, but the judgment was for the

Field v. Lumbard.

value of the property only, and not in the alternative, for a return thereof or its value, as the statute requires; and the defendant herein, the surety on the bond, asserted that he was discharged because of this irregularity. A consideration of this question renders unnecessary an examination of the other questions involved.

It was in one case suggested, without decision, that the provision for an alternative judgment is solely for the benefit of the defendant, and that the plaintiff cannot on that account complain. (*Goodman v. Kennedy*, 10 Neb. 270.) That suggestion was contrary to two prior decisions, holding the requirement mandatory. (*Hooker v. Hammill*, 7 Neb. 231; *Moore v. Kepner*, 7 Neb. 291.) The doctrine of the earlier cases has since several times been reaffirmed. (*Singer Mfg. Co. v. Dunham*, 33 Neb. 686; *Manker v. Sine*, 35 Neb. 746.) It must now, therefore, be taken as established that the requirement is mandatory, and that either party may insist upon its observance. It was further held in *Goodman v. Kennedy* that before the plaintiff can be heard to complain that the judgment was absolute, he must make it appear that a return is practicable. This case was cited on this point in the recent case of *Eickhoff v. Eikenbary*, 52 Neb. 332, but the point was not there considered necessary to a decision, and was guarded accordingly. In *Manker v. Sine* the burden of proof was otherwise stated, and it was made the duty of the defendant to show that a return could not be had. In the case before us nothing appears to show whether or not a return could be had; but we do not think it necessary here to determine where, in a suit between the parties, the burden of proof lies; because, where the action is against the surety on the bond, other principles govern. If, in the original action, the burden is upon plaintiff, it must be because the information and means of proof lie especially in his possession,—a consideration which does not apply to his surety. In *Dorrington v. Meyer*, 8 Neb. 211, it was held that the sureties cannot complain because the judgment is not in the alternative.

The opinion treats this point very briefly, giving as a reason that the sureties may appear in the replevin suit and have judgment properly entered, and if they fail to do so they are bound. The question recurred in *Lee v. Hastings*, 13 Neb. 508, and the judgment was reversed apparently for the reason that the replevin judgment was not in the alternative. In *Lee v. Hastings* the parties to the replevin suit stipulated for an absolute judgment, but this was not considered as distinguishing the case from *Dorrington v. Meyer*, because the argument seems rather to have been that the stipulation had the opposite effect, for the court said: "Even where such a stipulation is entered into it does not preclude the necessity for a formal judgment in the form required by statute." The decision was reasoned wholly on the theory that the statute formed a part of the obligation and that the sureties were entitled to have their contract construed according to its terms; that their liability could not be enlarged by any disregard of the requirements of the law. The same judge wrote both opinions, and in *Lee v. Hastings* he says that *Dorrington v. Meyer* "has no application to the facts of this case." As the difference was clearly not found in the fact that there was a stipulation in the later case, we can only account for that language by supposing that the fact that the bond in *Dorrington v. Meyer* was given, and perhaps the replevin judgment there considered was rendered, before the enactment of the statute requiring an alternative judgment, was what controlled the court in the former case. In that view *Lee v. Hastings* rules this case without any conflicting case to embarrass us; in any other view *Lee v. Hastings* must be treated as having overruled *Dorrington v. Meyer*, and so governing the present case, as being the later expression. Moreover, we think the doctrine of *Lee v. Hastings* the better. As there said, the sureties contract with a view to an alternative judgment if the plaintiff should be unsuccessful. They are discharged, *pro tanto* at least, by a return of the property if the judgment be regular; but

if the judgment be absolute, a return of the property
would not satisfy it, and their liability would be thereby
increased. Nor do we think that it is their duty to
appear in the replevin suit and see that the judgment is
proper. It is rather the duty of the defendant therein
to see that the judgment is such that it will protect him,
than for the sureties, who are not parties, to appear and
see that it is of such a character that it will bind them.
Eickhoff v. Eikenbary, above referred to, is not opposed to
this view. It was there held that the execution need not
be in the alternative, because the statute does not so
provide, and because it is the plaintiff's affirmative duty
to return the property. The sureties can nevertheless insist that the judgment, by following the statute, makes it
possible for the plaintiff to perform that duty and so
satisfy the judgment. The judgment of the district court
being in accordance with this opinion, it is

AFFIRMED.

PHŒBE REBECCA ELIZABETH ELWINA LINTON ET AL.,
APPELLEES, V. JOHN WHITTAKER COOPER ET AL.,
APPELLANTS.

FILED JANUARY 8, 1898. No. 7646.

1. **Conveyances:** ACKNOWLEDGMENT. As between the parties an acknowledgment is not essential to the validity of a conveyance,
unless the property be a homestead, or for the purpose of barring
dower.

2. ———: ———: MARRIED WOMEN. A conveyance by a married
woman of her separate property, not her homestead, is valid between the parties although not acknowledged.

8. **Evidence:** CONVEYANCES: ACKNOWLEDGMENT. A valid acknowledgment permits a conveyance to be received in evidence without
further proof; but one not acknowledged may be received in evidence if its execution and delivery be otherwise proved.

4. **Husband and Wife:** MORTGAGES: CONSIDERATION. A married
woman may pledge her separate estate to secure an indebtedness
of her husband, but there must be a new consideration to sustain
a mortgage to secure his antecedent debt.

5. ———: ———: ———. The making of further advances to the husband is a sufficient consideration to sustain a mortgage by the wife of her separate property to secure an antecedent debt. In such case the repayment of the subsequent advances does not discharge the mortgage.

6. **Mortgages**: CONSIDERATION: EVIDENCE. Evidence examined, and *held* to conclusively show a delivery of the mortgage in suit, and a valid consideration therefor.

APPEAL from the district court of Douglas county. Heard below before FERGUSON, J.   *Reversed.*

Charles A. Goss and *John L. Webster,* for appellants.

John T. Cathers and *William A. Redick, contra.*

IRVINE, C.

This action was begun by Phœbe Rebecca Elizabeth Elwina Linton, and her husband, Adolphus Frederick Linton, against John Whittaker Cooper and others, composing the firm of Brown, Janson & Co., bankers in London, the object being to have declared void and canceled a mortgage to secure £10,000, purporting to have been made by the Lintons to Brown, Janson & Co. on fifty acres of land in Omaha, and also a deed purporting to convey certain other lands in Omaha, from the Lintons to Brown, Janson & Co.   Brown, Janson & Co. answered, and by cross-petition sought the foreclosure of both instruments, alleging that the deed had been executed to secure the payment of a debt.   On the trial the plaintiffs dismissed their petition, and the defendants abandoned all claim under the deed, so that the case proceeded as one by the defendants against the plaintiffs to foreclose the mortgage on the fifty acres.   There was a finding for the plaintiffs, and a decree denying foreclosure and cancelling the mortgage.   The defendants appeal.

Although both in the district court and in this the burden lies upon the defendants to establish the mortgage, the case can be best developed by stating the defenses relied on by the plaintiffs.   These, while volu-

30

minously pleaded, may be briefly analyzed as follows:
(1) That the mortgage was never delivered; (2) that it
was not acknowledged according to law; (3) that, if given
at all, it was to secure only the past due indebtedness
of Mr. Linton, and covered the separate property of Mrs.
Linton, and was without consideration as to her.

Mrs. Linton is of American birth, the daughter of John
Borland Finlay. Mr. Linton is a British subject; and
the two seem to reside in England, although their letters
in evidence are dated from London, Brighton, Ostend,
and Aix-la-Chappelle. Mrs. Linton is the owner in her
own right of a considerable amount of property in and
about Omaha, including the fifty acres in controversy.
Mr. Linton had an account, in 1889, with the banking
firm of Brown, Janson & Co., the defendants. On the
face of this account he was in October of that year in
debt to the bank in a large sum, apparently something
over £12,000. An effort is made to show that at least
£10,000 of this debt was not really his, but that of Coates,
Son & Co. We need not pay much attention to this
branch of the case. In the light most favorable to Mr.
Linton it would seem to be a debt for which both he and
Coates, Son & Co. were liable, and the only question
would be which is the principal debtor and which the
surety. There is in the record a judgment at law in England from which it appears that Linton has been adjudicated the debtor of the bank to the amount claimed.
It is the theory of the defendants that the mortgage was
delivered October 21, 1889, to cover the existing indebt-
ness of Linton to the bank, together with future advances. The mortgage is dated April 15, 1889. It is
clear that it was not originally executed for the purpose
of covering this debt, but was, on the contrary, executed
with a view to obtaining other advances from the bank
for different purposes. The negotiations for this loan
resulted in its rejection by the bank, and the mortgage
was returned to Mr. Linton without delivery. How it
again got into the possession of the bank raises the cru-

cial question in the case so far as it concerns the delivery
of the mortgage. Mr. Cooper seems to have transacted
all the business on behalf of the bank; he was present
at the trial, and we have his testimony. According to
him, Mr. Linton, being heavily indebted, as already
stated, and desiring further advances, offered to give
security in the form of this mortgage. Mr. Cooper desired some assurance from Mrs. Linton that the arrangement was satisfactory to her. The conversation on this
subject occurred October 18, 1889. Accordingly, Mr.
Linton returned on October 21, bearing the following
letter, which, it is admitted, was signed by Mrs. Linton:

"CABARSTON HOUSE, Oct. 18th, '89·

"SIR: My husband tells me that you are under the impression that I have trustees in America. The only one
I have is for the property left me by my mother, which
is all in Pennsylvania, and is now being contested, as I
am advised by counsel that he has no right to hold the
property, as the will was invalid. The whole of the Linton estate in Omaha belongs to my husband and myself.
My husband has my authority to make arrangements
with your bank about the property, and any arrangement made by him I will agree to. I am *not* an *American*,
as Mr. Van Wagner stated, but a *British subject*, and all
documents signed by me must be judged by the *English
courts* alone.

"Believe me, truly yours,

ELWINA LINTON."

Relying on this letter Mr. Cooper accepted the mortgage on October 21, and on the faith thereof made a
further advance to Mr. Linton of £3,800. These facts are
denied by the Lintons. In order to explain their theory
it is necessary briefly to recur to the former transactions.
They claim that after the former negotiations had failed,
the mortgage was returned to Mr. Linton. Colonel Finlay was during the summer in England; Linton was
about, in his presence, to destroy the mortgage, when

Finlay dissuaded him. Negotiations were then in progress looking towards a loan of £50,000 on the security of
Mrs. Linton's American property; abstracts and other
documents had been placed in the hands of a Mr. Van
Wagner, an American lawyer in London, for the purpose
of procuring from him an opinion as to title, and as to the
form of the securities, and Colonel Finlay desired to submit this mortgage to Mr. Van Wagner to ascertain
whether is was in proper form for the securities which it
was contemplated giving. An opinion was rendered by
Mr. Van Wagner to Messrs. Janson, Cobb, Pearson &
Co., solicitors, of London, and the papers returned to
them. The mortgage in question happened thus to come
into the hands of these solicitors, who represented
Brown, Janson & Co., and in some way passed from them
to the bank. A great deal of the evidence is devoted to
tracing the mortgage between the time of its execution,
in April, and the 21st of October. We need not inquire
very closely into this, because we take it that although
the mortgage was originally intended for another purpose and was not in fact delivered for its original purpose, still, if it came properly into the hands of Brown,
Janson & Co. in October by delivery by the mortgagors
with the intention of having it operate as security as
alleged by the bank, it would be a valid instrument for
that purpose. Mrs. Linton testified that she never authorized such a delivery. Mr. Linton testified that he
never so delivered it. Ordinarily this would create such
a conflict in the evidence that we would not be at liberty
to disturb the finding of the trial judge thereon,—the
credibility of witnesses being generally a matter for the
determination of the triers of fact in the district court.
This rule is not, however, so rigid as to compel us to
accept the statement of a witness in the district court,
where it is absolutely demonstrated to be false or mistaken. We would not be compelled to approve a finding
that two and two make five, or that on a certain morning
the sun rose in the west, although some witness may have

so testified and honestly believed it to be the fact. The letter already quoted goes far to show that Mrs. Linton did at the time intend that the mortgage should be delivered, and that she granted to Mr. Linton full authority in the premises. This letter is explained by both on the theory that they had in view the consummation of the larger loan, and that the letter referred to those negotia· tions and not to this mortgage. Their subsequent conduct conclusively repels that theory.

Before referring to the evidence as to subsequent events it may be proper to say that the plaintiffs contend that the subsequent conduct of Mr. Linton could in nowise tend to bind Mrs. Linton. Whether this is true, in view of the very broad and general authority conferred by the letter of October 18, we need not inquire. Mr. Linton's subsequent conduct and admissions were admissible in evidence for the purpose of impeaching his own testimony if for no other purpose. On December 19 he addressed to Coates, Son & Co. a letter, in which he says: "If you will get me a loan of say £20,000, with which I can pay off my loan of Brown, Janson & Co. of £10,000 (of San Sebastians and £16,000 mortgages on the Omaha property), I will, besides handing you the above security, give you a further collateral security of," etc. There was executed in April not only the £10,000 mortgage, but also another of £6,000 not involved in this case, and the "£16,000 mortgages on Omaha property" could only have referred to these two. February 3, 1890, he addressed to Mr. Shard, of the firm of Janson, Cobb, Pearson & Co., a letter, in the course of which he says: "My only objection to your putting the mortgage of the Omaha property on record is that it will destroy or interfere with our position there, as we have never had a mortgage on the property before, and it is only necessary for the bank to receive payment or further cover. It does seem to me important that mortgage should not be upon record unless we are unable within the next few days to settle with the bank." Some time, apparently near the end of February, he again addressed Mr. Shard a letter, in which he says: "I am sorry you did not understand me about the mortgage on the Omaha property. I have no objection to giving a new one properly dated. My wife thought Cooper wanted to take the Omaha property for the stocks." In March another letter to Mr. Shard says: "I sent you a wire this morning about the Omaha mortgage. My wife is of opinion that Colonel Finlay would raise trouble if it is recorded. The mortgage was to have been for advances to be made. You cannot use it at present as cover." During the whole interval there was continued correspondence between him and Janson, Cobb, Pearson & Co. Letters on both sides referred to this mortgage as a subsisting incumbrance, and this last letter contains the first protest by Mr. Linton on the subject. We are not certainly unreasonably reluctant to accept Mr. Linton's bare denial on the trial, in the face of these contemporaneous documents. With Mrs. Linton the case is no better. On April 2, 1890, Mr. and Mrs. Linton executed to Cooper and others a deed absolute in form on their property in Omaha, being the deed referred to in the statement of the case, and nowhere is the evidence of the defendants contradicted that the purpose of this deed was to replace the mortgage in suit. At the same time they wrote a letter intended to operate as a defeasance, beginning "We having to-day executed an absolute conveyance to three of your partners on three pieces of land at Omaha, it is understood that such land is to be held by you as security for all moneys at any time owing by us, or either of us, to you." On the 20th of May, 1890, the Lintons joined in a mortgage to Greenwell & Co., which, it recites, shall "charge the property heretofore described subject to a mortgage already existing thereon in favor of Messrs. Brown, Janson & Co., bankers of London, England, dated the 15th April, one thousand eight hundred and eighty-nine, for securing £10,000 and interest." This was followed by a covenant "that the aforesaid premises are unincumbered except as to the above mentioned mortgage of the 15th of April, one thousand eight hundred and eighty-nine, to Messrs. Brown, Janson & Co. for £10,000." This mortgage to Greenwell & Co., it seems, was afterwards avoided by decree of the district court of Douglas county; but counsel err in assuming that the avoidance of the mortgage destroyed its probative force. It could not in any event operate as an estoppel in favor of Brown, Janson & Co. Whether valid or not, it was nevertheless a solemn and distinct admission by Mrs. Linton of the validity of the mortgage in suit. Somewhat later Brown, Janson & Co. instituted bankruptcy proceedings against Mr. Linton, and concerning these proceedings Mrs. Linton wrote them from Ostend August 6, 1891, a long letter, in the course of which she says: "The bank in London have two securities registered in Omaha against my estate, the two documents are for about £16,000. Mr. Shard holds the deeds of my property." In the face of these repeated admissions, formal and informal, it is impossible to believe that the mortgage did not pass into the hands of Brown, Janson & Co. with the intention on the part of both Mr. and Mrs. Linton to make it a valid security. In justice to the trial court we should say that the opinion of the district judge discloses that his decision was not based on any finding that the mortgage was not delivered, but was, on the contrary, based on his views as to the sufficiency of the consideration. The decree contains a finding that it was not delivered, and this finding must be, and is, accepted in the review of the case. The statement as to the opinion is made as a matter of fairness to the judge, and not as influencing our decision.

The mortgage was acknowledged before an official describing himself as consular agent. It is contended that such an official has no authority to take an acknowledgment, and that the deed being that of a married woman, a legal acknowledgment is necessary to its validity. In support of that proposition we are cited to numerous

authorities* in other states where the subject is governed
by statutes not like ours, and which are therefore inap-
plicable.   We are also cited to *Roode v. State*, 5 Neb. 174.
In that case it was said that an instrument purporting
to be the deed of a *feme covert* without her acknowledgment is void as to her.   The deed there involved purported to be the conveyance of her husband and her name
seems to have been inserted in it for the sole purpose of
barring dower.   For that purpose an acknowledgment
is necessary.   (Compiled Statutes, ch. 23, sec. 12.)   An
acknowledgment is also essential for the purpose of conveying a homestead.   (Compiled Statutes, ch. 36, sec. 4.)
For other purposes an acknowledgment is not in this
state necessary as between the parties to an instrument.
(*Stevenson v. Craig*, 12 Neb. 464; *Missouri Valley Land Co.
v. Bushnell*, 11 Neb. 192; *Kittle v. St. John*, 10 Neb. 605;
Weaver v. Coumbe, 15 Neb. 167; *Connell v. Galligher*, 39
Neb. 793; *Horbach v. Tyrrell*, 48 Neb. 514.)   Except in the
special instances referred to, the office of an acknowledgment is twofold merely: to entitle the instrument to
record, and to permit its admission in evidence without
further proof of its execution.   (*Burbank v. Ellis*, 7 Neb.
156; *Horbach v. Tyrrell, supra.*)

It is argued that without an acknowledgment the mortgage should not have been received in evidence; but the
statute merely makes a proper acknowledgment sufficient
proof to admit the instrument, and it does not make that
method of proof exclusive.   An unacknowledged instrument, as shown by the cases already cited, may be received in evidence, provided its execution and delivery
be proved, as they were in this case.   The married
woman's act (Compiled Statutes, ch. 53, sec. 2) provides
that a married woman "may bargain, sell, and convey her
real and personal property, and enter into any contract

Clark v. Graham, 6 Wheat. [U. S.] 577; *Runfelt v. Clemens*, 46 Pa. St.
455; *Warren v. Brown*, 25 Miss. 73; *Clark v. Thompson*, 12 Pa. St. 274;
Graham v. Long, 65 Pa. St. 385; *Tully v. Davis*, 30 Ill. 103; *Myers v. Boyd*,
96 Pa. St. 427; *Rogers v. Adams*, 66 Ala. 600; *Dewey v. Campau*, 4 Mich.
565; *Buell v. Irwin*, 24 Mich. 145; *Keller v. Moore*, 51 Ala. 340.

with reference to the same in the same manner, to the same extent, and with like effect as a married man may in relation to his real or personal property." Under the authorities cited there can be no doubt then that the deed or mortgage of a married woman of her separate estate is valid between the parties although not acknowledged. The validity of this acknowledgment is, therefore, not a question necessary to be decided.

We now come to the question of the consideration. The condition of the mortgage names no time for the payment of the debt. It may be assumed that it was due presently, or upon demand, and that there was, therefore, no consideration by way of extending time on the antecedent debt of the husband. The defendants contend, however, that on the faith of the mortgage there was an advancement made upon its delivery of £3,800, and that there were two other comparatively small loans made at a later period. The plaintiffs show conclusively that at the time of the delivery of the mortgage Mr. Linton's current account was overdrawn about £2,300 and that, of the £3,800 passed to Linton's credit on the delivery of the mortgage, £2,300 was absorbed in covering this overdraft. This, without an extension of time, was not a new consideration. They further contend that of the remaining £1,500, £1,000 represented the profits accruing to Linton from a sale that day made of stock held by him in the Imperial Bank of Persia; that £500 was the result of a discount or purchase of a "sold note" of Coates, Son & Co. of stock in the Pahang Exploration Company; that of the two later advances one was a similar transaction in the stock of the United States Debenture Corporation, and the other in shares of the Canadian Meat Company. There is evidence fairly tending to sustain all these assertions, and they meet but a qualified denial from Mr. Cooper. It must, however, be remembered that if the mortgage was delivered at all, it was as a general cover for past debts and future advances; and every one of the subsequent transactions is of such a character that it is hardly probable that the bank would enter into it with a man already deeply in debt to them, as was Mr. Linton, without further security than the items to which they severally relate. The Persian stock transaction was this: Linton was about to go on the Continent and desired to dispose of the Persian stock before he went, as it was then at a considerable premium. It was ascertained that he could close it out at a profit of £1,250. Brown, Janson & Co. desired to make the sale for him, as they had arrangements by which they could divide the commissions with the brokers, and thus realize a profit to themselves. Linton proposed that they give him credit for £1,000 and accept the remaining £250 as the commission to be so divided. This was done, and the £1,000 immediately passed to his credit. While this was perhaps a very short loan, it was, in effect, a discount of his profits, because it was done before the sale was made and the proceeds realized. With regard to the "sold note," the transaction was that the sold note was immediately delivered and its amount placed to Linton's credit. It would seem from the evidence that it was not realized on by Brown, Janson & Co. for some weeks, and was then short a few pounds of the amount advanced. The Debenture Company transaction seems to have been an absolute loan to Linton on behalf of a friend with the understanding that the shares bought with the money should be deposited as collateral. Linton says he does not know whether this was done. The Canadian Meat Company item was a similar transaction. Thus, while Brown, Janson & Co. obtained, or were to obtain, other security for each of these items, they were all, in effect, advances, and, as we said, such advances as would hardly be made on behalf of a man who already owed more than £12,000 largely unsecured. The security afforded by the £10,000 mortgage was the inducement to make these advances, according to the testimony of Cooper, and even according to Linton there must have been some close connection between them, because in spite of the efforts

of his counsel to draw out from him his story with regard
to the £1,000 and £500 of October 21 as separate transactions, his mind worked in such a manner that he kept
reverting to Cooper's demand for a letter from Mrs. Linton authorizing him to act with reference to the Omaha
property, and he over and over again states the facts in
regard to the procurement of that letter as if they were
inseparably connected in his mind with the procuring of
the advances. The law on the subject is not difficult.
It is settled that a married woman may become surety
for her husband, and that a present advance or the extension of an antecedent debt is a sufficient consideration
for her so doing. (*Stevenson v. Craig, supra; Buffalo
County Nat. Bank v. Sharpe*, 40 Neb. 123; *Smith v. Spaulding*, 40 Neb. 339; *Briggs v. First Nat. Bank of Beatrice*, 41
Neb. 17; *Watts v. Gantt*, 42 Neb. 869.) But there must be
a new consideration if the mortgage be given to secure
an antecedent debt. (*Kansas Mfg. Co. v. Gandy*, 11 Neb.
448.)

The trial court seems to have viewed the facts as we
do, but proceeded on the theory that a subsequent payment had been made sufficient to discharge any indebtedness created at the time, or after the mortgage was given;
that it was therefore discharged. In this we think there
was error. It would seem that the rule for the application of payments, where no direction is given by the
debtor and no special application has been made by the
creditor, is directly contrary to that applied by the trial
judge; and payments should be applied first to the satisfaction of the earlier debts. (NORVAL, J., in *State v. Hill*,
47 Neb. 456.) But irrespective of this, there was a confusion by the trial judge between the consideration for
giving the mortgage and the debt secured thereby. The
debt secured was the whole of the debt of Linton to the
bank, past and future, to the extent of £1,000. The new
consideration was present and future advances, and the
repayment of such present and future advances did not
defeat the consideration which had by such advances

already been executed, nor did it discharge the mortgage. To reduce this transaction to its simplest form
will at once elucidate our meaning. If A owes B $100,
which is not secured, and if C agrees that if B will lend
A a further sum of $5, C will pledge his property as
security for the $100 already owed, the further advance
is a new consideration which will sustain the pledge,
which can then only be discharged by the repayment of
the $100.

· There is a final contention that no part of the consideration passed to Mrs. Linton, and that the contract was
not made with reference to her separate estate. No discussion is needed to dispose of this argument. The cases
already cited show that she need not be a party to the
consideration, and the mortgage itself was an express
charge on her separate estate.

The judgment of the district court is reversed, and the
case is remanded with directions to take an account of
the amount due from Linton to the bank, and enter a
decree of foreclosure for an amount in money of the
United States equivalent to that debt, but not exceeding £10,000, with interest at six per cent from October 21,
1889.

REVERSED AND REMANDED.

FRED RADZUWEIT, APPELLEE, v. JOHN B. WATKINS ET
AL., APPELLANTS.

FILED JANUARY 3, 1898. No. 7681.

1. **Judgments:** EQUITABLE RELIEF. A court of equity, in granting relief against judgments, is not restricted to cases where the court
entering the judgment complained of was without jurisdiction,
but will extend its assistance in cases where jurisdiction was obtained, but the defendant, without fault or negligence on his part.
but by accident or misfortune, was prevented from making his
defense, provided it be further shown that he had a good defense to the merits.

2. ——: ——. Where judgments were rendered in the county court
and transcripts thereof filed in the district court and the lands
of the defendant were levied upon and advertised for sale, all
before he learned of the pendency of the suit and when he had
a good defense to the merits, *held*, that the remedy by proceedings in the county court to vacate the judgments under section 602
of the Code was inadequate and injunction a proper remedy.

APPEAL from the district court of Douglas county.
Heard below before KEYSOR, J. *Affirmed.*

Lake, Hamilton & Maxwell, for appellants.

C. A. Baldwin, contra.

IRVINE, C.

Radzuweit, by this suit, sought to restrain the defendants from enforcing against him two judgments recovered by the defendants Watkins and Hoagland against
Radzuweit and one Zimmatt in the county court of Douglas county. The district court granted a perpetual injunction, and the defendants appeal. They do not contend that the evidence did not tend to establish such
allegations of the petition as were put in issue, but they
assert that the petition itself was insufficient to warrant
the relief granted. We need not, therefore, inquire beyond the averments of the petition and their legal sufficiency.

The petition alleges, in substance, that on March 21,
1893, Watkins and Hoagland began two suits against
plaintiff and A. Zimmatt and C. Zimmatt in the county
court of Douglas county, each suit being to recover on
certain promissory notes alleged to have been made by
the Zimmatts and Radzuweit to Watkins and Hoagland.
A summons was issued and returned as personally served
on A. Zimmatt and not served on C. Zimmatt, and as
served on Radzuweit by leaving a copy of the same at his
usual place of residence. Thereafter in due time a default was taken as to Radzuweit and judgment entered
in both cases against him April 7, 1893. Thereafter, on

April 11, transcripts of said judgments were filed in the office of the clerk of the district court, writs issued thereon and a lot belonging to Radzuweit levied upon and advertised for sale to satisfy the judgments. The petition further alleges that Radzuweit did not execute the notes, did not authorize any one to execute them on his behalf, and did not know of their existence until he learned that the lot was advertised for sale to pay the judgment. At the time the actions were begun Radzuweit was absent from home from early in the morning until late at night and he did not know that there had been such service, did not know that his name was on the notes, did not know that he had been sued, did not know that judgment had been rendered until three days before this suit was begun, and after the lot had been advertised for sale, when a neighbor called his attention to the published notice. This petition certainly alleges a good defense to the law actions and shows that plaintiff had no actual knowledge of the proceedings in time to interpose that defense. It also shows that he was personally guilty of no negligence. It is, however, contended that the service of summons was in law good, and equivalent to a personal service, and that being so equity can afford no relief. There can be no question that the service was good and conferred jurisdiction upon the county court. The return was that a copy had been left at Radzuweit's usual place of residence and the petition does not deny, but rather admits, that the return was true. The right of a court administering equity to prevent the enforcement of a judgment is not, however, confined to cases where the judgment was void for want of jurisdiction. It extends to all cases where the defendant in the law action, without negligence or fault of his own, was prevented from making his defense, and where he has a good defense which would, had it been interposed, have prevented the judgment, and where relief cannot be had at law or in the original action. In other words, it is sufficient to show that the judgment is inequitable and that the defendant has been at no fault and has no other remedy.

In *Horn v. Queen*, 4 Neb. 108, and 5 Neb. 472, a summons issued by a justice of the peace had been served by leaving a copy at the defendant's residence. He was then absent, but returned on the return day. He was then taken sick and was unable to attend to business affairs for twenty days. He had a defense to the action. It was held that he had shown grounds for the interposition of equity. Here there was no doubt as to the jurisdiction of the court. In the first report MAXWELL, J., said: "And in general the absence of a party from unavoidable circumstances, where it is apparent he had a defense to the action, will be sufficient to authorize a new trial," and that where it would have been proper for the law court to grant a new trial, if it still had authority to do so, it is proper for a court of equity to interfere after that authority has lapsed. In the second report GANTT, J., said: "When a party, from some unavoidable circumstance, and without any laches or want of reasonable diligence on his part, is prevented from appearing and making his defense to a suit, courts will relieve him upon being satisfied that there is reasonable ground to believe injustice has been done to him by a trial in his absence."

In *Young v. Morgan*, 9 Neb. 169, relief was also given where there was no question of jurisdiction involved, but where the defendant had allowed the case to go by default because he supposed it to be founded on a note which he owed, whereas it turned out to be based on a note similar thereto but forged.

In *Morse v. Engle*, 28 Neb. 534, a doctrine was announced which seems to be directly opposed to the foregoing cases and which if adhered to would doubtless govern this case in favor of the defendants. There the original action had been against a husband and wife, and it was asserted that the summons, left at the residence, had been received by the husband and secreted, and that the wife was kept in ignorance thereof. It was

held that this afforded no ground for relief, the court saying that the service was in accordance with the statute,
and that where this is so "nothing connected with or incident growing out of such service can be held to be an
unavoidable casualty or misfortune preventing the party
from defending." It will be seen at once that the attention of the court was there drawn to the legal sufficiency
of the service. The service being good, the court held
there could be no relief, overlooking entirely the well
known and almost elementary rule that although jurisdiction is complete, relief may be had where by fraud,
accident, or even mistake, and without fault of the defendant, an unjust judgment has been rendered. In *Holliday v. Brown*, 34 Neb. 232, *Morse v. Engle* was reviewed,
and while the court there again seems to have lost sight
of the rule that to authorize relief the jurisdiction of the
court in the original case need not necessarily be involved, and although *Holliday v. Brown* has been much
criticised and is peculiarly reasoned on another point, it
may justly be regarded as having practically overruled
Morse v. Engle.

It is also contended that Radzuweit had his remedy by
proceeding, under section 602 of the Code, in the county
court to vacate the judgments, and for that reason is not
entitled to relief in this action. But before he knew of
the proceedings at all the county court judgments had
been entered by transcripts in the district court, his land
had been levied upon and was about to be sold. Merely
proceeding in the county court to have the judgments
there vacated would not dispose of the record in the
district court and would not prevent the sale of his land.
The remedy under section 602 was not adequate and injunction was, under the circumstances, the proper
remedy.

AFFIRMED.

J. D. MACFARLAND V. WEST SIDE IMPROVEMENT ASSOCIATION.

FILED JANUARY 3, 1898.   No. 7635.

1. **Corporations:** STOCK: LIABILITY OF SUBSCRIBER. The capital stock of a corporation must be fully subscribed before an action will lie against a subscriber to recover assessments thereon, unless by law or charter provision the corporation is permitted to proceed with its main design with a less subscription. (*Livesey v. Omaha Hotel Co.*, 5 Neb. 50.)

2. ——: ——: ——: ESTOPPEL. A subscriber may, however, by his conduct, either waive or estop himself from setting up such a defense.

3. ——: ——: ——. One who acts as treasurer of a corporation, receives payment of assessments from other subscribers, himself pays certain assessments, and disburses the funds of the corporation in carrying out its main object, is estopped to set up that the stock has not all been subscribed, although at the time of such acts he was ignorant of the deficiency.

4. ——: KNOWLEDGE OF AGENT: LIABILITY OF PRINCIPAL. One elected treasurer of a corporation, who with the consent of its promoters permits an agent to perform all the active duties of the office, but in the name of the treasurer, is responsible for the consequences of the agent's acts as if they were his own, and is charged with notice of all facts learned by the agent by reason of his performance of such duties.

ERROR from the district court of Lancaster county. Tried below before TIBBETS, J. *Affirmed.*

A. G. Greenlee and *Lambertson & Hall,* for plaintiff in error.

Ricketts & Wilson, contra.

IRVINE, C.

The West Side Improvement Association recovered a judgment against Macfarland for certain unpaid assessments on shares of its capital stock alleged to have been by him subscribed. While several defenses were pleaded, the questions here presented relate only to one,

31

—that the full amount of the capital stock, as fixed by the articles of incorporation, had not been subscribed. The capital stock was fixed at $200,000, and only a little more than $100,000 was subscribed. The general principle is well settled that a subscription does not become obligatory until the whole amount has been subscribed, unless the law or some provision of the articles permits the corporation to begin its effective work at an earlier stage. (*Livesey v. Omaha Hotel Co.*, 5 Neb. 50; *Hale v. Sanborn*, 16 Neb. 1; *Hards v. Platte Valley Improvement Co.*, 35 Neb. 263.) Everywhere a qualification is recognized in connection with this rule, and that is, that a subscriber may, by his conduct, lose the right to insist on its observance, and the crucial question here is whether Macfarland has so conducted himself as to lose that right. There is but little conflict in the evidence on this point. Macfarland subscribed for stock to the amount of $2,500, and paid two small assessments thereon. He was chosen treasurer of the corporation, and about that time was informed by some of its promoters that his services were desired in that capacity, and that he had been, or would be, elected. He did not desire the office, and so stated. He was then president of the First National Bank of Lincoln, and one Miller was a subordinate officer of the bank. Macfarland conceived that the corporation desired that the bank should have its account, and informed the promoters that if such was their wish Mr. Miller would take care of the money; that he, Macfarland, found his time fully occupied. He then said to Mr. Miller that he had been elected treasurer and had no time to attend to the business, and that if Miller would do so he might have any compensation that might accrue. Several witnesses testify to these conversations, and their accounts vary so slightly that the differences are clearly attributable to differences in the habits of expression of the witnesses, so that it would be dangerous to attribute any special force to the form of words employed by any one of them.

From the testimony of all, the inference, evidently drawn by the trial court, is readily deducible that Macfarland did not decline the office, but accepted it with the understanding that Miller was to perform its active duties, receiving any compensation it might afford. Clearly, under such circumstances, Macfarland became the responsible officer, charged with whatever duties the office entailed, and trusting to Miller as his own agent, not that of the corporation, for the performance of those duties. Just here a matter of importance in the case, but presenting no legal difficulty, may appropriately be disposed of. Miller, being Macfarland's agent, Miller's acts as treasurer were in law those of Macfarland, and Miller's knowledge, acquired through his performance of those acts, is to be imputed to Macfarland himself. An account was opened with the bank in the name of Macfarland as treasurer. A note, made by some of the promoters, was discounted at the bank to obtain money to begin the work of the corporation, and its proceeds were credited to Macfarland in that account. Assessments were made on the capital stock received by Miller, and also deposited in this account. Among them were the two payments made by Macfarland himself. The object of the corporation was to erect buildings for and maintain a normal school near Lincoln. With the money so obtained the corporation proceeded to erect a large building, and for many weeks Miller, by checks drawn in the name of Macfarland, disbursed money in the payment of vouchers which showed on their face that they were for expenses incurred in the building operations. Macfarland was thus charged with notice that the corporation was proceeding with its main object. He did not know, and it does not appear that Miller knew, that the full amount of capital stock had not been subscribed.

It will be seen that Macfarland participated in the acts of the corporation by holding the office of treasurer, receiving subscriptions, and disbursing money for the purpose of carrying out its main object. Such participa-

tion is generally said to waive the requirements of full
subscription, or else to estop a subscriber from insisting
thereon. The language of the cases has often been in
this respect ambiguous, yet it is here very important to
ascertain whether the liability arises in such case from
waiver or by estoppel. If from waiver, which has in this
connection been defined as the intentional relinquishment of a known right (*Livesey v. Omaha Hotel Co.*, *supra*),
Macfarland is not here precluded from making the defense, because he was ignorant of the deficiency in the
subscriptions. We think that the loose use of language
in the adjudicated cases has been due to a consciousness
in the minds of the judges that the defense might be lost
either by waiver or estoppel, and because it has not, in
most cases, been necessary to distinguish between them,
knowledge of all the facts and circumstances creating
an estoppel concurring. There can be no doubt that a
subscriber may waive the defense. So, too, when there
has been no waiver because of ignorance of material
facts, he may so conduct himself as to raise an estoppel.
In *Musgrave v. Morrison*, 54 Md. 161, it was held that
active participation in proceeding with the work of the
corporation charged a subscriber, irrespective of his
knowledge that the whole capital had not been subscribed. An instructive case is that of *President v. Mc-
Conaby*, 16 S. & R. [Pa.] 140. The case antedates any we
have seen cited directly on the subject, but the principle
involved is the same. There a subscriber defended on
the ground that the charter had been obtained by means
of fictitious subscriptions for part of the stock. The
court held that so far as the fraud was upon the state,
the state alone could be heard to complain of it, and that
so far as it affected the defendant, he could not be heard
to complain if he had acted upon the charter, advertised
the election of officers, and assisted, as the court says,
"in putting the charter in motion;" that if he so acted,
he was bound, although ignorant of the fictitious character of the subscriptions. We find nothing really opposed

to this view. While many cases speak of knowledge as an essential, they are cases where there was knowledge, or where the conduct of the subscriber had not been such as to create an estoppel *in pais*. While Macfarland undoubtedly acted in good faith, and without any intention of deceiving others, and while it is not shown that any particular person was induced to alter his position because of Macfarland's acts, still it is evident that every subscription paid, every obligation assumed by the corporation, every hour's work upon the building, was the resultant of the combined acts of defendant and other officers, who by proceeding held out the corporation as fully organized, with a lawfully available capital. The fact that others may have been induced to act is sufficient. (*Masonic Temple Ass'n v. Channell*, 43 Minn. 353.) It would be manifestly impossible in most cases to show that any particular subscriber had paid, or that any particular person had contracted with the association on the faith of the defendant's acts alone, and yet it is clear that his acts combined with others' influenced every dealing with the corporation. Although he was ignorant of the deficiency in subscriptions, he was ignorant when he might have known, and must bear the consequences. Any other rule would be highly inequitable.

Other questions argued are either rendered immaterial by the conclusion reached on this, or are so distinctly corollary thereto that they do not require separate notice.

Submitted with the case on its merits is a motion to strike from the record certain portions of the bill of exceptions. This motion is aimed at matter inserted by the trial judge in pursuance of an order made by this court remanding the record for the trial judge's action according to the facts. (*Macfarland v. West Side Improvement Ass'n*, 47 Neb. 661.) The proceedings seem to have been in accordance with the opinion and direction of this court as there expressed, and the motion is therefore overruled. The judgment of the district court is

AFFIRMED.

CASES

ARGUED AND DETERMINED

IN THE

SUPREME COURT OF NEBRASKA.

JANUARY TERM, A. D. 1898.

PRESENT:

Hon. T. O. C. HARRISON, CHIEF JUSTICE.
Hon. T. L. NORVAL, } JUDGES.
Hon. J. J. SULLIVAN, } JUDGES.
Hon. ROBERT RYAN, }
Hon. JOHN M. RAGAN, } COMMISSIONERS.
Hon. FRANK IRVINE, }

THOMAS DOWNS v. JAMES B. KITCHEN.

FILED JANUARY 19, 1898. No. 7758.

Negligence: DANGEROUS BUILDING: LIABILITY OF OWNER. Following *Kitchen v. Carter*, 47 Neb. 776, the judgment of the district court is affirmed.

ERROR from the district court of Douglas county. Tried below before AMBROSE, J. *Affirmed.*

Connell & Ives, for plaintiff in error.

George E. Pritchett and *J. C. Cowin, contra.*

PER CURIAM.

The facts in this case are substantially the same as those in *Kitchen v. Carter*, 47 Neb. 776, and upon the authority of that case the judgment of the district court in this is

AFFIRMED.

M. F. LAMASTER, APPELLEE, V. C. C. ELLIOTT AND WILL-
IAM BARR, APPELLANTS.

FILED JANUARY 19, 1898.   No. 7496.

1. **Receivers**: JOINT OWNERS OF PROPERTY: ILL WILL. That there exists a feeling of ill will or hostility or a disagreement between
joint owners of property is not sufficient to warrant a court in
appointing a receiver to take charge of the property unless such
fact prevents a beneficial use of the property or practically operates an exclusion of one of the joint owners from the benefit and
use of the property.

2. ———: ———. *Held*, That the facts as established by the findings
of the referee herein and the further finding of the court did not
disclose such a condition of affairs in regard to property owned
jointly by two of the parties hereto as to warrant the decree of
the court appointing a receiver thereof.

3. **Costs**: MOTION TO RETAX: REVIEW. If the question of the liability
of the respective parties to an action to pay costs therein is one
which was directly considered and determined by the trial court,
no motion in that court to retax costs is necessary to entitle a
party to have a judgment against him for the costs or any part
thereof reviewed in this court.

APPEAL from the district court of Lancaster county.
Heard below before HALL, J.   *Reversed.*

Morning & Berge, for appellants.

Mockett & Polk, contra.

HARRISON, C. J.

It appears that during the year 1894 M. F. Lamaster
was the owner of lot 6, block 58, in the city of Lincoln,
and William Barr owned the adjoining lot 5.   On these
lots stood a brick building, one-half on each lot, of which
Barr owned the portion erected on his lot and Lamaster
the part of the building which was on his lot.   The building had two large rooms on the ground floor, one on each
lot.   There was a common stairway running up immediately over the division line to floors above, of which there
were two, each divided into a number of rooms, and each

floor having a common hall in the center. The building was heated with steam, and in the basement of the building, placed immediately over the dividing line of the lots, was the furnace and boiler of the heating apparatus, the whole of such apparatus being owned jointly or in common by the owners of the building. It was put into the building by the parties under an agreement that each should pay one-half the expense in all respects of its operation at all times and to be equally interested and represented in such operation. One C. C. Elliott claims that during the year 1894, and prior to the time that artificial heat was required for that year, he entered into a contract with the owners of the building by which he was to attend to the heating apparatus during the years 1894 and 1895. On November 22, 1894, Lamaster commenced this action, alleging in his petition that Elliott had not been employed by him, nor had he joined in hiring Elliott nor consented that he be employed, but that Barr had employed Elliott against the wishes and contrary to his, Lamaster's, protests; he also pleaded that Elliott was incompetent and had failed to properly attend to the heating apparatus, by reason of which the rooms belonging to Lamaster had not been heated properly, but had been cold and uncomfortable and rendered almost untenable; that Elliott was insolvent. It was also pleaded that Lamaster and Barr were unable to agree on a person who should be employed to attend to the heating apparatus. It was of the prayer of the petition that a receiver be appointed to take charge and employ a competent person to operate the heating apparatus until such time as the differences between the owners should be adjusted; also, that Elliott be restrained from operating the heating apparatus and that Barr be restrained from further retaining Elliott in his employ for such purpose, and, also, from the employment of any other person for the work except as might be ordered or directed by the court. A temporary restraining order was granted and issued. Separate answers were filed for appellants, in each of which the allegations of appellee's petition were denied and it was alleged that the hiring of Elliott was participated in and was the act of both Barr and Lamaster; that he was a competent man for the work and was doing it properly, and that the trouble was occasioned by the fact that Elliott had rented rooms of Barr in the building to be heated and was occupying the same with his family. For the appellants there was filed a motion that the restraining order be dissolved. After issues were joined the court appointed Hon. M. B. Reese referee to hear the testimony and to make and report findings of fact and conclusions of law to the court. By stipulation of parties the testimony was presented in the form of affidavits. After a full hearing the referee reported as follows:

"First—That the said Barr and Lamaster are each the separate and several owners of lots 5 and 6, and of their buildings thereon, but which buildings constitute one block, known as the Barr-Lamaster Block, the said William Barr being the owner of lot 5 and the plaintiff being the owner of lot 6, in block 58, in the city of Lincoln.

"Second—That each building is furnished and provided with a system of pipes and radiators, used for the purpose of supplying said buildings and the different rooms thereof with heat by steam, but that the steam for both is supplied from one boiler.

"Third—That the furnace and boiler provided and used for generating steam are owned by the said plaintiff and the said William Barr in common, and that each of them have the right to the use of the same; and that the furnace and boiler have been provided for the joint use of both in furnishing steam and heat for said buildings, and that the rights of both in and to said furnace and boiler are equal.

"Fourth—That it is necessary for the accommodation of the owners and tenants of said building that during the winter season of the year some competent person be employed to operate said furnace and boiler.

"Fifth—That the defendant C. C. Elliott is a capable engineer and is competent to operate said furnace and boiler, and has a certificate of qualification issued to him by competent authority of the city of Lincoln.

"Sixth—That the said C. C. Elliott was employed for the season of 1894-5 by William Barr to take charge of the said heating apparatus, and that such employment was with the knowledge and (originally) the consent of plaintiff, and that he has never been discharged by the act of both Barr and Lamaster, and that at the time of the commencement of this suit he was engaged in the discharge of the duties of his employment; that on the 22d day of September, 1894, the notice set out in plaintiff's petition signed by plaintiff was caused to be served upon him by plaintiff.

"Seventh—That sufficient heat has not been furnished the occupants of the Lamaster side of said block at all times, but the proof is unsatisfactory as to the cause of the failure or who was at fault.

"Eighth—That the furnace and boiler are capable of furnishing sufficient heat for the block if they and the radiators are properly managed.

"Ninth—That the said defendant C. C. Elliott has wrongfully excluded plaintiff from exercising the necessary acts of ownership over said furnace and boiler and other portions of his property in the basement of the said building and has prevented him from entering therein and thereto, and that plaintiff should be permitted to have free access to the same.

"Tenth—That there is at present no necessity for the appointment of a receiver.

"CONCLUSIONS AT LAW.

"First—That as to the defendant William Barr this action should be dismissed.

"Second—That as to the defendant C. C. Elliott a perpetual injunction should be awarded restraining and enjoining him from interfering with or preventing plaintiff from exercising acts of ownership over and having access to his property, including the furnace and boiler and other property in connection therewith or owned by plaintiff, but not to restrain the said Elliott from discharging his said duties as engineer of said building.

"Third—That the costs in this case should be equally divided between the plaintiff and the defendant C. C. Elliott, each one paying one-half.

"To all of which the plaintiff excepts, and to that part awarding an injunction against C. C. Elliott he excepts."

For the appellants a motion was made for confirmation of the report of the referee and judgment in accordance therewith. To the report the appellee made many objections and urged exceptions. The court, on hearing of the motion for confirmation and the exceptions, overruled the exceptions to the fifth and seventh findings of fact and sustained the exception to the tenth and also sustained the exceptions to the first and third conclusions of law and as was stated in the decree, "In all other respects and in the fifth, sixth, and seventh findings of fact, the said referee's report is by the court duly confirmed, as supported by the evidence and the law." It was further stated in the decree: "From the evidence the court finds that between the plaintiff and defendant Barr exists a feeling of ill will and hostility that renders impossible any unity of action in the control and management of their joint property, the heating plant in the Barr-Lamaster Block, located on lots 5 and 6, block 58, in the city of Lincoln, and that for the proper use of said heating plant to warm the separate property of each, said Barr and said Lamaster, a necessity does now exist for the appointment of a receiver over their said joint property, the said heating plant." A receiver was appointed to take charge of the heating apparatus, Elliott was reinstated in his position, the restraining order was vacated, and the costs of the cause, including fees of referee, were adjudged to be paid one-half by Lamaster and one-half by Barr. From the judgment Barr has appealed to this court.

It is urged that the facts established were insufficient to warrant the decree by which a receiver was appointed and placed in charge of the property. By reverting to the findings of fact reported by the referee, and to which the court overruled exceptions, it appears that Elliott was competent and qualified to perform the work for the doing of which he had been employed; that his employment was by the joint owners of the property; that though sufficient heat had not at all times been furnished in the rooms of the Lamaster portion of the building, the proof did not satisfactorily disclose the cause or who was in fault. Courts are very slow to interfere between joint owners of property, joint tenants, or tenants in common. It has been said that where the facts constitute a clear case of the use and enjoyment of the property by one to the entire exclusion of another a receiver will be appointed, not, however, when the appointment will subject the co-tenant to inconvenience and expense, without corresponding benefit to the complainant. (*Low v. Holmes*, 17 N. J. Eq. 148; Beach, Receivers [2d ed.] sec. 494; 20 Am. & Eng. Ency. Law 52-53.) The court in this case made a finding additional to the ones made and reported by the referee to the effect that there existed a feeling of ill will and hostility between the joint owners of the property so intense that it prevented any unity of action in the control and management of the property. Conceding this conclusion to be a sound one, without discussing it or the evidence on which it was based, it was not sufficient to warrant the court in placing a receiver in control of the property unless such fact operated the exclusion from the property or its use and enjoyment of one of the joint owners, and unless this feeling was the cause of the failure of Lamaster to enjoy the use and benefit of the heating apparatus,—and we must here remember that there was the finding of fact approved by the court that there was no satisfactory proof of the cause of the failure of the apparatus to properly heat all the building and that the proof did not disclose who was at fault. Clearly there was no such condition of facts as warranted a court in interfering with the rights of the joint owner to wrest the property from the possession of both and place it in the hands of a receiver when the finding of facts showed that it could not be said that there was any fault of the joint owner, a cause of the complainant's trouble. The decree herein was unsupported by the facts as established by the findings and must be reversed.

In the district court there was a motion by Barr and Elliott that judgment be rendered on the findings of fact and conclusions of law, from which it may be said that said parties had nothing to urge against such a judgment being entered; and without an examination of any of the questions which might be presented relative to all portions of such a decree being warranted by the facts, no objections having been made other than have been settled herein, a decree will be entered in accordance with the conclusions announced in the report of the referee. It is, however, urged that relative to the costs the decree must remain as announced by the district court, inasmuch as the appellants presented in such court no motion to retax the costs. In the case of *Burton v. State*, 34 Neb. 125, in regard to a similar contention, it was stated: "It is urged by the county attorney in his brief that a motion to retax costs was necessary in order to give plaintiff standing in this court. We cannot agree with this view. Ordinarily the taxing of costs is a clerical act performed by the clerk, and the presumption is that the action of the clerk has not been called to the attention of the court; hence this court will not, as a rule, review an order taxing costs until a motion to retax has been made and the trial court given an opportunity to correct the errors, if any have been made. In this case the court has considered the question of the liability of plaintiff in error and deliberately determined that he is liable for the costs of prosecution. Here the reason of the rule is wanting. It would be an idle and useless form to ask the court to correct on the theory of a mistake or inadvertence of the clerk that which the record shows to have been the deliberate act of the court." The matter of the costs in the case at bar is within the doctrine announced in that case, from which it follows that no motion to retax was necessary. (See, also, *Hartford Fire Ins. Co. v. Corey*, 53 Neb. 209.)

Judgment of the district court reversed and judgment ordered as hereinbefore stated.

JUDGMENT ACCORDINGLY.

JAMES CARRALL ET AL. V. STATE OF NEBRASKA.

FILED JANUARY 19, 1898.   No. 9574.

53	431
55	301
52	431
158	322
58	431
60	22
53	431
61	430

1. **Summoning Jurors.** The provisions of section 664 of the Code of Civil Procedure in regard to summoning jurors, "Whenever at any general or special term or at any period of a term for any cause there is no panel of * * * petit jurors," are broad enough to cover and include any and all possible reasons for which at any term of a court there may be no panel of jurors present for the trials of causes.

2. ————: CRIMINAL CASES. The provisions of the section to which reference has just been made are applicable in relation to jurors for trials of criminal causes. (Criminal Code, sec. 466.)

3. ————: ————. During the pendency of a term of district court, for which no panel of jurors had been provided for service by the proper officers, a crime was committed and an information filed by the county attorney charging parties with the commission of the crime and the accused were brought before the court for trial. *Held*, To be a condition of affairs within the import of section 664 of the Code of Civil Procedure, and the action of the trial court in ordering jurors summoned as prescribed in said section was proper.

4. **Names.** The names "Mrs. Fred Steinburg" and "Mrs. Fred Steenburg," the first indorsed on an information as the name of a witness, and the second appearing in testimony as her name, are *idem sonans*.

5. **Witnesses: NAMES: INFORMATION.** It is allowable, though probably not the best practice, to indorse the name of a married woman on an information as a prospective witness in a criminal case by

the use of her husband's surname and prefixed thereto the appellative abbreviation "Mrs." and the Christian name or names of her husband or the initial letter or letters thereof.

6. ——: ——: ——. The law does not recognize other than the one or first Christian name, but where a person as a matter of fact has a second or middle Christian name and is commonly known or identified by the use of such middle Christian designation, if his wife's purposed use as a witness in a criminal cause is evidenced by an indorsement of her husband's surname and the abbreviation "Mrs.," together with the middle Christian appellation of the husband, it is sufficient where it does not appear or there is no complaint that the accused person was misled thereby or lacked information of what person was to be produced as a witness.

7. ——: ——: ——. The main purpose of the requirement that the names of witnesses be indorsed on the information in a criminal action is to convey to the accused information or knowledge of the identity of witnesses to be produced on behalf of the state at the trial.

8. Harmless Error: EVIDENCE. The admission of immaterial testimony is not sufficient ground for the reversal of a judgment where not prejudicial to the rights of the complaining party.

9. Instructions: REASONABLE DOUBT. A portion of an instruction, worded as follows: "You are not at liberty to disbelieve as jurors if you believe as men. Your oath imposes on you no obligation to doubt where no doubt would exist if no oath had been administered,"—*held* not objectionable and erroneous when read and construed with the further portions of the same instruction and the other paragraphs of the charge in that the first sentence did not read, "You are not at liberty to disbelieve as jurors if from the evidence you believe as men," instead of as it did with the omission of the reference to the evidence.

10. Burglary: INSTRUCTION: DEFINITION. The statute defining burglary states, among other things, "If any person shall * * * willfully, maliciously and forcibly break and enter," etc. If in an instruction, in which it is purposed to embody a statement of the elements which constitute the crime and necessary to be proved, the word "maliciously" in reference to the breaking and entering is omitted, it is sufficient if other words, or another word, identical in meaning or expressing the same meaning be used.

11. Instructions: REPETITIONS. It is not error to refuse to give instructions if their substance is embodied and given in the charge to the jury.

12. ——: REVIEW. The actions of the trial court in refusing to give certain requested instructions examined and approved.

13. Burglary: EVIDENCE. The evidence *held* sufficient to sustain the verdict.

ERROR to the district court for York county. Tried below before SEDGWICK, J. *Affirmed.*

M. S. Gray and *F. C. Power,* for plaintiffs in error.

C. J. Smyth, Attorney General, and *Ed P. Smith, Deputy Attorney General,* for the state.

HARRISON, C. J.

In an information filed in the district court of York county the plaintiffs in error were charged with the commission of the crimes of burglary and larceny, and on trial were convicted and sentenced to terms of imprisonment in the penitentiary. To obtain a reversal of the judgment, error proceedings have been prosecuted to this court in their behalf.

The crime of which the plaintiffs in error were convicted was alleged to have been committed in the night-time of the 22d day of May, 1897. The term of court during the continuance of which they were tried had its commencement on April 19, 1897. The information against these parties was filed June 28, 1897. No regular panel of jurors had been drawn or summoned for service during the term of court. The time of the term was apparently, probably according to prior expectation or arrangement, being devoted to the disposition of causes in which the services of jurors were not required. When the information was presented in this cause of the commission of the crime subsequent to the time the court convened it became necessary, if the accused were to be tried during the existing term of court, that a jury be provided for the trial. To meet this exigency the court by order directed the sheriff to summon jurors, the number being fixed at twenty-four. The sheriff complied with the order and the attendance of the required jurors was procured. To a trial by this special panel the ac-

32

cused interposed objections, which were overruled, and
they were placed on trial before a jury selected from the
jurors summoned in the manner we have indicated.

As one of the assigned errors it is urged that the jurors
were not procured for service in a method provided by
law; that this branch of the proceedings of the trial of
the accused was without warrant of law, was irregular;
hence the judgment should be reversed. It is not
claimed that the jury was unfair, or that any degree of
prejudice resulted to the rights of the parties through
the selection of the jurors in the way stated; but whether
that there is no such complaint might be to any extent
governing in the question we need not in this cause and
do not determine. It may be solved on another ground.
In section 466 of our Criminal Code it is provided: "In
all [criminal] cases, except as may be otherwise expressly provided, the jury summoned and impaneled according to the provisions of the laws in force relating to
the summoning and impaneling of juries in other cases
shall try the accused." And in section 664 of the Code
of Civil Procedure: "Whenever the proper officers fail to
summon a grand or petit jury, or when all the persons
summoned as grand or petit jurors do not appear before
the district courts, or whenever at any general or special
term or at any period of a term for any cause there is no
panel of grand or petit jurors, or the panel is not complete, said court may order the sheriff, deputy sheriff, or
coroner to summon without delay good and lawful men.
having the qualifications of jurors, and each person summoned shall forthwith appear before the court, and if
competent, shall serve on the grand jury or petit jury as
the case may be, unless such person may be excused from
serving or lawfully challenged." The provisions of this
section are broad enough to cover and include any and
all possible reasons for which at any term of court there
may be no panel of jurors present for the trial of causes,
and the contingencies of the present case are entirely
within its scope. The term was convened and progressed

without a panel of jurors, the acts which constituted the alleged crime were committed and the information of them presented to the court after the commencement of its term, and the cause brought before the court was one the disposition of which demanded a jury. There being none, the court could exercise the power granted it by the section we have quoted. (*People v. Coughlin*, 11 Western Rep. [Mich.] 556, 35 N. W. Rep. 72; *Bennett v. Tintic Iron Co.*, 34 Pac. Rep. [Utah] 61; *Smith v. Bates*, 28 S. W. Rep. [Tex.] 64; *Western Union Telegraph Co. v. Everheart*, 32 S. W. Rep. [Tex.] 90; *St. Clair v. United States*, 14 Sup. Ct. Rep. 1002; *Smith v. State*, 21 Tex. App. 277; *Ohio & M. R. Co. v. Trapp*, 30 N. E. Rep. [Ind.] 812; *State v. Page*, 12 Neb. 386.) The argument that this construction of this section of the statute clothes the district courts with great or too much power might have force or effect if addressed to the legislature, the lawmakers; but where the language is as direct and unambiguous in its import as is employed in this section, courts may not construe it and give it a different meaning to avoid a possible difficulty, or abuse of its grant or power. Moreover, it is not to be presumed that the district courts, or the judges thereof, will abuse any of the powers conferred on them, but rather that they will use them as intended by the legislators.

It is of the assignments that the trial court erred in allowing one of the witnesses called for the state to testify, for the reason that her name was not indorsed on the information. The name of this witness, as it appeared on the back of the information, was as follows: "Mrs. Fred Steinburg." The court reporter has given it in his notes "Mrs. Fred Steenburg." Whether this is a mistake in the spelling of the name by the county attorney in the indorsement on the information or of the reporter we cannot say. It is not disclosed by the record. But, however this may be, we think the two words may be fairly said to be *idem sonans*. (See 16 Am. & Eng. Ency. Law 112, and note.) As an exposition of the doc-

trine of *idem sonans* in regard to names in a warrant we
will quote from the decision in the case of *People v. Gosch*,
46 N. W. Rep. [Mich.] 101, as follows: "It is also claimed
that the warrant was void for the reason that it did not
properly name the respondents.   In the warrant the first
name of Gosch was spelled 'Amel' instead of 'Amiel,' and
the name of 'Brearly' was spelled therein 'Brailey.' This
claim is scarcely worthy of notice.   The names are *idem
sonans.*"   The name of this witness, as appears from the
record, is "Alena Mary Steenburg," and her husband's
name "Paul Fred Steenburg."   The statute requires the
"names of witnesses" to be indorsed on the information.
(Criminal Code, sec. 579.)   It is argued that "Mrs. Fred
Steinburg" was not the name of the witness, and this
being the name written on the instrument was insufficient,—did not fulfill the requirements of the law.
It must be said that in a strict sense or meaning this
was not the name of the witness.   A married woman
takes her husband's surname, and by a social custom
which so largely prevails that it may be called a general one she is designated by the use of the Christian
name or names, if he has more than one, of the husband, or the initial letter or letters of such Christian name or names of the husband, together with
the appellative abbreviation "Mrs." prefixed to the surname, and all married women, there may be possibly a
few exceptions, are better known by such name than
their own Christian name or names used with their husband's surname, and their identification would be more
perfect and complete by the use of the former method
than the latter.   That knowledge of the identity of the
witnesses to be produced against him be conveyed to the
accused person is the main object to be accomplished by
the indorsement of the names of witnesses on the information.   This is the aim and purpose of the law by
which such act is required.   (*Stevens v. State*, 19 Neb. 647;
Parks v. State, 20 Neb. 515; *State v. Everett*, 45 Pac. Rep.
[Wash.] 150.)   To comply with the strict letter of the

law the names of witnesses should be indorsed on the information, and it would no doubt be better practice for county attorneys to follow the law as strictly as possible; but we think it allowable to give notice that a married woman will be called as a witness for the state, that her name be indorsed on the information as was the one in the case at bar. It is further urged in this connection that the name of the husband of this witness was "Paul Fred Steenburg" and that the law disregards all Christian names except the first; hence in law the husband's name was Paul Steenburg, and indorsing his surname with the prefixes "Mrs. Fred" was not a compliance with the statutory requirement, because it was not, strictly speaking, her name, nor was "Fred" in law recognized as of her husband's name. The evidence disclosed that the husband was known as "Fred Steenburg," and the wife, in her testimony, when being interrogated directly on this point, stated that her name was "Mrs. Fred Steenburg," from which it appears that the indorsement on the information was of her a sufficient identification, one which met the purpose of the statute, notwithstanding the law does not recognize a second or other than first Christian name. This appellation "Fred" was that by which the husband was known and identified, and it indicated the wife when applied to her in the manner of its indorsement with the other name and term on the information. Had it appeared that the accused were misled and thereby lacked information of one of the witnesses to be produced at the trial by the state, or that any prejudice had in fact resulted to their rights by reason of the form of this indorsement of the witness, a different question would be presented; but this is not even claimed in argument.

It is argued that there was error committed in the admission of the testimony of E. J. Wightman, called as a witness by the state. This witness was cashier of the First National Bank at York, Nebraska, and testified in regard to the manner in which silver moneys were placed in rolls or packages in said bank and in what amounts, etc. It further appeared in evidence that the money alleged to have been stolen by the accused in the course of the charged burglary consisted in the main of silver and had been sent by the First National Bank of York to the bank which suffered the loss, and in rolls or packages as described by this witness. The evidence of this witness on the subject indicated, if in any sense improper, was but immaterial, and we do not believe it can have been in any degree prejudicial to the accused; hence it furnishes no ground for a reversal of the judgment.

It is urged that the court erred in giving instruction numbered 16 of its own motion. This was an instruction relative to a reasonable doubt. The portion of it to which objection is urged reads as follows: "You are not at liberty to disbelieve as jurors if you believe as men. Your oath imposes on you no obligation to doubt where no doubt would exist if no oath had been administered." A similar instruction, substantially the same as this, was approved in *Barney v. State*, 49 Neb. 515; *Willis v. State*, 43 Neb. 102. (See also *Bartley v. State*, 53 Neb. 310.) In some of the instructions approved in the cases cited there was a variation in the wording from the one in the case at bar and in some the words "if from the evidence" appeared in the one sentence as follows: "You are not at liberty to disbelieve as jurors if from the evidence you believe as men." In the case at bar they were not used, but in other portions of the instructions that all findings or beliefs of the jurors must be from the evidence was strongly stated, and must, we think, have been so impressed on the minds of the jurors that the omission of the words to which we have referred in the particular connection stated could not have misled the jury or worked any prejudice to the rights of the accused. The practical effect of the instruction on the minds of the jurors, when considered in connection with other instructions on the same and other subjects, must have been as if these words had been inserted in the portion of the instruction where it is urged they should have been.

In the section of the statute defining burglary it is stated: "If any person shall, in the night season, willfully, maliciously, and forcibly break and enter." Instruction number 4, given in the case at bar, was a statement of the material elements of the crime charged, of which proof was necessary before a conviction could result, and it omitted the word "maliciously" in reference to the breaking and entering. In the instruction it was said of the breaking and entering, that they must be "willfully, feloniously, and forcibly." The words used fully expressed and included the meaning of the word "maliciously," and this being true, the instruction was sufficient. This is within the doctrine approved by this court relative to a statement in a charge of a crime in an indictment, and it is equally applicable to a statement in an instruction descriptive of a crime. (*Whitman v. State*, 17 Neb. 224; *Hodgkins v. State*, 36 Neb. 160; *Wagn r v. State*, 43 Neb. 1.) And what was further stated in the opinion in the case last cited is equally applicable here, viz.: "This is especially true in view of section 412 of the Criminal Code, providing that no indictment shall be deemed invalid, nor shall the trial, judgment, or other proceedings be stayed, arrested, or in any manner affected for any defect or imperfection which does not tend to the prejudice of the substantial rights of the defendant upon the merits." It follows that the objection to this instruction is unavailing.

The refusal of the court to give an instruction numbered 3, requested by counsel for the accused, is assigned for error. While the precise words of one portion of this instruction were not used in the charge to the jury, its substance and the idea to be conveyed by it were given in effect by paragraphs numbered 9, 10, and 11 thereof.

Of the argument in regard to the refusal to give the requested instructions 7 and 9, it suffices to say that the principles embodied therein, or the essential elements of the instructions, were included in portions of the charge of the court.

Instruction numbered 8, of the refusal to give which error is urged, was defective, in that it wholly ignored the proposition that the jury must be governed by the evidence, and its refusal was not an error.

In view of the verdict returned there was no prejudicial error in refusing to give the requested instruction numbered 9½.

Instruction numbered 13, requested for the accused, was to the effect that the evidence was insufficient to warrant a verdict of guilty of larceny, and that numbered 14 was, to the same effect, relative to the charge of burglary, and they were properly refused. It is insisted that the evidence was insufficient to sustain the verdict, which must be viewed as one of guilty of the charge of burglary. The evidence was in its nature circumstantial and, when carefully analyzed, is sufficient and satisfactory as to every element charged, and ample to support the verdict. It follows that the judgment of the district court will be

AFFIRMED.

JAMES H. PERKINS ET AL. V. CHARLES TILTON.

FILED JANUARY 19, 1898. No. 7742.

1. **Rulings on Evidence:** REVIEW: OFFER OF PROOF. An offer to prove, to lay the foundation for the proper presentment of error in the exclusion of proposed testimony as answer to a question to which an objection is sustained, must be of matter which would have been admitted as relevant, responsive, and pertinent in answer to the rejected interrogatory.

2. **Exchange of Realty:** JOINDER OF PARTIES: REVIEW. Error assigned of the giving of an instruction examined and the action of the trial court approved.

3. ———: ———. *Held*, That the plaintiffs in error were properly jo ned as defendants in the action.

ERROR from the district court of Hitchcock county. Tried below before WELTY, J. *Affirmed.*

W. S. Morlan, for plaintiffs in error.

J. W. Cole, contra.

HARRISON, C. J.

On October 5, 1891, the defendant in error was the owner of a tract of land in the state of Illinois, and James H. Perkins, of plaintiffs in error, was the owner of the northwest quarter of a section of land situate in Hitchcock county, this state, and his wife, Ann Perkins, owned five quarter-sections of adjoining land. The whole tract of six quarter-sections constituted one farm. On the date stated a contract was entered into between the parties for the exchange of the two tracts of land. The negotiations for the trade and the contract with which they closed were between James H. Perkins and the defendant in error, Ann Perkins not then actively or personally appearing in the transaction or in any manner participating except as she may have been represented by her husband, and we must conclude that she was so represented, for she claimed, and in this suit claims, the benefits and rights conferred by the transaction. After the consummation of the exchange the defendant in error instituted this action to recover the value of certain improvements which he asserted plaintiffs in error wrongfully removed from the farm in Nebraska; an amount of taxes due on said farm which he alleges plaintiffs in error agreed to, but failed to pay; also a sum which he claimed his due by reason of a shortage in the number of acres of land contracted to be conveyed and the number of acres actually transferred to him. The contract of the parties appears to have been evidenced by a written instrument, but this had been lost, destroyed, or could not be produced. A trial of the issues resulted favorably to the defendant in error,

and the cause is presented here for review in error proceeding on behalf of James H. Perkins and Ann Perkins.

There are but three assignments of error noticed in
argument, the first of which relates to the trial court's
action in excluding testimony.   During the examination
of James H. Perkins he was interrogated at some length
in relation to a trip which he had made with defendant
in error from Nebraska to the land in Illinois and what
he did and saw while in Illinois, and in this connection
was further questioned, with the results as follows:

Q. What, if any, acquaintance did you have with this
man before you went there?

A. Not any.

Q. What acquaintance had you with that part of the
country?

A. None at all.

Q. When you got there what kind of weather was it?

A. Dry.

Q. What, if any, did Mr. Tilton represent to you as to
quality and value of the land?

To the question last quoted an objection was interposed, which was sustained.   There was then for the
plaintiffs in error an offer to prove, which of type-writ-
ten matter occupies some two and one-half pages of the
paper ordinarily used, and which, in substance, embodied
an offer to prove, that of date December 17, 1891, and
between defendant in error and Ann Perkins, there was
a modification, verbally, of the contract for the exchange
of the land; also certain statements then made by defendant in error to Ann Perkins in regard especially to
the value of the land in Illinois which she claims were
false, but were guarantied by him to be true; and further, of certain representations in relation to the quality
and value of said land made to James H. Perkins and
by him conveyed to Ann Perkins which were false; and
further, that the whole of these matters were relied upon
by Ann Perkins and she was thereby induced to make

the exchange of lands. It was of the evidence that the
contract provided that James H. Perkins should go to
Illinois and see the land there, and if after an examination he was satisfied with it, the trade should be concluded. Whether this was of the contract or not, Perkins did, almost immediately after it was made, October
5, 1891, go in company with defendant in error to the
land in Illinois and examined it, returned therefrom to
his home, and the trade was afterward completed. This
examination was for himself and his wife, the parties
concerned. With this fact in view and an application of
the rules of law which would govern and settle the
question of the relative positions and rights of the parties, there was little, if any, of the offer to prove which
could have been admitted in answer to the question propounded as either responsive or in any degree material
or relevant. This being true, the offer of proof was as
if none had been made and the record of the action of
the court in not allowing the question to be answered
presents no noticeable error. (*Dunphy v. Bartenbach*, 40
Neb. 143.)

Another assignment of error which is urged in argument is in relation to the third instruction requested
for defendant in error and given. The record is not in
a very satisfactory condition wherein it refers to the
instructions. Under the heading of "Instructions asked
by plaintiff" (defendant in error) there are three paragraphs numbered, presumably, by the person who prepared the copy of the record for this court as follows:
1st, 3rd, 5th. These designations were evidently made
with the typewriter. The one designated "3rd" has also
with a lead pencil been marked "2," and the one numbered "5th" has been marked with lead pencil "3." We
are not certain as to which marking we should accept
as the true one, but without stopping to decide this matter, accepting the conclusion which we must that this
was a contract for the benefit of plaintiffs in error jointly
and by which they were jointly bound to defendant in

error, it is not material which of the numbered instructions we consider as the "3rd" and its giving assigned for error, for, in this view of the contract and the relations in which by its terms the parties were placed, either paragraph was properly given.

What we have just said in regard to the contract also disposes of the third branch of the argument, which is a contention that the plaintiffs in error were not jointly or equally bound by the contract, but only to the extent it involved the land belonging to each or any matters or things pertaining thereto, and that they were improperly joined in this action. The land of the plaintiffs in error was all contracted to be exchanged as one piece for the benefit of the two parties and on the same terms as to both and such terms equally binding on each and both. It follows that the judgment of the district court will be

AFFIRMED.

CHARLES E. PERKINS, TRUSTEE, APPELLANT, V. EDWARD POTTS, APPELLEE.

FILED JANUARY 19, 1898. No. 9235.

Landlord and Tenant: ATTORNMENT TO STRANGER: ADVERSE POSSESSION. The conclusions and decision announced on the former hearing in this cause (52 Neb. 110) approved and followed.

REHEARING of case reported in 52 Neb. 110. Reaffirmed.

Warren Pratt and T. M. Stuart, for appellant.

Dryden & Main, contra.

HARRISON, C. J.

This cause was appealed to this court from an adjudication in the district court of Buffalo county of the matters in controversy and submitted under the provisions of rule 2 (44 Neb. ix), and the judgment of the district court was affirmed. A motion for a rehearing was filed and sustained and the case has been again presented and submitted. The opinion of the court rendered on the former hearing was written by Commissioner RAGAN and is reported in 52 Neb., 110. ·

It appears that the appellant was, on November 1, 1887, the owner of a tract of land in Buffalo county, this state, and on said date, by written contract with one Kilgore, agreed to sell to Kilgore the tract of land. The land was to be paid for at a date fixed in the contract of sale at ten years subsequent to the date of the contract, and it was further provided that there should be annual payments of interest on the principal sum, the consideration for the sale, from the inception of the agreement to its fixed termination. It was further of the contract that the vendee should pay the taxes which might be assessed against the land. The payments provided for were to be made according to the terms of the contract; if not, a forfeiture of the vendee's rights thereunder was to ensue. There were assignments of the contract by the vendee and assignees until by assignment the appellee claimed to be entitled to the benefit of its provisions. January 30, 1896, one Knox was in actual possession of the land as lessee of the appellee, and on said day an agent of appellant went to the land and induced Knox to accept a lease thereof from the appellant. Knox remained on the land and during the farming season of 1896 raised a crop of grains thereon. After the maturity of at least some of the crops, the appellee took into his possession and removed from the land 120 bushels of oats which had been grown on the land during that season. To recover these the appellant commenced an action of replevin, and also this action in the district court of Buffalo county, stating in the petition in this that he was the owner in fee of the land and in possession thereof, also the owner of the crops grown thereon du-·

ing the year 1896, and that appellee had wrongfully entered upon the premises and taken therefrom the grain before mentioned; that it had been replevied and the action of replevin was pending; also that it was threatened by appellee that he would again go upon the premises and take therefrom all crops grown during the year 1896, which threats would be executed unless appellee was restrained; and further that appellee was insolvent. The prayer of the petition was that appellee be perpetually enjoined from entering upon said premises and doing any of the threatened and purposed acts. The district court dismissed the petition. For a more extended statement see the opinion in 52 Neb. 110.

This court in the decision formerly rendered held:

"1. One who takes possession of real estate as the tenant of another cannot hold said real estate adversely to his lessor without first having actually or constructively surrendered the premises to him.

"2. Where a tenant in possession without his landlord's consent attorns to a third party,—the latter not having acquired the interest of the landlord in the real estate either by grant or operation of law,—the possessory rights of the landlord are not thereby affected, as such an attornment is void.

"3. The vendee of an executory contract for the sale of real estate by virtue of such contract entered into possession, made certain improvements upon the premises, and partly performed his contract of purchase. Afterwards the vendee, while in default in the performance of his part of the contract of purchase, leased the premises to a tenant for one year, and put him in possession. The vendor by reason of the default of the vendee, and in pursuance of the provisions of the contract of sale, declared the same forfeited, and demanded possession of the premises from the vendee. The possession was not surrendered, and thereupon the vendor went upon the premises, and induced the tenant, without the vendee's knowledge or consent, to accept a lease from

him (the vendor) for said premises.   The vendee forcibly
entered and removed part of the crops grown by his tenant, and threatened to enter and remove the remainder,
and the vendor applied to the district court for a perpetual injunction to restrain the vendee's entrance upon
the premises.   Held, that the application was properly
denied."

We have carefully re-examined the questions upon the
determination of which the appellant's right to institute
and successfully maintain this action depends, and are
strengthened in the views we before entertained and
which were embodied in the opinion heretofore rendered.
That the appellant induced Knox, the tenant of appellee
in the manner disclosed by the facts herein, to receive
a lease of the land he occupied from the appellant, to
attorn to him, did not give appellant any greater possession of the premises than he possessed before such act,
and did not dispossess the appellee.   The possession of
the lessee, Knox, remained the possession of his landlord
to whom he first attorned, of whom he had received the
possession which he had never abandoned or surrendered.
Change of possession of lands cannot be so readily and
easily effected.   Where a tenant disclaims holding under
his landlord and attorns to a stranger the attornment
is void and does not operate a dispossession of the landlord.   (*Blue v. Sayre*, 2 Dana [Ky.] 213; *Rogers v. Boyn-
ton*, 57 Ala. 501; *Springs v. Schenck*, 6 S. E. Rep. [N. Car.]
405; Taylor, Landlord & Tenant [7th ed.] sec. 705.)   "A
tenant cannot repudiate the title of the landlord under
whom he originally entered, and claim to hold the premises under another, until he has first surrendered possession to his original landlord.   It is not enough that
he has abandoned the premises for a time, and afterwards entered under the new title, unless he has given
notice of such abandonment to the original landlord."
(*Juneman v. Franklin*, 3 S. W. Rep. [Tex.] 562.)   As supporting the first portion of the doctrine announced, there
is cited: *Rector v. Gibbon*, 4 Sup. Ct. Rep. 606; *Killoren v.*

Murtaugh, 5 Atl. Rep. [N. H.] 769, and note; *Pengra v. Munz,* 29 Fed. Rep. 830. Approving and applying the doctrine announced in *Rector v. Gibbon,* see *Goode v. Gaines,* 12 Sup. Ct. Rep. 839. "A tenant cannot defeat the possession of his landlord by merely going out of the house, taking a lease from another, who claims title thereto, and going back professedly under the new lease." Such action did not end the landlord's possession and give the other party of whom the later lease was accepted possession. (*State v. Howell,* 12 S. E. Rep. [N. Car.] 569.) "Where, under a contract for the sale of land, the vendor executes to the vendee the usual bond for titles, and delivers to him the possession of the premises, even if the latter fail to pay the purchase-money at maturity, he may, nevertheless, retain possession, either by himself or his tenant, until such time as he shall be legally evicted therefrom by the vendor; and the tenant who enters under the vendee cannot, without first surrendering his possession to the latter, attorn to the vendor upon any supposed right of the latter, without the consent of the vendee to rescind the contract of sale." (*Broxton v. Ennis,* 22 S. E. Rep. [Ga.] 945.) The further conclusion of the former opinion follows that a resort to action of injunction was not allowable to determine the conflicting claims of the parties to the possession of the premises.

The counsel for appellant in the brief filed in support of the motion for a rehearing requested that certain other questions be at this time decided, though the court might conclude to adhere to the opinion formerly rendered as to the points therein considered. This we would be pleased to do, but their discussion and determination here would scarcely be proper or pertinent since they are not directly involved, and in a contest between the parties in another form of action they might be involved. The decree of the district court is

REAFFIRMED.

JENNIE SHAFFER V. SAMUEL S. VINCENT.

FILED JANUARY 19, 1898.   No. 7675.

1. **Bill of Exceptions**: AUTHENTICATION. A bill of exceptions, to be available in the supreme court, must be authenticated by the clerk of the district court.

2. ——: ——. A certificate by the clerk of that court merely stating that the original bill was filed in his office on a certain date, is insufficient to identify a document contained in the transcript as being either such original bill or a copy thereof.

ERROR from the district court of Harlan county. Tried below before BEALL, J. *Affirmed.*

R. L. Keester, for plaintiff in error.

John Everson, contra.

NORVAL, J.

This was an action by Samuel S. Vincent against Jennie Shaffer and others to obtain the cancellation of a deed to certain real estate in Harlan county, on the ground that the same was procured by misrepresentation and fraud. A decree was entered for Vincent as prayed. A motion for a new trial was filed by Jennie Shaffer, which was overruled by the court, and she alone has brought the record here for review.

The assignments of error call in question the sufficiency of the evidence to sustain the findings and decree, the decisions of the court below upon the admission of testimony, and the ruling upon the motion for a new trial. These assignments are not available, because the document attached to the transcript is not authenticated by the certificate of the clerk of the trial court as being either the original bill of exceptions in the cause or a copy thereof. The district clerk merely certifies that the original bill of exceptions was filed in his office on a certain date, which is insufficient for the purpose of au-

33

thentication. As none of the questions argued can be considered without the aid of a bill of exceptions, the decree must be

AFFIRMED.

LAURA F. FUNK, APPELLEE, V. KANSAS MANUFACTURING COMPANY ET AL., APPELLANTS.

FILED JANUARY 19, 1898. No. 7701.

1. **Judgments:** EQUITABLE RELIEF: NEGLIGENCE. A court of equity will not afford relief against a judgment or decree obtained against a party through the negligence of his attorney.

2. ——: ——: EVIDENCE. Evidence *held* insufficient to support the decision of the trial court vacating a former decree in another action between the same parties.

APPEAL from the district court of Lancaster county. Heard below before STRODE, J. *Reversed.*

Ricketts & Wilson, for appellants.

Doty & Haggard, contra.

NORVAL, J.

The Kansas Manufacturing Company recovered several money judgments against Ancil L. Funk, on which executions were issued, which were returned by the sheriff of Lancaster county *nulla bona.* Alias executions were thereupon issued on said judgments, and levies were made thereunder upon certain real estate as the property of Funk, which prior thereto he had conveyed to his brother-in-law T. W. Thornburg, who likewise conveyed it to Laura F. Funk, the wife of said judgment debtor. Subsequently, and after the levy of said executions, the Kansas Manufacturing Company commenced a suit in the court below, in the nature of a creditor's bill, against Ancil L. Funk, Laura F. Funk, and T. W. Thornburg, to set aside the deeds to said real estate, and to subject the property to the payment of said judgments. On May 11, 1893, Laura F. Funk filed an answer and cross-petition therein, which not only denied many of the material averments of the creditor's bill, but pleaded matters upon which she asked affirmative relief. On June 19, 1894, the plaintiff therein replied to said answer and cross-petition and filed a supplemental petition setting up the recovery by it on that day of another judgment against said Ancil L. Funk. On June 20, which was a day in the April term, 1894, of the district court of Lancaster county, the cause was tried in the absence of Mrs. Funk, and in nine days later a decree was entered cancelling the conveyances, and awarding the plaintiff therein a lien upon the real estate. An order of sale was issued thereon, and the property was advertised for sale, but prior to the day fixed for the sale, and on August 28, 1894, Mrs. Funk instituted this action against the sheriff, Fred A. Miller, and the Kansas Manufacturing Company to enjoin the sale and to vacate and set aside the decree of June 29. From the decree awarding Mrs. Funk the full measure of relief demanded in her petition the defendants prosecute this appeal.

The evidence adduced tended to prove that Mrs. Funk had a meritorious defense against the creditor's bill. Therefore we are limited in our investigation to the question whether sufficient cause existed for setting aside and vacating the decree which canceled the conveyances to the real estate in controversy. Relief was asked upon two grounds: First—That her attorneys failed to properly look after her interest in the action or to notify her of the time when the cause would be reached for trial; and second—that she was misled as to the time of the trial by an agreement made with the Kansas Manufacturing Company that the cause should not be heard during the April term, 1894, of the district court. Assuming, without deciding the point, or intimating that the facts warrant such an inference, that Mrs. Funk's attorneys were negligent, such fact constituted no justification for vacating the decree. It is well settled that equity will not relieve a party against a judgment on account of his own negligence or that of his attorney. The fault or negligence of an attorney is in law regarded the neglect of the client. (Weeks, Attorneys [2d ed.] sec. 294; 1 Black, Judgments secs. 500-503; *Jones v. Leech*, 46 Ia. 186; *Drinkard v. Ingram*, 21 Tex. 650; *Lee v. Green*, 28 Atl. Rep. [N. J.], 904; *Yates v. Monroe*, 13 Ill. 213; *Kern v. Strausberger*, 71 Ill. 413; *Clark v. Ewing*, 93 Ill. 572; *Barrow v. Jones*, 1 J. J. Marsh. [Ky.] 470; *Ganzer v. Schiffbauer*, 40 Neb. 633; *Scott v. Wright*, 50 Neb. 849; *Losey v. Neidig*, 52 Neb. 167.)

Plaintiff and her husband on and prior to April 10, 1894, resided in the city of Lincoln and on that date they moved to Alcovia, Wyoming. There were then pending two suits in the district court of Lancaster county in favor of the Kansas Manufacturing Company, one against Ancil L. Funk for the recovery of a money judgment, and the other was the creditor's bill already mentioned. Ancil L. Funk testified that about a week prior to the removal of himself and wife to Wyoming he interviewed H. H. Wilson, one of the attorneys for the plaintiff in the last named suit, as regards the trial thereof, and his version of the conversation which then took place is here reproduced in his own language: "I met Mr. Wilson near the corner of Eleventh and O and told him that I was going to Wyoming before long, and would necessarily be some distance from the railroad, and I would like to be sure that this case was put off until fall. He said that he was not particular about the equity case, but the law case he should press—he had put that off and would not put it off again—but the equity case he was not particular about, and would not take any undue advantage of my absence, or my wife's." Mr. Funk further testified that had it not been for this conversation and the reliance placed thereon, he and his wife would have attended the trial. H. H. Wilson testified positively that no conversation of the import narrated by Mr. Funk was ever had, and Mr. Wilson is corroborated by other testimony appearing in the record. Moreover, if the conversation occurred as testified to by Mr. Funk it is insufficient to sustain the allegation in the petition that there was a definite agreement that the cause should not be tried during the term of the district court at which it was heard. At most it cannot be claimed that Mr. Wilson agreed to anything more than that no undue advantage should be taken of the absence of Mr. Funk or his wife. The record fails to disclose that any undue advantage was taken of the absence, since the Funks, by letters received from their attorney, were advised that the equity case was on the call for the April term and urged upon them the necessity of their being present at the trial. In no reply to these letters was it suggested that there was an agreement that the cause should not be tried at that term of court. Counsel for Mrs. Funk consented to the setting of the case down for trial, and when it was reached asked for no postponement of the hearing, and made the very best defense possible without the assistance of either client or witness. It is manifest that no sufficient cause was shown for vacating the decree of June 29, 1894. The decree of the court below herein is reversed, and the action dismissed.

REVERSED AND DISMISSED.

CHICAGO, BURLINGTON & QUINCY RAILROAD COMPANY, APPELLEE, V. CITY OF NEBRASKA CITY ET AL., APPELLANTS.

FILED JANUARY 19, 1898. No. 8419.

1. **Municipal Corporations:** ANNEXATION OF TERRITORY. Ordinance No. 226 of Nebraska City was ineffectual of itself to annex adjacent territory to said city or to extend the territorial limits of the municipality.

2. ——: TAXATION. A city cannot levy a tax on property where its
situs is not within the corporate limits.

3. **Taxation**: INJUNCTION. A court of equity will enjoin the collection
of a tax which is absolutely void.

APPEAL from the district court of Otoe county. Heard
below before CHAPMAN, J. *Affirmed.*

C. W. Seymour, for appellants.

John C. Watson, J. W. Deweese, and *F. E. Bishop, contra.*

NORVAL, J.

Action was instituted by the Chicago, Burlington &
Quincy Railroad Company to enjoin the collection of a
city tax assessed in 1893 by the authorities of Nebraska
City upon the west half of plaintiff's bridge spanning
the Missouri river at or near said city. From a decree
awarding the company a peremptory injunction the defendants appeal.

The tax in question is claimed by the plaintiff to be
invalid upon two grounds: First—The bridge in question is a part of plaintiff's line of railroad, and the portion of the structure lying within this state is not subject
to taxation by the local assessing and taxing officers,
but the state board of equalization alone has jurisdiction
to assess the same. Second—No portion of said bridge
is within the corporate limits of Nebraska City, and
therefore the municipal authorities thereof had no power
to tax the same for any purpose whatever.

The first contention is in the teeth of the decision of
this court in *Cass County v. Chicago, B. & Q. R. Co.,* 25
Neb. 348, where it was distinctly ruled that the west half
of the railroad bridge across the Missouri river at Plattsmouth was subject to taxation by the local assessor and
not by the state board of equalization. That decision
is vigorously assailed as being unsound, and standing
alone as a precedent upon the question therein considered. An investigation of the subject anew is sought

herein. In the opinion of the writer, any discussion of that decision at this time, or of the first ground above stated for relief in this case, would be mere *obiter*, since the trial court found, and its finding is sustained by the proofs, as will hereafter appear, that no portion of the railroad bridge at Nebraska City is included within the geographical limits of such city. It will be soon enough to approve or overrule the decision alluded to when the question therein determined shall fairly arise in a pending cause.

The facts upon which the second ground for relief are predicated are substantially these: The territorial legislature of Nebraska in 1855 passed an act incorporating Nebraska City, the first section whereof provided "that all the territory within the geographical limits of Nebraska City, as designated upon the plat of said city, together with all the additions that may be hereafter made thereto according to law, is hereby declared to be a city by the name of Nebraska City." (Session Laws 1855, p. 391.) At the same session of the legislature there was enacted a law incorporating as Kearney City all the territory included in the boundaries of such city as designated upon the plat thereof. (Session Laws 1855, p. 417.) These two cities were consolidated by legislative enactment in 1857, and declared to be a corporation by the name and style of Nebraska City. (Session Laws 1857, p. 53.) The recorded plats of the two cities thus consolidated show a strip of land 160 feet wide lying between their eastern boundaries and the west bank of the Missouri river, which strip is designated on the plats as "Levee 160 feet wide." The west end of the railroad bridge is 120 feet east of the east boundary line of Nebraska City, as shown by the plats aforesaid, so that no portion of the bridge is within the limits of such city, unless the corporate boundaries were legally extended by ordinance No. 226 passed by the mayor and council on December 5, 1892, the first section of which follows:

"Section 1. That the following described land and
territory be, and the same is hereby, included in the
corporate limits of the city of Nebraska City, Otoe
county, state of Nebraska, and the said limits are hereby
extended so as to embrace and to include the same,
to-wit: Commencing at the city limits on the quarter-
section line running east and west through section ten
(10), township eight (8), in range fourteen (14) east of
the sixth principal meridian, in Otoe county, state of
Nebraska, thence east to the middle of the channel of
the Missouri river; thence down said channel until it
intersects north and south line 350 west, and parallel
to the north and south eighty-acre line in the southwest
quarter of section ten (10); thence south to the city
limits; thence in a northwesterly direction along the city
limits to the place of beginning; also the surface of
the ground and the accretion thereto lying between the
corporation line of said city and the Missouri river
within the above described line, being a part of section
ten (10), in township eight (8), in range fourteen (14)
east of the sixth principal meridian, in Otoe county,
state of Nebraska, and containing less than five acres."

The adoption of said ordinance was wholly insufficient
to change the boundaries of the municipality. The statute at that time in force designated the mode for the annexation of adjacent territory to a city of the first class
having less than 25,000 inhabitants. (Compiled Statutes
1891, ch. 13a, art. 2, secs. 4, 6.) The one for which provision is made in said section 4 permits such annexation
to be accomplished by the passage of an ordinance by
the mayor and council extending the corporate limits so
as to include territory contiguous or adjacent to the city,
which by the authority or acquiescence of the owner has
been subdivided into tracts or parcels containing not
to exceed five acres. The record fails to establish that
the real estate sought to be annexed by the ordinance
in question had been subdivided by the owner into parcels of the size specified by said section 4. It is true the

amount of land attempted to be added to the city does not exceed five acres, but that is an unimportant consideration, and does not meet the legislative requirement that the contiguous territory must have been subdivided by the proprietor into parcels of not to exceed five acres, in order to entitle the same to be attached to the corporation by the mere passage of an ordinance ordering it to be annexed. It is a familiar doctrine that municipal corporations can exercise only such powers as are conferred by law, either expressed or implied. Where the statute points out the mode of procedure for the extension of the boundaries of a city, the same must be substantially followed, else it will be of no validity. It does not appear that the method provided in section 4 for the extending of the boundaries of a city of the class of Nebraska City has been pursued. The other statutory mode of annexation of adjacent real estate has not been observed, since it is not claimed that the land embraced within the description contained in the ordinance has been by the proprietor or owner thereof laid out into lots, blocks, avenues, and alleys or other grounds, nor has a plat thereof been made, acknowledged, and recorded as section 6 contemplates and requires. The ordinance was therefore in and of itself ineffectual to extend the limits of the municipality.

It is suggested that the boundaries of the city were enlarged so as to include the said strip of land 160 feet wide lying immediately east of the platted territory, by ten years' adverse usage by the city authorities. Doubtless, the mayor and council entertained a different view, else the ordinance to which reference has been made would most likely never have been adopted. They hardly would have attempted to annex territory which was already regarded as embraced within the boundaries of the city. Moreover, this record fails to show that the city limits were changed to include this adjacent territory by virtue of any adverse use or occupancy of the premises. No part of the bridge being within the geographical limits or boundaries of Nebraska City, the taxes levied and assessed thereon by the municipal authorities are unauthorized and void. (*Chicago, B. & Q. R. Co. v. Cass County*, 51 Neb. 369.)

In argument it is said that plaintiff has an adequate remedy at law, and that injunction will not lie to restrain the collection of the tax. It is true a court of equity will not interfere to prevent the enforcement of a tax merely because the assessment was irregular, but injunction may be resorted to where the whole tax is absolutely void and the enforcement thereof would be inequitable and against conscience. (*Touzalin v. Omaha*, 25 Neb. 817; *South Platte Land Co. v. Buffalo County*, 7 Neb. 253; *Bellvue Improvement Co. v. Bellvue*, 39 Neb. 876; *Chicago, B. & Q. R. Co. v. Nemaha County*, 50 Neb. 393; *Chicago, B. & Q. R. Co. v. Cass County*, 51 Neb. 369.) As the authorities of Nebraska City had no jurisdiction to impose the taxes in controversy plaintiff may invoke the aid of a court of equity to prevent the collection thereof. For the reason stated, the decree of the district court is right and it is

AFFIRMED.

WILLIAM M. ELLIOTT V. CARTER WHITE-LEAD COMPANY.

FILED JANUARY 19, 1898. No. 7673.

1. **Pleading and Proof:** VARIANCE. There can be no recovery if there is a material variance between the allegations and the proof. The *allegata* and *probata* must agree.

2. **Trial:** DIRECTING VERDICT. Where the evidence is uncontradicted, and all reasonable men must draw the same conclusion therefrom, it is not error for the court to direct a verdict in favor of the party entitled thereto under the pleadings and proofs.

3. **Review:** ORAL INSTRUCTIONS. Error in giving an oral instruction is not available in this court where no exception was specially taken on that ground in the trial court at the time the instruction was given.

ERROR from the district court of Douglas county. Tried below before BLAIR, J. *Affirmed.*

Weaver & Giller, for plaintiff in error.

I. R. Andrews, contra

NORVAL, J.

William M. Elliott sued the Carter White-Lead Company to recover for personal injuries. At the close of the plaintiff's testimony the jury, in obedience to an oral instruction of the trial court, returned a verdict for the defendant. A motion for a new trial was overruled, and judgment was entered against the plaintiff in accordance with the verdict. Subsequently, on motion of the defendant, an order was entered requiring that security for costs be given by the plaintiff, who prosecutes this error proceeding.

The defendant is the owner and operator of a factory in the city of Omaha for the manufacture of white lead, and plaintiff was in its employ. An inclined wooden elevator was used by the defendant to hoist pigs of lead from railway cars up and into a vat on the inside of the company's building. This elevator consisted of two pine planks about fourteen feet long, nine inches wide, two inches thick on the upper edge and three inches on the lower, fastened or bolted parallel to each other, and about two feet apart, so as to permit the passage between them of an endless chain with an apron attachment. This elevator stood at an angle of about 45 degrees, with one end resting on the foundation of the building and the other passing through the floor above into the room containing the vat. A pig of lead weighing about 100 pounds being placed on the lower part of the elevator was pushed or slid up and along the upper edges of said planks by the apron attached to the endless chain to the top of the elevator, where it fell into the vat, the apron continuing on around; and on reaching the bottom at each revolution another pig of lead was placed on the apron, which in like manner was elevated to the vat in the room above. The continual sliding of the pigs of lead had worn several scallops on the surface of the upper edges of the two planks to the depth of about one-fourth of an inch. A few hours prior to the injury hereafter mentioned the elevator was repaired by nailing on the upper edge of each plank, for the entire length, a strip of iron two inches wide and about one-eighth of an inch in thickness. These strips of iron were fastened with eight-penny nails driven about nine inches apart and near the center of the scallops. Shortly after said repairs were completed plaintiff assisted in unloading a car of lead. His portion of the work was to carry the pigs of lead from the car and place them on the elevator, one at a time, in proper position to be pushed up by the apron. After he had been thus at work between three and four hours, a pig of lead, which he had placed on the elevator, was carried in the usual way by the apron until it was within a short distance of the top, when one end thereof, it is claimed, caught upon a protruding nail which threw the pig of lead down the elevator and upon the foot of plaintiff, causing the injury which is made the basis of this action.

It is urged that the elevator was defective and out of repair, and that the defendant was negligent in not instructing the plaintiff in the use of the same and in not apprising him of the danger and hazard of the work he was called upon to perform. By the undisputed testimony it was established that the elevator had just been repaired and placed in a safe condition for use, and that the pig of lead which caused the injury was the first one to fall after the making of the said repairs. Moreover, the specific act of negligence charged in the petition is that the nails used for fastening the iron bands to the planks were so small that they worked loose, and protruded and extended above the upper surface of said bands, enabling the nails to catch the lead

and causing it to fall upon plaintiff's foot. This averment is not sustained by a scintilla of evidence. On the
contrary, it is claimed in the brief of plaintiff that the
accident was occasioned by the weight of the pig of lead
depressing the iron strip down into one of the scallops
already mentioned, causing the nail to protrude and
catch one end of the pig of lead, whereby it was thrown
down the elevator. The petition does not charge that
the injury resulted in any such manner. If it occurred in
the mode suggested, it is remarkable that some one of
the several hundred pigs of lead which plaintiff had
placed on the elevator prior to the accident, during the
same evening, was not also caught on the protruding
nail and thrown down, since the pigs of lead were shown
to be nearly all of the same size and weight. As to the
failure of defendant to instruct plaintiff in the method
of operating the elevator and of the danger and hazard
of the employment, it is sufficient to say that no negligence in that regard is imputed to the defendant in the
petition. A recovery cannot be had for acts of negligence not alleged in the petition. The rule is the *allegata*
and *probata* must agree. (*Worth v. Buch*, 34 Neb. 703;
Imhoff v. House, 36 Neb. 28; *Luce v. Foster*, 42 Neb. 818.)

Doubtless, where different minds may honestly draw
from the evidence different conclusions as to whether
negligence or the absence thereof is established, the
question as to the conclusion to be reached is a proper
one for the jury, and not for the trial court. It is likewise firmly settled in this state that where the evidence
is uncontradicted and all reasonable men must draw the
same inference therefrom, the question of negligence is
one of law for the court, and in such case it is not error
for it to direct a verdict in favor of the party entitled
thereto under the proofs adduced. (*Chicago, B. & Q. R.
Co. v. Landauer*, 36 Neb. 642; *Woolsey v. Chicago, B. & Q.
R. Co.*, 39 Neb. 798; *Dehning v. Detroit Bridge & Iron
Works*, 46 Neb. 556; *Slayton v. Fremont, E. & M. V. R. Co.*,
40 Neb. 840.) It was unfortunate that the plaintiff re-

ceived the injury, but it was one of the risks incident
to his employment, and which he assumed. An examination of the evidence set forth in the bill of exceptions
reveals that no other verdict in the case could have been
properly returned; hence it was proper practice for the
trial court to direct a finding for the defendant.

It was urged that it was error for the trial judge to
instruct the jury orally. There are two ready answers
to this contention. The error was without prejudice,
inasmuch as under the pleadings and evidence the defendant was entitled to have a verdict directed. (*Zittle v.
Schlesinger*, 46 Neb. 844.) In the next place the action of
the court cannot be reviewed, as no objection was specifically taken to the instruction at the time it was given
on the ground that it was not in writing. (*Worback v.
Miller*, 4 Neb. 31; *City of Chadron v. Glover*, 43 Neb. 732;
Jolly v. State, 43 Neb. 857; *Omaha & Florence Land Co. v.
Hansen*, 32 Neb. 449.)

After judgment, the court below sustained a motion
made before trial requiring the plaintiff to give security
for costs on the ground that he was a non-resident.
Why the court did not pass upon the motion at an
earlier period is not disclosed. It may be possible that
the ruling was obtained before judgment, and that the
date of the decision was erroneously stated in the transcript. For present purposes, however, the transcript
must be treated as correct. Conceding the position contended for by plaintiff to be sound, that the defendant
waived its right to have security given by the delay in
having the motion called to the attention of the court,
nevertheless the sustaining of the motion will not authorize a reversal, because plaintiff was not in the least
prejudiced by the ruling. Judgment for costs had already been entered against him and the action dismissed.
The court did not attach any penalty to the failure of
plaintiff to comply with the order relating to security
for costs, nor has such security been given. The judgment is

AFFIRMED.

EDWARD LORENZ V. STATE OF NEBRASKA.

FILED JANUARY 19, 1898.   No. 9508.

1. **Criminal Law:** EVIDENCE: OPINION OF ATTORNEY GENERAL. A conviction in a criminal case will ordinarily be reversed where the attorney general declines to file a brief on the ground that the evidence is insufficient to sustain the judgment.

2. **Homicide:** EVIDENCE. The evidence in the case examined, and *held* not sufficient to support the verdict.

ERROR to the district court for Red Willow county. Tried below before NORRIS, J. *Reversed.*

W. R. Starr, for plaintiff in error.

C. J. Smyth, Attorney General, and *Ed P. Smith, Deputy Attorney General,* for the state.

NORVAL, J.

The defendant below, Edward Lorenz, a boy sixteen years old, was tried and convicted of murder in the first degree, and sentenced to imprisonment in the penitentiary for life. The petition in error, among other assignments, alleges that the verdict is not sustained by the evidence. The attorney general has declined to file a brief in the cause, giving as a reason therefor that he is convinced, upon an examination of the record, that said assignment is well taken; therefore, upon the authority of *George v. State,* 44 Neb. 757, and *McAleer v. State,* 46 Neb. 116, we would be justified in reversing the judgment and sentence. A careful perusal of the evidence adduced by the state on the trial, and none was introduced by the defense, satisfies us that it is insufficient to sustain a verdict of guilty. It may be the accused committed the crime charged, but if so, the state has failed to prove it.

REVERSED AND REMANDED.

STATE OF NEBRASKA V. JOSEPH W. THOMAS, RECEIVER OF MIDLAND STATE BANK, APPELLEE, AND LEPHA J. McCARGAR, APPELLANT.

FILED JANUARY 19, 1898. No. 9252.

Banks and Banking: INSOLVENCY: TRUSTS: AGENCY. When an agent, in accordance with a long course of business, deposits in his own name as agent moneys of his principal with his knowledge and consent in a bank which becomes insolvent, the moneys so deposited will not be declared a trust fund in favor of the latter, and established as a preferred claim.

APPEAL from the district court of Douglas county. Heard below before SCOTT, J. *Affirmed.*

The facts are stated in the opinion.

B. N. Robertson, for appellant:

The right of appellant under her mortgage is not limited to the chattels described therein, but extends to the proceeds of the property. (*Union Stock Yards Bank v. Gillespie,* 137 U. S. 411; *McLeod v. Evans,* 66 Wis. 401; *Capital Nat. Bank v. Coldwater Nat. Bank,* 49 Neb. 786; *Baker v. New York Nat. Exchange Bank,* 100 N. Y. 31.)

Agency of the bank in closing out the hardware stock was established. The hardware stock was impressed with a trust in favor of Mrs. Jones and appellant. (*People v. City Bank,* 96 N. Y. 32; *Hamer v. Sidway,* 124 N. Y. 538; *National Bank of Fishkill v. Speijht,* 47 N. Y. 668; *Wilson v. Dawson,* 52 Ind. 513.)

The Midland State Bank was a collecting agent, and acquired no title to the proceeds of the draft. (*Branch v. United States Nat. Bank,* 50 Neb. 470; *Drovers Nat. Bank v. O'Hare,* 119 Ill. 646; *Nurse v. Satterlee,* 46 N. W. Rep. [Ia.] 1102; *State v. State Bank of Wahoo,* 42 Neb. 896; *Davenport Plow Works v. Lamp,* 45 N. W. Rep. [Ia.] 1049; *In re Knapp,* 70 N. W. Rep. [Ia.] 626; *State v. Midland State Bank,* 52 Neb. 1; *Independent District of Boyer v.*

King, 45 N. W. Rep. [Ia.] 908; *Myers v. Board of Educati.n*, 51 Kan. 87; *Overseers of Poor v. Bank of Virginia*, 2 Gratt. [Va.] 547; *First Nat. Bank of Central City v. Hummel*, 14 Colo. 259; *Cady v. South Omaha Nat. Bank*, 46 Neb. 756; *Third Nat. Bank v. Stillwater Gas Co.*, 30 N. W. Rep. [Minn.] 440; *San Diego County v. California Nat. Bank*, 52 Fed. Rep. 62.)

John L. Kennedy, contra.

NORVAL, J.

This is an appeal from an order of the district court refusing to order the receiver of the Midland State Bank to pay the amount of the claim of Lepha J. McCargar as a preferred claim.

The facts upon which the right to a preference is based may be summarized as follows: On January 13, 1896, Alexander M. McCargar, who was engaged in the hardware business in the city of Omaha, executed on his stock and fixtures three chattel mortgages, one in favor of Mrs. William H. Jones for $1,957.13, one to his wife, Lepha J. McCargar, securing $500, and the third to the Midland State Bank for $1,280. The mortgages had priority in the order named. The mortgagees took possession of the chattels under their mortgages, advertised and sold the property at public sale on February 7, 1896, to the Midland State Bank for $2,650, but it failed to pay the amount of its said bid. Thereupon a written agreement was entered into between the three mortgagees to the effect that the property was to be placed in the possession of said A. M. McCargar for the purpose of sale under the direction of the parties, the proceeds arising therefrom to be applied in paying off the mortgages in the order of priority, and the stock remaining was to belong to the bank. In pursuance of said agreement, A. M. McCargar took possession of the mortgaged property and continued to dispose of the same at retail until September 6, 1896, the proceeds being deposited

34

as received in the Midland State Bank to the credit of
"A. M. McCargar, Agt. for mortgagees." The moneys
were subsequently drawn by McCargar upon his checks
and applied according to the terms of the agreement, in
payment of the expenses and on the mortgage of Mrs.
Jones. The debt of the latter was thereby reduced to
$902.15, but nothing had been paid on the other two
mortgages. On the date last mentioned the entire remainder of the mortgaged stock was sold to George Mortimer, of Shelton, this state, for $1,929.07, who drew a
sight draft for said sum on a bank at Shelton payable
to the order of the Midland State Bank, which the latter
bank forwarded to the Shelton bank, and on September
8, 1896, received as proceeds of the same a draft drawn
by the Shelton bank on the First National Bank of
Omaha. The Midland State Bank on the following day
deposited this draft in the Union National Bank of
Omaha, received credit for the amount thereof, and on
the same day the draft was paid by the said First National Bank. On September 8 the Midland State Bank
credited the account of "A. M. McCargar, agent for mortgagees," with the amount of said draft, and two days
later McCargar as agent drew a check on the account
in favor of his wife, Lepha J. McCargar, for the amount
due on her mortgage, which check was the same day
delivered to Mrs. McCargar, who retained the same without presentation for payment until after the Midland
State Bank closed its doors on September 15. McCargar as agent also drew a check on said account for
$902.15 in payment of the balance due on Mrs. Jones'
mortgage, and another check to the Midland State Bank
for the amount of the balance of the proceeds of the
mortgaged chattels remaining in said bank. Mrs. Mc-
Cargar was aware that the money realized from the sale
of the property was being deposited by her husband in
said bank.

The question involved is whether Mrs. McCargar, under the facts just stated, is entitled to have a trust in her

favor enforced against the funds of the Midland State Bank in the hands of the receiver. Said bank was not the agent or trustee of Mrs. McCargar in the disposal of the hardware stock. On the contrary, by the written agreement entered by the three mortgagees, Mr. McCargar was appointed to represent all of them for the purpose of disposing of the mortgaged property and applying the proceeds arising from the sale to the satisfaction of the mortgages in the order of the priority of the liens. That McCargar converted the property into money in accordance with the terms of the trust is undisputed. But instead of paying Mrs. Jones and Mrs. McCargar the amounts due them respectively, as under the terms of the tripartite agreement it was his duty to do, he, with the knowledge of his wife, deposited the proceeds of the sales, from time to time as the same were received, in the Midland State Bank on open account to the credit of "A. M. McCargar, Agt. for mortgagees." These deposits having been made with her knowledge and consent, the legal effect is precisely the same as if they had been made to Mrs. McCargar in person. In that case the relation of debtor and creditor would have been created and the money thus deposited would not have been impressed with the character of a trust fund. Had the money been deposited by McCargar without the knowledge of his wife or her subsequent ratification of his action in the premises a trust could have been enforced in her favor against the bank, since it received the funds with full information of their trust character.

It is urged that the Midland State Bank was a collecting agent of the draft drawn in its favor by Mr. Mortimer, the purchaser of the remainder of its stock, and that the bank acquired no title to the proceeds of the draft. It is undoubtedly true that the draft was collected through the agency of the bank, and on its receipt of the proceeds of the collection, it was its duty to pay over the same to A. M. McCargar, as the agent of the mortgagees. This was done, and the amount deposited to the credit of McCargar as such agent, precisely in accordance with the manner in which McCargar had conducted the business of the trust for several months preceding, and with the full knowledge of his wife. She subsequently recognized the deposit by accepting a check for the amount of her mortgage debt on the bank drawn by McCargar as agent. We are convinced the appellant is not entitled to have a trust declared in her favor, and that the court below did not err in refusing to order the receiver to pay the amount due Mrs. McCargar as a preferred claim. The case is unlike *State v. State Bank of Wahoo*, 42 Neb. 896. In that case the money was deposited without the knowledge or consent of the owner, and there was no subsequent ratification, while here the converse was true. The other decisions cited in brief of appellant are no more nearly in point than the one just mentioned. The decree is

AFFIRMED.

THEODORE WIDEMAIR V. WILLIAM H. WOOLSEY, SHERIFF.

FILED JANUARY 19, 1898. No. 7687.

1. **Exemption.** Under section 521 of the Code of Civil Procedure, a judgment debtor, who is the head of a family and has no homestead—*i. e.*, owns neither lands, town lots, nor houses subject to exemption under the homestead laws of the state—may claim as exempt from forced sale on execution personal property to the value of $500.

2. **Homestead.** The words "subject to exemption as a homestead," as used in said section 521, do not refer to "houses" alone, but apply to "lands" and "town lots" as well.

ERROR from the district court of Johnson county. Tried below before BUSH, J. *Reversed.*

Davidson & Giffen, for plaintiff in error.

J. Hall Hitchcock and *Hugh La Master, contra.*

NORVAL, J.

This suit was brought for damages for the conversion of certain goods, wares, harness, and merchandise belonging to plaintiff. The district judge directed a verdict for defendant. The facts which must control the decision of the cause are, briefly stated, as follows: Plaintiff was a married man, residing with his family in the town of Cook, this state, where he was engaged in the business of making harness. His entire personal property did not exceed in value the sum of $500. He owned the lot on which his harness-shop was located, but did not reside thereon. His wife was the owner of three vacant and unoccupied lots in the town of Cook. Plaintiff and his wife lived in rented property, and at no time since their marriage did they reside upon, or occupy as a home, any real estate belonging to them, or either of them. The defendant, as sheriff of Johnson county, levied upon, took into his own possession, and sold, the goods in dispute under and by virtue of two executions issued upon two separate judgments recovered against plaintiff, and the proceeds of the sale were applied towards the satisfaction of said executions and judgments. Prior to the sale plaintiff filed with the defendant, in accordance with the provisions of section 522 of the Code of Civil Procedure, an inventory, under oath, of the whole of the personal property owned by plaintiff, and demanded that the same be appraised and released from the levies as exempt, with which request defendant refused to comply.

The point presented for consideration is whether the property levied upon was exempt under the laws of the state. The question is one of statutory construction. Section 521 of the Code of Civil Procedure is as follows:

"Sec. 521. All heads of families who have neither lands, town lots, or houses subject to exemption as a homestead, under the laws of this state, shall have exempt from forced sale on execution the sum of five hundred dollars in personal property."

The contention of defendant is, which was the view
taken by the trial court, that the words "subject to exemption as a homestead," as employed in said section,
apply alone to "houses." In other words, a debtor is
not entitled to the benefits of the provisions of said section 521 if he owns either lands or town lots or any real
estate whatever, although the same may be vacant and
unoccupied. We cannot yield assent to such doctrine.
Homestead and exemption laws are invariably construed
liberally in favor of the debtor who claims the protection
of their provisions. The exemption of $500 in personal
property was given by the legislature to every judgment
debtor, being the head of a family, who owns no homestead. Such provision was made in lieu of a homestead.
If such debtor owns any real estate, either lands or town
lots, or any houses so impressed with the character of a
homestead as to render the same exempt from levy and
sale on execution, he cannot invoke the protection of
section 521. On the other hand, he is entitled to the
exemption of $500 in personal property if he has no real
estate, or house, which is exempt from judicial process,
even though he owns unoccupied lands or town lots in
which no right of homestead exists. This is the plain
meaning of the law, and is in accord with the construction placed upon said section 521 of the Code in *Hamilton
v. Fleming*, 26 Neb. 242. That was an action to recover
exempt personal property levied upon by the sheriff under a writ of attachment. It was urged that the petition
did not state a cause of action. The court sustained the
pleading, saying: "Upon an examination of the petition,
we find that it is alleged that at the time the said order
of attachment was levied upon the goods of defendant in
error she was a resident of this state and the head of a
family, and not the owner of a homestead, and had filed
her inventory of said property with plaintiff in error, and
notified him that she selected said property to hold
exempt from levy and sale under the laws of this state.
While these allegations do not follow strictly the lan-

guage of the statute, yet they must be held sufficient. There is no allegation in terms that defendant was not the owner of 'lands, town lots, or houses subject to exemption as a homestead' as in section 521 of the Civil Code; but the allegation that she was not the owner of a homestead must be treated, when assailed after verdict, as equivalent to the use of the language contained in the statute. By the section of the Code above referred to, a homestead may consist of lands or town lots with the necessary buildings thereon, or of houses, and they are all included within the term 'homestead' as used in the petition; and the averment must be taken as negativing the ownership of a homestead of either character."

In construing the provisions of said section 521, in *Stout v. Rapp*, 17 Neb. 470, the court observed: "In order to secure the benefit of this section it must appear that the 'head' of the family has no real estate exempt. If the head of the family has a home in which the family resides, the exemption provided for by this section does not exist. They cannot have both. (*Axtell v. Warden*, 7 Neb. 182.) If he had no homestead, he would not only be entitled to this exemption, but either party (husband or wife) might select it from the personal property of the husband."

In *Williams v. Golden*, 10 Neb. 434, COBB, J., speaking of the intention of the legislature in enacting said section 521, said: "Evidently it was their intention to give the landless debtor an exemption of personal property in lieu of the more wealthy debtor's homestead exemption."

There is no room to doubt that every head of a family in this state is entitled to claim personal property to the value of $500 as exempt from sale under execution where he has no real estate or house constituting a homestead, or in respect of which exemption from judicial process could be successfully asserted. Under the undisputed facts in the case at bar no homestead character had been impressed upon either the business property owned

by the plaintiff or the lots belonging to his wife. He
having "neither lands, town lots, or houses subject to
exemption as a homestead," the personal property seized
by the defendant is exempt from levy and sale under the
executions, and, therefore, the district court erred in directing a verdict for the defendant.

We have been urged to enter a judgment in this court
in favor of the plaintiff in accordance with section 594
of the Code of Civil Procedure, for the minimum value
placed upon the property by the witnesses. An examination of the evidence discloses that this is not a proper
case for the enforcement of the provisions of said section,
as there are controverted facts which should be determined by the trial court, or a jury. The judgment is
reversed and the cause remanded for further proceedings.

REVERSED AND REMANDED.

E. G. WEST ET AL., APPELLEES, v. W. H. REEVES, IM-
PLEADED WITH F. A. REYNOLDS, APPELLANT.

FILED JANUARY 19, 1898.   No. 7764.

1. **Mechanic's Lien**: VENDOR'S LIEN: PRIORITY. The lien of a person
who furnishes material for the erection of a house upon land in
possession of the vendee under an executory contract of purchase
is subordinate to the lien of the vendor who retains the legal title
to secure deferred installments of the purchase price, except in
cases where the vendor himself promotes the improvement or
causes it to be made.

2. ———: WAIVER OF VENDOR'S LIEN. A vendor who retains the legal
title to land sold does not, by mere silence and inaction, waive
his right to a purchase-money lien in favor of one who furnishes
building material to improve the property.

APPEAL from the district court of Dawson county.
Heard below before HOLCOMB, J. *Reversed.*

W. D. Giffin and *Warrington & Stewart,* for appellant.

W. J. Trotter, contra.

SULLIVAN, J.

On April 16, 1892, the defendant Reynolds, being the fee owner of certain real estate in Gothenburg, sold the same to his co-defendant, Reeves, who paid a portion of the purchase price, executed promissory notes for the balance, took a bond for a deed, and entered into possession of the property. Afterwards, Reeves bought on credit from the plaintiff material for the purpose of, and which he used in, building an addition to the dwelling-house on the premises. Within the time limited by the statute, a mechanic's lien for the amount remaining due for this material was filed in the proper office. In this action, which was brought by the plaintiff to foreclose his lien, he contends that it is entitled to priority over the lien of Reynolds for the deferred installments of the purchase price of the land. The improvement in question was not made in compliance with any obligation imposed on Reeves by the terms of the contract of purchase. The contract for the material was not made with Reynolds nor with his agent; it was made with Reeves alone, and the lien resulting therefrom can only attach to Reeves' interest in the land.

It is argued on behalf of the appellee that Reynolds waived his right to a prior lien by reason of his silent observation of the improvement as it progressed. This claim is not backed by the citation of any authority and is not, we think, entitled to serious consideration. Reeves had a right to improve the property and charge his interest therein with the cost of the improvement whether Reynolds consented or objected. His consent would have been immaterial and his objection impertinent. It follows that the defendant Reynolds is entitled to a first lien for the unpaid purchase-money, and that the court erred in subordinating his lien to that of the plaintiff. This conclusion is sustained by the following decisions: *Birdsall v. Cropsey*, 29 Neb. 672; *Irish v. Lundin*, 28 Neb. 84; *Pickens v. Plattsmouth Investment Co.*, 37 Neb. 272;

Bohn Mfg. Co. v. Kountze, 30 Neb. 719. The judgment of the district court is reversed and the cause remanded for further proceedings.

REVERSED AND REMANDED.

CHARLES H. ROHMAN V. WILLIAM GAISER.

FILED JANUARY 19, 1898. No. 7778.

1. **Contract**: PROVISION FOR BENEFIT OF THIRD PERSON. A provision in a contract between the state and a person contracting with it for the erection of a public building is valid which imposes on the contractor the duty of paying for material furnished and used in the erection of such building.

2. **Sales**: DELIVERY: PLEADING. Statements in the answer construed in connection with an allegation of the petition and held to import an admission of the delivery of the material for the price of which this suit was brought.

3. **Action**: CONTRACT: PARTIES. One not a party to a contract may maintain an action thereon when such contract was made for his benefit or the benefit of a class to which he belongs.

ERROR from the district court of Lancaster county. Tried below before TIBBETS, J. *Affirmed.*

Daniel F. Osgood, for plaintiff in error.

Benjamin F. Johnson, contra.

SULLIVAN, J.

This action was brought to recover a balance alleged to be due the defendant in error for material furnished to John Lanham and used by him in the erection of a chapel and dormitory for the Home for the Friendless at Lincoln. The action was upon a bond to the board of public lands and buildings executed by Lanham as principal, and J. C. McBride and the plaintiff in error as sureties. Said bond was conditioned as follows:

"The condition of this obligation is such that, whereas,

the above bounden, John Lanham, has been awarded a
contract to build, erect, construct, and complete a chapel
and dormitory for the Home for the Friendless located
at Lincoln, Lancaster county, Nebraska; and, whereas,
the said John Lanham has agreed to furnish all work,
labor, and materials necessary for the building, erecting,
and completing of said chapel and dormitory, and has
agreed to settle and pay in full for all work and labor
performed, and has agreed to settle for and pay all ma-
terial-men, for any and all material actually furnished in
the erecting, constructing, building, and completing said
chapel and dormitory: Now, therefore, if the said John
Lanham shall well and truly keep and perform each and
every covenant, stipulation, and agreement contained in
said contract and according to the plans and specifica-
tions on file in the office of the commissioner of public
lands and buildings, and shall pay in full for all work
done and labor performed, and shall pay all laborers'
and mechanics' wages, and shall settle in full and pay
for all material actually furnished in the constructing,
erecting, and completing said chapel and dormitory of
the Home for the Friendless, according to the terms of
the contract, then this obligation to be void, otherwise
to remain in full force and effect.   ·

"JOHN LANHAM.

"J. C. McBRIDE.

"CHARLES H. ROHMAN."

There was a trial in the district court which resulted
in a verdict and judgment for Gaiser, whereupon Rohman brought the case here for review by petition in error.

The principal contention of the plaintiff in error is
that the clause in the bond requiring the contractor to
pay for material used was inserted without statutory
authority therefor, and hence did not create a valid obligation. This precise question was before this court in
the case of *Sample v. Hale*, 34 Neb. 220, where it was
held that such a provision was valid and that the sureties on the contractor's bond would be liable for all debts

arising thereunder. The doctrine of that case was subsequently approved in *Korsmeyer Plumbing & Heating Co.
v. McClay*, 43 Neb. 649, *Kaufmann v. Cooper*, 46 Neb. 644,
and in other cases.* The provision in Lanham's contract with the board for the payment of all material used
in the construction of the Home for the Friendless inured to the benefit of Gaiser. It is a proposition firmly
established in the jurisprudence of this state that one
not a party to a contract may maintain an action thereon,
when such contract is made for his benefit or the benefit
of a class to which he belongs. (*Cooper v. Foss*, 15 Neb.
515; *Shamp v. Meyer*, 20 Neb. 223; *Doll v. Crume*, 41 Neb.
655; *Barnett v. Pratt*, 37 Neb. 349.)

It is also assigned for error that the verdict is not sustained by sufficient evidence. The petition charges that
Gaiser furnished material to Lanham to the amount of
$875. In addition to a general denial, the answer states
"that the plaintiff has been paid in full for all claims
and demands for material furnished the defendant John
Lanham, as alleged in plaintiff's petition. This is, in
effect, an admission of the furnishing of the material as
the plaintiff in his petition claims it was furnished,
coupled with an attempt to avoid the consequent liability
by pleading that the same has been paid for. (*Blumen-
thal v. Mugge*, 43 Mo. 427; 1 Ency. Pl. & Pr. 795.) It follows that no proof upon this point was necessary. The
judgment is

AFFIRMED.

---

*Habig v. Layne, 38 Neb. 743; *Lyman v. City of Lincoln*, 38 Neb. 794;
Doll v. Crume, 41 Neb. 655; *Hickman v. Layne*, 47 Neb. 177; *Fitzgerald v.
McClay*, 47 Neb. 816; *King v. Murphy*, 49 Neb. 670.

53 4
54 4

ANDREW D. RICKETTS V. FREDERICK J. ROGERS.

FILED JANUARY 19, 1898.　No. 7757.

1. **Contract**: CONSTRUCTION: QUESTION FOR COURT. When the meaning
of a written contract can be ascertained without the aid of extrinsic evidence, its interpretation belongs to the court and not
to the jury.

2. ——: ——: ——. Contract in suit examined in connection
with the undisputed evidence and *held* to present no reason for
committing its interpretation to the jury.

ERROR from the district court of Lancaster county.
Tried below before HALL, J.　*Reversed.*

Ricketts & Wilson, for plaintiff in error.

References: *Sanford v. Sornborger,* 26 Neb. 295; *Pryor
v. Hunter,* 31 Neb. 678; *Treitschke v. Western Grain Co.,* 10
Neb. 358; *Hamley v. Doe,* 36 Neb. 398; *Slade v. Swedeburg
Elevator Co.,* 39 Neb. 600; *Swartz v. Duncan,* 38 Neb. 782;
Hall v. Wheeler, 37 Minn. 522, 35 N. W. Rep. 377; *City of
Muscatine v. Keokuk Northern Line Packet Co.,* 45 Ia. 185;
Regan v. Baldwin, 126 Mass. 485; *Harbach v. Miller,* 14
Neb. 9; *Treat v. Price,* 47 Neb. 875; *Wagner v. Ladd,* 38
Neb. 161; *Weber v. Kirkendall,* 44 Neb. 766.

Lamb & Adams, contra.

SULLIVAN, J.

This was an action in the district court for Lancaster
county. A trial resulted in a verdict and judgment
against Ricketts, who brings the case to this court for
review by petition in error.

The facts are these: In July, 1892, Rogers sold Ricketts a half-section of land in Lancaster county subject
to the right of way of the Fremont, Elkhorn & Missouri
Valley Railroad Company. The purchase price agreed
upon was $12,300, of which $600 was cash. The balance
was to be paid March 1, 1893, when possession was to be
delivered, an abstract of title furnished, and deed of con-

veyance executed to the purchaser. At the appointed time the parties came together to carry out their agreement. It was then discovered that Rogers had previously conveyed to the railroad company, in addition to the right of way, a strip 130 feet wide and 1,000 feet long out of the northeast corner of the land aforesaid. On account of Rogers' inability to make title to this strip Ricketts demanded a rescission of the contract or a suitable abatement from the purchase price. Thereupon a discussion ensued touching the damage occasioned by the loss of the three-acre strip. Ricketts insisted that the damage was $500 and Rogers maintained that it did not exceed $120, and offered to compromise for that sum. The evidence is conflicting as to the terms on which the transaction was consummated, but it is not disputed that an agreement was reached, in pursuance of which Rogers delivered the deed for the land, received the purchase price, except $250, and took from Ricketts the written contract here set out:

"RICKETTS & LYON, GRAIN.
"A. D. Ricketts.
"References: First National Bank, American Exchange National Bank.
"LINCOLN, NEB., March 1, 1893.

"Mr. F. J. Rogers has left in my hands two hundred and fifty dollars to cover damages for a strip of land 130 feet wide and 1,000 feet long, along the right of way of the Fremont & Elkhorn Valley R. R., which strip commences on the north line of west half of section 18, town 11, range 7, Lancaster county, Nebraska, and runs 1,000 feet south on west side of right of way of said railroad. The condition of this contract is this: If Mr. F. J. Rogers makes A. D. Ricketts a good warranty deed for said strip of land, then the said Ricketts is to refund the $250 to Rogers.   A. D. RICKETTS."

As to whether the $250 was retained as agreed compensation for the loss of the three-acre strip or as an indemnity for actual damages to be thereafter ascertained is a question about which the parties do not agree. The contract quoted was executed after the delivery of the deed and payment of the purchase-money, except the sum of $250. It was executed at Rogers' request, expressed in this language: "You give me something in black and white to show that you owe me $250 on the purchase price of the farm." The entire controversy between the parties related to the amount of the purchase-money which Ricketts should retain as compensation for the loss of the three-acre strip; and thus it appears that the written contract was made and delivered as the final repository and appropriate evidence of the conclusion reached upon the matter in dispute.

At the trial the court declined to construe the contract and submitted it to the jury for construction. In view of the conceded facts this was error. This agreement recites that $250 is left in Ricketts' hands to cover damages, and clearly prescribes the condition on which Rogers shall be entitled to receive it. Its essential terms are not ambiguous or obscure, and extrinsic evidence was not needed to aid in its exposition. The judgment of the district court is reversed and the cause remanded for further proceedings.

REVERSED AND REMANDED.

CORTELYOU, EGE & VANZANDT ET AL. V. JUSTIN McCARTHY, SR.

FILED JANUARY 19, 1898. No. 7759.

53   4
55
53   4
56
53
59

1. **Action on Supersedeas Bond**: PLEADING. The averments of the petition *held* to sufficiently state a cause of action on a supersedeas bond.

2. ———: ———. In an action on a supersedeas bond, *held* unnecessary to allege the issue and return of an execution *nulla bona*.

3. **New Trial**: JOINT MOTION. A motion for a new trial should be overruled as to all the parties joining therein if it is not available to any one of them.

ERROR from the district court of Holt county. Tried below before KINKAID, J. *Affirmed.*

H. M. Uttley, for plaintiffs in error.

H. E. Murphy and *M. F. Harrington*, *contra.*

RYAN, C.

On November 6, 1890, Justin McCarthy, Sr., recovered a judgment against the firm of Cortelyou, Ege & Vanzandt in the district court of Holt county. This judgment was affirmed in the supreme court (*Cortelyou v. McCarthy*, 37 Neb. 742), and this action was brought upon the supersedeas bond given in the original action. From a judgment rendered as prayed the principals and sureties on the bond prosecute error to this court.

It is first urged that the petition failed to state a cause of action against the parties to the bond. The petition recited the pendency of the action, the rendition of judgment, the giving of the bond copied in the petition, and its approval, the affirmance of the judgment, the issuance of a mandate and the fact that said mandate had been spread upon the records of the aforesaid district court. It was averred that no part of the judgment had been paid, except a sum for which credit was given in the petition, and that there remained, and still continued due, the sum of $1,480, for which amount judgment was prayed. This we think sufficiently stated a cause of action.

There were averments in the petition disclosing the issuance and return *nulla bona* of an execution on the judgment after its affirmance, but this we have purposely omitted, because such averments are not required in an action on an undertaking of the nature of that herein sued upon. (*Flannagan v. Cleveland*, 44 Neb. 58; *Johnson v. Reed*, 47 Neb. 322.) This renders it unnecessary to consider. whether or not there was error in permitting the sheriff to amend his return, a matter with respect to which plaintiffs in error have complained in their petition in error and in their brief.

It is contended that there was error in sustaining a demurrer to certain defenses pleaded in the amended and substituted answer. This alleged error is not now available, for the reason that after this ruling was made the defendants in the district court withdrew their said amended and substituted answer and elected to stand upon a single designated defense in the original answer.

We cannot determine that there was error in the refusal of the district court to grant the application of the defendants for a continuance, because the affidavits on which such application was founded were not preserved by a bill of exceptions.

The motion for a new trial was jointly made by the defendants in the district court; hence that motion is available to none of the said defendants unless it is available to all. (*Long v. Clapp*, 15 Neb. 417; *Boldt v. Budwig*, 19 Neb. 739; *Hoke v. Halverstadt*, 22 Neb. 421; *Hagler v. State*, 31 Neb. 144; *Dorsey v. McGee*, 30 Neb. 657; *Scott v. Chope*, 33 Neb. 41.) This consideration renders unavailable the argument that there was no proof of the execution of the supersedeas bond, for there was direct undisputed evidence that said bond was signed by Mr. Cortelyou.

There is found no error in the record and the judgment of the district court is

AFFIRMED.

LIFE INSURANCE CLEARING COMPANY V. MARGUERITE ALTSCHULER.

FILED JANUARY 19, 1898. No. 7727.

1. **Insurance:** WAIVER OF CONDITION: EVIDENCE. The evidence in this case examined, and *held* to have justified the jury in finding that there was a waiver of a condition precedent with respect to the delivery of a policy, the existence of such condition not having been communicated to the insured.

35

2. **Appearance:** REVIEW: RECORD. A special appearance must be assumed to have been properly overruled when the affidavit upon which it was founded does not appear in the record in the supreme court.

3. **Continuance:** SUFFICIENCY OF APPLICATION: REVIEW. An application for a continuance which failed to disclose the names of absent parties whose testimony was desired, and the nature of their testimony, *held* properly to have been denied.

ERROR from the district court of Adams county. Tried below before BEALL, J. *Affirmed.*

Tibbets, Morey & Ferris, for plaintiff in error.

M. A. Hartigan, contra.

RYAN, C.

In this case there was recovered a judgment against the plaintiff in error in the district court of Adams county in the sum of $2,513.65, upon an insurance policy held by defendant in error on the life of her husband, Sigmund Altschuler. This policy was dated April 5, 1893, and Sigmund Altschuler died August 14 of the same year. We shall not undertake an analysis of the pleadings, but shall refer to such portions thereof as shall become necessary whenever the necessity arises.

James Hale testified that in 1893 he was one of the general agents of the Equitable Life Insurance Society at Grand Island for the western half of this state, and that by reason of the prospectus of the plaintiff in error soliciting the submission to it of rejected applications for examination he had become acquainted with said plaintiff in error. With such policies as plaintiff in error would issue there was always sent to said witness a certificate of health, filled out ready to be signed by the applicant, or rather the policy holder, and by the doctor who had examined the applicant when the first application was made. This certificate was intended to show that the condition of the party to be insured had continued as it was when the original application was

made. Mr. Hale, when the policy on the life of Mr. Altschuler was received by him at Grand Island, also received the health certificate to be brought up to the date
of the policy, which, only upon the bringing forward of
such certificate, he was authorized to deliver. It is not
pretended that this condition precedent was known by
Mr. Altschuler or any one acting for him. Mr. Hale forwarded the policy and certificate to his brother in Hol-
drege, by whom these documents were entrusted to a Mr.
Feeney. It seems that Mr. Feeney lost the certificate
which ought to have been signed, but he did not fail to
deliver the policy, and the first quarter's premium, $53.95,
was remitted by draft to Hale. This draft was cashed by
Hale and its proceeds held by him until after the death of
Mr. Altschuler. This amount he then tendered to the
defendant in error, who refused to receive it. Whether
or not there was a waiver of the condition with reference
to the health certificate was submitted to the jury upon
conflicting evidence as a question of fact, and we cannot
interfere with its conclusion. We must therefore accept
the policy as one binding upon the plaintiff in error.

It is urged that the acceptance of the second premium
of $53.95 was brought about by the fraud of Mrs. Altschu-
ler in leading plaintiff in error to believe her husband
was not ill when, in fact, he was at the point of death.
If the policy had been issued before the time this alleged
misrepresentation took place we cannot understand why
this policy should be invalidated by the fact that Mr.
Altschuler, since the issue of the policy, had sickened
and was about to die. If there was any such misrepresentation and fraud as, under proper conditions, might
be available, it cannot be considered on this branch of
this case, for neither fraud nor misrepresentation was
pleaded with reference to the acceptance of this payment.

Plaintiff insists that the district court erroneously
held that proper service of summons had been made
upon the insurance company. The return of the sheriff

showed service upon O. H. P. Hale as its agent in Adams county. In support of the objections to the service made by a special appearance for that purpose alone there seems to have been filed certain affidavits, but they are not to be found in the record; hence the ruling of the district court must be sustained.

Before the trial began there was an application for a continuance on account of the alleged absence of material witnesses. This application is recited to have been founded upon an affidavit made by Mr. Ferris, one of the attorneys for plaintiff in error. There is no such affidavit in the record. The motion itself fails to disclose the names of the absent witnesses and what would be the testimony of each. It is obvious that we cannot say in view of these omissions that the district court erred in denying a continuance. At a later date, but while the trial was in progress, there was another application, which was oral, and in this the request was but for a short time to permit of a search in the restaurants and hotels of Hastings for O. H. P. Hale and P. M. Feeney. It was not disclosed by the record that these parties were to be used as witnesses, much less was there a suggestion with reference to the nature of the testimony they would give. The court did not err in denying this request.

We have carefully considered the instructions in the light of the printed briefs for plaintiff in error and have discovered no just ground for complaint. The judgment of the district court is

AFFIRMED.

JOSEPH AINSWORTH, EXECUTOR, APPELLEE, V. JOSEPH H. TAYLOR, APPELLANT.

FILED JANUARY 19, 1898.   No. 9399.

1. **Appeal in Equity:** RULINGS ON EVIDENCE: REVIEW. An appeal of an equitable action to the supreme court pursuant to the provisions of section 675, Code of Civil Procedure, does not present

for review the correctness of a ruling of the district court excluding proffered evidence; such ruling must be presented as prescribed by section 584 *et seq.*

2. **Executors**: ACTIONS: EVIDENCE. Evidence *held* sufficient to sustain
the judgment of the district court.

APPEAL from the district court of Douglas county.
Heard below before KEYSOR, J. *Affirmed.*

C. A. Baldwin, for appellant.

G. W. Shields, contra.

RYAN, C.

There has already been a description of the issues involved in this case upon a former consideration thereof
on a petition in error. (*Taylor v. Ainsworth,* 49 Neb. 696.)
There has now been another trial of these issues in the
district court of Douglas county which resulted in a
similar judgment to that already reversed, and the defendant again seeks a reversal; this time, however, by
appeal. We have carefully examined the evidence adduced and feel satisfied that there was sufficient to sustain the judgment entered by the district court, and
there might be an affirmance but for the fact that there
are complaints in the brief of appellant as to the rulings
of the district court whereby were excluded various matters of evidence. One of these will serve to illustrate
our views with regard to all, and we shall therefore consider but one of the rulings which appellant in argument
insists was erroneous.

The action was by an executor to recover money in her
lifetime entrusted by his testatrix to the defendant.
There was no attempt to deny the receipt of the money,
but Taylor, the defendant, pleaded that he should not
be required to pay it to the executor because of an arrangement between himself and said testatrix, the nature of which is sufficiently indicated by a portion of the
bill of exceptions, to which we shall refer in this connec-

tion. J. L. Shivers, a witness in no way disqualified, was under examination and had testified that he was acquainted with the testatrix and had talked with her concerning the transaction pleaded in the answer in this action. The bill of exceptions describes the further examination of this witness in this language:

"Q. Now state, if you please, what that conversation was.

"Mr. Shields: Now I object to that, as incompetent, irrelevant, and immaterial, and as calling for testimony tending to vary the terms of a written agreement between the deceased and the defendant, and for the further reason that it appears from the question that the contract, if any was made, was in the nature of a will disposing of property after the death of the decedent and, not being in writing witnessed by two witnesses in the form of a will, is void."

"Counsel for the defendant thereupon offered to show by the testimony sought to be elicited by the question objected to that the testatrix had told witness that the money had been by her entrusted to Taylor upon an agreement between them that Taylor would pay testatrix $80 each year as interest and such portions of the principal as she would require, and, that when she died, whatever balance had not meantime been paid to her was to become the property of Taylor. The objection was sustained and the proposed evidence was excluded. We are asked to consider the alleged error in this ruling of the court, notwithstanding the fact that there has been filed neither a motion for a new trial in the district court, nor a petition in error in this court. The question thus presented is, whether or not an erroneous ruling of the district court, assuming that the ruling was of that class, can be urged on an equitable appeal as ground for the reversal of a judgment when such alleged error has neither been challenged by a motion for a new trial nor by a petition in error. Section 675 of the Code of Civil Procedure provides: "In actions in equity either party may appeal from the judgment or decree rendered, or final order made by the district court, to the supreme court of the state; the party appealing shall within six months after the date of the rendition of the judgment or decree, or the making of the final order, procure from the clerk of the district court and file in the office of the clerk of the supreme court a certified transcript of the proceedings had in the cause in the district court, containing the pleadings, the judgment or decree rendered or final order made therein, and all the depositions, testimony and proofs offered in evidence on the hearing of the cause, and have said cause properly docketed in the supreme court; and on failure thereof the judgment or decree rendered or final order made in the district court shall stand and be proceeded in as if no appeal had been taken." In this section there is no requirement that errors shall be assigned. If a party elects to appeal from a judgment in an equitable action, his election seems to imply that he is content to retry the cause in the supreme court upon the evidence actually considered by the district court. Section 582 of the Code of Civil Procedure is as follows: "A judgment rendered, or final order made, by the district court may be reversed, vacated, or modified by the supreme court for errors appearing on the record." Section 584 of the same Code, referring to the provisions of section 582 and others immediately preceding it, contains this language: "The proceedings to obtain such reversal, vacation, or modification, shall be by petition entitled 'petition in error' filed in a court having power to make such reversal, vacation, or modification, setting forth the errors complained of, and thereupon a summons shall issue," etc. These provisions clearly contemplate only the consideration of errors appearing on the record and require that each alleged error shall be specially set forth in the petition in error. The strictness with which the requirements of specific assignments has been enforced is amply illustrated in every volume of the reports of the opinions of this court. Not only must the errors be pointed out in the petition in error, but even this is unavailing, if there has been a failure to file a motion for a new trial even in equity cases. (See *Scroggin v. National Lumber Co.*, 41 Neb. 196, and the authorities therein cited.) There is perceived no reason why all this strictness should be dispensed with, merely because an unsuccessful litigant chooses to have his case docketed as an appeal case rather than as an error proceeding in the supreme court. Because of the statutory provisions above indicated and of the reasonableness of the requirement that errors must be specifically pointed out, we are precluded from considering the errors argued in the brief of appellant and the judgment of the district court is

AFFIRMED.

SAMSON BURKHOLDER V. McKINLEY-LANNING LOAN & TRUST COMPANY ET AL.

FILED JANUARY 19, 1898. No. 7751.

Review: SUFFICIENCY OF EVIDENCE. In this case but one question is presented, and that is the sufficiency of the evidence to sustain the judgment of the district court. An examination of all the evidence disclosing that this objection is not well taken, said judgment is affirmed.

ERROR from the district court of Kearney county. Tried below before BEALL, J. *Affirmed.*

John W. Tipton and *Ed L. Adams,* for plaintiff in error.

Tibbets Bros., Morey & Ferris, contra.

RYAN, C.

The McKinley-Lanning Loan & Trust Company brought this action for the foreclosure of a mortgage executed to said plaintiff by Samson Burkholder and his wife to secure payment of ten promissory notes made

by Samson Burkholder to said company, each of which
said notes was for the sum of $17.50.   There was made
defendant A. P. Tillinghast, by whom a cross-petition
was filed asking the foreclosure of a mortgage likewise
made by Samson Burkholder and his wife to said company to secure payment of a note for $1,400 executed by
Mr. Burkholder to said company, by which company it
had been transferred to Tillinghast.   The notes secured
by the two above described mortgages, as well as the
mortgages themselves, bore date September 28, 1892.
The notes for $17.50 fell due in succession at intervals of
six months reckoning from their date.   The $1,400 note
was due in five years from its date and the interest
thereon at six per cent per annum was evidenced by ten
semi-annual coupon notes.   In the petitions for foreclosure it was averred, and by the answer admitted, that
the first semi-annual payments due the respective holders
of the mortgages sought to be foreclosed had not been
paid when foreclosure proceedings were instituted.   In
each of the mortgages there was a provision that a failure to make any semi-annual payment thereby secured,
for a period of ten days after the same fell due, rendered
the whole amount secured due and subject to collection.
The contention of plaintiff in error was that the loan was
really made at the rate of eight and one-half per cent
per annum; that for two and one-half per cent per annum distinct coupons were made, and that, if the foreclosure was permitted for the amount of the ten notes of
$17.50 each at the end of the first year of the term of
the loan, the amount would include interest at a higher
rate than ten per cent per annum, and that the loan under such circumstances was usurious.   The claim of the
holders of the mortgage was that the notes for $17.50
each simply represented the commission which Mr. Burkholder had agreed to pay for obtaining the loan at the
rate of six per cent per annum, and that these notes were
not for any portion of interest.   On conflicting evidence
the district court adopted the contention of plaintiff, and

this conclusion having support in the evidence cannot be
disturbed.   The petition in error presents no other question and the judgment of the district court is

AFFIRMED.

JOHN THOMPSON, APPELLANT, V. JAMES THOMPSON,
APPELLEE.

FILED JANUARY 19, 1898.   No. 9482.

1. **Quieting Title:** REVIVOR OF ACTION: RENTS. In an equitable action
   by a devisee to quiet title and obtain possession of real property
   it was sought to recover the rental value of the land which had
   accrued previous to the revivor of the action in the name of such
   devisee.   Whether or not the devisee under any circumstances
   would be entitled to such recovery of rent is not determined, because neither put in issue by the pleadings nor argued by counsel.

2. **Improvements:** QUIETING TITLE: RENTS. An action of the nature
   above indicated was pending several years before the death of a
   testator who was the original plaintiff.   The devisee, in whose
   name the action was revived upon the death of the testator, on
   his petition recovered for rent until the time of the filing of said
   petition as though the defendant had during his entire possession
   been the tenant of the devisee.   Supported by sufficient evidence
   in the same case there were findings that the possession of the
   defendant had been taken and held in good faith and that lasting
   and valuable improvements had been made during such possession
   by such defendant under circumstances which justified him in
   making them. *Held*, That the district court properly charged the
   land finally adjudged to belong to plaintiff with the fair value of
   such improvements even though some of said improvements were
   made after the commencement of the suit by the testator.

APPEAL from the district court of Lancaster county.
Heard below before HOLMES, J.   *Affirmed.*

Sawyer, Snell & Frost, for John Thompson.

References: *Thompson v. Thompson*, 30 Neb. 492, 49 Neb.
157; *Goble v. O'Connor*, 43 Neb. 59; *Carter v. Brown*, 35
Neb. 675; *Jackson v. Loomis*, 4 Cow. [N. Y.] 168; *Fletcher
v. Brown*, 35 Neb. 660.

Samuel J. Tuttle, contra.

References: *Gallagher v. Mars*, 50 Cal. 23; *Fairchild v. Rasdall*, 9 Wis. 350; *Callanan v. Judd*, 23 Wis. 343; *Gould v. Lynde*, 114 Mass. 366; *Osborn v. Osborn*, 29 N. J. Eq. 385; *Russ v. Mebius*, 16 Cal. 350; *Courvoirsier v. Bouvier*, 3 Neb. 52; *Hansen v. Berthelsen*, 19 Neb. 433; *O'Brien v. Gaslin*, 20 Neb. 347; *Kelley v. Palmer*, 42 Neb. 423; *Dailey v. Kinsler*, 31 Neb. 340; *City of Hastings v. Foxworthy*, 45 Neb. 676; *Merriam v. Goodlett*, 36 Neb. 384; *Skinner v. Skinner*, 38 Neb. 756.

RYAN, C.

The history of this case serves to illustrate the bitterness which is ordinarily the characteristic of a family quarrel. On September 20, 1887, John Thompson, senior, began this litigation by filing his petition in the district court of Lancaster county. On a trial of the issues joined thereon in that court he was unsuccessful and, on an appeal to this court, the judgment against him was reversed. (*Thompson v. Thompson*, 30 Neb. 489.) A lifetime of eighty years' duration was not long enough to enable plaintiff to see this litigation closed, for during its pendency this court has been required to affirm the probate of the will of this octogenarian. (*Thompson v. Thompson*, 49 Neb. 157.) On November 21, 1896, this action was revived in the name of John Thompson, junior, a son of the elder Thompson above referred to, and, by his will, the sole devisee of the land in controversy. After this revivor there was filed a new petition, which we shall now describe, premising, however, that while we might have doubts of the right of the devisee as such to the entire relief prayed by him, we do not deem it advisable to consider this question, which has neither been put in issue by the pleadings nor argued by counsel.

The averments of the petition necessary to be considered were, in effect, that John Thompson, senior, on

April 14, 1881, obtained from the Burlington & Missouri River Railroad Company an executory contract, by the terms of which he was entitled to receive a deed of conveyance of the land herein in controversy upon making certain payments; that in April, 1887, for the sole purpose of obtaining a loan to make the last of said payments, the said holder of said executory contract assigned the same to the defendant James Thompson; that the said James Thompson had refused to reconvey said land to John Thompson, senior, during his lifetime, or to John Thompson, junior, as devisee of John Thompson, senior, though often requested so to do. The final paragraph and prayer of this petition were as follows:

"13. That the rental value of said land during the time that the defendant has been in possession of the same as aforesaid is $300 a year and the defendant has not paid or accounted for the same to this plaintiff or the said John Thompson, senior, in his lifetime, and there is now due and owing from the defendant to the plaintiff, as rent for the use and occupation of said land, the sum of $2,400. Wherefore plaintiff prays that the defendant may be decreed to have no claim, title, estate, or interest whatsoever in or to said land, and that the title of the plaintiff to said land may be adjudged to be made valid as against any and all claims of said defendant; that the defendant be forever enjoined and barred from asserting any claim whatsoever in and to said land adverse to the plaintiff, and that plaintiff's title to said land may be confirmed and quieted and the sheriff directed to put him in possession thereof; also that plaintiff may have and recover a personal judgment against the defendant for the sum of $2,400 and for such other, further, and different relief as may be just and equitable, including costs of suit."

By an answer and reply such issues were joined as rendered pertinent this finding of the district court:

"6. That at or about the time of the procurement of the said loan, John Thompson, senior, in accordance with

his plans and promises in that behalf made, and as he
then particularly desired, without any undue influence,
unfair practices, or fraud on the part of any one, and
more particularly of the defendant James Thompson,
made and executed his last will and testament wherein
he bequeathed to the defendant all of his property, both
real and personal,—his real property consisting only of
the land now in controversy herein,—and delivered the
same to the keeping of the said son James, the defendant; that the defendant James Thompson, believing that
he was to be the owner of the land upon the death of his
father, and at his father's request, in good faith, and
being in the lawful possession of said land, erected a
dwelling house and made other lasting and valuable improvements thereon, the value thereof being as hereinafter found, paying the interest on the mortgage loan
and the taxes on said land and has continued so to do
up to the present time."

The items found were for breaking the land, $160;
dwelling house, stable, and other buildings, $902.30;
labor in making improvements, $400; other improve-
ments, $231.71. The total value of these improvements
made by James was $1,694. In addition to the above
sum of $1,694 for improvements the district court cred-
ited James Thompson with the interest on the mortgage
loan, which he had paid, $900, and taxes on the real prop-
erty in dispute, $217.66. The grand total of the allow-
ances in favor of James was, therefore, $2,811.66, and
against this there was charged for rent the sum of
$1,800. For the difference, $1,011.66, James was decreed
entitled to a lien against the real property in controversy.
The evidence satisfies us that the figures above set out
were substantially just and will, therefore, be so accepted. It is urged, however, that James should be dis-
allowed payment for improvements made on the land
after suit had been brought to set aside his title. In
this case, as shown by the above quoted finding, there are
special features which render inequitable the rule in-

voked. James was rightfully in possession when he
made the improvements and they were made at the request of his father. The evidence shows that this request was made because the father of James contemplated making his home for the remainder of his life
with James in the house erected at the instance of the
father. The court found that the other improvements
were made under the same circumstances, and that all
these were made upon the faith of an existing will entrusted to the keeping of James, in which will James was
named as sole devisee. A subsequently executed will
substituted John Thompson, junior, as sole devisee, but
this, while it was finally probated as the controlling will
of the father, did not alter the fact that James, in reliance on the provisions of the will first executed and the
request of his father in connection with the making
thereof, acted in good faith in improving the raw prairie
land as he did. Aside from this consideration there is
another of great weight, and that is, that in the petition
of plaintiff it was sought to hold James liable for the
rent of the property up to that time just as though he
had been a tenant of plaintiff. In making proofs of this
rental value of the land the witnesses for plaintiff increased their estimates, year by year, as they themselves
stated, because of the increased improvements which,
meantime, had been made. Under all these circumstances we are of the opinion that the district court was
merely requiring equity to be done in charging the land,
of which John was decreed the owner, with the value of
these improvements, even though some of them were
made after the commencement of this action.

On behalf of James Thompson, on his appeal, we are
urged to reconsider some of the views expressed by this
court determining the former appeal, but this we do not
think the facts justify. It may be possible that some
conclusions differing from those of the district court
might perhaps have been reached by us had we originally
passed upon the evidence, but this question we need not

determine, for there was sufficient to justify the result actually attained, and the judgment of the district court is therefore

AFFIRMED.

VESTA HAGENSICK, APPELLEE, V. TOBIAS CASTOR ET AL., APPELLANTS.

FILED JANUARY 19, 1898.   No. 7750.

1. **Estoppel by Deed**: QUITCLAIM. The general rule is that an ordinary quitclaim deed vests only in the grantee such title or estate as the grantor was at the time of the execution and delivery of the deed possessed of; and if a grantor in such a deed subsequently acquires the title to the real estate thereby conveyed, that title does not inure to the grantee in the quitclaim deed.

2. ———; RECITAL OF ESTATE CONVEYED. Whatever be the form or nature of the conveyance of real property, if the grantor therein sets forth on the face of such instrument by way of recital or averment, either in express terms or by necessary implication, that he is seized or possessed of a particular estate in the premises conveyed, then such grantor and all persons claiming under him are ever afterward estopped from denying that he was so seized and possessed at the time he made such conveyance.

3. ———: ———. Such an estoppel operates upon the estate and binds an after-acquired title as between parties and privies. *Van Rensselaer v. Kearney*, 52 U. S. 297, followed.

4. ———: DESCRIPTIO PERSONÆ. In 1887 George H. Ohler was absent from home and had been for several years, and his children, believing him dead, partitioned among themselves his real estate. They effected this by quitclaim deeds from one to another, each deed reciting that the grantor "being one of the three heirs of George H. Ohler." In 1891 Ohler died owning this real estate and it descended to his heirs, the three children who had already partitioned it. *Held*, (1) That the recital in the quitclaim deeds, "being one of the three heirs of George H. Ohler," was not a mere *descriptio personæ* of the grantor, but an assertion by such grantor that he was then an heir at law of Ohler; (2) that the grantors in said quitclaim deeds had by such recital estopped themselves and those claiming under them from asserting that they were not heirs of George H. Ohler in 1887, and estopped from asserting the title to the land which they acquired by his death in 1891, against the grantees in said quitclaim deeds and those claiming under them.

APPEAL from the district court of Saline county.
Heard below before HASTINGS, J.   *Affirmed.*

The opinion contains a statement of the case.

Griggs, Rinaker & Bibb, for appellants:

The quitclaim deeds do not work an estoppel because
they contained no covenants, and conveyed only the interest of grantors in the premises. (*Lavender v. Holmes,*
23 Neb. 345; *Holbrook v. Debo,* 99 Ill. 372; *White v. Bro-
caw,* 14 O. St. 339; *Gibson v. Chouteau,* 39 Mo. 536; *Gates
v. Hunter,* 13 Mo. 365; 7 Am. & Eng. Ency. Law 10, 11;
Hanrick v. Patrick, 119 U. S. 156.)

The quitclaim deeds work no estoppel, because the
word "heirs," as used therein, evidently means children.
(*Heard v. Horton,* 1 Den. [N. Y.] 165; *Conger v. Lowe,* 124
Ind. 368; *Levengood v. Hoople,* 124 Ind. 29.)

The truth that grantors were not heirs at the time they
made their quitclaim deeds appears in the record without objection and by solemn admission and stipulation of
all parties.   There is therefore no estoppel by virtue of
the deeds. (Bigelow, Estoppel [3d ed.] 298; 7 Am. &
Eng. Ency. Law 5; *Pelletreau v. Jackson,* 11 Wend. [N.
Y.] 110.)

J. H. Grimm and *Hastings & McGintie,* also for appellants.

Halleck F. Rose and *Webster, Rose & Fisherdick,* for appellee:

When a deed sets forth on its face by way of recital or
averment that the grantor is seized or possessed of a particular estate, or where the seizure or possession of a particular estate is affirmed in the deed, either in express
terms or by necessary implication, the grantor and all
persons in privity with him shall be estopped from ever
afterwards denying that he was so seized of such estate

at time of conveyance. The estoppel works upon the estate and binds an after-acquired title between parties privies. (Rawle, Covenants for Title [5th ed.] sec. 245; Bigelow, Estoppel [5th ed.] 396; 2 Herman, Estoppel, secs. 640, 647; *Van Rensselaer v. Kearney*, 11 How. [U. S.] 325; *Bush v. Cooper*, 18 How. [U. S.] 83; *French v. Spencer*, 21 How. [U. S.] 240; *Clark v. Baker*, 14 Cal. 629; *Root v. Crock*, 7 Pa. St. 378; *Bachelder v. Lovely*, 69 Me. 38; *Magruder v. Esmay*, 35 O. St. 231; *Lindsay v. Freeman*, 83 Tex. 264; *Hannon v. Christopher*, 34 N. J. Eq. 459; *Goodtitle v. Bailey*, Cowp. [Eng.] 597; *Nixon v. Carco*, 28 Miss. 414.)

The tenants derive title from a common ancestor, and having gone into a partition of the property on certain terms, by mutually releasing and conveying to each other certain allotments in severalty, the law annexes a warranty of title, from the fact that the transaction was a partition of a common estate, and as between the parties and privies this implied warranty is a complete estoppel against each of the other heirs to claim any estate in the portion set off in severalty to plaintiff. (Bigelow, Estoppel [3d ed.] 346; 1 Washburn, Real Property 431, 432; *Tewksbury v. Provizzo*, 12 Cal. 21; *Morris v. Harris*, 9 Gill [Md.] 26; *Patterson v. Lanning*, 10 Watts [Pa.] 135; *Venable v. Beauchamp*, 3 Dana [Ky.] 321; *Feather v. Strohoecker*, 3 P. & W. [Pa.] 505.)

Where lands are conveyed by deed, which ordinarily operates only to transfer vested interests, such as a quitclaim, or deed of bargain and sale, but it distinctly appears on the face of the deed that it was intended to transfer any future or expectant interest which the grantor might acquire, equity will treat the deed as an executory agreement to convey, and compel the grantor to convey the subsequently-acquired interest. (2 Story, Equity Jurisprudence [13th ed.] sec. 1040b; *Hannon v. Christopher*, 34 N. J. Eq. 467; *McWilliams v. Nisly*, 2 S. & R. [Pa.] 509; *Powers' Appeal*, 63 Pa. St. 443.)

RAGAN, C.

In 1875 George H. Ohler resided in Saline county, Nebraska, and was seized in fee-simple of a tract of land therein containing 280 acres. At this date Ohler left home and never returned, although he seems to have been heard from by members of the family from time to time. In June, 1887, his three children, Vesta Hagensick *née* Ohler, James Ohler, and Electa Wheeler *née* Ohler, partitioned among themselves the father's real estate. This partition was effected by quitclaim deeds executed by the children, one to the other, each of the deeds reciting that the grantor therein "being one of the three heirs of George H. Ohler." Each child took possession of that part of the real estate allotted to him under the partition. In 1891 the ancestor died, and soon after that two of his heirs, James Ohler and Electa Wheeler, conveyed to Tobias Castor by warranty deed all the real estate which the decedent owned in his lifetime, except eighty acres thereof. The Castor conveyance by its terms included the part of the decedent's estate allotted to Vesta Hagensick in the partition thereof made by the decedent's children in 1887. On the 8th of July, 1892, Castor deeded to one Rosamond B. Westervelt the lands conveyed to him by the two children, and on the same day Westervelt, by another conveyance, became invested with the title to the eighty-acre tract above mentioned which had been allotted to Electa Wheeler in the partition made of the father's real estate by his children in 1887. In the district court of Saline county Vesta Hagensick brought this action against Castor and others to have quieted and confirmed in her the title to the real estate allotted to her by the partition made thereof by Ohler's children in 1887. She had a decree as prayed and Castor and others have appealed.

1. The district court found, and the evidence sustains the finding, that the quitclaim deeds made by the children of George H. Ohler to one another in June, 1887, of his

real estate were made and accepted by said children with
the purpose and intent of effecting among themselves a
voluntary partition and division of the lands of their
father, they then believing him to be dead, and believing
that they were then seized of said lands as his heirs at
law; that each of said children entered into the possession
of the portion of the lands allotted to him by the partition made thereof and held and occupied such lands in
severalty to the commencement of this suit; that in each
of said quitclaim deeds made by said children the grantor
therein recited that he or she was one of the three heirs
of George H. Ohler; that by such recital such grantor intended to define the estate conveyed to be an estate of
inheritance vested in him as an heir at law of George H.
Ohler. As a conclusion of law the court found that the
said parties who had executed said quitclaim deeds, and
all persons claiming through or under them, were, by reason of the recital in said deeds that the grantors therein
were heirs of George H. Ohler, estopped to dispute that
assertion, and consequently were estopped from claiming
the title to such real estate, which had descended to said
parties, as heirs of George H. Ohler on his death in 1891.

Was this conclusion of the district court correct? We
think it was. The general doctrine undoubtedly is that
an ordinary quitclaim deed vests only in the grantee
such title or estate as the grantor was, at the time of the
execution and delivery of the deed, possessed of; and that
if a grantor in such deed subsequently acquires the title
to the real estate thereby conveyed, that title does not
inure to the grantee in the quitclaim deed. (Compiled
Statutes, ch. 73, sec. 51, and cases hereinafter cited.)
The conveyance made to Vesta Hagensick by her brother
and sister in June, 1887, of the real estate in controversy
was a quitclaim deed; the grantors in that deed had no
title to the real estate which it attempted to convey and,
therefore, Vesta Hagensick acquired no title by that
deed. In 1887 George H. Ohler was still alive, and his
two children who conveyed a part of his real estate to

Vesta Hagensick were not then his heirs, and as such had no title to the real estate they attempted to convey; but the two children who made this conveyance to Vesta Hagensick subsequently thereto by the death of their father in 1891 became invested as his heirs with the title to two-thirds of all the real estate of which George H. Ohler died seized. In other words, the two children who executed the quitclaim deed to Vesta Hagensick subsequently acquired title to that real estate, and this title so subsequently acquired would not inure to the benefit of or vest in Vesta Hagensick, if the conveyance made to her by her brother and sister, and the contract on which such conveyance was predicated, was, and was intended by the parties thereto to be, nothing more than a quitclaim of any interest which the grantors therein possessed or were supposed to possess to the real estate conveyed. But the district court has found, and the evidence sustains it, that the conveyance made to Vesta Hagensick by her brother and sister was intended by the parties thereto to vest in her the title which the grantors in those deeds had to the land as heirs of their ancestor, they then believing him to be dead; and the conveyance made to Vesta Hagensick by her brother and sister is not only a quitclaim deed, but it contains the solemn recital or statement that the grantors in those deeds were then and there heirs of George H. Ohler. This statement is not, as counsel for appellants seem to argue, a mere *descriptio personae* of the grantors. The statement is written in the body of the deed following the description of the real estate conveyed. Nor by any reasonable construction can the statement be construed to mean that the grantor was one of the children of George H. Ohler; but it is a recital, a statement, an asseveration, and representation of the grantor that he was then and there an heir at law of George H. Ohler; and this conveyance was accepted and acted upon in the belief that the statement made was true.

The question then is, can these grantors or those claim-

ing under them now be-heard to assert the fact that they
were not then heirs of Ohler as against the representation made by them in their deed? We think the most
respectable authorities in the country answer this question in the negative. A case which so answers the question under consideration, and in which it was most
thoroughly considered, is *Van Rensselaer v. Kearney*, 52
U. S. 297. The court said: "On the part of the complainant it is insisted that the conveyance is a deed of bargain
and sale, and quitclaim, without any covenants of title
of warranty, and therefore could operate to pass only the
estate for life of which the grantor was then seized; that
it contains no appropriate words, when taken together,
by force of which the subsequently acquired title inured
to the benefit of the grantee, or those claiming under him,
or that can estop the heirs from denying that he had any
greater estate than the tenancy for life; and that the
deed purports on its face to grant and convey simply the
right, title, and interest which the grantor possessed in
the premises at the time, and nothing more. * * *
The general principle is admitted, that a grantor, conveying by deed of bargain and sale, by way of release or
quitclaim of all his right and title to a tract of land, if
made in good faith, and without any fraudulent representations, is not responsible for the goodness of the title
beyond the covenants in his deed. * * * A deed of
this character purports to convey, and is understood to
convey, nothing more than the interest or estate of which
the grantor is seized or possessed at the time, and does
not operate to pass or bind an interest not then in existence. The bargain between the parties proceeds upon
this view, and the consideration is regulated in conformity with it. If otherwise, and the vendee has contracted for a particular estate, or for an estate in fee, he
must take the precaution to secure himself by the proper
covenants of title. But this principle is applicable to a
deed of bargain and sale by release or quitclaim, in the
strict and proper sense of that species of conveyance;

and, therefore, if the deed bears on its face evidence that the grantors intended to convey, and the grantee expected to become invested with, an estate of a particular description or quality, and that the bargain had proceeded upon that footing between the parties, then, although it may not contain any covenants of title in the technical sense of the term, still the legal operation and effect of the instrument will be as binding upon the grantor and those claiming under him, in respect to the estate thus described, as if a formal covenant to that effect had been inserted; at least, so far as to estop them from ever afterwards denying that he was seized of the particular estate at the time of the conveyance." The court, after citing and reviewing the authorities, proceeds as follows: "The principle deducible from these authorities seems to be that, whatever may be the form or nature of the conveyance used to pass real property, if the grantor sets forth on the face of the instrument by way of recital or averment, that he is seized or possessed of a particular estate in the premises and which estate the deed purports to convey; or what is the same thing, if the seizin or possession of a particular estate is affirmed in the deed, either in express terms or by necessary implication, the grantor and all persons in privity with him shall be estopped from ever afterwards denying that he was so seized and possessed at the time he made the conveyance. The estoppel works upon the estate, and binds an after-acquired title as between parties and privies. The reason is that the estate thus affirmed to be in the party at the time of the conveyance must necessarily have influenced the grantee in making the purchase; and hence the grantor and those in privity with him, in good faith and fair dealing, should be forever thereafter precluded from gainsaying it. The doctrine is founded, when properly applied, upon the highest principles of morality, and recommends itself to the common sense and justice of every one. And although it debars the truth in the particular case, and therefore is not unfrequently characterized as odious, and not to be favored, still it should be remembered that it debars it only in the case where its utterance would convict the party of a previous falsehood; would be the denial of a previous affirmation upon the faith of which persons had dealt and pledged their credit or expended their money. It is a doctrine, therefore, when properly understood and applied, that concludes the truth in order to prevent fraud and falsehood, and imposes silence on a party only when in conscience and honesty he should not be allowed to speak." This case expresses our views in far better language than any we are able to command. To the same effect see *Bush v. Person*, 59 U. S. 82; *Lessee of French and Wife v. Spencer*, 62 U. S. 228; *Clarke v. Baker*, 14 Cal. 612; *Magruder v. Esmay*, 35 O. St. 221; *Hannon v. Christopher*, 34 N. J. Eq. 459; *Wells v. Stickleberg*, 52 Neb. 597. Following the rule laid down in these cases, we hold that the grantors in the quitclaim deeds made to Vesta Hagensick, by reciting therein that they were then and there the heirs of George H. Ohler, have forever estopped themselves and all persons claiming under them from disputing that assertion. The decree of the district court is

AFFIRMED.

W. J. WILLIAMSON V. HEINRICH GEORGE.

FILED JANUARY 19, 1898.   No. 7770.

Covenants: EVIDENCE. Evidence examined, and *held* to sustain the finding of the jury that the recitals of the deed in controversy do not express the actual contract made between the parties.

ERROR from the district court of Hamilton county. Tried below before WHEELER, J. *Affirmed.*

Hainer & Smith, for plaintiff in error.

John A. Whitmore, contra.

RAGAN, C.

W. J. Williamson brought this suit in the district court
of Hamilton county against Heinrich George.   The latter
had a verdict and judgment and Williamson brings the
same here for review on error.

In his petition in the district court Williamson alleged
the purchase by him of a quarter section of land in Kansas from George; that the latter executed to him a deed
of conveyance for said land warranting the same to be
free of all incumbrance except the taxes and a mortgage
of $500 on the land which Williamson assumed and
agreed to pay as a part of the consideration for such conveyance; that at the time of said conveyance the land was
incumbered by a mortgage for $100 in addition to the $500
mortgage assumed by Williamson.   George in his answer
admitted the sale of the land to Williamson and the execution and delivery to him of a deed therefor, but he interposed as a defense to the action that the contract between him and Williamson was that he would sell and
convey his equity only in this land to Williamson for
$100; that he was a Russian unable to read or write the
English language, and could understand but very little of
it when spoken; that Williamson paid him the $100 and
he, George, and his wife executed the deed of conveyance,
but that Williamson caused to be fraudulently inserted
therein the covenant against incumbrance contrary to
. the agreement between the parties.

Several complaints are made in the brief of counsel for
the plaintiff in error here as to the action of the district
court in the admission and exclusion of evidence on the
trial.   We have carefully examined this record and it
must suffice to say that we do not think any action of the
district court in that respect was prejudicial to the plaintiff in error.

Complaints are also made by the plaintiff of the action
of the district court in giving and refusing to give certain
instructions.   We have likewise examined these and

reached the conclusion that the plaintiff in error was not prejudiced by any instruction given or refused by the district court. The serious question in the case, and the one that has given us the most trouble, is whether this finding of the jury is supported by the evidence. The evidence on the part of Williamson tends to show that the contract between him and George is fairly expressed in the deed of conveyance made by the latter. On the other hand, the evidence of George, who testified at the trial through the medium of an interpreter, tends to show that he owned the land subsequently conveyed to Williamson; that it was heavily incumbered; that he was unable to pay the incumbrance; that he had been advised by a friend in Kansas that he could get $100 for his equity in the land; that this information was conveyed to George by a letter and the letter was shown to Williamson; that Williamson then contracted with George to buy the latter's equity in the land for $100, which sum he paid; that Williamson explained in German, which language George understood, the contents of this deed after it was drawn and before it was executed, and that he made such an explanation of it that George understood, not that he was warranting the title of this land to be free from incumbrance, but that he was simply parting with his equity in the land for $100. The evidence for the defendant in error is very meager and somewhat unsatisfactory, but, after giving the record the most careful study of which we are capable, we are constrained to say that we think the evidence sustains the finding of the jury to the effect that the deed executed by George and his wife does not recite the actual contract made between the parties. The judgment of the district court is

AFFIRMED.

CREIGHTON UNIVERSITY, APPELLEE, V. EDWARD C. ERFLING ET AL., APPELLANTS.

FILED JANUARY 19, 1898. No. 7772.

Review: EVIDENCE. The record presents for consideration no disputed question of law. Evidence examined, and *held* to sustain the decree of the district court.

APPEAL from the district court of Douglas county. Heard below before DUFFIE, J. *Affirmed.*

Arthur C. Wakeley, for appellants.

Frank T. Ransom, contra.

RAGAN, C.

Edward C. Erfling and others appeal from a decree of the district court of Douglas county foreclosing an ordinary real estate mortgage against their property. The appeal is based upon the contention of the appellants that they were not allowed by the district court certain credits to which they claim they were entitled. The record presents no disputed question of law. It would subserve no useful purpose to even summarize the evidence here. In our opinion the contentions of the appellants are untenable. The evidence justifies the decree of the district court and it is

AFFIRMED.

JOHN E. CASTILE V. BENJAMIN F. FORD ET AL.

FILED JANUARY 19, 1898. No. 7779.

1. **Defect of Parties:** OBJECTION. A defect of parties plaintiff appearing on the face of the petition must be objected to by demurrer on that ground, or it will be waived.

2. **Executions:** EXEMPT PROPERTY: WRONGFUL SEIZURE: DAMAGES. The seizure and retention of exempt property, known by the officer to be exempt, and after its exempt character has been legally established, constitute an abuse of process for which the officer is liable. The judgment plaintiff will be liable also, if, knowing the facts, he advised the seizure or retention or participated in the officer's acts.

3. ——: ——: ——: ——. In such case the ultimate return of the property goes only in mitigation of damages; it is no defense to the action.

ERROR from the district court of Douglas county. Tried below before BLAIR, J. *Reversed.*

B. N. Robertson and *C. W. Young,* for plaintiff in error.

Cavanagh & Thomas, contra.

IRVINE, C.

Castile alone brought this action against Ford and Daley, who were constables, the Consolidated Coffee Company, and William Preston & Co., alleging in the petition that on the 5th day of December, 1892, the Consolidated Coffee Company and Preston & Co., each having judgments against Matilda Castile, the wife of plaintiff, caused executions to be issued thereon and placed in the hands of Daley for service; and that "on the —— day of December, 1892," Daley levied upon certain chattels "of plaintiff and Matilda Castile." Facts are stated constituting such property exempt from execution, and it is alleged that the defendants, confederating together to oppress and harass the plaintiff, and knowing the property to be exempt, seized and withheld it, and threatened to

sell it. Plaintiff obtained from the district court of
Douglas county an injunction perpetually restraining
Daley from selling the property; whereupon the defendants caused Daley to deliver it to Ford who levied upon it
by virtue of other executions issued at the instance of the
coffee company and Preston & Co. Plaintiff filed the
appropriate affidavit and inventory to procure its release,
and the defendants, in pursuance of said combination and
confederation, refused to surrender it; whereupon, at the
suit of plaintiff, a writ of mandamus was issued by the
district court requiring the release of the property on the
"—— day of January, 1893." Special damages are
pleaded by way of injury to the goods, because of their
detention, for loss of time, and for attorneys' fees expended in procuring the release of the goods. Early in
the trial objection was made to the introduction of any
evidence on the ground that the petition did not state
a cause of action, in that it alleged that the property was
the joint property of husband and wife while the husband
sued singly. The court sustained the objection and a dismissal followed. The action of the trial court cannot
be sustained on the ground stated in the objection. The
defect suggested was, at most, a defect of parties plaintiff. This appeared on the face of the petition and was
waived by failure to demur on that ground. (Code of
Civil Procedure, secs. 94, 96.) We need not, therefore,
consider whether the point would have been well taken
had it been seasonably raised. Otherwise there can be
no doubt that a cause of action was stated. The petition
alleged a willful and malicious attempt to seize and sell
property known to be exempt, and a second attempt after
the first failed. Whether or not an officer is liable for
seizing exempt property in the absence of a claim for exemption, there can be no doubt that he is liable for withholding it after the exemption is established, or for seizing
it again for the same debt. The petition in this respect
charges a flagrant abuse of process, and charges that it
was the result of a conspiracy in which all the defendants

participated. They would in such case be jointly liable with the officer. (*Murray v. Mace*, 41 Neb. 60.) In such case the fact that the goods were ultimately returned goes only in mitigation of damages; it is not a defense. Plaintiff would still be entitled to recover all other damages available in cases of trespass. We need not determine whether a recovery could be had for all the special damages here pleaded. The district court did not proceed far enough to reach that question. There could certainly be a recovery for the detention of the property, and for injuries done to it while in the defendants' possession. It is asserted that there is no allegation of any withholding, but in this assertion counsel err. The petition in effect alleges a withholding from the "—— day of December, 1892," to the "—— day of January, 1893." While these dates are not certainly stated and the petition in that respect may have been open to motion, the averments are sufficient against a general objection on the trial.

REVERSED AND REMANDED.

SAMUEL M. MELICK v. CYRUS D. KELLEY.

FILED JANUARY 19, 1898.   No. 7737.

Contracts. To establish an express contract there must be shown what amounts to a definite proposal and an unconditional and absolute acceptance thereof.

ERROR from the district court of Lancaster county. Tried below before STRODE, J. *Affirmed.*

J. L. Caldwell, for plaintiff in error.

Webster, Rose & Fisherdick, contra.

IRVINE, C.

Kelley brought this action against Melick to recover an unpaid portion of a promissory note executed by defendant to plaintiff.   The defense was that the note was given as part consideration for the sale by plaintiff to defendant of certain real estate; that after it became due a contract had been entered into whereby the note was to be surrendered upon the defendant's executing to plaintiff a reconveyance of the real estate, and sending the deed to a bank in Cheyenne for delivery to plaintiff, upon plaintiff's surrender to the bank of the note; that defendant had complied with his part of the contract, but plaintiff had refused to accept the deed or surrender the note. The plaintiff had judgment and the defendant prosecutes this proceeding in error.

It would be useless to rehearse the evidence in detail. It wholly fails to disclose the consummation of any contract between the parties, such as the defendant pleads. The negotiations were entirely by means of letter.   The first letter, which apparently contained a proposition from Kelley to Melick, is not in evidence, nor is there any proof of its contents.   Nowhere in the evidence does there appear any proof as to what lands were to be reconveyed.   If all which Kelley had conveyed to Melick were contemplated, it appears that the offer was not complied with, because, while the deed tendered covered all the property, it appears that two lots had by Melick been conveyed to a stranger, and the deed was to be delivered only on the erasure of the descriptions of those two lots. Furthermore, the deed was sent with a demand that Kelley should agree to refund all taxes which Melick had paid.   This coupled the acceptance of Kelley's proposition with a condition, which for its enforcement required a counter-acceptance by Kelley which was not given.   In any view, assuming for the proposal all that defendant claims, there was no absolute, unconditional acceptance thereof, and the contract was not completed.   To establish an express contract it is necessary to show a definite proposal and an unconditional and absolute acceptance thereof.

AFFIRMED.

HOMER D. WAGER ET AL. V. PHILIP S. WAGONER.

53 5
61

FILED JANUARY 19, 1898. No. 7692.

1. **Insane Persons**: SUITS: NEXT FRIEND. One who is insane, but who has not been so adjudged, and who has no guardian, may sue by his next friend.

- 2. **Review**: INCOMPETENT EVIDENCE: HARMLESS ERROR. A judgment in a case tried to the court without the intervention of a jury will not be reversed because of the admission of incompetent or immaterial evidence when there was sufficient competent evidence to sustain the finding.

3. **Insane Persons**: DEEDS: AVOIDANCE. In order to avoid the deed of an insane person, it is unnecessary to prove that there was fraud or other wrong-doing inducing its execution.

4. ——: ——: ——: CONSIDERATION. The deed of an insane person may be set aside without returning the consideration, at least when it does not appear that a return in specie is practicable.

ERROR from the district court of Boone county. Tried below before KENDALL, J. *Affirmed.*

J. S. Armstrong and *Charles Riley,* for plaintiffs in error:

An action by an insane person should be brought by a properly-appointed guardian, and not by a next friend. (*Covington v. Neftzger,* 30 N. E. Rep. [Ill.] 764; *Dorsheimer v. Roorback,* 18 N. J. Eq. 438; *Nichol v. Thomas,* 53 Ind. 42; *Tiffany v. Worthington,* 65 N. W. Rep. [Ia.] 817; *Row v. Row,* 41 N. E. Rep. [O.] 239.)

Duffie & Van Dusen and *Howell & Spear, contra.*

IRVINE, C.

This action was brought in the name of Philip S. Wagoner by William J. Wagoner as his next friend, against Homer D. Wager and two others. The petition alleged that Philip S. Wagoner was, on August 25, 1893, insane and wholly incapable of contracting, that he was the owner of certain described land in Boone county, and that the defendants conspired together to defraud him thereof,

and procured him to convey said land to Wager for a
grossly inadequate price. The answers were in effect
general denials. There was a trial to the court and a
general finding for the plaintiff, followed by a decree requiring Wager to reconvey to the plaintiff.

The first question presented is whether the action may
be maintained by a next friend. It is both pleaded and
proved that there had been no adjudication of insanity
and no guardian appointed. Under such circumstances
we have no doubt that the action was properly brought
by a volunteer as the next friend of the insane person.
One is not an outlaw, although insane, and the courts will
interfere to protect his rights of person and of property
at the instance of one who volunteers on his behalf. This
does not open up the way to vexatious litigation by irre-
sponsible persons, because the court would in such case
have the power, expressly reserved in the case of infants,
to discontinue the suit if it turn out to be not in the interest of the plaintiff to have it prosecuted, to substitute another person by appointment for the volunteer if he
should be deemed unsuitable, or to substitute the duly
appointed guardian if one should be appointed *pendente
lite*. To hold that a suit may not be so maintained would
frequently deprive lunatics of all protection, because it
may often happen that the time occupied in procuring the
appointment and qualification of a guardian would render all relief impracticable. The cases holding that a
lunatic may not sue by next friend are for the most part
those where a guardian or committee has been appointed,
or where, as in Ohio and in Illinois, a statute makes adequate provision for suing in another manner. (*Row v.
Row*, 41 N. E. Rep. [O.] 239; *Covington v. Neftzger*, 30 N.
E. Rep. [Ill.] 764.) In the latter state, perhaps before
the statute was passed, but certainly on a consideration
of the law independent of statute, it had before been
held that a next friend might sue. (*Chicago & P. R. Co. v.
Munger*, 78 Ill. 300.) In New Jersey it was once held that
a next friend might sue at law, but not in equity. (*Dor-*

sheimer v. Roorback, 18 N. J. Eq. 438.)   This was because
the chancellor thought there was no semblance of authority for such a proceeding in equity except one or two
loose *dicta* referred to in the opinion.   He must have
overlooked *Nelson v. Duncombe*, 9 Beav. [Eng.] 211, and
Light v. Light, 25 Beav. [Eng.] 248, both earlier cases.
There was also suggested a distinction between cases of
total and partial incapacity, but we think there can be
no ground for proceeding differently merely because
of the degree or duration of the mental derangement.
Nor is there in this state any room for a distinction
in this respect between law and equity.   The procedure is the same.   The practice here resorted to is supported by the English cases already cited as well as by
Jones v. Lloyd, L. R. 18 Eq. Cas. 265, *Rock v. Slade*, 7 Dowl.
22, and in this country by *Plympton v. Hall*, 56 N. W. Rep.
[Minn.] 351, *Reese v. Reese*, 15 S. E. Rep. [Ga.] 846, *Edwards v. Edwards*, 36 S. W. Rep. [Tex.] 1080, *Holzheiser v.
Gulf W. T. & P. R. Co.*, 33 S. W. Rep. [Tex.] 887, *Dudgeon
v. Watson*, 23 Fed. Rep. 161, *Whetstone v. Whetstone*, 75 Ala.
495, and *Chicago & P. R. Co. v. Munger, supra.*

It is next argued that the court erred in finding under
the evidence that Philip Wagoner was insane at the time
of his making the deed to Wager.   We have examined
the voluminous evidence in the case and are satisfied that
there is sufficient competent testimony to preclude any
interference with the finding of the trial court.   In this
connection attention is called to the fact that the court
received in evidence the record of certain proceedings before the insanity board of Douglas county, whereby an
inquiry had been made under chapter 40, Compiled Statutes.   It was held in *Dewey v. Algire*, 37 Neb. 6, that the
record of such proceedings is not admissible in a case
like this for the purpose of proving insanity; but it is
established by repeated decisions of this court that, in a
case which has been tried by the court without a jury, the
judgment will not be reversed because of the admission of
incompetent or immaterial evidence, when there was suf-

37

ficient competent evidence to sustain the finding. Moreover, this record could hardly have prejudiced the defendants because it showed that the plaintiff was not adjudged insane.

It is asserted next that the charge of conspiracy made in the petition is not sustained by the evidence. It is not necessary to the relief granted that it should be. If the plaintiff was insane, his deed was void and might be so decreed, although there was no conspiracy and no fraud. This issue might affect the liability of Wager's co-defendants, against whom, as well as Wager, the judgment went for costs, but we cannot consider any question affecting them alone, because all the defendants joined in the motion for a new trial and the petition in error. and if the judgment was correct as to one it must be affirmed as to all. (*Dorsey v. McGee.* 30 Neb. 657.)

Finally it is contended that Wager should receive restitution of the consideration by him paid. This, in the case of an insane person, is not essential as a condition of granting relief. (*Dewey v. Algire, supra; Rea v. Bishop.* 41 Neb. 202.) It did not appear that the ability existed to restore the consideration in specie. The right to recover it back as money had and received or otherwise was not a question involved in the case and is not now open to consideration.

AFFIRMED.

OMAHA & REPUBLICAN VALLEY RAILWAY COMPANY v.
GRANITE STATE FIRE INSURANCE COMPANY.

FILED JANUARY 19, 1898.   No. 7678.

Actions: RAILROAD COMPANIES: FIRES: INSURANCE: ESTOPPEL. Property partially insured was burned by the negligence of a railroad company. The insurer paid to the insured the amount of the policy and took from him an assignment of his cause of action against the railroad, to the extent of the insurance paid. The insured then sued the railroad company for the remainder of his loss. The railroad company knew of the insurance company's rights and pleaded the assignment, but abandoned the defense and stipulated that judgment should go against it. *Held,* That the insurance company was not precluded by its knowledge of the pendency of that suit, nor by the settlement thereof, from afterwards maintaining an action against the railroad to recover the amount of the insurance by it paid.

ERROR from the district court of Lancaster county. Tried below before HALL, J. *Affirmed.*

The opinion contains a statement of the case.

J. M. Thurston, W. R. Kelly, and *E. P. Smith,* for plaintiff in error:

The cause of action arising from the negligence of the railroad company is indivisible. The claim of the insurance company should have been presented in the action by the insured. The insurer cannot maintain a separate action against the railroad company for the amount paid under its policy. (*Rockingham Mutual Fire Ins. Co. v. Bosher,* 39 Me. 256; *Mobile & M. R. Co. v. Jurey,* 111 U. S. 584, 593; *Hall v. Railroad Co.,* 13 Wall. [U. S.] 370; *Phœnix Ins. Co. v. Erie & Western Transportation Co.,* 117 U. S. 312; *Gales v. Hailman,* 11 Pa. St. 515; *British & Foreign Marine Ins. Co. v. Gulf, C. & S. F. R. Co.,* 21 Am. & Eng. R. Cas. [Tex.] 112; *The Propeller Monticello v. Mollison,* 17 How. [U. S.] 153; *Smith v. Jones,* 15 Johns. [N. Y.] 229; *Willard v. Sperry,* 16 Johns. [N. Y.] 121; *MacDougall v. Maguire,* 35 Cal. 274; *Ætna Ins. Co. v. Hannibal & St. J. R. Co.,* 3 Dill. [U. S. C. C.] 1; *Swarthout v. Chicago & N. W. R. Co.,* 49 Wis. 625; *Hundhausen v. Bond,* 36 Wis. 29-41; *Yates v. Whyte,* 4 Bing. N. C. [Eng.] 272; *Randal v. Cockran,* 1 Ves. Sr. [Eng.] 98; *Peoria Marine & Fire Ins. Co. v. Frost,* 37 Ill. 333; *First Presbyterian Society of Green Bay v. Goodrich Transportation Co.,* 7 Fed. Rep. 257; *Marine Ins. Co. v. St. Louis, I. M. & S. R. Co.,* 41 Fed. Rep. 643; *Norwich Union Fire Ins. Society v. Standard Oil Co.,* 59 Fed. Rep. 984; *Continental Ins. Co. v. Loud & Sons Lumber Co.,* 93 Mich. 139; *Pratt v. Radford,* 52 Wis. 118; *Home Mutual Ins. Co. v. Orc-*

gon R. & N. Co, 26 Pac. Rep. [Ore.] 857; *Watson v. Milwaukee & M. R. Co.*, 57 Wis. 339; *Hustisford Farmers Mutual Ins. Co. v. Chicago, M. & St. P. R. Co.*, 66 Wis. 58; *State Ins. Co. v. Oregon R. & N. Co.*, 20 Ore. 563; *North Shore R. Co. v. McWillie*, 5 Mont. Q. B. [Can.] 122.)

Insurer did not by subrogation acquire the right to maintain suit in its own name. (*Brighthope R. Co. v. Rogers*, 8 Am. & Eng. R. Cas. [Va.] 710-12; *Grubbs v. Wysor*, 32 Gratt. [Va.] 131; *Hart v. Western R. Co.*, 13 Met. [Mass.] 99-105; *Mason v. Sainsbury*, 3 Doug. [Eng.] 61; *Clark v. Inhabitants of the Hundred of Blything*, 2 B. & C. [Eng.] 254.)

The insured sued the railroad company and recovered a judgment, which defendant paid. The insurer had notice of the pendency of that action and was estopped from afterward maintaining a suit against the railroad company for the amount paid under the policy. (*City of Boston v. Worthington*, 10 Gray [Mass.] 496; *Chicago v. Robbins*, 2 Black [U. S.] 418; *Clarke v. Carrington*, 7 Cranch [U. S.] 322; *Pierce v. Chicago & N. W. R. Co.*, 36 Wis. 284; *Stanley v. Goodrich*, 18 Wis. 534; *Pratt v. Donovan*, 10 Wis. 320.)

The insurer having refused to be made a party to the suit by insured, the judgment in favor of the latter is *res judicata*. (*Miller v. Covert*, 1 Wend. [N. Y.] 488; *Guernsey v. Carver*, 8 Wend. [N. Y.] 493; *Bendernagle v. Cocks*, 19 Wend. [N. Y.] 209; *Trask v. Hartford & N. H. R. Co.*, 2 Allen [Mass.] 331; *Rittenhouse v. Levering*, 6 Watts & S. [Pa.] 197; *Newcomb v. Cincinnati Ins. Co.*, 22 O. St. 382; *McCormick v. Irwin*, 35 Pa. 117; *Gosviler's Estate*, 3 Pen. & W. [Pa.] 203; *Kernochan v. New York Bowery Fire Ins. Co.*, 17 N. Y. 436.)

Charles O. Whedon, contra:

The settlement of insured's claim by the railroad company did not affect the rights of insurer. If so intended it is a fraud upon the insurer and does not impair its rights or remedies. (*Connecticut Fire Ins. Co. v. Erie R. Co.*, 73 N. Y. 399; *Clark v. Wilson*, 103 Mass. 223; *Mon-*

mouth County Mutual Fire Ins. Co. v. Hutchinson, 21 N. J. Eq. 107; *Graff v. Kipp*, 1 Edw. Ch. [N. Y.] 618; *Hart v. Western R. Co.*, 13 Met. [Mass.] 99; *Ætna Fire Ins. Co. v. Tyler*, 16 Wend. [N. Y.] 397; *Gracie v. New York Ins. Co.*, 8 Johns. [N. Y.] *237; *Timan v. Leland*, 6 Hill [N. Y.] 237; *Trask v. Hartford & N. H. R. Co.*, 2 Allen [Mass.] 331; *Mayor v. Stone*, 20 Wend. [N. Y.] 139; *Rockingham Mutual Fire Ins. Co. v. Bosher*, 39 Me. 253; *Perrott v. Shearer*, 17 Mich. 48; *Atlantic Ins. Co. v. Storrow*, 1 Ed. Ch. [N. Y.] 621.)

Upon payment of insured's claim under the policy insurer acquired a right of action against the railroad company. (24 Am. & Eng. Ency. Law 306; 2 May, Insurance sec. 454; Harris, Subrogation [1st ed.] sec. 624; Wood, Insurance [1st ed.] secs. 473, 474.)

The insurer may maintain the action in its own name. (Code of Civil Procedure, sec. 30; *Connecticut Fire Ins. Co. v. Erie R. Co.*, 73 N. Y. 399; *Garrison v. Memphis Ins. Co.*, 19 How. [U. S.] 317; *Marine Ins. Co. v. St. Louis, I. M. & S. R. Co.*, 41 Fed. Rep. 643; *Home Ins. Co. v. Pennsylvania R. Co.*, 11 Hun [N. Y.] 182; *Hustisford Farmers Mutual Ins. Co. v. Chicago, M. & St. P. R. Co.*, 66 Wis. 58; *St. Louis, A. & T. R. Co. v. Fire Ass'n*, 55 Ark. 163; *London Assurance Co. v. Sainsbury*, 3 Doug. [Eng.] 245; *Mills v. Murry*, 1 Neb. 327; *Seymour v. Street*, 5 Neb. 93; *Hicklin v. Nebraska City Nat. Bank*, 8 Neb. 463; *Hoagland v. Van Etten*, 22 Neb. 684.)

Charles E. Magoon, also for defendant in error.

IRVINE, C.

From admissions in the pleadings and from the stipulation of facts whereon this case was tried we gather the following facts: One Erickson was the owner of land along the line of the railroad owned by the plaintiff in error, on which were certain buildings and personal property of the value of $3,900, which were wholly destroyed by fire set out by the negligence of the railroad company. Erickson had insurance on the property, written by the defendant in error, to the amount of $1,000. The insurance company paid the loss and Erickson assigned to it his cause of action against the railroad company to the extent of $1,000. Erickson then brought suit against the railroad company, alleging the loss of his property through its negligence, its value as $3,900, and the insurance and payment to him of $1,000 by the insurance company, and prayed damages for $2,900. The railroad company answered in that case, alleging the assignment to the insurance company, and another assignment to a stranger of the remainder, and that Erickson was, therefore, not the real party in interest. After issues were so joined a settlement was made between the railroad company and Erickson, whereby it was agreed that judgment should be entered in favor of Erickson for $1,750. A jury was impaneled, a verdict returned in accordance with the stipulation, judgment entered thereon and paid. Pending this suit the railroad company had notified the insurance company of its pendency, and the insurance company had refused to intervene, notifying the railroad company at the same time of its intention to hold the railroad company under the assignment. After the judgment in favor of Erickson was entered and paid, this suit was begun by the insurance company to recover to the extent of $1,000 and interest. The railroad pleaded the foregoing facts. The case was submitted to the court without a jury, on a stipulation of facts, which left no issue to be determined from evidence. The court found for the insurance company and entered judgment accordingly. The assignments of error relied on relate to the correctness of the conclusions of law reached by the district court.

Certain propositions contended for by the railroad company are undoubtedly correct, and any consideration of the case must proceed from the starting point thereby established. At common law a chose in action, with certain exceptions not here material, was not assignable, so as to permit the assignee to sue in his own name.

The right of an insurance company to recover against a wrong-doer, whose negligence has subjected the insurance company to a liability, whether the company's right be based on an equitable subrogation or an express assignment, is traced through the insured; that is, no cause of action can exist on behalf of the insurer, unless it existed in favor of the insured. Any defense available against the insured is equally available against the insurer, except as to acts of the insured after payment of the loss and with notice to the wrong-doer of the insurer's rights. That principle goes no farther. A cause of action for tort, such as this, is indivisible without the consent of the defendant. A person injured cannot, by assignments of portions of his damages, subject the defendant to a multiplicity of suits for the same wrong. The authorities cited by the railroad company really tend to establish nothing more than the foregoing principles.

We take it that this case is controlled by the following considerations: Under our Code of Civil Procedure actions must, with a few express exceptions not relating to this case, be brought in the name of the real party in interest. (Code, sec. 29.) The assignee of a chose in action may maintain an action thereon in his own name without the name of the assignor. (Code, sec. 30.) The original cause of action being indivisible, unless by the consent of the defendant, Erickson should have joined the insurance company as a plaintiff in his action. If the company refused to so join, it might have been made a defendant. (Code, secs. 40, 41, 42.) The railroad's answer in the Erickson suit was therefore good, and stated a valid defense; its abandonment of the defense and stipulation for judgment against it amounted then to a waiver of a good defense and a voluntary payment. Knowing, as it then knew, of the rights of the insurance company, it is not protected, by that voluntary payment of Erickson's claim, against a valid claim of the insurance company not included in that settlement. Its action was equivalent to express consent to a splitting of the cause of action, and it can claim no estoppel against the insurance company because it acted with full knowledge of its rights and of its intention to assert them.

Not a single case cited conflicts with the views expressed. In *London Assurance Co. v. Sainsbury*, 3 Doug. [Eng.] 167, Langdale had suffered a loss through the riots of 1780. He sued the inhabitants under the riot act. Allowance was made in that suit for the insurance by him received, and he had judgment for the difference. The insurance company then brought suit. The case was, therefore, much like this. It was held by a divided court that the insurance company could not sue. Lord Mansfield, who with Mr. Justice Buller formed the majority, held that this was so because the common law forbade an assignee to sue in his own name, but said: "If by law either Langdale or the plaintiffs might sue, I have no doubt that it may be shown, from what passed at the trial, that the sum sought to be recovered was not included in the damages, otherwise the plaintiffs might recover against Langdale and show the verdict as conclusive evidence." With us an assignee may sue, and we have therefore in this case, not an authority against the insurance company, but the great weight of Lord Mansfield's opinion that under a state of the law like ours, the action would lie under precisely similar circumstances.

Some cases, such as *Ætna Ins. Co. v. Hannibal & St. J. R. Co.*, 3 Dill. [U. S.] 1, and *Norwich Union Fire Ins. Society v. Standard Oil Co.*, 59 Fed. Rep. 984, state the rule generally that where the loss is greater than the insurance the insurer may not sue. These were cases where the insurer attempted to sue before payment to the insured, and are merely authority for the proposition that the claim is indivisible, and that the railroad company should therefore have insisted on its defense against the partial action of Erickson. The former case holds that the rule applies not only to the common law, but the statute of Missouri, but cites the statute as permitting only the assignment of actions based on contract. With us the right of assignment extends to torts. In *State Ins. Co. v. Oregon R. & N. Co.*, 20 Ore. 563, the rule was stated that in such case the insurance company must not sue alone. This does not conflict with our views as a general statement, but it is perhaps worthy of notice that that decision is based on the premise that in Oregon the distinction between actions at law and suits in equity has not been abolished and that the statutory provision permitting an unwilling party, who should be plaintiff, to be made a defendant, applies only to equity cases.

In Wisconsin it is held that the insurance companies must join in one action, and the insured with them if he retains any interest. (*Swarthout v. Chicago & N. W. R. Co.*, 49 Wis. 625; *Pratt v. Radford*, 52 Wis. 114.) That the court was only deciding what we have said, that in the first case the railroad company might have defended on the ground that all were not joined, and not that a confession or settlement of the first suit would bar another by parties not included in the first, is manifest from the language of Lyon, J., in *Pratt v. Radford*: "Had the defendants paid the plaintiff the damages claimed, knowing that the latter had received from the insurance companies the amounts insured, the defendants would still be liable to an action by such companies to recover the amounts so paid, and the release of the plaintiff would be no defense to the action."

In *Connecticut Fire Ins. Co. v. Erie R. Co.*, 73 N. Y. 399, it was held that if the wrong-doer pays the assured after payment to him by the insurer, and with knowledge of that fact, it is a fraud on the insurer, and will not protect the wrong-doer from liability to him.

AFFIRMED.

JAMES W. HORKEY V. W. W. KENDALL, SHERIFF.

FILED JANUARY 19, 1898. No. 7718.

1. **Affidavit:** VERIFICATION: NOTARY PUBLIC. A notary public who is the attorney of one of the parties to an action is not permitted to take the affidavit of his client for the purpose of procuring an attachment.

2. **Attorney and Client:** VERIFICATION OF PLEADING: STATUTES. The amendment of 1887 to section 118 of the Code, notwithstanding its general language, cannot be held to apply to affidavits, other than those verifying pleadings, without giving the amending act a construction which would render it violative of section 11, article 3, constitution.

3. **Affidavit for Attachment:** VERIFICATION. An affidavit to procure an attachment, sworn to before a notary who is also plaintiff's attorney, is not a nullity, but a mere irregularity which cannot be attacked collaterally.

4. **Attachment:** PLEADING: EVIDENCE. The rule that an officer attaching property in the possession of a stranger claiming title must, in order to justify, not only prove that the attachment defendant was indebted to the attachment plaintiff, but that the attachment was regularly issued, does not require that strict regularity in all the attachment proceedings must be shown, but only that there was such a substantial compliance with every essential requirement as to create a valid lien.

5. ——: ——: ——: REPLEVIN. An officer from whom goods held under attachments have been replevied may prove the attachments under a general denial; and, although he adds to the general denial a special plea of one attachment, he may nevertheless prove other attachments.

ERROR from the district court of Howard county. Tried below before THOMPSON, J. *Affirmed.*

T. T. Bell and *Henry Nunn,* for plaintiff in error.

Frank J. Taylor and *F. H. Woods, contra.*

IRVINE, C.

This was an action of replevin by Horkey against Kendall, who was sheriff of Howard county, for certain chattels, part of which Horkey claimed to own absolutely, and part under a chattel mortgage from one Dobry, the general owner. As to the first portion he was successful; as to the mortgaged chattels there was a judgment against him for their return or their value, and of the latter portion of the judgment he complains.

The district court received in evidence, over the objection of the plaintiff, an affidavit filed by the Western Manufacturing Company to procure an attachment against Dobry. The defendant justified under the writ issued thereon. By other documents offered in evidence at the same time it appeared that Frank J. Taylor, the notary public before whom the affidavit was made, also appeared in the attachment suit as the attorney of record of the plaintiff. The objection was based on that fact. Section 370 of the Code of Civil Procedure prescribes the purposes for which an affidavit may be used, among them the obtaining of a provisional remedy. Section 371 prescribes what officers may take such affidavits; to-wit, "any person authorized to take depositions." Immediately following are certain sections with reference to depositions. Sections 374 and 375 designate the officers who may take them, among them notaries public. Section 376 is as follows: "The officer before whom depositions are taken must not be a relative or attorney of either party, or otherwise interested in the event of the action or proceeding." These sections must be construed together, and their joint effect is to prohibit the attorney for either party from taking the affidavit whereby a provisional remedy is obtained. It is claimed, however, that section 118, as amended in 1887, has modified the foregoing provisions. Prior to 1887 the material portion of section 118 was as follows: "The affidavit verifying pleadings may be made before any person before whom a deposition might be taken." Chapter 93 of the Laws of 1887 is entitled "An act to amend section 118 of title 7 entitled 'Pleadings in Civil Actions' of the Code of Civil Procedure of the state of Nebraska, and repeal said original section." By this act the material portions of section 118 are amended to read as follows: "The affidavit verifying pleadings may be made before any notary public or other officer authorized to administer oaths * * * and nothing herein shall be construed to prohibit an attorney at law, who is a notary public, from swearing a client to any pleading or other paper or affidavit in any proceeding in the courts of the state." As indicated by the title to the act of 1887, title 7 of the Code, of which section 118 forms a part, is entitled "Pleadings in Civil Actions." Section 91 enacts that the only pleadings allowed are the petition of the plaintiff, the answer or demurrer of the defendant, the demurrer or reply of the plaintiff, and the demurrer of the defendant to the reply. Subsequently come the well-known requirements as to verification of pleadings of fact, and section 118 appears in that connection. The pleadings therein referred to were evidently pleadings in the specific, technical sense, as defined by section 91. We refer to this because it is asserted that this court, in *Jordan v. Dewey*, 40 Neb. 639, has declared such affidavits as the one in question to be pleadings. In that case the court was dealing with the method of trying motions to dissolve attachments, and stated that on the trial of such motions the affidavit for the attachment and that traversing the averments of that affidavit constitute the pleadings on which such motion is to be tried. That is, the issues of fact are to be found from an inspection of these two affidavits. The word "pleading" was not there used in its specific or technical sense, and the court was not attempting to amend section 91 or section 118. In *Payne v. Briggs*, 8 Neb. 75, Judge COBB, speaking for the court, criticised quite severely the practice of taking depositions in the office of an attorney in the case, and sometimes before a notary who is his clerk. In *Collins v. Stewart*, 16 Neb. 52, the court had reversed a judgment because the trial court had refused to strike from the files certain affidavits offered as evidence on a motion to dissolve an attachment, but sworn to before one of the attorneys. In the light of those decisions it is not improbable that the legislature intended, by the last clause of the amendment of 1887, to entirely remove the disability resting on an attorney who happens also to be a notary public, at least so far as it prevented him from taking his own client's affidavit in any proceeding. But, if that was the object of the legislature, it endeavored to effect it by unconstitutional means. The constitution provides (art. 3, sec. 11) that no bill shall contain more than one subject, which shall be expressed in its title, and no law shall be amended unless the new act contains the section or sections so amended, and the section or sections so amended shall be repealed. This requires that an act, not complete in itself, and being in effect amendatory of other acts, shall expressly recite and repeal the sections amended. (*Smails r. White*, 4 Neb. 353; *Sovereign r. State*, 7 Neb. 407; *Holmberg v. Hauck*, 16 Neb. 337; *State r. Lancaster County*, 17 Neb. 85; *Touzalin r. Omaha*, 25 Neb. 817; *Stricklett r. State*, 31 Neb. 674; *Trumble v. Trumble*, 37 Neb. 340; *City of South Omaha v. Taxpayers' League*, 42 Neb. 671.) And, although the title of "an act to amend" a certain other act is sufficient for the purpose indicated by that title, it does not indicate the purpose of engrafting by amendment upon that act provisions not germane to its original subject. (*City of Tecumseh v. Phillips*, 5 Neb. 305; *White v. City of Lincoln*, 5 Neb. 505; *Burlington & M. R. R. Co. v. Saunders County*, 9 Neb. 507; *Miller v. Hurford*, 11 Neb. 377; *State r. Pierce County*, 10 Neb. 476; *Trumble v. Trumble, supra*; *State r. Tibbets*, 52 Neb. 228.) Applying these tests to the act of 1887, the scope claimed for it, and perhaps indicated by its text, would make it operate as an amendment of section 371, as explained by sections 374, 375, and 376. It does not refer to, recite, or repeal any of those sections. Its title indicates only a purpose to amend section 118, which embraced only the subject of verifying pleadings. We cannot, without permitting a violation of the constitution, give it any broader effect as amended.

But it does not follow because the affidavit was irregular, and might have been quashed on motion for that purpose in the attachment suit, that the plaintiff in this case can avail himself of the defect. In *Oberfelder v. Kavanaugh*, 21 Neb. 483, this court laid down the following rule: "When an officer attaches property found in the possession of a stranger claiming title, in an action for such taking, the officer, in order to justify it, must not only prove that the attachment defendant was indebted to the attachment plaintiff, but that the attachment was regularly issued." Several times since has this language been repeated with approval; but in each case with regard to a substantial defect in the proof of the attachment, one that would not only lead to a reversal on petition in error by the attachment defendant, but one reaching to the very validity of the lien acquired or sought to be acquired. Thus in the leading case there was no proof of any affidavit. An attachment without an affidavit would be void. In *Williams v. Eikenberry*, 22 Neb. 210, and in *Paxton v. Moravek*, 31 Neb. 305, the writ of attachment itself was not offered in evidence. In *Williams v. Eikenberry*, 25 Neb. 721, the pendency of the action to which the attachment was ancillary was not proved. In *Bartlett v. Cheesebrough*, 32 Neb. 339, the debt was not proved. In *Spaulding v. Overmire*, 40 Neb. 21, there was no competent evidence of any of the proceedings. The court did not, in any of the cases, hold or intend that there could be no justification if some inconsequential irregularity was made to appear. On the contrary, the object is to establish an interest founded on a valid lien, and the proof is sufficient if this be shown. Irregularities not going to the existence and validity of the lien are not open to such a collateral attack. (*Scrivener v. Dietz*, 68 Cal. 1.) The provisions of our Code as to the competency of officers administering oaths to affiants are substantially declaratory of the common law, and both at the common law and under statutes like ours it is very generally held that the making of an affidavit before an attorney in the case, if he be an officer generally authorized to take affidavits, is an irregularity merely, which must be attacked at once by motion, or it will be waived; and that such an affidavit is not a nullity. (*Gilmore v. Hempstead*, 4 How. Pr. [N. Y.] 153; *Smith v. Ponath*, 17 Mo. App. 262; *Linck v. City of Litchfield*, 141 Ill. 469; *Swearingen v. Howser*, 37 Kan. 126; *Haward v. Nalder*, Barnes [Eng.] 60.) In *Wilkowski v. Halle*, 37 Ga. 678, an attachment was held void where the affidavit was made before one of the attorneys who was a notary, but in that state notaries not only take the affidavit, but they approve the bond and issue the writ. This attorney had done all three acts, and the reasoning of the court was entirely directed against permitting him to approve the bond and issue the writ. In *Owens v. Johns*, 59 Mo. 89, the clerk of the court was plaintiff and made the affidavit before his own deputy. This was held void. It was the same as if he had taken his own affidavit. In *Greenvault v. Farmers & Mechanics Bank*, 2 Doug. [Mich.] 498, the affidavit was taken before an officer not authorized to take any affidavits. As pointed out in *Swearingen v. Howser, supra*, there is a clear distinction between the administration of an oath by one not authorized to administer oaths, and the administration of an oath by one generally authorized, but forbidden to do so in a particular case. In the first case no power exists, and the act is a nullity; in the other the power exists, but it has been wrongfully exercised. We have found no cases other than the three commented upon which tend to support the theory that the affidavit was void. We are convinced that it was not and that it was properly received in evidence.

The defendant in his answer pleaded specially a justification under a writ of attachment sued out by the Continental National Bank. He also pleaded by general denial, and offered in evidence the attachment at the suit of the Western Manufacturing Company. It is argued that the court erred in receiving this evidence. It is admitted that the evidence would generally be relevant under a general denial, but it is asserted that the defendant having elected to plead specially, should be restricted to the special matter pleaded. *Westover v. Vandoran*, 29 Neb. 652, is cited as supporting that contention. In the case cited there was no general denial, and the question was as to the necessity of replying to the special matter pleaded. In *Williams v. Eikenberry*, 22 Neb. 210, it was held that the general denial and special plea of justification were not inconsistent, and that an election between them could not be required, although the special matter might be proved under the general denial. That case rules this. Although the special plea was here superfluous, it did not render irrelevant to the general denial matter which would have been relevant in the absence of the special plea.

There are a few other assignments of error, but they are not discussed in the briefs.

AFFIRMED.

WILLIAM MACK v. CHARLES PARKIESER.

FILED FEBRUARY 2, 1898.   No. 7809.

1. **New Trial:** OBJECTIONS TO INSTRUCTIONS. Objections to instructions must be specifically and separately assigned in a motion for a new trial.

2. **Instructions:** REVIEW. Instructions must be read and construed together, and if so considered they state the law applicable to the case and without confusion or conflict, a single paragraph is not erroneous for the reason that in and of itself it may be incomplete.

3. **Trial:** MOTION TO DIRECT VERDICT: WAIVER OF ERROR. If there is interposed for defendant at the close of the evidence in chief for the plaintiff a motion that the court instruct the jury to return a verdict for defendant and such motion is overruled, by the introduction of evidence for defendant in support of the defense error in the overruling of the motion, if any, is waived.

ERROR from the district court of Douglas county. Tried below before KEYSOR, J. *Affirmed.*

William A. Redick, for plaintiff in error.

C. P. Halligan, contra.

HARRISON, C. J.

This action was instituted by defendant in error in the district court of Douglas county to recover damages which he alleged had been suffered by him by reason of the breach of the covenants of a warranty deed executed and delivered to him by plaintiff in error in the conveyance of certain lands. Pleadings were filed by which issues were joined, and a trial thereof resulted in a verdict and judgment favorable to defendant in error. The cause is presented here by error proceeding on behalf of the unsuccessful party in the trial court.

One assignment of error to which attention is directed in the argument in the brief filed is that the court erred in giving paragraph numbered 5 of its charge to the jury. In the motion for a new trial the assignment in regard to error in giving instructions was as follows: "That the court erred in giving to the jury paragraphs numbered 1, 2, and 5 of the charge of the court on its own motion." This method of grouping in one assignment several numbered paragraphs, of the giving of each of which it is desired to assign error, has repeatedly been considered by this court, and it has been as often held that if any one of the group is unobjectionable the assignment will be no further examined. These portions of the charge were not all, if any, erroneous and the assignment is unavailing. No objection is urged against any except the one numbered 5; further than this, paragraph 5, when read in connection with other paragraphs of the charge, was not open to the complaint urged against it.

There is but one other question argued which it is stated was raised by the court's refusal at the close of the evidence introduced for defendant in error to instruct

38

the jury to return a verdict for the plaintiff in error.
This, it appears, was a verbal request or motion to the
effect just stated and which was refused by the court.
It is unnecessary to examine this question as, for the
plaintiff in error on the overruling of this motion, there
was offered and received evidence in support of his defense; and the error, if any, in overruling the motion was
thus waived.

This disposes of all the errors urged in the argument
here, and it follows that the judgment of the district
court must be

AFFIRMED.

NORVAL, J., not sitting.

P. L. JOHNSON, APPELLEE, V. MARGARET A. ENGLISH ET
AL., APPELLANTS.

FILED FEBRUARY 2, 1898.   No. 7812.

1. **Evidence:** DOCUMENTS: INDORSEMENTS: OFFER.   An offer and reception in evidence of a certificate of purchase at tax sale, if it have
an indorsement of an assignment thereon, do not include and
carry with them as evidence such assignment, unless the offer
and reception were sufficiently broad to and did include such indorsement.

2. ———: CONSTRUCTION OF STIPULATION.   Certain of the words employed in a stipulation of the parties examined and construed, and
held not to be an admission or statement that the original purchaser at tax sale was the assignor of the party asserting ownership of the certificate of purchase at tax sale by assignment
thereof to him by such purchaser, and not an admission or statement that such an assignment had been made.

APPEAL from the district court of Douglas county.
Heard below before FERGUSON, J. *Reversed.*

James P. English, for appellants.

Ralph W. Breckenridge, Saunders, Macfarland & Dickey,
and *George E. Pritchett, contra.*

HARRISON, C. J.

The appellee, P. L. Johnson, commenced this action in the district court of Douglas county to foreclose a tax lien against a lot in Hanscom Place addition to the city of Omaha. It was of the allegations of the petition that one E. B. Baer had on a stated date purchased the designated property at tax sale and received a certificate of such tax sale and that he subsequently paid certain taxes which were assessed against the property. It was also pleaded that the appellee Johnson became the owner of the tax sale certificate by purchase from E. B. Baer and its due assignment and transfer by the latter. Andrew J. Hanscom, who was of the parties defendants in the district court, answered, and among the matters pleaded set forth the execution and delivery to him and his ownership of a mortgage of the premises in controversy and prayed its foreclosure and establishment as a first lien on the property. The appellants answered, setting forth certain matters by reason of which it was asserted the claimed lien of appellee Johnson was of none effect and denied the assignment of the certificate to him and his ownership thereof. The trial resulted in the appellee Johnson being accorded a lien as claimed and it was allotted priority to that of Andrew J. Hanscom, of which there was a foreclosure decreed.

In this, an appeal to this court on behalf of the holders of the title to the lot involved in the suit, it is contended that there was no evidence that Johnson was the owner of the certificate of purchase at tax sale—that it was not shown to have been assigned to him. The fact of assignment of the certificate and Johnson's consequent ownership thereof was of the issues raised by the pleadings, and it devolved on him to produce the proof of such fact. The certificate of purchase at tax sale is a creature of the statute and the law by which it was created also prescribed the manner in which its sale or assignment might be evidenced. See sections 116 and 117 of article

1, chapter 77, Compiled Statutes, in the latter of which it
is stated: "The certificate of purchase shall be assignable
by indorsement, and the assignment thereof shall vest in
the assignee, or his legal representative, all the right and
title of the original purchaser; and the statement in the
treasurer's deed of the fact of the assignment shall
be presumptive evidence of such assignment." Whether
it may be sold and its transfer proved in a manner other
than provided in the statutory law we need not now discuss or determine. In this action a transfer by indorsement was alleged and relied on, and whether established
by proof is to be our inquiry.

It is of the findings of the court embodied in its decree
that "The court further finds that on or about the first
day of February, 1894, the said E. B. Baer sold, assigned.
and transferred the said tax certificates, together with
all his right, title, and interest therein and to the taxes
paid thereon, to P. L. Johnson, this plaintiff, who is now
the owner and holder thereof," etc., from which we
would be induced to expect the record to disclose the
evidential facts to warrant such conclusion. The bill
of exceptions does not purport to contain all the evidence introduced during the trial. All evidence of a
documentary character is, we presume, omitted therefrom. The following stipulation appears in said bill:
"In order to avoid incumbering the record by attaching
copies of the exhibits referred to in the bill of exceptions.
it is hereby stipulated by and between all of the parties
to this suit, that all the taxes and special assessments
set out and mentioned in the petition of the plaintiff
were duly, legally, and regularly assessed and levied.
and were valid liens upon the real estate set forth in the
petition, and that said taxes and special assessments
were paid by E. B. Baer, the party mentioned in the petition. As plaintiff assignor." The certificate was offered and received in evidence, and it was stated in argument that as the certificate is not contained in the bill of
exceptions. and the court has stated in its finding that

the certificate was duly assigned, it is fair to presume that the assignment from Baer to Johnson did appear indorsed thereon, but even if it did, this would not be sufficient, for the offer and reception of the certificate would not and did not carry with it and include the reception of the indorsement as substantive evidence of the assignment. To effect this it was necessary that the indorsement be identified, offered, and received in and of itself independently as testimony of the certificate. No offer or reception as testimony of the indorsed assignment, if it existed, was made or had during the trial and it was not of the evidence. See *Schroeder v. Neilson*, 39 Neb. 335, where, in an action on a promissory note by the indorsee or assignee thereof, the note was introduced with the indorsement thereon, but without any direct reference to or proof of the latter, it was stated in an opinion in an error proceeding to this court in regard to whether the introduction and proof of the indorsement were thus accomplished as follows: "The answer of Neilson denied Schroeder's ownership of the note. The note was drawn payable to the order of Ingolsbe & Co. It was indorsed 'Ingolsbe & Co., O. Ingolsbe.' There was no proof offered that the indorsement 'Ingolsbe & Co.' was made by that firm, a member thereof, or by anyone else. The note was offered and admitted in evidence, but that did not prove that the indorsement thereon was that of the payee." See also *Cummins v. Vandeventer*, 52 Neb. 478, an action for the foreclosure of a mechanic's lien, on the trial of which the original account and claim of lien with the indorsement of the county clerk of the filing thereof was offered and received in evidence without reference to or including in the offer and reception the filing as substantive testimony in and of itself. It was held that the offer and reception of the lien did not include and carry with it the indorsement. See to the same effect *Noll v. Kenneally*, 37 Neb. 879. It follows that the assignment was not shown and the right of Johnson to maintain the action did not appear, and the finding of the court on this point was without support in the evidence.

It is further argued in this connection that it is admitted in the stipulation, which we have quoted herein, that the assignment had been made. The stipulation, we gather from the record, was in type-writing to and including the words petition, after which there was a period; following this mark there was written in the stipulation with pen and ink the words, "as plaintiff assignor." The contention for appellee is that these words are used in the stipulation of Baer, the original owner of the certificate of tax sale, in a descriptive sense and indicative of the relation which he bore to Johnson, the appellee, and amount to an admission that he was plaintiff's assignor and assigned the certificate to appellee. This to us is a strained construction of the stipulation. Taking the words to which we have referred in the connection in which they were placed by the writer and reading them as it seems proper to, all things considered, they must be construed to mean and to refer to Baer as the party mentioned in the petition as the assignor of plaintiff, now the appellee Johnson. This being true, there is nothing in the record to show that Baer had assigned the certificate to Johnson or the latter's ownership of said instrument.

The decree of the district court to the extent it awarded appellee Johnson a lien and the foreclosure thereof must be reversed and the case remanded to the district court for further proceedings.

REVERSED AND REMANDED.

JOSEPH STOREY ET AL. V. MACHA M. BURNS.

FILED FEBRUARY 2, 1898.　No. 7821.

Proceedings in Equity: REVIEW. A review by petition in error of
the proceedings during the trial in the district court of an equity
cause cannot be obtained in this court if no motion for a new
trial was filed in the trial court; and in a case so presented here,
the record will be examined no further than to ascertain whether
the pleadings state a cause of action or defense and support the
judgment or decree.

ERROR from the district court of Adams county. Tried
below before BEALL, J. *Affirmed.*

Capps & Stevens, for plaintiff in error.

Batty, Dungan & Burton and *M. A. Hartigan, contra.*

HARRISON, C. J.

This action was commenced by the defendant in error
in the district court of Adams county December 29, 1893,
to procure the foreclosure of a real estate mortgage.
Issues were joined, and on June 23, 1894, as a result of a
trial, the defendant in error was awarded a decree.

The cause is presented to this court by petition in
error on behalf of the defendants in the district court.
There was no motion for a new trial filed for plaintiffs in
error in the trial court. It is the rule that to obtain a
review in this court by petition in error of the proceedings during the trial of such an action as this a motion for
a new trial must be made in the trial court as in a law
action. (*Carlow v. Aultman,* 28 Neb. 672; *Hansen v. Kinney,* 46 Neb. 207.) In an error proceeding to this court,
where it appears that no motion for a new trial was filed
in the district court, no further examination will be made
than to ascertain whether the pleadings state a cause of
action or defense and support the judgment or decree
rendered. (*Hansen v. Kinney, supra.*) The petition in the

present case states a cause of action and supports the decree. The latter must therefore be

AFFIRMED.

IOWA LOAN & TRUST COMPANY, APPELLEE, V. ROBERT C. STIMPSON ET AL., APPELLANTS.

FILED FEBRUARY 2, 1898. No. 7801.

1. **Executions: APPRAISEMENT: FRAUD.** If a sale of real estate under order of sale or execution is attacked on the ground of a fraudulent appraisement, no active fraud being claimed or attempted to be shown except in the low value placed on the property as compared with a value given in evidence adduced on the subject, to support the objection the discrepancy must be so great as in and of itself to raise a presumption of fraud in making the appraisement.

2. ———: ———: **NOTICE TO DEBTOR.** There is no requirement of the law that notice be given the debtor of the making of an appraisement.

APPEAL from the district court of Buffalo county. Heard below before SINCLAIR, J. *Affirmed.*

F. G. Hamer, for appellants.

Fred A. Nye, contra.

HARRISON, C. J.

In this, an action to foreclose a real estate mortgage, the proceedings were prosecuted to a decree and, after stay, a sale of the mortgaged premises, which was confirmed. From the order of confirmation an appeal to this court has been perfected.

In the brief filed for the appellant it is argued that the sale should not have been confirmed for the reasons: First, the appraisement of the property was so low as to raise the presumption of fraud; second, no notice was given the debtor of the appraisement of the property. In regard to the first of these reasons it appears from the record that it rests solely on the differences in value of the property which were placed on it by persons called for the purpose in the three appraisements which were had before a sale was made and in the testimony in affidavits of parties filed for appellant. The point argued is of a matter of which complaint must first be addressed and presented to the district court, or a judge thereof, and determined on the evidence adduced, and the resultant finding, as embodied in and shadowed by the decree or order, must govern and be allowed to prevail, unless manifestly wrong. After an examination of all the evidence herein we cannot disapprove the finding of the district court, cannot say that it was palpably wrong in the conclusion which it must have reached, that there was not such a great discrepancy between the appraisal value of the property and the values stated in the affidavits as to raise a presumption of fraud. This being true, there is nothing in this branch of the argument which calls for a reversal of the order of the district court.

In regard to the second stated reason it must be said that the appraisement was one of the steps prescribed by law to be taken by the officer conducting the sale and of the occurrence of which the statute does not require any notice to be given. It is a part of the proceedings of which parties must take notice. (*Smith v. Foxworthy*, 39 Neb. 214.) The argument that notice should be given the debtor of the time of the appraisement might with propriety be addressed to the legislature. Courts can but enforce the law as made, not read into it what may suggest itself as proper or probably beneficial. It follows that the order of the district court must be

ＡＦＦＩＲＭＥＤ.

NORTHWESTERN MUTUAL LIFE INSURANCE COMPANY, AP-
PELLEE, V. JOHN MULVIHILL ET AL., APPELLANTS.

FILED FEBRUARY 2, 1898. No. 7785.

1. **Foreclosure of Mortgage:** MASTER COMMISSIONER. Power is conferred on the district court in section 852 of the Code of Civil Procedure to authorize in a decree of foreclosure of a mortgage
against real estate some person to execute the decree to the extent it orders a sale of the real property, and such person is referred to in sections 451, 452, and 453 of the Code as a "master
commissioner."

2. ——: ——: POWERS. Sections 451, 452, and 453 of the Code, section 852, and the sections in relation to sales of real estate under
levy of an execution are to be read and construed connectedly,
and when this is done power is conferred thereby on the person
designated by the court in a decree of foreclosure of a real estate
mortgage to make the sale, to conduct the same in the manner
prescribed in the Code for making sales under levy of execution,
including that of administering the oath to the parties called to
make the appraisement of the property.

3. ——: ——: OATH. There is no requirement of statute that the
person designated by the court in its decree of foreclosure of a
mortgage on real estate to make the sale be sworn or take, subscribe, and file an oath.

4. ——: ——: ——. Where such person is acting or has acted
and the appraisement or the sale is attacked by motion to set
aside, if that an oath had been taken, or taken and subscribed,
was an essential requirement, on hearing, it must be presumed
in the absence of a showing to the contrary that there had been
a compliance with the requirement.

5. ——: ——: ——. Semble. A district court should in the decree by which it authorizes the person to make a sale of real
estate under mortgage foreclosure also require that such person
take, or take and subscribe, an oath and also give a bond for the
true performance of the assigned duty. (*Omaha Loan & Trust Co.
v. Bertrand*, 51 Neb. 508.)

6. ——: APPRAISEMENT. The evidence introduced on the point of
objection to a sale of real estate under decree of foreclosure of a
mortgage, that the value fixed in the appraisement was too low,
held sufficient to sustain a finding of the district court of a tenor
contrary to that of the objection.

APPEAL from the district court of Douglas county.
Heard below before KEYSOR, J. *Affirmed.*

Gregory, Day & Day, for appellants.

Wharton & Baird, G. W. Shields, J. W. West, Frank Heller, Silas Cobb, Montgomery & Hall, Guy R. C. Read, John W. Lytle, and *Frank T. Ransom, contra.*

HARRISON, C. J.

In this, an action commenced in the district court of Douglas county to foreclose a mortgage on real estate, a decree of foreclosure was entered in which was included the appointment of a special master commissioner to execute the portion of the decree in reference to a sale of the property. A stay was effected by request filed; at its expiration order of sale issued and the master commissioner proceeded with the preliminaries attendant as prescribed by law on all sales of the character of this one. As one of the steps an appraisement was made which, on motion of the appellants herein, was set aside. A second appraisement was then made, to which objections were filed, presented, and, on hearing, overruled, and the sale was proceeded with to a completion. A return of the sale was made, and on motion for confirmation and hearing on objections to the sale the sale was confirmed; from which order this appeal was taken.

The points urged in argument are, first, that the master commissioner never qualified, did not take or subscribe an oath in the proceedings; second, that the appraisers were never sworn to make appraisement as required by law, in that the oath was administered to them by the acting special master commissioner, who had never qualified by taking the oath of office and was not authorized in any manner to administer an oath to the appraisers; third, that all proceedings had herein and acts committed or done by the acting special master commissioner were without force or effect and not binding in law upon the appellants; fourth, that the valuation given the property in the appraisement was so much lower than its true value that the appraisement and sale should have been set aside.

It may be said that the third point, as stated in the brief of appellants, but embodies the conclusion or the result of the establishment of the point designated "First," and will need no separate discussion. A question which arises under the first point urged is, was the person appointed by the court in its decree to make the sale required to take and subscribe an oath? It is claimed in argument that he was "an especially appointed officer" within the meaning of section 1, chapter 10, Compiled Statutes 1897, in which it is stated: "All state, district, county, precinct, township, municipal, and especially appointed officers, except those mentioned in section 1, article 14, of the constitution, shall before entering upon their respective duties, take and subscribe the following oath, which shall be indorsed upon their respective bonds. * * * If any such officer is not required to give bond, the oath shall be filed in the office of the secretary of state, or of the clerk of the county, city, village, or other municipal subdivision of which he shall be an officer." It seems from a reading of the provisions of this section, including that which prescribes where the oath shall be filed, that it refers to state, district, county, precinct, township, or municipal officers either elected or appointed and not to a person who has by the decree of a court been appointed to make a sale provided for in the decree and for no other purpose. Such a person cannot be called an officer in a proper sense or use of the term. The person designated by the decree to execute it to the extent it directed a sale was not an elected or appointed officer of the state or any subdivision enumerated in the section and was not by reason of its existence required to take, subscribe, and file an oath therein set forth. The authority of the court to appoint a party to make a sale in an action of foreclosure of a real estate mortgage is conferred by section 852 of the Code of Civil Procedure, which is as follows: "All sales of mortgaged premises under a decree in chancery shall be made by a sheriff, or some other person authorized by the court in the county where the premises or some part of them are situated, and in all cases where the sheriff shall make such sale he shall act in his official capacity and he shall be liable on his official bond for all his acts therein, and shall receive the same compensation as is provided for by law for like services upon sales under speculation [execution]." There is no requirement in the section just quoted that the one designated by the court to make the sale shall be sworn, nor is there any provision of our statutory law in which such requirement appears; and we conclude he may act without being sworn. (To the same effect see *Omaha Loan & Trust Co. v. Bertrand*, 51 Neb. 508.) Whether the court might not, in its decree by which authority is given the party to act, also demand of him to take, subscribe, and file an oath and further to give bond conditioned for the faithful performance of the duties assigned him, it would seem in all good reason should be answered affirmatively. It has been held by this court that an officer, a moderator of a school district, may hold the office and perform the duties thereof without being sworn, the office being one established by law and there being no provision of statute that an oath be taken by such officer. (See *Franz v. Young*, 30 Neb. 360. See also *Laird v. Leap*, 42 Neb. 834; 16 Am. & Eng. Ency. Law 1021, note 3; *Commonwealth v. Cushing*, 99 Mass. 592; *Commonwealth v. Dugan*, 53 Mass. 233; *McAlister v. Commonwealth*, 6 Bush [Ky.] 581.) There is another reason why this point in the argument must be determined adversely to the contention of counsel for appellants on the subject of whether the party who made the sale had been sworn. There was no showing, other than a certificate of the clerk of the district court, that "no oath of special master commissioner has been filed in above entitled case." This is attached to the bill of exceptions, but was not made a part of it, and it but established that no oath of the party referred

to had been filed in the case, and not that he had not
taken the oath; and if the law had required it, in the absence of a showing to the contrary, the presumption
would prevail that the party designated in the decree to
make the sale and acting, or who had acted, had been
duly qualified.   (16 Am. & Eng. Ency. Law 1021, note 3;
Nelson v. People, 23 N. Y. 293; *Dayton v. Johnson*, 69 N. Y.
419.)

The second point argued, and to which we have hereinbefore specifically alluded, is to the effect that the
appraisement was void for that the appraisers had not
been sworn.   The basis of this is that the party assigned
in the decree to make the sale was not authorized to
administer an oath, and if he would have been so empowered had he prior to the appraisement taken an oath, he
had not done so and the attempt by him to administer
the oath to the appraisers was without force or effect.
It is said in the brief: "He can only act within the spirit
and letter of the statute;   unless he is authorized to
administer an oath, the attempt to qualify freeholders
by him, without an oath, renders such an appraisement
absolutely void, and we have this anomaly of the present proceedings: an officer of the statute performing a
high judicial office, without the solemnity of an oath, and
undertaking to perform the function of a judicial officer
in administering an oath, when he has not been qualified
by taking the oath upon his own part."   In section 852
of the Code of Civil Procedure, which we have hereinbefore quoted, the power is conferred on the court to
designate the party who shall make the sale.   Sections
451, 452, and 453 provide as follows:

"Sec. 451. Real property may be conveyed by master
commissioners as hereinafter provided: First—When by
an order or judgment in an action or proceeding, a party
is ordered to convey such property to another, and he
shall neglect or refuse to comply with such order or
judgment.   Second—When specific real property is required to be sold under an order or judgment of the
court.

"Sec. 452. A sheriff may act as a master commissioner under the second subdivision of the preceding section. Sales made under the same shall conform in all respects to the laws regulating sales of land upon execution.

"Sec. 453. The deed of a master commissioner shall contain the like recital, and shall be executed, acknowledged, and recorded as the deed of a sheriff, of real property sold under execution."

In the opinion in the case of *State v. Holliday*, 35 Neb. 327, these three sections of the Code and section 852 were quoted, and it was in effect held that each and all of the sections refer to the same person who is denominated in sections 451-453 as a master commissioner, but is not so named in 852 or given any appellation other than a general one of person. In *McKeighan v. Hopkins*, 14 Neb. 361, sections 451 and 452 were quoted and construed in connection with sections 491a-491d and 495 of the Code relative to appraisements and sale of real estate under writ process or order of court, and it was said: "These provisions apply to all sales of real estate under the process of the court, whether upon execution or order of sale." It seems clear from a perusal of all the sections of the Code that they should be read and construed connectedly, as we have seen has been done; and if so, it is further evident that the person authorized by the court to make the sale is to proceed therein as stated in the manners indicated in the sections of the Code to a number of which in relation to the particular subject we have herein more or less directly referred. In one of them, 491a, it is stated: "Whenever, hereafter, execution shall be levied on any lands and tenements, the officer levying the same shall call an inquest of two disinterested freeholders, who shall be residents of the county where the lands taken on execution are situated, and administer to them an oath impartially to appraise the interest of the person, or persons, or corporation against whom the execution is levied, in the property so levied upon." This confers the power to administer the oath to the appraisers, and, by force of the sections connectedly, on the person who makes the sale by authorization of the court; nor is this an unheard-of anomaly (if such it may truly be called), or one which stands alone in our statutory law. Of the legislative enactments, in regard to elections, in sections 15 and 16, chapter 26, Compiled Statutes, it is provided:

"Sec. 15. Previous to any vote being taken, the judges and clerks of election shall severally take an oath or affirmation according to the form prescribed in chapter on official bonds.

"Sec. 16. In case there shall be no judge or justice of the peace present at the opening of the polls, it shall be lawful for the judges of election to administer the oath or affirmation to each other and the clerks of election; and the person administering such oath or affirmation shall cause an entry thereof to be made and subscribed by him, and prefix to each poll book."

Here oaths are required to be administered by persons who have not been sworn. We must conclude that the party who was designated in the decree to make the sale could administer the oath to the parties called as appraisers.

In relation to the further objection that the value of the property sold, fixed by the appraisers, was too low, and so much so that it furnishes a sufficient reason for setting the sale aside, it must be said that this was a question submitted to the trial court on evidence adduced on behalf of the parties appellants and appellee; and after examination of the evidence, in which there was, as is usual in such cases, quite a considerable difference of opinion, we cannot say that the finding of the district court thereon was manifestly wrong. There was ample evidence to support the finding, hence it will not be disturbed. The order of the district court is

AFFIRMED.

AULTMAN, MILLER AND COMPANY, APPELLANT, V. ALFRED   53 545|
L. BISHOP ET AL., APPELLEES.   57 746|

FILED FEBRUARY 2, 1898.   No. 7730.

1. **Subrogation.** "The doctrine of subrogation is not administered
by courts of equity as a legal right, but the principle is applied
to subserve the ends of justice and to do equity in the particular
case under consideration. It does not rest on contract, and no
general rule can be laid down which will afford a test in all
cases for its application. Whether the doctrine is applicable to
any particular case depends upon the peculiar facts and circumstances of such case." *South Omaha Nat. Bank v. Wright*, 45 Neb.
23, and *Rice v. Winters*, 45 Neb. 517, followed.

2. ———: PARTIES. The party to whom the debt of another has been
paid, the payment of which furnishes the basis of the claim for
subrogation, is a proper and necessary party to the action for
subrogation.

3. ———: MORTGAGES: ATTACHMENT. One Bishop, engaged in business, gave a mortgage on his stock in trade and other personal
property to D., W. & Co. A., M. & Co., to whom Bishop was indebted, very soon afterward began an action against him in which
it procured a writ of attachment to issue and its levy on the
stock in trade and personal belongings of the tradesman. D., W.
& Co., predicating its right and title to the property on the mortgage by Bishop to it, commenced an action in a court of Iowa
wherein it alleged the conversion of the property by A., M. & Co.
The plaintiff recovered a judgment for the value of the property,
such value being fixed by the verdict. The judgment was paid by
A., M. & Co. One of the grounds for attachment in the suit in
this state was the alleged fraudulent transfer or disposal of the
property by Bishop, the mortgages to D., W. & Co. furnishing the
basis for said allegation. A motion was filed to discharge the
attachment, which, on hearing, was overruled, and subsequent to
the judgment rendered against it in Iowa, A., M. & Co. prosecuted the suit and attachment in this state to final judgment.
After payment of the judgment rendered by the Iowa court, A.,
M. & Co. instituted this action in the same court in which it had
its judgment and order to sell the property under attachment.
The object sought in this action was its subrogation to the rights
of D., W. & Co. under the mortgages under which the last mentioned company had asserted and been accorded rights in the
suit in Iowa. *Held*, That the subrogation was properly allowable
as to the right to subject the property to the payment of the sum
which A., M. & Co. had paid to extinguish the Iowa judgment, but
not to receive a deficiency judgment against Bishop or enforce

39

payment by him personally of any balance of such amount remaining after the application of the proceeds of the property to the payment thereof.

APPEAL from the district court of Hamilton county. Heard below before WHEELER, J. *Affirmed.*

Hainer & Smith, for appellant.

Howard M. Kellogg, contra.

HARRISON, C. J.

The plaintiff in its petition filed in this action in the district court of Hamilton county pleaded that Alfred L. Bishop, of defendants, was for two years prior to November 24, 1890, engaged in business in the city of Aurora, in this state, selling at retail agricultural implements, musical instruments, sewing machines, buggies and wagons, etc., and that on the said date he was indebted to plaintiff in sums aggregating about $1,600 for purchases of it of certain portions of the articles which he had in stock for sale; that Deere, Wells & Co., of Council Bluffs, Iowa, did business in this state, and under the same firm name and style and on the 17th of December, 1890, the defendant Bishop executed and delivered to Deere, Wells & Co. two chattel mortgages, each, according to its words and figures, being for the purpose of securing the payment to the designated mortgagee the total sum of $13,115.22 in stated sums and at fixed dates. In one of the mortgages as the property thereby subjected to a lien there was described specifically the articles which the mortgagor then had, as a dealer, for sale and in the other certain enumerated stock of the horse kind. It was also alleged that on December 26, 1890, the plaintiff instituted an action in the district court of Hamilton county against said Bishop to recover an alleged balance then its due from him in the sum of $1,673.44, and at the same time filed in said action its affidavit in attachment, stating therein, among other things, that the defendant had made a fraudulent disposition of his property; that plaintiff procured a writ of attachment to issue and to be levied on certain property, which was that included and described in the mortgages to Deere, Wells & Co.; and that on March 27, 1893, during the pendency of a term of the said district court, on a full hearing of the cause on its merits, Bishop was adjudged indebted to plaintiff in the sum of $1,031.90 and the attached property was ordered to be sold and the proceeds applied in satisfaction of the judgment; that said judgment is still in full force and effect; that no appeal has been taken therefrom and no part has been collected or paid.   It was further averred that during the year 1891, Deere, Wells & Co. commenced an action against plaintiff in a district court of Iowa to recover of and from the plaintiff the value of the property which had been taken for plaintiff under the writ of attachment in this state in its action against Bishop; that Deere, Wells & Co. claimed ownership of the property under and by virtue of the two chattel mortgages executed and delivered to it by Bishop; that issues were joined in the action in the Iowa court and a trial had which resulted in a judgment in favor of Deere, Wells & Co. in the sum of $3,500, which the plaintiff of the present action afterwards paid in full, together with the costs, $155.46; and that Deere, Wells & Co. had received the amount of the judgment from the clerk of the court, to whom it was paid by the plaintiff herein; that Alfred L. Bishop attended at the trial of the cause in Iowa and was a witness therein on behalf of Deere, Wells & Co., "and aided, abetted, and assisted Deere, Wells & Co. in obtaining the said judgment." The prayer of the petition was as follows: "Wherefore plaintiff prays that it may be ordered, adjudged, and decreed by this court that plaintiff by operation of law succeeded to all the rights of the defendant Deere, Wells & Co. under and by virtue of the terms of said chattel mortgages as to all of such property that said Deere, Wells & Co. procured the value of in the action of conversion tried in said district court of Pottawattamie county, and that plaintiff be subrogated to each and all of the rights of said Deere, Wells & Co. and be permitted and allowed to foreclose said chattel mortgages so far as relates to the property which was taken into consideration upon the trial of said action of conversion; that said defendants, and each of them, may be barred and foreclosed of all equity of redemption and other interest in or to said mortgaged property; that an account may be taken of the property now in the hands of the sheriff and being held under and by virtue of the order of attachment issued in the cause pending in this court, and that said property may be sold according to law and out of the proceeds thereof the plaintiff be allowed a credit upon the amount he paid to said Deere, Wells & Co. upon the judgment aforesaid, and that defendant Alfred L. Bishop be adjudged to pay any deficiency which may remain after applying the proceeds of said sale toward the payment of the amount of said judgment, together with interest and costs; that it further be ordered that the sheriff of this county sell said property under the order of this court in this cause; that the property be released from the order made in the case wherein the plaintiff was plaintiff and the defendant Alfred L. Bishop was defendant and heretofore tried in this court, and that an order releasing said property from the attachment proceedings as heretofore alleged be made without prejudice to any right of plaintiff to enforce said judgment for the full amount thereof and to the same extent as if no order had been made for the sale of the attached property, and for such other, further, or different relief as may be just and equitable in the premises."

To this petition for Alfred L. Bishop there was the following answer: "The defendant Alfred L. Bishop, for answer to the petition of the plaintiff herein, admits that he was in business in Aurora, Nebraska, prior to November 24, 1890, as alleged; admits the bringing of a suit against him by plaintiff, the issuance and service of an attachment therein, the seizure of goods thereon, and the rendition of final judgment in this court in said action as alleged. He admits that Deere, Wells & Co. commenced an action against this plaintiff in Pottawattamie county, Iowa, and that he testified as a witness in said action, and that the judgment rendered therein has been paid by the plaintiff. He alleges that in the action brought against him in this court by the plaintiff, the pleadings, record, and proceedings in which are made a part of the petition herein, he filed a motion and affidavit for the discharge of the attachment theretofore issued; that a full hearing was given thereon, upon both affidavits and oral testimony; that to sustain the attachment and the allegation in their affidavit, as a ground therefor, that this defendant had disposed of his property with intent to defraud his creditors, the plaintiff claimed, and introduced evidence to prove, that the mortgages now set out in the plaintiff's petition were fraudulent both in fact and law; that said claim was controverted by this defendant; that a full hearing was had upon said question, the same was argued to the court by counsel; that this court expressly found and decided in said proceedings that said mortgages, set up in plaintiff's petition, were in law, though not in fact, fraudulent and void as against the other creditors of this defendant; that the lien of the plaintiff's attachment was superior to the lien of said mortgages, and upon that ground the court sustained said attachment and, on final judgment being given in said case, ordered the attached property sold for the payment of the same, from which judgment and order no appeal or proceedings in error were prosecuted by either party. Wherefore this defendant submits to the court that both plaintiff and this defendant, parties to said action, are bound and concluded by said finding and decision of this court therein, that the plaintiff is barred and estopped from claiming that the mortgages set out in the petition constitute any lien upon, or give any claim whatever to, the goods conveyed by the attachment and described in

the petition herein; that, as between the plaintiff and
this defendant, all questions as to the ownership of the
property seized under said attachment, and all questions
as to the priority of right as between said mortgage and
attachment liens has been fully adjudged and finally settled by the order of this court in said action. This defendant therefore prays that the plaintiff's petition be
dismissed at its costs, and for such other or different relief as may be equitable in the premises."

To this answer the plaintiff filed a general demurrer.
For Deere, Wells & Co. there was filed a general demurrer to the petition. On hearings the demurrer of
Deere, Wells & Co. to the petition was overruled and
that of plaintiff to Bishop's answer was sustained. Subsequently a stipulation was entered into between the
plaintiff and Bishop and filed which was as follows: "It
is hereby stipulated and agreed, by and between the parties to the above entitled cause, that the plaintiff shall
take into its possession the property now held by the
sheriff of Hamilton county, Nebraska, under and by virtue of a writ of attachment issued in a certain cause heretofore pending in this court, wherein the plaintiff herein
was plaintiff, and the defendant herein, Alfred L. Bishop,
was defendant; that said plaintiff shall be required to
account for the sum of $1,450 in lieu of said property, and
that the making and entering into this stipulation shall
in nowise or manner abridge or affect any of the rights
of either of the parties to this action, and that any judgment or order made in this cause shall operate upon said
amount, and that the plaintiff shall be required to apply
said amount as may be finally adjudged in said cause, in
the same manner and to the same extent as any such
judgment or order might be made as against said property."

Deere, Wells & Co. elected to stand on their demurrer
and Bishop to stand on his answer and to plead no further; and on final submission of the cause the court adjudged that the plaintiff be subrogated to the rights of

Deere, Wells & Co. in and to the property taken under the writ of attachment in the former case of plaintiff against Bishop; that the property be released from the lien and levy of the attachment; and it was further stated in the judgment as follows: "The parties to this action having stipulated in writing, which stipulation is on file in this cause, that said property was of the value of $1,450 and that the same has been turned over to the plaintiff, it is ordered that said plaintiff make no further account for said property. Plaintiff then moved the court for judgment, and the award of execution for any deficiency yet remaining after applying said $1,450 upon the amount of said judgment for $3,500, together with its interest to this date, which motion the court overruled, and refuses to require said defendant Alfred L. Bishop to make further accounting, or be liable for the amount paid to said Deere, Wells & Co. other than the payment of said $1,450."

It is insisted that as to Deere, Wells & Co. the petition did not state a cause of action, hence it was an error to overrule its demurrer thereto. The contention on this point is to the effect that Deere, Wells & Co. was not further interested in the matter and was neither a proper nor necessary party to the action. Creditors to whos' rights a party seeks to be subrogated are necessary parties to an action to obtain such subrogation. (*Harris r. Watson*, 20 S. W. Rep. [Ark.] 529; *Bond v. Montgomery*, 20 S. W. Rep. [Ark.] 525; *Kyner v. Kyner*, 6 Watts [Pa.] 227.)

Coming now to the main question raised and argued, viz., Was the appellant entitled to be subrogated to the rights of Deere, Wells & Co. under its mortgages as against Bishop, the mortgagee, and if so, to what extent? we will call attention to this: That it arises under a demurrer to the answer in which it is claimed that the appellant's attachment in an action in the same court in which this was instituted, and in which all parties in this were also parties, was adjudicated to be the superior lien;

that the mortgages by Bishop to Deere, Wells & Co. were, as to creditors of whom appellant was one, fraudulent and void; that having obtained such an adjudication the appellant cannot now assert to the contrary and enforce the mortgages. Whatever adjudication, if any, of the question of the liens on the property of the appellant's attachment and the mortgages of Deere, Wells & Co. prior to the trial of the action of conversion in the court in Iowa of the rights of the same parties, it being that taken under appellant's attachment and also mortgaged to Deere, Wells & Co., was, on the hearing of a motion to dissolve the attachment, overruled and there was no final order or judgment in the original action in this state until a date subsequent to the judgment rendered in the Iowa court. Appellant obtained a final judgment in the original action here prior to payment of the judgment in Iowa. The judgment in the original action in this state did not affect the question of the validity of the mortgages as between the immediate parties to them, the mortgagor and mortgagee; as between them they were not adjudged void or in any manner or degree disturbed or touched by the adjudication.

The right of subrogation is a creation of equity and independent of any contractual relations between the parties. (*Memphis & L. R. Co. v. Dow*, 120 U. S. 287, 7 Sup. Ct. Rep. 482.)

In *Ætna Life Ins. Co. v. Town of Middleport*, 8 Sup. Ct. Rep. 625, it was said: "The doctrine of subrogation in equity requires (1) that the person seeking its benefit must have paid a debt due to a third party before he can be substituted to that party's rights; and (2) that in doing this he must not act as a mere volunteer, but on compulsion, to save himself from loss by reason of a superior lien or claim on the part of the person to whom he pays the debt, as in cases of sureties, prior mortgagees, etc. The right is never accorded in equity to one who is a mere volunteer in paying a debt of one person to another."

In the case of *South Omaha Nat. Bank v. Wright*, 45 Neb.

23, this court said: "The doctrine of subrogation is not administered by courts of equity as a legal right, but the principle is applied to subserve the ends of justice and to do equity in the particular case under consideration. It does not rest on contract, and no general rule can be laid down which will afford a test in all cases for its application. Whether the doctrine is applicable in any particular case depends upon the peculiar facts and circumstances of such case." See also *Rice v. Winters,* 45 Neb. 517, where the doctrine announced in *Bank v. Wright* was followed, and it was further stated: "A person seeking the benefit of subrogation must have paid a debt due to a third party before he can be substituted to that party's right; and in doing this he must not act as a mere volunteer, but on compulsion to save himself from loss by reason of a superior lien or claim on the part of the person to whom he pays the debt. The right of subrogation is never accorded in equity to one who is a mere volunteer in paying a debt of one person to another."

We think that by the adjudication in the Iowa court in the action of conversion (it must be borne in mind that this occurred prior to any final order or adjudication in the court in this state of the respective rights of the litigants, the appellant and Deere, Wells & Co.) the appellant became entitled to the right and title of Deere, Wells & Co. by virtue of its mortgages to the property; this for the reason that in order to maintain its possession of the property it had been compelled to pay its value to Deere, Wells & Co. Bishop had transferred the property to Deere, Wells & Co. and was not further interested than that its value, its proceeds, should be applied in the extinguishment partially or wholly of his indebtedness to Deere, Wells & Co. The last mentioned party received its value, and to the appellant it seems but fair to accord the continued possession of the goods, and such right or title as it had, by paying the Iowa judgment paid a consideration for to Deere, Wells & Co.,—this was the right to the value or proceeds of the property. (See

Adler v. Lang, 28 Mo. App. 440.) The matters litigated in
the Iowa action were the right to the possession of the
property and its value, by being adjudged to pay its
value to Deere, Wells & Co., and complying therewith
appellant but became entitled to enforce the mortgages
under which Deere, Wells & Co. had recovered, and this
only against the property and to apply its proceeds to the
payment of the amount which it had paid to Deere, Wells
& Co. It had the property under its attachment, and by
reason of such possession it was summoned to the Iowa
court and there participated in a trial in which it was
declared to be a wrong-doer and to make restitution to
the party wronged. The value of the property was a
matter directly in issue and, presumably after a full presentation, was fixed by the judgment of the court as between the two litigant companies. The property of
Bishop was in effect applied at a determined valuation
on his indebtedness to Deere, Wells & Co. The appellant
became entitled by payment of the judgment to proceed
against the thing involved as the bone of contention—
the property; and to exhaust it in his repayment of the
amount it had been forced to pay. Bishop could not
and cannot complain, for it is but a payment of the
debt which, by the execution and delivery of the mortgages, he said it should be taken to pay, in case of his failure or default in satisfying the same; but to allow the appellant to apply the property on the amount it paid to
Deere, Wells & Co., the judgment of the Iowa court, and
in a sum less than the value fixed by such judgment, and
to recover from Bishop any sum a balance of the amount
it paid, would be to take Bishop's property and to pay his
debt with it in a stated sum and further require that he
pay again a portion of the same debt. We are satisfied
that appellant could claim and be accorded subrogation
to the extent the property would satisfy the amount it
paid Deere, Wells & Co., but not to enforce any part
of it as a personal claim against Bishop. Bishop was
not a party to the case in the Iowa court and could not

be and was not bound by any portion of the adjudication there, and might be heard to complain of the valuation placed on the property if so disposed; nor did the fact, as pleaded in the petition, that he was in attendance there at the trial as a witness, coupled with the further statement of the conclusion that he aided, abetted, and assisted Deere, Wells ·& Co. in obtaining the judgment, present any matter which can avail to bind him. (See *Schribar v. Platt*, 19 Neb. 625.)

It is argued for appellees that a long time elapsed between the date of the payment of the Iowa judgment by appellant and the time of this action, and the property was of such a character that it had greatly depreciated in value; hence it would be unfair to Bishop to have it applied at the depreciated valuation and he be compelled to pay the balance. This cannot be considered, for the reason that it is not of the pleadings and, consequently, has no place in the case. It is true that the parties stipulated that the appellant should be required to account for the sum of $1,450 in lieu of said property, but it was also of the stipulation that it should in nowise or manner abridge or affect any of the rights of either of the parties to the action, and no argument is made that it did so affect or change any of the rights of the parties, and we will leave it where the parties themselves have been content to leave it, with no particular comment on or discussion of it or its effect.

It follows from what has been said herein that the judgment of the district court was correct and will in all things be

AFFIRMED.

STATE OF NEBRASKA, EX REL. DOUGLAS COUNTY, V. JOHN
F. CORNELL, AUDITOR OF PUBLIC ACCOUNTS.

FILED FEBRUARY 2, 1898. No. 9812.

1. **Taxation:** PURPOSES: STATUTES. The legislature may authorize taxation for a public purpose, but a tax imposed for an object in its nature essentially or strictly private is invalid.

2. **Constitutional Law:** PUBLIC PURPOSE. It is for the legislature in the first instance to decide what is and what is not a public purpose, but its determination of the question is not conclusive upon the courts.

3. **Taxation:** VALIDITY OF STATUTE. A tax law will not be declared invalid on the ground that the tax is not for the benefit of the public, unless it was imposed for the furtherance of an object or enterprise in which the public has palpably no interest.

4. ———: ———: INTERSTATE EXPOSITIONS: COUNTY BONDS. Chapter 24, Laws 1897, authorizing counties to participate in interstate expositions, to issue bonds for such purpose, and to provide for the levy of a tax for their payment, does not contravene the constitution on the ground that the object of the statute is to advance individual interest merely and not to promote the public welfare.

5. ———: ———: ———: ———: PROCEEDS. An appropriation of the money arising from the sale of the bonds issued under said act for the erection of suitable buildings, and maintaining the same, and a county exhibit at the Trans-Mississippi and International Exposition to be held in the city of Omaha in 1898, is for a public purpose or use, and not in violation of the constitution.

6. **Statutes:** CONFLICT: CONSTRUCTION. It is a well settled rule of construction that special provisions in a law relating to particular subject-matter will prevail over general provisions in other statutes so far as there is a conflict.

7. **Counties:** BONDS: INTERSTATE EXPOSITION. An affirmative vote of two-thirds of all of those cast on the proposition is sufficient to carry county bonds issued under chapter 24, Session Laws 1897, for the purpose of making a county exhibit at an interstate exposition.

ORIGINAL application for a writ of mandamus to compel the auditor of public accounts to register bonds issued by relator for the purpose of raising funds for an exhibit at the Trans-Mississippi and International Exposition. *Writ allowed.*

Howard H. Baldrige, H. L. Day, and *Montgomery & Hall,* for relator.

C. J. Smyth, Attorney General, and *Ed P. Smith, Deputy Attorney General, contra.*

NORVAL, J.

This was an original application to this court for a peremptory writ of mandamus, on the relation of Douglas county, to compel the respondent, as auditor of public accounts, to register in his office 100 certain coupon bonds of said county, aggregating $100,000, voted for the purpose of raising money to enable it to participate in the Trans-Mississippi and International Exposition to be held in the city of Omaha during the year 1898. In 1897 the legislature of this state passed an act entitled "An act to authorize counties to participate in interstate expositions, to issue bonds for such purpose, and to provide for a tax for the payment of such bonds." (Session Laws 1897, p. 192, ch. 24.) The first three sections of said law are here reproduced:

"Section 1. Whenever one thousand (1,000) voters of any county in the state of Nebraska having over one hundred thousand population shall petition the board of county commissioners or the board of supervisors to that end, any such county shall be and hereby is authorized to issue the bonds of such county, to become due twenty (20) years from the date thereof, and to bear interest at the rate not to exceed five (5) per cent per annum, to provide for the expenses of promoting the interests of such county by participating in any interstate exposition held in the state of Nebraska and making at such exposition a county exhibit, improving or beautifying the grounds, and erecting or aiding in the erection of a suitable building or buildings therefor, and maintaining the same during such exposition, to an amount to be determined by the board of county commissioners or board of supervisors, not exceeding one hundred thousand dollars

($100,000); *Provided*, The board of county commissioners or board of supervisors shall first submit the question of the issuing of such bonds to a vote of the legal voters of such county at a general or special election, such question to be submitted entire after notice to such voters published in any newspaper of general circulation in such county for four (4) weeks next prior to such election; and *Provided*, That such interstate exposition shall first have been recognized by the congress of the United States by an appropriation of a sum not less than one hundred thousand dollars ($100,000).

"Sec. 2. The proposition when submitted shall contain a statement of the amount necessary to be raised each year for the payment of the interest of said bonds and for the payment of the principal thereof at maturity.

"Sec.. 3. If two-thirds ($\frac{2}{3}$) of the votes cast on such proposition at any such election be in favor thereof, the said bonds shall be authorized and the proper officers of the county shall thereupon issue said bonds and the same shall be and continue a subsisting debt against such county until they are paid."

Section 4 of said act provides for the levying of a sufficient tax by the proper county officers upon all of the taxable property of the county to pay the principal and interest upon said bonds as the same become due and payable.

The relation shows that the proposition to issue the bonds in question was submitted to the electors of the county, and the same was adopted by them in strict conformity to the provisions of the said legislative enactment. The respondent has declined to register the bonds for the reason their legality is questioned; but he has not, by answer or otherwise, advised the court of the particular grounds upon which their validity is assailed, nor has he submitted any authorities in opposition to the issuance of the writ. Counsel for relator, in the briefs and at the bar, have argued two propositions, to which attention will be given, namely: First—

Whether the bonds were voted for a lawful object or purpose. Second—Did the proposition to issue them receive the requisite affirmative vote of the electors of the county?

The following principles are too well established by the authorities to require discussion at this time:

First—The legislature may authorize taxation for a public purpose, but a tax imposed for an object in its nature essentially private is void. (1 Dillon, Municipal Corporations sec. 508; Cooley, Taxation [2d ed.] 55, 103; 25 Am. & Eng. Ency. Law 87, and the numerous cases cited in note 2 on said page.)

Second—It is for the legislature in the first instance to decide whether the object for which a tax is to be used or raised is a public purpose, but its determination of the question is not conclusive. (*Supra.*)

Third—To justify a court in declaring a tax invalid on the ground that it was not imposed for the benefit of the public, the absence of a public interest in the purpose for which the money is raised by taxation must be so clear and palpable as to be immediately perceptible to every mind. (*Turner v. Althaus*, 6 Neb. 54; *Board of Directors of Alfalfa Irrigation District v. Collins*, 46 Neb. 411; *Brodhead v. City of Milwaukee*, 19 Wis. 658; *Sharpless v. Mayor of Philadelphia*, 21 Pa. St. 150; *People v. Common Council of East Saginaw*, 33 Mich. 164; *Walker v. City of Cincinnati*, 21 O. St. 14; *Stockton & V. R. Co. v. City of Stockton*, 41 Cal. 147; *Weismer v. Village of Douglas*, 64 N. Y. 91; *Loan Association v. Topeka*, 20 Wall. [U. S.] 664.)

In the last case it was said: "It is undoubtedly the duty of the legislature which imposes or authorizes municipalities to impose a tax to see that it is not to be used for purposes of private interest instead of public use, and the courts can only be justified in interposing when the violation of this principle is clear and the reason for interference cogent. And in deciding whether in a given case the object for which the taxes are assessed falls upon the one side or the other of this line, they must be governed mainly by the course and usage of the government, the objects for which taxes have been customarily and by long course of legislation levied, what objects or purposes have been considered necessary to the support and for the proper use of the government, whether state or municipal. Whatever lawfully pertains to this and is sanctioned by time and the acquiescence of the people may well be held to belong to the public use, and proper for the maintenance of good government, though this may not be the only criterion of rightful taxation."

The language of Folger, J., in his opinion in *Weismer v. Village of Douglas*, 64 N. Y. 99, deserves to be reproduced here: "It is a general rule that the legitimate object of raising money by taxation is for public purposes and the proper needs of government, general and local, state and municipal. When we come to ask, in any case, what is a public purpose, the answer is not always ready, nor easily to be found. It is to be conceded that no pinched or meager sense may be put upon the words, and that if the purpose designated by the legislature lies so near the border line that it may be doubtful on which side of it it is to be domiciled, the courts may not set their judgment against that of the lawmakers."

In *Board of Directors of Alfalfa Irrigation District v. Collins*, 46 Neb. 420, occurs this language: "While all agree that the legislature cannot, without the consent of the owner, appropriate private property to purposes which in no way subserve public interests, the rule is quite as firmly settled that the courts will not interfere by declaring acts invalid simply because they may differ with the lawmaking power respecting the wisdom or necessity thereof. For if, by any reasonable construction, a designated use may be held to be public in a constitutional sense, the will of the legislature should prevail over any mere doubt of the court."

In the light of the principles already stated, is the

legislation, under which the bonds in question were
voted, illegal on the ground that it authorized the imposing of burdens upon the public, by way of taxation, in
aid of a private enterprise, and not in furtherance of an
object which is public in its character? The answer
must be in the negative. The statute under review does
not attempt, or purport, to authorize the issuance, or
donation, of the bonds to private individuals, or the corporation under whose auspices the exposition is to be
held. Nor does the act contemplate that the money derived from the sale of the bonds shall be devoted to
promote the interest of a few; but the intention of the
law was to enable any county availing itself of its provisions to raise the means with which to meet the
expenses of erecting a suitable building or buildings, and
maintaining the same, and an exhibit of the resources of
the county at the Trans-Mississippi and International
Exposition to be held in the city of Omaha in 1898. The
proceeds of the bonds are to be disbursed, for the purpose
mentioned in the law, by Douglas county, through its
officers and agents. We cannot determine judicially
that such an object is purely private, and not public in
its character, especially in view of the legislation and
adjudication in this state now to be mentioned. The
legislature in 1891 appropriated $50,000 "to provide for
a presentation of the products, resources, and possibili-
ties of the state of Nebraska at the World's Columbian
Exposition." (Session Laws 1891, p. 395, ch. 57.) An
additional appropriation of $35,000 was subsequently
made for the same purpose. (Session Laws 1893, p. 380,
ch. 41.) Both of those amounts were paid by the state
treasurer, and the money was expended without any one
challenging the legality of the appropriations on the
ground that they were not made for the public good.
Our legislature appropriated $100,000 at the last session
for the purpose of defraying the expenses of the state
in making a proper exhibit of its resources and products
in the said Trans-Mississippi and International Exposi-
40

tion. (Session Laws 1897, p. 369, ch. 88, sec. 4.) Section
3, article 1, chapter 2, Compiled Statutes, provides that
$2,000 shall be paid annually out of the state treasury to
the state board of agriculture to be used in payment of
premiums awarded by said board at the state fair; and
section 10 of the same article and chapter authorizes the
payment to the state horticultural society of $1,000 an-
nually for the use and benefit of said society. The legislature has each session made the appropriations required
by said sections, for the purposes therein indicated, and
the same have been paid, without a suggestion from any
source that the money was not devoted to a public use.
Section 16 of the same article and chapter authorizes a
county, under certain restrictions, to appropriate and
pay to the county agricultural society not exceeding $100
for every thousand inhabitants in the county, "to be expended by such society in fitting up such fair grounds,
but for no other purpose." This section has never been
assailed as being invalid, although it has remained upon
the statute books for nearly twenty years. Section 12,
article 1, of said chapter 2, authorizes the payment by
county boards, to agricultural societies complying with
the provisions thereof, of a sum equal to three cents for
each inhabitant in the county from the county general
fund. In *State v. Robinson*, 35 Neb. 401, it was ruled that
this section authorized the appropriation of money for a
public purpose, and the expenditure was permissible
under the constitution. That case is not distinguishable
in principle from the one at bar. The adjudication of
other courts fully sustains the same doctrine.

The city of Philadelphia appropriated $50,000 to meet
the official contingent expenses incidental to the Centennial Exposition. It was held that this appropriation
was valid. (*Tatham v. City of Philadelphia*, 11 Phila. 276.)

An appropriation by a town made in pursuance of a
statute to celebrate the centennial anniversary of its incorporation has been upheld. (*Hill v. Easthampton*, 140
Mass. 381.) Likewise an appropriation of money by a

city for the celebration of holidays is held to be for a public purpose. (*Hubbard v. City of Taunton*, 140 Mass. 467.)

• The legislature of California made an appropriation of $300,000 for the purpose of making a state exhibit at the World's Fair Columbian Exposition. The supreme court of that state, in *Daggett v. Colgan*, 92 Cal. 53, held the appropriation was for public use, and was constitutional.

In *Norman v. Kentucky Board of Managers of World's Columbian Exposition*, 93 Ky. 537, it was decided that an appropriation of $100,000 to enable the state to participate in the World's Fair at Chicago was a valid exercise of legislative power under a constitution which provided that "taxes shall be levied and collected for public purposes only."

The legislature of the state of Tennessee, in 1895, passed an act authorizing the several counties of the state to appropriate money to provide for an exhibit of the resources at the Tennessee Centennial Exposition to be held at Nashville. The county of Shelby, in that state, appropriated $25,000 in pursuance of said act, but the proper county officer refused to issue a warrant against said appropriation, claiming that the act was invalid. On an application for a writ of mandamus the supreme court, in *Shelby County v. Exposition Co.*, 96 Tenn. 653, overruled the contention, saying: "To our minds it is entirely clear that an exhibition of the resources of Shelby county at the approaching State Centennial Exposition is a county purpose. In view of the fact that the event to be celebrated is one of no less note and importance than the birth of a great state into the American Union, and of the further fact that the exposition is reasonably expected to attract great and favorable attention throughout the country, and be participated in and largely attended by intelligent and enterprising citizens of numerous other states at least, it is beyond plausible debate that such an exhibition is well calculated to advance the material interests and promote the general welfare of the people of the county making it. It will excite industry, thrift, development, and worthy emulation in different avenues of commerce, agriculture, manufacture, art, and education within the county; thereby tending to the permanent betterment and prosperity of her whole people. In short, it will encourage progress, and progress will ensure increased intelligence, wealth, and happiness for her people, individually and collectively. Undeniably, that which promotes such an object and facilitates such a result in any county is, to that county, a county purpose in the truest sense."

No case in conflict with the foregoing has come under the observation of the writer. Decisions, however, are to be found in the books holding the appropriation of moneys for celebrations of public events to be invalid, but such decisions turn on the question of statutory authority rather than on the right of the legislature to confer such power. (See *Hood v. Mayor and Aldermen of Lynn*, 83 Mass. 103; *Tash v. Adams*, 64 Mass. 252; *City of New London v. Brainard*, 22 Conn. 552.)

In *Hayes v. Douglas County*, 92 Wis. 429, it was ruled that a county tax levied for the purpose of defraying the expenses of placing blocks of stones from the county in the Wisconsin state building at the Columbian World's Fair was unauthorized and void. The ground for this holding does not appear in the report of the case, as the only reference to the subject in the body of the opinion is in the language following: "The Columbian Fair stone tax was altogether unauthorized and void." We presume that the power to impose the tax in that case was not conferred by statute. Upon principle and authority we are constrained to hold that the bonds were voted for a public purpose, one for which the money of the county may be lawfully devoted.

Attention will now be given to the question whether the proposition to issue these bonds received the requisite number of affirmative votes. Sections 27 to 30, inclusive, of article 1, chapter 18, Compiled Statutes, relate

generally to the submission of questions to a vote of the
electors of the county. Said section 30 declares: "If it
appears that two-thirds of the votes cast are in favor of
the proposition, and the requirements of the law have
been fully complied with, the same shall be entered at
large by the county board upon the book containing the
record of their proceedings, and they shall then have
power to levy and collect the special tax in the same manner that the other county taxes are collected." This section has been construed as requiring, to adopt a proposition involving the issuance of bonds, an affirmative vote
of two-thirds of the electors participating at the election
at which the same is submitted. (*State v. Anderson*, 26
Neb. 517; *Stenberg v. State*, 50 Neb. 127.) So that if the
provisions of said section 30 apply to the bonds in question, they failed to carry, since they did not receive two-
thirds of the votes cast at the election, although more
than two-thirds of those voting on the proposition were
in favor of the bonds. It is very evident that said section
30 cannot be invoked here, because it is embraced in the
statute which provides generally for the submission of
questions to a vote of the county, and must give way to
any special act upon the same subject. The law under
which the bonds in controversy were voted relates specifically to the subject of issuing bonds to enable counties
to participate in interstate expositions, and the provision
therein as to the vote necessary to carry that class of
bonds governs and controls, for the obvious reason it is
a special law in relation to a particular subject. This
principle has been recognized by a long line of decisions
in this state. (*McCann v. McLennan*, 2 Neb. 286; *People v.
Gosper*, 3 Neb. 310; *Albertson v. State*, 9 Neb. 429; *Richardson County v. Miles*, 14 Neb. 311; *Fenton v. Yule*, 27 Neb.
758; *State v. Benton*, 33 Neb. 823, 834; *Richards v. Clay
County*, 40 Neb. 51; *Merrick v. Kennedy*, 46 Neb. 264; *Van
Horn v. State*, 46 Neb. 62; *State v. Moore*, 48 Neb. 870.) It
follows that these bonds were carried by the requisite
vote, and no valid objection having been urged against

their registration, a peremptory writ of mandamus is ordered as prayed.

WRIT ALLOWED.

WYLER, ACKERLAND & COMPANY V. E. ROTHSCHILD & BROS. ET AL.

FILED FEBRUARY 2, 1898. No. 7726.

1. **Statute of Frauds:** ORAL CONTRACT OF SALE. To take an oral contract for the sale of personal property of over $50 in value out of the statute of frauds, when no part of the purchase-money has been paid, delivery and acceptance of the property, or some portion thereof, by the vendee are necessary.

2. ———: ———· DELIVERY TO CARRIER. A delivery of goods. under a verbal contract of sale, to a common carrier for transportation, the receipt and acceptance of the goods by the purchaser at the place of destination, and the payment of the freight charges thereon, operate to take the contract out of the statute of frauds.

3. **Sale:** ACCEPTANCE OF GOODS. The execution and delivery of a chattel mortgage on goods by a vendee shortly after their receipt by him are such an assertion of ownership as will constitute an acceptance of the goods.

ERROR from the district court of Webster county. Tried below before BEALL, J. *Affirmed.*

A. D. Ranney and *J. S. Gilham,* for plaintiff in error.

James McNeny, contra.

NORVAL, J.

This was replevin for a lot of clothing. The verdict and judgment were against the plaintiffs. Wyler, Ackerland & Co., wholesale dealers in clothing, were the owners of goods in controversy. In the summer of 1893 they received through their traveling salesman an order, unsigned, from Louis Schumann, of Blue Hill, for a bill of clothing of the value of over $1,100, for fall delivery. In August of that year the goods replevied were shipped

by plaintiffs to Schumann at Blue Hill, who received the
same, paid the freight charges thereon, and placed them
in his store.   His clerk, Mr. Lepin, opened one or more
of the boxes, took out two suits of the clothing, one of
which had been sent complimentary to Mr. Lepin, and
then closed the boxes, as it was then too early to place
the goods on the shelves for the winter trade.   Three
days after the receipt of the goods by Schumann he executed a mortgage to E. Rothschild & Bros. for $200 and
another mortgage for $3,500 to State Bank of Blue Hill
on the mortgagor's entire stock of goods and fixtures,
"and all kinds of merchandise and chattels of every kind
and description now contained and being in my clothing
store in Blue Hill."   These mortgages were given to secure *bona fide* debts, and when they were executed and
delivered the clothing in controversy was in the store.
Possession of the property was taken by mortgagees,
whereupon plaintiffs instituted this suit.

The contention of plaintiffs is that the title to the replevied property had not passed to Schumann prior to
the making of the mortgages, but that the clothing was
shipped by the plaintiffs to the mortgagor subject to his
approval, and that he never accepted the same.   Edward
Weinstein, plaintiffs' traveling salesman, who took the
order for the clothing, testified that he sold Mr. Schumann
the goods with the privilege of acceptance or refusal on
their arrival at Blue Hill, and that the consignee declined
to accept them.   This is positively contradicted both by
Mr. Schumann and Lepin, his clerk, and the conflict in
the testimony was resolved by the jury against the contention of plaintiffs.   Paying the freight on the goods,
opening the boxes in which they were shipped and taking
therefrom two suits of clothing, and the execution of the
mortgages on the goods constituted a full and unqualified
acceptance thereof by Mr. Schumann.   That the order
given for the clothing was unsigned by Schumann does
not render the sale void under the statute of frauds, since
there was a delivery and acceptance of the goods.   (*Leg-*

gett & Myer Tobacco Co. v. Collier, 89 Ia. 144; *Sullivan v. Sullivan*, 70 Mich. 583.)

It is urged that the court erred in not permitting A. D. Ranney to testify that Mr. Schumann had informed witness he had not accepted the goods and had no intention of mortgaging them. Mr. Schumann was not a party to this suit; therefore the testimony was admissible only for the purpose of impeachment, and the proper foundation was not laid for the introduction of the excluded testimony.

Complaint is made of the giving of the instruction following: "If the jury find from the evidence that Schumann did accept the goods in controversy, prior to making the mortgage, then you should find for defendant." It is urged that it requires more than the mere acceptance of goods to take the sale out of the statute of frauds. It is true, delivery and acceptance both were indispensable. (*Powder River Live-Stock Co. v. Lamb*, 38 Neb. 339.) The undisputed testimony shows that the clothing was delivered to Schumann; hence it was unnecessary for the court to submit to the jury the question of delivery of the goods. There was no error in the two other instructions criticised by counsel. The judgment is

AFFIRMED.

MARY R. HARRIS V. JOHN BARTON.

FILED FEBRUARY 2, 1898. No. 7816.

1. **Bill of Exceptions:** AUTHENTICATION. A bill of exceptions will not be considered unless authenticated by the clerk of the trial court.

2. ———: ———: REVIEW. Assignments of error which are unavailing without a bill of exceptions will be disregarded where such bill is not authenticated according to the statute.

ERROR from the district court of Saline county. Tried below before HASTINGS, J. *Affirmed.*

Smith & McCreary and *J. D. Pope,* for plaintiff in error.

Charles H. Sloan, contra.

NORVAL, J.

This was an action of replevin by Mary R. Harris against John Barton to recover a number of buggies and wagons. From a verdict and judgment for the defendant the plaintiff prosecutes this proceeding.

The petition in error contained nine assignments. Three relate to rulings on the evidence, five are based on the giving and refusing of instructions, and one relates to the overruling of the motion for a new trial. These assignments are unavailing, for the reason their consideration involves an examination of the bill of exceptions, and the document attached to the transcript purporting to be the bill of exceptions is not authenticated by any certificate of the clerk of the trial court, as either the original bill or a copy thereof. (*Moore v. Waterman,* 40 Neb. 498; *Wax v. State,* 43 Neb. 18; *Yenny v. Central City Bank,* 44 Neb. 402; *Martin v. Fillmore County,* 44 Neb. 719; *Union P. R. Co. v. Kinney,* 47 Neb. 393; *Romberg v. Fokken,* 47 Neb. 198; *Derse v. Straus,* 49 Neb. 665.) For the reason stated the judgment is

AFFIRMED.

DAVID VAN ETTEN ET AL. V. WILLIAM MEDLAND ET AL.   53
56

53
58

FILED FEBRUARY 2, 1898.   No. 7712.

53
61
61

1. **Taxation:** ACTION TO ENFORCE LIEN: NOTICE TO REDEEM. It is the settled rule in this state that a purchaser at a tax sale is not required to give the notice to redeem mentioned in section 3, article 9, of the constitution, to maintain an action to enforce a tax lien.

2. **Pleading:** DEFINITENESS: WAIVER. The filing of a demurrer to a petition is a waiver of the right to insist that the allegations of the pleading shall be made more definite and certain.

3. **New Trial**: EXCEPTIONS: REVIEW. An exception in the trial court to an order denying a motion for a new trial is necessary to obtain a review in this court of questions properly included in such motion.

ERROR from the district court of Douglas county. Tried below before FERGUSON, J. *Affirmed.*

David Van Etten, for plaintiffs in error.

Henry W. Pennock, A. C. Troup, Francis A. Brogan, Switzler & McIntosh, and *B. F. Cochran, contra.*

NORVAL, J.

This is a proceeding to review the decree of the district court foreclosing a tax lien.

The first assignment is that the trial court erred in overruling the demurrer to the petition. It is insisted that the petition is fatally defective, inasmuch as it is not alleged therein that notice to redeem from the tax sale had been served upon the occupants of the land. Section 3, article 9, of the constitution is invoked to sustain the contention, which provides: "The right of redemption from all sales of real estate, for the non-payment of taxes or special assessments of any character whatever, shall exist in favor of owners and persons interested in such real estate, for a period of not less than two years from such sales thereof; *Provided,* That occupants shall in all cases be served with personal notice before the time of redemption expires." The foregoing provision has been frequently under consideration by this court, and it has been uniformly ruled that the redemption notice is essential only where a tax deed is sought, and that service of such notice is unnecessary to maintain an action to enforce a tax lien. (*Bryant v. Estabrook,* 16 Neb. 217; *Lammers v. Comstock,* 20 Neb. 341; *McClure v. Lavender,* 21 Neb. 181; *Helphrey v. Redick,* 21 Neb. 80.) This construction of the constitution has been adhered to so long as to now become a rule of property, and we do not feel at liberty to investigate the question anew.

After the demurrer was overruled, the defendants assailed the petition by a motion to make the pleading more definite and specific by attaching copies of the receipts for taxes paid. The motion was denied, and the ruling is urged as a ground for reversal. The motion was made too late to be of any avail. It should have been presented prior to the filing of the demurrer. (*Fritz v. Grosnicklaus*, 20 Neb. 413.)

Another contention is that plaintiff permitted the real estate to be sold for taxes before the expiration of the last day of the second annual sale occurring after the date of plaintiff's purchase, and therefore section 120, article 1, chapter 77, of the Compiled Statutes should control the case. The record discloses that plaintiff's purchase was on October 17, 1888, and that the real estate was again sold to one Pilot on November 10, 1891, which was during the third annual sale after the one at which plaintiff bid in the land at tax sale. The section of the statute invoked by the defendant, therefore, has no application here.

It is finally insisted that there was error in the assessment in the amount of recovery. This question was raised by the motion for a new trial, but it is unavailing in this court, for the reason no exception was taken in the court below to the overruling of such motion. (*Lowrie v. France*, 7 Neb. 191; *Murray v. School District*, 11 Neb. 436; *Burke v. Pepper*, 29 Neb. 320.) The decree is

AFFIRMED.

STATE OF NEBRASKA, EX REL. WILLIAM MEDLAND, V. CUNNINGHAM R. SCOTT.

FILED FEBRUARY 2, 1898.   No. 9538.

1. **Time to Present Bill of Exceptions for Allowance.** When forty days are given to prepare and serve a bill of exceptions, the draft of the bill and proposed amendments are submitted to the trial judge in time, if presented to him within sixty days after

the final adjournment of the term at which the decision was rendered.

2. ———. The third division of the syllabus in *Schields v. Horbach*, 40
Neb. 103, disapproved.

ORIGINAL application for a writ of mandamus to compel the respondent, as one of the judges of the district
court of Douglas county, to sign a bill of exceptions.
Writ allowed.

·*Henry W. Pennock,* for relator.

Connell & Ives, contra.

NORVAL, J.

This is an original application for a peremptory writ
of mandamus to compel the respondent, one of the judges
of the district court of Douglas county, to sign and settle
a bill of exceptions in a cause tried before him wherein
relator was plaintiff and Henry Schlueter and others
were defendants.   The respondent insists that the proposed bill of exceptions was not presented to him for
allowance within the time prescribed by law, and his
refusal to allow the bill is placed upon that ground alone.
The decree in the cause in which the bill of exceptions
is sought was entered at the February term, 1897, of the
district court, and which term adjourned *sine die* on April
10, 1897.   Forty days from such final adjournment were
allowed relator by the court within which to prepare and
serve a bill of exceptions.   The proposed bill was served
upon counsel for the defendants in said cause on May 19,
1897, who returned the same to plaintiff's counsel on the
29th day of the same month with one proposed amendment.   On June 4, 1897, relator served notice upon defendants' counsel that on the 9th day of said month the
draft of the bill would be submitted to respondent for
settlement and allowance, and it was presented to him
at the time and place designated in said notice.   Whereupon counsel for defendants objected and protested

against the settling of said bill on the ground that it had not been submitted to the respondent within the period fixed by statute.

It will be observed that the proposed bill was not submitted to the respondent for allowance within ten days from the time it had been returned to relator's counsel with the proposed amendment thereto, but was presented to the trial judge within sixty days from the final adjournment of the term at which the decree was rendered. It is argued by counsel for respondent that the law requires a proposed bill of exceptions to be submitted to the trial judge for his signature within ten days from the time the draft is returned to the party seeking the allowance of the bill. *Schields v. Horbach,* 40 Neb. 103, supports this contention, but such holding is in direct conflict with the earlier and later decisions of this court construing section 311 of the Code of Civil Procedure. In *First Nat. Bank v. Bartlett,* 8 Neb. 321, the court says: "The party excepting has fifteen days from the rising of the court in which to reduce his exceptions to writing, and submit the same to the adverse party without an order of the court. If he desires a longer period of time in which to prepare and submit the same to the adverse party, the court may extend the time not to exceed forty days from the rising of the court. In such case, the bill must be submitted to the adverse party within the period prescribed in the order. The adverse party then has ten days in which to propose amendments and return the bill to the party excepting. The party seeking the settlement of the bill has ten days after the time limited for the return of the bill to him, with the proposed amendments, in which to present the same to the judge for his signature, making sixty days in all from the rising of the court. But where a shorter period is fixed upon, when the bill must be prepared and presented to the adverse party for examination and amendment, the twenty days within which the bill must be signed by the judge dates from that period and cannot be extended beyond.   *   *

The design of the law evidently is to allow a fixed period for the presentation of a bill to the adverse party for the proposal of amendments, and for presenting the amended bill to the judge for his approval and signature, being analogous, in that regard, to the return and answer day of a summons." This case has been cited with approval and followed in *Sherwin v. O'Connor*, 23 Neb. 221; *State v. Gaslin*, 25 Neb. 71. Those decisions were not referred to or commented upon in *Schields v. Horbach, supra;* and in *Conway v. Grimes*, 46 Neb. 288, the doctrine announced in *First Nat. Bank v. Bartlett* and the cases following it was reaffirmed. My associates are of the opinion that where forty days are allowed to prepare and serve a bill of exceptions, the draft and proposed amendments may be presented to the trial judge for his signature upon proper notice at any time within sixty days from the final adjournment of the term of court at which the decision was rendered, while the writer adheres to the rule stated in the third division of the syllabus in *Schields v. Horbach*, 40 Neb. 103. It follows that the proposed bill was submitted to the respondent within the statutory period, and should be allowed by him as the bill of exceptions in the case. As the respondent was induced to withhold his signature from the bill by reason of the decision in *Schields v. Horbach, supra*, the writ will be allowed without costs.

WRIT ALLOWED.

GRAND ISLAND BANKING COMPANY ET AL., APPELLANTS,
V. MARY E. WRIGHT ET AL., APPELLEES.

FILED FEBRUARY 2, 1898.   No. 6538.

1. **Married Women**: CONTRACTS. The common-law disability of a married woman to contract is in force in this state, except as abrogated by statute.

2. ———: ———: SEPARATE ESTATE. She may make contracts only

in reference to her separate property, trade or business, or upon the faith and credit thereof and with the intent on her part to thereby charge her separate estate.

3. ——: ——: ——. Whether a contract of a married woman was so made is a question of fact.

4. ——: ——: ——: ACTION ON NOTE: BURDEN OF PROOF. When a married woman signs a note there is no presumption that she intended thereby to fasten a liability upon her separate estate, but in an action on such note, where coverture is pleaded as a defense, and proved, the burden is upon the plaintiff to establish that it was made with reference to, and upon the credit of, her property, and with the intent to bind the same. .

5. ——: SURETYSHIP: MORTGAGES: DEFICIENCY JUDGMENT. Where a husband gives a note for his own indebtedness, and the wife signs the same as surety merely and executes a mortgage to secure the payment thereof upon her own real estate, a personal judgment cannot be rendered against her on foreclosure for any deficiency after sale of the premises, where it is not disclosed that in executing the note and mortgage it was the intention to bind her property generally.

APPEAL from the district court of Hall county. Heard below before HARRISON, J. *Affirmed.*

Charles G. Ryan, for appellants.

W. H. Thompson, contra. •

NORVAL, J.

The Grand Island Banking Company and John Lang each brought a separate action in the district court of Hall county against Mary E. Wright and Frederick Wright, wife and husband, to foreclose two real estate mortgages upon the same property, given by the defendants to secure promissory notes executed by them. Subsequently the suits were consolidated by consent of parties, a decree of foreclosure was entered, and the mortgaged premises were sold thereunder; but the proceeds were insufficient to pay the amount due upon the mortgages. Applications for deficiency judgments were made by the plaintiffs, which were denied as to the defendant Mary E. Wright, but such judgment was rendered against the said Frederick Wright in favor of each of the plaintiffs for the full amount due them respectively, after applying the proceeds arising from the sale of the mortgaged property. Plaintiffs appeal from the decision denying their applications for judgments in deficiency against Mary E. Wright. The sole question in the case is whether she was liable to a personal judgment upon either of the notes secured by the mortgages. It is undisputed that the notes and mortgages were signed by both defendants, that the real estate covered by the mortgages at the time they were executed was owned by Mary E. Wright, who was then a married woman living with her husband, and that in neither of the notes or mortgages is there any stipulation to the effect that they were given with reference to her separate property, or that her estate generally should be bound for the payment of the debts secured by said mortgages. There is to be found in the bill of exceptions evidence tending to establish that the notes were executed to obtain loans made to the husband alone for his individual use and benefit; that no part of the debts was contracted by the wife, or in her behalf; that she signed the notes as surety merely for Mr. Wright, there being no agreement or understanding of any kind, nor any fact or circumstances proven, from which an inference can be drawn that her property, other than that covered by the mortgages, if any she possessed, which is not shown, should be liable for the payment of the notes. We are persuaded that the evidence adduced was sufficient to authorize the trial court in finding that the notes were not made with reference to Mrs. Wright's separate estate, or that she agreed or intended to bind the same, except to the extent of the property actually pledged by the mortgages. Under the facts disclosed by this record was either of the plaintiffs entitled to a deficiency judgment against Mrs. Wright?

The important question that confronts us in this case is the liability of a married woman on her contracts of suretyship. The solution of this question depends upon

the extent of the power conferred upon her by the legislature to create debts to be paid out of her separate
property, since, at common law, a married woman is
wholly incompetent to contract in her own name, and
this rule is in force in this state unless it has been abrogated in whole or in part by statute. By section 1, chapter 53, Compiled Statutes, the property which a woman
may own at the time of her marriage, and the rents,
issues, and profits, or proceeds thereof, as well as any
property subsequently acquired by descent, devise, or the
gift from any person except her husband, are her sole and
separate property, and not subject to the disposal of her
husband or liable for his debts, except for necessaries furnished the family, and not then until execution against
the husband for such indebtedness has been returned unsatisfied for want of property whereon to make a levy.
Section 2 declares: "A married woman, while the marriage relation subsists, may bargain, sell, and convey her
real and personal property, and enter into any contract
with reference to the same in the same manner, to the
same extent, and with like effect as a married man may in
relation to his real and personal property." Section 3 provides: "A woman may, while married, sue and be sued, in
the same manner as if she were unmarried."   Section 4 is
in this language: "Any married woman may carry on
trade or business, and perform any labor or services on
her sole and separate account; and the earnings of any
married woman, from her trade, business, labor, or services, shall be her sole and separate property, and may be
used and invested by her in her own name."

Thus it will be observed the legislature has to some extent removed the common-law disability of a married
woman.   In this state she may acquire and hold property
in her own right, and may engage in business on her separate account, and her earnings derived either from such
trade or business or from her labor or services she owns
in her own right.   The implied power of a *feme covert* to
contract is given by the last section quoted; but this only

41

extends to her separate trade or business and to contracts
with reference to her personal services. The express au
thority conferred upon married women to enter into contracts is to be found in section 2 copied above. But this
statute does not expressly, nor by implication, enlarge a
wife's capacity to contract generally. She can buy and
sell property in her own name and upon her own account,
and enter into valid contracts with reference to her separate estate the same as if she were a *feme sole*, or as a married man may in relation to his property. The statute
does not undertake to confer upon a married woman an
unrestricted power to make contracts, but such right is
limited to contracts made with reference to, and upon the
faith and credit of, her separate property or estate. Upon
such contract she is liable, but all her other engagements
and obligations are void as at common law. To hold un-
qualifiedly that a married woman has the same right to
enter into contracts, and to the same extent, as a man
would be to disregard the qualifying clause of said section 2, which confers upon her the authority to "enter
into any contract with reference to the same [her prop-
erty] in the same manner, to the same extent, and with
like effect as a married man may in relation to his real
and personal property." If the legislature had intended
to wholly remove the common-law disabilities of a married woman, and give her general power to make contracts of all kinds, this intention, doubtless, would have
been expressed in apt and appropriate language. It
would have expressly enacted that she could bind herself
and her property by her general engagements whether
made or entered into for the benefit, or on account of, her
separate property or not, instead of empowering her to
contract alone with reference to her own property, trade,
and business. In construing this statute it is important
to bear in mind that the legislature was not attempting
to impose disabilities upon married women, but was engaged in removing some of those already existing. She
can contract only so far as her disabilities have been so

removed by the legislature. The statute requires that
contracts, to be valid, must be entered into with reference
to her separate property, and it is for the courts to so construe this enactment as to carry out the legislative will.
It is true section 3 permits a married woman to sue and
be sued, but this does not authorize the recovery of a judgment against her when no cause of action exists, nor
does it attempt to declare what contracts of hers will
support an action; what are valid or what are nugatory.
The construction we have given the statute is in accord
with numerous decisions of this court. (*Davis v. First
Nat. Bank of Cheyenne,* 5 Neb. 242; *Hale v. Christy,* 8 Neb.
264; *Spaun v. Mercer,* 8 Neb. 357; *State Savings Bank v.
Scott,* 10 Neb. 83; *Barnum v. Young,* 10 Neb. 309; *Gillespie
v. Smith,* 20 Neb. 455; *Eckman v. Scott,* 34 Neb. 817; *Godfrey v. Megahan,* 38 Neb. 748; *Buffalo County Nat. Bank v.
Sharpe,* 40 Neb. 123; *McKinney v. Hopwood,* 46 Neb. 871.)

Hale v. Christy, cited above, was an action to foreclose a
mortgage given by the defendants, husband and wife, to
secure their promissory note. The trial court found that
the wife was personally liable for the debt. This court
held she incurred no personal obligation by executing the
note. The third paragraph of the syllabus reads as follows: "Under sections 42 and 43, chapter 61, General
Statutes, a married woman may sell and convey real
estate, or any interest she may have therein, the same
as if she were single. As to her other contracts she is
liable only to the extent that they are made with reference to, and on the faith and credit of, her separate
estate." It is suggested that the holding in that case as
to the personal liability of Mrs. Christy was mere *obiter*
for the reason the question did not then arise, and could
not until the court came to render a deficiency judgment.
The finding in the decree of foreclosure that Mrs. Christy
was personally liable for the debt would have bound her,
unless set aside, so that the decision on that proposition
was not *obiter.* This is the effect of the decision in *Stover
v. Tompkins,* 34 Neb. 465. We quote the first clause of

the syllabus of the case: "Where a grantee of real estate
has assumed in the deed of conveyance a certain mortgage as part of the consideration, and in an action to foreclose had been made a defendant and a decree rendered
against him that he should be liable in case of deficiency,
which decree remained unreversed and without modification, he will not be permitted, when judgment for deficiency is sought, to set up facts which existed when the
original decree was obtained and should have been
pleaded to show that he was not liable."

State Savings Bank v. Scott, 10 Neb. 83, was an action
upon a joint and several promissory note signed by W. D.
Scott and S. A. Scott, husband and wife. The coverture
of Mrs. Scott was pleaded. The trial court found that
she executed the note as surety for her husband, and was
not liable for its payment. This court affirmed the judgment, the last clause of the syllabus being in the following language: "A wife is bound by her contracts when
made with reference to or upon the faith and credit of
her separate estate, but she is not bound as surety upon
a promissory note unless it appears that she intended
thereby to bind her separate estate." The same doctrine
was again stated in *Eckman v. Scott*, 34 Neb. 817.

Barnum v. Young, 10 Neb. 309, was a suit against a married woman upon her promissory note, the sole question
involved being whether her coverture relieved her from
liability for its payment. From a verdict in her favor
the plaintiff prosecuted error. This court affirmed the
judgment, and approved, as containing a fair expression
of the law, the following instructions given upon the
trial:

"1. The defendant being a married woman at the time
she signed the note in question, she will not be liable for
the payment thereof unless it was given with reference
to, and on the faith and credit of, her separate property
and estate.

"2. You are instructed by the court that under the law
and evidence of this case the material question for you to

settle from the evidence is, Did the defendant, at the time she gave the note to John G. Compton, contract with reference to and upon the faith and credit of her separate estate? If she did so contract, then she would, under the law of this case, be liable for the full amount of the note. But if from the evidence you find that she did not so contract with reference to, and upon the faith and credit of, her separate estate, then you must find for the defendant."

Godfrey v. Megahan, 38 Neb. 748, was a suit against a husband and wife upon a promissory note executed by them for a pre-existing debt of the husband, the wife signing the same as surety merely. She pleaded her coverture, and that the note was not executed with reference to her separate property, trade, or business, but at the request of her husband as surety for him. Upon a trial to the court this defense was sustained and the action dismissed as to Mrs. Megahan, which judgment was sustained upon a review of the record by this court. The propositions decided in that case are clearly stated in the syllabus of the opinion prepared by RAGAN, C., as follows:

"1. The disability of a married woman to make a valid contract remains the same as at common law, except in so far as such disability has been removed by our statutes.

"2. The statute has removed the common law disability of a married woman to make contracts only in cases where the contract made has reference to her separate property, trade, or business, or was made upon the faith and credit thereof, and with intent on her part to thereby bind her separate property.

"3. Whether a contract of a married woman was made with reference to her separate property, trade, or business, or upon the faith and credit thereof, and with intent on her part to thereby bind her separate property, is always a question of fact."

In *Buffalo County Nat. Bank v. Sharpe*, 40 Neb. 123, it

was held that where a married woman executes a mortgage on her real estate to secure the debt of her husband, her separate estate to the extent of the property mortgaged is bound for the payment of such debt. Of the same purport is the case of *Watts v. Gantt,* 42 Neb. 869.

In *Smith v. Spaulding,* 40 Neb. 339, it was decided that a married woman may contract as surety for her husband, but that decision did not overrule or modify the prior adjudications of this court relative to the liabilities of married women on their contracts, as an examination of the opinion will disclose. This court held that the trial court in that case erred in refusing an instruction embodying the proposition enunciated in the syllabus in *Barnum v. Young,* 10 Neb. 309.

In *Briggs v. First Nat. Bank of Beatrice,* 41 Neb. 17, it was ruled that a married woman is liable on a note which she signed as surety, when the note contained a clause pledging her separate estate for its payment.

This court has not in any instance decided that a married woman is personally liable on her general engagements, or that all the common-law disabilities of a *feme covert* have been abrogated in this state. On the contrary, the rule has been steadfastly adhered to that her contracts to be valid must be made with reference to, and upon the faith and credit of, her separate property. Her intention to charge such estate must be disclosed. If the rule laid down in the decisions mentioned above so long adhered to is to be abrogated, it should be by legislative enactment.

There is much confusion and conflict in the decisions of the courts of the different states upon the proposition whether the intention to charge the separate estate by the giving of a promissory note must be expressed on the face of the instrument, or whether it may be established by parol evidence. It is not necessary in this case that we should decide between the two rules, since it does not appear from the note itself, nor was it established by other testimony, that it was her intention to bind her own property, other than that covered by the mortgage.

It is claimed that when a *feme covert* executes a note the presumption arises that she intended thereby to charge her separate estate or property. To this doctrine we cannot assent. A married woman cannot contract generally, and the burden is cast upon the one seeking to enforce a contract against her to show that it is an obligation she was authorized to make under the statute. An infant is not liable on his contract as a general rule, except for necessaries, but in an action against him on a contract, it is a good defense to establish his minority, unless the plaintiff shows the debt was for necessaries furnished the minor. The burden is not upon the infant to show that the indebtedness was not incurred for necessaries. (*Wood v. Losey*, 15 N. W. Rep. [Mich.] 557.) So in a suit against a married woman when her coverture is pleaded and proven, it devolves upon the plaintiff to show that the contract was made with reference to and upon the credit of her separate estate. (*Vogel v. Leichner*, 102 Ind. 55; *Cupp v. Campbell*, 103 Ind. 213; *Jouchert v. Johnson*, 108 Ind. 436; *Stillwell v. Adams*, 29 Ark. 346; *Fisk v. Mills*, 62 N. W. Rep. [Mich.] 559; *Fechheimer v. Peirce*, 70 Mich. 440, 38 N. W. Rep. 325; *Kenton Ins. Co. of Kentucky v. McClellan*, 43 Mich. 564, 6 N. W. Rep. 88; *Schmidt v. Spencer*, 87 Mich. 121, 49 N. W. Rep. 479; *Haydock Carriage Co. v. Pier*, 74 Wis. 582, 43 N. W. Rep. 502; *Buhler v. Jennings*, 49 Mich. 538, 14 N. W. Rep. 488; *Menard v. Sydnor*, 29 Tex. 257; *Trimble v. Miller*, 24 Tex. 215; *Haynes v. Storall*, 23 Tex. 625; *Corington v. Burleson*, 28 Tex. 368; *Baird v. Patillo*, 24 S. W. Rep. [Tex.] 813; *Early v. Lar*, 20 S. E. Rep. [S. Car.] 136; *Litton v. Baldwin*, 8 Humph. [Tenn.] 209; *Hughes v. Peters*, 1 Cold. [Tenn.] 67; *Law v. Traders Deposit Bank*, 21 S. W. Rep. [Ky.] 756; *Halenicht v. Rawls*, 24 S. Car. 461; *West v. Laraway*, 28 Mich. 464.)

Fechheimer v. Peirce, 70 Mich. 440, was an action upon a promissory note, signed by Ella G. Peirce and Grand

Peirce, husband and wife. The instrument purported to be signed by the husband as surety. It was shown on the trial that the note was given for a loan of money made to the husband. The check for the money was delivered to him, although it was payable to the order of his wife. The jury returned a verdict against both makers, and a judgment rendered thereon was reversed by the supreme court. Campbell, J., in delivering the opinion of the court, said: "We think there was nothing to go to the jury against defendant. It is the law of this state that a married woman can make no obligation except on account of her own separate property, and that anyone seeking to hold her must make out an affirmative case. * * * The signing of a note by a married woman creates no presumption of consideration, but it must be proved."

While there are authorities which hold that when a married woman signs a note, the presumption arises that she intended thereby to charge her separate property, it is believed that the rule we have adopted is more consistent with sound principle and the weight of authority.

It is argued that if Mrs. Wright is not liable in this case for the deficiency remaining after the sale of the property, because of her coverture, the entire debt was void as to her, and the mortgages upon her real estate given to secure the same indebtedness were not enforceable. The argument is fallacious. She pledged certain of her separate estate to the payment of this indebtedness, and for that reason, to the extent of the proceeds of such property, her separate estate was bound. Further than that she never agreed nor was it her intention that her property should stand as security for the debts of her husband. A wife may make a valid mortgage upon her real estate to secure a note executed by the husband, for his indebtedness, since the intention to charge her own property is manifest. (*Nelson v. Bevins*, 19 Neb. 715; *Buffalo County Nat. Bank v. Sharpe*, 40 Neb. 123; *Watts v. Gantt*, 42 Neb. 869.) But it does not follow that she is liable on the contract of suretyship where such contract was not made upon the faith and credit of her separate estate, and where she did not intend that such estate should be bound for the payment of the debt. Plaintiffs were not entitled to a personal judgment against Mrs. Wright. (*Gaynor v. Blewett*, 86 Wis. 399; *Johnson Co. v. Rugg*, 18 Ia. 137; *Rogers v. Weil*, 12 Wis. 741; *Wolff v. Van Metre*, 19 Ia. 134; *Salinas v. Turner*, 33 S. Car. 231; *Greig v. Smith*, 29 S. Car. 426; *American Mortgage Co. of Scotland v. Owens*, 72 Fed. Rep. 219, 18 C. C. A. 513.)

AFFIRMED.

HARRISON, C. J., having presided in the trial court, took no part in the above opinion.

SULLIVAN, J., and RAGAN, C., concurring.

RYAN, C., dissenting.

In the opinion prepared by NORVAL, J., it is said that it is undisputed that the notes and mortgage securing said notes were signed by both Mary E. Wright and her husband Frederick Wright, and that in neither is there a stipulation that said instruments were given with reference to the wife's separate property, or, that her estate generally should be bound for the payment of the debts secured by said mortgage. It is also stated that there was evidence tending to establish the fact that the notes were executed to obtain a loan made to the husband alone for his individual benefit, and that the wife signed the said notes solely as surety for Mr. Wright. The notes signed by Mrs. Wright were in the following language:

"$115.00.　　GRAND ISLAND, NEB., August 1, 1889.

"February 1st, 1891, after date, for value received, we, or either of us, promise to pay to the order of the Grand Island Banking Company one hundred and fifteen and no 100 dollars at the bank in Grand Island, Nebraska, with interest at ten per cent per annum payable from maturity. It is expressly understood that all the makers of this note are principals thereon. The indorsers severally waive presentment for payment, protest, and notice of protest and notice of non-payment of this note and all defense on the ground of any extension of the time of its payment, or any part thereof, that may be given to the holder or holders to them or either of them. Secured by mortgage of even date herewith on lots 7 and 8, block 98, in Railroad Addition to Grand Island, recorded in Hall county, Nebraska.

"MARY E. WRIGHT.

"FREDERICK WRIGHT."

The only note made to John Lang was in the following language:

"$2,300.00.

"GRAND ISLAND, NEBRASKA, August 1st, 1889.

"On the first day of August, 1894, I promise to pay John Lang, or order, twenty-three hundred and no 100 dollars, with interest from this date until paid at the rate of 7 per cent per annum, payable semi-annually as per coupon attached. Value received. Principal and interest payable at the office of the Grand Island Banking Company in Grand Island, Nebr. Should any of the said interest be not paid when due, it shall bear interest at the rate of ten per cent per annum from the time same becomes due, and upon failure to pay any of said interest within thirty days after due, the holder may elect to consider the whole note due and it may be collected at once. It is expressly agreed and declared that these notes are made and executed under, and are in all respects to be construed by, the laws of the state of Nebraska.   MARY E. WRIGHT.

"FREDERICK WRIGHT."

In respect to the mortgages to secure the notes it was stipulated that the legal title of the mortgaged property was, when the mortgages were made, held by Mary E. Wright.

Section 2, chapter 53, Compiled Statutes, is in this language: "A married woman while the married relation subsists may bargain, sell, or convey her real and personal property, and enter into any contract with reference to the same, in the same manner, to the same extent, and with like effect as a married man may in relation to his real and personal property." Section 3 of the same chapter provides: "A woman may, while married, sue and be sued in the same manner as if she were unmarried." By section 1 of the aforesaid chapter it is provided that any property that a woman in this state may own at the time of her marriage and any property that she may afterwards acquire from any person, except her husband, shall be her separate property. The provisions of these sections are supplemented by those of section 4, which section is in this language: "Any married woman may carry on trade, or business, and perform any labor or service on her sole and separate account; and the earnings of any married woman from her trade, business, labor, or services shall be her sole and separate property, and may be used and invested by her in her own name."

The power of a married woman to bind her estate in the same manner as a man might do, would, under the above provisions, exist without room for any question whatever, but for the supposed limitations found embodied in section 2 in this language, "and enter into any contract with reference to the same." One view, and that adopted in the aforesaid opinion, as I understand it, is that by reason of these qualifying words there should be contained in every contract made by a married woman express words to the effect that by her said contract she intends to bind her separate estate. In view of our statutes I shall now consider the cases cited in support of this proposition and such other decisions of this court as bear upon this subject. It is not questioned that the statute under consideration was enacted to relieve married women of their common-law disabilities. The words of limitation found in section 2 might, therefore, be held necessary because in the statute the status of married women's property alone was under consideration. If from section 2 there should be dropped the words "and enter into any contract with reference to the same" and the corresponding words "in relation to," it would read thus: "A married woman, while the marriage relation subsists, may bargain, sell, or convey her real or personal property in the same manner, to the same extent, and with the same effect as a married man may his real and personal property." This would empower her only to bargain, sell, or convey her property. She could make no other contract with reference to it. To avoid this result the general enabling clause, "and enter into any contract with reference to the same," was inserted. Let us now consider section 2 simply with reference to this clause. For this the parts involved are as follows: "A married woman * * * may * * * enter into any contract with reference to the same (her real and personal property) in the same manner, to the same extent, and with like effect, as a married man may in relation to his real and personal property." If the limitation under consideration requires that a married woman, in order to contract with reference to her real and personal property must, in such contract, expressly so recite, what shall be said of the language "may * * * contract with reference to the same in the same manner * * * as a married man, in relation to his real and personal property"? No one would claim that a married man could render liable to his debts his real and personal property only by expressly stating in his promissory note that he intended thereby to bind such separate real and personal property. This, however, must be the logical effect of the above provision, if it is so construed as to make this requirement in relation to the property of married women, for, by statute, the property, real and personal, of each is to be bound in the same way as is the like property of the other. The

fact that the legislature intended in the chapter to con-
fine its effects to the contractual capacities of a married
woman and used the guarded language which it did with
regard to the rights of a married woman to contract with
reference to her property, so that it would not be mis-
understood as changing her marital status and duties
toward her husband, is manifested from the consideration that her right to contract is the same as the right of
a married man, that is to say, such duties and liabilities
as the marriage relation implies between the parties
thereto, remain unaffected by this chapter. By virtue of
section 2, chapter 53, Compiled Statutes, there exists
such a correlation between the contractual powers of a
married woman and those of a married man, with respect
to their property rights, that, unless we are willing to
say that married men do not contract with reference to
their separate property unless their promissory notes or
other evidences of indebtedness so state in express language, we cannot consistently insist upon that requirement in relation to the contracts of a married woman.
Notwithstanding the confident language to the contrary
in the opinion filed as to the construction which should
be placed upon this chapter of the Compiled Statutes
defining the contractual rights of married women, I
think we are not enlightened by a clear uniformity in
the adjudications of this court.

In *Webb v. Hoselton*, 4 Neb. 308, MAXWELL, J., said in
effect that, at common law, the husband and wife were
treated as one person, and that during coverture her
legal relation and existence were treated as though suspended, but that, in equity, a married woman, as to contracts with reference to her separate property, was regarded as *feme sole*. Following this observation there
occurred in the opinion this language: "And the fact
that a debt has been contracted during coverture either
as principal or as surety for herself or husband or
jointly with him, seems ordinarily to be held *prima fa ie*
evidence of an intention to charge her separate estate"

without any proof of a positive agreement or intention
to do so. (*Bullpin v. Clarke*, 17 Ves. [Eng.] 365; Story.
Equity Jurisprudence 1400; *Murry v. Barlee*, 4 Sim.
[Eng.] 82; *Owens v. Dickerson*, 1 Craig & Ph. [Eng.] 48;
Norton v. Turrill, 2 P. Wm. [Eng.] 144.) Our statutes
provide that 'a married woman, while the marriage relation subsists, may bargain, sell, or convey her real and
personal property and enter into any contract with reference to the same in the same manner, to the same
extent, and with like effect as a married man may in
relation to his real and personal property. A married
woman may carry on any trade or business and perform
any labor or services on her sole and separate account,
and the earnings of any married woman from her trade,
labor, business, or services shall be her sole and separate
property and may be used and invested by her in her
name.' In the case of *Yale v. Dederer*, 22 N. Y. 450, where
a wife signed a note with her husband as surety, she
having a separate estate, the court held that unless the
consideration of the contract was one going to the direct
benefit of the estate the intention to charge the separate
estate must be stated in, and be a part of, the contract
And the court refused to permit parol proof to establish
that intention. That decision, in our opinion, cannot
be sustained on either principle or authority." There
was more than one proposition discussed in *Webb v.
Hoselton*, and GANTT, J., dissented as to the result, without giving his reasons or directing attention to the particular branch of the discussion which met his disapproval of the holding of the court in *Yale v. Dederer*, 22
N. Y. 450.

In *Davis v. First Nat. Bank of Cheyenne*, 5 Neb. 242, the
opinion was by Judge GANTT, who, after a brief reference to the scope of the act under consideration, said:
"It is not necessary now to inquire into the wisdom of
the act in regard to the extent it goes in legalizing the
contracts of married women, or in regard to the right of
action by or against her, as though she were a *feme sole*.

The statute confers upon her the right and power to make legal and binding contracts; it gives her the legal right to sue, and makes her legally liable to be sued on her contracts, in the same manner as if she were unmarried, and the court must expound the law as it finds it made by the constitutional lawmaking power. But the rule must be observed that all such contracts of a *feme covert* must be with reference to, and upon the faith and credit of, her separate estate." The above quotation contains the entire discussion in which was formulated the proposition that a contract which would bind a married woman must be one with reference to, and upon the faith of, her separate estate.

In *Hale v. Christy*, 8 Neb. 264, the language of Judge LAKE upon this proposition was as follows: "It is urged by counsel for Mrs. Christy that owing to her coverture she incurred no personal liability by signing said note. This, no doubt, is true, and the finding of the court below that she was liable cannot be upheld. Even under the very liberal provisions of our more recent legislation respecting the rights of married women, this court has already held that to bind her the contract must be made with reference to, and upon the faith and credit of, her separate estate. (*Davis v. First Nat. Bank of Cheyenne*, 5 Neb. 242.) She was not liable on the note. But while the finding of the court that Mrs. Christy was indebted on the note cannot be upheld, inasmuch as the decree does not go to the extent of adjudging that she shall pay it, no injury was done." Following the above language it was said that as Mrs. Christy could not be held liable at law, her property could not be taken to satisfy a deficiency judgment if the mortgaged property should not thereafter sell for enough to satisfy fully the amount thereby secured. The language quoted, therefore, amounts to mere *ol iter*, for it touched no proposition involving the liability of Mrs. Christy as presented in the case as it stood at the time the above opinion was delivered.

In *State Savings Bank v. Scott*, 10 Neb. 83, MAXWELL, then chief justice, quoted from *Davis v. First Nat. Bank of Cheyenne* this language of GANTT, J.: "But the rule must be observed, that all such contracts of the *feme covert* must be with reference to, and upon the faith and credit of, her separate estate." Following the above quotation the chief justice said: "And the same doctrine is affirmed in *Hale v. Christy*, 8 Neb. 264. This being the construction given to this statute more than three years ago, it has become a rule affecting the rights and liabilities of individuals, and, if unsatisfactory, should be changed by the legislature and not by the court."

In *Barnum v. Young*, 10 Neb. 309, COBB, J., while intimating that his views might be different if the question was an open one, declared that he felt bound by the case of *State Savings Bank v. Scott, supra*, and the two cases which it followed.

In *Gillespie v. Smith*, 20 Neb. 455, it was held that a married woman, by limiting her defense to the allegation that the notes she signed were not a charge upon her separate estate, too much restricted it to avoid liability, for the reason that the negative pleaded did not amount to the allegation that her contract did not concern her separate property, trade, or business. In the language of the opinion: "The reason is, that her non-liability can only arise from her inability to contract, and this she must clearly allege." ●

In the case of *Bowen v. Foss*, 28 Neb. 373, the action had been brought and a recovery had against E. A. Bowen, the wife of D. Bowen, upon their promissory note of which the following is a copy:

"$100.   CRETE, NEB., Nov. 27, 1882.

"On or before the 27th day of Nov., 1883, for value received in one spring buggy, we promise to pay F. I. Foss, or order, one hundred dollars, with interest at ten per cent from date, payable at the State Bank in Crete. The express condition of the sale and purchase of the above property is such that the ownership does not pass

from said ——— until this note and interest are paid in
full; that the said ——— has full power to declare this
note due, and to take possession of said property at any
time that they may deem themselves insecure, even before the maturity of the note.   D. BOWEN.

"E. A. BOWEN."

The defense was that Mrs. Bowen was a married
woman living with her husband, D. Bowen, and was sick
at the time, and that she signed said note as surety for
her husband. Upon these issues there had been judgment against Mrs. Bowen. The discussion of the facts
is in the following language of MAXWELL, J., who delivered the opinion of this court: "The testimony of the
defendant in error tends to show that the indebtedness
in question was incurred for a new buggy; that at the
time of the purchase the plaintiff in error was in ill
health and could not bear the fatigue of riding in a
lumber wagon; that the defendant in error had in his
hands for collection certain debts due her in Ohio
amounting to about $400; that the husband of the plain-
tiff in error was not in a condition, financially, to pay
the debt, and therefore the credit was not given to him,
but to his wife. This testimony is denied by the plaintiff
in error and her husband, but we find no denial of the
charge in substance, that the husband had no means to
pay a debt of this kind. This, we think, is a material
circumstance in the case in considering to whom the
credit was given, as Mr. Foss testifies that he knew that
the wife was abundantly able, while the husband was
not. There are other circumstances tending to corrobo-
rate the testimony of Foss and the verdict seems to be in
accord with the justice of the case."

In *Godfrey v. Megahan*, 38 Neb. 748, the general proposition is again stated, that a married woman's disability
to contract has been removed only in cases where her
contract has reference to her separate property, trade,
or business or was made upon the faith and the credit
thereof and with intent on her part thereby to bind her

separate property. The third paragraph of the syllabus of the case last referred to would seem amply sustained by the reasoning in *Bowen v. Foss, supra*. This paragraph is as follows: "Whether a contract of a married woman was made with reference to her separate property, trade, or business, or upon the faith and credit thereof, and with the intent on her part to thereby bind her separate property, is always a question of fact."

In *Davis v. First Nat. Bank of Cheyenne, supra*, GANTT. J., speaking of the enactments above referred to, said: "These statutes have legalized the contracts of married women, and, so far as her separate property is concerned, she is *feme sole*, and can legally contract and deal with her property as she pleases. She can bind it by general engagements; but 'it should appear that the engagement is made with reference to, and upon the faith and credit of, her estate; and the question, whether it is so or not, is to be judged by the court.' (Perry, Trusts sec. 659; *Frary v. Booth*, 37 Vt. 78; *Todd v. Lee*, 15 Wis. 400; *Same v. Same*, 16 Wis. 506.)"

It would seem from this language that the proposition that the determination of the intention of the wife in making her contracts was one to be determined by the courts—that is, that it is a question of law—must have been lost sight of in *Bowen v. Foss, supra*, and has met with direct disapproval in *Godfrey v. Megahan, supra*. With reference to this proposition it is difficult to classify *Eckman v. Scott*, 34 Neb. 817, for in that case the language of MAXWELL, C. J., is as follows: "The testimony shows that M. A. Scott is the wife of W. T. Scott; that the debt in this case was that of the husband and did not in any manner relate to the business of the wife, and that she signed the note as surety for him. In a number of cases this court has held that where the contract did not relate to her separate business or estate, a married woman was not bound as surety on a promissory note unless it appeared that she thereby intended to bind her separate estate. (*State Savings Bank v. Scott*, 10 Neb. 84; *Hale v.*

Christy, 8 Neb. 265; *Barnum v. Young*, 10 Neb. 309; *Davis v. First Nat. Bank of Cheyenne*, 5 Neb. 242; *Payne v. Burnham*, 62 N. Y. 74.) The wife, therefore, was not liable on the note."

It will hereafter be shown that whether or not a married woman's contract is with reference to, or upon the faith and credit of, her separate property is a question of law or of fact depends upon circumstances; that sometimes it is one, and sometimes it is the other, or, possibly, sometimes both. In *Smith v. Spaulding*, 40 Neb. 339, it was held that a married woman in this state may contract as surety for her husband (citing *Stevenson v. Craig*, 12 Neb. 464), and that the extension of the time of payment of her husband's past due indebtedness is a sufficient consideration to support her contract as his surety for such debt. In *Buffalo County Nat. Bank v. Sharpe*, 40 Neb. 123, it was held that where the consideration was as in the case last cited, and the security for her husband's debt by way of a mortgage on the wife's property, that the consideration was sufficient and that the property mortgaged was duly bound for the payment of the debt secured. This case was approved and followed in *Watts v. Gantt*, 42 Neb. 869. The doctrine of *Smith v. Spaulding* was restated and followed in *Johnson v. Guss*, 41 Neb. 19, and it was held, furthermore, that the cases cited had established in this state the rule that the wife is not liable on her contracts unless they are made with reference to her separate estate, or an intention is shown to bind such separate estate.

While it may be possible that we have not reviewed all the cases cited by this court with relation to the liability of a married woman upon her contracts, it is believed that there is no case omitted which could do more than restate one, or perhaps more, propositions noted already. It can scarcely escape observation that there has never been any attempt to analyze section 2, chapter 53, of the Compiled Statutes. The first attempt to state its scope was this remark of GANTT, J.: "But the rule must be observed, that all such contracts of the *feme covert* must be with reference to, and upon the faith and credit of, her separate estate." (*Davis v. First Nat. Bank of Cheyenne*, 5 Neb. 242.) In the next case in point of time (*Hale v. Christy, supra*) this remark was approvingly quoted, but immediately afterwards it was disclosed that in the case under consideration it had no practical application. In *State Savings Bank v. Scott* and in *Barnum v. Young*, both reported in the 10th Nebraska, the remark of GANTT, J., was not only approved in the abstract as correct, but was declared to have stood as the law of the state so long that it would be improper for the courts to change it. Cases which followed the four last referred to simply reiterated the same remark as though it had been made independently of the general proposition which immediately preceded it, which was to the effect that the statute had conferred upon a married woman the right and power to make legal and binding contracts and had given her the right to sue, and had made her liable to be sued, in the same manner as though she was unmarried, and that the court must expound the law as it finds it made by the constitutional law-making power. It has the sound of a legal proposition pregnant with meaning to say that all contracts of the *feme covert* must be with reference to, and upon the faith and credit of, her separate estate, but under our statute what is meant by it? In *Davis v. First Nat. Bank of Cheyenne, supra*, GANTT, J., said: "But the settled doctrine of the common law is that the general engagements of a married woman, in respect to her separate property, could only be enforced in equity; and this, not upon the ground that she could make valid contracts in law or equity, but because her honest engagements ought to be answered; and hence it is said that 'intimately connected with the right of a married woman to dispose of her separate property is the right or power of such *feme covert* to contract debts and charge her separate estate, either by special agreements in relation to it, or by general engagements   *   * and her separate estate will be bound to make good her contracts, and it may be reached.by proper proceedings, though she is not personally liable.' (Perry, Trusts secs. 596, 657, 662; *Pentz v. Simonson*, 2 Beas. [N. J. Eq.] 232; *Glass v. Warwick*, 40 Pa. St. 140.)"

Already there has been quoted from *Webb v. Hoselton, supra*, language to the same effect as the above with regard to the equitable liabilities of a married woman's property, upon her contracts with reference to it. If, by our statute, the property of a *feme covert* can be subjected only by pleading and proving as an independent substantive fact that the owner contracted with reference to, or upon the faith and credit of, it, in what respect or to what extent have these statutory enactments changed the status of a married woman's property? In both *Webb v. Hoselton* and *Davis v. First Nat. Bank of Cheyenne*, connected with the statement of the rule in equity with reference to the power to subject the property of married women, there was an epitome of the provisions of chapter 53, Compiled Statutes, from which it might be inferred that in the mind of the writer of each of those opinions there existed a sense of close relationship of some kind between the equitable rule as it was and the statutory rule as it is. From the rule of the statute that "A woman may, while married, sue and be sued in the same manner as if she were unmarried" (Compiled Statutes, ch. 53, sec. 3), it seems open to no question that the intention of the law-makers was, at law, to hold personally liable a married woman upon her contracts, instead of compelling a resort to equitable proceedings to subject her separate property. The general rules of pleading are to such an action applicable, for a married woman may be sued during coverture as though she were unmarried. The fact that a married woman has contracted with reference to her separate property, or upon the faith and credit of it, is by no express provision required to receive more attention in the petition against her than though the suit was one against

her husband to charge him in respect to his separate
property. In practice, however, the difficult question
and one which there seems never to have been any attempt to meet in this state and the one upon which I
cannot agree with the views of Norval, J., is, as to the
manner in which proof shall be made as to how the wife
contracted on the faith and credit of her separate estate.
In *Coquillard v. Horcy*, 23 Neb. 622, occurs this language:
"As we understand the rule for the construction of contracts, it is that, if a contract is to be construed by reference to its terms alone, and without calling in the aid
of extrinsic facts and circumstances, it is the duty of the
court to interpret it. But if the construction must depend upon the proof of other and extrinsic facts, then
these questions of fact should be submitted to the jury,
under proper instructions from the court. (*Begg v.
Forbes*, 30 Eng. Law & Eq. 508; *Etting v. United States
Bank*, 11 Wheat. [U. S.] 74; *First Nat. Bank of Springfield v. Dana*, 79 N. Y. 108; *Edelman v. Yeakel*, 27 Pa. St.
26.)" Ordinarily the question, whether a contract is
with reference to a married woman's separate estate or
employment, would probably be a question of fact dependent, for instance, upon the circumstances that goods
were purchased for her original stock, or afterward to
replenish it, or that clerks or other employés were hired
to assist her in conducting her business. But there
might be such circumstances surrounding the making of
a contract by her upon the faith and credit of her separate property, but not with reference to it, that, as a
question of fact, it should be submitted to the jury. In
either of these two cases, where there is no writing, the
contentions are liable, in a pre-eminent degree, to be
dependent upon questions of fact. But where the contract of a married woman is in writing, how are we to
ascertain and enforce her liability? There has been no
change in the rules of construction or evidence on account of the act in relation to married women. Whenever to the legislature there has appeared a necessity of

a change of rules of evidence in any class of cases that its provisions may be rendered effective, there has been no hesitancy in that respect, as has been instanced by the proviso in section 5, chapter 44, Compiled Statutes, that the agent who acts for the borrower shall also be deemed the agent of the loaner, and the enactment as to the presumption of the value of the real property insured under the provisions of our valued policy law. Indeed, it may be said that all statutory provisions which provide for constructive notice and defines its effect are of this nature. It is therefore worthy of note that in the act relating to married women there is no provision by which is changed the existing rules of evidence and construction, for thereby is evidenced an intention that they shall be given their ordinary meaning and force.

The supreme court of Ohio, in the very instructive case of *Williams v. Urmston*, 35 O. St. 295, had under consideration an appeal from a decree which independently of statute subjected the separate estate of a married woman who had signed an ordinary promissory note with her husband. In respect to the correct deductions to be drawn from the fact that a married woman had signed a note with her husband there was used the following apposite language: "What inference is to be drawn from the act of a married woman, having an estate to her sole and separate use, in signing the promissory note of another, as surety, as respects her intention or purpose in so doing? In view of the fact that in the act of signing she incurs no legal liability, the question admits of but one rational answer, and that is, in the absence of proof showing fraud or imposition, that she intended thereby to make the debt a charge upon her separate estate. Unless this inference is drawn, her act becomes wholly vain and frivolous and entirely destitute of a purpose or a meaning. That such is the natural implication from the act of signing has been distinctly affirmed in numerous cases. In *Bell v. Kellar*, 3 B. Mon. [Ky.] 381, the rule was stated as follows: 'If a *feme covert*, having a separate estate, make or indorse a note, the presumption is that it was the intention, and the effect is, to charge her separate estate.' In *Cowles v. Morgan*, 34 Ala. 535, it was held that 'a promissory note executed by the wife during coverture, jointly with her husband, is a charge upon her separate estate created by contract.' So in *Burnett v. Hawpe*, 25 Gratt. [Va.] 481, it was held that 'if the wife contracts a debt for herself or for her husband, or jointly with him, the instrument executed by her is sufficient to charge her separate estate without any proof of a positive intention to do so or even a reference to such estate contained in the writing.' In *Metropolitan Bank v. Taylor*, 62 Mo. 338, it was held that 'in reference to her separate estate a married woman is to be treated as a *feme sole*, and the giving of a note, or making of a written contract by her, raises the presumption that she intends to bind her separate estate.' This case was on a note executed by the wife as surety for her husband. The same rule prevails in Kansas. (*Deering v. Boyle*, 8 Kan. 523; *Wicks v. Mitchell*, 9 Kan. 80.) Judge Story, in commenting on the subject, says: 'Indeed it does seem difficult to make any sound or satisfactory distinction on the subject as to any particular class of debts, since the natural implication is, that if a married woman contracts a debt she means to pay it, and if she means to pay it, and she has a separate estate, that seems to be the natural fund which both parties contemplated as furnishing the means of payment.' (2 Story, Equity Jurisprudence sec. 1400. See also to the same effect 1 Bishop, Married Women sec. 873.) In *Avery v. Van Sickle*, *ante* 270, we held, that where a married woman executed a promissory note for property acquired by her an implication arises, in the absence of proof showing a different understanding, that she thereby intended to charge her separate estate with its payment. If she executed the note upon the understanding that her separate estate was not to be bound for its payment, its enforcement against her would operate a fraud upon her.

No one would pretend that this could be done. But when she executes a note, either as principal, maker, or surety, and has not been deceived in so doing, nor subjected to any undue influence, we think a just inference arises that she thereby intended to deal on account of her estate, and to bind the same in equity for the payment of the note; and that, as a necessary result, a court of equity will give effect to such intention by subjecting the estate to the payment of the note in the mode prescribed by the statute for enforcing claims against the separate estate of a married woman. Her liability, or rather that of her estate, does not depend on whether or not the debt incurred on its account is beneficial to her or otherwise. If made, and no fraud or imposition is shown, the court cannot refuse relief from the mere fact that the engagement entered into proves unprofitable or injurious."

In the foregoing case, in which there were satisfactory citations of authorities as to the presumption which should be held naturally to arise upon proof that a married woman had signed a promissory note, either as principal or otherwise, are clearly, forcibly, and, I believe, correctly stated, not only as applying in an action in equity to subject a married woman's separate property as that was, but as well in an action at law, under our statute, in fixing her personal liability.

IRVINE, C., concurs in the foregoing opinion of RYAN, C.

BEALS, TORREY & COMPANY V. WESTERN UNION TELEGRAPH COMPANY.

FILED FEBRUARY 2, 1898.   No. 7706.

Right to Dismiss Action. A plaintiff has an absolute right to dismiss his action at any time before the final submission of the cause, subject alone to compliance with conditions precedent, such as the payment of costs, etc., as may be imposed by the court.

ERROR from the district court of Brown county. Tried below before BARTOW, J. *Reversed.*

J. C. McNerny and *Macfarland & Altschuler,* for plaintiff in error.

Estabrook & Davis, contra.

NORVAL, J.

This action was for the recovery of damages sustained by the plaintiff for the failure of the defendant to correctly transmit and deliver a message. Before the final submission of the cause plaintiff asked leave to withdraw a juror, which motion was denied by the court, as was likewise overruled the application of plaintiff for leave to dismiss the cause without prejudice to a future action. A verdict, under a peremptory instruction of the court, was returned for the defendant, and the judgment entered thereon is before us for review.

It appears from the record that before the final submission of the cause to the jury plaintiff asked permission to dismiss the action without prejudice, which application the court denied. This ruling was clearly erroneous. By section 430 of the Code of Civil Procedure the right is given a plaintiff to dismiss his action without prejudice to a future suit at any time prior to final submission, upon such equitable terms as the court may impose. (*Sheedy v. McMurtry,* 44 Neb. 499; *Dayton & W. R. Co. v. Marshall,* 11 O. St. 502; *Hancock Ditch Co. v. Bradford,* 13 Cal. 637.) There was an abuse of discretion under the circumstances in refusing to allow plaintiff to discontinue his action. The judgment is accordingly reversed, with directions to the court below to enter an order of dismissal without prejudice to the right of plaintiff to institute another action for the same cause.

REVERSED.

STATE INSURANCE COMPANY OF DES MOINES V. LOLA M. HUNT.

FILED FEBRUARY 2, 1898.   No. 7796.

Insurance: WITHDRAWAL OF DEFENSE FROM JURY. It is error to withdraw from the consideration of the jury any valid defense which the evidence tends to establish.

ERROR from the district court of Dakota county. Tried below before NORRIS, J. *Reversed.*

C. J. Garlow, for plaintiff in error.

Mell C. Jay and *Jay & Beck, contra.*

SULLIVAN, J.

On April 11, 1891, the State Insurance Company issued a policy of insurance to Lola M. Hunt for a term of five years on a dwelling-house located in South Sioux City, in this state. The premises were occupied by the assured when the policy was issued. Subsequently, however, she removed to Sioux City, Iowa, and one O. A. Anderson, with his family, entered into possession of the property and continued to occupy it until August 23, 1893. On the morning of the following day it was entirely destroyed by fire. In an action brought to recover for the loss sustained the company alleged and relied on a violation of the following provisions of the policy: "Or if without written consent hereon * * * the risk be increased by any means; or if there is any change in the occupant or occupancy of the premises insured; or if the buildings or either of them become vacant, * * * then in every such case this policy shall be void." There was a verdict and judgment in favor of Hunt, and the insurance company has brought the case here for review by petition in error.

On the trial the company offered to prove that when Hunt vacated the property it remained unoccupied for a period of ten days or more. This offer was refused and the defendant excepted. In stating the issues the court instructed the jury that "Defendant, the insurance company, answering, admits that the policy was issued; that the premium was , aid, and that the dwelling-house was destroyed by fire while such policy was in force, and that proof of loss was duly made, resting its defense upon the alleged fact that the plaintiff procured or caused the fire that destroyed the dwelling-house to be set for the purpose of securing the insurance money from this and other companies, and also, that the hazard to the building had been increased by the act of the plaintiff by leaving said house vacant at the time it was burned." Upon the giving of this instruction as well as upon the rejection of the offer above mentioned error is assigned. That the instruction complained of withdrew from the consideration of the jury the defenses based on change of occupants and non-occupancy must be conceded, and the action of the court in this regard cannot be justified on the assumption that there was no evidence tending to establish these defenses or either of them. The judgment of the district court is reversed and the cause remanded for further proceedings.

REVERSED AND REMANDED.

CHARLES BEST, APPELLANT, V. GEORGE C. ZUTAVERN ET AL., APPELLEES.

FILED FEBRUARY 2, 1898. No. 7788.

1. **Alimony:** LIEN ON HOMESTEAD: HUSBAND AND WIFE. A judgment for alimony in favor of a wife, rendered in an action for divorce, is a lien on the family homestead, the title whereof is in the husband.

2. **Real Estate:** POSSESSION. Actual possession of land is notice to the world of the possessor's ownership or interest therein.

3. **Executions:** PURCHASE BY APPRAISER OF LAND: SHERIFF'S DEED.

In an action to quiet title, a sheriff's deed made in pursuance of an execution sale will not be canceled merely because the purchaser was one of the appraisers of the land for the purpose of sale, neither actual fraud being charged nor offer made to reimburse such purchaser.

4. **Limitation of Actions:** DEMURRER. It is ground for demurrer that an action is barred by the statute of limitations only when it affirmatively so appears on the face of the petition.

APPEAL from the district court of Johnson county. Heard below before BABCOCK, J. _Affirmed._

Davidson & Giffen, for appellant.

T. Appelget, J. Hall Hitchcock, Griggs, Rinaker & Bibb, and _L. .C. Chapman, contra._

SULLIVAN, J.

From the petition filed in the district court it appears that Best was the patentee of 160 acres of land in Johnson county, which he occupied with his wife and children from 1863 till 1887. In the latter year his wife sued him for a divorce, which she obtained, together with a judgment for $1,250 alimony, which was made a specific lien on the family homestead and ordered to be paid in installments. Best continued to occupy the land with his minor son, who was dependent upon him for support. When the first installment of alimony became due an execution was issued and forty acres of the homestead sold for its satisfaction. At this sale Zutavern, who had acted as one of the appraisers, became the purchaser. The bid, however, was made by the defendant Shaw, and the title first taken in his name. On the maturity of the second installment of alimony a second execution was issued and another forty of the land sold to satisfy it. Zutavern was also the purchaser of this forty. Afterwards, and while Best was still in possession, Zutavern mortgaged the land to the Smith Bros. Loan & Trust Company and conveyed it by deed to Appelget. Watrous is an assignee of part of the debt secured by the mortgage

to the loan and trust company. The defendants, except
Appelget, severally demurred to the petition on the
ground that it did not state a cause of action and because
the action attempted to be stated was barred by limitation. The demurrers were sustained and, from a judgment dismissing the petition, the plaintiff appeals.

Upon the record two questions are presented for consideration: (1.) Were the execution sales void? (2.) Was
the action to quiet title barred by the statute of limitations? Best's possession of the land was constructive
notice to the world of his interests therein. (*Uhl v. May,*
5 Neb. 157; *Kahre v. Rundle,* 38 Neb. 315; *Pleasants v.
Blodgett,* 39 Neb. 741; *Monroe v. Hanson,* 47 Neb. 30.)
Therefore, the other appellees acquired no better title
than Zutavern had. By section 26 of the divorce act it
is provided that "judgments and decrees for alimony or
maintenance shall be liens upon the property of the husband, and may be enforced and collected in the same
manner as other judgments of the court wherein they are
rendered." (Compiled Statutes, ch. 25, sec. 26.) So, if
the judgment for alimony was a lien, the procedure to
collect it was authorized and regular. We think it was
a lien because the court, having jurisdiction of the parties
and authority to adjust their rights growing out of the
marital relation, made it so. This action of the court
may have been irregular, but it was not void. We think
it was a lien for another reason, and that is, that the land
was not exempt to Best under the provisions of the homestead law. The husband's right to an exempt homestead
cannot, we think, be asserted against the wife who has
been forced by his aggression to leave his domicile, and
who, in an action for divorce, has obtained a judgment
for alimony against him. The homestead law is a family
shield and cannot be employed by either spouse to wrong
the other. The supreme court of Kansas, under a statute which authorized the court upon granting a divorce
to award the wife such share of the husband's real or
personal estate as shall be just and reasonable, held that

the court has power to award the wife possession of the
family homestead, the title to which is in him. (*Brandon
v. Brandon*, 14 Kan. 342.) And, in a later case, it was
decided by the same court that a decree which was declared to be a lien on all the husband's realty was a valid
lien on the family homestead. (*Blankenship v. Blankenship*, 19 Kan. 159.) The logic of these decisions is that
exemption statutes are not designed to protect the husband against the wife's claim for alimony. To the same
effect are the cases of *Mahoney v. Mahoney*, 59 Minn. 347,
61 N. W. Rep. 334, and *Daniels v. Morris*, 54 Ia. 369. From
these considerations it results that the sale on the second
execution was clearly valid. But the other sale was
void. It was made so by the express terms of section
503 of the Code of Civil Procedure, which reads in part
as follows: "No sheriff or other officer making the sale
of property, either personal or real, or any appraiser of
such property, shall, either directly or indirectly, purchase the same; and every purchase so made shall be
considered fraudulent and void."

Assuming that the sale of the first tract was void, Best
contends that the court should have cleared his title
from the cloud created by such sale. In this he is wrong.
There is no charge in the petition that the appraisement
was fraudulent in fact or even that the valuation fixed
was too low. It is not claimed that Zutavern made the
appraisement in contemplation of becoming a purchaser,
or that he was guilty of any wrongful conduct whatever
touching the appraisement or sale. There was no offer
to reimburse him; and for this reason the petition fails
to present a case for equitable relief. True, in the case of
Goble v. O'Connor, 43 Neb. 49, it was held that a purchaser
at a judicial sale who has chilled bids is not entitled in
an action to cancel his deed to the benefit of the rule that
"he who seeks equity must do equity." It was there
said—and it is the rule everywhere—that the maxim
quoted cannot be invoked to protect one from the consequences of his own fraudulent conduct. While this is

the settled rule in cases of actual fraud, it has no application to cases of constructive fraud. (*Ex parte James*, 8 Ves. [Eng.] 351; *White v. Trotter*, 14 S. & M. [Miss.] 30. 53 Am. Dec. 112.) On grounds of public policy, the statute has disqualified appraisers of real estate taken on execution from becoming purchasers at the sale; and one who becomes such purchaser in disregard of this statutory prohibition is guilty of a constructive fraud and can acquire no title. He has no standing in a court of law. But, if he be innocent of actual fraud, the owner of the land cannot invoke the aid of a court of equity to cancel his deed without offering to reimburse him. (*McCaskey v. Graff*, 23 Pa. St. 321.)

Upon the question of the statute of limitations little need be said. More than four years intervened between the execution sales and the commencement of this action. Consequently, the claim for relief, so far as it pertained to the land last sold, was barred. When Best discovered the fraud in the first sale of which he complains does not appear. That an action is barred by limitation is ground for demurrer only when it affirmatively so appears on the face of the petition. (*Peters v. Dunnells*, 5 Neb. 460; *Hurley v. Estes*, 6 Neb. 386; *Hurley v. Cox*, 9 Neb. 230.) The judgment of the district court was right and is

AFFIRMED.

BANK OF BLADEN, APPELLANT, V. ISAAC DAVID ET AL., APPELLEES.

FILED FEBRUARY 2, 1898. No. 7808.

1. **Homestead.** A homestead whose value, after deducting incumbrances, does not exceed $2,000, is exempt from seizure and sale for the satisfaction of its owner's ordinary debts.

2. ————: CONVEYANCE FROM HUSBAND TO WIFE. Land constituting a statutory homestead when conveyed by a husband to his wife

does not become liable for his then existing debts by subsequently losing its homestead character, even when the transfer was voluntary.

APPEAL from the district court of Webster county. Heard below before BEALL, J. *Affirmed.*

A. M. Walters, for appellant.

Case & McNitt, contra. .

SULLIVAN, J.

This was a creditor's bill, filed in the district court of Webster county, to subject certain real estate owned by Mary J. David to the payment of a judgment recovered by the Bank of Bladen against her husband, Isaac David. There was a general finding and judgment in favor of the defendant, and the plaintiff brings the case to this court by appeal.

The land in question was occupied by the Davids as a family homestead for several years prior to the fall of 1890, when they removed from Webster county to Galesburg, Illinois. In August, 1890, David conveyed the homestead to his wife through one Sheen, who served as a conduit for the title. The consideration for the conveyance to Mrs. David was an agreement on her part to support the family and pay her husband's debts, including a mortgage on the land in question amounting to $1,000. The debt, upon which the bank's judgment is based, existed, but had not matured, at the time of the conveyance of the homestead to Mrs. David.

It is contended that the consideration for the conveyance is not sufficient to sustain it against the claims of creditors. Conceding the point without discussion, we are still constrained to hold that the judgment of the district court was the only one that could rightfully have been rendered in the case. The land was a homestead, and, after deducting the indebtedness secured by mortgage thereon, its actual value at the time of its convey·

43

ance was less than $2,000. It was exempt from levy and
sale for the satisfaction of David's debts. (*Munson v.
Carter*, 40 Neb. 417; *Hoy v. Anderson*, 39 Neb. 38 5; *Roberts
v. Robinson*, 49 Neb. 717; *Mundt v. Hagedorn*, 49 Neb. 409.)
It, therefore, did not concern the appellant whether
David retained the title or transferred it to his wife. It
was not injured by the transfer and has no grievance
even if such transfer was without consideration and
made to defraud creditors. (*Smith v. Rumsey*, 33 Mich.
183; *Vaughan v. Thompson*, 17 Ill. 78; *Vogler v. Montgomery*,
54 Mo. 577; *Wood v. Chambers*, 20 Tex. 247; *Butler v.
Nelson*, 72 Ia. 732.)

But it is contended that, when the land lost its homestead character, it became liable for the satisfaction of
the bank's judgment. A sufficient answer to that contention is that it was not then the property of the judgment debtor. The conveyance which vested the title in
Mrs. David infringed none of the legal rights of David's
creditors. It was valid when made. It was not vitiated
by Mrs. David's subsequent change of domicile. It is
valid still. Even Jove himself could not change the
nature of a past transaction. Whether Mrs. David
agreed to pay the bank's claim is quite immaterial. That
question is not an issue in this case. If she has so contracted there is an obvious and adequate remedy at law.
When her liability shall be judicially ascertained, the
appellant will be able to reach this land without the aid
of a court of equity. The judgment of the district court
was manifestly right and is

AFFIRMED.

SYLVIA ELVA PALMER, BY HER GUARDIAN AND NEXT
FRIEND, EMMA D. PALMER, V. MISSOURI PACIFIC
RAILWAY COMPANY.

FILED FEBRUARY 2, 1898.   No. 7818.

Railroads: HIGHWAY-SIGNALS: INJURY TO INFANT: INSTRUCTIONS. In
an action for personal injuries inflicted by a passing locomotive
at a railway crossing it is error to instruct the jury that the question of whether the bell was rung or the whistle sounded is immaterial in case they find that the injured party by reason of her
tender age could not understand the meaning of such signals.

ERROR from the district court of Adams county. Tried
below before BEALL, J.   *Reversed.*

A. H. Bowen, for plaintiff in error.

W. P. McCreary, J. C. Watson, J. W. Orr, and *B. P. Waggener, contra.*

SULLIVAN, J.

This action was brought in the district court of Adams
county on behalf of the plaintiff, an infant then about
two years old, by her next friend to recover for injuries
received by her at a crossing on the defendant's line of
road in said county from a locomotive passing along and
over the same: Among other alleged negligent omissions of the defendant to which the plaintiff attributes
her injury, she avers that the employés of the defendant
in charge of the locomotive failed to ring the bell or
sound the whistle on approaching the crossing in question. This was denied by the defendant, and upon this
issue, among others, the cause was submitted to the jury,
who returned a verdict for the defendant. There was
judgment on the verdict and the plaintiff prosecutes
error to this court.

One of the grounds relied upon for a reversal of the
judgment of the district court is the giving of the following instruction at the request of the defendant:

"If you find from the evidence that at the time of the alleged injury the plaintiff, by reason of her tender age, could not understand the meaning of the warning of danger if given by the ringing of the bell or the blowing of the whistle, then you are instructed that it is imma- terial in this case whether or not the bell was rung or the whistle blown and in such case you are instructed to disregard any evidence on that point."

This instruction is erroneous. It is not always essen- tial to the effectiveness of such warnings that they be given to those of sufficient intelligence to understand their meaning. They are usually held to be for the pro- tection of domestic animals as well as men. (*Chicago, R. I. & P. R. Co. v. Reid*, 24 Ill. 144; 4 Am. & Eng. Ency. Law [1st ed.] 925.) Such warnings are not given to domestic animals upon the theory that they understand their meaning, but upon the theory that their attention will be arrested, their fears aroused thereby, and that their natural instincts will urge them to seek safety in flight. The attention of children is as quickly arrested, their fears as easily aroused, and their instinct of self- preservation as strong as those of domestic animals. With respect to children of tender years and immature judgment, a railroad corporation, to say the least, owes the duty which the law exacts from it in respect to domestic animals straying upon its track. (*Gunn v. Ohio River R. Co.*, 36 W. Va. 165; 32 Am. St. Rep. 842.) But it is urged that the evidence upon this point on behalf of the plaintiff was insufficient to warrant its submission to the jury and that the giving of this instruction, if error, was error without prejudice. It is sufficient to say that we have examined the evidence and are satisfied that the question should have been submitted to the jury. For the error mentioned the judgment of the district court is reversed and the cause remanded for a new trial.

REVERSED AND REMANDED.

GENEVA NATIONAL BANK V. RICHARD DONOVAN ET AL.

58
58

FILED FEBRUARY 2, 1898.   No. 7813.

1. **Transcript of Journal Entry:** REVIEW. Where there is expressly excepted from the certificate of a clerk of the district court authenticating a transcript the journal entry of that court on the motion for a new trial, such entry must be treated as though not appearing in the transcript.

2. **Ruling on Motion for New Trial:** REVIEW. On a petition in error in this court alleged errors of the district court committed during the progress of the trial, or in the rendition of its judgment, cannot be considered when in the district court there appears to have been no ruling on the motion for a new trial.

ERROR from the district court of Fillmore county. Tried below before HASTINGS, J. *Affirmed.*

F. B. Donisthorpe, for plaintiff in error.

Ong & Wilson, contra.

RYAN, C.   •

The Geneva National Bank brought this action in the district court of Fillmore county for the foreclosure of a mortgage securing payment of a note made by Richard Donovan and Catherine Donovan. The defendants interposed the defense of usury, which, upon a trial, was sustained to the amount of $275.40, which sum was accordingly credited upon the principal, and for the balance a decree was entered. By its petition in error the bank seeks to set aside the finding of the existence of usury.

The certificate of the clerk of the district court attached to the transcript is in this language: "I, H. F. Putlitz, clerk of the district court within and for the county of Fillmore, state of Nebraska, do hereby certify that the above and foregoing is a true and correct transcript of the plaintiff's petition, answer of Richard Donovan and Catherine Donovan, reply of plaintiff herein,

journal entries, except on demurrer and motion for a
new trial, as the same appear on file and of record in the
office of said clerk in the within entitled action. Witness my hand," etc. Since there is expressly excepted
from this certificate the journal entry on the motion for
a new trial, the transcript must be considered as though,
therein, that ruling did not appear. Under such circumstances the errors alleged to have occurred on the trial,
or in the rendition of the judgment, cannot be reviewed
in this court. (*Leach v. Reniwald*, 45 Neb. 207, and authorities therein cited.) The judgment of the district court
is therefore

AFFIRMED.

JOSEPH H. NASH v. JAMES A. COSTELLO.

FILED FEBRUARY 2, 1898. No. 7784.

Fraudulent Conveyances: EVIDENCE. The evidence in this case examined and *held* insufficient to sustain the verdict of the jury.

ERROR from the district court of Hall county. Tried
below before THOMPSON, J. *Reversed.*

W. T. Thompson, O. A. Abbott, and *Abbott & Caldwell,* for
plaintiff in error.

W. H. Thompson, Charles B. Keller, and *W. A. Prince,*
contra.

RYAN, C.

The sheriff of Hall county levied several writs of attachment issued out of the district court of said county
on a stock of goods in the possession of Joseph H. Nash.
As the owner of said goods, Nash, in the same court,
replevied them from the sheriff. A trial to a jury resulted in a verdict in favor of the sheriff, upon which a

judgment was rendered, of which Nash, upon proceeding in error in this court, seeks a reversal.

On the trial of this cause in the district court Nash introduced in evidence the following written memorandum: .

"In consideration of eight thousand three hundred dollars to us in hand paid, the receipt of which is hereby acknowledged, we, each for ourselves individually, and jointly and separately, do hereby sell and convey unto Joseph H. Nash our entire stock of general merchandise, together with all furniture and fixtures, also all notes due to us and all book accounts and other bills receivable due to us, said goods, chattels, and merchandise now in the storeroom situated upon lot numbered six (6), in block numbered five (5), in the town of Mason City, county of Custer, state of Nebraska, and the title to the same we will, and our heirs and assigns shall, defend against all lawful claims of any nature whatever. In witness whereof, we have hereunto set our hands at Mason City, Nebraska, this 3d day of November, A. D. 1892.   J. M. PERSINGER.

                        "A. B. WARRELL & CO."

     "In presence of
        "DENNIS RUNYON."

N. R. Persinger, on behalf of plaintiff, testified that during 1892 he was the president of the Central City Bank, of Central City, Nebraska, and was acquainted with certain obligations held by the bank against A. B. Warrell, John M. Persinger, and the Merrick County Mercantile Company. One of these he identified and it is of the descriptions following, to-wit: A promissory note dated September 22, 1892, payable ninety days after date to the Central City Bank of Central City, for $4,000, with ten per cent per annum interest after maturity, made by the Merrick County Mercantile Company, per J. M. Persinger. Another obligation which was held by Joseph H. Nash was identified by this witness, of which the description was as follows: A promissory note dated

June 30, 1892, executed by the Merrick County Mercantile Company to Joseph H. Nash, for $1,075, drawing ten
per cent interest per annum from date, due by its terms
six months after date. The third obligation identified
by this witness was a promissory note of date September
22, 1892, due ninety days after date to the aforesaid Central City Bank, for $3,300, drawing ten per cent per
annum interest from maturity, executed by A. B. Warrell. These three notes, N. R. Persinger testified, constituted the consideration named in the above memorandum. There was no effort made to show that these notes
evidenced an indebtedness which had no real existence.
N. R. Persinger further testified that on the date of the
above memorandum, at the request of Mr. Nash, he took
the above described promissory notes to Mason City,
where A. B. Warrell was running a store, and induced
him to execute the above memorandum and transfer the
possession of the personal property therein described to
a person sent by Mr. Nash to take possession thereof immediately upon Mr. Nash being notified that the memorandum had been signed. This witness testified that the
notes due the bank were transferred to Mr. Nash, by
whom, soon after the date of the memorandum, all three
notes were delivered to A. B. Warrell as having been
paid. He also testified that the note made to Mr. Nash
was for money individually loaned by Mr. Nash, independently of the bank or of his relationship thereto as
its cashier, and there was no evidence offered contradictory of this statement.

The fraud sufficient to vitiate the transfer to Mr. Nash,
of which the attaching creditors asserted the existence,
was based upon the alleged identity of A. B. Warrell, A.
B. Warrell & Co., and the Merrick County Mercantile
Company with the Central City Bank and its cashier, Mr.
Nash. To an understanding of this contention it is
necessary that a short history of certain transactions be
given in this connection. The predecessor of the Central City Bank held notes made by John M. Persinger,

by his wife, by his wife's father, and by A. B. Warrell,
aggregating in amount $6,500.   These, it seems, had
been given for an indebtedness really owing by John M.
Persinger.   Immediately after N. R. Persinger had
organized the Central City Bank there was organized the
Merrick County Mercantile Company as a corporation.
To this corporation the cashier of Central City Bank
loaned $1,000 to enable it to effect an exchange of some
real property for a stock of goods.   The Merrick County
Mercantile Company, it seems, succeeded John M. Persinger in business, and at its organization he was made
its president and A. B. Warrell its secretary and treasurer.   These official relations, so far as the record discloses, have never ceased.   About September 15, 1891,
A. B. Warrell, with the knowledge and assent of the
Central City Bank, took a portion of the goods of the
Merrick County Mercantile Company of about the value
of $3,800 to Mason City and there opened a store in his
own name and proceeded to dispose of the goods with
which he had been entrusted.   For a fair proportion of
the indebtedness of the Merrick County Mercantile Company Mr. Warrell, when he had selected the goods he
was to take with him, made his own promissory note to
the Central City Bank,—the mercantile company gave its
note to the bank for the balance.   In August the remainder of the stock of the Merrick County Mercantile
Company was removed to Mason City.   This portion, together with what had been previously under the management of A. B. Warrell, from this time forward constituted a single stock, which was managed under the name
of A. B. Warrell & Co.   As we understand the evidence,
the note hereinbefore described as being for $3,300 was a
renewal of the proportion for which A. B. Warrell gave
his promissory note in 1891, and the notes for $4,000 and
$1,075 were for the amounts due the bank and Mr. Nash
respectively from the Merrick County Mercantile Company.   It is urged by the defendant that the capital
stock of the Merrick County Mercantile Company was

never disposed of, but was held almost exclusively by
the Central City Bank. We understand from the evidence that there were issued at least five and perhaps
fifteen shares of this stock of the par value of $10 per
share to parties outside the bank and the president and
secretary of the mercantile company. The certificates
for the remainder of the capital stock, the secretary testified, were signed up in blank and left with the Central
City Bank. N. R. Persinger testified that the certificates
were left with the bank, but not as collateral. This is
all the light we have on this subject, and while it shows
a very loose mode of doing business, we have not been
able to see how the bank, by acting as custodian of the
certificates of stock, is chargeable with a fraudulent intent towards creditors of the mercantile company or
towards A. B. Warrell or A. B. Warrell & Co., even if the
individual and firm last indicated should be regarded as
entities distinct from the mercantile company. In argument, however, the relations between the bank on the
one hand and the mercantile company, A. B. Warrell, or
A. B. Warrell & Co. on the other hand, it was insisted,
showed that the bank was in fact the owner of the goods
at every stage of the proceedings, and that when the bill
of sale was made to Nash the transaction was merely
an open assumption by the bank of a secret ownership
it all along had held of the goods in question. There is
in the record no evidence which justifies this contention.
The removal of the goods from Central City, it was testified, without contradiction, was to find a market in which
such goods would meet with a readier sale than at that
place. Under the management of Mr. Warrell this expectation, to some extent, seems to have been realized.
It is not disclosed why this condition did not continue
after a large addition had been made to the stock and
the management had become that of A. B. Warrell & Co.
The credits given by the bank and Mr. Nash seem, from
the first, to have been injudicious, but we can find no
evidence that these credits were fraudulently extended.

The bank or its cashier had the same right that any other creditor had to obtain satisfaction of the indebtedness owing to it or to him and this right seems not to have been fraudulently exercised. The judgment of the district court is therefore reversed and the cause is remanded for further proceedings.

REVERSED AND REMANDED.

HARRISON, C. J., not sitting.

CHARLES BEST V. GEORGE C. ZUTAVERN.   53
                                                         462 6

FILED FEBRUARY 2, 1898. No. 7799.

1. **Executions**: OBJECTIONS TO CONFIRMATION OF SALE. An objection to a confirmation of a sale on execution, on the ground of a mere irregularity in the appraisement, comes too late when first urged after the return of such completed sale by the officer conducting the same.

2. ————: SALE OF HOMESTEAD. The homestead right of exemption of real property under the laws of this state is not a proper subject for consideration upon proceedings for the confirmation of a sale of the alleged homestead on execution.

3. ————: CONFIRMATION OF SALE. The only matter settled and adjudicated in the proceedings and order of confirmation is as to the proceedings of the sheriff and those acting under and with him in the levy, appraisement, advertising, making, and returning of said sale. In so far as the principle thus stated in *Schribar v. Platt*, 19 Neb. 625, is in conflict with the reasoning in *Berkley v. Lamb*, 8 Neb. 392, the later case considered is *held*, in effect, to have overruled the earlier case.

ERROR from the district court of Johnson county. Tried below before BABCOCK, J. *Affirmed*.

Davidson & Giffen, for plaintiff in error.

J. Hall Hitchcock and *L. C. Chapman*, contra.

RYAN, C.

By his petition in error Charles Best questions, in this court, the correctness of the order of the district court of

Johnson county whereby were overruled his two objections to the confirmation of a sale of certain of his real property. These objections were not filed until after the sale had been made and returned for confirmation.

The first objection urged no fraud, but merely an alleged irregularity in the appraisement and was properly overruled. (*Vought v. Foxworthy*, 38 Neb. 214; *Burkett v. Clark*, 46 Neb. 466; *Overall v. McShane*, 49 Neb. 64; *Kearney Land & Investment Co. v. Aspinwall*, 45 Neb. 601; *McMurtry v. Columlia Nat. Bank*, 53 Neb. 21; *Ecklund v. Willis*, 44 Neb. 129.)

The second objection, briefly stated, was that the property sold by the sheriff was the homestead of Charles Best, and, therefore, being exempt from sale on execution, a confirmation of such sale should have been denied. In *Schribar v. Platt*, 19 Neb. 625, among other questions, there was determined the effect of a confirmation of a sale on execution over the objections of the execution defendant that the property sold was his homestead and as such was exempt from sale on judicial process. With respect to the contention of the adverse party that the confirmation of the sale was conclusive in a collateral proceeding, COBB, J., in the delivery of the opinion of this court, said: "The learned district court seemed to be of the opinion, and so found, that the question of title was involved in and settled by the proceedings for the confirmation of the said execution sale. In that, I think, the court erred; and that the only thing settled or adjudicated in the proceedings and order of confirmation, so called, was as to the proceedings of the sheriff and those acting under and with him in the levy, appraisement, advertising, making, and returning of said sale." It is true this view is hardly reconcilable with the reasoning in *Berkley v. Lamb*, 8 Neb. 392, but as it is the later and has been acquiesced in for several years it must prevail and *Berkley v. Lamb, supra*, to that extent must be deemed overruled. On principle the holding in *Schribar v. Platt, supra*, is evidently correct, for this court has held that, at chambers, a judge may confirm a judicial sale (*B a'rice Paper Co. v. Beloit Iron Works*, 46 Neb. 900; *McMurtry v. Tuttle*, 13 Neb. 232), and this is hardly consistent with the idea that at such a hearing there may be an adjudication of rights ordinarily determinable only by courts in the exercise of their jurisdiction as such. On principle the language above quoted from *Schribar v. Platt, supra*, finds direct support in the reasoning in *Quigley v. McErony*, 41 Neb. 73. (See also *Baumann v. Franse*, 37 Neb. 807.) The ruling of the district court, we therefore conclude, was right, and accordingly it is

AFFIRMED.

JOHANNA OLSEN V. MARY JACOBSON ET AL.

FILED FEBRUARY 2, 1898.   No. 7806.

Affirmance where all the questions presented are based on an unauthenticated bill of exceptions.

ERROR from the district court of Washington county. Tried below before KEYSOR, J.   *Affirmed.*

W. S. Cook, D. Z. Mummert, and *Frick & Dolezal*, for plaintiff in error.

Davis & Howell and *E. R. Duffie, contra.*

RYAN, C.

All the questions presented by the petition in error in this case depend upon the contents of an alleged bill of exceptions, and as it is not authenticated, the judgment of the district court is

AFFIRMED.

GEORGE E. COON ET AL. V. HUGH M. MCCLURE.

FILED FEBRUARY 2, 1898. No. 7761.

1. **Witnesses:** INSTRUCTIONS. An erroneous instruction that where a party litigant offers in evidence the testimony of a witness he is bound by such testimony, *held* not justified by the alleged fact that there was no testimony on the trial differing from that of said witness.

2. **Attachment:** GROUNDS: INSTRUCTIONS. An instruction which required the concurrence of an intent to hinder, delay, and defraud creditors, to render void transfers of a certain class, *held* erroneous where the provision of the statute is that the intent may be either to hinder, delay, or defraud.

3. ———: ———. The mere fact that in justifying the levy of an attachment in a replevin action the defendants in their answer alleged that the transfer, under which the plaintiff claimed title, was made with intent to hinder, delay, and defraud creditors did not vary the provisions of the statute.

ERROR from the district court of Webster county. Tried below before BEALL, J. *Reversed.*

Warren Switzler, for plaintiff in error.

M. A. Hartigan, contra.

RYAN, C.

This was an action of replevin for certain goods brought in the district court of Webster county, in which action there was a judgment in favor of the plaintiff. The defendants prosecute this error proceeding.

The possession of the defendants, a sheriff and his deputy, before the institution of this action was by virtue of a writ of attachment under which a levy had been made in an action wherein the Nebraska Moline Plow Company was plaintiff and O. C. Clingman & Co., a partnership firm, was defendant. The question was whether or not the transfer of the replevied property from Clingman & Co. to Hugh M. McClure was fraudulent as against the Nebraska Moline Plow Company, a creditor of O. C. Clingman & Co. The evidence relied upon to sustain the charge that the goods had been transferred in fraud of the said rights of a creditor was largely circumstantial in its nature. Mr. McClure was a witness in his own behalf and from him were elicited admissions tending to cast doubt upon the good faith of the transfer under and by virtue of which he claimed title. The plaintiffs in error called as their own witness O. C. Clingman, a member of the firm of O. C. Clingman & Co., and examined him with reference to the financial condition of the firm of which he was a member when the aforesaid transfer was made, the disposition of its assets, and other circumstances tending to cast discredit upon the claim that such transfer was in good faith. On rebuttal defendant in error examined A. D. McNeer, another member of the firm of O. C. Clingman & Co., for the purpose of explaining why he had drawn certain sums from the partnership funds, how he had replaced them, and the part he had taken with reference to the transfer to McClure. The following instructions were given to the jury:

"8. The court instructs the jury that when a party to an action calls a witness, they indorse such witness before the court and jury as a truthful person and entitled to credit, and they are bound by the evidence of such witness."

"5. The court instructs the jury that before the defendant in this action can question the act of the plaintiff McClure in purchasing the stock of goods it must not only appear from a preponderance of the testimony that the firm of O. C. Clingman & Co. was insolvent and that it sold its stock of goods to the plaintiff McClure with the fraudulent purpose of cheating, defrauding, and delaying its creditors, and it must further appear by the preponderance of the testimony that McClure not only knew these facts and, knowing them, he deliberately and willfully entered into the contract of purchase of the stock of goods with the purpose to aid and assist the firm of O. C. Clingman & Co. to cheat and defraud and delay its creditors."

The proposition that a party by offering the testimony of a witness vouches for his credibility has been approved by this court in *Blackwell v. Wright*, 27 Neb. 269, and in *Nathan v. Sands*, 52 Neb. 660. The proposition that such party is bound by the evidence of such witness is defended on the theory that there was no other evidence than that to the same effect as was the testimony of Clingman. We have carefully considered the bill of exceptions and find that there were circumstances shown by the testimony of witnesses called by the defendant in error from which the jury properly might have drawn inferences unfavorable to the good faith of the transfer by virtue of which McClure claimed title. That part of the instruction which assumed to tell the jury what effect must be given the evidence of Clingman was erroneous. (*Murphey v. Virgin*, 47 Neb. 692.)

Section 17, chapter 32, Compiled Statutes, is in this language: "Every conveyance or assignment, in writing or otherwise, of any estate or interest in lands, or in goods, or things in action, or of any rents or profits issuing therefrom, and every charge upon lands, goods, or things in action, or upon the rents and profits thereof, made with the intent to hinder, delay, or defraud creditors or persons of their lawful rights, damages, forfeitures, debts, or demands, and every bond or other evidence of debt given, suit commenced, or decree or judgment suffered, with the like intent as against the person so hindered, delayed, or defrauded, shall be void." The fifth instruction required that the jury must find the intent to hinder, delay, and defraud creditors was entertained by Clingman & Co. to render the transfer void. This was more than the statute required, for, under its provisions above quoted, it was sufficient if there existed an intent to hinder, delay, or defraud. Defendant in error seeks to justify this departure from statutory requirements by the fact that in the answer filed by plaintiff in error the justification of the attachment was that there had been a transfer with intent to hinder, delay, and defraud, and hence, it is argued, it was not erroneous in the instruction to adopt the same phraseology. If the averments of the answer had been of an intent to hinder, delay, or defraud, that pleading would have been faulty. The proper language is given by the statute and it should have been followed by the court in its instruction. For the errors indicated the judgment of the district court is reversed.

REVERSED AND REMANDED.

J. ABBOTT THOMPSON, APPELLEE, V. S. H. KYNER ET AL., APPELLANTS.

ELIZABETH P. AVERY, APPELLEE, V. S. H. KYNER ET AL., APPELLANTS.

WATSON GIBBONS, APPELLEE, V. S. H. KYNER ET AL., APPELLANTS.

FILED FEBRUARY 2, 1898.   NOS. 7715, 7716, 7717.

Payment of Mortgage to Mortgagee's Agent Not Made: EVIDENCE. The evidence in the case of Thompson against Kyner examined, and *held* to sustain the judgment of the district court; and upon stipulation of the respective parties interested the judgment in each of the three cases is affirmed.

APPEALS from the district court of Brown county. Heard below before BARTOW, J.   *Affirmed.*

J. S. Davisson and *W. J. Courtright,* for appellants.

C. C. Flansburg, contra.

OPINION by RYAN, C., in the case next following.

WATSON GIBBONS ET AL. V. S. H. KYNER ET AL.

FILED FEBRUARY 2, 1898.   No. 8312.

New Trial: EVIDENCE. The evidence on which a petition for a new trial was granted examined and *held* insufficient.

ERROR from the district court of Brown county. Tried below before BARTOW, J. *Reversed.*

C. C. Flansburg, for plaintiffs in error.

J. S. Davisson and *W. J. Courtright, contra.*

RYAN, C.

In the district court of Brown county, J. Abbott Thompson filed his petition for the foreclosure of a certain mortgage and note securing payment of the same. both of which were executed to him by Harvey McMunn on May 20, 1885. The loan thus evidenced and secured was for the term of five years. The mortgaged premises were purchased on November 3, 1885, by Kyner. The principal defense pleaded by Kyner was the payment of said note in the year 1890. On the issues joined there was decreed a foreclosure as prayed. There were two other cases tried in the same court, to-wit, Gibbons against Kyner, No. 7717, and Avery against Kyner, No. 7716, on the same issues and with the same result reached in the case of Thompson against Kyner, and by appeal all three are now pending in this court. (See *ante,* p. 625.) In effect the parties have stipulated that the same judgment shall be rendered in this court in each of these cases; hence, Gibbons against Kyner and Avery against Kyner need receive no further notice in this case than is necessary to carry into effect this stipulation.

Mr. Kyner's testimony was to the effect that when the interest became due he paid it to the Farmers & Merchants National Bank at Fremont until the Nebraska Mortgage & Investment Company notified him, after which time he paid the interest to the company last named. The notices sent by the Farmers & Merchants Bank were signed by C. H. Toncray, cashier, and recited that the interest was due and payable at that bank. As a matter of fact the note given by McMunn, as well as each of the coupons, recited that it was payable at the First National Bank of Hartford, Conn. In such notices as were sent by the Nebraska Mortgage & Investment Company there was no statement with reference to the place at which either principal or interest was required to be paid. In his testimony Mr. Kyner identified a postal card sent to him by the said investment company whereby was acknowledged the receipt of $44 in which was included the amount of interest paid on this loan at or about that time, which was November 27, 1889. In this communication Mr. Kyner was informed that the coupons paid by the $44, above mentioned, would later be sent to him, and they were, ordinarily, within from eight to thirty days after payment. The principal sum was paid to the Nebraska Mortgage & Investment Company soon after it fell due and was never remitted to Mr. Thompson. The testimony of Mr. Thompson and C. H. Smith was taken by deposition and offered by Mr. Kyner. In his deposition Mr. Thompson stated that an application for a loan was submitted to him by Tiffany & Smith, that on this application he advanced the money to be loaned Mr. McMunn, and in due time received back the note and mortgage sued on. He further testified that after the receipt of the principal note and coupons in connection therewith he retained the same in his possession in his safe, and if the money was sent to Tiffany & Smith or their successor, C. H. Smith & Co., he would bring the coupon down, and that he knew nothing of a claim of payment of the principal until about the month of March, 1893. He furthermore testified that he did not object to receiving payment of coupons through Tiffany and C. H. Smith & Co., and did not know whether they had a western agency or not, and he thought that most

of the coupons were paid to him through the First Na
tional Bank of Hartford, Connecticut, though of this he
was not certain.   On his cross-examination Mr. Thompson testified that he never gave C. H. Smith & Co., C. H.
Smith, senior, or C. H. Smith, junior, any authority concerning the collection of moneys on account of the Mc-
Munn loan, and never authorized any person to represent
him in Nebraska in connection with this loan.   The testimony of C. H. Smith was consistent with that of Mr.
Thompson. He explained that for fifteen years preceding January 1, 1887, he had been engaged in business
under the name of E. D. Tiffany, and since that date as
a member of the firm of C. H. Smith & Co.   He testified
that this business was dealing in investment securities,
including western loans; that he had never known Mr.
Toncray personally until October, 1890, and had no business relations with him except receiving drafts for payments of interest on loans negotiated by the Farmers &
Merchants National Bank.   He further testified that the
firms of which he was a member never made any western
farm loans, but sold applications made by correspondents for which the firm of which he was a member received a commission.   In such cases when the papers
were completed and delivered there was no obligation to
render further services for any one, though, if applied to
by customers the firms of which he was a member would
attend to making collections of interest.   When such
collections were made at Fremont, Nebraska, they were
received by C. H. Smith & Co. and E. D. Tiffany through
the Farmers & Merchants National Bank of that place,
until the date of the organization of the Nebraska Mortgage & Investment Company, after which time they were
received through the last named company.   At the request of customers the firm of C. H. Smith & Co. would
write to correspondents with reference to the probability
of payments of principal or interest already in default,
but Mr. Smith testified that he did not think these customers knew anything about these correspondents.

There was a large number of letters introduced in evidence in the deposition of Mr. Smith. These were written by the firm of which he was a member to its correspondent in Fremont, but they were entirely consistent with the testimony above quoted. We are clearly of the opinion that the judgment of the district court was in harmony with the views of this court expressed in the following cases: *First Nat. Bank of Omaha v. Chilson*, 45 Neb. 257; *South Branch Lumber Co. v. Littlejohn*, 31 Neb. 606; *Bull v. Mitchell*, 47 Neb. 647; *Richards v. Waller*, 49 Neb. 639; *Thomson v. Shelton*, 49 Neb. 644; *City Missionary Society v. Reams*, 51 Neb. 225.

There was, however, filed subsequently to the rendition of said judgment a petition for a new trial on the ground of newly-discovered evidence material to the issues which had been determined by such judgment; and, on a hearing, the prayer of this petition was granted and a new trial was awarded. To test the correctness of this ruling a petition in error has been filed in this court wherein the case was docketed as "Gibbons et al. v. Kyner et al. No. 8312." The evidence claimed to be material was contained in an affidavit made by George W. E. Dorsey, in which, in substance, he stated that he had been the president of the Nebraska Mortgage & Investment Company from its organization in 1888 until some time in 1891; and that, while acting as such president prior to June 1, 1890, affiant had a conversation with Charles H. Smith, of the firm of C. H. Smith & Co., in regard to the manner of doing business between that firm and the Nebraska Mortgage & Investment Company. The portion of this affidavit claimed to be material is probably to be found within the following quotation, but just where the writer hereof is unable to determine: "The manner of doing business between said C. H. Smith & Co. and the Nebraska Mortgage & Investment Company was all discussed and the manner of doing business between other people under like circumstances was fully discussed and compared. By other people doing a like

business I refer to the business of making and collecting
real estate loans where the western correspondent deals
with the borrower, and the eastern correspondent deals
directly with the lender, and where the money in making
the loan passes from the lender to the eastern correspondent, thence to the western correspondent, thence to the
borrower, and where, when collections are made, the
money passes from the mortgagor to the western correspondent, thence to the eastern correspondent, thence
to the mortgagee or lender.   And the manner of making
collections by such western correspondent was also discussed, and the trouble and expense that the Nebraska
Mortgage & Investment Company was to in sending out
notices to the borrowers from time to time, and that the
principal and interest was about to mature and requests
for prompt remittances of same in loans negotiated by it
and its predecessor through Smith & Co., and in the collection and remittance of such interest and principal by
said Nebraska Mortgage & Investment Company should
thereafter be entitled to deduct exchange at the time of
making such remittances as compensation to said Nebraska Mortgage & Investment Company for its work
and expense in making such collections.   And Mr. Smith
expressed himself as a part of said conversation to the
effect that, everything considered, other western correspondents did not deduct such exchange at the time of
remitting, and that the Nebraska Mortgage & Investment Company should conform to the general custom
and not deduct any such exchange, and it was agreed, as
a part of said conversation between Mr. Smith as a member of the firm of C. H. Smith & Co. and myself acting as
president of the Nebraska Mortgage & Investment Company, that said Nebraska Mortgage & Investment Company should look after the collection and remittance of
the principal and interest of the loans negotiated
through said Nebraska Mortgage & Investment Company
and its predecessor and C. H. Smith & Co. without any
charge therefor for exchange or otherwise."

The weak point in the defense of Mr. Kyner, originally, was the failure to show that C. H. Smith & Co. or the Nebraska Mortgage & Investment Company was the mortgagee's agent for receiving and paying interest or principal to such mortgagee. The mortgagee held in his possession the note and each coupon until some one was ready to pay them to him, and when one was paid he merely surrendered it as being paid. The inconsequential talk preceding the agreement of Mr. Dorsey to forbear exacting exchange was irrelevant to this question of agency. If it was intended to contradict C. H. Smith merely for the purpose of discrediting him it was likewise inadmissible, under the ruling of this court in *Nathan v. Sands*, 52 Neb. 660. In any view, the proposed testimony of Mr. Dorsey could not in the least strengthen the weak point in Mr. Kyner's defense; hence the petition for a new trial should have been denied and the order of the district court on this branch of the case is therefore reversed. It was in effect stipulated that on this branch the same judgment should be rendered in Avery against Kyner, No. 7716, and in Gibbons against Kyner, No. 7717, as in this case in this court. It is accordingly ordered that the judgments sought to be reviewed by Mr. Kyner as appellant be affirmed and that the orders granting new trials in such cases be reversed and that these cases be remanded to the district court for the entry of these judgments and orders.

JUDGMENTS ACCORDINGLY.

MINNIE L. JAYNES v. OMAHA STREET RAILWAY COMPANY.

FILED FEBRUARY 2, 1898.   No. 5370.

1. **Dedication:** TITLE TO STREETS. Where land is conveyed and platted into an addition to a city in pursuance of the statute the fee-simple title to the streets and alleys of such addition thereby vests in the public.

2. ———: ———. But the public holds the title to such streets and alleys in trust for the use for which they were dedicated.

3. ———: ———. Such a grant construed, and *held* that it contemplated the right of the public to use the streets for the purpose of passage by such means as it might see fit to employ; but the grant did not contemplate that any person should exclusively and permanently appropriate any portion of a street to his own use to the continued exclusion of the remainder of· the public therefrom.

4. **Eminent Domain:** ADDITIONAL BURDEN. Whether the use made of a street is an additional burden upon the easement does not depend upon the motive power which moves the vehicles employed in such use, but depends upon whether the vehicle and appliances used in and necessary to effectuate the purpose permanently and exclusively occupy a portion of the street to the continued exclusion of the rest of the public therefrom.

5. ———: ———: ELECTRIC RAILWAYS: DAMAGES. A corporation constructed in a street its railway tracks and set poles, at stated distances apart, on either side of said tracks near the margin of said streets; on these poles it placed wires and used these poles and wires for the moving of its cars on said tracks by electricity. An abutting lot-owner sued the railway company for damages, alleging in his petition that the continued existence· in the street opposite his property of the poles and wires interfered with his ingress to, and egress from, his premises and depreciated them in value. *Held,* That the petition stated a cause of action.

6. ———: ———: ———: ———. What acts, omissions, facts, and circumstances are competent evidence of damages to be considered by a jury are questions of law for the court; but whether such acts, omissions, facts, or circumstances affect an owner's property and damage it, and the amount of such damages, are for the jury.

7. ———: ———: ———: ———. It seems that, by reason of article 1, section 21, of our constitution, it is not absolutely essential that the poles and wires of an electric street railway company should be held, as a matter of law, to be an additional burden upon the easement, in order to entitle the abutting lot-owner to compensation for the depreciation to his real estate, caused by the permanent and continued presence in the street in front thereof of such poles and wires.

ERROR from the district court of Douglas county. Tried below before IRVINE, J. *Reversed.*

The opinion contains a statement of the case.

H. C. Brome and *Brome, Andrews & Sheean,* for plaintiff in error:

Whenever the location, construction, and use of a public improvement occasion a direct disturbance of a

physical right which the owner enjoys in connection with
his property, and the result of such interference is to
lessen the market value of the property, then that property is damaged within the meaning of our constitution
and the owner entitled to compensation commensurate
with the injury sustained.   (*Gottschalk v. Chicago, B. & Q.
R. Co.*, 14 Neb. 550; *Rigney v. City of Chicago*, 102 Ill. 64;
City of Pekin v. Winkel, 77 Ill. 56; *City of Pek'n v. Brereton*,
67 Ill. 477; *City of Elgin v. Eaton*, 83 Ill. 535; *City of
Shawneetown v. Mason*, 82 Ill. 337; *Stock v. City of East St.
Louis*, 85 Ill. 377; *Chamberlain v. West End of London & C.
P. R. Co.*, 2 Best & S. [Eng.] 605; *Beckett v. Midland R.
Co.*, 3 Common Pleas L. R. [Eng.] 81; *Mollandin v. Union
P. R. Co.*, 14 Fed. Rep. 394; *Republican V. R. Co. v. Fellers*,
16 Neb. 169; *Chicago, K. & N. R. Co. v. Hazels*, 26 Neb. 364;
Omaha & N. P. R. Co. v. Janecek, 30 Neb. 276; *Reardon v.
City and County of San Francisco*, 66 Cal. 492; *City of Den-
ver v. Bayer*, 7 Colo. 113; *City of Montgomery v. Maddox*, 89
Ala. 181; *Omaha H. R. Co. v. Cable Tram-Way Co.*, 32 Fed.
Rep. 727; *City of East St. Louis v. O'Flynn*, 119 Ill. 200;
City of Denver v. Vernia, 8 Colo. 399; *Hogan v. Central P.
R. Co.*, 71 Cal. 83; *Town of Longmont v. Parker*, 14 Colo.
386; *Gainesville, H. & W. R. Co. v. Hall*, 14 S. W. Rep.
[Tex.] 259.)

Use and occupation of a public street or highway by
an electric street railway with its poles, wires, and tracks
were not contemplated or authorized by the original
dedication of the street to the public, and if such use and
occupation decrease the market value of adjacent lots
by a physical interference with the use and enjoyment of
the streets by the owner in connection with his property,
then his property is "damaged" within the meaning of
that word in our constitution, and he is entitled to compensation.   (*Southern P. R. Co. v. Reed*, 41 Cal. 256; *Imlay
v. Union B. R. Co.*, 26 Conn. 249; *South Carolina R. Co. v.
Steiner*, 44 Ga. 546; *Cox v. Louisville, N. A. & C. R. Co.*, 48
Ind. 178; *Indianapolis, B. & W. R. Co. v. Hartley*, 67 Ill.
439; *Phipps v. Western M. R. Co.*, 66 Md. 319; *Grand

Rapids & I. R. Co. v. Heisel, 47 Mich. 393; *Chamberlain v.
Elizabeth Cordage Co.*, 41 N. J. Eq. 43; *Lawrence R. Co. v.
Williams*, 35 O. St. 168; *Carl v. Sheboygan & F. DuL. R. Co.*,
46 Wis. 625; *Hastings & G. I. R. Co. v. Ingalls*, 15 Neb. 123;
Burlington & M. R. R. Co. v. Reinhackle, 15 Neb. 279.)

John L. Webster, contra:

The construction or operation of a street railway along
the streets cannot be made the foundation of an action
for damages by an abutting property owner. (*Taggart v.
Newport S. R. Co.*, 19 Atl. Rep. [R. I.] 326, 7 L. R. A. 205;
Williams v. City Electric Street R. Co., 41 Fed. Rep. 556;
Halsey v. Rapid Transit S. R. Co., 20 Atl. Rep. [N. J.] 859;
Koch v. North Avenue R. Co., 15 L. R. A. [Md.] 377; *Texas
& P. R. Co. v. Rosedale Street R. Co.*, 64 Tex. 80.)

The construction and operation of a street railway
do not cast any additional servitude upon the street, and
a railway company is not liable to the abutting property
owner for damages arising from the construction and
operation of the road. (*Attorney General v. Metropolitan
R. Co.*, 125 Mass. 515; *Fulton v. Short Route Railway Transfer Co.*, 85 Ky. 640; *Grand Rapids & I. R. Co. v. Heisel*, 38
Mich. 62; *Briggs v. Lewiston & A. H. R. Co.*, 79 Me. 363;
Hobart v. Milwaukee City R. Co., 27 Wis. 194; *Elliott v.
Fair Haven & W. R. Co.*, 32 Conn. 579; *Citizens Coach Co.
v. Camden Horse R. Co.*, 33 N. J. Eq. 267; *Carson v. Central
R. Co.*, 35 Cal. 325; *Newell v. Minneapolis, L. & M. R. Co.*,
35 Minn. 112; *Kellinger v. Forty-second Street & G. S. F. R.
Co.*, 50 N. Y. 206; *Finch v. Riverside & A. R. Co.*, 25 Pac.
Rep. [Cal.] 765.)

RAGAN, C.

Minnie L. Jaynes brought this suit in the district court
of Douglas county against the Omaha Street Railway
Company, hereinafter called the railway company, a corporation organized under the laws of the state and owning and operating an electric street railway in the streets
of the city of Omaha by permission of the city's authority.

Jaynes in her petition alleged, among other things, that she was the owner of lot 8, in block 15, in R. V. Smith's Addition to the city of Omaha; that said lot was a tract of land 243 feet in length east and west and 66 feet in width north and south; that it was bounded on the east by Sixteenth street and on the south by Clarke street; that the railway company had constructed its railway over and upon and along the surface of said Sixteenth and Clarke streets in front of her property, and was operating its cars thereon, the motive power being electricity; that the railway company, for the purpose of so operating its cars, had erected poles on either side of said streets adjacent to her premises, and placed a wire upon said poles parallel to the railway track, and had strung wires across said streets on said poles; that by reason of such construction and operation of said railway on said tracks adjacent to said premises the value of the latter had been greatly depreciated; that the location of the poles and wires of the railway company in said streets interfered with Jaynes' ingress to and from her property, and thereby depreciated its value. There was a prayer for a judgment for damages. To this petition the railway company filed a general demurrer, based on its contention that the petition did not state facts sufficient to constitute a cause of action. The district court sustained the demurrer and dismissed the petition and Jaynes brings that judgment here for review on error.

1. By sections 104, 105, and 106, article 1, chapter 14, Compiled Statutes 1897, it is made the duty of every original owner or proprietor of any tract of land who shall subdivide the same for the purpose of laying it out in an addition to a city to cause a plat of such subdivision to be made with reference to known or permanent monuments, and in such plat give the dimensions and the courses of all streets and alleys established thereby, and to execute and acknowledge this plat before some officer authorized to take acknowledgments of deeds, and when so executed, to file such plat for record in the office of

the register of deeds of the proper county. The acknowledgment and record of such an instrument are equivalent
to a deed in fee-simple of such portion of the premises
platted as is on such plat set apart for streets and other
public purposes. Assuming that Smith was the original
owner of the lands out of which the lots of Jaynes were
carved, that he complied with the statute just quoted
and thereby dedicated these streets to the public and
thereby conveyed the fee-simple title of these streets to
the city of Omaha, we have the question, for what purpose was this dedication or grant made? The particular
purposes which were in the mind of the owner at the
time he made this dedication or grant are not expressed
therein; and the question therefore is, for what purpose
does the law imply or presume the owner granted these
streets to the public? Is the construction and operation
of such an electric railway as the one here on the surface
of these streets embraced in the purposes for which the
original owner dedicated these streets to the public?
Or, in the language of the law books, is the construction
and operation of this street railway an additional burden
or servitude on the easement granted?

It is said by Booth, in section 83 of his work on Street
Railways, that the courts of last resort of the country to
which the question has been presented have all decided
that the construction and operation of such a street railway as the one in question here was not an additional
servitude to those embraced in the original grant. The
courts referred to by this author are Kentucky, Michigan,
Maryland, New Jersey, Pennsylvania, Rhode Island,
Utah, and the United States circuit court for the district
of Arkansas. We shall briefly examine these cases.

The Kentucky case was decided in 1893 and is the
Louisville Bagging Mfg. Co. v. Central P. R. Co., 95 Ky. 50,
4 Am. Electrical Cases 202. It was an application for
an injunction by the owner of a lot fronting on a street
to enjoin the construction and maintenance of an electric
street railway on two grounds: (1) That it would inter-

fere with the lot owner's accustomed use of the street for backing vehicles up to his warehouse; (2) would be dangerous to those residing or doing business on the street. The *nisi prius* court denied the application for injunction, and its judgment was affirmed by the court of appeals; but the question as to whether the construction and operation of the street railway was an additional burden is not mentioned in the case; nor is the question as to whether the street railway company would be liable to damages for the injury done to the lot owner's property by the construction and operation of the railway either argued or discussed in the opinion; and though the question as to whether electric street railways were additional burdens had prior to that date been presented to several courts of last resort, no case of any court is cited in the opinion.

The case from the United States circuit court for the district of Arkansas is *Williams v. City Electric Street R. Co.*, 41 Fed. Rep. 556. In that case the United States circuit court held that the construction and operation of a street railway on the streets of a city was not an additinal burden simply because of the fact the cars were moved by steam. That was the only point in the case. No such question as the one here was involved in the Arkansas case.

The Utah case referred to is *Ogden City R. Co. v. Ogden City*, 26 Pac. Rep. 288. This case was decided in 1891 and was an application for an injunction by the Ogden City Railway Company against Ogden City and another railway company to enjoin Ogden City from carrying into effect an ordinance granting to this other railway company permission to lay a double-tracked street railway in a certain street of Ogden City; the contention of the Ogden City Railway Company being that in 1883 Ogden City, by ordinance, had granted it permission to lay down a double-tracked street railway in said streets, that it had already constructed a single track with turnouts in that street, and that if the other railway com-

pany was granted permission to construct another
double-track railway in the same street, the streets would
be so obstructed by the four tracks as to interfere with
other modes of travel; and that if the defendant street
railway company, in constructing its track, should use
poles and wires, the plaintiff street railway's property
would be greatly damaged thereby. The injunction was
denied. The court said: "The allegations of fact are not
sufficient to warrant an injunction on the ground that
the construction of the defendant's railway would damage the abutting property by materially interfering with
rights appurtenant thereto." We do not think this is an
adjudication that the construction and operation of an
electric street railway in the streets of a city is not an
additional burden; and though that question had prior
to that time been before the courts of Rhode Island and
New Jersey, the opinions in those cases are not referred
to, nor is there an opinion of any other court mentioned.

The earliest case that we have been able to find in
which the question under consideration was decided is
Taggart v. Newport Street R. Co., 19 Atl. Rep. [R. I.] 326,
decided in January, 1890. This was an application for
an injunction by abutting property owners to enjoin the
street railway company from erecting poles and wires
as concomitants of their street railway in front of the
complainants' property. It appears that prior to the
time the suit was brought the street railway company
had been using horses to move their cars and were about
to substitute electricity as a motive power. In the opinion the court enumerates the grounds upon which the
injunction was asked, as (1) that the street railway company had not given certain notices required by the law
of its incorporation; (2) that the use of electricity was
illegal, as the statute creating the street railway company authorized it to use as a motive power "steam,
horses, or other power as the city councils of said city
and towns may from time to time direct;" (3) that the
erection of the poles was prohibited by the act incor-

porating the street railway company, as that act provided that the street railway should be used, constructed, and operated so that "such corporation shall not incumber any portion of the streets occupied by such tracks." The court held that the company had given the notice required by statute; that the use of electricity as a motive power was expressed within the law creating the corporation; and that the poles in the street were not an incumbrance within the meaning of the act creating the corporation, taking Webster's definition of the word "incumber." The court denied the injunction and said, in the fifth point of the syllabus: "The change of the power by which a street railway is operated from horse-power to electricity, and the erection of poles necessary for its operation, does not impose an additional burden on the abutting property owners." The court reached this conclusion, that the street railway with its poles and wires was not an additional burden, by finding that the electric street railway company did not occupy the streets any more exclusively than it would if operated by horse-power. There is no question that the law of the case was correctly laid down, if the evidence, or the record on its face, sustains the finding of fact made by the court that the electric street railway no more exclusively occupies the street than an ordinary horse railway.

The Rhode Island case just noticed was quoted as an authority for the proposition that an electric street railway is not an additional burden, by the supreme court of New Jersey in December, 1890, in *Halsey v. Rapid Transit Street R. Co.*, 47 N. J. Eq. 380, 20 Atl. Rep. 859. In this case an abutting lot owner sought to enjoin a street railway company from building its track in a street opposite his premises and from erecting certain iron poles in the center of the street to be used in the operation of its cars. The court denied the injunction and held that the placing of the poles in the middle of the street for the purpose of using electricity for street car propulsion did not impose a new servitude on the land in the street. But it would seem from a reading of the opinion that the complainant's application for an injunction was denied on the ground of the court's doubt as to whether the complainant's property had been or would be damaged by the erection of these poles in the center of the street opposite his property. The court said: "It is true there is a very small space in the middle of the street over which a wagon approaching the entrance cannot pass, but it may pass on either side. Besides the distance of the pole from the entrance renders it very improbable, as it seems to me, that a wagon, in passing from the street to the entrance, would, if there was no pole there, pass over this space one time in fifty. Certain it is that, even if it be true that the pole diminishes the complainant's means of access to the entrance, the diminution is so insignificant as to lay no ground for relief in equity. A doubt as to whether the complainant's land in the street has been appropriated to a purpose for which the public has no right to use it will, at this stage of the cause, be fatal to his claim to an injunction. * * * 'It is impossible to emphasize too strongly the rule so often enforced in this court, that a preliminary injunction will not be allowed where either the complainant's right, which he seeks to have protected *in limine* by an interlocutory injunction, is in doubt, or where the injury, which may result from the invasion of that right, is not irreparable.' "

The supreme court of Pennsylvania, in January, 1891, in *Lockhart v. Craig Street R. Co.*, 21 Atl. Rep. 26, referred to the Rhode Island case as being directly in point, and, if good law, controlling the case under consideration. The Pennsylvania case was an application for an injunction by abutting property owners to restrain the street railway company from constructing and operating its road in a street in front of the complainant's property. The court denied the injunction and stated the question to be whether the construction of the street railway with its poles and wires amounted to a taking of the property of the complainant without compensation. The court said: "The placing of the wires over the streets does not appear to be a taking of plaintiff's property. The streets are dedicated to public use, and he has certain special rights as an abutting owner, but I cannot see how a wire run through the air above the streets can be said to be a taking, injury, or destroying his property. But another question arises in reference to the posts placed in the ground for the support of the wires by means of which the cars are moved. * * * And it may be now taken as settled that the owner's rights of abutting property are subject to the paramount right of the public, and the rights of the public are not limited to a mere right of way, but extend to all beneficial legitimate street uses, as the public may from time to time require. * * * The case of *Taggart v. Railway Co.*, 19 Atl. Rep. 326, is directly in point, and, if good law, covers the case in hand. My own impression is that the use of poles, wires, and other necessary appliances, such as proposed being used by defendants, is not, in any respect, a greater interference with the ownership of the adjoining property owner on a street than the use of streets for fire-plugs, horse-troughs, etc. * * * To my mind the power in the Craig Street Railway Company to construct and maintain a railroad in compliance with the terms of the act under which it was incorporated is clear, and that these defendants have shown a legal right to proceed and construct the railway contemplated by them, unless the failure to provide means by which the plaintiffs may have such damages as they may sustain assessed and paid or secured in advance renders the act unconstitutional. Upon this question I am not free from doubt, but the decided inclination of my mind is that the act is not unconstitutional for that reason, because the use of the streets for the purpose of applying motive power in the manner proposed is not such a new use as in cities should be treated as outside the proper use for which streets will be held to have been originally

45

dedicated to the public use. *Taggart v. Railway Co.*, before cited, is exactly in point. The case presented by plaintiffs is certainly not so clear from doubt that a chancellor should grant an injunction summarily stopping a great public improvement before final hearing, more particularly if the position taken by plaintiffs is correct, and defendants have no legal right to take possession of the streets, as they are about to do, a common law action will compel them to pay all damages arising to plaintiffs and thereafter equity would probably afford a complete remedy by which the wrong done them could be fully corrected." It seems from this that the supreme court of Pennsylvania did not decide, at least in this case, that an abutting property owner was remediless if the construction of the street railway in front of his property damaged it, but denied the abutting property owner an injunction to restrain the erection of the improvement, leaving the question as to whether he was damaged, and if so, how much, to the law courts.

In *Detroit City Railway v. Mills*, decided in May, 1891, 48 N. W. Rep. [Mich.] 1007, the street railway company was erecting its poles and constructing its track in a street in front of a lot owner's property. The lot owner cut the poles down and threatened to continue to do so as long as they were erected, and thereupon the railway company enjoined the lot owner from interfering with its construction of its railway. The *nisi prius* court made the injunction perpetual. The property owner appealed and the supreme court affirmed the judgment. The question as to whether the proposed erection of the poles and wires and tracks on the street constituted an additional burden upon the easement seems to have been much discussed in the case. In the syllabus the court said: "The use of the street for street railways in such a way as not to interfere with the right of a lot-owner as one of the public to pass and repass thereon, or with the right of ingress or egress to and from his lot, does not impose a new burden and servitude, addi-

tional to what was implied by the dedication, which it
is beyond the power of the city to authorize without
additional compensation to the abutting lot-owners."
The court was composed of five judges. Two of these
judges seem to have been of opinion that the street railway involved in the action, as it was proposed to be constructed, was not or would not be an additional burden
upon the easement. Two of the judges dissented from
that opinion and the third concurred in affirming the
judgment of the lower court, but said: "I am not prepared to say that the construction of a street railroad
track in a street is of itself no additional burden or
servitude upon the street. I think it is, but to what extent depends upon all the facts and circumstances under
which it is imposed." The cases heretofore alluded to
from Kentucky, New Jersey, and Pennsylvania are referred to in the majority opinion as authorities for the
proposition that an electric street railway track with its
wires and poles is not an additional burden. But the
most that can be said for the Michigan case is that
whether such a street railway is or is not an additional
burden is a question of fact depending upon whether or
not, it is so operated and constructed as to interfere with
the lot-owner's right of ingress and egress to and from
his property and his free use of the street.

The Maryland case referred to by Booth is *Koch v.
North A. R. Co.*, 23 Atl. Rep. 463, decided in January,
1892. It was an application by abutting lot owners to
enjoin a street railway company from constructing its
road in a certain street in front of their property. The
application was based upon four grounds: (1) that the
defendant was not lawfully incorporated; (2) that it had
no right to lay tracks of its own outside of tracks already
laid in the street by street railway companies; (3) that
the city of Baltimore had no authority to authorize the
railway company to use electricity as a motive power;
(4) that the road proposed to be built was an elevated
road within the meaning of the statute which provided

that no elevated roads should be built in that street. The court overruled each of these contentions and denied the injunction. The cases already alluded to from Rhode Island, New Jersey, Pennsylvania, and the federal district of Arkansas are referred to in the opinion, and it is said of them that "they proceed on the principle that a street is a way set apart for public travel and that the use of electricity for propelling street cars is but a new and improved motive power in no manner inconsistent with the uses and purposes for which streets were opened and dedicated as ways for public travel;" and the court decides that the use of electricity as a motive power for street cars does not impose a new servitude upon the streets so as to entitle the abutting owner to compensation. But the question as to whether poles and wires placed in a street in front of an abutting owner's premises constituted an additional servitude entitling him to compensation was neither presented to nor decided by the court.

In *Limburger v. San Antonio Rapid-Transit Street R. Co.*, 30 So. Rep. 533, the supreme court of Texas held that "the use of a street for an electric railway does not impose an additional burden or servitude to that implied by the dedication." That was an action by an abutting property owner against a street railway company to recover damages which he alleged his property had sustained by the construction of a street railway track between the curb of the street and another railway track in the street. The cases hereinbefore referred to were cited by the supreme court of Texas as authorities for the conclusion reached by it. But it is to be noticed that in the Texas case there is not one word on the subject of poles and wires. It does not appear whether or not this street railway company used any poles and wires for the operation of its road. So far as the opinion discloses the whole complaint of the abutting property owner was the presence in the street in front of his property of the tracks and the cars thereon.

These are all the cases which I have been able to find which hold, if they do, that an electric street railway with its concomitants of poles and wires is not an additional burden, and if the abutting owner's property is damaged by the use of the streets for such poles and wires that he has no remedy for such damages. The leading case is the Rhode Island case, and the conclusion reached there was predicated upon the court's finding that the electric street railway did not occupy any more exclusively any portion of the street than an ordinary horse railway would. If all the other cases follow the Rhode Island case, and if it can be said that these cases are authority for the proposition contended for here, that an electric street railway with its wires and poles is not an additional burden, then it is worth while to observe that the principle upon which the cases rest is the one mentioned by the Rhode Island court, namely, not an exclusive and continued occupation of a part of a street to the exclusion of the rest of the public. That principle is sound. But in the case at bar there is no room for the conclusion that the street railway company by the poles and wires which it has placed in the street does not exclusively occupy a portion of that street to the exclusion of the rest of the public. Looking at the original platting of Jaynes' property and the dedication made by the then owner of the lots of a part of it for a street, we think the true construction of the grant made is this: that the grantor intended that the street should be used for the purpose of enabling the public to pass and repass thereon; that it might pass on foot, on horseback, or in vehicles, and that whether the motive power of the vehicles should be steam, electricity, horse-power, compressed air, or any other power. The grant contemplated the right of the public to temporarily use any part and all of these streets for the purpose of passing over them in any manner that it might choose and by such means as it might see fit to employ. But the grant did not contemplate that any person or corporation might exclusively and permanently appropriate any part of these streets to its use to the continued exclusion of the rest of the public. In the case at bar the railway company with its poles and wires has exclusively appropriated a portion of these streets to its own use to the exclusion of the rest of the public. If the railway company were moving its cars on the surface of these streets by electric power without so permanently and exclusively occupying any portion of the street, we do not think the mere fact that the motive power used was electricity would take the use out of the purpose contemplated by the original grant. The use made of these streets by the railway company is not one common with that of the public generally; its poles and wires remain and must remain and exclusively occupy particular portions of the street and continuously exclude the public from such portions. Whether a use made of a street is an additional burden upon the easement we do not think depends upon the motive power which moves the vehicle employed. It depends upon the question whether the vehicle and appliances used in and necessary* to effectuate that purpose permanently and exclusively occupy all or a portion of the street to the continued exclusion of the rest of the public. If they do not, then it is not an additional burden. If they do, it is.

It has been almost universally held, we think, that an ordinary street railway whose cars were moved by horses was not an additional burden. See, among others, the following authorities: *Attorney General v. Metropolitan R. Co.*, 125 Mass. 515; *Citizens Coach Co. v. Camden Horse R. Co.*, 33 N. J. Eq. 267; *Hobart v. Milwaukee City R. Co.*, 27 Wis. 194; *Texas & P. R. Co. v. Rosedale Street R. Co.*, 64 Tex. 80; *Elliot v. Fair Haven & W. R. Co.*, 32 Conn. 579. These decisions rest upon the principle that the street was originally dedicated to the public for the purposes of travel thereon; that a car is a vehicle, the same as a coach or a wagon, and that the

track of a street railway company is laid upon a level
with the surface of the street and in such manner as not
to obstruct the street and prevent people from freely passing and repassing thereon.   In other words, the horse-car
and its track is not a continued exclusive appropriation
of any part of the street to the continued exclusion of the
rest of the public from that part of the street.

The city of Shawneetown, Illinois, built a levee in a
street of that city for the purpose of protecting it against
the overflow waters of the Ohio river.   The levee was
some ten feet high, but so constructed that the top
thereof could be used as the street had been.   An abutting lot owner sued the city for damages, claiming that
his lot had been depreciated in value by the presence in
front of it of this levee, as it hindered his free ingress
and egress to and from his property, and the supreme
court of Illinois, in *City of Shawneetown v. Mason*, 82 Ill.
337, held that the levee was an additional burden and
the city liable.

The city authorities of East St. Louis, Illinois, authorized a bridge company which owned a bridge across
the Mississippi river at that point to construct an approach to this bridge in a public street.   An abutting
lot owner sued the city for damages, claiming that the
approach to the bridge interfered with his free ingress
and egress to and from his property and depreciated it
in value, and the supreme court of Illinois, in *Stack v.
City of East St. Louis*, 85 Ill. 377, held that the approach
to the bridge was an additional burden and the city
liable for damages which its presence caused the abutting lot owner.

The city of New York, prior to May, 1773, caused one
of its engineers to survey and lay out into lots certain
territory.   Upon the plat the engineer left a space for
streets.   The conveyance made of these surveyed lots to
the grantors of one Story contained a covenant that the
grantee in such deed would "build and erect" at his
own expense certain streets, among others the streets on

which Story's property fronted. 'The deed also declared that the streets marked on the survey or plat
"shall forever thereafter continue and be for the free
and common passage of and as public streets and ways
for the inhabitants of the said city and all others passing and returning through or by the same in like manner
as the other streets of the same city now are or lawfully
ought to be." Story became the owner of one of the
lots so surveyed and marked out on said plat. The New
York Elevated Railroad Company was about to construct in this street, under proper municipal and legislative authority, a trestle-work fifteen feet high. On
this they were intending to lay tracks and on these
tracks operate passenger cars. Story sought to enjoin
the railroad company from such use of the street until
he should be awarded the damages which his property
would sustain thereby. The case went to the court of
appeals of New York and is reported in *Story v. New
York E. R. Co.*, 90 N. Y. 122. It was insisted by counsel
for the railroad company that the construction and
operation of the railroad as contemplated was within
the purpose of the original grant or dedication of the
land for the street; but the court of appeals held that
the proposed railroad would impose an additional
burden upon the easement, and the principle upon which
it based its decision is that the trestle-work would
amount to a permanent and exclusive occupation of a
portion of the street to the continued exclusion of the
public from such portion. To the same effect see *Lahr v.
Metropolitan E. R. Co.*, 104 N. Y. 288.

It is quite generally held that an ordinary steam railroad in a city street or country highway constitutes an
additional burden, and this is because the track of a
steam railroad is of such a nature and so constructed
that it exclusively and continuously occupies a portion
of the street or highway to the continuous exclusion of
the rest of the public from such part of said street or
highway. See, among others, *Hastings & G. I. R. Co. v.*

Ingalls, 15 Neb. 123; *Indiana, B. & W. R. Co. v. Hartley*, 67 Ill. 439, and cases there cited.   Railroad cars are as much vehicles for the transportation of passengers enabling the public to pass and repass from one part of the city or country to another as are horse-cars or carriages and buggies; but the rails of an 'ordinary railroad are laid upon ties, and these rest upon an elevation, and the road-bed is of such a nature and construction that it obstructs the street or highway in which it is placed and debars the rest of the public from the use of that part of the street or highway occupied by its track.

It is also very generally held that telegraph and telephone poles in city streets or rural highways constitute additional burdens entitling the abutting property owner to compensation.   See, among others, the following cases so holding: *Board of Trade Telegraph Co. v. Barnett*, 107 Ill. 507; *Chesapeake & P. Telegraph Co. v. Mackenzie*, 21 Atl. Rep. [Md.] 690; *American Telephone & Telegraph Co. v. Smith*, 18 Atl. Rep. [Md.] 910; *Western Union Telegraph Co. v. Williams*, 11 S. E. Rep. [Va.] 106; *Eels v. American Telephone & Telegraph Co.*, 143 N. Y. 133. The principle upon which all these cases rest is the sound one that the highway or street is dedicated to the public for the purpose of enabling the public to pass and repass thereon. and that the erection of the poles in the streets by the telephone or telegraph companies is a permanent and exclusive occupation of the streets by such companies to the continued exclusion of the remainder of the public, and in that sense the poles are a continued obstruction in the streets.

The supreme court of Pennsylvania, in *Pennsylvania R. Co. v. Montgomery County P. R. Co.*, 167 Pa. 62, held that an electric street railway, such as the one involved in this case, built in a public highway outside of the city was an additional burden entitling the adjacent land owner to damages.   We think that the poles and wires of the electric railway company are an additional servitude or constitute an additional burden upon the streets in which they are placed, and that the abutting lot owners of such streets are entitled to whatever damages their property has sustained by reason thereof.

2. Thus far we have considered this case with reference to the question as to whether the original dedication made of the street contemplated that the city might use or authorize the use of the streets for the purpose of placing poles and wires therein in connection with the operation of a railway. But our constitution, article 1, section 21, provides that the property of no person shall be taken or damaged for public use without just compensation. The writer is of opinion that if it be assumed that the original owner of this street in dedicating it to the public contemplated that it might be used for the erection of poles and wires therein in connection with the operation of a passenger street railway, nevertheless if the city, in applying the street to that use, or authorizing it to be so applied, damages the property of the adjacent owner, he is by virtue of the constitution entitled to damages. This court, with nearly all other courts in which the state constitution is like ours, has held that an abutting lot owner is entitled to compensation if his lot is depreciated in value by reason of the changing of the grade of the street in front of it. Now, when the land owner plats it into an addition to a city, leaves a space for a street, he not only dedicates that space to the public for the purpose of a street, but he knows, or must know, that the municipality may work such street, keep it in repair, pave it, grade it, curb it, and may change the grade. And where the courts have awarded damages to abutting lot owners because of a change in the grade of a street, it has not been upon the principle that such a change of grade was not contemplated at the time the grant was made; but it has been because of the constitutional inhibition that the public for its use shall not damage the citizen's property without compensation. Such is the *City of Elgin v. Eaton*, 83 Ill. 535. Most of the old constitutions contained a provision that private prop-

erty should not be taken for public use without just compensation, and it was quite generally held by the courts that this provision of the constitution did not entitle an abutting lot owner to compensation for damages which his property had sustained by reason of a change of grade in the street. These cases rest upon the principle that a change of grade of a street was within the purview of the original grant of the land for the street. Suppose that A, owning a block in a city, shall deed one-half of it to that city for any public purpose. By such a grant the city may devote that to any city purpose it may choose, and A could not be heard to say that the purpose to which the city had devoted the grant was not within it; but nevertheless, if the city, in the use it makes of the granted property, shall injure the remainder of A's property, it would be liable for the damages, because in accepting the grant it did so subject to the constitutional provision, and though it might devote it to any public purpose it chose, yet if in so doing it damages A's property, or any other citizen's property, it must make good such damages. It seems to me, therefore, that in order to enable the plaintiff in error in this case to recover damages from the street railway company, it is not absolutely essential that the poles and wires of the street railway company should be held, as a matter of law, to be an additional burden upon the easement.

3. The petition in this case alleges that the permanent existence in the street opposite this property of the poles and wires of the railway company interferes with the plaintiff's ingress and egress to and from her property and have depreciated its value. Are these facts evidence competent to go to the jury for the determination of the question as to whether the plaintiff's property has been damaged within the meaning of the constitution just quoted?

In *Gottschalk v. Chicago, B. & Q. R. Co.*, 14 Neb. 550, the railroad company constructed its tracks in an alley with

the consent of the city authorities. The owner of the
abutting lot sued the company for damages. The court,
in speaking of the constitutional provision in reference
to damage to property for public use, said: "The constitutional provision, therefore, is that private property
shall not be taken or injuriously affected without just
compensation therefor. The evident object of the
amendment was to afford relief in certain cases where,
under our former constitution, none could be given. It
was to grant relief in cases where there was no direct
injury to the real estate itself, but some physical disturbance of a right which the owner possesses in connection with his estate, by reason of which he sustains
special injury in respect to such property in excess of
that sustained by the public at large. To this extent
the property owner is entitled to recover. It is not
necessary to entitle a party to recover, that there should
be a direct physical injury to his property if he has sustained damages in respect to the property itself whereby
its value has been permanently impaired and dimin-
ished."

In *City of Omaha v. Kramer,* 25 Neb. 489, it is said:
"The words 'or damaged' in section 21, article 1. of the
constitution, include all damages arising from the exercise of the right of eminent domain which cause a
diminution in the value of private property."

In *Chicago, K. & N. R. Co. v. Hazels,* 26 Neb. 364, the
railway company took no part of Hazels' property and
no part of the street in front of his lot was occupied by
the railway company's track, and yet the court held that
if Hazels' property was damaged because of the location
of the tracks he was entitled to recover.

In *Omaha & N. P. R. Co. v. Janecek,* 30 Neb. 276,
Janecek sued the railroad company for damages which he
alleged he had sustained by reason of the depreciation in
value of his real estate as the result of the construction
and operation of the railroad in front of his premises.
Janecek owned block 16, and also a small tract of land

lying immediately south thereof. His residence was on
the west end of this small tract of land. West of block 16
and the small tract of land was Atlantic street, and west
of this was block 15. The railroad company constructed
its road through this latter block. No part of the railroad was on any part of Janecek's property, nor was any
part of the railroad's property in the street on which his,
Janecek's, property abutted. The court, speaking
through NORVAL, J., said: "The plaintiff's right to recover is based upon section 21, article 1, constitution of
this state, which provides that 'The property of no person shall be taken or damaged for public use without
just compensation therefor.' It has become the settled
law of this state that under this provision of our constitution it is not necessary that any part of an individual's
property should be actually taken for public use in order
to entitle him to compensation. If the property has
been depreciated in value by reason of the public improvement, which the owner has specially sustained, and
which is not common to the public at large, a recovery
may be had." To the same effect is *City of Pekin v.
Winkel*, 77 Ill. 56; *Stack v. City of East St. Louis*, 85 Ill.
377; *Rigney v. City of Chicago*, 102 Ill. 64. In this last
case Rigney recovered damages from the city of Chicago
because it had permitted the construction of a viaduct
over the intersection of Kinzie and Halsted streets 220
feet west of Rigney's property. Rigney claimed that
the construction of this viaduct cut off his communication with Halsted street, except by means of a pair of
stairs at the intersection, and that because of this im-
pairment of communication his real estate had been
damaged. The supreme court said: "'Property' in its
appropriate sense means that dominion or indefinite right
of user and disposition which one may lawfully exercise
over particular things or objects, and generally to the
exclusion of all others, and doubtless this is substantially the sense in which the word is used in the constitution, as to the taking or damaging of private property

for the public use. But the word is often used to indicate the subject of the property or the thing owned.
* * * The restriction of the remedy of the owners of
private property to cases of actual physical injury to the
property was under the constitution of 1848, which simply provided that private property should not 'be taken
or applied to public use' without just compensation, etc.
The constitution of 1870, however, provides that 'private
property shall not be taken or damaged for public use
without just compensation,' thus affording redress in
cases not provided for by the constitution of 1848, and
embracing every case where there is a direct physical
obstruction or injury to the right of user or enjoyment of
private property, by which the owner sustains some
special pecuniary damage in excess of that sustained by
the public generally which by the common law would, in
the absence of any constitutional or statutory provision,
give a right of action."

Applying the principles enunciated in the foregoing
cases to the facts of the case at bar, we are of opinion
that if Jaynes' property is depreciated in value by reason of the exclusive use of a part of the streets in front
thereof by the railway company's poles and wires and
the continued presence in such streets of said poles and
wires, she is entitled to compensation for such damages.
As an abutting property owner she has the right to free
ingress and egress to and from this property and to and
from the street, a right to an unobstructed view of the
property from the street and an unobstructed view of the
street from the property, and if poles and wires of the
railway company in the street in front of this property
permanently and continuously infringe these rights, and
she is damaged thereby, she is entitled to compensation
therefor. If a railway company, without responsibility
to the abutting lot owner, may build and maintain in the
street one track, it may construct and maintain any
number. If it may with impunity place and maintain in
the street in front of the lot owner's property poles fifty

feet apart, it may place them five feet apart, or closer, until the premises, with poles and wires in front, will resemble the pictures one sees of the staked corral of the South African Zulu. Such a staking in of premises would, of course, impair their value; and yet the difference in the case supposed and the one under consideration is one of degree only. This difference does not affect the owner's right of action, but goes only to the *quantum* of his damages. What acts, omissions, facts, or circumstances are competent evidence of damages to be considered by a jury are questions of law for the court; but whether such acts, omissions, facts, and circumstances affect an owner's property and damage it and the amount of such damages are for the jury.

The judgment of the district court is reversed and the cause remanded with instructions to overrule the demurrer of the street railway company and permit it to answer.

REVERSED AND REMANDED.

IRVINE, C., not sitting.

RYAN, C.

I desire to place my concurrence in the result in this case on grounds rather more limited than those above given. In this case a general demurrer was sustained to the petition, upon which, the plaintiff having elected to stand, there was a judgment for the defendant. The demurrer, for present purposes, must be assumed to have admitted such facts as were well pleaded, and it therefore is necessary that the averments of the petition should be stated with more than ordinary fulness. The defendant was described as a corporation engaged in the maintenance, construction, and operation of street railways in the city of Omaha, and was described as the successor of another street railway company in rights and liabilities with respect to the street railway along plaintiff's premises, hereinafter more particularly described. The condition of the streets affected and their appropriation and use by the predecessor of the defendant, as well as by the defendant itself, were described in the petition in this language: "That said lot (owned by plaintiff) is a strip of ground 240 feet in length east and west and 60 feet in width north and south, bounded on the east by Sixteenth street, on the south by Clarke street, in the city of Omaha; said Sixteenth street east of said premises and Clarke street south of said premises, at the time of the happening of the grievances hereinafter complained of, were, and for a long time prior thereto had been, public streets of said city of Omaha, but not occupied, used, or obstructed by steam, electric, or horse railways in any manner whatever; that on or about the first day of September, 1889, a corporation known as the Omaha Motor Railway Company constructed a line of street railway over and upon Clarke street, immediately south of said premises, and over and upon Sixteenth street, immediately east of said premises, and commenced the operation of said line of railway over and upon said streets adjacent to said premises, the motive power used upon said street railway at the time of the construction thereof being electricity, poles for the purpose of supporting overhead wires being set in the ground along said streets and adjacent to said premises and overhead wires being attached thereto along said streets adjoining said premises. Plaintiff further says that ever since the construction of said street railway the same has been operated as an electric street railway, cars and motors passing over the line of said railway immediately adjacent to said premises and over Clarke street immediately south of said premises and Sixteenth street immediately east of said premises at intervals of about five minutes. Plaintiff further says that by reason of the location, construction, and operation of said line of street railway over and upon Clarke street immediately south of said premises and over and upon Sixteenth street immediately east of said premises and adjacent thereto, said premises have been greatly depreciated, the location of the tracks, poles, and wires of said street railway upon said Clarke and Sixteenth streets, as hereinafter described, greatly interfering with the egress from, and ingress to, said premises from said streets and obstructing the view from said premises looking toward said streets, the passage of trains over said street railway upon said streets in front of and adjacent to said premises also greatly interfering with the ingress to and egress from said premises, rendering the same difficult and dangerous, and the noise and vibration incident to the use of said tracks by said defendant company greatly interfering with the comfort and convenience of persons occupying said premises, said premises having been lessened and depreciated in value, on account of the construction and operation of said street railway, in the sum of $20,000."

The facts upon which the plaintiff predicates his right of recovery are the taking possession of, and the using for, a street railway operated by electricity of two streets adjacent to his property. The first class of the elements of damages claimed refers to the effect of locating the tracks, poles, and wires as obstructions to ingress and egress and of the view from the premises of plaintiff looking toward the street. The other elements are the passage of trains over the track, interfering with, and rendering dangerous, egress from and ingress to plaintiff's premises, and the noise and vibration incident to the use of the tracks which interfere with the comfort and convenience of persons occupying said premises. In respect to the last two, it may be said that it is now the settled doctrine in this country that, an ordinary street railway upon which cars are moved by horse-power is not an additional burden. (*Citizens Coach Co. v. Camden Horse R. Co.*, 33 N. J. Eq. 267; *Hobart v. Milwaukee City R. Co.*, 27 Wis. 194; *Carson v. Central R. Co.*, 35 Cal. 325; *Texas & P. R. Co. v. Rosedale Street R. Co.*, 64 Tex. 80; *Elliott v. Fairhaven & W. R. Co.*, 32 Conn. 579; *Chicago, B.*

46

& Q. R. Co. v. West Chicago S. R. Co., 40 N. E. Rep. [Ill.] 1008; Merrick v. Intramontaine R. Co., 24 S. E. Rep. [N. Car.] 667.) For the occupation and use of the street for ordinary street railway purposes it must, I think, be conceded that the defendant was not liable to plaintiff in damages upon the authority of these cases, hence I omit the allegations as to the occupation and use of the street by a track, for it is common to all street railways, whether operated by horse-power or electricity.

I shall now consider the respects in which the petition charges that the defendant's use of the street differed from that of an ordinary street railway operated by horse-power and in what respects this different use has caused damage to be suffered by the plaintiff. These factors we have already grouped under the first class of elements of damages, and they are the locating of poles and wires which obstruct ingress and egress and interfere with view from plaintiff's premises across the street. The manner in which real property may be injuriously affected without being physically disturbed or entered upon is well illustrated by the following adjudicated cases: The city of Shawneetown, Illinois, built a levee in a street of that city for the purpose of protecting it against the overflow waters of the Ohio river. The levee was about ten feet high, but was so constructed that its upper surface could be used as the street had been before the construction of said levee. An abutting lot owner sued the city for damages, claiming that his lot had been depreciated in value by the presence in front of it of this levee, for the reason that it hindered his free ingress and egress to and from his property, and the supreme court of Illinois held the city liable. (City of Shawneetown v. Mason, 82 Ill. 337.) The construction of the approaches to a bridge in such a manner as to obstruct the ingress and egress of an owner to and from his property was held to be such an injury as entitled such owner to maintain an action for damages. (Stack v. City of East St. Louis, 85 Ill. 377.) In Merrick v. Intramontaine R. Co., supra, it was said by Faircloth, C. J., delivering the opinion of the supreme court of North Carolina: "If the street railway should be so constructed—for instance, if it should shut out or shut off the abutter with embankments, and thus materially impair his rights—this would seem to be an additional burden and subject the company to damages." These adjudicated cases serve to illustrate the fact that in plaintiff's petition the averments that the location of the poles and wires of the street railway upon Clarke and Sixteenth streets in such a way as to interfere with plaintiff's ingress and egress and his view from his premises towards said streets, in connection with the allegation that thereby his real property had suffered depreciation in value, sufficiently stated a cause of action in view of section 21, article 1, of the constitution of this state, which is as follows: "The property of no person shall be taken or damaged for public use without just compensation therefor." As further illustrating the applicability and purpose of this constitutional provision, see also *Gottschalk v. Chicago, B. & Q. R. Co.*, 14 Neb. 550; *City of Omaha v. Kramer*, 25 Neb. 489; *Chicago, K. & N. R. Co. v. Hazels*, 26 Neb. 364; and *Omaha & N. P. R. Co. v. Janecek*, 30 Neb. 276. I have considered this case as it was presented by the averments of the petition which the demurrer admitted to be true, and, tested by the requirements of liberal construction laid down in *Roberts v. Samson*, 50 Neb. 745, there was stated a cause of action. If there exist facts which should serve to change or modify our views, these facts, I think, should be pleaded by the defendant, for we cannot assume their existence. For the reasons above stated I concur in the conclusion. The judgment of the district court should be reversed.

BANKERS LIFE INSURANCE COMPANY OF LINCOLN, NE-
BRASKA V. THOMAS L. STEPHENS.

FILED FEBRUARY 2, 1898. No. 7807.

Insurance: CONSTRUCTION OF CONTRACT FOR COMPENSATION OF AGENT.
The contract between an insurance company and one Stephens provided for the appointment of the latter as the insurance company's
agent for an indefinite time; that his compensation for services
rendered as agent should be a certain per cent of the premiums
collected and remitted on risks written by him. Further, the contract recited: "For the first fifteen months we will give you a
salary of $200 per month, and should your income from the com-
mission part of your contract run more than your salary, you
shall be entitled to the benefit of the same. In consideration of
the contract as a whole you agree to turn into the company of
insurance accepted and paid for $200,000 the first fifteen months."
Held, (1) That the agent was entitled to a salary of $200 per
month and the stated per cent of premiums collected for the first
fifteen months he served the company; (2) that the salary was
payable monthly; (3) that the agent's writing $200,000 insurance
during the first fifteen months of his employment was not a condition precedent to his right of $200 per month and the percentage
on premiums collected during that time.

ERROR from the district court of Lancaster county.
Tried below before STRODE, J. *Affirmed.*

Ames & Pettis, for plaintiff in error.

John A. Davies, R. D. Stearns, and *E. C. Strode, contra.*

RAGAN, C.

January 20, 1892, the Bankers Life Insurance Company
of Lincoln, Nebraska, and Thomas L. Stephens entered
into a contract in writing in and by which Stephens was
appointed agent of the insurance company for an indefinite time. The contract was in words and figures as
follows:

"Thomas L. Stephens, Glenwood, Iowa: You are hereby
appointed an agent of the Bankers Life Insurance Company of Nebraska, for field work under the management
of said company, with authority to secure applications

for insurance, collect and remit first premiums, and to perform such other duties as may be required of you in this behalf, subject to all the rules and regulations of this company and such other instructions as shall be communicated to you from time to time by said company. It shall be your duty:

"First—To thoroughly inform yourself of the company's plans and advantages, and to make them publicly known throughout the limits of your agency.

"Second—To use your best efforts and your greatest skill in promoting the company's business by canvassing personally for acceptable applications for insurance in said company, and in guarding its interests generally.

"Third—To receive all moneys and other securities received by you on account of said company in a fiduciary trust, and transmit the same to the home office at once, together with a report in detail, embracing every item of business done by or through you not previously reported.

"Fourth—To execute and maintain in behalf of said company a bond in the sum of $500, with good and sufficient sureties, conditioned for the faithful performance of all your obligations under this appointment.

"You are not authorized to alter, make, or discharge contracts, or to bind the company in any way.

"The compensation to be allowed for services properly rendered under this appointment shall be a commission upon the premiums actually collected and remitted upon the policies secured by it through you as follows: Sixty per cent of the first year premiums on fifteen and twenty payment life, twenty year endowment, ordinary life, ten year renewal, and twenty year bond; fifty per cent on ten payment life and fifteen year endowment. Also a ten per cent annual renewal interest on each policy written by or through you for four years succeeding the first year, and this shall be construed to mean that a ten per cent renewal interest shall be paid each year for four years on all policies written by or through you when premiums have been collected and paid for, said four years to commence one year from date of policy. (But all your interest under this contract shall cease at any time your connection with this company is severed, except that if such severance is made by the company you shall be entitled to, and the company hereby agrees to pay you, two annual renewals of ten per cent each on all premiums collected and paid for on all policies written by or through you or your sub-agents, such payment being in lieu of the four ten per cent annual renewals specified herein.) Neither sickness or death shall annul any of your interest under this contract.

"You are hereby authorized to hire sub-agents, and any difference between what you pay them and your contract will be credited to your account.

"This appointment may be revoked at any time upon one year's previous notice in writing, should you fail to comply with any of its conditions, or should the amount of new business secured by you not prove remunerative, or should the business not be conducted in a satisfactory manner.

"For the first fifteen months we will give you a salary of $200 per month, and should your income from the commission part of your contract run more than your salary, you shall be entitled to the benefit of the same. In consideration of the contract as a whole, you agree to turn into the company of insurance accepted and paid for $200,000 the first fifteen months in any or all of the following kinds of policies: Ten, fifteen, and twenty payment life; fifteen and twenty year endowment; twenty year bond; ten, fifteen, and twenty payment life, with extended insurance.

"I hereby accept the foregoing appointment and agree to comply with its terms and conditions."

In the district court of Lancaster county Stephens brought this suit against the insurance company, alleging that he entered upon the duties contracted to be performed by him by virtue of such contract and continued in the performance of such duties for the insurance company for a period of ten months immediately after January 20, 1892; that at the end of that time the insurance company, having wholly failed to perform its part of the agreement, wrongfully discharged him from its employ, and then and thereafter refused to permit him to longer continue in its employ; that he was at all times during the fifteen months immediately following the date of such contract able, ready, and willing, and repeatedly offered and held himself out as being ready and willing, to do and perform all the duties and obligations required of him by said contract. By this action Stephens sought to recover from the insurance company fifteen months' salary at $200 per month. He had a verdict and judgment, and the insurance company brings the case here for review on error.

The only contention of the plaintiff in error, which we notice, is that the district court erred in the construction placed by it upon the contract between the parties. The insurance company's construction of the contract is that Stephens was to be paid for the first fifteen months of his employment a compensation at the rate of $200 per month, provided that during said time he wrote and turned into the insurance company risks accepted by the company, and on which the premiums had been paid, aggregating $200,000. On the other hand, Stephens' construction of the contract was and is that in any event he should be paid a compensation of $200 per month for the first fifteen months that he served the company and the commissions provided by the contract on all risks procured during that time. A further contention of Stephens was that this salary of $200 per month was payable monthly. The district court adopted the construction of the contract contended for by Stephens. We are of opinion that the construction placed upon the contract by the district court was the correct one, and its judgment is

AFFIRMED.

JOHN L. SCHIEK ET AL. V. NANCY SANDERS ET AL.

FILED FEBRUARY 2, 1898. No. 7827.

1. **Intoxicating Liquors**: ACTION AGAINST SALOON-KEEPER: DAMAGES. Damages awarded *held* not excessive under the evidence.

2. ————: EVIDENCE OF INTOXICATION: LICENSE. Evidence examined, and *held* to sustain the finding of the jury that the deceased, at the time he was injured, was intoxicated from drinking liquor furnished him by the plaintiff in error, and that plaintiff in error was a licensed saloon-keeper at the time of furnishing the deceased such liquor.

3. ————: EVIDENCE OF LICENSE. In a suit by a widow against a saloon-keeper to recover damages for loss of support resulting from her husband's death, alleged to have been caused by his intoxication from drinking liquors furnished by plaintiff in error, when the issue is whether the plaintiff in error was a licensed saloon-keeper, proceedings of the city council showing the granting of a liquor license to the plaintiff in error, and the record of liquor licenses kept by the city clerk, showing that a liquor license had been granted to the plaintiff in error, are competent and sufficient evidence to sustain a finding that the plaintiff in error was a licensed dealer in intoxicating liquors. To prove the affirmative of such an issue the production in evidence of the actual license issued is not essential.

4. ————: SALES: LIABILITY OF SALOON-KEEPER AND SURETIES. A licensed dealer in intoxicating liquors, and the sureties upon his bond, are liable for the loss of support sustained by the widow and children of a decedent, whose death was contributed to by intoxicating liquors drank by the deceased and which were furnished him by the liquor dealer.

ERROR from the district court of Gage county. Tried below before BUSH, J. *Affirmed.*

Alfred Hazlett and *Fulton Jack*, for plaintiffs in error.

George Arthur Murphy and *William C. Le Hane, contra.*

RAGAN, C.

On the evening of April 14, 1893, E. J. Sanders boarded a passenger train of the Rock Island Railway Company at Beatrice, Nebraska, for the purpose of going to his

home at Harbine, a station near by, and while alighting
or attempting to alight from the train at Harbine he was
injured, from the effects of which he died on the 17th of
the same month.   His widow, Nancy Sanders, in behalf
of herself and her four minor children, in the district
court of Gage county, brought this suit against John L.
Schiek and others, being licensed dealers in intoxicating
liquors and the sureties on their bonds, for damages for
loss of support and maintenance which she and her children had sustained by reason of the death of the husband
and father, basing her action upon the ground that the
saloon-keepers had sold or furnished to said Sanders at
Beatrice, Nebraska, on the date of his injury, intoxicating
liquors, which he there drank and which caused his intoxication, and that the injuries from which he died
resulted from his being intoxicated by the liquors so sold
and furnished him.   Mrs. Sanders had a verdict and
judgment, and the defendants below, who were held
liable, have brought the same here for review on error.

1. The first argument is that the damages awarded
Mrs. Sanders by the jury are excessive, appearing to
have been given under the influence of passion or prejudice.   The jury awarded Mrs. Sanders $850 damages.
The amount prayed for in the petition was $5,000.   The
evidence shows, without conflict, that Sanders, prior to
his injury, was a healthy man, thirty-eight years of age;
that he was a mechanic capable of earning, and had been
earning for some years immediately prior to the time of
his injury, about $3 per day; that he devoted his earn-
ings to the support and maintenance of his family, consisting of his wife and four minor children, the oldest
being twelve years of age; that his death left his widow
and children without means of support, except what the
widow earned by washing.   Sanders' expectancy of life
at the time of his death was more than twenty-five years.
We find nothing in the record which indicates that the
jury was influenced by passion or prejudice, at least
against these plaintiffs in error, in making this award,

The evidence would have sustained a verdict for all claimed in the petition.

2. A second argument is that the verdict is not sustained by sufficient evidence. One of the contentions on which this is based is that one Blanchard, a brother-in-law of the deceased, was a witness for the plaintiff below, and plaintiffs in error contend that they impeached his testimony. Blanchard testified on the trial in behalf of Mrs. Sanders to being in company with the deceased in Beatrice. most of the day on which he was injured; that he was present with him in the saloons of the plaintiffs in error, and that Sanders drank from fifteen to twenty drinks of whisky and a number of drinks of beer; in short, that he was in the saloons of the plaintiffs in error on the day he was injured, drank intoxicating drinks therein which were furnished him by the plaintiffs in error, and was drunk from the effects of the liquor drank at the time he left Beatrice, about 8 o'clock in the evening, for his home at Harbine. Certain witnesses testified on behalf of the plaintiffs in error that Blanchard testified at the coroner's inquest held over the body of Sanders on April 17 to the effect that Sanders was not drunk in Beatrice on the 14th; or, in other words, witnesses testified to statements made by Blanchard on April 17 and other times which tended to contradict the testimony he gave on the trial of this case. But we cannot say 'that the verdict lacks evidence to support it because of this attack upon the credibility of Blanchard. Notwithstanding the attack upon his testimony the credibility of his evidence was still for the jury. Furthermore, if the entire evidence of Blanchard be eliminated from the record, the evidence still sustains the finding of the jury that the plaintiffs in error furnished Sanders liquor on April 14 from which he became intoxicated, and that his intoxication caused the injury from which he died. Various witnesses testified that Sanders and Blanchard were together in Beatrice on April 14; were in the saloons of plaintiffs in error drink-

ing intoxicants as late as 5 o'clock in the evening. Mrs. Blanchard testified that her husband and the deceased were at her house between 1 and 2 o'clock in the afternoon and that they were both drunk at that time; that they returned later in the evening, about 6 o'clock, and that Sanders was drunk at that time; that she tried to induce him to remain at her house over night because of his intoxicated condition. Other witnesses testified to Sanders being in a store in the afternoon and buying or negotiating for a jacket or blouse which he tried on; that he was then intoxicated and acted foolishly, and that he attracted the attention of the lady clerks to his intoxicated condition by remarking that he looked well enough in that jacket for a Sunday school superintendent. Another disinterested witness testified to meeting Sanders near 6 o'clock P. M. in the saloon of the plaintiffs in error; that Sanders drank intoxicants in the saloon at that time; that he was drunk, and though he was a stranger to the witness he shook hands with him and called his attention to the fighting qualities of a dog he had with him. This is not all the evidence, but it is sufficient to show that the finding of the jury that Sanders was drunk in Beatrice on the evening of April 14 from drinking liquors furnished him by the plaintiffs in error is sustained by the evidence.

A second argument under the contention that the verdict lacks evidence to sustain it is this: The petition alleges that the plaintiffs in error were licensed saloon-keepers. The answer denies this. The plaintiffs in error insist that the record contains no proof that they were licensed saloon-keepers on April 14, 1893. This contention is untenable. On the trial there were introduced in evidence the applications made by the plaintiffs in error for license to sell intoxicating liquors for the year ending May 1, 1893, the public notices given by them of such application as required by the statute, the bonds executed by the saloon-keepers in pursuance of the provisions of the statute, the proceedings of the city

council granting them licenses to sell intoxicating liquors
for the ensuing year, and the "license book" kept by the
city clerk which recited that licenses had been issued to
the plaintiffs in error, the date thereof, the amount of
the license fee, and when the license expired. It is true
that the actual paper, certificate, or license, if one was
actually issued by the city council or the clerk and delivered to the plaintiffs in error, was not produced in
evidence; but if such a paper existed it did not belong
in the office of the city clerk; if it had ever been issued,
it was delivered to the plaintiffs in error and was presumably in their possession. The evidence offered by
the plaintiffs below upon this subject was sufficient to
sustain the jury's finding that the plaintiffs in error
were on April 14, 1893, duly licensed saloon-keepers in
the city of Beatrice.

3. The third argument is that the court erred in giving
to the jury the following instruction: "The court instructs the jury that it is not necessary in order to warrant a recovery in this case that the intoxication of E. J.
Sanders, deceased, by means of intoxicating liquors sold
or given away by any of the defendants herein to him
be the direct, natural, and proximate cause of the death
of said E. J. Sanders; but if the jury shall find that the
use of intoxicating liquors, directly or indirectly, contributed towards or assisted in producing the death of
said E. J. Sanders, and that all or any part of the intoxicating liquors so used by the said E. J. Sanders were
sold or given away to him by defendants, *   *   * or
any of them, then your verdict shall be in favor of the
plaintiffs and against the defendants, or such of them as
were guilty of such wrongful act." The criticism upon
this instruction is that it lays down the rule that a
saloon-keeper and the sureties on his bond are liable to
the widow and children of a decedent for their loss of
support if the decedent's death was contributed to by
intoxicating liquors drank by the decedent which were
furnished him by the saloon-keeper. The contention of

the plaintiffs in error is that the liability of the saloon-keeper only attaches where it is shown that he furnished liquor to the decedent and his drinking of the same and his intoxication therefrom were the direct and proximate causes of his death. But by an unbroken line of decisions of this court in construing the liquor law of the state (Compiled Statutes, ch. 50) it is now established that a saloon-keeper and the sureties upon his bond are liable for the loss of support sustained by a widow and children of a decedent whose death was contributed to by intoxicating liquors drank by the deceased and which were furnished him by the saloon-keeper. The court did not err in giving this instruction. (See, among others, the following authorities: *Roose v. Perkins,* 9 Neb. 304; *Kerkow v. Bauer,* 15 Neb. 150; *Elshire v. Schuyler,* 15 Neb. 561; *McClay v. Worrall,* 18 Neb. 44; *Wardell v. McConnell,* 23 Neb. 152; *McManigal v. Seaton,* 23 Neb. 549; *Jones v. Bates,* 26 Neb. 693; *Sellars v. Foster,* 27 Neb. 118; *Uldrich v. Gilmore,* 35 Neb. 288; *Chaelir v. Sawyer,* 42 Neb. 362; *Cornelius v. Hultman,* 44 Neb. 441; *Gran v. Houston,* 45 Neb. 813.)

4. A final argument is that the court erred in refusing to instruct the jury that no evidence had been adduced before them showing that the plaintiffs in error were on April 14, 1893, licensed saloon-keepers in the city of Beatrice, and that they should therefore return a verdict in their favor. For reasons already stated the court did not err in refusing to so instruct the jury.

There is no error in the record and the judgment of the district court is

AFFIRMED.

A. U. Wyman, Receiver, Appellee, v. L. B. Williams
et al., Appellants.

Filed February 2, 1898. No. 7634.

1. **Corporations:** Insolvency: Directors. The directors of an insolvent corporation cannot lawfully appropriate its assets to the payment of debts due them from it to the entire exclusion of other corporate creditors.

2. ———: Action by Receiver: Subscribers to Stock. A suit by the receiver of a corporation against subscribers to its stock to recover their unpaid stock subscriptions will not lie until the amount justly due from the corporation has been ascertained and the corporate property exhausted.

3. ———: ———: ———. When the directory of a corporation, before it is put into the hands of a receiver, makes a call or assessment on the stock subscribers for all or a part of their unpaid stock subscriptions, such calls become at once corporate property or assets of the corporation and may be sued for and collected by a receiver subsequently appointed as any other asset of the corporation.

4. ———. *Globe Publishing Co. v. State Bank of Nebraska*, 41 Neb. 175, and *State v. German Savings Bank*, 50 Neb. 734, reaffirmed and distinguished.

Motions for rehearing of case reported in 52 Neb. 833. *Overruled.*

Hall & McCulloch, Warren Switzler, and *J. W. West*, for the motion.

Ragan, C.

This is a motion for rehearing of *Wyman v. Williams*, 52 Neb. 833. It is not necessary to state all the facts, as they are sufficiently stated in the former opinion.

The parties filing the motions for rehearing are S. R. Johnson, George F. Wright, and Henry W. Yates. These parties were subscribers to the stock of the Nebraska Insurance Company and paid in cash for the stock subscribed by them fifty per cent of its face value, and by the articles of incorporation the remainder of the subscription was payable on the call of the directors. Some time after the corporation began business the directors of the corporation made a call or an assessment upon their stockholders of eighty-three and one-fourth per cent of the amount of the unpaid stock subscriptions for the purpose of raising money to pay the debts and expenses of the corporation. Subsequently the insurance company was placed in the hands of a receiver and he brought this action against the parties filing this motion, and the other stockholders of such insurance company, and sought to recover the full amount of their unpaid stock subscriptions. The decree of the district court, so far as it affects the parties moving here, resulted in a personal judgment against them in favor of the receiver for the amount of the assessment or call made against them by the stockholders. We will first dispose of Mr. Yates' motion. He was made a party defendant to the receiver's action, and it seems that he appeared therein, demurred to the petition, and that his demurrer was overruled. If he filed an answer in the case, the fact is not disclosed by the record. This being the case, he could only be heard on this appeal as to the correctness of the district court in overruling his demurrer; but a copy of this demurrer is not in the record, and we do not know upon what grounds the demurrer was urged below. We must therefore overrule the motion.

Johnson and Wright make three arguments in support of their motion for a rehearing. The first is that the district court, by its decree, found that prior to the time the call or assessment was made for unpaid subscriptions they had advanced to the insurance company a large sum of money, and they insist that these advancements were made by them under an agreement existing between them and the insurance company that the advancements made by each of them should be applied on their unpaid stock subscriptions. There is some evidence in the record on behalf of Johnson and Wright which tends to support this contention, but whether these

advancements of money made by them to the insurance
company were made in pursuance of an agreement that
they should be applied on their stock subscriptions and
were as a matter of fact payments on their unpaid stock
subscriptions was a question of fact for the district court.
That tribunal has resolved that question of fact against
these appellants and we cannot say that its conclusion
is not supported by sufficient evidence.

The second argument is that the directors, among
whom were Wright and Johnson, at the time they levied
the assessment and made the call for the payment of
part of the unpaid stock subscriptions, then and there
agreed that the moneys which Johnson and Wright had
before that time advanced or loaned to the insurance
company, and which the insurance company was then
owing them, should be set off against what would be due
from them as stockholders of the corporation on the assessment levied upon their unpaid stock subscriptions.
This argument is somewhat inconsistent with the contention of appellants that the moneys that they had prior
to that time advanced to the insurance company were
payments upon their stock subscriptions. But it is insisted that the receiver could not adopt that part of the
action of the directors making the assessment or call
without also adopting the disposition which the directors
made of the assessment so far as appellants are concerned. The argument is this, as we understand it: That
at the time the assessment was levied or the call made
the insurance company was largely indebted to Johnson
and Wright and that the directors had the right to apply
or to cancel the assessment of Wright and Johnson to the
extent the insurance company owed them; but, as already stated, Johnson and Wright were part of the directory of this corporation; it was at that time insolvent,
and they could not take advantage of their position to
obtain a preference of debts owing by the corporation
to themselves. (See *Gordon v. Plattsmouth Canning Co.,*
36 Neb. 548; *Ingwersen v. Edgecombe,* 42 Neb. 740; *Tillson*

v. Downing. 45 Neb. 549.) If the insurance company was indebted to Johnson and Wright, they had the right, and perhaps have still, to file their claims with the receiver against the corporation and have them paid out of its assets, but they had no right, being directors of the corporation, to use its assets for the purpose of discharging the corporation's debt to themselves to the entire exclusion of other corporate creditors.

The third argument is that a suit by a receiver against the stock subscribers of a corporation to recover unpaid stock subscriptions will not lie until after the corporate property shall have been exhausted. This is true. (See Constitution, art. 11, sec. 4; *Globe Publishing Co. v. State Bank of Nebraska,* 41 Neb. 175; *State v. German Savings Bank,* 50 Neb. 734.) But this action of the receiver was brought for the very purpose of collecting in the assets of the corporation. After the directors had made the call or the assessment on the stockholders, such a call and assessment became an asset of the corporation, or, in the language of the constitution, became corporate property, and if the corporation had continued to exist and do business, it might have maintained an action in its own name against the stockholders for such assessment; and when it went out of business and was put into the hands of a receiver, he could sue to recover these calls or assessments because they were assets of the corporation, as much so as he could have sued upon a promissory note which the corporation owned. It is true that the receiver in this case by his petition sought to recover from the stockholders all their unpaid stock subscriptions, but by the decree of the district court his recovery was limited to the amount of the call or assessment made by the directors. The motions for rehearing are overruled.

REHEARING DENIED.

CITY OF FRIEND V. FRED N. BURLEIGH, EXECUTOR.

FILED FEBRUARY 2, 1898. No. 7777.

1. **Death by Wrongful Act:** PETITION. A petition in an action based on chapter 21, Compiled Statutes, which avers that the defendant by his wrongful act, neglect, or default caused the death of a person, that the plaintiff is such person's duly-appointed personal representative, and that the deceased left a widow and children, states a cause of action.

2. **Evidence:** DECLARATIONS. A declaration, to be a part of the *res gestæ*, need not necessarily be coincident in point of time with the main fact proved; but such fact and the declaration concerning the same must be so clearly and closely connected that the declaration in the ordinary course of affairs can be regarded as the spontaneous explanation of the fact.

3 **Death by Wrongful Act:** EVIDENCE: DECLARATIONS. Where the negligence of a city causes the death of one, and his personal representative sues such city to recover for the benefit of the widow and next of kin of the deceased damages to compensate them for the pecuniary loss they have sustained by reason of his death, the exclusion from evidence of the declaration of the deceased that his injury was the result of his own carelessness, *held* not prejudicial.

4. ———: CARLISLE TABLES. In such suit the "Carlisle tables" are admissible in evidence for the purpose of showing the expectancy of life of the deceased and to admeasure the pecuniary loss to his widow or next of kin resulting from his death.

5. **Executors:** ASSETS OF ESTATE. Such a cause of action is not an asset of the estate of the decedent.

6. **Negligence.** The doctrine of comparative negligence is not in force in this state.

ERROR from the district court of Saline county. Tried below before HASTINGS, J. *Affirmed.*

J. D. Pope, E. E. McGintie, F. I. Foss, and *W. R. Matson,* for plaintiff in error.

Charles O. Whedon and *J. Palmer, contra.*

RAGAN, C.

On the night of December 4, 1890, David B. Burleigh, while on his way to his residence in the city of Friend, stepped or fell off a sidewalk in said city, at a point where the walk crossed a ravine some ten feet deep and fifty feet wide, receiving certain injuries from such fall from which he subsequently died. In the district court of Saline county his executor brought this suit against the said city of Friend to recover the pecuniary damages which, he alleged, the deceased's widow and next of kin had sustained by his death; the basis of the executor's action being that the proximate cause of Burleigh's death was the negligent failure of the city to provide the sidewalk, where it crossed said ravine, with railings, or to keep displayed at night on said walk at said place some light or signal. The executor had a verdict and judgment, and the city has brought the same here for review on error.

1. The first argument is that the petition does not state a cause of action. The gist of this contention is that the facts stated in the petition do not show that the widow and next of kin of the deceased have sustained any special pecuniary loss by reason of his death. The petition alleges that the deceased at the time of his death was fifty-eight years old; that he was before the injury a strong and vigorous man; that he was engaged in mercantile business, and that he left surviving him a widow and six children, to whom he devised his property. The action is brought under Compiled Statutes, chapter 21, corresponding to Lord Campbell's Act, and giving to a personal representative an action on behalf of the widow and next of kin for pecuniary injuries by them sustained through the death of the decedent where such death has been caused by the wrongful act, neglect, or default of another under such circumstances that the person injured might himself have maintained an action. In *Burlington & M. R. R. Co. v. Crockett*, 17 Neb. 570, it was held that in such cases the petition must allege that there survived a widow or next of kin. Clearly so, because if there were no persons entitled to the proceeds of the action there could be no such proceeds. There could

be no pecuniary loss unless there was some one within
the designated class to sustain it. In *Anderson v. Chicago,
B. & Q. R. Co.*, 35 Neb. 95, the question was one of evidence and not of pleading, and it was held that the jury
was warranted in returning a verdict for an insignificant sum, as the evidence did not show a pecuniary
loss. There the next of kin were adult brothers and
sisters and the deceased was not shown to have so conducted himself as to warrant an inference that his
continued existence would have been for their pecuniary
advantage. There was no legal obligation in their favor.
In *Kearney Electric Co. v. Laughlin*, 45 Neb. 390, the petition alleged that the deceased left a widow and certain
children and that they were wholly dependent upon him
for support. This was held sufficient. In *Orgall v. Chicago, B. & Q. R. Co.*, 46 Neb. 4, it was held that a petition
must show that the beneficiaries sustained a pecuniary
loss. There again the next of kin was one not legally
dependent upon the deceased for support. On the contrary, the deceased was the daughter of the next of kin.
The rule deducible from these cases, as well as from the
weight of cases elsewhere, is that the petition must show
facts from which a pecuniary loss is inferable. In the
case of collaterals or others not legally dependent upon
the deceased, at least where they are not heirs at law,
facts must be pleaded showing an actual pecuniary interest in his life. Where, however, it is pleaded that the
next of kin sustain such a relationship to the deceased
that the law imposes upon him a duty to support them
and that practical ability existed to enable him to perform that duty, a pecuniary interest is pleaded. Its extent is a question for the jury. Here the allegations of
good health of the deceased, that he was actually engaged in business, and that he left a widow and children.
are sufficient to answer the requirements of any of the
cases.

2. On the trial the city offered to prove that Burleigh.
after his injury, stated that his injury was the result of

his own carelessness and that nobody was to blame for it but himself. The refusal of the district court to permit this evidence is the second assignment of error argued here. It is first insisted that the evidence offered was competent as part of the *res gestæ*. This term means a thing or things done in and about—as a part of—the transaction out of which the litigation in hand grew and on which transaction such litigation is based. (*Collins v. State*, 46 Neb. 37.) And in *Missouri P. R. Co. v. Baier*, 37 Neb. 235, it was held: "A declaration, to be a part of the *res gestæ*, need not necessarily be coincident in point of time with the main fact proved. It is enough that the two are so clearly connected that the declaration can, in the ordinary course of affairs, be said to be a spontaneous explanation of the real cause." In this case the declarations of the decedent made a few moments after the accident and explanatory of it were held admissible as part of the *res gestæ*. In *Omaha & R. V. R. Co. v. Chollette*, 41 Neb. 578, the remarks of a brakeman on the train, made at the time an accident occurred, as to the cause of the accident, were held admissible as *res gestæ*. In *Collins v. State, supra*, the declarations of the deceased made two and one-half hours after he was shot, as to who shot him, were held not admissible as *res gestæ*. In the case at bar the deceased was injured on the night of December 4, 1890, and died on the 19th day of the following February. The witness by whom it was proposed to prove the declarations of the deceased visited him several times between the date of his injury and his death; spent four nights with him. At some of these visits the deceased made the declaration offered in evidence, but it does not appear how soon after the injury the declaration proposed to be proved was made. Under these circumstances we think that the injury sustained by the deceased and his declarations concerning the same were not so clearly and closely connected that the declarations, in the ordinary course of affairs, can be regarded as the unpremeditated explanation of the injury, and therefore the declaration was not part of the *res gestæ* and on that ground was properly excluded. It is not necessary to determine whether this declaration of the deceased was admissible in evidence on any other principle, since the record discloses that the court permitted witnesses for the city to detail alleged conversations had with the deceased, in which he stated all the facts relating to his injury. The city, then, was not prejudiced by the exclusion from the jury of the alleged declaration of the deceased that his injury was the result of his own negligence.

3. A third argument is that the court erred in permitting to be introduced in evidence the Carlisle tables of expectancy of life. It is not claimed that these tables were not of themselves competent evidence, but it is insisted that there is no evidence to show that the benefit of the services or earnings of the deceased, had he lived, would have inured to his next of kin, and for that reason the tables were incompetent. The expectancy of the deceased at the time of his death was fifteen years. At that time he was engaged in mercantile business, which seemed to have been a prosperous one, his sales amounting to about $9,000 a year; and his expenses from $1,000 to $1,500 a year. His expenses included the support of his family. Prior to his death he lived with his family. If the family consisted of simply the husband and wife, then upon the death of the husband the widow was deprived of the profits and earnings which the husband made and which prior to his death he devoted to her support and maintenance. Of course the administrator was entitled to recover only the amount of the pecuniary loss which the widow and next of kin had sustained by reason of the death of the deceased, and these Carlisle tables were admissible in evidence for the purpose of showing the number of years which the deceased would probably have lived and to admeasure the loss to his widow and next of kin resulting from his death. If it were true that the next of kin of the deceased, before his

death, had married and moved away from the family and
were supporting themselves, and all the earnings and
profits of the deceased were devoted to his wife, then
the administrator would recover for the benefit of the
widow a sum which would recompense her for the
pecuniary loss resulting to her from her husband's death,
and this loss would be the support and maintenance
measured in money furnished the wife by the husband.
The fact, if it be a fact, that the next of kin were supporting themselves during the life of the deceased and
that none of his earnings and profits were devoted to
their support would not render the Carlisle tables incompetent evidence.

4. A fourth argument of the city is that the court
erred in refusing to permit it to prove that prior to the
accident to Burleigh the sidewalk in question was in
constant use by the citizens of Friend both day and night
and that no other accident was ever known to happen on
that walk. We do not see how this evidence would have
tended to prove or disprove any issue in the case.

5. A fifth argument of the city is that the district
court erred in refusing to permit it to prove that the
inventory of the property of the decedent filed in the
county court of Saline county by the executor did not
contain the claim sued for here. There was no error in
this ruling of the court. This cause of action did not
belong, and does not belong, to the estate of the decedent. It belongs to his widow and next of kin, and
was not and is not, and can never become, an asset of his
estate.

6. The city requested the court to instruct the jury as
follows: "If the widow and children were as well off
financially after the death of said Burleigh as before his
death, then the plaintiff is not entitled to recover." The
court added to this instruction the following: "On account of the death of David B. Burleigh." The city now
complains that the court erred in modifying the instruction. The modification made by the court to the in-

struction did not change its force and effect. The
instruction was substantially the same after it was
modified as before. We doubt whether the city was entitled to such an instruction, but if there was any error
in giving this instruction it was an error committed in
favor of the city and of which it cannot complain.

7. Another argument of the city is that the court
erred in refusing to give the following instruction to the
jury: "You are further instructed that the deceased was
bound to exercise ordinary care for his personal safety
while passing along the streets of the defendant; and
if the jury find from the evidence that plaintiff's slight
negligence, if any, contributed directly to the alleged
injury, then you will find for the defendant." The court
did not err in refusing to give this instruction. Such
expressions as "slight negligence" and "slight want of
ordinary care" should not be used in instructions, as
they tend to obscure and confuse what should be stated
in plain and concise language. The doctrine of comparative negligence is not in force in this state. Our
courts do not recognize degrees of negligence. The rule
is that if a person himself in the exercise of ordinary
care is injured through the negligence of another he
may recover; but if his own negligence contributed to
or was the proximate cause of the injury he cannot recover. (*Village of Culbertson v. Holliday,* 50 Neb. 229.)

The foregoing embrace all the assignments of error
which we think it worth while to notice. There are other
complaints about the action of the district court in giving and refusing to give certain instructions. We have
examined carefully the entire record and it must suffice
to say that we think the court committed no error of
which the city can complain. The judgment of the district court is

AFFIRMED.

CLAUS MATTHEIS V. FREMONT, ELKHORN AND MISSOURI
VALLEY RAILROAD COMPANY.

FILED FEBRUARY 2, 1898.   No. 7760.

1. **Eminent Domain:** CONDEMNATION PROCEEDINGS: TRIBUNAL. The
proceeding for condemning real estate for right of way of a railway company provided for by section 97, chapter 16, Compiled
Statutes, is not instituted in nor conducted by the county court.

2. ———: ———: ———. Such a proceeding is conducted by the county
judge, the sheriff, and the appraisers selected by the former. These
constitute a tribunal not to try a civil action pending between
the land-owner and the railway company, not to pronounce a
judgment, but simply to assess the damages which the land-
owner will sustain by reason of the appropriation of his land for
the railroad's right of way.

3. ———: ———: ———. The powers conferred upon the county
judge and the duties required of him by that act are not judicial
powers and duties but purely ministerial ones.

4. ———: ———: VACATING AWARD. The county court has no jurisdiction of an action brought under section 602 of the Code of Civil
Procedure to vacate such a condemnation proceeding on the
ground that the award of damages made therein was procured by
fraud.

5. ———: ———: ———: COUNTY COURT. The county court has no
jurisdiction of a suit in equity to vacate such a condemnation proceeding.

6. ———: ———: ———: ———. Whether a county judge has jurisdiction to set aside an award of damages made in such a condemnation proceeding for any cause or at any time not decided.

7. ———: ———: ———: ———. But, if the county judge has such
jurisdiction, an application to him to set aside an award of damages made in such a proceeding under such statute, solely on the
grounds that the damages were inadequate, and the award procured by fraud of the railroad company, should not be entertained when the application was made more than five years after
the condemnation proceeding occurred, the condemnation money
awarded the applicant had all that time been in the hands of
the county judge for the applicant's use, the railroad company
had built and was operating its road on the easement condemned;
the application not averring that the applicant had no legal
notice of such condemnation proceeding whether he appealed or
attempted to appeal from the award made, nor that he was deprived of his appeal by fraud, accident, or some circumstance
beyond his control.

ERROR from the district court of Douglas county. Tried below before DUFFIE, J. *Affirmed.*

Warren Switzler, for plaintiff in error.

William B. Sterling, Benjamin T. White, and *James B. Sheean, contra.*

RAGAN, C.

In June, 1887, the county judge of Douglas county, at the request of the Fremont, Elkhorn & Missouri Valley Railroad Company, hereinafter called the railroad company, which desired to obtain a right of way across the land of Claus Mattheis, selected six disinterested freeholders of said county, caused them to be summoned by the sheriff thereof, and they made an assessment of the amount of damages which Mattheis would sustain by reason of the appropriation of a part of his land for right of way by the railroad company and duly reported their assessment to such county judge, who certified the same under his seal of office and transmitted it to the county clerk of said county for record. In October, 1894, Mattheis filed against said railroad company in the county court of Douglas county a petition praying the county court to set aside and vacate the condemnation proceeding upon the ground that the assessment of damages made by the appraisers in such proceeding was procured by the fraud of the railroad company. The county court sustained a general demurrer to this petition and dismissed the same, and Mattheis prosecuted a petition in error from that judgment to the district court of said county, which affirmed the judgment of the county court, and Mattheis has brought here for review on error the judgment of the district court.

1. As we understand from his argument counsel for the plaintiff in error insists that this action can be maintained upon one of three theories. The first theory is that the condemnation proceeding was had in the county

court and was a judicial proceeding; and that the condemnation proceeding which resulted in awarding damages to the plaintiff in error was a judgment or an order made by the county court; and under sections 602, 603, and 610 of the Code of Civil Procedure they are entitled to have that court set such condemnation proceeding aside, because procured by fraud of the railroad company. But was this condemnation proceeding had in the county court, and was the proceeding in any sense, a judicial one? Section 97, chapter 16, Compiled Statutes, provides that if a railroad company desires to locate its road across certain real estate, and the owner thereof refuses to grant the right of way, then, upon application of either the railroad company or the land-owner, the county judge shall select six disinterested freeholders and direct them to be summoned by the sheriff of the county; that these freeholders so selected shall inspect and view the real estate sought to be appropriated for the right of way by the railroad and assess the damages which the land owner will sustain by reason of the appropriation of his land for such right of way, and make a report of their assessment in writing to the county judge of said county; that he shall, after certifying such report under his seal of office, transmit the same to the county clerk of said county for record; that the clerk shall file and record said report, and it shall thereafter have the force and effect of a deed from the land owner to the railroad company for the easement appropriated. The section also provides that either party may have the right to appeal from the assessment of damages made by the freeholders to the district court of the county in which the lands are situate within sixty days after the date of the assessment, and in case such an appeal be taken, the finding and decision of the district court shall be transmitted by the clerk thereof, duly certified, to the county clerk, to be there filed and recorded. Section 97 of the chapter provides that in case of the default, absence, refusal, or neglect of any freeholder to act as a

commissioner or appraiser the sheriff shall, upon the selection of the county judge, summon other freeholders to
complete the panel. It is to be observed that the county
court has nothing whatever to do with this proceeding.
It is not a proceeding instituted in the county court.
The appraisers are not selected by the county court. The
summons is not returnable to the county court, and with
the report of the appraisers the county court has no concern whatever; and the statute does not even require that
a report of the proceedings of the appraisers shall be kept
in the county court. The entire proceeding is conducted
by the county judge, the sheriff, and the appraisers selected by the former. These constitute a tribunal not
to try a civil action pending between the land owner
and a railroad company, not to pronounce a judgment,
but simply to inquire and report to the county judge
what damages the land owner will sustain by reason of
the appropriation of his land for the railroad's right of
way. The power conferred by the act upon the county
judge and the duty required of him by that act are not
judicial powers or duties, but purely ministerial powers
and duties. (*Illinois C. R. Co. v. Rucker*, 14 Ill. 353; *Chicago, B. & Q. R. Co. v. Wilson*, 17 Ill. 123; *People v. McRob-
erts*, 62 Ill. 38, which were mandamus cases, one to compel the county judge to appoint the appraisers to assess
the damages of the land owner which the railroad company desired for right of way, and the other two mandamus proceedings to compel circuit judges to appoint
such appraisers.) Looking at the action in the case at
bar as one brought under section 602 of the Code of Civil
Procedure in the county court of Douglas county, invoking its powers to vacate and modify one of its own judgments or orders made by it because obtained by fraud,
it cannot be maintained, for the simple reason that the
condemnation proceeding which the action seeks to have
the county court vacate and set aside did not occur in
the county court; and if the result of the condemnation
proceeding can in any sense be regarded as a judgment

or an order made, then the county court did not render such judgment or make such order.

2. A second theory upon which counsel for plaintiff in error seeks to maintain this action is that the county court is invested with equitable jurisdiction, and that this action is brought to that court, invoking its equity powers to set aside the condemnation proceeding because procured by fraud; but this theory, like the other, assumes that the condemnation proceeding occurred in the county court. It may be conceded that the county court, as a court of record, is invested with equitable powers and jurisdiction in any case before it when by the constitution or the laws of the state that court is invested with jurisdiction of the subject-matter out of which the case or proceeding in hand grows. But neither the constitution, nor any statute of this state, invests the county courts with general equitable jurisdiction; and if this condemnation proceeding was procured by fraud practiced upon the county judge and the appraisers, the county court is not invested with any equitable jurisdiction to vacate it. If in a suit brought before the county judge sitting as a justice of the peace one party by fraud should obtain a judgment, it certainly would not be contended that the county court was possessed with equitable jurisdiction to set that judgment aside. The county court, then, had no jurisdiction or authority to grant the relief prayed for in this action, viewing it as purely an equitable action invoking the equity powers of the county court.

3. We do not determine whether the county judge, because of the power conferred upon him and the duties required of him by the statute in the condemnation of real estate for railway purposes, is invested with the authority to set aside for any reason at any time an appraisement made in such a proceeding. Certainly the statute in express terms invests him with no such power; but assuming for the purposes of this case that the county judge has jurisdiction to set aside an appraise-

ment made because procured by fraud and that the proceeding at bar is an application addressed to him invoking his exercise of such power, we are of opinion that the application was by him properly denied. The record discloses that the plaintiff in error in this case had personal notice of the condemnation proceeding. For aught the record discloses he was present when the appraisement was returned, and the only injury which he claims to have sustained by the alleged fraud of the appraisers is that the damages awarded him were inadequate. The record does not disclose that he appealed from the award made, nor that he made any attempt to appeal, nor that he was prevented from appealing by any fraud, accident, casualty, or circumstance beyond his control—in other words, the application does not aver facts which show that the plight of the plaintiff in error is not the result of his own laches; and, conceding the authority of the county judge in the premises, we also think that this application was made too late. The record discloses that the railway company paid to the county judge for the use of the plaintiff in error the amount of damages awarded; that this money is still in the hands of the county judge. The railway company took possession of its right of way, constructed its road thereon, and has been operating the same over such right of way for years before this application was made. In any view, then, which we are able to take of this case the judgment of the district court is right and is

AFFIRMED.

NORVAL, J.

I concur in the judgment just entered on the sole ground that the county court had no jurisdiction of the subject-matter of the action.

WILLIAM A. CLEGHORN, EXECUTOR, APPELLEE, V. SIMON
OBERNALTE ET AL., APPELLANTS.

FILED FEBRUARY 2, 1898. No. 7791.

1. **Husband and Wife**: TITLE TO REALTY: TRUSTS. A husband and his
family resided on a rented farm. The husband worked at his
trade of plasterer, was an habitual drunkard and squandered his
earnings, devoting none of them to the support of his family. The
wife and children conducted the farm, she doing the labor of a
farm hand. During this time she purchased, on executory contract, a piece of land and made the first payment thereon out of
the earnings of her labor. She and her husband then moved on
the land purchased. The husband continued to conduct himself,
and the wife to labor and manage the new farm, as before, and
from her earnings thereon, with his consent, she made the deferred payments on the land purchased, when the vendor, by inadvertence or mistake, deeded the land to the husband. *Held*, (1)
That the money earned by the wife was her property; (2) that the
land purchased belonged to the wife; (3) that the husband held
the legal title to said land in trust for her; (4) that said land was
not liable for a debt of the husband contracted before the date of
the conveyance to him.

2. ——: ——: ——: ESTOPPEL. Where land is paid for with a
wife's money, but deeded to the husband, he will hold the title in
trust for her; and she is not estopped from claiming the land as
against her husband's creditors unless her conduct in the premises
induced them to believe that the husband was the actual owner of
the land and to extend credit to him on the strength thereof.

APPEAL from the district court of Cass county. Heard
below before CHAPMAN, J. *Reversed.*

Byron Clark, for appellants.

Beeson & Root, contra.

RAGAN, C.

William A. Cleghorn, executor of Frank Stander,
brought this suit in the district court of Cass county
against Simon Obernalte, Lena Obernalte, his wife, and
Simon Hansen, praying for a decree setting aside a conveyance of certain real estate made by Obernalte and

wife to Hansen, and another conveyance made by Hansen
of the real estate to Obernalte's wife, and to subject said
real estate to the payment of a judgment in favor of the
executor against Simon Obernalte. The executor had a
decree and the parties made defendants in the court below
have appealed.

1. The petition in this case is one in the nature of a
creditors' bill and is framed upon two theories, the first
being that the real estate was the property of Simon
Obernalte at the time he became indebted to the executor's testator, and that the conveyances were made for
the purpose of placing the title to the real estate in Obernalte's wife and thus hindering and delaying Obernalte's
creditors. But the evidence in the record will not sustain a decree based upon this theory of the petition. The
evidence shows, without conflict, that at the time of the
trial of this action, in 1894, Obernalte and his wife had
been married some twenty-five years; that they then had
seven children, the youngest of these being five years of
age and the oldest twenty-four, and that some of these
children were males; that Mrs. Obernalte, prior to her
marriage, worked for wages as a domestic and saved her
earnings and seems to have invested them in an acre
tract of land in the city of Plattsmouth. Some years
after their marriage Obernalte and his family moved
upon a rented farm near Weeping Water, in Cass county,
and remained there until about 1880. During this time
Obernalte, who was a plasterer and brick mason, did
little, if any, work upon the farm. When he did work he
worked at his trade, and, being then and down until 1892
an habitual drunkard, squandered his earnings. During
these years prior to 1880 Mrs. Obernalte and the children
conducted the rented farm, she performing regular farm
labor, such as caring for stock, harvesting, and husking
corn and other such work as is usually done by men. In
the meantime she sold the acre lot she owned in Plattsmouth for cash, and about 1880 she purchased from some
person or corporation in the city of Lincoln the 160 acres

of land in controversy, receiving a contract for a deed, though this contract seems to have run to the husband. At the time of this purchase she made the first payment of $150 cash, and of this sum her husband contributed $25 only, and never at any time contributed any further sum towards the payment of the land. The Obernalte family then moved upon the land purchased. Obernalte continued to conduct himself as he had been doing up until 1892, when he seems to have reformed; but from the time of the purchase of this land until this trial Mrs. Obernalte and the children remained upon it and cultivated it, Mrs. Obernalte performing the labor usually performed by a man in the cultivation and conduct of the farm, and from the earnings and proceeds of this farm she made the annual payments upon the land purchased under contract, until in September, 1889, the vendor of the land conveyed it by deed to Simon Obernalte. In the same month he and his wife made the deed attacked in this action to Hansen, and in the following January Hansen conveyed to Mrs. Obernalte. The evidence shows that the deed of this land to Simon Obernalte was by mistake or inadvertence; that it should have been made to Mrs. Obernalte. The debt on which the judgment against Simon Obernalte is based was contracted on November 12, 1888. At that date Simon Obernalte signed a note to one Stander, as surety for some other parties. Mrs. Obernalte had no knowledge of the existence of this debt until the year 1892, about a year before judgment was rendered upon the note. It will thus be seen that on November 12, 1888, at the time Obernalte became surety on the note, he did not have even the legal title to the real estate in controversy, and he never at any time owned the equitable title to this real estate. The equitable title to this real estate was purchased and paid for by Mrs. Obernalte with her money, except the $25 furnished by the husband, and when Obernalte became possessed of the legal title to the land in September, 1889, he held the title in trust for his wife, and since he was never the

48

owner of the real estate it was never liable for his debts. This case falls within the principle of *Mosher v. Neff*, 33 Neb. 770. In that case Neff purchased certain land with money belonging to his wife, but took the deed therefor in his own name. Afterwards he signed a note as surety, on which judgment was rendered against him. After the recovery of the judgment Neff conveyed the land through a trustee to his wife, and the court held that the husband held the legal title of the land in trust for his wife and it was not liable for his debts, since the record showed that the debt upon which the judgment was rendered was not contracted by Neff upon the faith of his being the owner of the real estate. In *Hews v. Kenney*, 43 Neb. 815, it was held that where a husband uses the money of his wife in paying for land the title to which he takes in his own name, a trust will arise in favor of the wife which a court of equity will protect against the husband's creditors, unless it is made to appear that such creditors gave the husband credit on the faith of his being the actual owner of the property of the wife the title to which was in his own name. Neither of these cases, nor the conclusion which we reach here, that Simon Obernalte, while he held the legal title to this real estate held it in trust for his wife, are opposed to *Brownell v. Stoddard*, 42 Neb. 177. That was an action by judgment creditors to subject to the payment of their judgments lands conveyed by a debtor through a third party to the debtor's wife. The district court subjected the lands to the payment of the husband's debt; but in that case the husband acquired the title to the land in 1871 and the conveyance to his wife occurred in 1887; and at the time the land was purchased the wife had furnished her husband $1,000 of the purchase money, and the court allowed her a lien upon the land prior to the lien of the husband's creditors for this $1,000 and interest. This was the feature of the decree which was complained of, and the court held that the wife was not entitled to this lien, since there was no evidence to show that there was any agreement or intention between· herself and husband at the time she furnished the money that he should repay it or she have an interest in or lien upon the land by reason thereof.

2. A second theory upon which the petition in this case is framed is that though Mrs. Obernalte was the equitable owner of this land, she has estopped herself from claiming the land as against her husband's creditors because of her conduct in allowing the title of the land to remain of record in her husband's name, and that he was enabled to contract the debt made the basis of this proceeding upon the belief of the creditor that he was the actual owner of the real estate. This theory has no support whatever in the record. In the first place there is not a particle of testimony to show that Stander extended credit to Obernalte because he believed him to be the owner of the real estate in controversy. In the second place, at the time the debt was contracted in November, 1888, the legal title to this land was of record in the name of the person who afterwards conveyed it to Obernalte, and this conveyance was not made until September, 1889.

The decree of the district court is reversed and the action dismissed.

REVERSED AND DISMISSED.

JOSEPH G. SLOAN, SHERIFF, v. REBECCA FIST.

FILED FEBRUARY 2, 1898.   No. 7763.

1. **Evidence: WRITINGS.** In order to render written instruments admissible in evidence, their execution or genuineness, unless admitted, must be established by proof, except in cases within statutory exceptions.

2. ——: ——: EXCEPTIONS: ASSIGNMENTS OF ERROR. An exception taken or assignment in error against the admission in evidence of a group of documents, offered together, is not waived by confining the discussion in the briefs to a single document comprised within the group, the objections urged being good against all.

ERROR from the district court of Pawnee county. Tried below before BABCOCK, J. *Reversed.*

Story & Story and *Griggs, Rinaker & Bibb*, for plaintiff in error.

Francis Martin and *Lindsay & Raper, contra.*

IRVINE, C.

This action was replevin, by Rebecca Fist, claiming the chattels in controversy as vendee of Herman Fist, against the sheriff of Pawnee county, who had seized them under writs of attachment sued out against Herman Fist. The plaintiff prevailed in the district court.

We shall consider only one assignment of error, but in order to do so a brief outline of the facts is essential. Herman Fist was as early as 1889 engaged in the mercantile business at Pawnee City. His brother, Emanuel Fist, the husband of the plaintiff, resided in Hastings. Emanuel was for a time engaged there in mercantile pursuits, but in 1887, as the result of a fire, he ceased to transact business on his own behalf, and entered the treasurer's office as an employé, Rebecca becoming the capitalist of the family. The claim on the part of the plaintiff is that Herman, in 1889, began to appeal to his brother for financial assistance, which was afforded him out of plaintiff's means, and from time to time, until the debt reached the sum of $7,400. Then an arrangement was made, in October, 1893, whereby Herman transferred to Rebecca, in discharge of the debt, a half interest in his stock and business. The business was for some time thereafter conducted under the name of Herman Fist & Co., but Herman having largely overdrawn his account and having involved the firm in debt, Rebecca took the remaining half from him in satisfaction of her own claim and in consideration of her paying the partnership debts and another debt covered by a separate contract. Both these transfers are assailed as fraudulent. Their *bona fides* was the issue on which the case really turned. A material inquiry was of course as to the advances made by Rebecca to Herman and the manner in which they had been made. Emanuel had conducted most of the business, and testified that the money was obtained by checks or drafts on banks in Hastings, some drawn by Rebecca herself, others by Herman directly on the banks, and paid out of the credits of Rebecca by her direction. After so testifying Emanuel was asked: "Have you checks showing the payment of these amounts?" He answered in the affirmative. He was then asked: "What are these papers here?" and answered, "These are checks." "Showing the payment of the amount you first named?" "Yes, sir." The checks, eleven in number, were then offered in evidence, with all the indorsements and canceling marks thereon, and without any further proof received, over defendant's objection that they were incompetent and that no foundation had been laid for their introduction. The indorsements were of a character to indicate that their proceeds had been obtained by Herman at Pawnee City, and that the checks had then passed through banks at St. Joseph, Omaha, and other points, finally reaching Hastings and being there paid. A portion of them appear to be checks drawn by Herman upon the Adams county bank, and would in nowise tend to show any advancement by Rebecca except for a pencil memorandum appearing thereon as follows: "Chg. R. Fist ac." These documents, if genuine, would, it will be seen, afford potent evidence to establish the transactions as Emanuel had narrated them, but such instruments do not prove themselves, and Emanuel's testimony that they were checks showing the payment was insufficient to prove the genuineness of a single signature or indorsement. There was no testimony whatever as to who made the memorandum "Chg. R. Fist ac.," when it was made, or why. Yet the materiality of the checks bearing that memorandum depended entirely upon its force. The checks were received without sufficient proof of their authenticity, and the error was clearly prejudicial. The checks were offered *en masse*, the same objection was interposed to all, and in the petition in error a single assignment covers all the checks. In the brief, however, complaint is made only of admitting one of the Herman Fist checks, and that because of the failure to prove the memorandum referred to. It is contended that the plaintiff in error has thus abandoned the rest of his assignment, and thus admitting that the other checks were properly admitted he is in the position of having made his objection and assignment of error too broad. The rule is that the court will not consider assignments of error not discussed in the briefs. They are treated as waived. By so waiving them we do not think plaintiff in error estops himself from taking advantage of exceptions taken at the trial with special reference to the waived assignments, but pertinent also to matters insisted upon. The failure to discuss an assignment merely indicates that it is not considered of sufficient importance, in view of the whole record, to ask the court's attention to. The objection to all the checks was good. The assignment in error directed against all was well taken. That being so, plaintiff in error is not precluded from its benefit because in his brief he selects for attack only a portion of the field covered by that assignment.

REVERSED AND REMANDED.

· ———————————·

BERTHA LEOLA MARTIN, APPELLEE, v. IDA A. LONG ET AL., APPELLANTS.

FILED FEBRUARY 2, 1898. No. 7810.

Parent and Child: ADOPTION: INHERITANCE. An infant was adopted by strangers The articles of adoption provided that if she should remain with them until her majority she should receive $500. The articles for her bestowed on her "equal rights and privileges of children born in lawful wedlock." *Held,* That the first provision was not exclusive as to property rights, but that on the death of the foster parents intestate, before the child reached her majority, she was entitled to inherit as if their own.

APPEAL from the district court of Cass county. Heard below before CHAPMAN, J. *Affirmed.*

Byron Clark and *C. S. Polk*, for appellants.

Abbott & Caldwell and *Beeson & Root*, contra.

IRVINE, C.

In 1885 Bertha Leola Martin, an infant, was adopted by Shadrach Cole and Agnes, his wife. During the minority of the child Shadrach Cole died, Bertha remaining with his widow until the latter's death severed the relationship, when Bertha returned to her mother, with whose consent the Coles had adopted her. In the course of settlement of Shadrach Cole's estate an order of distribution was made, whereby $700 was set apart for Bertha, and the remainder apportioned among the children of her foster parents. Thereafter this proceeding was begun in the county court wherein the adoption had been effected and the estate of Shadrach Cole was administered, by Bertha Martin, through her mother as guardian, to set aside the order of distribution and award to Bertha the same rights of inheritance as rested in her foster brothers and sisters. The basis of the proceeding was that there had been no service of notice of the hearing of the application for the order of distribution other than by publication, and that Bertha had not been represented by guardian *ad litem*. That such was the fact was conceded. The county court refused to vacate the original order, but the district court on appeal set it aside and awarded to Bertha her proportionate share in the estate, as if she were a daughter in fact. This appeal is from that order.

It is suggested that the action was not properly brought. The contention is that the right to vacate erroneous proceedings against infants exists in favor of the infant concerned, and can be exercised by him alone after reaching his majority and within the statutory period; that there is no authority in the guardian to so proceed while the minority of the infant continues. We cannot see what policy could be subserved by such a construction of the law; and the statute invoked, section 609 of the Code of Civil Procedure, being a statute of limitations, and having manifestly for its object the extension of time within which suits may be brought by persons under disabilities, and not fixing a time when causes of action shall be deemed to accrue, we are not disposed, in the absence of authority, to so construe it as to postpone the opportunity to apply for the correction of judicial errors. The point is really not insisted upon, as counsel say in their brief that they do not desire that the case be dismissed without an adjudication of the merits.

The law with reference to the adoption of children is found under title 25 of the Code. It has been amended since the relations in question were created. As it then stood it provided in effect that the parents should file with the probate judge a signed and sworn statement relinquishing all right to the custody and control over the child and all claim to services and wages "to the end that such child shall be fully adopted by the party or parties" desiring to adopt such child. The person adopting was required to file a similar statement that he freely and voluntarily adopted the child as his own, "with such limitations and conditions as shall be agreed upon by the parties," and then, as a proviso, was added this language: "Whenever it shall be desirable the party or parties adopting such child may, by stipulations to that effect in such statement, adopt such child and bestow upon him or her equal rights, privileges, and immunities of children born in lawful wedlock." (Code of Civil Procedure [Compiled Statutes 1895], sec. 797.) A subsequent section (799) provided for the entry of a decree "in accordance with the conditions and stipulations of such statement," reserving to the judge the right to refuse the decree if satisfied that the adoption would not be for the best interest of the child.   Then it was provided that the decree should be conclusive, that the child should take the surname of the foster parents "and all relations of parent and child, agreeable to such stipulations and the decree of the probate court, shall attach, and such child or children, if so stated in such decree, shall be subject to the exclusive control and custody of such parent or parents, and shall possess and enjoy all the rights, privileges, inheritance, heirships, and immunities of children born in lawful wedlock." (Code of Civil Procedure [Compiled Statutes 1895], sec. 800.) In this case the relinquishment was simple and absolute in form.   The declaration of the foster parents was as follows:

"We, Shadrach Cole and Agnes Cole, being first duly sworn, depose and say that we are residents of Cass county, Nebraska.   That we do freely and voluntarily adopt Bertha Leola Martin, a female child four years of age, the daughter of Mary Martin (the only surviving parent of Bertha Leola Martin) as our own, with the following limitations, to-wit:

"First—If Bertha Leola Martin remains with us until she arrives at her majority, she shall receive from us the sum of five hundred dollars.

"Second—If we should both die prior to her majority, her mother if living shall have control over her,— and we bestow upon her equal rights and privileges of children born in lawful wedlock.

"SHADRACH COLE.
"MRS. AGNES COLE."

The decree, after a bare recital of the proceedings, was as follows:

"It is therefore considered and adjudged by me that the right to the custody of, and power and control over, said Bertha Leola Martin, and to her services and wages by her mother, Mary Martin, shall and do cease and determine from this date, and that said Bertha Leola Martin shall be the adopted child of said Shadrach Cole and Agnes Cole upon the conditions of the sworn statements made herein and shall * * * and be subject to their exclusive custody and control and shall possess all the rights and privileges of children born in lawful wedlock."

The question presented is whether the first stipulation of the articles of adoption, providing for a payment of $500, is an exclusive provision as to property rights, or whether, on the other hand, it is a cumulative positive provision, leaving to the adopted child also the privileges, with regard to inheritance, that actual children enjoy. An interesting field for discussion is thus opened up, but we agree with counsel for the appellants that "the action is dependent entirely upon the construction of the articles of adoption," and it therefore presents no question of general law justifying an extended opinion. It cannot be doubted that under the statutes it was perfectly competent for the foster parents to bestow upon the child rights of inheritance as full as if she were their own, - -a child born in lawful wedlock, in the awkward phraseology of the statute. Some stress is laid upon the varying terms of the section regarding the articles of adoption and that regarding the decree. The claim is that the child is only entitled to the right of inheritance when it is so stated in the decree. Whether the phrase "if so stated in such decree" applies to such matters as the rights of the child or only to the custody we need not inquire, because the preceding section requires the decree to follow the articles of adoption; and it could hardly be contended that the court would be authorized by decree to confer such rights except as expressly or impliedly conferred by the articles of adoption. This decree incorporates the provisions of the articles by reference thereto, and expressly confers, in the language of both the articles and the statute, the rights and privileges of children born in lawful wedlock. The omission of the word "immunities" can have no significance. The right of inheritance is an affirmative privilege. It is not an immunity. Nor, as intimated, can the omission of the word "inheritance" be significant. The articles followed the section with relation thereto, and that section contained no such word. The use of the word in the section relating to the decree, in view of the fact that the proceeding is one contractual in its nature, and that the court could not impose an obligation not assumed by the parties, indicates, if it indicates anything, that its meaning was comprehended within the term "rights" or "privileges" employed in the section with reference to the articles whereby the obligations are by the foster parents assumed. What, then, did the foster parents mean by the articles in this case? The statute does not enlighten them and there is no extrinsic evidence as to the situation of the persons concerned which is of any assistance. It is doubtful if any competent evidence of that character could be offered. It is not doubtful that the last clause of the articles standing alone would be sufficient to confer rights of inheritance. If such was not the intention, it must be because a contrary intent is to be gathered from the first clause. In considering this it must be borne in mind that the mother of the child was a party to the proceeding and was surrendering her child to others, and that the right to inherit is not absolute, but may be defeated by will. To give an adopted child in that respect the rights and privileges of children proper would be an empty form if all such rights could be defeated by will. The most natural impulse of a mother so situated, and yielding to others the care of a child, presumably from motives touching only the child's welfare, would be to guard in this respect by requiring a stipulation for something certain when the wardship should cease; an obligation enforceable as a contract, not one resting in the mere volition of others. If this language was meant to be exclusive, it is hardly conceivable that the broad language would have been used at the close. The foster parents, if not intending to confer property rights, would not have employed language, the most obvious import of which, as determined by usage, relates thereto. We think that it was the intention to confer upon the child all the rights of children proper, and, in addition thereto, to secure to her in any event, upon her majority, the sum specified in the first clause.

AFFIRMED.

JULIUS C. SHARP ET AL., APPELLEES, V. CITY OF SOUTH OMAHA ET AL., APPELLANTS.

FILED FEBRUARY 2, 1898.   No. 9660.

1. **Municipal Corporations: Gas Companies: Franchises.** It is within the power of cities of the first class having less than 25,000 inhabitants to grant the right to a gas company to lay and maintain its pipes and mains under the streets and other highways of the city for the purpose of supplying its inhabitants with gas, and to regulate the charge therefor.

2. ———: ———: ———. The authority to grant such a franchise is not restricted to persons or companies authorized to erect works within the city for the manufacture of gas, nor need such franchise be limited to the period of five years.

3. ———: ———: ———. Subdivision 15 of section 68 of chapter 13a, article 2, Compiled Statutes, is not a restriction upon subdivision 16, but a concurrent provision relating to another subject, the former to laying mains on the streets, the latter to lighting the streets.

APPEAL from the district court of Douglas county. Heard below before SCOTT, J.   *Reversed.*

George E. Pritchett, for appellants.

J. M. Woolworth and *Congdon & Parish, contra.*

IRVINE, C.

The council of the city of South Omaha passed, and the mayor approved, an ordinance purporting to grant to the South Omaha Gas Light Company, its successors and assigns, authority, for a period of twenty-five years, to sell and supply gas within the city, and to lay and maintain pipes and mains under the surface of the streets, alleys, and other public highways of the city. In pursuance of provisions in the ordinance the South Omaha Gas Light Company assigned its rights, through an intermediate grantee, to the Omaha Gas Company. The Omaha Gas Company was proceeding to lay its mains in the streets of South Omaha when this suit was begun by three taxpayers of South Omaha, who alleged in their petition the foregoing facts and asserted that the ordinance was void. The prayer was for an injunction restraining the gas companies from laying their pipes and the defendants, the city and the two gas companies, from performing any acts in pursuance of the ordinance. The city did not appear in the action, and its default was entered. The two gas companies answered, denying many of the averments of the petition. A decree was rendered reciting that the cause was "submitted to the court upon the petition of the plaintiffs Julius C. Sharp, Harry Sharp, and Louis Schroeder, and the answer and demurrer of the defendants the South Omaha Gas Light Company and the Omaha Gas Company, without evidence, and was argued by counsel, on consideration whereof the court finds upon the issues joined between the plaintiffs * * and defendants * * * in favor of the plaintiffs," and granting a perpetual injunction as prayed. This finding is not so unwarranted as would appear at first blush, because the averments of the petition were largely conclusions of law, and most of the denials in the answer were denials of those conclusions. Where issues of fact were joined their materiality is doubtful. The real question is the power of the mayor and council to enact such an ordinance, its passage, approval, and terms being admitted.

The charter provisions invoked on either side as bearing on the question, are the following, from article 2, chapter 13a, Compiled Statutes:

Sec. 35. "The mayor and council shall have the care, supervision, and control of all public highways, bridges, streets, alleys, public squares, and commons within the city, and shall cause the same to be kept open and in repair and free from nuisances."

Sec. 68, sub. 15. "To make contracts with and authorize any persons, company, or association to erect gas works, electric or other light works in said city, and give such persons, company, or association the privilege of furnishing lights for the streets, lanes, and alleys of said city for any length of time not exceeding five years; to purchase or provide for, establish, construct, maintain, operate, and regulate, for the city, any such gas works, electric or other light works; or to condemn and appropriate for the use of the city, gas works, electric or other light works and plants in a manner and form as provided in subdivision nineteen of this section; and to levy a tax not exceeding five mills on the dollar in any one year for the purpose of paying the cost of lighting the streets, lanes, and alleys of said city, or for the purpose of buying or establishing, extending, and maintaining such gas works, electric or other light works; and where the amount of money which would be raised by the tax levy provided for in this section would be insufficient to establish or pay for a system of gas, electric, or other light works, to borrow money and pledge the property and credit of the city upon its negotiable bonds or otherwise to an amount not exceeding fifty thousand dollars for the purpose of establishing or paying for, maintaining, and operating such gas, electric, or other light works, authority therefor having first been obtained by a majority vote of the people at an election upon a proposition submitted in a manner provided by law for the submission of propositions to aid in construction of railroads and other works of internal improvement; and when any such bond shall have been issued by the city, to levy annually upon all the taxable property of the city such tax as may be necessary (not exceeding one mill for twenty thousand dollars of bonds so issued) for a sinking fund for the paying of the accruing interest on such bonds and the principal thereof at maturity; to provide for the office of light commissioner, and to prescribe the duties and power of such office; *Provided*, That in cities having a water commissioner, such water commissioner shall be ex officio light commissioner."

Sec. 68, sub. 16. "To provide for the lighting of streets, laying down of gas pipes, and erection of lamp posts, and to regulate the sale and use of gas and electric or other lights and the charge therefor, and rent of gas meters within the city, and to require the removal from the streets, avenues, and alleys, and the placing under ground of all telegraph, electric, and telephone wires."

The ordinance attacked provides in its first section that the South Omaha Gas Light Company, its successors and assigns, are authorized, for a period of twenty-five years, "to sell and supply gas in the city of South Omaha, Douglas county, Nebraska, and to use, lay, and maintain pipes and mains, with all necessary and proper attachments, connections, and appurtenances below the surface of the highways, sidewalks, streets, alleys, lanes, avenues, boulevards, and public places, and on bridges and viaducts in said city," etc. By the second section the quality of gas to be furnished is specified, and it is provided that it shall be sold at a certain maximum rate. By section 3 it is provided that the company shall furnish gas to the city for its public buildings at the rate of $1 per 1,000 cubic feet. Other provisions regulate in detail the manner of laying pipes, and provide for the payment to the city of five cents for each thousand cubic feet of gas sold and paid for. A forfeiture is provided in case of the company's failure to perform any of the conditions of the ordinance. Provision is made for the city's requiring the company to extend its mains, and in this connection is the following: "The South Omaha Gas Light Company, its successors and assigns, shall be required to extend its mains upon like requests whenever the city shall enter into contract with it for lighting and furnishing with gas not less than four street lamps for every 1,000 feet of such extension," etc. It will be observed that the ordinance does not expressly authorize the construction of gas works within the city. It only authorizes the use of the streets and other public highways for the laying and maintenance of mains. Nor is there involved in the ordinance any contract for the lighting of the streets. The clause last quoted merely anticipates the probability of such a contract in the future, and in view of that probability reserves a power to require a further use of the franchise than the grantee might see fit to make of its own accord. It is alleged in the petition, denied in the answer, and without evidence by the court found to be true, that the assignee, having already gas works in Omaha, intends to supply the city of South Omaha from such works. We shall assume as the district court did, that the ordinance did not contemplate the erection of works for the manufacture of gas in South Omaha.

It is admitted by the plaintiffs that the general power of control over the streets, conferred by section 35, would be sufficient, if that section stood alone, to authorize such an ordinance as the one under consideration. It is practically admitted that subdivision 16 of section 68, standing alone, would not restrict the power conferred by section 35, even if it did not itself grant the power. It is, however, contended that subdivision 15 is a specific grant on the subject, which prevails against and limits the more general provisions, and restricts the power of the city in the premises to the granting of the right to lay pipes in the streets to such persons, companies, or associations as have already or contemporaneously been authorized to erect gas works in the city, and that then the franchise cannot endure for more than five years. In support of this argument attention is called to the subsequent provisions of subdivision 15, for the acquisition, by construction, purchase, or condemnation, of gas works. The argument is that the language of the grant of power

is confined to persons or corporations which shall have
gas works in the city, and that a reason is found for the
restriction in a manifest policy of the act to provide for
ultimate municipal ownership.   It is said that effective
exercise of those provisions demands that private plants
should be wholly within the city.   The force of this argument is entirely destroyed by reference to the fact that
previous to 1895, subdivision 15 began as at present, but
ended with the words "not exceeding five years."   The
provisions for municipal construction, purchase, and condemnation were added by amendment in that year.   (Session Laws 1895, ch. 13.)   The peculiar language of the
first part of the statute could not, therefore, have been
adopted with any reference to the policy of municipal
ownership.   We must ascertain the force of the provisions by looking to their original form.   The new words
do not affect this case.   There was then a general supervision and control of the streets vested in the council.
This was followed by a grant of power to authorize "any
person * * * to erect gas works * * * in said
city, and give such persons, * * * the privilege of
furnishing lights for the streets * * * for any length
of time not exceeding five years."   Then there came a
grant of power, referring again to the lighting of streets,
but also to keeping them free from electric wires, and
also to provide for the laying down of gas pipes, and regulate the sale and use of gas and the charge therefor.   Subdivision 15 relates solely to the lighting of highways.
Subdivision 16 relates, among other things, to the furnishing of gas to private consumers and the use of the
streets for that purpose.   They are separate provisions
relating to different subjects, not intended the one to
nullify the other, but intended to exist concurrently and
each to control with reference to its own subject-matter.
We need not consider whether contracts may be made
for lighting the streets with persons who have not gas
works within the city.   Entirely distinct from the provisions on that subject there is an ample grant of power,

49

unqualified as to persons, method, or time, to regulate
the laying down of mains, the sale and use of gas, and
the rate to be charged therefor.　The ordinance in question
extends only to that subject and is within the power.

* REVERSED AND DISMISSED.

JOHN V. FARWELL, JR., V. CHICAGO, ROCK ISLAND AND
PACIFIC RAILROAD COMPANY.

FILED FEBRUARY 17, 1898.　No. 7505.

Eminent Domain: DAMAGE TO CITY LOTS: EVIDENCE.

REHEARING of case reported in 52 Neb. 614.

Cornish & Lamb and *Tibbets, Morey & Ferris,* for plaintiff
in error.

L. W. Billingsley and *R. J. Greene, contra.*

PER CURIAM.

This is a rehearing of the case reported in 52 Neb. 614.
The former opinion is adhered to, and for the reason
therein stated the judgment of the district court is reversed
and the cause remanded.

REVERSED AND REMANDED.

FRED LEWON v. THOMAS P. HEATH.

FILED FEBRUARY 17, 1898. NO. 7844.

1. **Descent and Distribution.** Lands of which a person dies seized, and which he has not devised, descend to the heirs, and the title vests in them, subject, however, to the debts of the ancestor.

2. **Ejectment:** ACTION BY HEIR. An heir may bring and maintain an action of ejcc ment relative to lands of which his ancestor died seized against any and all persons except the administrator of the e tate and such as have a right or rights thereto derived from the administrator, and this the heir may do during the pendency of the administration proceedings and prior to final settlement or any decree of distribution.

3. **Adverse Possession.** "To establish title to real property in this state by virtue cf the operation of the statute of limitations there must have been maintained by the party asserting it an actual, continuous, notorious, and adverse possession of the premises under claim of ownership during the full period required by the statute." (*Twohig v. Leamer*, 48 Neb. 248; *Gatling v. Lane*, 17 Neb. 77; *Lantry v. Parker*, 37 Neb. 353.)

4. ——: EVIDENCE. No definite or fixed rule can be framed in relation to what shall constitute *indicia* of adverse possession; such evidences must necessarily vary and be in accord with the conditions existent in the portion of the political division or subdivision in which the property to which it is claimed applicable is situate in regard to age of settlement, the extent and prevailing manner of cultivation, or use of lands, also the purposes for which the lands are or may be by nature adapted.

ERROR from the district court of Douglas county. Tried below before AMBROSE, J. *Reversed.*

C. A. Baldwin, for plaintiff in error.

L. D. Holmes, contra.

HARRISON, C. J.

The defendant in error commenced this, an action of ejectment, in the district court of Douglas county to recover the possession of a certain forty-acre tract of land at the time in the possession of the plaintiff in error. One of the defenses interposed was that of adverse possession for more than the statutory period of ten years.

After issues joined and on the trial thereof it was of the instructions to the jury,—

"First—That the plaintiff has shown a complete legal title to the premises in controversy, and is in law the legal owner of the premises described in the petition, and is entitled to the possession thereof.

"Second—You are also instructed that upon the question of adverse possession, as set up in the defendant's answer, there has been a failure of proof upon his part, and that he has not shown such possession as the law contemplates to be adverse, open, notorious, and hostile for ten years prior to the commencement of this suit. You will, therefore, in rendering your verdict upon the question of the possession of the real estate described in the petition, find for the plaintiff."

It appeared in testimony that one William B. Lacey during the year 1860 obtained from the United States a patent conveying to him the land the recovery of the possession of which was sought in this suit. Lacey was a resident of the state of Ohio and there died leaving a widow and three sons, his heirs. After his death an administrator of his estate was appointed by the probate court of the proper county in Ohio, who entered upon the duties of the settlement of the estate of the deceased. Neither the intestate during his lifetime, his heirs, nor the administrator of his estate ever saw or had any actual physical possession of this land. The defendant in error introduced evidence of the conveyance by the widow to him of her interest in the land of date during the year 1888; also conveyances by the three sons of their interests respectively in and to the land, one of date during the year 1883, one 1884, and the other 1888. There was no competent evidence that a decree of distribution of the estate had ever been made by the probate court.

It is argued by counsel for plaintiff in error that in order to recover it devolved on the plaintiff in error, inasmuch as he claimed by conveyances from the heirs, to show a final settlement of the estate and a decree of distribution by the probate court having jurisdiction. The administrator of the estate has the right to possession of the real estate of which the decedent died seized and may collect the rents, issues, and profits thereof until the final settlement of the estate or until delivered to the heir or devisee by order of the probate court. (See section 202 of the law in regard to decedents, Compiled Statutes 1897, p. 527, ch. 23.) It is conceded that the construction of this section in connection with some others of our law relative to the same subject must govern the disposition of the point presented. Lands of which a person died seized, when not devised, descend to the heirs in the order designated in the statute, subject, however, to the debts of the deceased (Compiled Statutes 1897, p. 503, ch. 23, sec. 30); and it may be further said, subject to the administrator's statutory right of possession conferred by the section to which we have hereinbefore alluded. The title vests in the heirs as it did at common law. (*Shellenberger v. Ransom*, 41 Neb. 631; *Johnson v. Colby*, 52 Neb. 327.) There exists no reason or rule, aside from the statutes, which would seem potent in its call to us to declare that the heirs of a deceased person claiming title and possession of real estate of which their ancestor died seized, or a person claiming the title and right of possession of real estate by, through, or under them, shall not have the right to the possessory action of ejectment as against all persons in possession, except such as are so by right derived through, under, or from the administrator; nor, as we view and construe the provisions of the statutes on the subject separately or connectedly, do they furnish any forcible arguments or grounds for saying that to allow said heirs or their transferees the right to such action would place them as to their asserted rights and the administrator and his possessory rights in an irreconcilable or any conflict, or to hold that such heirs or persons may not enforce the right of possession by action as against all save and except the administrator or persons claiming by, through, or under him. If the title passes to and vests in the heirs, as it most certainly does, then the possessory right goes with it, except to the extent it is placed by law in the administrator, which is not exclusively or absolutely, but optionally with him, and for purposes indicated by statute and for none other; and such purposes may be subserved and fulfilled consistently with the right of the heirs or persons claiming under them to assert and obtain possession of any save parties who are in as of right derived from the administrator.

In the case of *Territory v. Bramble*, 5 N. W. Rep. [Dak.] 945, it was said, in reference to a section of the probate act of the territory, in the exact words of the section 202 of our law which we are considering: "Our statute was taken from Wisconsin, whence it was taken from Michigan, and was afterward enacted in Nebraska and Oregon. A similar statute is found in Alabama and Mississippi, in all of which states it has received a judicial construction; and under the rule that a legislature taking a statute from the laws of another state gives to the new enactment the same construction given to it by the courts of the state from which it was taken, we may, with profit, inquire what construction was placed upon this statute by the court of Wisconsin and Michigan."

In *Kline v. Moulton*, 11 Mich. 370, the administrator had sold the real property without obtaining license, as required by the statute, and the grantee under the deed, while admitting that he got no title to the land, contended that he got all the right the administrator had, to-wit, the right of possession; but the court denied the right, and held that the administrator had no right of possession that he could sell or transfer."

In *Marvin v. Shilling*, 12 Mich. 356, the court stated: "In *Streeter v. Paton*, 7 Mich. 341, we had occasion to consider the effect of this statute on the rights of the heir, and came to the conclusion that the statute did not interfere with the descent of the real estate to the heir, and his right to take possession, or bring ejectment therefor against any one, except the administrator or some one in possession under him, and that the object of the statute was to permit the personal representative of the deceased to take possession of the real estate and hold it until it should be sold by him under a license of the probate court, or the final settlement of the estate if he thought proper to do so, unless ordered to deliver it over to the heir by the probate court."

In the case of *Jones v. Billstein*, 28 Wis. 221, wherein from the facts it appeared that ân administrator had sold real estate of his decedent and the sale was void, the heir of the deceased brought an action of ejectment against the grantee who asserted that conceding that the sale did not pass the title to the land to him, yet the deed was not void, but conveyed to him the possessory right of the administrator, and if the deed was void the heir could not maintain the action, for the right of possession was in the administrator until the settlement of the estate and the administrator alone could bring ejectment. The court, in its opinion, stated on this subjèct: "It is claimed that the statute which gives to the executor or administrator the right to the possession of the real estate, and the power to receive the rents, issues, and profits thereof, necessarily deprives the heir of such right of possession until such time as the estate is settled or delivered over to him by order of the court. But we think that no such result necessarily follows. As we understand the statute, it gives the personal representative the power to reduce the real estate to his actual possession should he think proper, or should the probate court direct him so to do, but it does not imperatively require him to take possession thereof, and until he does so the common right of the heir to the possession remains unimpaired." (See also *Holbrook v. Campau*, 22 Mich. 288; *Flood v. Pilgrim*, 32 Wis. 376; *Filbey v. Carrier*, 45 Wis. 469; *State v. Reeder*, 5 Neb. 203; *King v. Boyd*, 4 Ore. 326.)

The doctrine announced in *Marvin v. Schilling, supra, Streeter v. Paton,* and *Campau v. Campau* was quoted with approval in *Dundas v. Carson*, 27 Neb. 640.

In the case of *Balch v. Smith*, 30 Pac. Rep. [Wash.] 648,
which is cited by counsel for plaintiff in error as sustaining his position and which does so, it is said: "Section
956, Code Proc., provides that the administrator may take
possession of the real estate of his intestate, and maintain
possession thereof, with the responsibility of ownership,
until the same shall have been delivered over by order of
the probate court. And it is contended on the part of the
respondents that this shows clearly the intent on the part
of the legislature that, before the heir gets such title as
he can enforce in the courts, the property claimed by him
must have been so delivered over; and that the simple
fact of his heirship, without the aid of such adjudication
by the probate court, is not sufficient to authorize him to
maintain an action against an adverse holder;" and, after
stating that the courts of Dakota, Michigan, and other
states hold a doctrine directly contrary to the contention
of counsel, further says: "But we should feel constrained
to hold with these decisions were this section 956 the only
provision of our statute relating to this subject. The
cases of which we have been speaking seem to have gone
off entirely upon the language of the section of the statutes of the respective states corresponding to our section
956, and if they had other provisions similar to the succeeding sections of our probate practice act, to which
we shall now call attention, such fact seems to have
escaped the attention of the courts, and we assume that
these further provisions of our statute were not contained in those under discussion when those cases were
decided. Our section 956, as we have already seen, simply gives the administrator permission to take possession
of the real estate,—at least, it uses the word 'may' instead
of the word 'shall,' and in the light of the cases above
referred to, we should construe such language as they
have done, were it not for such further provisions of our
law." The opinion announces the doctrine that title and
the rights incident thereto regularly pass to an heir only
by a decree of distribution of the court in which adminis-

tration proceedings are or have been pending.   This was
followed in the case of *Hazelton v. Bogardus*, 35 Pac. Rep.
[Wash.] 602, but, as fully appears, the rule announced
was based on the construction of the section of the statutes of Washington almost if not identical with ours in
terms connectedly with others; the effect of the whole
number so viewed forcing the conclusion.   But there are
no further provisions of our law which, read in connection
with section 202, call into existence such conditions as
confronted the Washington court; hence the opinions
cited are not in point and the doctrines therein stated
cannot be adopted or followed in the case at bar.

A second point discussed by the counsel for plaintiff
in error is that the court erred in instructing the jury to
the effect that the plaintiff in error had failed to produce
evidence sufficient to establish a title by adverse possession.   In regard to adverse possession and claim of title
by reason thereof it has been several times announced
by this court: "To establish title to real property in this
state by virtue of the operation of the statute of limitations there must have been maintained by the party
asserting it an actual, continuous, notorious, and adverse
possession of the premises under claim of ownership during the full period required by the statute."   In the opinion in the case of *Lantry v. Parker*, 37 Neb. 353, wherein
the adverse possession of land was in question, it was
said: "This evidence is, we think, sufficient to justify the
trial court in finding that defendant had the notorious,
continuous, and adverse possession of the land for the
statutory period.   The law does not require that possession shall be evidenced by a complete inclosure, nor by
persons remaining continuously upon the land and con-
stantly, from day to day, performing acts of ownership
thereon.   It is sufficient if the land is used continuously
for the purposes to which it may be, in its nature,
adapted." (See also *Twohig v. Leamer*, 48 Neb. 247.)   Taking into consideration the facts that this land was quite
hilly and rough, or what is commonly termed "broken

land;" that one portion of it was so sandy as to be used as a "sand pit," where persons procured sand for use in making mortar for plastering and other purposes; that not a great portion was arable land or fit for cultivation; also the conditions existent in this state during many of the years of plaintiff in error's alleged possession, relative to fencing, cultivation, and other of the well-defined and approved *indicia* of possession, and that many of them were not present where the possession was undoubted; also bearing in mind for what purpose this land was by nature adapted, we think the evidence adduced on the subject of the adverse possession of plaintiff in error was sufficient to demand that question be submitted under appropriate instructions to the jury for its consideration and determination, from which it follows that the court erred in giving the instruction it did, and the judgment must be reversed and the cause remanded.

REVERSED AND REMANDED.

N. N. BRUMBACK ET AL. V. AMERICAN BANK OF BEATRICE.

FILED FEBRUARY 17, 1898. No. 7865.

Trial: OPENING AND CLOSING. The party to an action upon whom rests the burden of the issues is entitled, on the trial of the cause, to open and close the evidence; also the arguments to the jury. *Hickman v. Layne*, 47 Neb. 177, followed.

ERROR from the district court of Gage county. Tried below before BUSH, J. *Reversed.*

J. E. Cobbey and *G. M. Johnston*, for plaintiffs in error.

C. E. White, contra.

HARRISON, C. J.

This action was instituted by the defendant in error in the district court of Gage county to recover of plaintiff, in error the amount alleged to be due defendant in error on a promissory note. Issues were joined, and as a result of a trial the bank received a verdict and judgment, and the opposite parties have presented the cause here for review in error proceeding.

At the inception of the trial a motion or claim was made for plaintiffs in error that they be allowed the opening and closing in the introduction of testimony and argument of the cause to the jury. This was overruled, to which action an exception was noted for the movers and it is of the errors assigned and argued. An examination of the pleadings discloses that if there had been no evidence introduced the plaintiff in the action would have been entitled to a judgment. The issues being thus joined the motion for plaintiffs in error should have been allowed and the action thereon was an error for which the judgment must be reversed. It is provided in section 283 of the Code of Civil Procedure: "When the jury has been sworn the trial shall proceed in the following order, unless the court for special reasons otherwise direct: * * Third—The party who would be defeated, if no evidence were given on either side, must first produce his evidence. * * * The parties may then submit or argue the case to the jury. In the argument, the party required first to produce his evidence shall have the opening and conclusion." (See *Vifquain v. Finch*, 15 Neb. 505; *Rolfe v. Pilloud*, 16 Neb. 21; *Omaha & R. V. R. Co. v. Walker*, 17 Neb. 432; *Osborne v. Kline*, 18 Neb. 344; *Rea v. Bishop*, 41 Neb. 202; *Hickman v. Layne*, 47 Neb. 177.)

There is but one brief filed, it being that which contains the argument on behalf of plaintiffs in error, and as the case must be remanded supposably for another trial, we do not deem it necessary at this time to discuss the other matters presented.

REVERSED AND REMANDED.

JASON R. GEORGE ET AL. V. WILLIAM CLEVELAND.

FILED FEBRUARY 17, 1898.   No. 7775.

Village Bonds: INTERNAL IMPROVEMENTS: COMPLIANCE WITH CONTRACT:
INJUNCTION. The electors of the village of Shelton, in Buffalo
county, by a favorable vote on the proposition, authorized the
issuance and delivery of the bonds of the village to two designated persons on the construction and operation by said persons
of a mill. The persons named did not build the mill but entered
into a copartnership with two other parties under the name and
style of the Shelton Milling & Grain Company, and the company
built and operated the mill. *Held*, That the voters of the village
could demand the strict or literal performance of the contract;
and the erection and operation of the mill by the copartnership
was not such a fulfillment of the compact and did not entitle
either the company or the two persons named in the proposition
approved by the voters at the election to demand and receive the
bonds.

ERROR from the district court of Buffalo county.
Tried below before NEVILLE, J.   *Affirmed.*

Marston & Nevius and *John M. Thurston,* for plaintiffs in
error.

Calkins & Pratt, contra.

HARRISON, C. J.

This action was instituted by defendant in error for
himself and others similarly interested to restrain the
issuance and delivery of the bonds of the village of Shelton, Nebraska, in the aggregate sum of $2,000, to Jason
George and Thomas Turney.   Pleadings were filed by the
parties, by which issues were joined, of which a trial resulted in a decree by which the delivery of said bonds was
perpetually enjoined and restrained.   From such decree
the present appeal has been perfected.

It appears that George and Stevens submitted for the
consideration of the citizens of Shelton the following
proposition, the date et cetera are shown in copy:

"We, the undersigned, herewith submit the following

proposition to the citizens of the village of Shelton, in Buffalo county, Nebraska, to-wit: In consideration of the voting and delivery of bonds by the said village of Shelton, in the sum of $2,000, we hereby agree with the said citizens of Shelton to build and fully equip and operate for five years a flouring mill with roller process, to be run by water-power and to do custom work, and have a capacity of 75 barrels per day; said mill shall be 24 by 40 feet, three stories high exclusive of basement, with addition 16 by 40 feet, and to cost not less than $15,000.

"And we further agree to produce flour equal in quality and yield to any flouring mill in the state. When said mill is completed and successfully run three months to the satisfaction of a citizens' committee of said village of Shelton, the said bonds to be turned over and delivered to us.

"Dated at Shelton, Nebraska, this 10th day of June, 1893.   J. R. GEORGE.
                                        "THOMAS TURNEY."

The authority for the issuance of any bonds of the char· acter involved in this litigation, if it exists, is contained in the provisions of our statute in relation to issuance of bonds in aid of works of internal improvements. A petition was presented to the county board and, pursuant to the prayer thereof, an election called for the purpose of taking a vote of the citizens on the question of the issuance of the bonds and their donation to the parties who had made the offer, in accordance with the terms and on their compliance with the conditions and obligations by the offer placed on them. The published call and notices of the election, the holding of which was fixed and occurred of date July 18, 1893, contained the following as of the essential portions of the proposition submitted:

"Shall the village of Shelton and state of Nebraska issue the bonds of the village of Shelton to the amount of $2,000, payable to J. R. George and Thomas Turney, or bearer, on the expiration of ten years from the date of same, and bearing interest at the rate of six per cent per

annum, payable annually, with coupons attached to said
bonds payable to bearer at the office of the treasurer of
Buffalo county, Nebraska?   And shall the county board
cause to be levied annually upon the taxable property of
the village of Shelton, in addition to the regular taxes,
an amount of taxes sufficient to pay the annual interest
on said bonds to-wit, one hundred and twenty dollars,
and two hundred dollars each year for ten years to pay
the principal?   Said bonds to be held in trust by the
trustees of the said village of Shelton, to be turned over
to the said J. B. George and Thomas Turney when they
shall have erected in the said village of Shelton a flouring
mill, with roller process, to be run by water-power and
to do custom work, three stories high, exclusive of basement, main part to be 24x40 feet with addition 16x40
feet with a capacity of seventy-five barrels per day, and
to cost not less than $15,000, provided that said bonds
shall not be so turned over by said trustees until said
mill has been fully equipped and successfully operated
for three (3) months."

The original petition presented (as is stated in short
in the brief filed for the defendant in error) the following
reasons why the bonds should not be delivered:

"1. That the notice of the election was not published
for four weeks as required by law.

"2. That no copy of the question submitted was posted
up at the place of voting during the election.

"3. That the petition for said election was not signed
by fifty freeholders.

"4. That no notice of the result of said election had
been published for two weeks or at all.

"5. That the mill for which said bonds were voted was
not a public mill within the provisions of section 27, chapter 57, Compiled Statutes, and that it did not and could
not grind for toll as required by said chapter 57, Compiled Statutes, concerning public mills.

"6. That the donees had not complied with the terms
of the proposition, in that they had not built a mill cost-

ing fifteen thousand dollars, nor any greater sum than ten thousand dollars."

During the trial it appeared in evidence (it was of the testimony given by Mr. George, one of the plaintiffs in error) that about August 1, 1893, or subsequent to the election, the result of which was favorable to the issuance of the bonds, and prior to the erection of the mill, Jason R. George and Thomas Turney, with two other persons, formed a copartnership under the name and style of the "Shelton Milling & Grain Company," a one-third interest in the mill property being conveyed to the two parties who joined in the copartnership with Mr. George and Mr. Turney, and the company builded and owned the mill by reason of the construction of which George and Turney claimed the right to demand the delivery of the bonds to them.   Leave was then asked for defendant in error to file an amendment to the petition to conform to the facts as proved, and to which we have just referred.   This was granted, and the amendment was prepared and filed. The trial court embodied in its decree the following findings:

"1. That the petition presented to the county board for calling of the election mentioned in the petition herein was in all respects legal and sufficient.

"2. That the publication of the notice of said election was full, complete, and in accordance with law.

"3. That a copy of the proposition contained in said notice was duly posted at the polling place in the said village of Shelton on the day of said election, as required by law.

"4. That the canvass of the return of said election was duly made by the proper officers, and report thereof made to the county board, and that said proposition was duly declared carried in accordance with law.

"5. The court doth further find that all the preliminary steps necessary to the validity of said bonds, if issued, were duly taken and had in accordance with the statute.

"6. That the said mill erected was an internal improvement, and public mill under the statute, under and by virtue of which the said preliminary proceedings were taken and had; that said bonds were duly issued, registered, and placed in the hands of the trustees of said village of Shelton, under the terms of said proposition.

"7. The court doth further find that the evidence in this case shows that a proposition was made in writing by the defendants J. R. George and Thomas Turney to construct and operate a mill of certain dimensions, character, and capacity, described in said proposition, and to cost not less than $15,000, and that the schedule showing the items of cost of said mill, in evidence, shows that among said items was one of $7,000 for the plant, which consisted of a water privilege, right of flowage, race, and superstructure of an old grist mill occupying the present site of the mill tendered as being constructed in accordance with the terms of said proposition. That there was no proper evidence showing that the taxpayers of said village voted upon said proposition with the knowledge that said 'old plant' was to be a part of the said sum of $15,000, which said proposed mill should cost, and the court therefore finds that by reason of the failure to embody the proposed use of said 'old plant' in the said proposition in writing was a failure to inform the legal voters of said village of the full terms and complete consideration offered for the issue of said bonds, and for that reason the delivery of said bonds should be restrained.

"8. The court further finds that after said election, and before the construction of said mill, the said Jason R. George and Thomas Turney, the beneficiaries named in said bonds, and about the first day of August, 1893, took into partnership with them two other persons and formed a copartnership under the name and style of the Shelton Milling and Grain Company, and conveyed to said two persons a one-third interest in said mill property, and that said copartnership constructed said mill. And the court finds that by such a proceeding the real beneficiaries in said bonds, and the donees thereof, were changed and that said mill was not constructed by the said Jason R. George and Thomas Turney as required by the terms of said proposition and contract on the part of the taxpayers of said village, and for that reason the delivery of said bonds should be restrained."

From which will be gathered that finding numbered 8 is one which in and of itself furnishes sufficient basis and support for the decree rendered. There can be no doubt of the propriety of such an amendment of the petition as was asked or the right of the court to allow it, or that it was an entirely correct action in the present case. The citizens, the electors, having been informed by the offer as first made in the petition circulated and presented to the county board, in a call for notices of the election, and in the proposition submitted, in fact at every stage of the proceedings, that the mill would be erected and operated by Jason R. George and Thomas Turney, this being the consideration to be received by them and which they had stamped with their approval and sanctioned by their votes, were entitled not only to expect, but to demand that the conditions and terms of the compact, for such it was, be exactly fulfilled—be literally performed. The construction and operation of the mill by the Shelton Milling & Grain Company was not a literal compliance with the contract and did not confer upon it the right to demand and receive the bonds; nor did it place George and Turney in a position to entitle them to the bonds, nor to receive them in part for their own benefit and in part for the benefit of their partners; nor to demand and receive them in their names but in reality for the company.

In the case of *Township of Midland v. County Board of Gage County*, 37 Neb. 582, it was sought to restrain the issuance and delivery of certain bonds of the township. The issuance of the bonds to a designated railroad company in aid of the construction of its railroad had been authorized by a vote of the electors of the township.

50

The designated company did not complete the railroad, but sold and transferred all its rights and interests to another company, which completed the railroad and claimed the bonds. The trial court, by decree, perpetually enjoined the issuance of the bonds. On appeal to this court, in its opinion this court said: "The petition presented to the board of supervisors by the freeholders of the township prayed the calling therein of an election and the submission to the electors of a proposition to aid the railroad company. The proposition submitted to the electors was to aid the railroad company. The electors voted to aid the railroad company and authorized the board of supervisors, on the completion of the improvement by the railroad company, to issue the bonds of the township and deliver them to the railroad company. Yet this railroad company did not · complete the improvement. It sold out its property and franchises, and its vendee built the improvement and now claims the bonds. This will not do. If one vendee can claim this aid successfully, any vendee of the railroad company can. * * * The electors of the township are entitled to stand on the very letter of their promise. If they promised a donation to A if he would build a certain improvement, it does not follow that B is entitled to the donation, though he builds the improvement; in other words, the township electors designated the donee and only the one designated can take the donation. The electors did not authorize the supervisors to deliver the bonds voted to the railroad company or its vendee, and had they, it would have been ineffectual and the bond invalid. (*Jones v. Hurlburt*, 13 Neb. 125; *Spurck v. Lincoln & N. W. R. Co.*, 14 Neb. 293; *State v. Roggen*, 22 Neb. 118.) The most that can be said for the appellees is that the electors of this township authorized their agents, the board of supervisors and the county clerk of Gage county, to issue the bonds of said Midland township and deliver them to the railroad company when it had built a certain improvement. The railroad company never complied with the condition coupled with the authority given by the township electors to its agents. The vendee of the railroad has complied with the condition to build the improvement, and it now claims these agents should deliver the bonds to it. Authority from a principal to an agent to do a specific act is limited to that act." (See also *State v. Commissioners of Nemaha County*, 10 Kan. 577.)

In the case of *Nash v. Baker*, 37 Neb. 713, in which the relief sought was to enjoin the collection of $75,000 of bonds which, by vote, the citizens of Kearney had donated in aid of the construction by the Kearney & Black Hills Railway Company of its railroad on the ground that it had been represented to the voters that the road when built would be and operate as an entirely independent line and not under the control of any other railroad or railway and that said statement was untrue, in the discussion of one of the questions presented this court states: "In the case under consideration the representation was of the existence of a fact of controlling weight with the electors called upon to vote bonds in aid of the enterprise projected. The voter could only know of the nature and object of the project to be assisted, by the representations of its promoters. These representations necessarily referred to future conditions, the power to establish which was lodged in the promoters of the scheme. The promise was, that the road, when built, should exist and operate in entire independence of the domination of another road already in existence. It might be that this independence was undesirable, useless, and worthless. That proposition, however, should have been argued to the voters. It cannot now be urged against them. In an opinion in this court, in *Township of Midland v. County Board of Gage County*, 37 Neb. 582, filed during the present term, it has been held that the electors of a township are entitled to stand upon the very letter of their promise, a wholesome rule which should be extended to the facts under consideration. In the case at bar it may be that the insistence upon independence of the Union Pacific Railway was without reason, and even merely whimsical, yet it was a condition which the voters had a right to insist upon as qualifying their proposed donations. The propriety of employing the power of taxation to making donations to enterprises in no way connected with the administration of government may well be doubted in any case. Such restrictive conditions as the voters see fit to insist upon must not be ignored by the proposed donee, especially after accepting the donation burdened with them." A rehearing was moved for and granted, and in a second opinion. reported in 40 Neb. 294, it was said: "The argument upon the rehearing is largely directed to the proposition that the evidence failed to establish some elements necessary to sustain a claim for relief on the ground of false representations. We think that each one of these elements is fairly established by the proof in the case, but if the case depended upon other principles the result would be the same. It is an incontrovertible fact that the contract of the voters, in view of the representations made and assurances held out, was for a railroad independent of other lines and not subject to the control of any other road. What they obtained was in fact a railroad practically owned and absolutely controlled by the Union Pacific Railroad Company, and bound to it by a close traffic agreement. Commenting upon certain language in the former opinion, as to the propriety of exercising the taxing power for such purposes, counsel insist that that question is for the legislative branch of the government and not for the courts. This may be conceded. but still, if taxes are to be imposed upon the whole body of taxpayers by a vote of a certain proportion of them for the purpose, not of exercising any legitimate function of government, but solely for the purpose of making a gift in aid of an enterprise quasi-public in its nature, but still of a business character, it is the duty of the courts to see that such power is not abused; that the donees bring themselves within the strict terms of the grant, and that the donors receive precisely what they bargain for."

The doctrines announced in the opinions of this court, from which we have quoted, are directly pertinent and applicable in and to the state of facts of the case at bar and must govern its decision.

There are other questions argued in the briefs, and they were also presented in the oral argument, but, in view of the disposition of the cause which must follow from the conclusion reached on the grounds which we have considered and determined, their discussion is unnecessary and will be omitted. The judgment of the district court is

AFFIRMED.

LEWIS E. KARNES V. GEORGE E. DOVEY ET AL.

FILED FEBRUARY 17, 1898.   No. 9754.

1. **Exemption:** WAGES. It is the purpose of the statutory law to absolutely exempt from forced application to payment of indebtedness the sixty days' wages of parties designated in the statute.

2. ———: ———: ASSIGNMENT OF CLAIM: DAMAGES. If an account, claim, or evidence of indebtedness has been sold and assigned by the party to whom it belonged, and in an action in the courts of this or another state or a territory the exempt wages of the debtor have been taken under process and applied to the payment of such indebtedness, in an action by the debtor against the original owner thereof to recover the amounts as provided by statute he may, if there are facts shown in evidence from which an inference or conclusion might be drawn that the assignment had been made without any intent or purpose on the part of the assignor to avoid or evade the effect of the exemption laws, the question of the existence or non-existence of such intention or purpose is one of fact to be determined by the jury under appropriate instructions; and an instruction requested to be given which ignores said proposition is erroneous and its refusal proper.

3. **Instructions:** ASSIGNMENTS OF ERROR. Errors in giving instructions and in refusals to give requested instructions must be separately assigned in the motion for a new trial and petition in error. Where this rule is violated and the trial court's action is deter-

mined to have been proper as to one of either of instructions given
or refused in relation to which errors have been assigned in gross,
the assignment need be no further considered.

ERROR from the district court of Cass county. Tried
below before RAMSEY, J. *Affirmed.*

D. O. Dwyer and *E. H. Wooley,* for plaintiff in error.

Beeson & Root, Byron Clark, and *C. A. Rawls, contra.*

HARRISON, C. J.

It appears herein that on and prior to August 19, 1892,
the defendants in error were, as partners, engaged in general mercantile business in the city of Plattsmouth, this
state, and the plaintiff in error on the date mentioned
was indebted to them on account; that said account was
then sold and assigned to a third party, who in a court
of the state of Iowa instituted an action thereon in which
a writ of attachment was procured to issue, accompanied
by a summons in garnishment against, and which was
served on, the Chicago, Burlington & Quincy Railroad
Company, owner and operator as assignee of the Burlington & Missouri River Railroad Company in Nebraska,
of which last mentioned company the plaintiff in error
was an employé; that as a result of said action in the
Iowa court the wages of the plaintiff in error, which he
asserts herein were by the laws of this state exempted
from forced application to the payment of his indebtedness of which was the account sold by defendants in
error, were taken and appropriated in payment of said account. The present action was commenced in the district
court of Cass county to recover of defendants the damages
alleged to have been suffered by plaintiff by reason of
the alleged assignment by defendants of the account and
the subsequent proceedings in the Iowa court and the
seizure and application therein of the exempt wages of
the plaintiff. Issues were joined, and in a trial the defendants were successful and the plaintiff presents the
cause to this court for review.

It is argued that the trial court erred in refusing to give in charge to the jury instruction numbered 2, requested for plaintiff, in terms as follows: "The court instructs the jury that if they believe from the evidence that plaintiff is the head of a family and a resident of this state, and that the money attached by the Iowa court was earned within the period of sixty days prior thereto, then and in that case your verdict should be for the plaintiff, and in this connection you are instructed that under the laws of Nebraska a creditor cannot lawfully assign a claim against a resident debtor of Nebraska to a person in another state and have exempt wages taken by such persons in the other state." And in this connection it is also urged that it was error of the court to give paragraph numbered 3 of its charge to the jury. The first would, if it had been read in connection with the other portions of the charge, have informed the jury, as is claimed in argument, that if an account against certain parties designated in our statutes was by the owner thereof assigned and by the assignee or other person to whom it might be further assigned taken to another state and suit thereon instituted in which the wages earned within the sixty days or time fixed by law were taken and applied in satisfaction of the account, an action would lie and could be successfully maintained against the original owner and assignor, and the verdict, regardless of the appearance of other fact or facts in evidence, should in this case be against the defendants. Paragraph numbered 3 given, and which, as we have stated, is attacked in this connection, was in effect the same as that numbered 2 requested for plaintiff, except in that it informed the jury if it further appeared in evidence that the account was sold and assigned without any intent or purpose on the part of the assignors of evading the exemption laws of the state the verdict should be for the defendants. It is provided in section 531*a* of the Code of Civil Procedure: "The wages of laborers, mechanics, and clerks who are heads of fam-

ilies, in the hands of those by whom such laborers,
mechanics, or clerks may be employed, both before and
after such wages shall be due, shall be exempt from the
operation of attachment, execution, and garnishee process; *Provided,* That not more than sixty days' wages
shall be exempt." And on the same subject, in section
531c: "That it be, and is hereby declared, unlawful for
any creditor of, or other holder of any evidence of debt,
book account, or claim of any name or nature against any
laborer, servant, clerk, or other employé of any corporation, firm, or individual in this state, for the purpose
below stated, to sell, assign, transfer, or by any means
dispose of any such claim, book account, bill, or debt of
any name or nature whatever, to any person or persons,
firm, corporation, or institution, or to institute in this
state or elsewhere, or prosecute any suit or action for
any such claim or debt against any such laborer, servant,
clerk, or employé by any process seeking to seize, attach,
or garnish the wages of such person or persons earned
within sixty days prior to the commencement of such
proceeding, for the purpose of avoiding the effect of the
laws of the state of Nebraska concerning exemptions."
In section 531c: "In any proceeding, civil or criminal,
growing out of a breach of sections one or two of this
act, proof of the institution of a suit, or service of garnishment summons by any persons, firm, or individual, in
any court of any state or territory other than this state
or in this state, to seize, by process of garnishment or
otherwise, any of the wages of such persons as defined in
section one of this act, shall be deemed *prima facie* evidence of an evasion of the laws of the state of Nebraska
and a breach of the provisions of this act on the part of
the creditor or resident in Nebraska causing the same to
be done." Also, in 531f: "Any persons, firm, company,
corporation, or business institution guilty of a violation
of sections one or two of this act shall be liable to the
party injured through such violation of this act, for the
amount of the debt sold, assigned, transferred, garnished,

or sued upon, with all costs and expenses and a reasonable attorney's fee, to be recovered in any court of competent jurisdiction in this state." The object of these and other provisions of statute on the subject, it is evident, is to exempt absolutely, if possible, the wages of the persons designated, to the extent or amount stated, and they should be construed in such manner as to render them effective of the expressed purpose. If we give the language used its ordinary and precise import, always bearing in mind the object sought to be accomplished by the law-makers who framed and enacted the portions of our law now under consideration, we think it is clear that if it appears in evidence that an account or claim has been assigned and an action instituted thereon by the assignee in a state other than this in which the exempt wages of the debtor have been seized and appropriated to the payment of the debt, and other facts have been shown from which the fair inference or conclusion might be drawn that the assignment by the original owner of the claim had been wholly without any intention or purpose of avoiding or evading the law of exemptions, the questions are of fact and to be submitted to the jury under proper instructions, and in this view of the matter the instruction requested and refused was erroneous, in that it ignored the proposition of the good faith of the assignors of the account at the time of such transfer; and the one given was correct, in that it noticed the proposition which was omitted from the requested instruction.

It is an established rule that alleged errors in regard to instructions given or refused must be specifically and separately assigned in both motion for a new trial and the petition in error; that if they be grouped in assignment in either pleading the errors indicated will be examined no further if it be ascertained that one of the errors of the group alleged is without force. (See *Graham v. Frazier*, 49 Neb. 90; *Johnston v. Milwaukee & Wyoming Investment Co.*, 49 Neb. 68; *Denise v. City of*

Omaha, 49 Neb. 750.) In this case errors were assigned in group in the motion for new trial in relation to several instructions given, and in the same manner in both motion for a new trial and the petition in error of instructions requested for plaintiff in error and refused, and having determined that one given was without error and of one refused the action was proper, we need consider no further alleged errors as to either group. There are no other objections presented in argument, and it follows that the judgment of the district court must be

AFFIRMED.

CHICAGO, BURLINGTON & QUINCY RAILROAD COMPANY V. JOHN POLLARD.

FILED FEBRUARY 17, 1898.   No. 7698.

1. **Railroad-Crossing**: DANGER: NOTICE.   A railroad-crossing is a place of danger, and all persons to whom negligence may be imputed are bound to take notice of that fact.

2. ———: ———: NEGLIGENCE.   A traveler on a street or public highway approaching a railroad-crossing thereof for the purpose of using it or going over must exercise ordinary care, or such care as would be exercised by a prudent man under all the facts and circumstances attendant upon and surrounding his approach to and crossing the track.

3. **Negligence**: QUESTION FOR JURY.   If different minds may reasonably draw different conclusions or inferences from the state of facts established by the evidence in a cause, whether such facts show negligence or contributory negligence is not a question of law for the court but must be submitted to the jury. *Omaha S. R. Co. v. Lochnessen*, 40 Neb. 37, followed.

4. ———: EVIDENCE.   The evidence in this case examined, and *held* not to establish conclusively and as matter of legal imputation contributory negligence on the part of the plaintiff.

5. ———: ———.   Actions of the trial court in giving and in refusing to give instructions in charge to the jury, and to which exceptions were urged, examined, and *held* not erroneous or not prejudicially so.

ERROR from the district court of Saunders county. Tried below before BATES, J. *Affirmed.*

J. W. Deweese and *F. E. Bishop,* for plaintiff in error.

Sawyer, Snell & Frost, contra.

HARRISON, C. J.

The plaintiff in this action, commenced in the district court of Saunders county, sought of the company a recovery of damages which he alleged became his due by reason of injuries to himself and the destruction of a wagon and harness, caused by the negligence and carelessness of the company's employés in the operation and running of a locomotive and passenger train of the company over and on its line of road through the village of Greenwood, this state; that by reason of such negligence and carelessness the said locomotive and train of the company struck the wagon in which, with team of horses attached, the plaintiff was crossing the railroad of the company at the regular street crossing thereof in said village, and threw the plaintiff from the wagon and inflicted on him the permanent injuries of which he complained, and destroyed his wagon and harness. The answer of the company placed in issue the material allegations of plaintiff's petition and alleged affirmatively that the injuries to himself and his property, if any occurred at the time and place claimed, were the results of his own negligence and carelessness. Of the issues joined there was a trial to the court and a jury. The verdict was returned favorable to plaintiff and judgment rendered thereon. The cause is presented to this court by error proceeding on the part of the company.

The discussion in the argument is, as was stated by counsel, confined to two or three points, the main one of which is that there was such contributory negligence on the part of plaintiff as to defeat a recovery on his part though the company might have been negligent. It is

insisted in this connection that the evidence in the case
shows conclusively, and as a matter of legal imputation,
negligence in the actions of plaintiff which must defeat
his action to recover for the alleged negligence of the
company.

This is one of the class of cases based on the incidents
of accidents at crossings of streets or public highways
and lines of railroads, in all of which as to the facts and
circumstances there is a general likeness or resemblance,
though in each there appears some particular and distinguishing facts or details not present in others. In
this case the plaintiff testified as follows:

Q. Were you in the village of Greenwood on the 8th of
April, 1893?

A. Yes, sir; in the afternoon.

Q. What did you take down, anything that day?

A. I took, I and my boy took, down a couple of loads
of corn.

Q. Did he drive one team and you another?

A. Yes, sir.

Q. In going from your place to the elevators there in
Greenwood did you cross any railroad track?

A. Yes, sir.

Q. On what street?

A. I think they call it First street.

Q. What did you do with the corn that you took to
town that day?

A. Dumped it in Railback's elevator.

Q. Where is that elevator?

A. It is south of Second street.

Q. After you had dumped the corn what did you do?

A. Drove around and weighed my wagon and started
for home.

Q. On what side of the railroad track were you after
you had dumped your corn?

A. On the southeast.

Q. In going from Second street, or near there, when
you had dumped your corn, how did you get to First
street?

A. By going north.

Q. Is there a wagon road along there?

A. Yes, sir.

Q. How does it run with reference to the railroad track?

A. Along-side of it.

Q. Now describe to the jury just what you did, what precautions you took in the way of looking for any trains on the way from Connor's elevator where you put your corn until you were struck by the train.

A. Used all the caution that I could use. The teams had not been in town for quite a bit; my boy had a team behind; I dumped my load first and I was watching for a train on account of his team, and also for myself, and when I got close to the track I saw smoke down towards Ashland, and I thought to myself, there is a train coming from that way, I just held the horses until I could see it was not a train, and I just turned in an instant,— it seemed only a few instants from the time, from the time I quit looking towards Lincoln, I had looked a few minutes towards Ashland——

Q. Was it minutes?

A. Not minutes; I just looked, just turned my head toward Lincoln, and there seemed to me to be an engine standing right there, and I just slashed the lines and let the horses loose from my hands, just let them have their heads, and that is all I know about it.

Q. What signals did you hear in the way of a bell or whistle?

A. I did not hear anything.

Q. Those two toots that some witness spoke about, did you hear that?

A. I did not catch it. My wagon was a loose box and may have stopped the noise; before the sound got to me the engine got to me, and if it did toot I did not hear it.

Cross-examination:

Q. How fast were you going that day?

A. I don't know; the team was walking along, going

on the railroad crossing. Well, I have timed them; they walk about four miles an hour.

Q. Probably three or four miles an hour?

A. Yes, sir.

Q. What kind of a team, did you have a quiet team?

A. Yes, sir; quiet.

Q. You were walking along on an ordinary walk?

A. Yes, sir.

Q. The team was quiet and paying no attention?

A. Yes, sir.

Q. There was no reason why you could not have stopped within twenty feet of it?

A. No, sir.

Q. You did not see the train until you were stepping on the crossing?

A. No, sir.

Q. The horses were stepping on the crossing?

A. Yes, sir; the horses were going over the last rail on the main line.

Q. Then you would be about over the first rail?

A. I think my wagon was; I don't know about myself, it was so quick I could not catch it.

Q. Where had you been looking?

A. Looking down toward Ashland and I saw a smoke down that way.

Q. Until you arrived at the crossing you had been looking toward Ashland?

A. Yes, sir; as the horses were starting over the switch I took my eye from toward Lincoln and turned toward Ashland, I saw smoke down there.

Q. Before you looked toward Lincoln?

A. Yes, sir.

Q. How long?

A. A few seconds.

Q. How many?

A. I could not hardly tell.

Q. Where did you begin to look toward Lincoln?

A. From the time I left the elevator.

Q. And you kept looking toward Lincoln from the time you left the elevator?

A. Yes, sir; until I looked the other way.

Q. You knew that this train was coming?

A. Yes, sir; I knew it was due about that time, the three o'clock flyer.

Q. You knew it did not stop?

A. Yes, sir; I knew it did not stop at Greenwood.

Q. You kept looking toward Lincoln until the horses stepped on the track?

A. Yes, sir; I saw smoke down there.

Q. How did you happen to see a smoke down there, looking toward Lincoln?

A. I turned my eye.

Q. You were not looking toward Lincoln all the time?

A. Maybe you know.

Q. You could not have seen a smoke toward Ashland if you had been looking toward Lincoln all the time?

A. If I had been looking direct there of course I could not, but I looked that way, and kind of cast my eye the other way and saw a smoke and held it there just a minute.

Q. Now, Mr. Pollard, as you drove along this street parallel to the railroad, you went along on an ordinary walk?

A. Yes, sir.

Q. You were not driving so that the wagon made much noise?

A. No, sir.

Q. Were you listening for the train?

A. Well, yes; my mind was on the train.

Q. You knew the train was due about that time?

A. About that time; I did not know just the time, I knew there was a "three o'clock flyer" about three o'clock.

Q. Did you know this was about three o'clock?

A. Yes, sir; about that.

Q. And your mind was on that train?

A. Yes, sir.

Q. You stood in the middle of the wagon?

A. Yes, sir; somewhere.

Q. How high would the line of your eye be from the ground as you drove along in that road?

A. I don't know.

Q. Eight feet?

A. Well, something like that, I expect; I never measured anything of that kind.

Redirect examination, by Mr. Snell:

Q. About what distance would you be in your wagon from the heads of your horses, how far from where you were standing in your wagon would it be to the heads of your horses did you say?

A. It would be about eighteen feet, I guess; somewheres near that, or sixteen feet; I never measured that.

Q. You speak of holding your eye toward Ashland a second or two, and you noticed something there. Why was it necessary to keep looking there? Was there any obstruction in the way?

A. The stock yard was there, and I think there was a box car there. I had looked to see if I was right or not, if a train comes up to switch in for the flyer to pass.

Q. As soon as you got where you could see clear by this box car there by the stock yards, then what did you do?

A. Then I turned my head to see if I could see down the track.

Q. Towards Lincoln?

A. Yes, sir; towards Lincoln.

Q. Now, what obstructions were there along the right of way, this wagon road, that prevented you from seeing towards Lincoln?

A. There was a little grain house there and an elevator office, two elevators and two offices and the depot. * *

Recross-examination:

Q. Where was this box car that you speak of?

A. I think there was one standing right by the hog shoot.

Q. Up toward Ashland?

A. Yes, sir.

Q. That is all, was it?

A. That is all that I seen.

It was stated by one of the witnesses called for the company:

Q. Did you see Pollard as he drove up to the track?

A. Yes, sir.

Q. I wish you would tell the jury what you saw.

A. I seen him make the turn in the road that parallels the railroad.

Q. As it goes to the crossing it makes the turn?

A. Just when he made the turn I seen him and watched him drive up on the crossing; he was in a lumber wagon, standing up, I believe; he drove up on the crossing, and seemed to be wrapped in his thoughts and oblivious of the surroundings. It appeared to me——

A. He stood looking down into his wagon and went up on the crossing and the horses crossed, and it seemed to me near the front end of the wagon struck the main line; he looked and seen the train coming, and he slashed the horses with the lines that way (indicating), and immediately the engine hit the wheel of the wagon, and that is the last I seen of him.

Q. What did he appear to be looking at as he drove up towards the crossing?

A. He was looking down in his wagon, as though he was studying about something.

Q. Did you see him look down toward the depot?

A. I did when the front end of his wagon hit the main line, he turned his head and seen it, and struck the horses with the lines, that way (indicating).

Q. Is that the first time he looked toward the depot?

A. Yes, sir; the first I seen.

Q. If he had been looking toward the depot, could you notice that?

51

A. Yes, sir; I never took my eyes off him since I first see him.

Q. Why was that?

A. When I seen the man driving on there and the train coming, when I heard the train coming, and he appeared to me to be oblivious of everything around him, I kept my eye on him until the train intervened, until the train hit the hind wheel of the wagon.

Q. Could you tell about where the train was when you heard it?

A. No, sir; I only saw him when he was probably forty feet from the main line. I did not notice the train until I seen the man that drew my attention, when I seen the man driving across, and I heard the train coming, heard the roaring.

And by another:

Q. What did Mr. Pollard appear to be paying attention to, if anything, as he drove up toward the crossing?

A. He didn't seem to be paying attention to anything more than the team; he was standing there driving along, and he didn't seem to notice anything.

Q. If he had had his face turned toward the south, could he have seen from where you were?

A. Yes, sir; I think he could very readily.

Cross-examination:

Q. Did he have his face turned toward the south?

A. No, sir; not when I saw him first.

Q. Then how did you come to the conclusion that he was not paying attention?

A. He stood there just driving the team along, and didn't seem to be looking either way to me.

Q. What part of his body could you see?

A. The back and side.

Q. Do you know where his eyes were, which way he was looking?

A. His face was turned toward the horses and I suppose he was looking at them.

Q. You suppose he was looking toward the horses?

A. Yes, sir.

It will be noticed that these witnesses, other than the plaintiff, but testify to what it seemed or appeared to them he was doing, and in regard to them it must be said that this is all they could do, as they were back of or behind plaintiff and could not see his eyes or know where he was looking except by the position of his head. The train which struck plaintiff's wagon was generally known along this portion of the line of railroad as the "flyer," did not stop at the station but passed through a portion of the village and until it struck the wagon at the street crossing its speed being estimated by one witness at twenty-five miles an hour and by the majority of the witnesses at forty or fifty; they were all, however, little if any, better than mere guesses, though all agreed that it was running quite rapidly. Between the depot and this crossing of First street (the depot was in the direction from the crossing from which this train came) stood on the company's right of way, two elevators, two grain dealers' offices, and one granary, at such distances apart and so situated as to obstruct (to what extent the witnesses were not all quite of the same opinion) the view of the track or railroad which would otherwise have been open to a person approaching the crossing along the street as the plaintiff did prior to the accident. A view of the track in the other direction was obstructed by stock yards, and on that particular day by a freight car. When a point thirty-five or thirty-six feet distant from the track was reached by one approaching to cross, the view along the line toward and beyond the depot was unobstructed for a considerable distance, one quite reliable calculation placed it half a mile. In the contrary direction the view of the line of railroad was obstructed by the stock yards and a freight car.

There are many cases cited by counsel which announce the doctrine in relation to the duty of a person about to go over a railroad track on a street or road crossing. This court, in reviewing one of this class of cases, *Omaha & R. V. R. Co. v. Talbot*, 48 Neb. 627, stated the rule as follows: "It is the duty of a traveler upon a public highway, when approaching a railroad crossing, to exercise ordinary care. All men must take notice of the fact that a railway crossing is a place of danger. And we are of opinion that a person who goes upon a railway crossing without first listening and looking for the approach of a train, in the absence of a reasonable excuse therefor, does not exercise ordinary care. We further think that the act of a party in going upon a railroad crossing without first listening and looking for the approach of a train, in the absence of a reasonable excuse therefor, admits of no other inference than that of negligence, and if such failure to look and listen contributes to the party's injury he cannot recover. *Pennsylvania R. Co. v. Rathgeb*, 32 O. St. 66, is a case very much like the one at bar. In that case Rathgeb was injured while attempting to cross the railroad track in a wagon. Before going upon the track he looked in one direction only. The district court charged the jury: I will not say to you that the plaintiff should have looked east along the track. I will only say that he was obliged to use his sense of sight in a reasonable manner, and it is for you to say whether he ought to have looked to the east along the track or not before he attempted to cross. But the supreme court held that the district court should have charged the jury that it was Rathgeb's duty to look to the east as well as the west along the track before attempting to cross it. In that case the court also held ordinary prudence requires that a person in the full enjoyment of the faculties of hearing and seeing, before attempting to pass over a known railroad crossing, should use them for the purpose of discovering and avoiding danger from an approaching train; and the omission to do so, without a reasonable excuse therefor, is negligence and will defeat an action by such person for an injury to which such negligence contributed. In the case at bar, Talbot did not look toward the southeast, the direction from which the train came which injured him. He alleges as a reason for not

looking in that direction that he supposed the train
bound northwest had already gone by, as it should have
done if it was on time; but this supposition of Talbot will
not excuse him for not exercising ordinary care in looking
both ways for the approach of a train. A traveler approaching a railway crossing has no right to assume that
cars are not approaching on the track, or that there is no
danger therefrom." And the question of contributory
negligence may on certain conditions of facts become one
of law for the court. (*Guthrie v. Missouri P. R. Co.*, 51
Neb. 746.) Also applicable in such cases we have the following principles and rules:

It is the duty of a traveler on a street or public highway about to cross a railroad track at a crossing to view
the track in both directions for the approach of a train.
(*Omaha & R. V. R. Co. v. Talbot, supra; Nixon v. Chicago,
R. I. & P. R. Co.*, 84 Ia. 331, 51 N. W. Rep. 157; *Schlimgen
v. Chicago, M. & St. P. R. Co.*, 90 Wis. 194, 62 N. W. Rep.
1045; *Railroad Co. v. Houston*, 95 U. S. 697; *Baker v.
Kansas City, Ft. S. & M. R. Co.*, 26 S. W. Rep. [Mo.] 20.)

It is the doctrine of this court that "Though it is true,
in many cases, that where the facts are undisputed the
effect of them is for the judgment of the court and not for
the decision of the jury, this is true in that class of cases
where the existence of such facts come in question rather
than where deductions and inferences are to be made
from them. And whether the facts are disputed or undisputed, if different minds may honestly draw different
conclusions from them, the case is properly left to the
jury." (*Atchison & N. R. Co. v. Bailey*, 11 Neb. 332. See
to the same effect *City of Lincoln v. Gillilan*, 18 Neb. 115;
Omaha, N. & B. H. R. Co. v. O'Donnell, 22 Neb. 475; *Johnson v. Missouri P. R. Co.*, 18 Neb. 690; *Miller v. Strivens*, 48
Neb. 458; *Union P. R. Co. v. Cobb*, 41 Neb. 120; *American
Water-Works Co. v. Dougherty*, 37 Neb. 373; *Omaha Street
R. Co. v. Craig*, 39 Neb. 601, and cases cited.)

"The policy of the law has relegated the determination
of such questions to the jury, under proper instructions

from the court. It is their province to note the special
circumstances and surroundings of each particular case,
and then say whether the conduct of the parties in that
case was such as would be expected of reasonable,
prudent men, under a similar state of affairs. When a
given state of facts is such that reasonable men may
fairly differ upon the question as to whether there was
negligence or not, the determination of the matter is for
the jury. It is only where the facts are such that all reasonable men must draw the same conclusion from them
that the question of negligence is ever considered as one
of law for the court." (*Grand Trunk R. Co. v. Ives*, 12 Sup.
Ct. Rep. 679.)

When the view of the road is so obstructed as to render .
it difficult to see an approaching train, the question
whether a traveler was wanting in due care is one for the
jury to determine; and it is also a question for the jury
under complicated circumstances, calculated to deceive
and throw the traveler off his guard. (Beach, Contributory Negligence [2d ed.] sec. 195.)

It was not for the trial court, and is not for this court,
to determine and say as a matter of law just what exact
point in the plaintiff's approach to the railroad he should
have looked in either direction on the track for a train,
or just at what instant he should have looked in either
direction for the same purpose. The question was, did
he, under his surroundings and all the circumstances, observe the care which ordinarily would have been taken
by a prudent person? It is insisted for the company
that the evidence discloses that it was impossible that
plaintiff looked and did not see the train approaching,
notwithstanding what he states on this subject in his testimony; that this appears so clearly that no two reasonable men considering the evidence could or can differ in
the conclusion drawn therefrom, and the question was
one of law for the court. Counsel for plaintiff contend
that there is presented herein a set of facts and circumstances which made the question of the contributory neg-

ligence one for the decision of the jury. The plaintiff states he looked along the track toward Lincoln, the direction from which the train came and from which he had reason to expect one at or about that time. His view of the track, in the direction just indicated, was partially, at least, and during some portions of his approach to the crossing wholly, obstructed by the buildings on the right of way, and until he was thirty-five or thirty-six feet from the main track to be crossed and on which the train came. His attention was attracted in the opposite direction by seeing some smoke there, which he conceived possibly to be proceeding from a train approaching from that direction. His view of the track looking toward the smoke was obstructed by stock yards and a freight car, and he states as soon as he obtained a clear view he turned again toward Lincoln and saw the train, but too late, as he thought, to avoid its striking him. It will be remembered that there were witnesses who stated that from where they saw the plaintiff as he approached the crossing, seemingly he was not looking either up or down the track or making any effort by use of either the sense of sight or hearing to ascertain whether there was a coming train by which he might be injured. This was a conflict in the evidence on this point. When the physical objects which were near, mainly the buildings on the right of way, their positions relatively to each other and to the track, the distance from it at which the view of the track was clear and unobstructed by the buildings to the plaintiff in his coming to the crossing, the time probably consumed by plaintiff in reaching and passing over so much of the crossing as he did, the speed of the train which while we do not think the evidence given definitely fixed it, it was conceded by all that it was running quite rapidly, that it was necessary plaintiff should look in both directions, which he says he did, that his attention was drawn away from the way from which the train was coming by smoke in the other direction, that his survey of the portion of the track to which he then turned his

eyes was obstructed, are all considered,—we cannot say
that there arises a certainty that he did not and had not
looked toward the approaching train, that it was impossible that he should have done so and not seen it and that
it was conclusively shown that he was negligent. It
might be said that in consideration of all the surroundings and complications, in the observation of ordinary
care, he should have stopped his team when he saw the
smoke toward Ashland, when it was within his knowledge that it was about the time a train, "the flyer," was
due from the other direction, and assure himself of safety
before starting over the track; but this would probably
properly have been for the jury to consider as an element
of the general question of whether the plaintiff, under all
the facts and circumstances and his situation on the day
he was injured, exercised ordinary care, was not urged
in argument, and we need not give it further notice.
From a full and careful examination and consideration of
all the evidence we conclude that contributory negligence
of plaintiff did not conclusively appear; that whether
the plaintiff's precautions to avoid danger were such as
prudence demanded, whether he exercised ordinary care
or such care as the somewhat distracting circumstances,
under all the attendant facts and circumstances demanded, was not a question of law, but one for the determination of the jury. (*Brown v. Edgerton*, 49 Pac. Rep.
[Kan.] 159; *Loucks v. Chicago, M. & St. P. R. Co.*, 18 N. W.
Rep. [Minn.] 651; *Moore v. Chicago, St. P. & K. C. R. Co.*,
71 N. W. Rep. [Ia.] 569; *Omaha, N. & B. H. R. Co. v.
O'Donnell, supra; Breckenfelder v. Lake Shore & M. S. R.
Co.*, 44 N. W. Rep. [Mich.] 957; *Nosler v. Chicago, B. & Q.
R. Co.*, 34 N. W. Rep. [Ia.] 850; *McDuffie v. Lake Shore &
M. S. R. Co.*, 57 N. W. Rep. [Mich.] 248; *Omaha S. R. Co.
v. Lochneisen*, 40 Neb. 37.)

It is complained that the court erred in refusing to read
to the jury an instruction numbered 1 prepared and requested for the company. This was to the effect that
there was conclusive evidence of contributory negligence

on the part of the plaintiff; hence he could not recover in the action, and the verdict should be for the defendant. The conclusion that we have hereinbefore reached, that under the evidence herein the question of contributory negligence on the part of plaintiff was one to be submitted to the jury for decision settles the point here presented, and it follows therefrom that it was not error to refuse the proffered instruction.

It is urged that the court committed error in giving in charge to the jury an instruction numbered 5, asked for plaintiff, which reads as follows: "In determining whether the plaintiff was guilty of contributory negligence, you can take into consideration whether he looked and listened for the train, the distance from the track at which he could first see it, the obstructions to his view, the smoke he saw, if any, in the direction of Ashland, and if from all the evidence you find that he exercised the care and caution in attempting to cross the track in question at the time he did that a prudent and careful man would have exercised under the same circumstances, then the plaintiff was not guilty of contributory negligence." It is said in the brief: "This instruction invades the province of the jury, according to the holdings of this court. One of the issues in the case was whether the plaintiff himself was guilty of contributory negligence, and in this paragraph the court groups a number of facts together, and tells the jury, not that these might be considered by them in determining whether the plaintiff was guilty of contributory negligence, but tells them that he was not guilty of contributory negligence." We do not think the instruction is open to the objection urged against it. It but states that the jury may take certain facts into consideration, which was entirely proper in this case, then referring the jury to all the evidence as a basis for a finding on the question, states in correct terms what it was necessary should appear had been done by plaintiff to avoid the imputation of contributory negligence, did not state that the plaintiff had not been guilty thereof, but that if the jury determined from all the evidence that his conduct and actions had been of a certain character, then it had decided that he had not been negligent. It might have been better to have defined contributory negligence generally and then further told the jury to ascertain from all the evidence including the consideration of the circumstances specifically set forth in the instruction quoted whether plaintiff had so acted as to be within the definition, but there was nothing misleading or prejudicially so, if erroneous, in the manner of statement employed.

The court instructed the jury of its own motion in the paragraph numbered 5 of its charge as follows: "The court instructs the jury that railroad companies, under their charters, have the same rights to use that portion of the public highway over which their track passes as the public have to use the same highway. Their rights and those of the public, as to the use of the highway at such point of intersection, are mutual and reciprocal; and, in the exercise of such rights both the company and those using the highway must have due regard for the safety of others, and use every reasonable effort to avoid injury to others." An instruction in the exact language of this appears in Sackett's Instructions to Juries [2d ed.] 403, sec. 29, over the following citations: *Indianapolis & St. L. R. Co. v. Stables,* 62 Ill. 313; Shearman & Redfield, Negligence sec. 463; *North Pennsylvania R. Co. v. Heilman,* 49 Pa. St. 60; *Cleveland, C. & C. R. Co. v. Terry,* 8 O. St. 570. This is but a general statement and might, if given alone on the subject, without other instructions modifying its import, be open to the objection that it is too general, not explicit enough, does not sufficiently explain the reciprocal rights of the parties as to the use of the highway at the crossing. It states in a certain sense the rule, and, with probably some limitations in regard to the manner and under what rules as to care and caution the use mentioned shall be exercised, may be proper in any case of the kind, but this need not be definitely determined here, as, at the request of the company, there were given some instructions, at least three, in regard to the duty of plaintiff when about to use this crossing, which, when read in connection with this one, we think fully cleared away any misunderstanding that could possibly have arisen in the mind of any juror through the giving of this instruction, and fully destroyed any misleading force it had, if any; hence its giving, if erroneous, was not prejudicial.

It is asserted that the several paragraphs of the instructions given were conflicting and confusing. The statement in argument on this point is that the court, in an instruction asked for plaintiff and given, informed the jury it should consider certain enumerated matters in arriving at a finding as to whether there had been any negligence on the part of the company, and in two paragraphs given at the request of the company told that body, if it should determine these matters did not affect the accident as elemental of its cause, they were robbed of any significance; and also that they might have occurred or existed and been of force as to the injury was of no consequence if the plaintiff was derelict in his duty to the extent of contributory negligence. The actions of the court as to these matters were without error; hence this objection fails. No prejudicial errors have been presented and the judgment of the district court must be

AFFIRMED.

MISSOURI PACIFIC RAILWAY COMPANY, APPELLEE, V.
ESTATE OF GEORGE JAY, APPELLANT.

FILED FEBRUARY 17, 1898. No. 8140.

Administrator: REVOCATION OF LETTERS. One sued by an administrator is not authorized to petition the county court to revoke plaintiff's letters of administration. *Missouri P. R. Co. v. Bradley*, 51 Neb. 596, followed.

APPEAL from the district court of Douglas county. Heard below before AMBROSE, J. *Reversed.*

Connell & Ives, for appellant.

B. P. Waggener and *James W. Orr, contra.*.

NORVAL, J.

The county court of Douglas county appointed an administrator of the estate of George Jay, deceased. Subsequently, the administrator instituted an action in the district court of said county against the Missouri Pacific Railway Company to recover damages on account of the death of his intestate. Thereupon the railway company petitioned the county court to revoke plaintiff's appointment as administrator, which application was denied, and on appeal to the district court the letters of administration were revoked. The estate has prosecuted an appeal to this court. In *Missouri P. R. Co. v. Bradley,* 51 Neb. 596, it was decided that one sued by an administrator is not entitled to petition the county court to revoke the letters of administration. Upon that authority the judgment of the district court is reversed and the proceedings dismissed.

REVERSED AND DISMISSED.

CHARLES S. ELGUTTER, ADMINISTRATOR, V. MISSOURI PACIFIC RAILWAY COMPANY.

FILED FEBRUARY 17, 1898. No. 7771.

1. **Appointment of Administrator:** COLLATERAL ATTACK. The appointment of an administrator may be collaterally attacked when the record affirmatively shows the court granting the letters acted without jurisdiction.

2. ———: APPLICATION. An application for administration must be regarded as abandoned where no action or step whatever is taken

by the court in the proceeding for nearly two years after the date fixed in the notice to the next of kin of the time and place of the hearing.

ERROR from the district court of Douglas county. Tried below before AMBROSE, J. *Affirmed.*

Connell & Ives, for plaintiff in error.

Lee S. Estelle, B. P. Waggener, and *James W. Orr, contra.*

NORVAL, J.

Ralph E. Gaylord, as administrator of the estate of George Jay, deceased, instituted this action in the court below to recover the sum of $5,000 damages on account of the death of his intestate, alleged to have been caused by the wrongful act, neglect, and default of the defendant. Subsequently, Gaylord was removed as administrator of said estate by the county court, and one Charles S. Elgutter was appointed administrator in his place, who was substituted as plaintiff herein by the district court. One of the defenses raised by the answer was that no administrator of the estate of Jay was ever legally appointed. The court below directed a verdict for the defendant on this ground, which ruling is presented for review.

The doctrine is firmly established in this state that the appointment of an administrator cannot be assailed collaterally where the county court did not exceed its jurisdiction in granting the letters of administration. (*Missouri P. R. Co. v. Lewis,* 24 Neb. 848; *Moore v. Moore,* 33 Neb. 509; *Bradley v. Missouri P. R. Co.,* 51 Neb. 653.) There is no room to doubt that the appointment of an administrator may be attacked collaterally where the record on its face discloses an entire want of jurisdiction by the county court to act in the premises. (*Moore v. Moore,* 33 Neb. 509; *Davis v. Hudson,* 29 Minn. 27; *Gillett v. Needham,* 37 Mich. 143.) Plaintiff's counsel insist that the facts necessary to confer jurisdiction upon the county court fully appear.

There is no dispute concerning the facts. It is disclosed that George Jay died in Douglas county on February 16, 1891, from injuries inflicted by one of defendant's engines; that five days later a petition in due form alleging the essential jurisdictional facts was presented to the county court of said county by a person claiming to be the widow of said decedent, although as a matter of fact she was not his widow, nor in any manner interested in his estate as a creditor or otherwise; that upon the filing of said petition an order was entered by the county court assigning April 24, 1891, as time for hearing of the application, and notice thereof was given by publication to all persons interested as required by law; that on said date no hearing was had, nor was any adjournment taken, and no other or further steps were had in the matter until February 3, 1893, when an application, setting forth no jurisdictional fact, was presented on behalf of the parents, brothers, and sisters of the decedent, to the county court of Douglas county, praying the appointment of an administrator of the estate of said George Jay, deceased; that no notice of this application was ever given, but on the day of the filing thereof Ralph E. Gaylord was appointed administrator, who qualified as such and received letters of administration, and on May 5, 1894, the county judge of his own accord revoked the appointment of Gaylord. and Charles S. Elgutter was substituted in his place, who duly qualified as administrator. The petition for the appointment of the administrator was sufficient in form and substance, and the statutory notice of the time and place fixed for the hearing was given, so the county court upon the face of the record at one time had jurisdiction to grant letters of administration upon the estate of the decedent. (See the decisions of this court heretofore cited.) The contention of the defendant is that the county court was ousted of its jurisdiction by reason of

its failure to take any step in the matter of the appointment of an administrator for nearly two years after the
giving of the notice of the hearing.   This position is un-
answerable.   In addition to a sufficient petition for administration, the statute requires notice of the application
"and of the time and place of hearing thereof to be given
by personal service on all persons interested, or by publication under an order of such court in such newspaper
printed in the state as he may direct." (Compiled Statutes,
ch. 23, sec. 195.)   The giving of notice is as essential to jurisdiction as is the filing of a sufficient application or petition for the granting of administration.   (*Davis v. Hudson*,
29 Minn. 27; *Gillett v. Needham*, 37 Mich. 143; *Palmer v. Oak-
ley*, 2 Doug. [Mich.] 433; *Dalton v. State*, 6 Blackf. [Ind.]
357; *Hart v. Gray*, 5 Sumner [U. S.] 339; *Seaverns v.
Gerke*, 3 Sawyer [U. S.] 353.)   The purpose of the notice
is to advise persons interested in the estate of the contemplated proceedings, so that they may appear and take
such action as shall best subserve their interests.   The
proper notice was given, it is true, but there was no appointment of administrator made at the time fixed in the
notice for the hearing, nor for almost two years thereafter; nor was the hearing of the application continued
or postponed.   On the contrary, the record shows that
the entire proceedings were abandoned, no steps looking
to the appointment of an administrator of the Jay estate
having been taken until February 3, 1893, when a new
application for the granting of administration, wholly
defective in substance, was filed, which was acted upon
by the county judge at once, without any notice whatever.   The proceedings were absolute nullities, and are
entirely valueless as authority for the administration.
(*Torrance v. McDougald*, 12 Ga. 526; *McGehee v. Ragan*, 9
Ga. 135.)   It follows that plaintiff had no authority to
maintain the action, and the judgment of the district
court is   .

AFFIRMED.

PHILIP BERGERON V. STATE OF NEBRASKA.

FILED FEBRUARY 17, 1898. No. 9618.

1. **Criminal Law**: INSTRUCTIONS. An instruction purporting to cover the whole case is erroneous which fails to include all the elements necessarily involved in the issues and within the evidence.

2. **Burglary.** By section 48 of the Criminal Code breaking and entering in the night-season are essential elements of the crime of burglary.

3. ———: INFORMATION: EVIDENCE. Where an information for burglary charges that the breaking and entering were effected with the intent to steal, it is necessary to prove that the property possessed some value and was within the building.

4. **Instructions**: REVIEW. A faultless instruction will not cure a misstatement of the law in another paragraph of the court's charge to the jury.

ERROR to the district court for Adams county. Tried below before BEALL, J. *Reversed.*

Thomas H. Matters and *Tibbets Bros., Morey & Ferris*, for plaintiff in error.

C. J. Smyth, Attorney General, and *Ed P. Smith, Deputy Attorney General*, contra.

NORVAL, J.

The object of this proceeding is to secure the reversal of a conviction of the crime of burglary. Of the several assignments in the petition in error, consideration will be given to those relating to instructions alone.

This prosecution was brought under section 48 of the Criminal Code, which declares: "If any person shall, in the night-season, willfully, maliciously, and forcibly break and enter into any * * * storehouse, * * with intent to kill, rob, commit a rape, or with intent to steal property of any value, or commit any felony, every person so offending shall be deemed guilty of burglary. and shall be imprisoned in the penitentiary not more than ten nor less than one year." The information charges that the accused burglariously broke and entered, in the night-season, a certain store building with the intent to steal specifically described chattels situate therein of the value of $30, belonging to Parmenter & Ellsworth.

The seventh instruction given at the request of the state is excepted to, which reads as follows:

"7. The court instructs you that it is not necessary for the state to prove beyond a reasonable doubt that the defendant stole and carried away all the property enumerated in the information, but if you believe from the evidence beyond a reasonable doubt that the defendant, Philip Bergeron, feloniously, burglariously, willfully, maliciously, and forcibly did break into and enter the building described in the information, and you further believe that said building was occupied by Parmenter & Ellsworth, and you further believe beyond a reasonable doubt that the said Philip Bergeron, being in said building in the second story thereof, by means of a pole, or any other instrument, reached through the skylight opening in the floor of the second story into the store room of Parmenter & Ellsworth below, in the night-season, and by means of said pole, or other instrument, took any property of value, however small, of Parmenter & Ellsworth, named in the information, and you further believe beyond a reasonable doubt that the said Philip Bergeron so took said property for the purpose and with the intent to steal the same, you are instructed that you shall find the defendant guilty, notwithstanding the fact that you may also believe from the evidence that the said Philip Bergeron did not steal and carry away all of the goods of Parmenter & Ellsworth mentioned in the information."

This instruction purported to include every element of the offense charged, and it told the jury, in effect, if they found the existence, from the evidence, of the enumerated ingredients of the crime, it was their duty to return a verdict of guilty. It is a familiar rule that an instruction is faulty which purports to cover the entire case, but which in fact fails to include all the elements necessarily involved in the case and within the evidence. (*Barnes v. State*, 40 Neb. 545; *McAleer v. State*, 46 Neb. 116.) The instruction quoted omitted important elements of the crime charged, namely, that the breaking and entering of the building occurred in the night-time, and with the intent to steal. Under the instruction the defendant could have been convicted of burglary, even though he broke and entered the building in the daytime for a lawful purpose, in case he subsequently, in the night-time, took property in the building belonging to the complaining witnesses, with the intent to steal the same. On account of the omissions indicated the instruction was erroneous. (*Ashford v. State*, 36 Neb. 38.)

Complaint is made of this instruction given on the request of the state:

"The court instructs the jury if they find beyond a reasonable doubt the defendant did at the time charged in the information, willfully, maliciously, burglariously, and forcibly break and enter said store building, with the intent then and there to steal, take, and carry away the property of the firm of Parmenter & Ellsworth, and although he did not steal, take, and carry away any of said property, yet you should find the defendant guilty."

The court by this instruction attempted to state what was necessary to be proven to entitle the state to a conviction, yet the paragraph of the charge omitted therefrom the question of the value of the property. The section of the Criminal Code already mentioned requires that the property must possess some value to constitute the offense of burglary when the information charges that the breaking and entering were effected with the intent to steal. The instruction likewise leaves out the element of ownership of the building, and fails to state that the property intended to be stolen must have been within the building. These were essential ingredients of the crime. (*Winslow v. State*, 26 Neb. 308.)

The second and eighth instructions on behalf of the state were also erroneous for the reasons already given.

The attorney general has suggested that instructions should be construed as a whole. This is undoubtedly the rule, and if when so considered they state the law correctly, they will be upheld. But this principle is not applicable here, since a good instruction will not cure one which attempts to cover the entire case, but which is palpably bad. (*Burlingim v. Baders*, 45 Neb. 673; *Farmers Bank v. Marshman*, 33 Neb. 445; *Ballard v. State*, 19 Neb. 609.) The judgment is reversed and the cause is remanded for further proceedings.

REVERSED AND REMANDED.

OSCAR BRYANT V. DAKOTA COUNTY.

FILED FEBRUARY 17, 1898. No. 7739.

$$\frac{\overline{53}}{54} \quad 7$$
$$\frac{\overline{53}}{61} \quad 7$$

1. **Statutes:** TITLES: CONSTITUTIONAL LAW: DEFECTIVE HIGHWAY: DAMAGES. The proviso clause of section 4, chapter 7, Laws 1889, which requires an action against a county for injury or damages resulting from a defective public highway to be brought within thirty days after the occurring of such injury or damages, is not inimical to that part of section 11, article 3, of the constitution which declares that "no bill shall contain more than one subject, and the same shall be clearly expressed in its title."

2. ———: REPUGNANCY. An act complete in itself is not unconstitutional, although it may be in conflict with, or repugnant to, a prior statute not referred to nor in express terms repealed.

ERROR from the district court of Dakota county. Tried below before NORRIS, J. *Affirmed.*

Daley & Jay and *Jay & Beck*, for plaintiff in error.

R. E. Evans, contra.

NORVAL, J.

This action was instituted in the court below against Dakota county to recover damages for personal injuries

alleged to have been sustained by the plaintiff by reason
of the defective condition of a certain public highway
which it was the duty of defendant to keep in repair.   A
demurrer to the petition was sustained, and the cause
dismissed; and to obtain a reversal of this ruling is the
purpose of this proceeding.

The record discloses that the suit was commenced more
than thirty days after the alleged injury and damages
occurred, which fact, the defendant insists, is sufficient
to defeat a recovery.   This contention is based upon section 4, chapter 7, Laws 1889 (Compiled Statutes 1897, ch.
78, sec. 117), which reads as follows: "If special damage
happens to any person, his team, carriage, or other property by means of insufficiency, or want of repairs of a
highway or bridge, which the county or counties are
liable to keep in repair, the person sustaining the damage
may recover in a case against the county, and if damages
accrue in consequence of the insufficiency or want of repair of a road or bridge, erected and maintained by two
or more counties, the action can be brought against all
of the counties liable for the repairs of the same, and
damages and costs shall be paid by the counties in proportion as they are liable for the repairs; *Provided, however,* That such action is commenced within thirty (30)
days of the time of said injury or damage occurring."
It is obvious that, if the proviso clause of said section is
valid legislation, the demurrer to the petition was properly sustained, since this suit was not commenced within
the designated period of thirty days.   It is argued by
counsel for plaintiff that said proviso contravenes section 11, article 3, of the constitution, which declares:
"No bill shall contain more than one subject, and the
same shall be clearly expressed in its title.   And no law
shall be amended unless the new act contain the section
or sections so amended and the section or sections so
amended shall be repealed."   It is suggested that the
said act of 1889 is inimical to the above provision for the
reason it embraces two distinct subjects of legislation,

and that one of them alone is expressed in the title. The act is designated as "An act relating to highways and bridges and liabilities of counties for not keeping the same in repair." Prior to the adoption of this piece of legislation there existed in this state no right of action against a county for the recovery of damages resulting from defective public highways or bridges (*Woods v. Colfax County*, 10 Neb. 552), while by the law under consideration the authority to bring such a suit was granted (*Hollingsworth v. Saunders County*, 36 Neb. 141; *Raasch v. Dodge County*, 43 Neb. 508). It is conceded that the purpose to confer such right of action is with sufficient clearness expressed in the title given to the law by the legislature, but it is insisted that such title is not broad enough to include the provision in the body of the act, limiting the period within which the action should be commenced. We are unable to yield assent to the proposition. The legislature had the undoubted right to give the remedy in question, or withhold as it saw proper. So, too, the law-making body had the power in conferring the remedy to attach as a condition that the action should be instituted within a specified length of time; and the remedy was given upon the express condition that it should be invoked within thirty days after the sustaining of the injury or damages. Such limitation was not an independent subject of legislation, but was germane to the principal object and purpose of the law, and was included in the title to the act. As was said in the opinion in *State v. Tibbets*, 52 Neb. 228, "The title to a bill may be general, and it is not essential that it specify every clause in the proposed statute. It is sufficient if they are all referable and cognate to the subject expressed. When the subject is expressed in general terms everything which is necessary to make a complete enactment in regard to it, or which results as a complement of the thought contained in the general expression, is embraced in and authorized by it. If the subject-matter is within the scope of the title, the constitutional require-

ment is met." Tested by this rule it is plain that the
title to the act before us was sufficiently broad and comprehensive to indicate the subject-matter of legislation.
and the requirements of the constitution were fully complied with.

Foxworthy v. City of Hastings. 23 Neb. 772, does not conflict with the views already expressed.   It was there held
that a provision in an act creating cities of the second
class. limiting the time to six months in which actions
may be brought for negligence against any city embraced within such class, was invalid, as being special
legislation. and not because such provision was passed in
violation of section 11. article 3, of the constitution.
Moreover, the act there under consideration created no
right of action. but the obnoxious clause was intended
as a new statute of limitation for an existing remedy or
right of action.

In *Weigel v. City of Hastings,* 29 Neb. 379, it was ruled
that the title of an act providing for the organization.
government, and powers of cities of the second class having over five thousand inhabitants was not sufficiently
comprehensive to include a provision exempting such
cities from liability for damages resulting from the
neglect of a street railway company to keep in a reasonably safe condition the street on which its line is being
constructed.   The provision of the act there condemned
was not germane to the subject-matter of the law expressed in the title, while in the statute under review
the remedy thereby conferred is conditioned upon the
proper steps being taken within a designated period, and
the clause limiting the time for bringing the suit was not
an independent subject of legislation, but was intimately
connected with the main purpose and subject of the act.

Lancaster County v. Trimble, 33 Neb. 121, is not in point
here.   In that case there was under consideration section 1. article 4, chapter 77, Compiled Statutes, which
authorized the foreclosure of tax liens by county commissioners where they have purchased for the county real

estate at tax sales, but limited such right of action to cases where the amount due on the tax certificate exceeds $200. It was decided that the limitation contravened section 4, article 9, of the constitution in that it had the effect to authorize the county commissioners to release the taxes upon lands where the amount of delinquent taxes thereon does not exceed the sum already named. Section 11, article 3, of the constitution was in no manner involved in that case.

The remaining three cases cited by counsel for plaintiff, *State v. Lancaster County*, 17 Neb. 85, *State v. Hurds*, 19 Neb. 323, and *Muldoon v. Levi*, 25 Neb. 457, merely announce the familiar doctrine that where a statute contains provisions which conflict with the constitution, if the valid and invalid portions are capable of separation, the latter alone will be disregarded, in case that it appears that the invalid part was not an inducement to the legislature to pass the remainder of the act.

It is urged that the act before us is bad because it modifies or amends the general statute of limitations contained in the Code, without in any manner referring to the same. A short answer to this line of argument is that the act is complete in itself, and therefore is not inimical to the constitution merely because it may be in conflict with, or repugnant to, some prior statute. For an able discussion of the question and citation of authorities see the opinion of RYAN, C., in *State v. Cornell*, 50 Neb. 526.

For the reason stated the district court did not err in sustaining the demurrer to the petition, and the judgment is accordingly

AFFIRMED.

CITIZENS NATIONAL BANK, APPELLANT, V. ISAAC D.
GREGG, APPELLEE.

FILED FEBRUARY 17, 1898. No. 7748.

1. **Costs:** TAXATION: REVIEW. Where costs have been illegally taxed, the appropriate remedy is by a motion to retax made to the court where the alleged mistake occurred.

2. ————: FEE BILL: INJUNCTION. A court of equity will not enjoin the collection of a fee bill where all the legal costs therein taxed have not been paid or tendered.

APPEAL from the district court of Howard county. Heard below before THOMPSON, J. *Affirmed.*

T. T. Bell, for appellant.

Paul & Templin, contra.

NORVAL, J.

This is an appeal from a decree refusing to enjoin the collection of a fee bill issued out of the district court of Howard county, in a replevin suit determined therein in which the Citizens National Bank was plaintiff and one William W. Kendall, sheriff, was defendant. The writ of replevin was executed by Noah Baxter, the county coroner, who returned the process into court with an itemized statement of his fees, amounting to $15.50. The replevin suit was decided against the plaintiff, and judgment was rendered against it for all costs. The fee bill was issued under section 3, chapter 28, Compiled Statutes, for the said sum claimed to be due the coroner, with seventy-five cents additional for issuing the fee bill. The contention of plaintiff is that the costs have never been taxed in the replevin suit, and furthermore that the total amount of costs was not inserted in the judgment at the time it was journalized. The record shows the rendition of a judgment against the plaintiff for the costs of suit; that the costs, including the amount due the coroner, had been taxed by the clerk of the district court and itemized upon the fee book prior to the issuance of the fee bill.   This was sufficient.   If a mistake was made in the taxation of the costs by the clerk, the appropriate remedy for correcting the error was by motion to retax. (*Woods v. Colfax County*, 10 Neb. 552; *Cozine v. Hatch*, 17 Neb. 694; *Whitall v. Cressman*, 18 Neb. 508; *Wilkinson v. Carter*, 22 Neb. 186; *Hoagland v. Van Etten*, 31 Neb. 293.) In no event could plaintiff enjoin the enforcement of the fee bill until it had first paid, or tendered, all the legal costs chargeable against it.   Unquestionably the sum of $3.75 was due from plaintiff as legal costs, of which amount $3 belonged to the coroner for serving the writ, and the remainder to the clerk for issuing the fee bill. Plaintiff paid all except seventy-five cents of said sum after the fee bill was in the hands of the coroner, but the bank could not invoke the aid of a court of equity, at least until it had paid all costs legally taxed against the bank.   The decree is right and is

AFFIRMED.

JONAS REYNOLDS V. STATE OF NEBRASKA.

FILED FEBRUARY 17, 1898.   No. 9805.

1. **Instructions**: NON-DIRECTION: REVIEW.   Mere non-direction by the court below affords no ground for reversal where a proper instruction covering the point was not requested.

2. **Statutes**: AMENDMENTS.   An act which in its purpose and scope is merely amendatory of a section of a prior statute must set out the new section and, in addition, contain a provision for the repeal of the old section sought to be amended.

3. ———: ———: CONSTITUTIONAL LAW: LARCENY.   The act of the legis'ature of 1875 amendatory of certain sections of the Criminal Co'e, including section 116 relating to stolen goods (Session Laws 1875, p. 1), is void, because it contains no provision for the repeal of the sections amended, as required by section 19, article 2, of the state constitution adopted in 1866.

ERROR to the district court for Hall county. Tried below before KENDALL, J. *Reversed.*

W. A. *Prince*, for plaintiff in error.

C. J. *Smyth, Attorney General,* and *Ed P. Smith, Deputy Attorney General,* for the state.

NORVAL, J.

Jonas Reynolds was convicted of the offense of receiving stolen goods, and he has brought the record of the trial to this court for review, assigning numerous grounds for reversal.

The first contention is that the court erred in not informing the jury, in its instructions, that the defendant had entered a plea of not guilty to the information. There are two ready answers to this suggestion: First, the accused tendered to the trial court no request to instruct the jury upon that point. The rule has been often announced and applied in this court in criminal cases that the mere failure to charge the jury upon a particular proposition is not reversible error, unless a suitable instruction has been tendered. (*Gettinger v. State,* 13 Neb. 308; *Hill v. State,* 42 Neb. 503; *Housh v. State,* 43 Neb. 163; *Barr v. State,* 45 Neb. 458; *Metz v. State,* 46 Neb. 547; *Pjarrou v. State,* 47 Neb. 294; *Johnson v. State,* 53 Neb. 103.) In the second place, the rights of the accused could not have been in the least affected by the failure to advise the jury in specific terms what plea the defendant had entered to the charge against him, since, in several of the instructions, the jury were, in plain and unequivocal language, told that the defendant was presumed to be innocent of the accusation contained in the information, should be acquitted if they entertained a reasonable doubt of his guilt, and that the verdict should be based alone upon the evidence adduced on the trial. In the light of the entire charge, no prejudicial error could possibly have resulted from the omission of the trial judge to state that the prisoner had pleaded not guilty.

Complaint is made of the giving of the fourth instruction, which is in the language following: "You are instructed that the law in this state is that if any person shall receive any goods or chattels of the value of thirty-five dollars or upwards, that shall be stolen or taken by robbers with intent to defraud the owner, every person so offending shall be imprisoned in the penitentiary no more than seven years nor less than one year." The foregoing is a substantial copy of section 116 of the Criminal Code of 1873, as attempted to be amended by the legislature of 1875, at least so far as the said amendatory section is applicable to the charge contained in the information. It is argued that it was reversible error to give the instruction quoted, because it was based upon a void amendment of section 116 of the Criminal Code, which objection was properly made in the court below. In the year 1873 the legislature passed an act entitled "An act to establish a Criminal Code." (General Statutes, p. 719, ch. 58.) Section 116 of said Code is here reproduced: "If any person shall receive or buy any goods or chattels of the value of thirty-five dollars or upward, that shall be stolen or taken by robbers, knowing the same to be stolen or taken by robbers, with intent to defraud the owner; or shall harbor or conceal any thief or robber, knowing him or her to be such, every person so offending shall be imprisoned in the penitentiary not more than seven years, nor less than one year."

The legislature in 1875, by an act entitled "An act to amend sections eight, * * * one hundred and sixteen, * * * of the Criminal Code, chapter 58 of the General Statutes of 1873," attempted to amend forty-one sections of the Criminal Code then in force, including said section 116 relating to the receiving or buying of stolen goods and the harboring or concealing of thieves or robbers. This act of 1875 is not, nor does it purport to be, entirely new legislation, creating a new offense, but is purely amendatory in its nature and character, and contains no provision for the repeal of any of the sections sought to be amended. The new act, it is claimed, is unconstitutional because it contains no repealing clause. The doctrine has been frequently asserted and applied in this state that an act, not complete in itself, but which is merely amendatory of a section of a statute, must set out the section amended and, in addition, contain a provision for the repeal of the old section so amended. (*Ryan v. State*, 5 Neb. 276; *Lancaster County v. Hoagland*, 8 Neb. 38; *City of South Omaha v. Taxpayers' League*, 42 Neb. 671; *State v. City of Kearney*, 49 Neb. 325; *State v. Tibbets*, 52 Neb. 228.)

The suggestion of the attorney general that the amended section 116 was enacted prior to the adoption of the present constitution is no sufficient answer to the objection urged against the validity of the section by counsel for the accused, since said act of 1875 contravened section 19, article 2, of the state constitution adopted in 1866, which declares that "no law shall be revived or amended, unless the new act contains the entire act revived, and the sections amended, and the section or sections so amended shall be repealed." The provision just quoted is substantially the same as the latter part of section 11, article 3, of the constitution of 1875. The amendatory section 116 of the Criminal Code was not adopted in the mode prescribed by the constitution of the state at that time in force, for the reason the amendatory act contained no provision for the repeal of the original section attempted to be amended, as required by said section 19, article 2, of the constitution of 1866. It follows that said amendatory section 116 is unconstitutional, and void, and the original section remains in full force and effect.

The amendatory section 116 did not contain the words "knowing the same to be stolen or taken by robbers," which were incorporated in the original section, nor does the amended section contain language of like import. Under the old section *scienter*, or knowledge of the accused that the property had been stolen or taken by robbers, was an element of the crime as originally defined, while the legislature by the latter act attempted to eliminate from the statute this feature of the offense. It requires no argument to show that the fourth instruction omitted to state one of the ingredients of the crime, and was accordingly prejudicial to the accused. Under that instruction the jury would have been justified in finding the defendant guilty, even though he had no knowledge that the goods described in the information had been stolen. It is true the record before us discloses that the trial judge, after verdict, but before passing sentence, read to the prisoner said original section 116 and the section as amended, and inquired of him whether he had anything to say why judgment should not be pronounced. It is obvious the reading of the original section at that time could not cure the error in giving the fourth instruction.

The conclusion reached makes unnecessary an examination or consideration of the other assignments of error. The judgment is reversed and cause remanded for a new trial.

REVERSED AND REMANDED.

JULIUS H. LANGHORST V. WILLIAM COON.

FILED FEBRUARY 17, 1898. No. 7740.

1. **Instructions:** REVIEW. An assignment of error against an entire charge is unavailing where one of the instructions is faultless.

2. **Review:** INSTRUCTIONS: ASSIGNMENTS OF ERROR. Errors in respect to refusing instructions must be separately assigned in the motion for a new trial and petition in error.

3. **Real Estate Agents:** COMPENSATION. Ordinarily a real estate broker, who for a commission undertakes to sell land on certain terms and within a specified period, is not entitled to compensation for

his services unless he produce to the owner a purchaser within the time limited who is able and willing to buy upon the terms prescribed in the contract of employment.

4. **Review: Conflicting Evidence.** A verdict based upon conflicting evidence will not be disturbed on review.

ERROR from the district court of Cass county. Tried below before CHAPMAN, J. *Affirmed.*

J. H. Haldeman. for plaintiff in error.

Beeson & Root, contra.

NORVAL, J.

Plaintiff sued to recover commissions for effecting the sale of real estate, and from the judgment rendered against him he prosecutes an error proceeding.

Complaint is made in the brief of the giving of five instructions. The charge of the court consisted of seven consecutively numbered paragraphs, and they were all grouped in a single assignment in the motion for a new trial, as well as in the petition in error. Two of the seven instructions are not assailed in the brief, and an examination of them convinces the court that they are faultless; therefore, the assignment relating to the giving of instructions will not be further considered. (*Union P. R. Co. v. Montgomery*, 49 Neb. 429; *Adams-Smith Co. v. Hayward*, 52 Neb. 79.)

Error is assigned for the refusal to give instructions 1 to 5 requested by plaintiff. Two of these requests are not included in the transcript, and the third was properly refused, because it was practically an instruction to return a verdict for plaintiff. Under the authorities the other requests need not be considered, since they were not separately assigned for error in the motion for a new trial and petition in error.

It is finally argued that the evidence fails to sustain the verdict. The testimony was conflicting. That introduced by plaintiff tended to show that he was employed by the defendant to procure a purchaser of the farm of the latter at a specified price, and was to receive as commissions for his services the sum of $400, and that in pursuance of such agreement plaintiff did induce one Peter Reutter to buy the land. On the other side, testimony was adduced to the effect that plaintiff was given two weeks in which to procure a purchaser for the farm, and that plaintiff was to receive for his services all in excess of $9,200; that at the expiration of that period he informed the defendant that he could not make the sale for said sum, and afterwards defendant himself sold the land to Reutter for said sum. The conflicting testimony was submitted to the jury under appropriate instructions, and the proofs are ample to sustain a finding in favor of the defendant. If the contract of employment was conditional, plaintiff could not recover without establishing that the conditions on his part to be performed had been fulfilled. (*Beatty v. Russell*, 41 Neb. 321; *Barber v. Hildebrand*, 42 Neb. 400.) It is a fact that plaintiff was instrumental in enabling defendant to dispose of his farm to Reutter, but plaintiff stipulated as to the terms upon which he was to receive a compensation, and these stipulations cannot be disregarded. The delay in making the sale was through no fault of defendant, so far as the record discloses. The judgment is

AFFIRMED.

STATE OF NEBRASKA, EX REL. SETH THOMAS CLOCK COMPANY, V. BOARD OF COUNTY COMMISSIONERS OF CASS COUNTY ET AL.

FILED FEBRUARY 17, 1898. No. 7859.

1. **Counties:** ALLOWANCE OF CLAIMS: MANDAMUS. One in whose favor a claim has been duly allowed by a county board may, by mandamus, compel the issuance of a warrant for the payment of such claim.

2. ——: ——: REVIEW. The validity of an order of a county board allowing a claim cannot be raised for the first time in this court in a case brought here by appeal or petition in error.

3. Corporation: EXISTENCE: PLEADING. A denial that the relator "is a corporation duly organized under the laws of the state of New York" does not put in issue the relator's corporate existence.

4. Payment: EVIDENCE. Evidence examined, and *held* insufficient to sustain respondents' plea of payment.

ERROR from the district court of Cass county. Tried below before CHAPMAN, J. *Reversed.*

A. W. *Agee* and *Byron Clark,* for plaintiff in error.

C. S. *Polk* and *H. D. Travis, contra.*

SULLIVAN, J.

By a petition in error filed in this court, the Seth Thomas Clock Company seeks a reversal of a judgment of the district court for Cass county denying its application for a peremptory writ of mandamus against the county commissioners and county clerk of said county. From an examination of the record it appears that in the year 1891 the county of Cass purchased of the relator a tower clock for use in its new court house, then in process of construction. The negotiations which resulted in the sale were conducted by one Charles Wickersham, who resided at Plattsmouth and managed his wife's jewelry business in that city. The wife's name was S. L. Wickersham. The clock company had no knowledge of either of the Wickershams, except what it gained through correspondence in relation to the transaction here in question. This correspondence was carried on in the name of S. L. or Susan L. Wickersham. The contract of sale was in writing. It was executed on behalf of the relator by Wickersham in the name of his wife. In due time the clock was forwarded to Platts-mouth, consigned to S. L. Wickersham, and some time later, with the assistance of an expert sent out by the relator, was set in place and accepted. Soon after the acceptance, a bill for $981, that being the contract price, was filed with the county clerk, allowed by the county board, and a warrant therefor, payable to the relator or bearer, was issued and delivered by the county clerk to Charles Wickersham, who converted it to his own use. To compel the issuance and delivery to it of another warrant for the amount of its claim the relator brought this suit.

The respondents attempt to justify the finding and judgment of the trial court on four distinct grounds. In their answer they pleaded payment of relator's claim "by delivering to S. L. Wickersham, the agent of relator, a warrant, No. 132, for the payment of $981;" and they now insist that this defense is established by the evidence. But we think otherwise. S. L. Wickersham was a real person; she resided, and was engaged in business, at Plattsmouth. She was the person the relator had in mind, and upon whom it conferred authority to act for it, in its dealings with Cass county. There is in the record no legal evidence whatever from which it could be inferred that Charles Wickersham was the owner of the jewelry business which was conducted in the name of S. L. Wickersham, or that the latter name was assumed and used by him for business purposes. The relator did not intend to make Wickersham its agent; it conferred upon him no authority, real or apparent. The contract of sale itself recites that it is made with S. L. Wickersham as agent of the relator; and the county clerk, at the time he delivered the warrant to Charles Wickersham, dealt with him, not as the agent of the clock company, but as the agent of his wife. We quote from the testimony of Frank Dixon, the county clerk:

Q. Now you never heard this Wickersham called anything but Charles Wickersham or C. W. Wickersham, did you?

A. Yes, sir; heard him called C. M. Wickersham.

Q. Now, the facts are, that your understanding of the

53

matter was that S. L. Wickersham was the wife of
Charles Wickersham of whom you have spoken, and acting as her agent in the transaction of the business in
which she was engaged in this city?

A. That was the understanding that I had.

Q. And you delivered to him this warrant, supposing
he was the agent of S. L. Wickersham, and transacting
all of her business for her?

A. Yes, sir.

Q. And that was the reason that you delivered it to
him?

A. Yes, sir.

While Wickersham had, doubtless, general authority
to manage his wife's business, she could confer upon him
no power to act for the relator in relation to its business.
(*Furnas v. Frankman*, 6 Neb. 429; *Ingraham v. Whitmore*,
75 Ill. 24; *Brown v. Railway*, 45 Mo. 221; *McKinnon v.
Vollmar*, 75 Wis. 82.) She had no actual authority to
appoint a subagent, and the nature of the business to be
transacted conferred no implied authority to do so. We,
therefore, conclude that the plea of payment was not
sustained.

It is urged as a second defense that if Wickersham was
not the agent of the relator, the delivery of the warrant
to him was a conversion of it for which there is a plain
and adequate remedy at law to which it must resort.
This position is obviously unsound. After the expiration of ten days from the allowance of the relator's claim.
it became entitled to receive from the respondents a warrant in due form, which it might present to the county
treasurer for payment. The duty to deliver the warrant
was one due to the relator from the respondents in their
official capacity and was enforceable by mandamus.
(*State v. Spicer*, 36 Neb. 469; *State v. Farney*, 36 Neb. 537;
Boasen v. State, 47 Neb. 245.)

It is next insisted that the claim allowed by the county
board was not verified, and hence the order of allowance
was null. Without conceding the correctness of the

legal proposition here contended for, it is sufficient to say that the answer having admitted the allowance of the claim, the respondents are not now in a position to question the validity of the order of allowance.

It is further urged, in support of the judgment, that the corporate character of the relator was not established by the proof, and that it, therefore, did not possess legal capacity to maintain this action. The application for the writ alleges that the relator "is a corporation duly organized under the laws of the state of New York." The answer denies "that the Seth Thomas Clock Company is a corporation duly organized under the laws of New York." This denial is a mere negative pregnant. It does not traverse the corporate existence of the relator, but only the regularity of the proceedings by which it was incorporated. (Boone, Code Pleading 61; Bliss, Code Pleading 332; *Harden v. Atchison & N. R. Co.;* 4 Neb. 521; *Leroux v. Murdock,* 51 Cal. 541.)

The evidence in the record conclusively establishes relator's right to a warrant for the amount of his claim as allowed by the county board, together with legal interest thereon. Therefore, the judgment is reversed, and the cause remanded.

REVERSED AND REMANDED.

UNITED STATES WIND ENGINE & PUMP COMPANY V. H. P. DREXEL ET AL.

FILED FEBRUARY 17, 1898.   No. 7843.

1. **Bonds:** VALIDITY: DEFECTS. A statutory bond is not void for want of a penalty nor because the beneficiaries are named as obligees therein, instead of a trustee according to the requirement of the statute under which it is given.

2. ——: APPROVAL: PUBLIC BUILDINGS. A bond for the protection of persons furnishing labor or material for the erection of a public building under the laws of the state of Iowa does not be-

come a binding obligation until accepted and approved by the officer charged by law with that duty.

3. ——: ——: DEFECTS. The approval of an irregular bond limited to certain beneficiaries named therein and based on an express waiver of their rights, is a rejection of such bond as to all other persons for whose benefit it was intended. HARRISON, C. J., and NORVAL, J., concur in the judgment for the reason stated in the third division of the syllabus alone.

ERROR from the district court of Douglas county. Tried below before HOPEWELL, J. *Affirmed.*

The opinion contains a statement of the case.

Cavanagh & Thomas, for plaintiff in error:

Obligors cannot escape liability, because the bond does not run to the county. (*Heatherington v. Hayden,* 11 Ia. 335; *Pursley v. Hayes,* 22 Ia. 29; *Huffman v. Koppelkom,* 8 Neb. 344; *Koppelkom v. Huffman,* 12 Neb. 95; *Thomas v. Hinkley,* 19 Neb. 324; *Riggs v. Miller,* 34 Neb. 666; *Fillows v. Gilman,* 4 Wend. [N. Y.] 414; *Faurote v. State,* 110 Ind. 463.)

The bond is not void for want of a penalty. (*Dodge v. St. John,* 96 N. Y. 260; *Williams v. Golden,* 10 Neb. 432; *Noble v. Himeo,* 12 Neb. 193.)

The defense that the bond was not delivered and accepted should not be sustained. If the bond was a statutory one, it was deposited where the statute directed. If the bond was a common law bond, placing it with the treasurer was a delivery. (*McCracken v. Todd,* 1 Kan. 148; *Green v. Wardwell,* 17 Ill. 278; *Ashkum v. Lake,* 12 Brad. [Ill. App.] 29.)

B. G. Burbank, H. C. Brome, and *A. A. McClanahan, contra.*

SULLIVAN, J.

The United States Wind Engine & Pump Company. by this proceeding in error, challenges the correctness of the order and judgment of the district court for Douglas county sustaining a demurrer to its petition and dismissing its action. The material allegations of the petition are in substance as follows:

1. It is the assignee and owner of a subcontractor's claim, amounting to $4,000, due for labor and material furnished in the erection of a court house for Montgomery county, in the state of Iowa.

2. The laws of Iowa give subcontractors a lien for all material and labor furnished in the erection of public buildings not owned by the state.

3. The statute giving such lien provides:

"Sec. 4. The contractor may at any time release such claim by filing with the treasurer of such corporation a bond to such corporation, for the benefit of such claimants, in sufficient penalty, with sureties to be approved by such treasurer, conditioned for the payment of any such sum which may be found due such claimant, and such contractor may prevent the filing of such claims by filing in like manner a bond conditioned for the payment of persons who may be entitled to file such claims."

4. In February, 1891, Richards & Co. as principal, with the defendants in this action as sureties, signed and delivered to the treasurer of Montgomery county a bond conditioned as follows:

"Now, therefore, we, Richards & Co., as principals, and H. P. Drexel, E. J. Refregier, E. A. Blum, J. H. Hulbert, and Albert Foll, as sureties, for the purpose of releasing the claim now on file with the auditor of Montgomery county, Iowa, in favor of the Northwestern Terra Cotta Company, which claim is a mechanic's lien against a public corporation, to-wit, Montgomery county, Iowa, and for the purpose of preventing the filing of any mechanic's lien for material furnished or work and labor performed in the building and erection of said court house, for which the persons furnishing said material and performing said labor would under the laws of the state of Iowa be entitled to file a mechanic's lien against said public corporation, to-wit, Montgomery county, Iowa, and for

the use and benefit of said Northwestern Terra Cotta
Company, and for the use and benefit of such other persons who now have or shall hereafter have a right to file
a mechanic's lien against said public corporation, Montgomery county, for materials furnished or work and
labor performed, and for the purpose of paying any and
all sum or sums found to be due the said Northwestern
Terra Cotta Company from Richards & Co. aforesaid.
and for the purpose of paying any and all sums due from
said Richards & Co. to any and all persons for materials
furnished or to be furnished, or for work and labor done
or to be done, for which any of said persons have now.
or may hereafter have a right to file a mechanic's lien
against said public corporation, Montgomery county,
Iowa, for said labor, work, or materials done or furnished, this obligation is executed, and we bind ourselves
and assigns to pay any such sum or sums so found to be
due said Northwestern Terra Cotta Company or any
other person or persons as hereinbefore mentioned.
This obligation is executed for the use and benefit of all
persons who now have or who may have hereafter a right
to file a mechanic's lien against said Montgomery county.
Iowa, under and by virtue of the provisions of sections
3322, 3327, 3328, and 3329 of McClain's Annotated Code
of Iowa, edition of 1888, being the laws of the 20 G. A.,
chapter 179, sections 1 to 4 inclusive, for materials furnished or to be furnished, or work or labor done or to be
done, in the building and erection of a court house at
Red Oak Junction, Montgomery county, Iowa, said court
house being erected and built by the said Richards & Co.
aforesaid."

Afterwards the county treasurer indorsed upon said
bond his approval in the following terms:

"It appearing to me that the Northwestern Terra Cotta
Company, of Chicago, Ill., has now and claims the right
to file a mechanic's lien or claim against Montgomery
county for materials furnished in the building of the
court house for said county;

"And it also appearing to me that Carnegie, Phipps & Co. claim to have the right now and hereafter to file a lien against said county for materials furnished and labor performed and to be hereafter furnished;

"And each of corporations and persons having consented in writing by me now held that non-resident sureties may file a bond:

"Now, as to the Northwestern Terra Cotta Company and Carnegie, Phipps & Co., the within and foregoing bond is now by me filed and approved this February 9th, 1891.   JOEL CAREY,
"Treasurer of Montgomery County, Iowa."

5. The labor and material which are the basis of this action were furnished in reliance upon the bond above mentioned; and plaintiff's assignor relying thereon, permitted Richards & Co., the principal contractor, to draw from Montgomery county the whole amount due according to the terms of the contract.

The bond in question was not in strict conformity with the provisions of the statute under which it was given, inasmuch as it fixed no penalty and failed to name Montgomery county as the obligee therein. But these defects would not vitiate it. They are mere irregularities affecting in no manner the substantial elements of the contract. (*Noble v. Himeo*, 12 Neb. 197; *Williams v. Golden*, 10 Neb. 432; *Dodge v. St. John*, 96 N. Y. 260; *Fellows v. Gilman*, 4 Wend. [N. Y.] 414; *Huffman v. Koppelkom*, 8 Neb. 344; *Koppelkom v. Huffman*, 12 Neb. 95; *Thomas v. Hinkley*, 19 Neb. 324; *Riggs v. Miller*, 34 Neb. 666.)

But was the bond delivered for the use and benefit of the plaintiff? That it was so tendered must be admitted, but to make it effective required not only a tender but an acceptance as well. To make it a binding obligation required that indispensable element of all valid contracts, a meeting of the minds of the contracting parties.

Richards & Co. presented to the county treasurer the contract in suit. The treasurer was an officer charged

by law with the duty of accepting such bond if found
sufficient in substance and form.   It was not sufficient
in form and he evidently was not satisfied with it because the sureties were non-residents of the state of
Iowa.   He, therefore, as appears from his indorsement
and as he rightfully might do, rejected it as a statutory
bond.   His acceptance of it "as to the Northwestern
Terra Cotta Company and Carnegie, Phipps & Co." was,
by the clearest implication, a rejection of it as to all others for whose benefit it was tendered.   In acting on this
bond he, in effect, declared: "This bond is not in conformity with the statute.   The sureties are non-residents
of the state, nevertheless, at the special instance of the
Northwestern Terra Cotta Company and Carnegie,
Phipps & Co., I accept and approve it for their benefit
only, reserving to all other subcontractors the right to
file their statutory liens."   To hold the defendants liable
in this case would be to charge them upon an unaccepted
offer of suretyship.   The judgment of the district court is

AFFIRMED.

AMOSKEAG SAVINGS BANK, APPELLEE, V. OLIVER ROB-
BINS ET AL., APPELLANTS.

FILED FEBRUARY 17, 1898.   No. 7803.

1. **Judicial Sales**: NOTICE: OBJECTIONS.   It is not a good objection to
   the confirmation of a sale of real estate made under a decree of
   foreclosure that the notice of sale did not accurately state the sum
   for the satisfaction of which the land would be sold.

2. ———: APPRAISEMENT: REVIEW.   The finding of the district court
   upon conflicting evidence that an appraisement was not fraudulent will, ordinarily, be sustained.

3. ———: ———: INCUMBRANCES.   When there is no error in the appraisement of land sold under a decree of foreclosure, the owner
   can not complain because the county clerk's certificate, furnished
   to the sheriff as required by section 491c of the Code of Civil Procedure, includes the mortgages which are the basis of the decree.

4. ————: SHERIFF'S RETURN: TIME. A foreclosure sale should be confirmed, notwithstanding the order of sale, issued by the clerk of the district court to the sheriff or other officer directing him to execute the decree, be returned more than sixty days from its date.

APPEAL from the district court of Buffalo county. Heard below before HOLCOMB, J. *Affirmed.*

Francis G. Hamer and *J. M. Easterling,* for appellants.

Dryden & Main, contra.

SULLIVAN, J.

This case is here on appeal from an order of the district court of Buffalo county confirming a sale of real estate made under a decree of foreclosure.

The first objection is that the notice of sale did not correctly state the amount due one Hawkins as fixed by the decree. The record shows that Hawkins was given a lien on the premises sold for $420, with ten per cent interest from December 22, 1893, while the notice of sale recites that the amount is $420, with interest thereon from December 22, 1892. We do not understand what baleful influence this variance had upon appellants' rights. We know of no law that requires the amount due on a decree of foreclosure to be stated in the notice of sale with mathematical accuracy. The notice would have fully answered the requirements of the statute without stating any amount whatever.

The claim that the appraisement was fraudulent was submitted to the district court upon conflicting evidence and we are bound by the conclusion reached.

It is next urged against the order of confirmation that the certificate of the county clerk shows both mortgages foreclosed in the action as prior incumbrances on the land in question. The clerk's certificate exhibits all the liens and incumbrances affecting this land appearing upon the records of his office. But these mortgages were not deducted from the gross value of the land in making the appraisement, so, of course, this objection is without merit.

Appellants contend, finally, that confirmation should have been denied because the order of sale was returned into court by the sheriff more than sixty days after it was issued. In the case of *Rector r. Rotton*, 3 Neb. 171, this question was considered and decided. In the opinion LAKE, J., uses the following language: "In case of foreclosure, which is a proceeding *in rem*, the decree of the court operates directly upon the mortgaged property; no writ or other process of the court is resorted to to bring it within its jurisdiction. By its judgment the court simply enforces a contract of sale voluntarily made by the owner. Nor is it at all necessary that an order of sale be issued by the clerk of the court to the officer charged with the execution of a decree; the judgment is his warrant of authority, and none other is required." The rule thus announced was subsequently affirmed in *Johnson v. Bemis*, 7 Neb. 224, in *Wyant v. Tuthill*, 17 Neb. 495, and in *Johnson r. Colby*, 52 Neb. 327. There has never been any departure from it. It is still the doctrine of this court. In the case of *Burkett v. Clark*, 46 Neb. 466, cited as supporting appellants' contention, the question whether an order of sale must be returned within sixty days from its date was neither presented by the petition in error nor argued in the briefs of counsel. Consequently, what is said on that subject is *obiter*. In that case the judgment of the district court confirming the sale was reversed because the land was advertised for sale before it was appraised, and for the further reason that the sheriff did not forthwith deposit in the office of the clerk of the district court a copy of the appraisement, including the certificates of liens and his application therefor. At page 474 of the opinion it is said: "The officer having levied upon the property, and having appraised the interest of the execution defendant therein, section 491*d* provides that he 'shall forthwith deposit a copy of' the appraisement made, together with the written application made by him to the clerk of the district court, county treasurer, and register of deeds, and the certificates furnished by them to him, in the office of the clerk of the court from which the execution which he holds was issued.   After this deposit has been made, the statute (Code of Civil Procedure, sec. 491*d*) provides that the officer 'shall immediately advertise the real estate.' It will thus be seen that the officer holding an execution for the sale of real estate has not authority to advertise the same for sale until he has levied upon it, caused it to be appraised, and deposited in the office of the clerk, from which the execution in his hands was issued, a copy of the appraisement made by him and the two freeholders, together with the application in writing for liens made by him to the clerk of the district court, the county treasurer, and the register of deeds, and the certificates which such officers furnished him in pursuance of said application."   The only point in the syllabus bearing upon this question is the 16th, wherein it is said: "An officer holding an execution and having levied the same upon real estate, whether he has offered it for sale or not, and if he has offered it for sale, whether he has sold it or not, must return the execution within sixty days from its date, stating what he has done under it."   The sale in this case having been made in pursuance of the decree and in strict conformity therewith, it cannot concern the appellants when the order of sale was returned or whether one was ever issued.   The judgment of the district court is

AFFIRMED.

GEORGE A. BENNETT, SHERIFF, v. C. A. WARNER.

FILED FEBRUARY 17, 1898.   No. 7845.

Attachment: FRAUDULENT CONVEYANCES: EVIDENCE. Evidence examined, and *held* sufficient to entitle the defendant to have the
case submitted to the jury on the theory that the sale in question
was mere'y colorable and made to hinder or delay a creditor in
the collection of his claim.

ERROR from the district court of Douglas county.
Tried below before BLAIR, J.   *Reversed.*

W. S. Shoemaker, for plaintiff in error.

Horton & Blackburn, contra.

SULLIVAN, J.

Under a peremptory direction of the trial court the
jury in this case returned a verdict for Warner, who was
plaintiff below.   To secure a reversal of the judgment
rendered on this verdict Bennett prosecutes error to this
court.   The facts are these: In 1893, and for several
years before that time, H. G. Gwynne was engaged at
Pocatello, Idaho, in buying hides and wool, which he
shipped for sale to his uncle, D. H. McDaneld, who was
engaged in the commission business in Chicago, Illinois.
As a result of their dealings Gwynne became indebted
to McDaneld in a sum claimed by the latter to be in the
neighborhood of $4,000.   A misunderstanding in regard
to this indebtedness having arisen between the parties,
their business relations were terminated some time prior
to July, 1893.   Some time in October of the same year
Gwynne left Pocatello for Chicago, instructing his man-
ager, McCarty, before starting, to call on Warner for
any money he might need during his absence.   Acting
on his instructions, McCarty did soon after obtain from
Warner $40 at one time and $50 at another time.   A
little later, on October 24, McCarty again applied to

Warner for an advancement. Warner, however, refused
to further respond in the way of a loan, but proposed to
buy a car-load of hides if McCarty had authority to sell.
McCarty thought he possessed the necessary power to
make the sale and accordingly made it, taking in payment Warner's check for the price agreed upon, less the
$90 previously loaned. The hides were then consigned
in Warner's name to John Miller & Co., a Chicago commission firm. While at Omaha, in transit, they were
seized by Bennett, sheriff of Douglas county, as the property of Gwynne, under an order of attachment, in an action commenced against him by D. H. McDaneld. The
alleged wrongful seizure of this property is the basis of
the judgment of which the plaintiff in error complains.

Warner had been at one time in the employ of Gwynne
in the hide and wool business, but, having been admitted
to the bar in 1891, he then engaged, and has since continued, in the practice of his profession at Pocatello.
He was the friend and legal adviser of Gwynne. He
knew the latter was indebted to McDaneld, and that, on
account of some misunderstanding in regard to that indebtedness, their business relations had been discontinued. He had talked with McDaneld about the matter and promised to use his good offices with Gwynne to
bring about an adjustment of the differences between
them. He knew that in the previous July, McDaneld
had sued Gwynne and attached a car-load of hides
owned by him and then in transit from Pocatello to the
city of New York. He knew that Gwynne was worth
about $20,000 and that McDaneld was his only creditor.
It does not appear that he had ever before advanced
Gwynne any money, or that he had bought any hides of
him or anybody else during the course of his professional
career. Neither does it appear why Gwynne expected
Warner to act as his bank during his absence or why it
became necessary to resort to him for loans with which
to conduct his ordinary business transactions. The
business of Gwynne was to buy hides at Pocatello and

sell them in the eastern markets, and it does not appear that either he or McCarty had ever before sold hides in the market where they were purchased. The defendant below tried the case on the theory that the sale to War- ner was colorable merely and made to prevent an attach- ment of the hides by McDaneld in Chicago or while in transit to that city. This theory was not without evi- dential support and should have been given to the jury under proper instructions. In the light of the evidence detailed, it was for the jury to say whether the transac- tion in question was an honest or corrupt one. *(Connelly v. Edgerton, 22 Neb. 82; Fitzgerald v. Meyer, 25 Neb. 77; Riley v. Melquist, 23 Neb. 474; Davis v. Scott, 22 Neb. 154.)* The judgment of the district court is reversed and the cause remanded.

REVERSED AND REMANDED.

PHENIX INSURANCE COMPANY OF BROOKLYN V. LOUIS SLOBODISKY.

FILED FEBRUARY 17, 1898. No. 7836.

Insurance: ACTION ON POLICY: PLEADING: EVIDENCE: BREACH OF CONTRACT: ESTOPPEL. Where an insurance company in its an- swer denies that it entered into a contract for the issuance of a policy of insurance on plaintiff's property in the usual or in any other form, such company cannot be permitted to offer in evidence a blank policy of the usual form for the purpose of showing the existence of certain conditions, restrictions, and warranties, with a view to showing such breaches thereof as, by the terms of the policy, operated to render it void.

ERROR from the district court of Douglas county. Tried below before KEYSOR, J. *Affirmed.*

Jacob Fawcett and *Greene & Breckenridge,* for plaintiff in error.

Parke Godwin and *John D. Howe, contra.*

RYAN, C.

This proceeding is for the reversal of a judgment rendered by the district court of Douglas county against
the Phenix Insurance Company of Brooklyn, New York.
The petition in said district court contained averments
to the effect that, February 14, 1893, plaintiff was the
owner of certain described personal property of which
the defendant agreed to become the insurer to an amount
equal to $2,000, but not in excess of $5,000, for a period
of one year, in consideration of the payment of $30, and
agreed to make and deliver to plaintiff a policy of insurance for $2,000 in the usual form of such policies is-
sued by the defendant. It was further alleged in the
petition that by the terms of the policies issued by the
defendant in the usual form the said defendant promised
to indemnify the assured against loss or damage by fire
of the property described to an amount not exceeding
the cash value thereof at the time of such loss, and in no
event to exceed the sum of insurance, and the said
amount to be paid by defendant sixty days after proofs
of loss of said property shall have been made by the assured and received by the defendant and the loss shall
have been ascertained by the arbitrators appointed and
the loss proved in accordance with the terms and provisions of such policy, or unless the company shall have
given notice of their intention to replace, rebuild, or repair the property damaged or destroyed within said sixty
days. It was further averred in the petition that, February 20, 1893, while the said agreement to insure was
in full force, the property insured was destroyed by fire
and that its value was $7,000, no part of which had ever
been paid by the defendant. It was also alleged in the
petition that plaintiff had furnished proofs of loss and
in all other respects complied with the conditions of said
agreement and policy on his part to be performed.
There was a prayer for judgment in the sum of $2,000,
with interest thereon from February 21, 1893. The an-

swer of the insurance company contained the following
averments: "It admits that on the 21st day of February,
1893, the dwelling-house and household furniture and
other personal property described in plaintiff's petition
were partially damaged by fire, but denies that the same
were totally destroyed by fire, and denies that said
household furniture and other personal property was of
the value set out in plaintiff's petition, and denies each
and every other allegation in plaintiff's petition contained. As a further defense to plaintiff's action the
defendant alleges that no completed contract of insurance was ever entered into between the plaintiff and defendant for the insurance set out in plaintiff's petition,
and that no policy of insurance was ever executed or
delivered to the plaintiff for any of the insurance set
out in plaintiff's petition; and that no money or premium of any kind was ever paid to the defendant by
plaintiff or any of the insurance set out in plaintiff's
petition." Following the above language there were
averments in the answer to the effect that the usual form
of policy which defendant was issuing on said February
17, 1893, to its patrons in Omaha contained certain conditions, restrictions, limitations, agreements, and warranties which were described at great length. By these
it was provided that the policies should become void if
the insured property should be sold, transferred, or incumbered, and it was provided that all representations
as to the condition of the title upon which the policy
issued should be deemed warranties, which, if broken,
should render the policy void. By its answer the insurance company pleaded that the property was incumbered February 17, 1893, etc., and upon these facts
pleaded that the policy was void. In the course of the
trial there was an offer in evidence of a policy by the
defendant of the usual form. The court refused to permit the introduction of this policy and the errors argued
in this case depend upon this ruling.

In making proof to entitle him to recover, plaintiff

followed the averments of his petition which have already been described. There was no cross-examination as to whether or not the usual form of policy contained the conditions, provisions, restrictions, or warranties set up in the answer. The proofs made by plaintiff, if believed by the jury, entitled him to recover. There was, therefore, no such condition as we can imagine might exist, when, under a denial, proof of the usual contents of a policy would be admissible. If it had been admitted in evidence, the usual form of policy could have subserved no purpose of the defendant, except to show that there were certain conditions, restrictions, and warranties, the breach of which destroyed plaintiff's cause of action. In other words, the introduction of the usual form of policy was material for only one purpose, and that was to serve as a basis for an affirmative defense. In *Home Fire Ins. Co. v. Fallon*, 45 Neb. 554, it has been held that where an insurance company, either before suit brought or by answer in the action, denies that the policy was in force when the loss occurred, it cannot avail itself of a provision in the policy that no action shall be brought until sixty days after proofs of loss and adjustment. The principle on consideration of which the conclusion just stated was reached is of controlling force with respect to the error herein assigned. A party cannot deny the existence of a contract and at the same time insist that such contract contained conditions for his protection. In other words, there must be a confession if he would avail himself of an avoidance.

There is found in the record no prejudicial error and the judgment of the district court is

AFFIRMED.

HELEN W. CHANDLER, APPELLANT, V. JAMES PYOTT ET
AL., APPELLEES.

FILED FEBRUARY 17, 1898.   No. 7826.

1. **Principal and Agent:** PAYMENT. A party who pays money to another to be applied on a note which such person has not in his possession, assumes the burden of showing the authority of such person to receive payment.

2. **Mortgages:** PAYMENT TO AGENT. The mere facts that a mortgagor had sent coupons, as they matured, to a certain person to whom the amounts thereby evidenced as due had been paid, and that the person so receiving such payments had delivered or even advanced the amount of such coupons to one to whom before maturity had been transferred the principal negotiable promissory note secured by mortgage, *held* not sufficient to satisfy the above requirement as to a payment to such person of principal and interest made before the same became due.

APPEAL from the district court of York county. Heard below before BATES, J. *Reversed.*

Sedgwick & Power, for appellant.

Harlan & Taylor and *J. W. Merriam,* contra.

RYAN, C.

In her petition filed in the district court of York county Helen W. Chandler prayed the foreclosure of a certain trust deed for the security of a certain negotiable promissory note of date April 1, 1889, by its terms due April 1, 1894. The payee named in this note was the Western Investment Bank of Chicago. The interest, at the rate of seven per cent per annum, was payable in semi-annual installments on the first days of April and October, respectively, as evidenced by coupons for $73.50 each. To secure the payment of said note and interest the makers thereof, Martha Pyott and James Pyott, executed a trust deed to William P. Kimball, by the terms of which, as trustee, Kimball was authorized, upon default of payment of principal or of interest existing for a certain time, to institute and prosecute foreclosure proceedings against the land described in the aforesaid trust deed, and on such proceedings to receive payment. There were paid to Kimball September 26, 1892, the sums of $1,000 as principal and $73.50 as interest. This money was never received by Mrs. Chandler, and the question in the district court was whether she must bear the loss or whether it must be borne by Wilhelm Gocke, who, meantime, had become the owner of the land described in the trust deed and had sent that money to Kimball. The judgment was in favor of the defendants.

William P. Kimball was president of the Western Investment Bank of Chicago until May 3, 1891, when said bank transferred its bankable assets to the Central Trust & Savings Bank. To close up the affairs of said Western Investment Bank its cashier, Mr. Vose, and James Frake were constituted a committee and so acted. After the transfer of the banking business above noted William P. Kimball conducted a loan business until August, 1893, when he failed. His testimony was to the effect that he never learned of the payment of the $1,073.50 above noted until his financial embarrassment did not admit of his making payment of the money to Mrs. Chandler. It is clear that, as trustee, Mr. Kimball was not authorized to receive payments unless they were made upon foreclosure proceedings instituted by him as trustee. The powers of the trustee were thus limited by the trust deed, and beyond this limitation the trustee as such had no power to act. (*Stark v. Olsen*, 44 Neb. 647.) His authority to receive the payment, concerning which this litigation has been carried on, if it existed, must therefore be found in his real or apparent agency for Mrs. Chandler, independently of his trusteeship. The testimony on behalf of Mrs. Chandler was that there was never such an agency, either real or apparent. Mr. Kimball testified that when the bank sold the note to Mrs. Chandler it was agreed between herself and himself that

the coupons and principal as they matured would be collected by the bank without expense to Mrs. Chandler.
This did not at all change the status of affairs material
to a consideration of this case, for there is no pretense
that the $1,073.50 in dispute was ever paid to the bank.
As a matter of fact, when this payment was made, the
bank had not been doing business for more than a year.
Mr. Kimball further testified that he always understood
that, while acting as president of the bank and while
doing business individually in these transactions, he was
acting as the agent of Joseph B. Chandler, who was acting as agent for his wife, Helen W. Chandler. The twen-
tieth interrogatory propounded to Mr. Kimball and his
answer thereto were as follows: "You may state how frequently you saw either the plaintiff or her husband and
talked with them with regard to the collection of loans
that you had in your charge." Answer: "Mr. Chandler
probably called seven or eight times or more per annum
at the bank, or later, at my office, usually coming a day or
two before the coupons became payable, bringing for collection whatever ones were maturing which belonged to
his wife or himself. Occasionally I gave him a check for
the total sum due before he left the office, at others the
check was mailed to his address." The evidence above
described, with that of an even less satisfactory nature, is
that upon which depends the correctness of the finding of
the district court in favor of the defendants. There is no
question that the husband of Mrs. Chandler received for
his wife all the payments which came into her hands and
transacted all the business pertaining thereto. He testified, unequivocally, that he, in no instance, entrusted a
coupon to Mr. Kimball, and that his surrender of coupons was always upon payment being made upon presentation, either to the bank or to Mr. Kimball. When
the payment of $1,000 on the principal, and the interest
then due was made, the note and coupon were in possession of Mrs. Chandler. The rule in such cases is that a
party who pays money to another to be applied on a note,

which such person has not in his possession, assumes the burden of showing the authority of such person to receive the payment. (*South Branch Lumber Co. v. Littlejohn*, 31 Neb. 606; *Bull v. Mitchell*, 47 Neb. 647; *Richards v. Waller*, 49 Neb. 639; *Thomson v. Shelton*, 49 Neb. 644; *City Missionary Society v. Reams*, 51 Neb. 225; *Greenman v. Swan*, 51 Neb. 81; *Frey v. Curtis*, 52 Neb. 406.) In *Porter v. Ourada*, 51 Neb. 510, it was held by this court that the mere fact that a mortgagee has been in the habit of collecting interest from the mortgagor and remitting it to an assignee of the mortgagor is not alone sufficient to authorize the conclusion that the mortgagee's agency was such as to authorize him to collect the entire unmatured mortgage debt, citing *Stark v. Olsen, supra*. The testimony of Mr. Kimball as to his understanding that he was acting as an agent for Mrs. Chandler was but the statement of his own deduction. The facts from which this deduction was drawn alone were proper to be stated as evidence. If his conclusion was based upon facts which he failed to state it would manifestly be unfair to give this conclusion any weight in the determination of this case. We can consider only the facts which he stated as justifying his conclusion, and these, above stated clearly, fall short of establishing his authority to receive the $1,073.50 payment for Mrs. Chandler. The judgment of the district court is reversed and this cause is remanded with instructions to the district court to enter a decree in conformity with the views above expressed.

                    REVERSED AND REMANDED.

HUGO E. NELSON V. STATE OF NEBRASKA.

FILED FEBRUARY 17, 1898. No. 9663.

Intoxicating Liquors: EVIDENCE OF UNLAWFUL POSSESSION. In a prosecution for having in his possession certain intoxicating liquors,
among which it was charged that there was beer, the defendant
introduced evidence tending to show that there was no beer and
that the liquid described in the information as beer was a tonic,
not intoxicating in its nature. The state offered in evidence a
search-warrant issued in an independent proceeding in which it
was recited that an information under oath had been filed by a
credible resident freeholder, whose name was given, that such
freeholder had reason to believe and did believe that the accused
had in his possion beer among other intoxicating liquors, kept
for the purpose of sale and which were being sold in violation of
chapter 50, Compiled Statutes of Nebraska. On this warrant there
was a statement in the return that the officer executing the same
had, upon search, found on the premises of the accused sixty-seven
bottles of beer. This warrant and return the court admitted in
evidence. *Held,* That, as the recitations of the warrant and return
were with reference to the essence of the crime for the commission
of which the accused was being tried, the admission of the warrant and return as independent evidence was prejudicially erroneous.

ERROR to the district court for Burt county. Tried
below before POWELL, J. *Reversed.*

H. H. Bowes and *Ira Thomas*, for plaintiff in error.

C. J. Smyth, Attorney General, and *Ed P. Smith, Deputy
Attorney General*, for the state.

RYAN, C.

In the district court of Burt county Hugo E. Nelson
was convicted of having in his possession on May 27,
1896, intoxicating liquors, to-wit, whiskey, beer, wine,
ale, alcohol, and brandy, kept and intended for sale, and
which were being sold without the license which is required in chapter 50 of the Compiled Statutes.

We shall consider but one assignment of error, which
is that the court erred in receiving in evidence Exhibit

1. This was identified by the officer by whom the return thereon was signed, as the warrant under which he had acted before the preliminary information was filed in this case. It was therefore executed in an independent proceeding, of the nature of which we are not advised, except that, as we gather from the oral testimony adduced in this case and the warrant and return hereinafter described, the proceeding was one under section 20, chapter 50, Compiled Statutes. The contents of the exhibit are as follows:

"In the County Court of Burt County, Nebraska.

"THE STATE OF NEBRASKA, ⎞
    COUNTY OF BURT.   ⎠

"To the sheriff or any constable of said county:

"Whereas, Chas. A. Patterson, a credible resident freeholder of said Burt county, has made complaint in writing and upon oath before me, Frank E. Ward, county judge in and for Burt county, Nebraska, that he has reason to believe, and does believe, that Hugo E. Nelson, of the county of Burt, state of Nebraska, on the 27th day of May, 1896, in the county aforesaid, then and there being, did then and there have, and now has, in his possession intoxicating liquors known as whiskey, beer, wine, ale, alcohol, in the cellar and building situated on lot thirteen (13), in block six (6), of the village of Oakland, Burt county, Nebraska, said place being kept by him, and that such intoxicating liquors were then and there, and are, intended for sale by said Hugo E. Nelson without a license as provided in chapter 50 of the Compiled Statutes of Nebraska for the year 1895: You are therefore commanded, with necessary and proper assistance, to enter in the daytime the said cellar and building kept by the said Hugo E. Nelson, situated on lot 13, in block 6, of the village of Oakland, in Burt county, Nebraska, and diligently search for said intoxicating liquors known as whiskey, beer, wine, ale, alcohol, and, if found, you shall seize said liquors with the vessels containing the same and keep the same securely until

final action be had thereon, and immediately **arrest the**
said Hugo E. Nelson, or the person in charge of **said**
liquors, and bring him before me for examination, to be
disposed of or dealt with according to law.

"Given under my hand and official seal, the 27th **day**
of May, A. D. 1896.

"[Seal county court, Burt county.]

"FRANK E. WARD,
"*County Judge.*

"STATE OF NEBRASKA, }
　BURT COUNTY. 　 }

"May 28th, 1896, I made diligent search for the **goods**
described in the within warrant and at the place mentioned therein, and have found the following: **One six**
gallon tin can containing about three gallons of alcohol,
one (1) gallon bottle full of whiskey, one and one-half
gallon bottles full of port wine, and one gallon **bottle**
full of blackberry wine, one gallon bottle two-thirds **full**
of brandy, and on the 28th day of May I researched the
premises and found sixty-seven bottles of beer.　I now
have said goods and chattels and the body of said Hugo
E. Nelson present in court.

"J. A. CLARK, *Sheriff.*
"By W. R. LANGFORD, *Deputy.*"

By the accused it was sought to be shown on the trial
of this case that the alcohol, wine, brandy, and whiskey
were necessarily used in his business as a druggist in the
preparation of tinctures, etc.　As to the nature of the
contents of the sixty-seven bottles taken on May 28,
there was direct conflict in the evidence—that for the
accused being to the effect that it was not beer, but was
what was called "Hospital Tonic," a preparation of the
nature indicated by its name and in its nature, as one
witness at least testified, not intoxicating.　With this
condition of evidence existing, the introduction of the
warrant and the return thereon disclosed that a person
not examined as a witness in this case, who, in the warrant, was described as a credible resident freeholder, **had**

made an affidavit to the effect that the accused in th's case was keeping certain intoxicating liquors, among which was beer, for the purpose of selling it in violation of law, and the return of the officer upon this warrant was that he had found sixty-seven bottles of beer upon the premises of the defendant. These facts, which the warrant and return tended to establish, were facts very material as against the accused, for by section 20, chapter 50, Compiled Statutes, the possession of intoxicating liquors by one not licensed to sell the same is presumptive evidence of the commission of the offense with which Nelson was charged. The officer by whom the above quoted return was made was examined and cross-examined as a witness in this case, and his testimony had much less of the positiveness than did his return wherein the contents of the sixty-seven bottles, unequivocally, were described as beer. Mr. Patterson, who filed the information upon which the search warrant issued, was not examined at all in this case; hence there was no opportunity to cross-examine him with reference to the sworn charges which by him had been made against Nelson. Independently of all the papers filed, the warrant recited what Mr. Patterson had alleged under oath, and these allegations were with reference to matters very important in determining this case. We conclude, therefore, that in admitting in evidence Exhibit 1 the district court erred, and accordingly its judgment is reversed and this cause is remanded for further proceedings.

REVERSED AND REMANDED.

H. GUND & COMPANY V. WILLIAM HORRIGAN ET AL.

FILED FEBRUARY 17, 1898. No. 7848.

Judgments: ENTRY NUNC PRO TUNC. If a judgment was in fact rendered and such judgment was not recorded, the court at any time afterward, in a proper proceeding, and upon a proper showing, may render such judgment *nunc pro tunc.* Following *Van Etten v. Test,* 49 Neb. 725.

ERROR from the district court of Adams county. Tried below before BEALL, J. *Affirmed.*

B. F. Smith, for plaintiffs in error.

T. J. Doyle, contra.

RYAN, C.

This action was begun in the district court of Adams county to subject to the payment of a judgment certain real property claimed by William and Catherine Horrigan as a homestead. On January 19, 1893, there was a trial, resulting in findings of certain facts, among which were the findings that William and Catherine Horrigan had a homestead interest in the real property, subject and second to a mortgage of $1,400 and accrued interest thereon; that a conveyance of William and Catherine Horrigan to their co-defendant, Peter Horrigan, was in fact and law a mortgage, which was subject and inferior to the claim of plaintiff, H. Gund & Co., and not a lien upon the premises. While these findings were followed by an order directing that judgment be entered upon them, there seems to have been no such judgment rendered at that time. On May 16, 1894, there was filed in this case a paper, which, though more pretentious in its designation and scope, may be treated as a motion for an entry of judgment *nunc pro tunc.* Notice of the pendency of this application was served on the attorneys for Gund & Co., by whom a special appearance was filed July

2, 1894, objecting to the jurisdiction of the court for the reason that no summons had been served on their client, and for the further reason that the court had lost jurisdiction of this case. On July 3, 1894, the record discloses that the cause was submitted to the court upon the evidence, oral, written, and documentary, which had been under consideration originally, and that the court thereon made a finding that the property was of the value of $3,400, and that because of the mortgage thereon of $1,400 there was no balance above the homestead exemption subject to the judgment in favor of H. Gund & Co. There was thereupon entered a decree that the judgment in favor of H. Gund & Co. was not a lien on the premises, and the homestead rights of William and Catherine Horrigan were quieted against said judgment. In *Van Etten v. Test*, 49 Neb. 725, it has been held that where, in fact, a judgment was rendered but not recorded, the court, at any time afterward, had power, independently of statutory authority, *nunc pro tunc*, to enter a proper judgment against the defendant upon due showing in a proper proceeding. The facts in this case justified the entry of a judgment *nunc pro tunc*, and in legal effect there was but the entry of such a judgment. There has been pointed out no irregularity in the exercise of this power, and we therefore conclude that no such irregularity exists. The judgment of the district court is accordingly

AFFIRMED.

ELSIE D. TROUP ET AL., APPELLEES, V. PAUL W. HORBACH ET AL., APPELLANTS.

FILED FEBRUARY 17, 1898. No. 9375.

1. **Corporations:** SALES OF STOCK: PAYMENT IN PROPERTY: LIABILITY OF PURCHASERS. Owners of property have a right, in disposing of it, to place such valuation thereon as they see fit; and if, with such property at an overvaluation, they pay for capital stock issued to

them by a corporation, the excess above the real value of the
property cannot subsequently be treated by creditors of the corporation as never having been paid, in the absence of fraud, misrepresentation, suppression of the truth, and the violation of the
obligations of law or morality, express or implied.

2. ———: ———: ———: ———. A purchaser of the capital stock of
a corporation from one who has fully paid for the same in property cannot be held liable to creditors of such corporation solely
on the theory that the property recognized as a proper medium of.
payment had been accepted as payment by the corporation at too
high a valuation.

3. **Attorney:** VERIFICATION OF PLEADING: ESTOPPEL. Where a defendant, an attorney at law, as such, signed the petition praying
judgment against himself, and verified such petition, in which it
was averred that he owed the plaintiff a certain sum, he cannot
in the face of these facts, on appeal, be relieved in the supreme
court.

APPEAL from the district court of Gage county. Heard
below before LETTON, J. *Reversed.*

The facts are stated by the commissioner.

John D. Howe, for appellants:

Purchase of stock and payment in property at more
than its real value will not enable a creditor giving credit
to the corporation with full knowledge of the facts to
charge the stockholder with the difference between the
real value of the property and the value at which it was
taken. (3 Thompson, Corporations sec. 2932; *Bank of
Fort Madison v. Alden,* 129 U. S. 372; *Thompson v. Bemis
Paper Co.,* 127 Mass. 595; *Hospes v. Northwestern Mfg. &
Car Co.,* 50 N. W. Rep. [Minn.] 1117; *Adamant Mfg. Co. v.
Wallace,* 48 Pac. Rep. [Wash.] 415; *First Nat. Bank v.
Gustin Minerva Consolidated Mining Co.,* 44 N. W. Rep.
[Minn.] 198; *Coit v. Gold Amalgamating Co.,* 119 U. S. 343;
Rickerson Roller-Mill Co. v. Farrell Foundry & Machine Co.,
75 Fed. Rep. 554.)

John A. Horbach was not a stockholder, as each party
must consent—the one to become a member, and the
other that he should become a member of the corpora.

tion. (*Essex Turnpike Corporation v. Collins*, 8 Mass. 299; Angell & Ames, Corporations sec. 527, and cases cited.)

Other references in an argument on the non-liability of appellants: *Gilke v. Dawson Town & Gas Co.*, 46 Neb. 333; *Wood v. Dummer*, 3 Mason [U. S.] 308; *Gorder v. Plattsmouth Canning Co.*, 36 Neb. 549; *Jackson v. Traer*, 64 Ia. 469; *New Albany v. Burke*, 11 Wall. [U. S.] 96; *Steacy v. Little Rock & Ft. S. R. Co.*, 5 Dil. [U. S. C. C.] 348; *Webster v. Upton*, 91 U. S. 65; *Upton v. Tribilcock*, 91 U. S. 45; *Phelan v. Hazard*, 5 Dil. [U. S.] 45; *Hart v. Lauman*, 29 Barb. [N. Y.] 410; *Moore v. Hudson River R. Co.*, 12 Barb. [N. Y.] 156; *Porter v. Buckfield B. R. Co.*, 32 Me. 539; *Memphis & L. R. Co. v. Dow*, 120 U. S. 287; *Peoria & S. R. Co. v. Thompson*, 103 Ill. 187; *Shaw v. Robinson*, 50 Neb. 403; *Morgan v. Brower*, 77 Ga. 627; *Flinn v. Bagley*, 7 Fed. Rep. 785; *Hatch v. Dana*, 101 U. S. 205; *Graham v. Railroad Co.*, 102 U. S. 148; *Gilman v. Gross*, 72 N. W. Rep. [Wis.] 885; *Coleman v. White*, 14 Wis. 762; *Hadley v. Russell*, 40 N. H. 109; *Farmers Loan & Trust Co. v. Funk*, 49 Neb. 353; *Adler v. Milwaukee Patent Brick Mfg. Co.*, 13 Wis. 57; *Griffith v. Mangam*, 73 N. Y. 611; *Morgan v. New York & A. R. Co.*, 10 Paige Ch. [N. Y.] 290; *Mann v. Pentz*, 3 N. Y. 415; *Pollard v. Bailey*, 20 Wall. [U. S.] 520; *Terry v. Little*, 101 U. S. 216; *Patterson v. Lynde*, 106 U. S. 519; *Niver v. Crane*, 98 N. Y. 40.

Charles Offutt, also for appellants:

The contracts between the Horbachs and the transit and power company were not frauds upon the creditors of the corporation, not a single creditor was injured by either of the contracts, John A. Horbach was never a shareholder either in fact or beneficially, and appellants are not liable. (*Fogg v. Blair*, 139 U. S. 118; *Christensen v. Eno*, 106 N. Y. 97; *Van Ostrand v. Reed*, 1 Wend. [N. Y.] 424.)

The shares of stock issued to Paul W. Horbach were not subscribed by either of the Horbachs or by Lantry. These shares had all been previously issued by the com-

pany to the original or other shareholders, and were by
the holders voluntarily surrendered to the company to
enable it to execute its agreement with Horbach.   Hence
the shares issued to Horbach were assets of the company
which it had the right to sell for what it could get, and
the purchaser or owner of such shares incurred none of
the liabilities of a subscriber to shares, nor any liability
to pay the difference between the par value of the shares
and what had been previously paid thereon.   (1 Cook,
Stock and Stockholders [3d ed.] sec. 29; *Ramwell's Case*,
50 L. J. Ch. [Eng.] 827; *Otter v. Brevoort*, 50 Barb. [N. Y.]
247; *People v. Albany & S. R. Co.*, 55 Barb. [N. Y.] 371;
Lake Superior Iron Co. v. Drexel, 90 N. Y. 87; *Morrow v.
Iron & Steel Co.*, 87 Tenn. 262; *Handley v. Stutz*, 139 U. S.
417; *Clark v. Bever*, 139 U. S. 96; *Van Cott v. Van Brunt*,
82 N. Y. 535.)

A transferee of shares is not liable for unpaid subscriptions on his shares unless he has agreed with the corporation to pay them.   If he has not promised he is not
liable.   (*Seymour v. Sturgess*, 26 N. Y. 143; 1 Cook, Stock
and Stockholders [3d ed.] sec. 46; *Foreman v. Bigelow*, 9
Fed. Cases 441; *Currie's Case*, 3 De Gex, J. & S. [Eng.]
367; *De Ruvigne's Case*, 5 L. R. Ch. D. [Eng.] 306; *Anderson's Case*, 7 L. R. Ch. D. [Eng.] 94; *Christensen v. Eno*,
106 N. Y. 97.)

Existing creditors were not injured by the contracts
with the Horbachs, and other creditors had knowledge
thereof.   Appellees cannot, therefore, complain of these
contracts.   (*First Nat. Bank of Deadwood v. Gustin Minerva Consolidated Mining Co.*, 42 Minn. 327; *Hospes v.
Northwestern Mfg. & Car Co.*, 48 Minn. 174; *Handley v.
Stutz*, 139 U. S. 417; 1 Cook, Stock and Stockholders [2d
ed.] sec. 46.)

E. R. Duffie and *A. H. Babcock*, also for appellants.

J. E. Cobbey and *G. M. Johnston*, contra:

Lantry having such notice as would put him on in-

quiry, the burden of showing himself an innocent pur-
chaser rested on him. (*Wishard v. Hansen*, 68 N. W. Rep.
[Ia.] 691; *Oswald v. Minneapolis Times Co.*, 68 N. W. Rep.
[Minn.] 15.)

The decree was correctly entered. (*Commercial Nat.
Bank v. Gibson*, 37 Neb. 750.)

Appellants are liable. (*Gilkie v. Dawson Town & Gas
Co.*, 46 Neb. 333; *Elyton Land Co. v. Birmingham Warehouse
Elevator Co.*, 9 So. Rep. [Ala.] 129; *Wishard v. Hansen*,
68 N. W. Rep. [Ia.] 691; *Globe Publishing Co. v. State
Bank*, 41 Neb. 175; *Gogebic Investment Co. v. Iron Chief
Mining Co.*, 47 N. W. Rep. [Wis.] 726; *Sanger v. Upton*,
91 U. S. 56; *Farmers Loan & Trust Co. v. Funk*, 49 Neb. 353;
State v. German Savings Bank, 50 Neb. 734; *Boulton Carbon
Co. v. Mills*, 43 N. W. Rep. [Ia.] 290; *Welles v. Larrabee*,
36 Fed. Rep. 866; *Preston v. Cincinnati, C. & H. V. R. Co.*,
36 Fed. Rep. 54; *Shields v. Casey*, 25 Atl. Rep. [Pa.] 619;
Davis v. Stevens, 17 Blatchf. [U. S.] 259; *Case v. Small*,
10 Fed. Rep. 722; *National Bank v. Case*, 99 U. S. 628;
McKim v. Glenn, 8 Atl. Rep. [Md.] 130; *Baines v. Babcock*,
27 Pac. Rep. [Cal.] 674.)

A transferee of stock is liable for the balance remaining unpaid upon stock which he purchases or receives,
knowing it to be unpaid, though it be issued as fully paid
and non-assessable. (*White v. Greene*, 70 N. W. Rep.
[Ia.] 182; *Henderson v. Turngren*, 35 Pac. Rep. [Utah]
495; *Peninsular Savings Bank v. Black Flag Stove Polish
Co.*, 63 N. W. Rep. [Mich.] 514; *Hastings Malting Co. v.
Iron Range Brewing Co.*, 67 N. W. Rep. [Minn.] 652; *Scoville v. Thayer*, 105 U. S. 225; *Calumet Paper Co. v. Stotts
Investment Co.*, 64 N. W. Rep. [Ia.] 782; *Carter v. Union
Printing Co.*, 16 S. W. Rep. [Ark.] 579; *Peck v. Elliott*,
79 Fed. Rep. 10; *Addison v. Pacific Coast Milling Co.*, 79
Fed. Rep. 459.)

All creditors becoming such after the corporation authorized the issue of stock may enforce the liability.
(*Handley v. Stutz*, 139 U. S. 417; *Webster v. Upton*, 91 U. S.
65; *Pullman v. Upton*, 96 U. S. 331.)

A. C. Troup, Griggs, Rinaker & Bibb, and *E. H. Hinshaw.*
also for appellees.

Ryan, C.

This appeal was advanced for hearing upon an agreement of parties in compliance with rule 2. (52 Neb. ix.)
The action was brought in the district court of Gage
county, wherein there were judgments against the several defendants conformably with the prayer of the petition. Plaintiffs alleged that they were creditors of the
Beatrice Rapid Transit & Power Company in various
sums which were described in separate paragraphs, and
in many instances were evidenced by judgments against
that company. They further alleged that under a decree of the United States circuit court for the eighth
circuit, district of Nebraska, all the property of the
Beatrice Rapid Transit Company had been sold and that
it was without any property for the payment of its aforesaid indebtedness. The prayer of the petition was as
follows: "Wherefore plaintiffs pray that each of said
defendants may be held liable for the several amounts
hereinbefore claimed due from them upon the stock of
the Beatrice Rapid Transit & Power Company, as hereinbefore alleged, and that said defendants, and each of
them, may be required to pay to these several plaintiffs
the amounts of their several claims; that the court may
adjudge the amount due from each may be held and decreed to be due to these several plaintiffs the full amount
of their respective claims, and that under the order of
this court the amounts so found due from said several defendants may be collected of them, severally, the full
amount found to be due to these plaintiffs, together with
the costs of this proceeding; that the said John A. Horbach and Paul W. Horbach may be held jointly and severally liable for the amount of stock issued to the said
Paul W. Horbach, as hereinbefore alleged, and that the
several plaintiffs may have such other further and dif-

ferent relief as in equity they may be entitled to, and for their costs." From this prayer it is clear that the defendants were proceeded against as being liable as holders of shares of the Beatrice Rapid Transit & Power Company capital stock on the assumption that these shares had not been paid for. Issues were joined by answers, except in the instances wherein there were defaults.

To illustrate the general theory on which it was sought to hold liable certain of the stockholders it will be sufficient to quote one sample paragraph of the petition. We shall also quote another paragraph which supplements the allegations of that already referred to. The two paragraphs above indicated are in this language:

"The defendant Beatrice Rapid Transit & Power Company issued to the defendant George R. Scott 115 shares of their capital stock of the par value of $11,500; that the only consideration paid by said Scott for the issuing of said stock was services rendered to the said rapid transit company, and real estate transferred by said Scott and wife to said rapid transit company, and that the total amount of said real estate and services did not exceed the amount of $7,000; that there is still due from said Scott on his said stock the sum of $4,500.

"The defendant Beatrice Rapid Transit & Power Company issued to the defendants William Ebright, E. S. Cushman, full Christian name unknown, L. F. Easterday, full name unknown, William Bozarth, Jacob Klein, William H. Tichnor, Jonathan S. Grable, John Ellis one or more shares each of its capital stock of the par value of $100 per share; that the only consideration paid therefor was the conveyance of certain real estate conveyed by each of them severally to the said rapid transit company, but these plaintiffs have not the records of said company and cannot give the exact amount of stock issued to each of them severally, nor the amounts in fact paid thereon, nor the value of the property given in pay-

55

ment therefor, but plaintiffs allege that they did not in fact pay the full par value of their said stock and that there is still due from each of said defendants a small amount on each of their said shares of stock so issued to them which plaintiffs ask they may be required, upon a hearing and accounting in this court, to pay to these plaintiffs. And plaintiffs allege that said defendants Schell, Brumback, Spencer, Beatrice Real Estate & Trust Company, Johnston, Davis, Blakely, Blakely, Scott, Ryan, Ebright, Cushman, Easterday, Bozarth, Klein, Tichnor, Grable, and Ellis, and each of them, had full knowledge that the respective shares of stock issued to them respectively, as alleged, had not been paid for in full and that the said property and services had been greatly overvalued, and that the payment for such stock by said property or services at such overvaluation was a fraud on the creditors of said rapid transit company."

In the petition there was no charge of fraud against the parties first named except the above language, and this, it is quite clear, was a mere conclusion of the pleader deduced from the facts alleged. Whether or not this deduction was correct is one of the questions which, later, we shall consider. With reference to the liability of Scott the court found in its decree as follows:

"The court further finds that 200 shares of the capital stock of the rapid transit and power company, being certificates 46 to 50 inclusive, were issued to George R. and W. W. Scott in consideration of the conveyance to said company by said George R. Scott of certain real estate; that said shares were of the value of $20,000, and that the property in exchange for which they were issued was of the fair cash value of $6,000; that said property was grossly overvalued."

In the decree there was a paragraph in this language:

"The court further finds that at the time that the aforesaid shares of stock were issued to the said L. E. Spencer, N. N. Brumback, G. M. Johnston, S. K. Davis, C. L. Schell, Jacob Klein, Nathan Blakely, Mrs. I. W. Funck,

J. S. Grable, John Ellis, H. C. Bozarth, William Tichnor, William Ebright, George R. Scott, Ira L. Ryan, Beatrice Real Estate & Trust Company, L. F. Easterday, Walter W. Scott, each and all of the persons had full knowledge that the property or services in consideration for which the said shares of stock were issued by the said corporation to said several persons respectively, was greatly disproportionate in value to the face of the shares of stock exchanged therefor, and that the officer of said corporation issuing said stock, and the parties receiving the same, both well knew that said great disparity in value existed, and each of the said issues of stock to each of the several persons aforesaid was made with the full understanding and knowledge that the property exchanged for said stock was worth for the most part only about one-half of the face value of said stock and was in fact of the value hereinbefore found by the court."

If we understand correctly the theory upon which the court proceeded in entering judgment pursuant to the above findings, it was that parties who purchased stock and in payment therefor transferred to the company real property, were only entitled to receive credit for the actual value of such real property at the time it was transferred. There was no evidence that there was any misrepresentation as to the value of this property upon which misrepresentation the company had acted to its injury, indeed, in most instances misrepresentation of value could scarcely have imposed upon the officers of the company, for the property was within the corporate limits of the city of Beatrice. It was not alleged that any of these purchasers of capital stock owed any duty to the company, or that they were in any way connected with it at the time that they exchanged real property for stock. We therefore assume that the theory was that at any subsequent time, within the limit fixed by the statute of limitations, it was the right of the company, and in case of its insolvency the right of its creditors, to institute an action against stockholders for the

difference between the par value of the stock and the
real value of property which the company had received
as full payment for such stock irrespective of the above
considerations. In this view we cannot concur. A
party, without fraud or misrepresentation, has the right
to fix whatever value he chooses upon his property, and
a corporation no more than a person can be relieved
against its own want of judgment in buying such property at the price named. In making this statement we
do not take into consideration fraud, breach of warranty,
misrepresentation, suppression of the truth, or other
proper grounds for relief which might be proper in some
cases to consider. These elements are purposely omitted,
for they were neither pleaded, proved, nor found to exist.
We are therefore of the opinion that the judgments of
the district court rendered in this case against Charles
L. Schell, N. N. Brumback, L. E. Spencer, Beatrice Real
Estate & Trust Company, S. K. Davis, William Ebright,
E. S. Cushman, L. F. Easterday, William Bozarth, D. W.
Morrow, Nathan Blakely, and George R. Scott must be
reversed. In the same class with the defendants just
named there were Jacob Klein, Alexander Moore, and
Ira Ryan, but the judgments against them cannot be
reviewed, for the reason that they were rendered upon
the default of said parties. ·

The judgment against G. M. Johnston must be affirmed
to the extent of $1,300, for reasons which shall now be
stated. In the petition it was charged that the Beatrice
Rapid Transit & Power Company had issued to Johnston
153 shares of its capital stock of the value of $15,300;
that the only consideration paid for this stock was
$14,000 in property and services; and it was alleged:
"That said Johnston still owes on said stock the sum
of $1,300." This petition was signed by Mr. Johnston as
an attorney for plaintiffs and was verified by him. The
affirmance of this portion of the judgment, to the extent
above indicated, is rendered necessary by the attitude
thus assumed by Mr. Johnston and by no other consideration.

A judgment in form seems to have been entered against Elsie D. Troup and J. C. Bozarth, but as they were not named in the petition as defendants, and as no relief was asked as against them, we assume that in reality there was no judgment against either of them.

The other defendants against whom judgments were rendered were John A. Horbach, Paul W. Horbach, and Victor G. Lantry, against whom the petition contained the following averments: "The said Beatrice Rapid Transit & Power Company issued to the defendant Paul W. Horbach 1,250 shares of said capital stock of the par value of $125,000; that said Paul W. Horbach paid no consideration whatever for said stock or any of it, but that the same was issued to him by the request of John A. Horbach, who had acquired said stock by virtue of an agreement with the Beatrice Rapid Transit & Power Company by which he was to loan the said Beatrice Rapid Transit & Power Company the sum of $20,000; that said $125,000 of stock was in the nature of a bonus to John A. Horbach and as an inducement to him to make said loan and was without consideration, and was issued to his son, Paul W. Horbach, for the illegal and collusive purpose of placing it beyond the attack of creditors of the Beatrice Rapid Transit & Power Company, and to relieve him, said John A. Horbach, from any liability on account of said alleged purchase of said stock; that afterwards said $125,000 of capital stock was by said Paul W. Horbach transferred to the said defendant Victor G. Lantry, who surrendered the original certificate issued to Paul W. Horbach and had the stock reissued to him. Plaintiffs believe and allege that the said transfer from said Paul W. Horbach to said Victor G. Lantry was wholly without consideration, but whether with or without consideration, said Victor G. Lantry never paid to said Beatrice Rapid Transit & Power Company the value of said stock or any part thereof, and said Victor G. Lantry, Paul W. Horbach, and John A. Horbach each knew, and had full notice of the fact, that said stock had been issued wholly without consideration, and that the said par value of said stock or no part thereof had been paid by them or either of them, or by any one at any time, to the said Beatrice Rapid Transit & Power Company, or to any one else for them, and each of said last named defendants had full knowledge that the said Beatrice Rapid Transit & Power Company was largely indebted at the time said stock was issued and at the several reissues thereof, and each of said three last named defendants knew that the issue of said $125,000 of stock was a fraud upon creditors of said rapid transit company, and upon the individuals and the public dealing with and extending credit to said rapid transit company, and these plaintiffs in particular; that the defendant Victor G. Lantry afterwards conveyed to the defendant D. W. Morrow and the defendant Alexander Moore, each, one share of said stock of the par value of $100, and that neither of said shares had been paid for, and which fact said defendants Morrow and Moore well knew, and said defendants well knew that said shares of stock so conveyed to them was issued without consideration and without being paid for in whole or in part by any person; that said defendants Paul W. and John A. Horbach, V. G. Lantry each became and still are liable for the full par value of said stock and said Morrow and Moore are each liable for the par value of one share of the said stock." With respect to these three defendants the finding of the district court was as follows:

"The court further finds that on about the 8th day of September, 1892, the defendant the Beatrice Rapid Transit & Power Company borrowed from one John A. Horbach, of the city of Omaha, Nebraska, the sum of $20,000 for one year, with interest at the rate of 8 per cent per annum, for the purpose of extending the lines, and completing and improving the plant of said company, and for the purpose of securing the payment of said loan at maturity the said Beatrice Rapid Transit & Power Company delivered to John A. Horbach, as collateral security, certain mortgage bonds of said company; that as an inducement to John A. Horbach for the making of said loan, said Beatrice Rapid Transit & Power Company through its directors agreed to procure and deliver to said John A. Horbach, as a bonus or premium in addition to the eight per cent interest which they agreed to pay on said loan, and for the purpose of allowing the control of said corporation to be in the hands of said Horbach, shares of stock representing one-half of the total capital stock of said company, to-wit, 1,250 shares of the par value of $125,000; that the agreement as to said shares was made with John A. Horbach in the first place, but that afterwards, at his instance and request, said shares of stock were issued to his son, Paul W. Horbach, of said city of Omaha; that at the time of making said loans, and as a part of the same transaction, it was agreed between John A. Horbach and Paul W. Horbach and the defendant Beatrice Rapid Transit & Power Company, in consideration of the sum of $20,000, that the said Paul W. Horbach should furnish the material and build the extensions, for the making of which said $20,-000 was borrowed, and that the provision with reference to the 1,250 shares aforesaid should be embraced in the contract made with Paul W. Horbach, which agreement was carried out.

"The court finds that said contract and agreement by which the said shares of stock were to be issued in the name of Paul W. Horbach, was made in fact for the benefit and protection of John A. Horbach, and for the purpose of avoiding any liabilities which the said John A. Horbach might incur by reason of the issuance of said stock to him in his own name.

"The court finds that thereafter, to-wit, on the 16th day of September, 1892, the said Beatrice Rapid Transit & Power Company, in pursuance of the said agreement with John A. and Paul W. Horbach, procured an issue to said Paul W. Horbach of 1,250 shares in said corporation, which said shares of stock were issued by virtue of certificate No. 86, and were issued upon no other consideration than heretofore stated.

"The court finds that the said John A. Horbach and Paul W. Horbach, prior to the time of the issuance of said stock to Paul W. Horbach, had full knowledge and notice of the financial condition, assets, property, and indebtedness of said Beatrice Rapid Transit & Power Company as it stood at the time said contracts or agreements with them were made, and had full knowledge of the manner in which stock had been issued to the persons then holding the stock of the corporation; that the fact that said stock, or a large portion thereof, was issued in excess for property and services which were grossly overvalued, and that none of said stock had ever been fully paid for in money and money's worth, was well known to them.

"The court finds that defendant Victor G. Lantry, who became the owner of the 1,250 shares of stock assigned to him by Paul W. Horbach, had sufficient knowledge to put a reasonable, prudent man upon inquiry as to the assets of said corporation, its condition, and whether or not said stock had ever been paid for, and that he is not such an innocent purchaser of said stock as to entitle him to be relieved from liability thereon. The court therefore finds that he is liable to the same extent as John A. and Paul W. Horbach upon the said 1,250 shares of stock.

"The court finds that certificate No. 86, issued to Paul W. Horbach, was made up and composed of shares of stock issued to the persons, and certificates, the numbers of which are hereinafter set forth, and that there remained due and unpaid upon each of said several shares of stock the amounts set opposite the name of each party in the following table, together with the total amount due as shown in said table:

Name of Source of Shares.	No. of Certificates.	Bal. per Share Unpaid.	No. of Shares to Horbach	Total Amount Due.
N. N. Brumback	4–5–7–9–............	$89 33	187½	$16743 87
L. E. Spencer......	13–14–16–17........	89 33	200	17866 00
G. M. Johnston	23 shares from No. 20;			
	21–22 2 from No. 26	60 00	215	12900 00
Elsie D. Troup..............	5 shares from No. 32..	50 00	5	250 00
Jacob Klein.................	29....................	62 50	5	312 50
J. S. Grable.................	36....................	57 50	5	287 50
John Ellis	37–60................	50 00	20	1000 00
H. C Bozirth...............	40....................	33 33	3	99 99
J. C. Bozarth	39....................	50 00	7½	875 00
William Tichnor............	41....................	50 00	7½	875 00
William Ehright............	38....................	50 00	8	400 00
F. L M. Easterday	57–59................	50 00	7	350 00
Ira L. Ryan...............	43–44–45............	47 55	30½	1450 00
George R. Scott & Walter				
Scott....................	46 to 50 inc..........	70 00	75	5250 00
N. N. Brumback, assigned to				
N. T. Brumback..........	No. 67 (26½ of this re-			
	issued to N N.Brum-			
	back)..............	89 33	73¾	6588 08
N. N. Brumback	73....................	33 33	10	333 30
I..W. Funck................	68....................	50 00	13	650 00
G. M Johnston.............	75–88................	33 33	30	999 90
L. E. Spencer, assigned to				
Mary B. Spencer..........	70 (58¾ of this cert.			
	reissued to L. E.			
	Spencer)..........	89 33	41½	3684 86
L. E Spencer	74–83................	33 33	30	999 90
S K. Davis.................	77....................	66 66	2½	166 65
C. L. Schell	79....................	83 33	47½	3958 17
Nathan Blakely	84....................	100 00	50	5000 00
George R. Scott...........	85....................	100 00	50	5000 00
Beatrice Real Estate & Trust				
Co., being reissue from No.				
6–15, part of Brumback &				
Spencer 1st issue	No. 92..............	89 33	50	4466 50
Paul W. Horbach...........	....	100 00	76	7600 00
			1250	$97112 72

"The court finds, as to defendants D. W. Morrow and Alexander Moore, that they are innocent purchasers without notice from the said Victor Lantry of the shares of stock held by them and that they are not liable for any amount whatsoever upon said shares of stock."

The above table shows who surrendered stock and in what amounts it was surrendered by individuals. Certificate No. 86 was simply an issue in place of stock thus surrendered. The transaction was but the regular and proper method of transferring the stock held by these individuals. We can find no evidence that either of the Horbachs or Mr. Lantry had actual knowledge of the manner in which this stock was issued to the individuals named in the table above given. We think unsustained by the evidence the finding that Lantry, when he became the owner of the 1,250 shares of stock assigned to him, had sufficient knowledge to put a reasonable, prudent man upon inquiry as to the assets of said corporation, its condition, and whether or not the stock had been fully paid for. The certificates issued to individuals, and those issued in their stead, recited that the shares were fully paid up and there were no facts contradictory of these recitations within the knowledge of Lantry, so far as the evidence shows, except such knowledge as was possessed by the public at large, and that was merely that the corporation was not in a prosperous financial condition. We have already found, however, that the original holders of the stock were not liable under the issues joined and there was therefore no unpaid subscription which could follow the stock. There was therefore no grounds for holding John A. Horbach, Paul W. Horbach, or Victor Lantry liable as successors in the ownership of stock when their assignors had already paid for the same, or at least must be deemed to have done so, under the issues tried in this case.

The judgment of the district court against G. M. Johnston to the extent of $1,300 is affirmed; the judgments against the other defendants not rendered upon defaults are reversed and the cause is remanded for further proceedings not inconsistent with the views above expressed.

REVERSED AND REMANDED.

VOL. 53] JANUARY TERM, 1898. 811

Horbach v. Troup. Phenix Ins Co. v. Fuller.

JOHN A. HORBACH, APPELLANT, V. ELSIE D. TROUP ET AL.,
APPELLEES.

FILED FEBRUARY 17, 1898. No. 9683.

New Trial: APPEAL: DISMISSAL.

APPEAL from the district court of Gage county.
Heard below before LETTON, J. *Appeal dismissed.*

John D. Howe, Charles Offutt, E. R. Duffie, and *A. H.
Babcock,* for appellant.

*J. E. Cobbey, G. M. Johnston, A. C. Troup, Griggs, Rinaker
& Bibb,* and *E. H. Hinshaw, contra.*

RYAN, C.

The record in this case presents for review the judgment of the district court of Gage county denying the
prayer of the petition of the appellant for a new trial in
the case of *Troup v. Horbach,* 53 Neb. 795. As the judgment in the case just referred to has been reversed we
need not inquire into the merits of this appeal, and accordingly it is dismissed at costs of appellant.

APPEAL DISMISSED.

PHENIX INSURANCE COMPANY OF BROOKLYN V. FRED A.
FULLER.

FILED FEBRUARY 17, 1898. No. 7862.

1. **Insurance:** TITLE TO INSURED PROPERTY: WAIVER OF CONDITION.
Where no inquiries are made of an insured as to the character or
condition of his title; where he makes no false representation as
to the character and condition of his title, relying upon which
the insurer is induced to and does insure the property; where the
insured has an insurable interest in the property, the insurer accepts and retains the premium and a loss occurs, then the insurer

cannot escape liability for such loss because of the fact that the
insured at the date of the policy was not invested with an absolute
and unincumbered title to the insured property, even though the
policy provides that it shall be of no validity unless the title of
the insured be an unconditional unincumbered one, as in such
case it will be conclusively presumed against the insurer that it
intended to and did insure the interest which the insured had in
the property and waived the provision in the policy providing for
its invalidity by reason of the imperfect title of the insured.

2. **Transcript for Review:** OPINION OF TRIAL COURT. Where a case is
tried to the court without a jury and a general finding made upon
which judgment is rendered, and, in addition thereto, the court
files a written opinion in the case, such opinion is not an essential part of the record of the case when it is brought here for
review.

3. ————. The judgment of the district court must stand or fall upon
the statutory record of the case—that is, the pleadings, the finding and judgment, and the bill of exceptions made a part of the
record.

4. **Trial to Court:** DECISION: REVIEW. In reviewing such case this
court will conclusively presume that the trial court considered all
the competent evidence before it and decided all the material and
necessary issues presented, though from the language of the written opinion the contrary should be made to appear.

ERROR from the district court of Douglas county.
Tried below before AMBROSE, J. *Affirmed.*

Jacob Fawcett and *Greene & Breckenridge,* for plaintiff in
error.

George W. Shields, contra.

RAGAN, C.

Fred A. Fuller sued the Phenix Insurance Company of
Brooklyn, New York, in the district court of Douglas
county to recover the value of certain property of his destroyed by fire, which property the insurance company
had insured against loss or damage by fire. Fuller had a
verdict and judgment, and the insurance company has
filed here a petition in error to review such judgment.

1. The policy contained this provision: "If the interest
of the assured in the property be other than an uncondi-

tional exclusive ownership, or if any other person or persons have any interest whatever in the property described, whether it be real estate or personal property, or if there be a mortgage or other incumbrance thereon, whether inquired about or not, it must be so notified to the company, and be so expressed in the written part of this policy, otherwise this policy shall be void." At the time of the issuance of the policy in suit the personal property of the insured was incumbered by a chattel mortgage. The insured did not notify the company of the existence of this mortgage, and no memorandum of its existence was written in the policy. The insurance company interposed as a defense to the action in the district court the existence of this chattel mortgage upon the insured property; and the first argument here is that the judgment of the district court is contrary to law, because the undisputed evidence shows that such a mortgage existed upon the insured property at the date of the issuance of the policy, and that the insurance company was not notified of the existence of such mortgage, and no memorandum of its existence was written in the policy. The evidence on behalf of the insured tends to show that the agent of the insurance company solicited this insurance. At the time the agent had no actual knowledge of the existence of the chattel mortgage upon the property, but made no inquiries of the insured as to whether the property was incumbered. In fact, the subject of an incumbrance upon the property about to be insured was not mentioned by either party, and while the insured kept silent upon the subject of the incumbrance, he did not do so with any sinister motive. In other words, the subject of the incumbrance upon the property was not mentioned, because it seems not to have been thought of either by the insured or the insurer. The premium for the insurance was paid by the insured and accepted and retained by the insurer. The evidence further shows that the value of the property at the date of its insurance exceeded the incumbrance thereon, and

at the date of the destruction of the property by fire the
incumbrance had been so reduced that the property destroyed exceeded in value both the insurance and the incumbrance thereon.   In *Ins. Co. of North America v. Bachler*, 44 Neb. 549, it was held that where the insured was
not questioned as to incumbrances on his property, and
did not intentionally conceal the existence of an incumbrance and did not keep silent in regard to the incumbrance from any sinister motive, the existence of a mortgage upon the property did not invalidate the policy.
And in *German Ins. Co. v. Kline*, 44 Neb. 395, it was held
that where the application for insurance is oral, and no
inquiry made as to the condition of the title of the property, the insured in fact had an insurable interest in the
property, the premium paid and accepted and retained,
the insurance company would be conclusively presumed
to have insured the insurable interest which the owner
had in the property and to have waived the provision in
the policy providing for its forfeiture by reason of the
existence of an incumbrance upon the property.   These
cases control the case at bar.

2. This case was tried to the court without a jury, and
the court found generally in favor of the insured and
against the insurance company and entered an ordinary
money judgment on such finding; but the learned district
judge also wrote an opinion in the case, and in this opinion he states that he did not deem it necessary to pass
upon the merits of the defense just considered and reserved the question presented by that defense.   A second argument here is that the judgment must be reversed
because the only issue in the case has not been passed
upon or decided by the district court; but this argument
assumes that the opinion of the district judge is an essential part of the record of the case brought here; but it is
not.   In reviewing a case brought here, either on error
or appeal, while this court is always pleased to have the
benefit of the written opinion of the trial judge, still the
judgment of the district court must stand or fall upon the

statutory record of the case—that is, the pleadings, the finding and judgment of the district court, and the bill of exceptions made a part of the record; and where general findings are made by a court and a judgment pronounced thereon, we must conclusively presume that the trial court considered all the competent evidence before it, and decided all the material and necessary issues presented by the pleadings, though from the language of the opinion the contrary should be made to appear. The judgment of the district court is

AFFIRMED.

MILWAUKEE MECHANICS FIRE INSURANCE COMPANY V. FRED A. FULLER.

FILED FEBRUARY 17, 1898.   No. 7863.

Insurance: TITLE TO INSURED PROPERTY: WAIVER OF CONDITION. The facts in this case and the law applicable thereto are the same as those in *Phenix Ins. Co. v. Fuller*, 53 Neb. 811, and on the authority of that case the judgment of the district court is affirmed.

ERROR from the district court of Douglas county. Tried below before AMBROSE, J. *Affirmed.*

Jacob Fawcett and *Greene & Breckenridge,* for plaintiff in error.

George W. Shields, contra.

RAGAN, C.

In the district court of Douglas county Fred A. Fuller sued the Milwaukee Mechanics Fire Insurance Company to recover the value of property insured by it and destroyed by fire. He had a verdict and judgment and the insurance company prosecutes here a petition in error.

The facts in this case are the same as those in *Phenix Ins. Co. v. Fuller,* 53 Neb. 811, and on the authority of that case the judgment of the district court pronounced in this is

AFFIRMED.

LOUIS SLOBODISKY V. PHENIX INSURANCE COMPANY OF BROOKLYN.

FILED FEBRUARY 17, 1898.   No. 7856.

1. **Insurance**: AUTHORITY OF AGENT: PREMIUMS. Whether the agent of an insurance company is invested with authority to waive the payment of the premium in cash and give the insured credit therefor, and whether he did so, are questions of fact.

2. ———: ———: ———. It seems that the authority of an insurance agent to waive the payment of the premium in cash and give the insured credit therefor may be inferred from the fact that the agent is authorized to negotiate contracts of insurance, to fill out and deliver insurance policies executed in blank and left with him for that purpose, and to receive and receipt for insurance premiums, and to make settlements from time to time with his principal for premiums collected.

3. ———: TITLE TO INSURED PROPERTY: WAIVER OF CONDITION. Where no inquiries are made of an insured as to the character or condition of his title; where he makes no false representation as to the character or condition of his title, relying upon which the insurer is induced to and does insure the property; where the insured has an insurable interest in the property, the insurer accepts and retains the premium and a loss occurs, then the insurer cannot escape liability for such loss because of the fact that the insured at the date of the policy was not invested with an absolute and unincumbered title to the insured property, even though the policy provides that it shall be of no validity unless the title of the insured be an unconditional and unincumbered one, as in such case it will be conclusively presumed against the insurer that it intended to and did insure the interest which the insured had in the property and waived the provision in the policy providing for its invalidity by reason of the imperfect title of the insured.

4. ———: OCCUPANCY. Because property is unoccupied at the date of its insurance, the insurer being ignorant thereof, of itself constitutes no defense to an action on the policy.

5. ———: DESCRIPTION: REPRESENTATIONS. The fact that an insured building is described in the policy as a dwelling-house is not a representation of the insured that the house was then and there occupied.

6. ———: INSURABLE INTEREST: JUDICIAL SALE. One may have an insurable interest in real estate though it has been sold at judicial sale, while such sale remains unconfirmed, as the title is not divested until the confirmation of such sale. *Greenlee v. North British & Mercantile Ins. Co.*, 71 N. W. Rep. [Ia.] 534, and *Hanover Fire Ins. Co. of New York v. Brown*, 25 Atl. Rep. [Md.] 589, followed.

ERROR from the district court of Douglas county. Tried below before BLAIR, J. *Reversed.*

John D. Howe, Parke Godwin, and *E. R. Duffie,* for plaintiff in error.

Jacob Fawcett and *Greene & Breckenridge, contra.*

RAGAN, C.

This is a suit upon an ordinary fire insurance policy brought in the district court of Douglas county by Louis Slobodisky against the Phenix Insurance Company of Brooklyn, New York. The jury, in obedience to an instruction of the court, returned a verdict for the insurance company, upon which a judgment of dismissal of Slobodisky's action was entered, and he brings that judgment here for review on error.

1. There is no dispute in the record as to the execution and delivery of the policy, nor that a fire occurred destroying some and damaging the remainder of the insured property. As a defense to the action the insurance company pleaded that the insured had failed and neglected to pay the premium for the insurance, and the policy in suit provided that the company should not be liable thereon until the premium for insurance was actually paid. Slobodisky replied to this defense that the agents of the insurer who issued the policy in suit were invested with authority to countersign, issue, and deliver policies; that for several years he had carried with said agents a line of insurance in various companies, including the insurance here; that such policies had been issued and delivered to him by said agents and a running account kept by said agents with him for the amount of the premiums on such policies, and that periodical settlements between the insured and said agents took place; that this policy was delivered by the agents of the insurer in the same manner that they had been accustomed to deliver other policies to the insured, the agents giving

56

the insured credit for the premium; and that shortly after
the fire the insured tendered the premium to the agents
and they refused to accept the same, giving as a reason
therefor that they were instructed not to do so by the insurer. At the trial the insured was called as a witness
and his counsel attempted to prove by him the facts
averred in his reply, but this evidence was excluded by
the court. The clause in the insurance policy that the
company should not be liable on the policy until the premium should be actually paid was a provision inserted in
the policy for the benefit of the insurer, and one which it
might waive. The facts stated by the reply of the insured in this case, if true, were sufficient to authorize an
inference or sustain a finding that the agents of the insurer did waive the payment of the premium in cash at
the time they issued the policy, gave the insured credit
for such premium, and that they had authority to do so.
Whether the agents of the insurer were invested with
authority to waive the payment of the premium in cash
and give the insured credit therefor, and whether they
did so, were questions of fact for the jury and the court
erred in not submitting those questions to the jury.
(*Nebraska & Iowa Ins. Co. v. Christiensen*, 29 Neb. 572;
Schoneman v. Western Horse & Cattle Ins. Co., 16 Neb. 404;
Pythian Life Ass'n v. Preston, 47 Neb. 374.) In *Angell v.
Hartford Fire Ins. Co.*, 59 N. Y. 171, it was held that where
an agent of a fire insurance company was authorized to
negotiate contracts of insurance, to fill up and deliver
policies executed in blank and left with him for that purpose, he had authority to make parol preliminary contracts to issue a policy, and that the payment of the
premium at the time of issuing the policy was not an
essential prerequisite to make the contract of insurance
binding upon the company; that if the agent gave credit
to the insured for the premium, the contract was binding.
In *Sheldon v. Connecticut Mutual Life Ins. Co.*, 25 Conn. 207,
it was held that an agreement made in good faith between an insurance company's agent having authority to

receive an insurance premium and the insured, that the agent should become personally responsible to his principal for the premium and the insured the agent's debtor therefor, constituted a payment of the premium as between the insured and the insurance company. To the same effect see *O'Brien v. Union Mutual Life Ins. Co.*, 22 Fed. Rep. 586; *Chickering v. Globe Mutual Life Ins. Co.*, 116 Mass. 321; *Harding v. Norwich Union Fire Ins. Soc.*, 71 N. W. Rep. [S. Dak.] 755; *Home Fire Ins. Co. v. Curtis*, 32 Mich. 402.

2. Another defense interposed was that the insured, at the date of the issuance of the policy in suit, had $5.500 of insurance upon the insured property, which added to the $2,500 embraced in this policy made the total insurance on the property $8,000, and that thereby the total insurance on the property was $3,000 more than permitted by the policy, as it only permitted $5,000 insurance upon the insured's property, inclusive of that embraced in the policy in suit. This defense is entirely overthrown by the policy itself, which was a risk of $2,500 placed by the insurer on a dwelling-house of the insured and the furniture therein, $500 being upon the dwelling-house and $2,000 upon the furniture. But the policy, on the face of it, provides that the total insurance permitted by the policy to be placed on the house is $5,000 and the total insurance on the furniture $5,000.

3. A third defense of the insurance company was that at the date of the issuance of the policy in suit the household furniture thereby insured was incumbered by a chattel mortgage, and that the insured wrongfully withheld from the agents of the insurer all knowledge of the existence thereof. The evidence shows that at the date of the issuance of the policy the household furniture was incumbered by a chattel mortgage, but that the value of the personal property, both at the date of the issuance of the policy and at the time of the fire, greatly exceeded the amount of the debt existing against the property which the chattel mortgage was given to secure. The

insured then at the date of the policy and at the time of
the loss of the property had an insurable interest therein.
The insured offered to show on the trial, under a proper
reply, that the agents of the insurer solicited this insurance, and at the time they issued the policy had actual
knowledge of the fact of the existence of the chattel
mortgage upon the household goods. This evidence the
court wrongfully excluded. But the record does not
show, nor was any attempt made to show, that the insured made a written application for this insurance. or
any application whatsoever; nor that he made any representation as to the character or condition of the title to
his property at the time of procuring the policy; nor that
any inquiries were made by the insurance agents of him
as to the character or condition of the title to the property. For aught that the record shows, no inquiries were
made by the insurance agents and no statements were
made on the subject of the character or condition of the
title to his property by the insured. He was silent upon
the subject, but there is not a word of evidence in the
record to show that the motive which inspired his silence
was a sinister one. Whatever may be the rule elsewhere,
the settled doctrine of this court is that when no inquiries
are made of an insured as to the character or condition of
the title to his property; where he makes no false representations as to the character and condition of his title,
relying upon which the insurer is induced to and does
insure such property; where the insured has an insurable
interest in the property insured, and the insurer insures
such property, accepts and retains the premium, and a
loss occurs, then the insurer cannot escape liability for
such loss because of the fact that the insured at the date
of the policy was not invested with an absolute and unin.
cumbered title to the insured property, even though the
policy provides that it shall be of no validity unless the
title of the insured to the property be an unconditional
unincumbered one; as in such a case it will be conclusively presumed against the insurer that it intended to

and did insure the interest which the insured had in the insured property and waived the provision in the policy providing for its invalidity by reason of the imperfect title of the insured. (*Ins. Co. of North America v. Backler*, 44 Neb. 549; *Slobodisky v. Phenix Ins. Co. of Hartford*, 52 Neb. 395; *German Ins. & Savings Institution v. Kline*, 44 Neb. 395; *Omaha Fire Ins. Co. v. Thompson*, 50 Neb. 580; *Phenix Ins. Co. v. Fuller*, 53 Neb. 811; *Hanover Fire Ins. Co. v. Bohn*, 48 Neb. 743.) This defense was not established.

4. A fourth defense of the insurance company was that the house insured by the policy in suit at the date of the policy stood upon leased ground; that is, that the insured did not own the fee-simple title to the lot upon which the insured building stood. The evidence shows that the insured, in 1889, leased this lot for twenty years and soon afterwards erected thereon a three-story brick and frame building, which is the one insured by the policy in suit; that he took possession of the leased property and was in possession of it under his lease at the date of the policy and at the time of the fire. In other words, the evidence shows that considering the building erected by him upon the leased lot as affixed to the land and being a part of the lot and therefore real estate, the insured, at the date of the policy and at the time of the loss, had an insurable interest in such property. What has just been said with reference to the third defense of the insurance company is applicable to this defense.

5. Another defense of the insurer was that by the terms of the lease between the insured and his lessor the rent reserved and the taxes upon the property were made a lien upon the insured's interest in this property and that at the time of the issuance of the policy in suit there were certain rents and taxes in arrears, and that these had become and were an incumbrance upon the insured's property, and that by reason of his default the insured's lessor had declared the lease forfeited. But the lessee had not been evicted, nor had any judgment of eviction

been pronounced against him by reason of his default in the payment of his rent. He was in possession and had an insurable interest in the property, and all that has been said of the third defense of the insurance company and the law applicable thereto is likewise applicable to this defense.

6. A sixth defense of the insurance company was that the insured building, at the date of the policy in suit, was unoccupied and that the insurer and its agents had no notice of that fact at the date of issuing the policy. Upon this subject the language of the policy is: "If during this insurance the above mentioned premises shall become vacant or unoccupied, * * * this policy shall cease and be of no force or effect." For the purposes of this case we assume that the evidence shows that the insured building was not occupied at the time of the issuance of the policy. But the defense of the insurer is that he had no notice of that fact when he issued the policy in suit. There is not a word of evidence in this record which establishes, or tends to establish, that fact; nor is there any evidence which shows, or tends to show, that the insured represented to the insurer that the building was occupied at the date of the policy, or that the insurer had any reason to infer from anything that the insured said or did that the building was occupied at the date of the policy. For anything that appears in this record the insurer issued the policy in suit on the building and its contents, then and there knowing that the building was unoccupied. We do not know of any law that prohibits an insurer from taking a risk upon unoccupied property. Whether the property was vacant at the date of the policy, whether the insurance company knew of its vacancy, whether the insured represented that it was occupied and thereby induced the insurer to take the risk, were questions of fact for the jury. But because the property was vacant and the insurer had no knowledge of these facts do not of themselves constitute any defense to this action. The fact that the insured building is de-

scribed in the policy as a dwelling-house cannot by any reasonable construction of language be tortured into a representation of the insured that it was then and there occupied. (*Browning v. Home Fire Ins. Co.*, 71 N. Y. 508.) This defense of the insurer, like the others noted above, was not established.

7. A final defense of the insurance company was that at the date of the issuance of the policy the insured building had been sold at a judicial sale to satisfy a mechanic's lien existing against it. The evidence on this subject shows, or tends to show, that a lien was filed against the property in 1890, nearly three years before the issuance of the policy in suit, for $97; that in June, 1892, a decree was rendered foreclosing this lien, finding the amount due thereon to be $115.72,—this was some eight months before the issuance of the policy in suit; that in June, 1892, an order of sale was issued, but nothing done under it until January, 1893, when a sale was made of the property. After the sale was made, to-wit, February 14, 1893, the policy in suit was issued, and in April, 1894, or more than a year after the issuance of the policy in suit, and after this controversy had arisen, this sale was confirmed. It further appears that this sale was subsequently set aside. But, notwithstanding the fact that the insured property had been sold at a judicial sale, which was presumably pending for confirmation at the date of the issuance of the policy in suit, the insured still had an insurable interest in this property, as his title to the property was not divested by that sale until it was reported and confirmed by the court under whose authority it was made. (See *Greenlee v. North British & Mercantile Ins. Co.*, 71 N. W. Rep. [Ia.] 534; *Hanover Fire Ins. Co. v. Brown*, 25 Atl. Rep. [Md.] 589.) Furthermore, as the sale was finally set aside, the insured property, at the date of the issuance of the policy, was, as a matter of law, incumbered only by the mechanic's lien judgment, and the evidence shows conclusively that at the date of this policy the value of the property exceeded by some thousands

of dollars the amount of this mechanic's lien judgment, and the amount of all liens for taxes and rents due upon the property. In other words, that the insured had an insurable interest in the house. The judgment of the district court is reversed and the cause remanded.

REVERSED AND REMANDED.

GEORGE W. MYERS ET AL. V. FARMERS STATE BANK OF EMERSON.

FILED FEBRUARY 17, 1898. No. 7815.

1. **Note: AVERMENT OF TRANSFER.** A petition on a promissory note alleged that the owner and holder of the note indorsed and delivered it to the plaintiff. *Held,* Equivalent to an express averment that the owner thereby transferred the title to the indorsee.

2. **Principal and Surety: NOTE: CHATTEL MORTGAGES.** Where the maker of a note secures its payment by chattel mortgage and the payee of the note indorses and delivers it to a third party, his failure to seize the mortgaged property for the purpose of satisfying the note even though requested so to do by the sureties of the maker will not of itself discharge them. (*Huff v. Slife,* 25 Neb. 448; *Eickhoff v. Likenbary,* 52 Neb. 332.)

ERROR from the district court of Dixon county. Tried below before NORRIS, J. *Affirmed.*

Jay & Daley, for plaintiffs in error.

J. J. McCarthy and *J. C. Robinson, contra.*

RAGAN, C.

In the district court of Dixon county the Farmers State Bank of Emerson, Nebraska, recovered a judgment against J. F. and R. R. Myers on certain promissory notes. To review this judgment the Myerses have filed here a petition in error.

1. The first argument is that the verdict is not supported by sufficient evidence. The bank in its petition

alleged that George W. Myers, J. F. and R. R. Myers executed and delivered the notes sued on to one John Kirwin, and on the date of the execution and delivery of
these notes to him he indorsed and delivered them to the
bank, guarantying in writing the payment thereof. J.
F. and R. R. Myers, as a defense to the action, admitted
the execution and delivery of the notes sued on, but alleged that they were sureties for George W. Myers; that
he had given the notes to Kirwin as a part of the purchase price for a certain race horse warranted by the
vendor to have great speed and to be a sound horse; that
the warranty had failed; that Kirwin as a matter of fact,
and not the bank, was the owner of the notes sued on;
that George W. Myers executed a chattel mortgage to
Kirwin on the horse to secure the payment of the notes
in suit, and that the mortgagor, with the consent of Kirwin and the bank, had removed the mortgaged horse out
of the state, and that neither the bank nor Kirwin had
made any attempt whatever to collect the notes by seizure and sale of the mortgaged property; and that the
bank knew that the plaintiffs in error were only sureties
for George W. Myers. The evidence shows, without contradiction, that the bank purchased these notes in the
ordinary course of business for a valuable consideration
before their maturity, and without any knowledge that
Kirwin had warranted the horse sold to George W. Myers, if such a warranty was made. If the fact is at all material here, we think the evidence fails to show that the
plaintiffs in error were sureties on these notes. The evidence does not show that the mortgagor of the horse removed him out of the state or jurisdiction of the court
with the knowledge or consent of the bank, if that fact is
at all material here. The evidence does tend to show
that the plaintiffs in error requested the bank to take possession of the mortgaged horse and dispose of him for
the purpose of raising money to satisfy the note sued on,
and that the bank neglected to do so. That question we
will notice later. But the evidence sustains the finding

of the jury that the bank purchased the notes in suit in the usual course of business before maturity, for a valuable consideration, without notice of any defense which the makers thereof had against the notes in the hands of the original payee.

2. A second argument is that the petition does not state a cause of action. The argument is founded upon the fact that the petition does not expressly allege that the bank is the owner of the notes. The petition alleges the execution and delivery of the notes by the Myerses to Kirwin and then alleges: "On the same day * * * Kirwin indorsed said note and delivered it to plaintiff. * * * The following is a copy of said note with the indorsement thereon." Here follows copy of the note, and then the indorsement in this language: "For value received I hereby guaranty the payment of this no e. * * * John Kirwin. No part of said note has been paid and there is due the plaintiff from defendants on this note the sum of $———." We think these recitals of the petition are equivalent to an express averment that the plaintiff was the owner and holder of the note. The averment that the owner and holder of the note indorsed and delivered it to the plaintiff implied that he thereby transferred the title of the instrument indorsed.

3. During their deliberation the jury came into court and stated that they had found from the evidence that the mortgagor had removed the mortgaged horse out of the state and that the plaintiffs in error had requested the bank to cause this mortgaged horse to be seized and returned to the state, and that the bank had neglected to do so, and they then propounded to the court this question: "Now the point of law upon which we would like to be informed is as to whether said J. F. Myers is still responsible after making this request." The court answered the query in writing as follows: "The evidence shows that all signers of the notes are makers, and the answer to your question is, yes." This action of the court is now assigned for error. The first complaint is

that the court in this answer to the jury assumed and decided that the plaintiffs in error were makers of the notes in suit, and not sureties thereon, and that this was one of the issues in the case; but as to whether they were sureties was a question of fact for the jury. As already stated, we think the undisputed evidence shows that these plaintiffs in error were makers of the notes, not sureties; but if they were sureties, and the court committed an error in saying that they were makers, the error was without prejudice to the plaintiffs in error, as, under the undisputed evidence in the case, they were liable on this note whether they were sureties or makers, and the effect of the instruction of the court was to tell the jury that the plaintiffs in error were liable upon this note notwithstanding the fact that they had requested the bank to cause the mortgaged property to be brought back into the state and the bank had neglected to do so. Where the maker of a note secures its payment by a chattel mortgage, and the payee of the note indorses and delivers it to a third party, the failure of the indorsee to seize the mortgaged property for the purpose of satisfying the note, even though requested so to do by the sureties of the maker, will not discharge them. (*Huff v. Slife*, 25 Neb. 448; *Eickhoff v. Eikenbary*, 52 Neb. 332.)

JUDGMENT AFFIRMED.

HOLT COUNTY BANK ET AL. V. HOLT COUNTY.

FILED FEBRUARY 17, 1898.   No. 7873.

1. **Pleading**: COPY OF WRITING. The requirement of section 124 of the Code of Civil Procedure is that a pleader shall state the facts which constitute his cause of action or defense; and if the suit is upon a written obligation then a copy thereof should be attached as an exhibit to the pleading.

2. ———: ———. But where a pleader copies into his pleading the entire written instrument upon which his action is based this sat-

isfies the requirements of the Code, as the purpose of the section
is to give the opposite party notice of the instrument upon which
the cause of action or defense is based.

3. ——: ——. A petition does not fail to state a cause of action
simply because the written obligation made the basis of the suit
is copied into and made a part of the petition instead of being
attached thereto as an exhibit.

4. **Constitutionality of Depository Law.** *Hopkins v. Scott,* 28 Neb. 661,
holding the depository law of 1891 (Session Laws, ch. 50) not unconstitutional for any of the reasons therein alleged, reaffirmed.

5. **Review:** EVIDENCE: JUDGMENT. Where the judgment is the only
part of the record of a former suit offered in evidence it will be
conclusively presumed that the court rendering the judgment had
jurisdiction of the parties thereto.

ERROR from the district court of Holt county. Tried
below before BARTOW, J. *Affirmed.*

H. M. Uttley and *R. R. Dickson,* for plaintiffs in error.

M. F. Harrington and *H. E. Murphy, contra.*

RAGAN, C.

The Holt County Bank in March, 1892, was a banking
corporation organized under the laws of the state and
domiciled at O'Neill, in said Holt county. On that date
it became a depository of county and public moneys in
pursuance of the provisions of chapter 50, Session Laws
of 1891, and executed a bond for the safe-keeping and
repayment of all moneys received by it as such depository from the county treasurer of said county. Holt
county brought this suit in the district court thereof
against the bank and the sureties on its depository bond
to recover a sum of money which it had received under
the depository law and under its bond and had not paid
over and accounted for to the treasurer of Holt county
on his demand therefor. It had a verdict and judgment,
and Adams, McBride, and Dwyer, sureties on the depository bond, bring that judgment here for review on error.

1. The first argument is that the petition does not
state a cause of action. This argument is based upon

counsel's contention that a copy of the depository bond
sued on must be attached to and filed with the petition.
Section 124 of the Code provides: "If the action * * *
be founded on * * * a * * * written instrument as evidence of indebtedness, a copy thereof must
be filed with the pleading." The plaintiff in this case did
not attach a copy of the depository bond to its petition
as an exhibit or otherwise, but copied the entire bond
into the petition and made it an integral part thereof.
This of course was not a literal compliance with the provisions of the Code, but the petition did not fail to state
a cause of action simply because the bond was copied
into, and made a part of, the petition, instead of being
attached thereto as an exhibit. *Ryan v. State Bank*, 10
Neb. 524, was a suit upon the official bond of a county
officer. It was there claimed that the petition was demurrable because no copy of the bond sued on was attached to it; but the court said that the objection was
untenable; that a failure to attach to the petition a copy
of the bond could not be reached by demurrer but by
motion. Conversely, *Pefley v. Johnson*, 30 Neb. 529, was
a suit on a written contract. In his petition the plaintiff alleged the making of the contract, "which is hereto
attached and made a part hereof," but in his petition,
aside from this exhibit, did not set out what the contract
was nor the breach of it, and it was held in that case that
while this style of pleading was not to be commended,
the exhibit must be read as a part of the petition. The
true meaning of the Code is that a pleader should state
in his pleading the facts which constitute his cause of
action or defense. If the suit is upon a written obligation, then a copy should be attached as an exhibit to the
pleading; but where a pleader sets out the entire written
instrument, upon which his action is based, in the pleading itself, it satisfies the requirements of the Code, as the
purpose of that section is to give the opposite party notice
of the instrument upon which the cause of action or defense is based.

2. The second argument is that the depository law of 1891 is unconstitutional. The validity of this act was assailed in this court in *Hopkins r. Scott*, 38 Neb. 661, upon the same grounds on which it is assailed here, and it was held that the act was not invalid for any of the reasons urged against it. It is not necessary to restate our reasons for the conclusions there reached.

3. It appears that the county, before the trial of this action, had obtained judgment against the Holt County Bank on the depository bond in suit here, and on the trial of this action the county introduced in evidence that judgment. It is now insisted by the plaintiffs in err_{or} that the court erred in permitting that judgment against the bank to be introduced in evidence in this case; and the only reason they urge as to why the judgment should not have been admitted in evidence is that it was void. as the court had no jurisdiction over the bank at the time it was pronounced. The court had jurisdiction of the subject-matter of the suit, and we have before us no part of the record of that case except the judgment itself. and we must indulge the presumption that the court had jurisdiction over the bank at the time it pronounced the judgment. It is said in the briefs that the summons in that case was not served upon the bank or upon any person upon whom a valid service might be made. We do not know whether the bank voluntarily entered its appearance in the action or whether a summons was served upon it, as none of these facts are disclosed by the record.

There are other minor objections made to the judgment, but we do not deem them of sufficient importance for consideration here. The judgment of the district court is the only one that could have been correctly rendered under the pleadings and the evidence, and it is accordingly

AFFIRMED.

EUGENE MOORE v. STATE OF NEBRASKA.

FILED FEBRUARY 17, 1898.   No. 9697.

53 831
56   37
*56   83
56   84
57 710

53 831
*59 531

53 831
62 445n

1. **State Officers:** FEES: CONSTITUTIONAL LAW.   Article 5, section 24, of
the constitution, providing that the officers of the executive department "shall not receive to their own use any fees, costs,
interest upon public moneys in their hands, or under their control, perquisites of office or other compensation, and all fees that
may hereafter be payable by law for services performed by an
officer, provided for in this article of the constitution, shall be
paid in advance into the state treasury," not only prohibits such
officers from receiving fees to their own use, but also prohibits
all executive officers except the treasurer from receiving fees at
all, and requires their payment in advance into the treasury by
the persons by whom they are payable.

2. **Insurance·Companies:** FEES: AUDITOR OF PUBLIC ACCOUNTS.   Chapter 43, section 32, Compiled Statutes, adopted in 1873, and relating
to fees paid by insurance companies for services performed for
them by the auditor, was so far modified by the constitution of
1875 as to require such fees to be paid in advance into the treasury, and prohibit the auditor from receiving them.

3. **Penal Statutes:** DESCRIPTION OF OFFENDERS.   When a penal statute
is made to apply only to a certain class of persons, the description of the class is so far descriptive of the offense, and that the
person charged is within the class is a substantive element of the
crime itself.

4. **Embezzlement of Public Moneys:** OFFICERS.   Section 124 of the
Criminal Code, relating to embezzlement of public moneys, applies
only to officers or persons charged by law with the collection,
receipt, safe-keeping, transfer, or disbursement of the public moneys, and those who aid or abet such officers or persons.

5. ———: AUDITOR OF PUBLIC ACCOUNTS.   The auditor of public accounts is not as such officer charged with the collection, receipt,
safe-keeping, transfer, or disbursement of any part of the public
moneys, and is therefore not within the descriptive terms of section 124 of the Criminal Code.

6. **Criminal Law:** ESTOPPEL.   In order to punish one as for a crime
the offense must be within the plain import of the words of the
statute creating or defining the crime.   An offense not within the
words cannot be adjudged a crime because within the reason or
spirit; and this principle cannot be evaded by holding that one
performing acts which are denounced as a crime when committed
by a particular class of persons is estopped from denying that he
is within that class.

ERROR to the district court for Lancaster county. Tried below before CORNISH, J. *Reversed.*

The opinion contains a statement of the case.

W. E. Reed, Barnes & Tyler, and *Brome & Burnett,* for plaintiff in error:

On the part of plaintiff in error it is respectfully submitted: (1) That under the laws of the state he cannot be adjudged guilty of the crime of embezzlement unless the money claimed to have been embezzled by him was by him lawfully and properly received by virtue of his office; (2) that under the law of the state as it existed when this embezzlement is alleged to have occurred, and as it now exists, the auditor of public accounts was not authorized to receive, and could not lawfully collect, any fees on account of and for issuing certificates of authority or for filing annual statements of insurance companies; (3) that to comply with the law it was necessary that every insurance company desiring to file an annual statement or procure a certificate of authority to be issued to its agent or agents should pay, or cause to be paid, the fees therefor in advance into the state treasury and that having so done, no other fees could be required of any such insurance company; and that the allegation contained in the information respecting the insurance companies therein referred to, to-wit, "That each of said insurance companies having then and there fully complied with sections 20, 23, 24, and 25 of chapter 43 of the Compiled Statutes of the state of Nebraska, and all provisions of the laws of the state," is an affirmative allegation that no money or fees was at that time due from these insurance companies to the state; (4) that the state cannot invoke the doctrine of estoppel. (*Ottenstein v. Alpaugh,* 9 Neb. 237; *State v. Holcomb,* 46 Neb. 629; *Lace v. City of Guthrie,* 44 Pac. Rep. [Okla.] 198; *Orton v. City of Lincoln,* 41 N. E. Rep. [Ill.] 159; *People v. Pennock,* 60 N. Y. 421; *San Luis Obispo County v. Farnum,* 41 Pac. Rep.

[Cal.] 445; *Hartford Fire Ins. Co. v. State*, 9 Kan. 210; *McAleer v. State*, 46 Neb. 117; *State v. Newton*, 26 O. St. 200; *State v. Meyers*, 47 N. E. Rep. [O.] 138; *Warswick v. State*, 35 S. W. Rep. [Tex.] 386; *State v. Bolin*, 19 S. W. Rep. [Mo.] 650; *State v. Johnson*, 49 Ia. 141; *United States v. Bixby*, 6 Fed. Rep. 375; 4 Lawson, Criminal Defenses 889; *State v. Moores*, 52 Neb. 770; *State v. Lovell*, 23 Ia. 304.)

C. J. Smyth, Attorney General, and *Ed P. Smith, Deputy Attorney General*, for the state:

(1.) Section 32, chapter 43, Compiled Statutes, requiring fees to be paid to the auditor, is not inconsistent with section 24, article 5, of the constitution; hence fees paid to him become in his hands the property of the state. Therefore, he was an officer charged with the receipt, safe-keeping, and transfer of public moneys. (2.) If the statute requiring payment of fees to the auditor is unconstitutional, the fees received by him from insurance companies belonged to the state, and, under section 24, article 5, of the constitution, it was his duty as an officer to pay such fees into the state treasury; and not having done so, but having converted the fees to his own use, he is guilty of embezzlement of public moneys. (3.) If the statute requiring payment of fees to the auditor is unconstitutional, the moneys paid to him by the insurance companies, with the intention of transferring the title to the state, and accepted by him with the intention of receiving the title for the state, became the property of the state, and, under section 21, chapter 10, Compiled Statutes, relating to liabilities of officers, he was responsible for such moneys as property of the state; and in failing to pay the fees into the treasury and in converting the same to his own use he was guilty of the crime charged. (4.) He is estopped to assert that he did not receive the moneys by virtue of his office. (*Beatrice Paper Co. v. Beloit Iron Works*, 46 Neb. 901; *Albert v. Twohig*, 35 Neb. 563; *State v. Smith*, 35 Neb. 24; *Pleuler v.*

57

State, 11 Neb. 547; *Hartford Fire Ins. Co. v. Sta'e*, 9 Kan. 210; *State r. Spaulding*, 24 Kan. 1; *State r. Leidtke*, 12 Neb. 171; *Thatcher v. Adams County*, 19 Neb. 485; *Laflin r. State*, 49 Neb. 616; *State v. Wallichs*, 16 Neb. 110; *United States r. Thomas*, 15 Wall. [U. S.] 337; *Welch r. Frost*, 1 Mich. 30; *Mason r. Fractional School District*, 34 Mich. 228; *Chandler r. State*, 1 Lea [Tenn.] 296; *Phelps v. People*, 72 N. Y. 334; *Village of Olean r. King*, 116 N. Y. 355; *Swan r. State*, 48 Tex. 120; *Morris v. State*, 47 Tex. 583; *Waters r. State*, 1 Gill [Md.] 302; *Commonwealth v. City of Philadelphia*, 27 Pa. St. 497; *Mayor r. Harrison*, 30 N. J. L. 73; *Ex parte Ricord*, 11 Nev. 287; *People r. Royce*, 37 Pac. Rep. [Cal.] 630; *State v. O'Brien*, 94 Tenn. 79.)

IRVINE, C.

The information in this case, omitting formal parts, allegations of time, and venue, and other averments not material to the questions presented for review, was as follows: "That Eugene Moore, * * * then and there being an officer, to-wit, auditor of public accounts of the state of Nebraska, and as such officer being charged with the collection, receipt, safe-keeping, transfer, and disbursement of the public money and a certain part thereof belonging to the state of Nebraska, and the property of the state of Nebraska, then and there unlawfully and feloniously did fraudulently convert to his own use, and embezzle of said public money the sum of twenty-three thousand, two hundred eight dollars and five cents in money, * * * the property of the state of Nebraska, which said money had then and there come into the custody and possession of said Eugene Moore by virtue of his office as auditor of public accounts as fees from insurance companies then and there doing business in the state of Nebraska, for services to be performed by the said Eugene Moore as said auditor of public accounts in filing by the said Eugene Moore as said auditor the annual statements of said insurance companies and in issuing certificates of authority by the said Eugene Moore as

said auditor to the agents of said insurance companies,"
etc. The remaining averments are chiefly in the way
of particularizing the services for which the money alleged to have been converted was received. To this information the defendant pleaded guilty, and then moved
in arrest of judgment on the ground that the information
charged no crime. The motion was overruled and the
defendant sentenced to imprisonment for eight years and
to pay a fine of twice the amount alleged to have been
embezzled.

A suggestion made in the argument, and reflected in
several places in the state's brief, is that the plea admitted the moral guilt of the defendant, and, to quote the
last sentence of the brief, "having pleaded guilty to all
the charges of the information, this court may well hesi-
tate before reversing his plea, and say he is not guilty
after he has said he is guilty." Surely the attorney general cannot mean to contend that because the defendant
has by his plea admitted the facts charged and therefore
a moral delinquency, he should be punished even if the
law does not denounce those facts as a criminal offense.
The question before us is not one of moral delinquency,
but simply whether the facts charged in the information
constitute a crime under the laws of this state. Defendant stands in no worse position in this respect than he
would on a demurrer to the information, which would,
for the purposes of the proceeding, involve the same admission.

While there are several different sections of the Criminal Code relating to embezzlement by different classes
of persons, it is conceded that the information in this
case was drawn with a view to section 124, and that it
does not charge an offense against any other section.
Section 124, so far as it is material, is as follows: "If any
officer or other person charged with the collection, receipt, safe-keeping, transfer, or disbursement of the public money, or any part thereof, belonging to the state, or
to any county or precinct, organized city or village, or

school district in this state, shall convert to his own use, or to the use of any other person or persons, body-corporate, association, or party whatever, in any way whatever, * * * any portion of the public money, or any other funds, property, bonds, securities, assets, or effects of any kind, received, controlled, or held by him for safekeeping, transfer, or disbursement, or in any other way or manner, or for any other purpose, * * * every such act shall be deemed and held in law to be an embezzlement," etc. It will be observed that this section refers only to the embezzlement of public money or property, and that it applies only to a particular class of persons—those charged with the collection, receipt, safekeeping, transfer, or disbursement of the public money or a part thereof. It goes almost without saying that no person is subject to the penalties of the statute unless he falls within the description of the class of persons to whom the statute is applicable. The description of the person against whom the penalty is denounced is to that extent descriptive of the offense. The allegation that the defendant was as auditor charged with the collection, receipt, safe-keeping, transfer, and disbursement of the public money is not an allegation of fact, admitted by the plea of guilty, but it is an allegation of law, and open to examination as such. We therefore address ourselves to the examination of that question. Unless the auditor, as such officer, was charged in one of the manners specified, the information fails to state an offense by failing to show that the defendant was within the class to which the statute applies.

In 1873 there was passed an act relating to insurance companies, section 32 of which was as follows: "There shall be paid by every company, association, person or persons, agent or agents, to whom this act shall apply, the following fees: For filing and examination of the first application of any company, and issuing of the certificate of license thereon, fifty dollars, which shall go to the auditor; for filing each annual statement herein required, twenty dollars; for each certificate of authority, two dollars; for each copy of paper filed as herein provided, the sum of ten cents per folio, and fifty cents for certifying the same and affixing the seal of office thereto; all of which fees shall be paid to the officer required to perform the duties." (Compiled Statutes, ch. 43, sec. 32.) It is under this section that the moneys alleged to have been embezzled were paid. In 1875 the present constitution of the state went into effect, and article 5, section 24 thereof, after fixing the salaries of the executive officers, proceeds as follows: "After the adoption of this constitution they shall not receive to their own use any fees, costs, interest upon public moneys in their hands, or under their control, perquisites of office or other compensation, and all fees that may hereafter be payable by law for services performed by an officer, provided for in this article of the constitution, shall be paid in advance into the state treasury." In our opinion this provision of the constitution so far modified the statute quoted as to require all fees for services rendered by the executive officers created by article 5 of the constitution, including, of course, fees payable by insurance companies under the statute, to be paid in advance into the treasury by the person or company by whom such fees are payable, and to prohibit the receipt thereof by the officer performing the service. It is argued that the effect of the constitution was simply to require the officer performing the services to pay the fees into the treasury, and that the statute is in necessary conflict with the constitution only in so far as it gave the fees to the officer to his own use. In this connection attention is called to section 21 of the same article of the constitution, which provides: "An account shall be kept by the officers of the executive department and of all the public institutions of the state of all moneys received or disbursed by them severally from all sources, and for every service performed, and a semi-annual report shall be made to the governor, under oath." It is said that this section plainly contemplates

the receipt by the executive officers of fees for services to be performed. The executive officers may be, and have been at times, entrusted with money by virtue of legislative appropriations, and as to them section 21 requires an account and report of such moneys. But it is said the section refers specially to fees for services performed. True, but it applies not only to the executive officers provided by the article of the constitution we are considering, but applies also to officers of all public institutions of the state, whereas section 24 is limited to the executive officers named in the first section of the article. It is only they who are prohibited from receiving fees for services performed. The legislature may in its wisdom permit officers of other state institutions to receive fees. Until 1881, the university had its own treasurer who received matriculation and other fees. Now we have a bureau charged with the inspection of oil and gasoline, and the inspectors in that bureau receive the fees fixed for the services performed by them. The provision in section 21 with reference to fees manifestly refers to fees received by those officers within the scope of section 21, and not within the prohibition of section 24. In no other way can the two sections be so construed as to give force to every part of each and create no conflict. Two former decisions of this court, *State v. Leidtke*, 12 Neb. 171, and *State v. Wallichs*, 16 Neb. 110, have some relevancy to this question, but they require more extended notice at another period of this discussion, and their effect will be considered later. Under the old constitution salaries were fixed for the various executive officers which seem parsimonious and ridiculously small even when compared with the present salaries of such officers. There was, however, no inhibition against an allowance of fees by way of further compensation, and the legislature, in imposing new duties, in several instances provided for the payment of fees to the officer as compensation for their performance. It is needless to say that this system opened the door for abuses, and section 24 of article 5

of the present constitution, having in view the vices of
the old system, sought to correct it by giving to the state
all such fees. This object was accomplished by the first
language quoted from section 24; and if that had been
the only object in view, section 24 would certainly have
ended with the prohibition against the officers described
receiving fees to their own use. But it was evidently
thought that a better system, and one more consonant
with the supervision and safety of public funds, could
be established by prohibiting the executive officers, other
than the treasurer, from receiving any fees at all. It
was therefore provided that all fees for services by them
performed should be paid in advance into the treasury.
This could conveniently be required in the case of the
executive offices, because they are all maintained at the
seat of government, where the treasury is located. Thus
no executive officer except the treasurer was charged in
any manner with the collection of fees, and their payment into the treasury was secured by requiring that
such payment should be made in advance of performing
the services. In only one of two ways can the construction contended for by the state be supported. One of
those demands that we should neglect altogether the
requirement that the fees shall be paid in advance; the
other is to assume that it was the intention of the constitution to require an executive officer, when a service is
demanded of him, to exact payment of the fee, then act
the role of a messenger by carrying the money to the
treasurer, then return to his own office and perform the
service. The former construction would violate the letter of the constitution; the latter is too absurd to be entitled to serious consideration. The rule is invoked that
before the court will hold a statute unconstitutional, a
construction will be given it in harmony with the constitution, although that construction be not the most natural or obvious one. But this is not a question of the
constitutionality of a statute. The statute was enacted
before the present constitution took effect and was in

every respect valid when passed. The schedule of the new constitution provides (article 16, section 1) that in order "that no inconvenience may arise ·from the revisions and changes made in the constitution of this state, and to carry the same into effect, it is hereby ordained and declared that all laws in force at the time of the adoption of this constitution, not inconsistent therewith, * * * shall continue," etc. Even if such a result would not follow in the absence of that provision, it is clear that its effect was to abrogate all existing laws in so far as they were inconsistent with the constitution. We are asked, in effect, not to give a strained construction to a statute in order to render it in harmony with the constitution, but to give a strained construction to the constitution in order to prevent its working a repeal or amendment of an antecedent statute which happened to be in conflict with the letter and policy of the constitution itself. The question is merely one of an implied amendment of a statute, and the purpose of the inquiry is simply to ascertain the intention of the constitution. We have no hesitation in holding that the intention is clearly evidenced of prohibiting the executive officers from receiving the fees payable for their official acts, and to require the persons paying such fees to pay them into the treasury.

The state asserts that if that be the effect of the constitution, the defendant was nevertheless charged with the safe-keeping and transfer of these fees, he having in fact received them. It is said that the embezzlement statute does not require that the person charged should be charged with the duty by statute, but that he may be charged in any one of four ways—by the constitution, by decisions of this court on equitable grounds, by the common law, and by statute. It will be seen that this is only another method of saying that he must in some way be charged by law. Let us assume the correctness of this analysis and see to what result it leads; for convenience, however, not proceeding exactly in the order indicated. The defendant, we have seen, was not charged by the constitution with the safe-keeping or the transfer of the money, but was forbidden thereby even to receive it. He was not charged by statute. The statute originally gave him the money to his own use, and the constitution, when it deprived him of the right to so hold it, also took away the right to receive it. After the constitution took effect that part of the statute was as if it had not existed, and neither its retention by the compilers in the compilations of statutes, nor the fact that the auditor undertook to act under it, gave it renewed vitality. We do not understand just what counsel mean by saying that an officer whose office and duties are alike created and limited by statute can be charged with the receipt, safe-keeping, or transfer of money by the common law; but assuming that thereby is meant that common-law principles will be applied in ascertaining and enforcing those duties, that subdivision becomes a part of the second, whereby it is claimed that he may be charged by decisions of the supreme court grounded on equitable considerations. The supreme court by its decisions creates no duties; it merely enforces existing duties, and by the two heads of argument adverted to it must be meant that a duty may arise from a consideration of the established principles of law and equity. So treated the argument under this head may be analyzed into two propositions: First, that the defendant having, although unlawfully, received the money, it did not thereby become his, but belonged thenceforth to the state, and that it was his duty to pay it to the treasurer; secondly, that he is estopped by the receipt of the money to deny the lawfulness of his act or the validity of the statute whereunder he acted.

The first proposition receives, at first impression, support from the cases of *State v. Leidtke* and *State v. Wallichs*, already referred to. Both were original applications for writs of mandamus, addressed to this court, both were submitted without briefs, and both serve to illustrate the dangers attendant upon a hasty examination of questions presented in original cases not properly prepared by counsel and decided without the benefit of full discussion. *State v. Leidtke* was an application by the attorney general for a writ of mandamus to compel the auditor to pay into the treasury certain fees designated as "office fees," and certain fees received as were the fees in this case, together with other fees paid by life insurance companies for preparing and publishing statements. The only defense alleged in the return was that the office fees had been paid into the treasury and that the fees received from insurance companies were paid for services performed as agent for the companies and not by virtue of his duties as auditor. No suggestion was made that if the services were a part of his official duties he was entitled to retain the fees, nor was it suggested that if the fees belonged to the state mandamus was not the proper remedy, because he was not enjoined as such officer with the duty of transferring them to the treasury. On this record the court stated that the only question involved was whether the insurance fees belonged to the state or to the auditor. The court then proceeded to give the constitution the same construction which we have given it, but to decide that the auditor having received the fees he held them in trust for the state and not to his own use. With this conclusion we are satisfied, with the reservation that the state is not bound to so treat them; but it does not follow that because an officer or a private individual owes the state money or holds money in trust for the state that he is therefore charged with its receipt, safe-keeping, transfer, or disbursement. It is not to the ordinary legal obligations flowing from express or implied contracts and the duty of fulfilling them that either the law relating to mandamus or the statute with regard to embezzlement of public funds applies; and the court did not in the case referred to otherwise decide. Whether the actual question which should have been decided was the public character of the serv-

ices, as the record shows, or the ownership of the money,
as the opinion states, the question was correctly decided;
and the court was not asked to consider, and did not consider, whether the payment of the money was a duty enjoined by law upon the respondent as auditor, and one
appropriate to be enforced by mandamus.   We cannot
give any force to the case as an implied decision of that
point when the record shows that it was not in fact considered.   *State v. Wallichs, supra,* was an application by
the commissioners of Gage county to require the auditor
to register certain refunding bonds issued by that
county.   The auditor based his refusal on the fact that
he had demanded fees and that payment had been refused.   As already said, there are no briefs in the case,
but an inspection of the opinion discloses that the county
contended it had the right to have the bonds registered
free of expense.   A statute passed prior to the adoption
of the constitution provided that "the auditor shall be
entitled to a fee * * * for each bond so registered,
to be paid by the holder thereof."   (Session Laws 1875, p.
170, sec. 3.)   The court said that this statute had not
been repealed, but, citing *State v. Leidtke,* that such fees
are not for the use of the auditor, but it is nevertheless
his duty to collect them.   If *State v. Leidtke* was to be
followed as holding that they must be turned in by the
auditor to the treasury—a question not involved in the
Wallichs Case—the court should not have overlooked the
other statement in the *Leidtke Case* that the fees should
be paid into the treasury in advance, the treasurer giving
proper vouchers therefor.   Here again the only question
really decided was that the fees must be paid; that the
county was for that purpose to be deemed the holder of
the bonds.   No fees had been tendered either auditor or
treasurer; so that whether they should be paid to the
treasurer or auditor the writ had in either case to be denied, and the remark of the court as to the duty of the
auditor to collect them was purely *obiter.*   We must
decline to accept either case as authority for the propo-

sition that this court has established a law imposing on
the auditor a duty in conflict with the constitution.

That where an officer receives money which he is not
by law authorized to receive, such money is not received
by him in his official capacity, and that any duty which
he may owe of paying the money is only that which rests
upon any debtor or bailee, is established by many cases.

San Luis Obispo County v. Farnum, 108 Cál. 562, was an
action on the bond of a county auditor to whom a tax
collector had paid money which should have gone to the
treasurer. The court said: "That the money in question,
having been collected by the tax collector for licenses,
belonged to the county is not questioned; but that it
came to the hands of the defendant Farnum as auditor
is a conclusion of law wholly unsupported by the facts
found. * * * Having received the money, it was
Farnum's duty to pay it over to the treasurer; but such
duty did not arise out of his office, nor was it at all different from the duty which would have rested upon him
to pay it over had he been a plain citizen not holding any
county office." (See also *People v. Pennock,* 60 N. Y. 421;
Orton v. City of Lincoln, 41 N. E. Rep. [Ill.] 159; *Lowe v.
City of Guthrie,* 44 Pac. Rep. [Okla.] 198; *Warswick v. State,*
35 S. W. Rep. [Tex.] 386; *State v. Johnson,* 49 Ia. 141;
People v. Cobb, 51 Pac. Rep. [Colo.] 523; *People v. Hilton,*
36 Fed. Rep. 172; *Rex v. Thorley,* Moody C. C. [Eng.] 343;
State v. Moeller, 48 Mo. 331; *Rex v. Hawtin,* 7 C. & P.
[Eng.] 281.)

A case very similar arose in Kansas, the question there
being whether a certificate issued to an insurance company was valid where the auditor had made a draft for
the money, then issued the certificate, and, after the proceeds of the draft were received, paid the money into the
treasury. The court held that the certificate was void,
saying: "The much more serious error is found in the
declaration that the auditor acted as the agent of the
state in drawing the draft, or in receiving the money
when it was paid. The limits of an officer's authority are

found in the law. * * * If the corporation chose to
pay this through the auditor, then for that purpose the
auditor was the agent of the corporation and not of the
state." (*Hartford Fire Ins. Co. v. State*, 9 Kan. 210.) It
is asserted that a distinction exists between that case
and the present, in that the law of Kansas made the payment of the money into the treasury a condition precedent to the performing of the services. The language
of the statute there was: "Before the auditor shall issue
any certificate of authority * * * there shall be
paid into the state treasury by the corporation," etc.
Our constitution says that the fees shall be paid into the
treasury in advance. We can see no difference. To pay
in advance means precisely the same as to pay before the
services are rendered. We are not unmindful that the
Kansas court, in *State v. Spaulding*, 24 Kan. 1, sustained
a conviction of embezzlement where a city clerk by custom had received certain license moneys which should
properly, under an ordinance, have been paid to another
officer. While there is some language in the opinion indicating that the court deemed a principle of estoppel
applicable, the conviction was sustained under a count
charging the receipt of the money by the defendant as an
agent of the city and not as clerk, the court holding that
while its receipt was no part of his official duties, there
was nothing to prevent the city by custom from appointing an agent for that purpose, and that he was to be
deemed such agent. The court cited *State v. Heath*, 8 Mo.
App. 99, which was afterwards reversed by the supreme
court (70 Mo. 565), and where the conviction was in a like
case sustained on the ground of agency, but not on the
ground of official station or duty, there being counts
charging the offense in each manner.

The statute of Ohio was precisely like ours with reference to embezzlement of public funds, and the supreme
court of that state held that it did not extend to a county
auditor because he was not as such charged with the collection and receipt of money. (*State v. Newton*, 26 O. St.

265.)   In a later case, but after some amendments of the
statute not material to the present inquiry, it was held
that a deputy treasurer was not within its provisions.
(*State v. Meyers,* 47 N. E. Rep. [O.] 138.)   These cases
are precisely in point.   The distinction urged by the
state, that in Ohio there was no law, valid or invalid, authorizing the officer to receive the money, does not exist,
but in effect concedes away the conviction here, because
after a law has been repealed it no longer exists so as to
impose future duties or confer future rights.   *State v.
Bolin,* 19 S. W. Rep. [Mo.] 650, is another case in point.

Nor do we think that there is any principle of estoppel
whereby the defendant is forbidden to deny that he is
within the class against which the penalties of the statute
are denounced.   For the purposes of this case we need
not inquire whether the same rules apply as to estoppel
in civil and in criminal cases, or whether a man may ever
be estopped to plead the law.   The cases cited as applying estoppels are for the most part cases where an officer
charged by law with the duty of collecting taxes has
actually collected them and then refused to turn them
over because illegally levied.   There the general duty of
collecting the money was imposed by law on the officer.
The money was paid.   The legality of the tax was a question solely between the public and the taxpayer, and the
latter having voluntarily paid the tax, it was no affair of
the collector whether he might have resisted the payment or not.   The matter was not one of an estoppel.
The issue was merely immaterial.   No one could defend
a charge of embezzlement as the agent of an individual,
on the ground that a third person had paid money
which he did not owe and could not have been compelled
to pay; but there is a multitude of cases holding that he
may defend if he had no authority to receive payment at
all.   Akin to these cases are those where a foreign corporation is prohibited from doing business except on
compliance with certain requirements, and an agent em-
bezzles its funds, and alleges in defense that the princi-

pal had no right to make the contracts leading to the
collection of the money. This is really a case of an immaterial issue, or if it be one of estoppel, it is an estoppel
to deny the facts giving the principal a right to do business. Where a criminal statute applies only to persons
of a certain class, the doing of the acts which the statute
forbids does not estop the defendant from denying that
he belongs to the class which is alone subjected to the
penalties. Yet that is at the last analysis the argument
of the state on this branch. A statute of this state
makes it rape for a male person of the age of eighteen or
upwards.to carnally know a female child under the age
of eighteen. Should it appear that a man had so carnally known a female child, he would not by that fact be
estopped from asserting that he was himself under the
age of eighteen. The description of the persons in such
statutes is a substantive element of the crime, and devolves upon the state to prove that the defendant is
within the class punishable. In *State v. Meyers, supra*,
the court, speaking of a statute essentially like this, said
that a statute defining a crime cannot be extended by
construction to persons or things not within its descriptive terms, although they appear to be within the spirit
and reason of the statute. In *State v. Lovell*, 23 Ia. 304,
Judge Dillon, after confessing that the criminal jurisprudence of this country is blemished with over-technical
niceties, said: "But the faults of the common-law tribunals in this regard are more than redeemed by their
stern determination not to admit or create constructive
crimes. This is among their noblest monuments." And
Chief Justice Marshall said in *United States v. Wiltberger*,
5 Wheat. 76, "To determine a case is within the intention
of a statute, its language must authorize us to say so. It
would be dangerous, indeed, to carry the principle, that a
case which is within the reason or mischief of a statute
is within its provisions, so far as to punish a crime not
enumerated in the statute, because it is of equal atrocity,
or of a kindred character, with those which are enu-

merated. If this principle has ever been recognized in expounding criminal law, it has been in cases of considerable irritation, which it would be unsafe to consider as precedents forming a general rule for other cases." The remark about "cases of considerable irritation" is aptly characteristic, we think, of the few cases called to our attention invoking principles of estoppel to prevent a man's defending on the ground that there is no law to convict him. It is precisely those cases of "considerable irritation" in which the courts should be particularly careful that the bulwarks of liberty are not overthrown, in order to reach an offender who is, but who perhaps ought not to be, sheltered behind them. The principle announced in the last cases cited is incorporated into the Criminal Code in order that the courts may not possibly depart from it. Section 251 provides that "no person shall be punished for an offense which is not made penal by the plain import of the words, upon pretense that he has offended against its spirit." To hold that the auditor is a person charged with the collection, receipt, safe-keeping, transfer, or disbursement of the public money, when the law expressly forbids him to receive it or handle it, would certainly go beyond the plain import of the words of the statute, and create a crime by construction in the plainest violation of the law.

REVERSED AND DISMISSED.

SULLIVAN, J., dissenting.

I do not concur in the conclusion of the majority and give here the reasons for my dissent.

The constitution of 1875 not only repealed that part of section 32 of the insurance law which authorized the auditor to appropriate to his own use the fees therein specified, but repealed, as well, so much of the section as authorized him to receive such fees for any purpose. These fees were, by the provisions of the constitution, required to be paid into the treasury of the state in advance of the rendition of the service which the statute made it the auditor's duty to perform. The money then, it must be conceded, was received without authority of law. Being so received, is the defendant guilty of embezzlement under section 124 of the Criminal Code, by reason of having converted it to his own use? Resolved into its elements the proposition is this: (1) Did this money belong to the state, and (2) does the defendant fall within the class of persons against whom the penalties of the section are denounced?

It is settled by a long line of decisions in other states that taxes or other public revenues collected by an officer acting under color of an unconstitutional law or void ordinance belong not to himself, but to the municipal or political corporation whose commission he bears. (*Chandler v. State*, 1 Lea [Tenn.] 296; *Village of Olean v. King*, 116 N. Y. 355; *Swan v. State*, 48 Tex. 120; *Morris v. State*, 47 Tex. 583; *Waters v. State*, 1 Gill [Md.] 302; *Commonwealth v. City of Philadelphia*, 27 Pa. St. 497; *Middleton v. State*, 120 Ind. 166; *Mayor v. Harrison*, 30 N. J. L. 73.) Here the defendant, acting under color of a statute originally valid, but repealed in part by implication on the adoption of the present constitution, collected fees due the state for official services rendered by him as auditor of public accounts; and now, after having rendered services to the insurance companies as the agent of the state, and after having assumed to act for the state in collecting the fees due for such services, he cannot be heard to deny that the fees so collected and received belong to, and are the property of, the state. The application of the doctrine of estoppel to the facts in this case has made the money in question the money of the state; and it must be so regarded whether its title be drawn in question in a civil or in a criminal case. The law does not require us to hold to-day in a criminal action that it is not the state's money, and to-morrow in a civil action that it is. In the case of *State v. Spaulding*, 24 Kan. 1, it was held that where a city officer, pursuant to a custom

58

of long standing, but without any other color of right. collected fees due to the city for services rendered by him. such fees belonged to the city. and that by their appropriation to his own use he was guilty of embezzlement.

But was the defendant one of the persons against whom section 124 of the Criminal Code is directed? Whatever may be the rule in other jurisdictions, the question is no longer an open one in this state.   It has been effectually set at rest by the decision in the case of *State v. Leidtke*, 12 Neb. 171.   The language of the section, "any officer or other person charged with the collection. receipt, safe-keeping, transfer, or disbursement of the public money," etc. (Criminal Code, sec. 124), is, unquestionably, descriptive of the persons who may be punished under its provisions. and is, therefore, descriptive of the offense.   It is, of course, true that the defendant was not charged by any valid law with the collection or receipt of the moneys here in question, but having collected and received them under color of his office, it became his duty to safely keep them and transfer them to the treasury of the state.   And this was not, as intimated in the case of *San Luis Obispo County v. Farnam*, 108 Cal. 562, 41 Pac. Rep. 445, a duty due from him as a private citizen, but one arising out of, and resulting from, his official station. Upon this point the *Leidtke Case* is direct authority; for. by the judgment of this court, a peremptory writ of mandamus was awarded against Leidtke to compel him to pay to the state treasurer fees collected by him as auditor under the provisions of section 32 aforesaid.   The writ could not have issued against him as a mere private debtor of the state. It could have issued only to coerce the performance of an official duty. (*Thatcher v. Adams County.* 19 Neb. 485; *Laflin v. State*, 49 Neb. 614.)

I am not prepared to say that I should agree to the rule established by the *Leidtke Case* were the question now presented for the first time.   But that decision has stood unchallenged for nearly twenty years.   It may be contrary to the weight of authority, but it has the support of sound reason; and, to say the least, it is not so serious an impediment in the way of justice as to call for a judicial repeal. The principle on which it rests has the sanction of very eminent authority. It is precisely the same principle which controlled the decision in the case of *State v. Spaulding, supra.* In that case the conviction was not sustained because Spaulding was agent of the city to collect license moneys. In truth he was not, and could not have been, such agent,—an exclusive agency for that purpose was, by ordinance, vested in the city treasurer; but having by an assumption of authority obtained the money which he embezzled, he was estopped from denying that such assumption was false. From the opinion written by Brewer, J., now of the supreme court of the United States, I quote as follows: "We do not affirm that the city was concluded by the defendant's acts, nor indeed that any one is estopped but himself. But we hold that when one assumes to act as agent for another, he may not, when challenged for those acts, deny his agency; that he is estopped not merely as against his assumed principal, but also against the state; that one who is agent enough to receive money is agent enough to be punished for embezzling it. An agency *de facto*, an actual even though not a legal employment, is sufficient. The language of the statute is, 'If any officer, agent, clerk, or servant of any corporation, or any person employed in such capacity.' * * * He [the defendant] voluntarily assumed full charge of this entire matter, including the receipt of the money and the issue of the license. The money was paid to him because of his office and to induce his official action, and he may not now say that it was not received 'by virtue of his employment or office,' or that its receipt was not one of the prescribed legal duties of such office. * * * He may not enter into the employment and then deny its terms or responsibilities. He is estopped from saying that this money which he embezzled is not the money of the city." It is no more true as a legal proposition that Spaulding was the agent

of the city, or, in the language of the Kansas statute,
"employed in such capacity," than it is that the defendant
in this case was "charged with the collection, receipt.
safe-keeping, transfer, or disbursement of the public
money." Nevertheless, he was convicted and the conviction sustained because the law did not permit him to
assert the truth and rely on it as a defense. So it seems
to me that the defendant Moore, having obtained the
money in question for the state by the exertion of his
official authority, should not be permitted to deny that he
held it in his official capacity. The remarks of Mr.
Bishop in his work on criminal law are pertinent here.
The author says: "In reason, whenever a man claims to
be a servant while getting into his possession the property to be embezzled, he should be held to be such on his
trial for the embezzlement. This proposition is not made
without considering what may be said against it. And
a natural objection to it is that when a statute creates
an offense which by its words can be committed only by
a 'servant,' an extension of its penalties to one who is not
but only claims to be such, violates the sound rule of
statutory interpretation whereby the words, taken
against defendants, must be construed strictly. But
why should not the rule of estoppel, known throughout
the entire civil department of our jurisprudence, apply
equally in the criminal? If it is applied here, then it
settles the question; for by it when a man has received
a thing of another under the claim of agency, he cannot
turn around and tell the principal, asking for the thing:
'Sir, I was not your agent in taking it, but a deceiver and
a scoundrel.' When, thereafter, the principal calls the
man under these circumstances to account, he is estopped
to deny the agency he professed, why also, if he is then
indicted for not accounting, should he not be equally
estopped on his trial upon the indictment?" (2 Bishop.
Criminal Law [7th ed.], ch. 16, sec. 364.) The rule thus
stated has been recognized and approved in *State r.
Spaulding, supra, State v. O'Brien*, 94 Tenn. 79, and *People*

v. Royce, 106 Cal. 173, 37 Pac. Rep. 630.   It has also received recent recognition from this court.   In the case of
Bartley v. State, 53 Neb. 310, the contention of the defendant that the depository act is unconstitutional is answered in the following language: "It is urged that the
court erred in assuming in the tenth, eleventh, and fifteenth paragraphs of the charge the validity of the depository law.   An elaborate argument is made in the
briefs against the validity of that piece of legislation on
grounds other than those heretofore considered by this
court.   We must be excused from entering upon a discussion of the subject at this time, as the defendant is
in no position now to assert that the public moneys of
the state were not rightfully on deposit in the Omaha
National Bank.   He recognized the validity of the statute by placing the moneys of the state in said bank, and
it would indeed be a reproach upon the law to permit
him to assail the depository law in a prosecution for the
embezzlement of the public funds so deposited by him.
It was the money of the state that went into the bank,
and it was likewise the money of the state that paid the
check, whether the bank was a lawful state depository
or not."   From these citations it appears that the
Leidtke Case does not stand solitary and alone.   The principle on which it was decided is not a pernicious one, to
say the least, and it should, in my judgment, be adhered
to.   The defendant, by his plea of guilty, has confessed
that he received the money embezzled as auditor of
public accounts, and I do not think we should either directly or by necessary implication overturn one of our
own decisions in order to hold that his confession is false.

INDEX.

Animals—*concluded*.

untary relinquishment thereof, or by such conduct as estops him from asserting it. *Id.*

3. A purchaser of live stock is charged with notice of an agister's lien. *Id.*

4. The owner's taking of live stock from possession of the agister without his consent does not divest him of his lien. *Id.*

5. That one purchased live stock for value without actual notice of an agister's lien, affords no protection against such lien. *Id.*

Appeal. See REVIEW.

Definitions of "appeal." *Nebraska Loan & Trust Co. v. Lincoln & B. H. R. Co*.. 248

Appearance.

1. A defendant who voluntarily submitted to the jurisdiction of the court cannot be heard afterward, by answer, to question such jurisdiction. *Shabata v. Johnston*................. 12

2. Upon review an order overruling a special appearance may be sustained where the affidavit upon which such appearance was based is not in the record. *Life Ins. Clearing Co. v. Altschuler* 482

Appraisement. See EXECUTIONS, 5-10.

Assessments. See CORPORATIONS, 1, 2. TAXATION.

Assignments. See ACTIONS, 4. EVIDENCE, 21. EXEMPTION, 3.

Assignments of Error. See REVIEW, 7-15.

Assumpsit. See MONEY PAID.

Attachment. See EXEMPTION, 3. SHERIFFS AND CONSTABLES.

1. Distribution of proceeds of chattel-mortgage sale of goods replevied by mortgagee from a sheriff who seized them under writs of attachment. *Sarpy County State Bank v. Hinkle* 108

2. n affidavit to procure an attachment, sworn to before a notary public who is plaintiff's attorney, is not a nullity, but an irregularity which cannot be attacked collaterally. *Horkey v. Kendall*.. 522

3. A notary public who is the attorney of one of the parties to an action is not permitted to take the affidavit of his client for the purpose of procuring an attachment. *Id.*

4. An officer from whom goods held under attachments have been replevied may prove the attachments under a general denial; and though he adds to the general denial a special plea of one attachment, he may prove other attachments. *Id.*

5. The rule that an officer attaching property in possession of

Contracts—*concluded.*

with it for the erection of a public building, a provision imposing on the contractor the duty of paying for materials used in the building is valid. *Id.*

3. Where the meaning of a written contract can be ascertained without the aid of extrinsic evidence, it should be interpreted by the court and not by the jury. *Ricketts v. Rogers.*. 477

4. To establish an express contract there must be shown what amounts to a definite proposal and an unconditional and absolute acceptance. *Melick v. Kelley.* 509

5. Construction of a contract providing for compensation of an insurance agent. *Bankers Life Ins. Co. v. Stephens.* 660

Conveyances. See ACKNOWLEDGMENT. ESTOPPEL, 2-5. VENDOR AND VENDEE.

Corporations. See INSURANCE, 6. MUNICIPAL CORPORATIONS.

1. The capital stock of a corporation must be fully subscribed before an action will lie against a subscriber to recover assessments thereon, unless, by law or charter provision, the corporation is permitted to proceed with its main design with a less subscription. *Macfarland v. West Side Improvement Ass'n* 417

2. A subscriber of capital stock may either waive or estop himself from setting up the defense, in a suit for assessments, that the entire stock has not been subscribed. *Id.*

3. Where a corporation's treasurer pays certain assessments, receives payment of assessments from others, and disburses funds of the corporation in carrying out its main object, he is estopped from asserting that the stock has not all been subscribed, though he was ignorant of the deficiency. *Id.*

4. Where the treasurer with consent of the promoters permits an agent to perform the active duties of the office, he is responsible for the agent's acts and is chargeable with notice of facts learned by the agent in the performance of such duties. *Id.*

5. The directors of an insolvent corporation cannot lawfully appropriate its assets to the payment of debts due them from it, to the exclusion of other creditors. *Wyman v. Williams* 670

6. A suit by the receiver of a corporation against subscribers to recover unpaid stock subscriptions will not lie until the amount justly due from the corporation has been ascertained and the corporate property exhausted. *Id.*

7. Where the directory of a corporation makes a call for unpaid subscriptions, such call becomes at once corporate property for which a receiver subsequently appointed may sue. *Id.*

8. A denial that relator is a corporation duly organized under the laws of the state of New York does not put in issue

Ejectment—concluded.

2. An heir may maintain ejectment for undevised lands of which his ancestor died seized, except as against the administrator and those claiming under him. *Lewon r. Heath....* 707

Election of Remedies. See INDICTMENT AND INFORMATION, 7-9.

Elections. See COUNTIES, 8.

1. Though a declaration of intention to become a citizen may constitute a resident alien an elector, this status does not extend to his son because the declaration was made before the son attained his majority. *Haywood v. Marshall........* 220

2. The intention of an elector must be ascertained from his ballot, and any inaccuracies in the preparation thereof cannot be urged for the first time after election, to defeat the clearly expressed intention of the voter. *Tutt v. Hawkins..* 367

Electric Railways. See EMINENT DOMAIN, 2-5.

Embezzlement. See PAYMENT, 2.

Prosecution.

1. A county attorney, without directions from the auditor of public accounts, may institute a criminal proceeding against a state treasurer for embezzlement of the state's money. *Bartley v. State.....................................* 310

Definitions. Elements of Crime.

2. Under section 124 of the Criminal Code, any person who advises, aids, or participates in an officer's embezzlement of public money is himself guilty of embezzlement. *Mills r. State ....* 263

3. The words "any person," used in section 124 of the Criminal Code relating to embezzlement of public money, are not confined in meaning to a person or persons, or officer or officers, in some manner intrusted with the collection, handling, or care of public money. *Id.*

4. Instructions in a prosecution for embezzlement *held* applicable to the evidence. *Id...................................* 261

5. The law for depositing state and county funds in banks (Session Laws 1891, p. 347, ch. 50) did not repeal section 124 of the Criminal Code, relating to the embezzlement of public money. *Whitney r. State...........................* 238

6. A county treasurer's deposit of public funds in a depository, pursuant to section 6, chapter 50, Session Laws of 1891, is not embezzlement. *Id.*

7. A state treasurer, who for an unauthorized purpose draws a check on a state depository bank having money of the state therein, which he delivers to the payee with intent to defraud the state, and the bank, on presentation of the check, places the amount thereof to the credit of a third party, whom the payee represents in the transaction, and at the same time charges the account of the state with a like

Intoxicating Liquors.

1. In prosecuting one for keeping intoxicating liquors for unlawful sale his possession of such liquors is presumptive evidence of guilt, in the district court, as well as before the examining magistrate. *Durfee v. State* 215

2. The council of a city of the second class having less than 5,000 inhabitants, when authorized by ordinance, may entertain a complaint against a saloon-keeper and, for proper cause, revoke his license, though he has not been convicted of a violation of the law relating to the sale of liquors. *Miles v. State* 305

3. A licensed saloon-keeper and the sureties upon his bond are liable for loss of support sustained by the widow and children of one whose death was contributed to by the drinking of intoxicating liquors furnished by the saloon-keeper. *Schiek v. Sanders*... 664

4. The fact that defendant was a licensed saloon-keeper may be shown by the proceedings of the city council and the license records, the production of the license issued not being essential. *Id.*

5. In a suit against a saloon-keeper for damages, evidence *held* to sustain a finding that plaintiff's husband was killed while under the influence of liquor sold by defendant, and that the latter was a licensed saloon-keeper at the time of the sale. *Id.*

6. Where a druggist charged with keeping beer for unlawful sale introduced evidence that he did not keep beer and that bottles found in his possession by the sheriff contained a non-intoxicating tonic, a search-warrant stating informer's belief that defendant kept beer and the return of the sheriff that he found bottles of beer in defendant's possession are inadmissible as independent evidence. *Nelson v. State*...... 790

Joinder. See NEW TRIAL, 3. PARTIES, 1. VENDOR AND VENDEE, 3.

Journal Entries. See EXECUTORS AND ADMINISTRATORS, 2. REVIEW, 58.

Judgments. See COURTS, 3, 4. DIVORCE. EXECUTORS AND ADMINISTRATORS, 1. HUSBAND AND WIFE, 9. MECHANICS' LIENS, 2. RECORDS.

Proceedings to Vacate.

1. Enforcement of a judgment by default, which is void for want of jurisdiction, should not be restrained by injunction on application of defendant unless he pleads and proves that he has a meritorious defense, has no adequate remedy at law, and was not negligent. *Bankers Life Ins. Co. v. Robbins* 45

2. In an action to restrain the enforcement of a void judgment, the remedies at law available to the party assailing the judgment, the adequacy of such remedies, and whether he was negligent, are discussed in the opinion. *Id.*

61

Physicians and Surgeons—*concluded.*

were not guilty of negligence in the treatment given the plaintiff nor in adopting and pursuing the method of treatment followed by them. *Id.*

5. Evidence that surgeons informed their patient that they would not return unless requested to do so, that they received no such request, and did not return, *held* relevant under the pleadings in an action for malpractice. *Id.*

6. In a suit for damages against a surgeon for alleged negligence in operating upon and treating plaintiff's fractured kneecap, text-books on surgery, though standard authority, cannot be read to the jury as independent evidence. *Id.*.... 29

Pleading. See ATTACHMENT, 4, 6. ATTORNEY AND CLIENT, 2. BONDS, 1, 3. CORPORATIONS, 8. EMINENT DOMAIN, 3. LIMITATION OF ACTIONS, 2. NEGOTIABLE INSTRUMENTS, 6. PARTIES, 1. REVIEW, 45.

1. A petition seeking to charge a trust on property in the hands of the receiver of an insolvent bank may allege that the bank obtained the property as bailee, and at the same time charge that it was obtained by fraudulent concealment of insolvency, and relief may be granted on the latter ground, though the former be not proved. *Higgins v. Hayden* 61

2. One pleading facts sufficient to constitute a cause of action may have proper relief, whether the case is denominated an action at law or a suit in equity. *Alter v. Bank of Stockham.* 223

3. A pleader should state the facts constituting his cause of action or defense. *Holt County Bank v. Holt County*......... 827

Amendments.

4. It is within the discretion of the trial court to allow an amendment of a petition in the course of a trial where such amendment does not change the original cause of action stated by the plaintiff. *Undeland v. Stanfield*................. 120

5. In an action on a policy of insurance, plaintiff's written demand for allowance of an attorney's fee, at the time of rendition of judgment, may be treated as an amendment of the prayer of the petition. *Hartford Fire Ins. Co. v. Corey.*. 209

Answer.

6. Statements in an answer *held* to import an admission of delivery of material for which suit was brought. *Rohman v. Gaiser* 474

Copy of Instrument.

7. In a suit upon a written obligation a copy thereof should be attached to the petition, but this requirement is satisfied where the pleader copies into his pleading the entire instrument upon which his cause of action is based. *Holt County Bank v. Holt County*....................................... 827

8. A petition does not fail to state a cause of action simply

Res Judicata.

1. A county board in passing on claims against the county acts judicially, and its judgment is final unless reversed on appeal. *Trites v. Hitchcock County* 79

2. A county board, in examining the reports and adjusting the accounts of a county officer, acts ministerially, and an adjustment so made is no bar to an action subsequently brought to recover moneys unlawfully withheld by the officer. *Id.*

3. In an action on the official bond of a county treasurer, answer *held* to plead an adjudication against the county by the allowance of a claim by the county board in its judicial capacity. *Id.*

Review. See INSTRUCTIONS. REMITTITUR.

1. Error cannot be predicated upon the overruling of a demurrer to a count subsequently eliminated by *nolle prosequi.* *Bartley v. State* 310

2. Error cannot be predicated upon the overruling of a challenge to a juror for cause, where the record fails to disclose that the complaining party exhausted his peremptory challenges. *Id.* 311

Amendment of Record.

3. A court of record has the inherent power to correct its own records, even after an appeal, so that such amended record may show correctly the history of the proceedings before the appeal was taken. *Andresen v. Lederer* 128
Andresen v. Carson 136

4. A trial court, after an appeal has been perfected, has no power to so correct its records that, in fact, a modification of the judgment appealed from shall be effected. *Id.*

Appeal and Error.

5. The method of reviewing judgments of the district court in proceedings by railroad companies in exercising the right of eminent domain is by petition in error and not by appeal. *Nebraska Loan & Trust Co. v. Lincoln & B. H. R. Co.* 246

6. In an equity case an appeal under section 675 of the Code relating to appeals in equity does not present for review the correctness of a ruling of the trial court in excluding evidence, but such a ruling may be presented under section 584 *et seq.* of the Code providing for review by proceedings in error. *Ainsworth v. Taylor* 484

Assignments of Error.

7. Alleged errors must be separately assigned. *Brinckle v. Stitts* 10

8. A joint assignment of errors, in a petition in error made by two or more persons, which is not good as to all who join therein must be overruled as to all. *Shabata v. Johnston*.... 12

9. Under an assignment that the verdict is not supported by

Statute of Frauds.

1. To take an oral contract for the sale of personalty worth over $50 out of the statute, where no part of the purchase money has been paid, delivery and acceptance of some portion of the property are necessary. *Wyler v. Rothschild* 566

2. Under a verbal contract of sale delivery of goods to a carrier, receipt and acceptance by the purchaser at the place of destination, and payment of the freight charges, take the contract out of the statute. *Id.*

Statute of Limitations. See LIMITATION OF ACTIONS.

Statutes. See MUNICIPAL CORPORATIONS, 6. TABLE, *ante*, p. lv. TAXATION, 6-9.

1. The law for depositing state and county funds in banks (Session Laws 1891, p. 347, ch. 50) did not repeal section 124 of the Criminal Code relating to the embezzlement of public money. *Whitney v. State* 288

2. Depository law (Session Laws 1891, p. 347, ch. 50) *held* valid. *Holt County Bank v. Holt County* 828

3. Special provisions in a law relating to particular subject-matter will prevail over general provisions in other statutes, so far as there is a conflict. *State v. Cornell* 556

4. An act complete in itself is not unconstitutional, although it may be in conflict with, or repugnant to, a prior statute not referred to nor in express terms repealed. *Bryant v. Dakota County* 755

5. Section 4, chapter 7, Session Laws of 1889, limiting to thirty days the time within which an action may be brought against a county for damages resulting from a defective highway, does not violate the constitutional provision that "no bill shall contain more than one subject, and the same shall be clearly expressed in its title." *Id.*

6. The amendment of section 118 of the Code (Session Laws 1887, p. 646) relating to verification of pleadings and stating that nothing in that section shall be construed to prohibit any attorney who is a notary public from swearing a client to any pleading or affidavit in any proceeding in the courts, cannot be held to apply to affidavits other than those verifying pleadings, without giving the amending act a construction which would render it violative of section 11, article 3, of the constitution relating to subjects and titles of bills. *Horkey v. Kendall* 522

7. The act of 1875 amending certain sections of the Criminal Code, including section 116 relating to stolen goods (Session Laws 1875, p. 1), is void because it contains no provision for the repeal of the sections amended, as required by section 19, article 2, of the constitution of 1866. *Reynolds v. State* .. 761

8. An act merely amendatory of a section of a prior statute must set out the new section and, in addition, contain a

Statutes—*concluded.*

provision for the repeal of the old section sought to be amended. *Id.*

9. Section 32, chapter 43, Compiled Statutes, was, by the constitution of 1875, modified so as to require insurance companies to pay in advance into the state treasury fees for services performed for them by the auditor of state, and to prohibit the latter from receiving such fees. *Moore v. State* 831

Stenographers. See NEW TRIAL, 1.

Stipulation.

Stipulation *held* not an admission that a purchaser at a tax sale was assignor of one claiming to be owner of the tax sale certificate. *Johnson v. English*......................... 530

Stock. See CORPORATIONS, 6, 7.

Stockholders. See CORPORATIONS, 3.

Street Railways. See EMINENT DOMAIN, 2-5.

Streets. See DEDICATION. MUNICIPAL CORPORATIONS, 6, 7.

Subrogation.

1. Doctrine of subrogation *held* applicable to case stated in the opinion. *Aultman v. Bishop*............................... 545

2. The right of subrogation not resting on contract, but being a mere equitable right, whether the doctrine should be applied depends upon the circumstances of each case. *Id.*

3. The party to whom the debt of another has been paid, the payment of which furnishes the basis of the claim for subrogation, is a proper and necessary party to the action for subrogation. *Id.*

Subscriptions. See CORPORATIONS, 1, 2, 6, 7.

Substitution. See PARTIES, 3.

Summons. See INSURANCE, 6.

Supersedeas. See REVIEW, 54, 55.

Suretyship. See BONDS. HUSBAND AND WIFE, 9. PRINCIPAL AND SURETY.

Surgeons. See PHYSICIANS AND SURGEONS.

Taxation. See COUNTY BOARD.

Void Taxes. Injunction.

1. One not guilty of laches may invoke the aid of a court of equity to restrain the collection of a void tax. *Harmon v. City of Omaha* 164
Chicago, B. & Q. R. Co. v. City of Nebraska City.............. 454

2. Void special assessments to pay for improving streets cannot be enforced solely on the ground of benefits by the im-

62

Lightning Source UK Ltd.
Milton Keynes UK
UKHW012129180219
337529UK00012B/1422/P